WOMEN AND POLITICS

The Pursuit of Equality

Australia • Brazil • Japan • Korea • Mexico • Singapore • Spain • United Kingdom • United States

WADSWORTH
CENGAGE Learning

Women and Politics:
The Pursuit of Equality
Third Edition
Lynne E. Ford

Senior Publisher: Suzanne Jeans

Executive Editor: Carolyn Merrill

Assistant Editor: Katherine Hayes

Editorial Assistant: Angela Hodge

Content Project Manager:
  Jessica Rasile

Senior Marketing Manager:
  Amy Whitaker

Marketing Coordinator:
  Josh Hendrick

Marketing Communications
Manager: Heather Baxley

Art Director: Linda Helcher

Senior Rights Acquisition
Account Manager: Katie Huha

Image Manager:
  Jennifer Meyer Dare

Print Buyer: Paula Vang

Production Service/Compositor:
  Carlisle

Cover Design: Rokusek Design

Cover Image: ©Masterfile

For product information and technology assistance, contact us at **Cengage Learning Customer & Sales Support, 1-800-354-9706**

For permission to use material from this text or product, submit all requests online at **cengage.com/permissions** Further permissions questions can be emailed to **permissionrequest@cengage.com**

Library of Congress Control Number: 2003110171

ISBN-13: 978-0-495-80266-2
ISBN-10: 0-495-80266-2

Wadsworth
20 Channel Center Street
Boston, MA 02210
USA

Cengage Learning is a leading provider of customized learning solutions with office locations around the globe, including Singapore, the United Kingdom, Australia, Mexico, Brazil and Japan. Locate your local office at: **international.cengage.com/region**

Cengage Learning products are represented in Canada by Nelson Education, Ltd.

For your course and learning solutions, visit **www.cengage.com**

Purchase any of our products at your local college store or at our preferred online store **www.CengageBrain.com**

Printed in the United States of America

Brief Contents

Contents

CHAPTER 5. WOMEN AS POLITICAL ACTORS: REPRESENTATION AND ADVOCACY

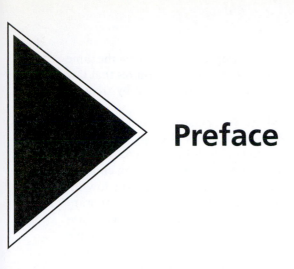

Preface

Women and Politics: The Pursuit of Equality, third edition, is intended to serve as a core text for undergraduate and graduate courses on women and politics. When I first developed the course in my own department nearly twenty years ago, a colleague joked, "What will you cover in the second week?" On the contrary, I have found that the biggest challenge in teaching a course on women and politics is to introduce students to the vast history of women's movements, to acquaint them with the scholarship on women as political leaders and political participants, and still leave time to address contemporary policy concerns. This is particularly true given the explosion of high-quality scholarship on gender and politics in the last two decades. Never satisfied with a single book, I usually ended up using parts of five or six books at a significant cost to my students. In *Women and Politics: The Pursuit of Equality,* third edition, I integrate the major topics related to women's political involvement into a single text. Although there are now several core texts in Women and Politics, very few provide thorough coverage of women's political participation and public policy issues in a single volume, as this one does. The history of women's entrance into the public sphere builds a strong foundation upon which the analysis of contemporary progress in politics and policy areas is considered.

To provide coherence, I have created a strong central organizing theme that links topics across chapters but remains flexible enough to permit individual instructors to organize their courses in a variety of ways. The book is organized around what I've termed the *paradox of gender equality*: the need to reconcile demands for equality with biological differences between women and men. I argue that, in trying to resolve the paradox, women have primarily followed two paths. One path advocates a *legal equality doctrine* based on the belief that women and men must be treated the same in order to achieve equality. Therefore, differences must be erased by laws and public policies before equality can be achieved. Just as viable, another path focuses on women's differences from men. Advocates of this approach believe that treating men and women the same when they are in fact different is unfair. The *fairness doctrine* requires that law and policy account for the consequences of biological difference by treating men and women differently, but fairly.

Resolving the paradox is complicated by the persistent and pervasive influence of the *separate spheres ideology*. Although this ideology impacts all women, it has affected different groups of women in different ways. Separate spheres ideology specifically excluded upper-class white women from employment and limited the type of employment opportunities and pay for low-income women and women of color in the workforce. Defining a contemporary role for women in the public sphere has been difficult because women's biological role in bearing children makes their traditional assignment to the home still seem "natural" to many people. Just as women's opportunities were once limited by the sharp demarcation between the private and public spheres, women today face conflicts created by a blurred line. Men and women alike are trying to sort out new gender roles. Presenting the paradox of gender equality within the context of separate spheres ideology enables students to examine their own preconceived notions of the "proper" roles for men and women and to connect events in their own lives with the theories and scholarship presented in the book. This approach also helps students understand why issues of gender equality seem to reappear for successive generations of political activists to tackle. In each chapter, a special effort is made to focus on the diversity of experiences among women of different races, economic classes, and political persuasions. The most compelling controversies of gender equality are often played out exclusively among women. Understanding how women differ from each other is as important as understanding how women are different from men. I've attempted to include as much scholarship as possible on the experiences of women of color, poor women, and women in other traditionally marginalized groups, including women who are opposed to equality altogether. Where such information is not available, I've challenged students to think carefully about why the gap in the research literature exists.

CHANGES IN THE THIRD EDITION

The third edition of *Women and Politics* maintains this solid framework, but includes significant updates to the scholarship, figures and tables, feature boxes, and current issues included throughout the text. New material has been added to explore the gendered impact of the economic recession on women and their families. The national candidacies of Hillary Rodham Clinton and Sarah Palin are explored in depth along with the media's gender bias throughout the campaign. Extensive coverage of the 2008 campaigns and general election is integrated within each chapter and goes well beyond women as voters and candidates to include coverage of ballot initiatives on reproductive issues and marriage equality; divisions among feminists over whom to support in the Democratic presidential primary; analysis of popular culture and socialization as forces responsible for the gender stereotypes in evidence during the campaign; new research on the "intersectionality" of race, class, sexual orientation, ethnicity and gender; the unprecedented levels of engagement among young people and first-time voters; the striking political geography of women's electability; new research on parity and the public's perception of gender balance in an "ideal government"; and preliminary analysis of the impact of the 2008 election outcomes for women through public policy.

Eight years of the Republican Bush administration, the ascendancy of social conservatives, wars on three fronts (Iraq, Afghanistan, and terror), and the threat of future terrorist strikes "remasculinized" politics in significant ways. Although still early in the new Obama administration, it is abundantly clear that the political landscape for women has shifted. In just five months, President Obama has signed the Lilly Ledbetter Equal Pay Act into law, reversed the global gag rule, reversed the ban on embryonic stem cell research, ensured that over-the-counter emergency contraceptives are available to women 17 years of age and older, reversed the previous administration's "conscience regulation," restored full funding levels to the United Nations family planning and maternal health initiatives, established the White House Council on Women and Girls, and announced that decisions about health policy will be driven by science and not political ideology. On the issue of abortion and reproductive choice specifically, Obama has emphasized that he will move away from scorched-earth rhetoric in favor of public discourse in search of common ground. In public statements he has reaffirmed women's agency in the moral and medical decisions related to reproductive health. But while elections matter and their consequences can sometimes be immediate as in the examples above, the fact that federalism empowers states to enact policy on a wide range of issues means that the pursuit of women's equality is multifaceted and takes place across the several levels of government. More extensive coverage of state policies affecting gender equity in education, employment, health, marriage and families, and fertility is included in the third edition.

In response to reviewer suggestions, the third edition includes more international comparative content in a number of ways. Scholarship drawing on international data, case studies, and comparative analysis has been integrated wherever possible throughout the book. A new feature found in Chapters 2 through 9 presents contrasts between women in the United States and elsewhere. These "Point of Comparison" boxes draw students' attention to empirical indicators of gender equality relevant to the content of each chapter and allow them to reflect on the ways in which the U.S. compares to other nations. Similarly, international content has been included in several of the "Encountering the Controversies of Equality" boxes.

Finally, the policy chapters have been updated to reflect the dynamics in education, work, and family and fertility politics. Title IX has withstood several direct challenges in the last decade and the proportion of women earning college and postgraduate degrees has steadily increased. Women's success in school has not, however, directly translated into a pipeline to top positions in the workplace. Increasingly, it is clear that women bear nearly the entire "cost" of having children and creating families. The lack of federal support for family leave, paid sick leave, and universal child care leaves women to cope as individuals. There is some evidence that working mothers are finding a public voice through organizations like MomsRising, but there has been no policy relief for the "double burden" women carry. The tension between work and family presents feminism with its greatest challenge in the twenty-first century and is perhaps the best example of the paradox of gender equality today.

TEXT ORGANIZATION

The two dominant paths women have taken in resolving the paradox—the pursuit of legal equality and the pursuit of fairness—offer a way to organize women's politics historically as well as to present students with the live controversies of gender equality. Chapter 1 lays out the origins of the separate spheres ideology, distinguishes between sex as a biological designation and gender as a social construction, and details the roots of the legal equality and fairness doctrines. Both paths are presented as reasonable ways to resolve the paradox of gender equality on many issues. This chapter also acknowledges that women disagree as to which approach is the better way to proceed, and presents an overview of the major strands of feminism and their critiques. Is feminism still relevant? The third edition includes a discussion of post-feminism and its implications for the pursuit of gender equality. Chapter 2 evaluates two major women's movements in the United States: suffrage and the Equal Rights Amendment. In both cases, the mechanism for change was a constitutional amendment. The contrast between the success of the suffrage movement and the failure to ratify the ERA illuminates the differences between a legal approach to equality and women's interest in fair accommodations for biological differences. The histories of both movements present students with examples of women's political activism and highlight the contributions of young women and women of color in both movements. In the third edition, efforts to resurrect the Equal Rights Amendment, now known as the Women's Equality Amendment, are evaluated.

Chapter 3 examines women as voters and political participants. Although initially slow to enter electoral politics, women are now registered at higher rates than men and have the power to dramatically shape elections. The Internet offers women new ways to access political information and has increased their likelihood of donating money to political candidates. Chapter 3 addresses a variety of questions: How do women evaluate candidates? Which issues mobilize women's participation? Can female candidates mobilize women voters? How do women in their twenties approach politics? Under what circumstances will women vote for other women? The third edition includes a substantial update on the impact and sources of the gender gap in presidential elections, in the battleground contests during the Democratic primaries, and in the 2008 general election. Expanded coverage of the ways in which political interest, political knowledge, and civic engagement inform women's participation is included. The impact of CODEPINK, a woman-founded antiwar organization has been included in the material on mobilizing forces for women. Trends in political party identification that differ by gender are explored as forces with potentially positive implications for female candidate in the future. Chapter 4 covers women as candidates for political office, evaluating the differences between male and female candidates, as well as differences among women in their approaches to running for elective office. Research demonstrates that when women run for office they are as likely as men to win, but they are substantially less likely to run in the first place—why? This edition includes the latest statistics on women officeholders at the local, state, and national levels, as well as the latest research on candidate emergence. The ways in which popular culture and socialization inform gender stereotypes is explored and then applied to evaluate the national candidacies of Senator Hillary Rodham Clinton and Governor Sarah Palin. New research on the political geography of women's electability is included in this chapter. Initiatives to recruit and train women candidates have been updated. Chapter 4 asks and explores the questions—why so few women in U.S. political office? Why has it taken so long for women to reach such a modest level of representation? The prospects for speeding up women's election to office through electoral gender quotas and gender gerrymandering are examined in this chapter. Chapter 5 evaluates women in public office—their behavior, their priorities, their style of governing, and their many accomplishments and challenges. The third edition includes updates on women officeholders and appointments throughout the executive branch and the judiciary. Nancy Pelosi's election as Speaker of the House of Representatives and other new leadership roles occupied by women in Congress are included here. An analysis of women's role in passing 2008–2009 federal stimulus legislation as well as the stimulus packages' likely impact on women is new to this edition. This chapter also looks at women as agents of change through avenues outside formal politics. Women have a long tradition of acting as political outsiders because they were excluded from mainstream politics. Now that there are more women on the inside, how do they and other advocates for women's interests work together to advance women's equality?

Chapters 6 through 8 focus on women and public policy. Chapter 6 examines education. Although Title IX is best known for opening athletic opportunities for women, it also opened doors to professional programs and eliminated quotas for women in "nontraditional" subjects such as math, science, and engineering. This chapter examines the link between education and income for women and men and explores the changing demographics of college admissions. New to this edition is a focus on STEM (science, technology, engineering, and mathematics) fields widely expected to offer the best prospect for high-paying jobs in the future, but areas where women are still underrepresented. Law-rence Summers's claim that women's absence from top science programs is due to their lack of intrinsic aptitude is explored in a new "Encountering the Controversies of Equality" feature. Chapter 7 is focused on work, wages, and women's broad participation in the economy, including a focus on the impact of the economic recession on women. This chapter addresses the pay gap and the surrounding controversies. While there is no question that women are paid less than men, is that because of sex discrimination or "choices" women make in prioritizing work and family responsibilities? What sort of help can individu-als expect from government in balancing the demands of work and family life? Why is the United States one of only four nations in the world not to provide government support for paid family leave? In this third edition, coverage of women in the military is expanded to reflect the evolution of their duties that *de facto* include combat even though *de jure* they are excluded from combat. This section also includes an examination of the challenges women in the mili-tary face including the risk of sexual assault, PTSD, their relative invisibility as veterans returning from war zones, and difficulties in combining military service with childbirth and motherhood. Chapter 7 also evaluates the impact that recent changes in the welfare system and proposed changes in the Social Security system have had on women. Chapter 8 is dedicated to family and fertil-ity issues. The definition of "family" has changed significantly in practice, but in many ways public policy regarding the family has not kept pace. The third edition includes new material on marriage equality, including a discussion of the states that permit same-sex marriage or civil unions and those that recog-nize marriages or unions made legal elsewhere. Although the federal Defense of Marriage Act remains in place and a majority of states have adopted laws or constitutional provisions to ban gay marriage, the political trend reflected in public opinion appears to favor marriage equality. This chapter examines the complex ways in which biology and gender intersect, shaping the roles men and women play in families. Should government be doing more to support families through paid leave and other social benefits? The third edition includes updated information on abortion politics, including federal and state policies restricting or regulating abortion and an extensive analysis of the U.S. Supreme Court's ruling in *Gonzales v. Carhart* (2007) that for the first time permits a ban on abortion without exceptions for the health of the woman. Implica-tions for access to abortion in the United States arising from the murder of Dr. George Tiller, pervasive clinic violence, and new regulations imposed by the states are explored in this edition. Finally, who gets to decide how many chil-dren a woman *should* have? The situation of Nadya Suleman (single mother of fourteen children conceived with the assistance of fertility technologies) is con-trasted with the philosophy of Quiverfull, a decidedly antifeminist conservative pronatalist movement. In conclusion, Chapter 9 evaluates women's progress in achieving equality and challenges students to think about issues relating to women and politics that they will face in their own lives. Material from through-out the book is drawn into the analysis of women's progress and students are invited to develop an equality agenda for the future. New in this edition is the "Taking Action" feature that links specific resources to the books summative conclusions and points students to direct action strategies to promote gender equality.

TEXT FEATURES

The third edition of *Women and Politics: The Pursuit of Equality* provides a number of features designed to encourage critical thinking. In each chapter, a box titled "Encountering the Controversies of Equality" presents students with a controversy or conflict generated by the paradox of gender equality and prompts them to consider how it could be resolved. These boxes are intended to clarify the concept of the paradox and to encourage students to appreciate the complexity of women's demands for gender equality. By having students grapple with contemporary issues related to the core themes of the text, the parallels between central issues facing women centuries ago and issues facing students today become quite clear. In Chapters 2 through 9, a new feature titled "Point of Comparison" specifically draws attention to the ways in which countries vary on political norms, processes, and/or empirical outcomes in issue areas related to the chapter's content. For example, the "Point of Comparison" in Chapter 4 focuses on a form of positive discrimination, electoral gender quotas, as a way to rapidly increase the proportion of women in elective office. When viewed alongside Table 4.2 listing the sixteen countries with the highest proportion of women serving in the lower house of the national legislature, students are able to think more critically about "quotas" and "discrimination"— words that in the context of American politics have negative connotations—as worthy of consideration in advancing women's political representation. In the policy chapters, the "Point of Comparison" features draw from a variety of publicly available data sources to compile empirical tables comparing nations across relevant indicators. For example, in Chapter 6, women's global educational attainment is featured and the table includes statistics on adult male and female literacy rates, girls' share of primary enrollment, and women's share of tertiary enrollment. Using the World Economic Forum's Global Gender Gap report, the top ten and the bottom ten countries are included as a point of comparison to the statistics from the United States. Finally, a new section has been added to Chapter 9 that suggests ways for students to take action directly to promote gender equality. Called "Taking Action: What Can You Do?," this feature points students to relevant resources that will enable them to get involved. In previous editions, this approach to encouraging direct engagement could be found on the companion Web site under "Paths to Action." The benefit to including this material in the final chapter (as well as on the Web site) is that it is more immediately tied to the summative information drawn from the previous eight chapters. As students are encouraged to develop a future agenda for women's equality and to find their unique role within that agenda, "Taking Action" gives them concrete steps to take.

Each chapter also relies on contemporary scholarship from a number of disciplines, including political science, history, sociology, psychology, anthropology, philosophy, and the natural sciences. The interdisciplinary approach enriches the analysis and makes the text appropriate for women's studies courses as well as courses in political science. Although politics changes daily, I have presented the most current data available, including figures for women's participation as candidates and voters in the 2008 national election. Internet resources in the text citations and the Suggested Readings, Web Resources, and Films section at the end of each chapter direct students to places where they can access the most current data, find additional information, and conduct independent research. The third edition includes a selection of relevant blogs in this list that for many people have taken the place of reflection journals and offer students a way to directly engage in dialogue about the issues covered in the text.

COMPANION WEB SITE

A Web site, accessible via www.cengage.com/politicalscience/ford/womenand politics3e, enhances and extends the theme and pedagogy of *Women and Politics: The Pursuit of Equality*, 3rd edition. The site provides chapter outlines, Web links, essay questions, and journal prompts for each chapter.

ACKNOWLEDGMENTS

I could not have completed this book without tremendous support from a variety of sources. The third edition was completed while on sabbatical, and I thank my colleagues in political science and at the College of Charleston for providing me with the luxury of extended time to read, research, and write. I owe my family—my husband, Frank Dirks, and my two children Grace and Samuel Ford-Dirks—an enormous debt of gratitude for their love, encouragement, and patience. Grace and Samuel are good reminders about the importance of role models in changing attitudes about gender-appropriate work. Both followed Hillary Clinton's quest for the Democratic presidential nomination in 2008 with great interest and enthusiasm. Their disappointment when Clinton ended her campaign was overwhelmed by their confidence that a woman will surely win the presidency "next time."

As this is the third edition of the book, I have benefitted greatly from the feedback generously offered by the students, faculty colleagues, and reviewers who have taken the time to carefully read and consider previous editions of the book. Many of the important new directions in this edition come directly from their input.

I would also like to extend special thanks to those scholars who provided their insights and useful suggestions for the development of this text: Marit Berntson, Roanoke College; Stefanie Chambers, Trinity College; Steven Greene, North Carolina State University; Kara Lindaman, Winona State University; Ruth Ann Watry, Northern Michigan University; and Julie Webber, Illinois State University.

L. E. F.

For Grace and Samuel

Two Paths to Equality

This is a book about women's use of politics and the political system in pursuit of gender equality. At its core, this book explores the complexity, tension, and controversy created by an overarching paradox in the unique nature of women's claims to equality. A paradox occurs when two apparently contradictory positions coexist. In this case, the paradox is this: How can demands for gender equality be reconciled with sex differences? Because "equal" often means "the same," how can men and women be the same if they are different?

The story of women's relationship to politics is therefore complex because the most direct path to gender equality is not clearly marked. In fact, this book argues that there are two well-worn paths women have travelled in pursuit of equality. On the one hand, women have argued that equality is only possible when the differences between men and women are erased by laws that require men and women to be treated equally. We will refer to this path as the *legal equality doctrine*. The other path consciously recognizes the differences between men and women and argues that women will always be disadvantaged if they are not somehow compensated for the social, economic, and political consequences of those differences. What matters most to advocates of this second approach is that women are treated fairly. Fairness may require laws, policies, and practices that treat women differently from men. We will refer to this path as the *fairness doctrine*.

The tension is evident in the disagreement among women themselves over which is the right path to take to improve women's status. Just because women share sex-linked biological characteristics with one another does not mean that they embrace a single understanding of gender equality, nor does it mean that

Encountering the Controversies of Equality

What Do Women Veterans Look Like?
What Should Women Veterans Look Like?

In 1999, the West Virginia Division of Veterans Affairs commissioned a statue honoring female veterans. When sculptor P. Joseph Mullins unveiled the design three years later, critics complained that it was not "feminine enough." The statue depicts a muscular woman wearing a casual uniform of pants and a t-shirt. "It would have been nice if we could have had a statue that looked more like a woman," said State Senator Anita Caldwell, vice chairwoman of the Senate Military Committee. State Senator Jon Blair Hunter, the committee's chairman, said the statue should "depict a woman in a skirt." The sculptor, himself a Vietnam veteran, said that depicting a woman in a skirt would have been inappropriate. The statue is "not a runway model and not a Playboy bunny," but rather a "nice, big, strong girl who's been through military training." Ten years, two wars, and two committees later, the statue is still not complete. The number of West Virginia female veterans has nearly doubled. The Division of Veterans Affairs has created a third committee primarily to identify a location for the statue, but the panel "could also reconsider the design."[1]

In New York, a 1998 statue in honor of female veterans located next to the State Museum is generating the opposite reaction. This statue, intended by its creator to invoke "Lady Liberty," appears in a clingy, flowing gown. A sash is draped over her left arm and a crown lies at her sandaled feet. State Senator Nancy Larraine Hoffman has asked the governor to move the statue to another location and to replace it with "something more representative of the sacrifices women veterans have made." She has said the statue "looks more like a Victoria's Secret ad." Margaret Bandy, one of the first women from New York to enlist in the Marines, says, "I think the statue misrepresents women in the military, especially today. I think the veterans deserve something less ethereal." Bandy enlisted in 1942 and served for three years as a drill instructor and company commander. "When you go to look at statues honoring men, they look like warriors. That's what we were too. I was fully willing to give up my life to defend my country."[2]

What do you think?

How is this controversy related to women's pursuit of equality and the paradox of gender? In both cases, the controversy stems from the collision of women's real contemporary roles with the image of women grounded firmly in the private sphere. What

In a Tuesday, March 1, 2005 file photo, P. Joseph Mullins of Charleston, W.Va., designer and sculptor of the Veterans Memorial at the state Capitol stands next to his model, front, and proposed sculpture still in a mold, honoring West Virginia's women veterans. The state Capitol Building Commission voted Wednesday, Sept. 9, 2009 to place the much-debated statue just southeast of the popular Veterans Memorial on the state Capitol grounds. (AP Photo/Jeff Gentner, File). *Jeff Gentner/ AP Photo.*

World War II Marine veterans Margaret Bandy, left, and June Worden, president of the Women Marines Association, look at New York's Women Veterans Memorial in Albany, N.Y. Tuesday, June 8, 2004. The women object to the portrayal in the center panel of the memorial and are urging the state to erect a different representation of New York's military women. (AP Photo/Tim Roske). *AP Photo/Tim Roske.*

is the appropriate visual representation of women's role in today's military? What does each visual tell us about women and men and the paradox of gender equality? What would you decide in each case and why?

1. "Agency Hopes New Committee Will End Flap over Veterans Statue," Associated Press State and Local Wire, July 19, 2004; "State Still Seeks Site for Female Veterans Statue," Associated Press, Charleston, W. Va., August 29, 2008; "Younger W. Va. Women Veterans Embrace Statue Design," *Herald-Dispatch* (Charleston, WV), September 15, 2008.
2. "Women Veterans Criticize Statue Honoring Them," Associated Press State and Local Wire, June 8, 2004.

they possess a group identity or group consciousness as *women* in a way that easily translates into political action. In this regard, *feminism* only adds to the tension. As an ideology, feminism has been ineffective as an organizing philosophy for women's movements because feminism itself incorporates the equality paradox. Feminism promotes unity among women while recognizing diversity, and it pursues equality even while recognizing differences.

Controversy is inevitable anytime one group makes demands that require another group to relinquish power, resources, control, or the privileges they currently enjoy. *Patriarchy* literally means "rule of" (*arch*) "fathers" (*patri*). More generally, patriarchy characterizes the pervasive control men exercise over social, economic, and political power and resources, not only in the United States, but also throughout the world. Feminism and women's movements directly challenge the privileged position of men and demand that women be viewed as individuals rather than simply derivatives of their relationships to men. The long-standing and persistent belief that men and women naturally occupy *separate spheres* strengthens the power of patriarchy. The separate spheres ideology promotes the belief that because of women's role in reproduction, they are best suited to occupy the private sphere of home and family. Alternatively, men are designed to occupy the public sphere of work and politics. Until the mid-1800s, common law, known as *coverture*, contributed to women's lack of power in the public sphere by defining married couples as one entity represented in civil society by the husband. Therefore, women could not vote, control property, or work for wages since they were indivisible from their husbands. Throughout the book, controversies about gender equality are most evident when women demand autonomy and work toward acquiring the rights and privileges that flow from eliminating the distinction between the public and private spheres.

This text employs the equality-difference paradox to examine women's historic and contemporary participation in politics. In doing so, it is important to state two caveats. First, accepting the equality-difference paradox as a framework for examining women's political integration in the United States does not mean that these are the only two positions one might adopt. Dichotomies can sometimes be limiting in that they accentuate, or exaggerate, the positions at either end of a spectrum, while giving little attention to the space in between. History suggests that neither polar position provides an entirely satisfactory approach to the pursuit of gender equality. Similarly, neither position will provide a full explanation of women's successes and failures in working toward gender equality. Rather it is the tension produced by the coexistence of the legal equality doctrine and the fairness doctrine that provides the most fertile ground on which to examine gendered society, women and politics, and the continuing controversies of equality. Second, equality is not the only goal of women's movements nor is the equality-difference framework the only way to understand women's pursuit of gender equality. This framework, however, does provide a very effective way to explore the multitude of controversies associated with the pursuit of gender equality and to examine the diverse perspectives among women, as well as differences between women and men. Many of the most interesting debates explored in this text, however, find women working in opposition to other women in defining and pursuing social, economic, and political goals. Finally, this is a book about women's engagement with politics in the United States, although insights drawn from women's experience in other political systems around the world can be found throughout the chapters.

POLITICS AND WOMEN'S PURSUIT OF EQUALITY

Why has it taken women so long to be recognized as important political actors? Why, in 2009, do women earn, on average, seventy-eight cents to a man's dollar, despite passage of the Equal Pay Act in 1963? Why do many women, young and old alike, shy away from using *feminism* as a label yet express support for feminist positions? Why was allowing women to vote seen as the most radical demand expressed in the *Declaration of Sentiments and Resolutions* adopted in 1848 at the first organized women's rights convention, in Seneca Falls, New York? Is the gender gap in contemporary electoral politics real, and if so, what does it mean? Why are women still petitioning government to address issues like child care, work, and family leave; pay equity; funding for women's health concerns; and rape and domestic violence when these very same issues were also on the agenda at the Seneca Falls Convention? Answers to these questions lie in the controversies of gender equality created by the equality-difference paradox. Although women have been citizens of the United States since its founding, they have never shared equally with men in the rights or obligations of democratic citizenship.[1] Instead, women have struggled for admission to full and equal citizenship even while many argued that their particular brand of citizenship would be distinctively different from that of men.

The paradox of women's equality suggests that two paths toward the same end can coexist. Advocates of both legal equality and fairness have seen politics and the political system as a means to their preferred ends. The result has been a long history of disagreement among women about the surest path to full integration into public life and even about whether full public participation itself is desirable. Because women themselves hold different attitudes and opinions about their appropriate roles, their ability to effectively practice interest-group politics has been greatly diminished. If women could present a united front, their numbers alone would demand considerable respect and attention within the economy and from politicians at all levels of government. In 2004, an unprecedented effort was undertaken to mobilize the twenty-two million single women who did not vote in the 2000 presidential election, in the hopes that a bloc vote might materialize.[2] Unable first to agree on unique sex and gender interests as women, and second to disentangle gender interests from the powerful cross-pressures of race, ethnicity, class, marital status, motherhood, and sexuality, women again found their interests allied with multiple groups and the bloc never materialized. In the 2008 presidential election, unmarried women made up 26 percent of the voting age population, outnumbering Hispanics and African Americans combined. Women's ability to speak with a single voice or act as a unified force on a single agenda is severely limited as a result. Thus women's relationship to politics and, more broadly, the development of women's movements have largely proceeded down two paths toward equality: one group advocating the legal equality doctrine and the other the fairness doctrine.

Feminists and nonfeminists alike find this division frustrating when a unified women's bloc would suit their needs. In 1920, both political parties worked feverishly to attract the female vote, and activists in the suffrage and women's rights movements worked diligently to turn out the women's vote in an effort to place their issues on the national policy agenda. When a coherent women's voice and vote failed to materialize, the parties eventually turned elsewhere, and activists were forced once again into an "outsider" strategy. More recently the media, trying to discover pivotal voting groups in the national electorate, have variously labeled female voters as "soccer moms" in the 1996 elections, "waitress moms" in the 1998 midterm elections, and, most recently, "security moms" in the 2004 election. Obviously, these characterizations do not describe even the barest majority of women in the electorate, but the desire to understand women's political behavior and contribution to the nation by reducing their entire identity to a variation on motherhood is nothing new. Motherhood and women's unique role in nurturing future generations of citizens have exercised a powerful defining (and limiting) influence on women's relationship to politics.[3] In 1914, Congress passed a unanimous resolution establishing Mother's Day. The resolution's language emphasized mothers' contribution to the nation:

> Whereas the service rendered the United States by the American mother is the greatest source of the country's strength and inspiration . . . Whereas the American mother is doing so much for the home, for moral spirits and religion, hence so much for good government and humanity . . . Therefore, be it resolved that the second Sunday in May will be celebrated as Mother's Day.[4]

Women's role in good government in 1914, expressed by Congress in this resolution, was not one of direct action or participation but rather was limited to their functions in the private sphere of the home and in their socially defined roles as mothers and nurturers. While the constitutional right to vote in 1920 gave women a powerful form of direct participation, they were not newcomers to politics even then.

DEFINING WOMEN'S POLITICS

Defining politics beyond the traditional scope of electoral, party, or institutional behavior allows a more complete examination of women's political behavior. Until at least 1920, women had been legally excluded from many

Defining Politics

Politics involves the authoritative allocation of values for a society. (Easton, 1953)

Politics: who gets what, when, and how. (Lasswell, 1936)

The art and science of governance; the means by which the will of the community is arrived at and implemented; the activities of government, politician, or political party. (Shafritz, 1988)

When gender is used as an analytic framework in the study of politics, politics itself needs to be redefined. Consider the following:

- Traditional definitions of politics make conflicts and terrain public, whereas many of the most significant issues and problems facing women are considered private. During the second wave of the women's movement, feminists adopted the slogan "the personal is political" to call attention to the public-private boundary that often excluded certain issues like rape, domestic abuse, and contraception from public policy discussions. The public-private dichotomy may also shape the way we understand and evaluate men's and women's political participation.
- Traditional definitions of politics focus on elite behaviors and attitudes, and dominant institutions. Feminists charge that this focus marginalizes the contributions, attitudes, and actions of multiple communities (people of color, women, the poor, lesbians, and gays). When marginalized groups are included in politics or political analysis, it is often in a way that ignores the challenges created by the many intersections of identity.
- Traditional definitions of politics ignore the power and ubiquitous nature of patriarchy.

Given these concerns, crafting a single definition of politics is challenging, but give it a try. Write down your definition of politics now, and then come back to it as you read more of this text. Is your definition comprehensive enough to include the many and varied forms of women's participation and the issues that most directly have an impact on women's daily lives?

conventional forms of participation. As a result, an *insider's* definition of politics, focusing exclusively on political party activity, voting, campaigning, seeking office, or making direct contact with public officials, does not prove very useful in examining women's activism prior to suffrage or in understanding the complexity of women's politics today. Defining "politics" is in itself a political exercise since any definition necessarily expresses some judgment about which participants, actions, and issues are legitimate. The pervasiveness of the separate spheres ideology and the power of patriarchy limited women's opportunities to engage in politics as it has been traditionally defined. Even though women were seen as *outsiders* prior to suffrage, the range of activities they undertook, the tactics they employed, and the issues they cared about were indeed political.

In pre-revolutionary America, women organized public demonstrations to protest the high cost of food and household goods, and boycotted English tea to protest high taxes. To promote these activities, they formed organizations such as the Daughters of Liberty and the Anti-Tea Leagues. During the Revolutionary and Civil Wars, women participated both on the battlefield and in more traditional tasks consistent with their gender role, such as nursing, cooking, and sewing clothes for soldiers. Although not yet seated in power, women nonetheless lobbied those closest to them for early political recognition. Abigail Adams issued the now famous plea to her husband John Adams to ". . . remember the ladies and be more generous and favorable to them than your ancestors. . . . If particular care and attention is not paid to the ladies, we are determined to foment a rebellion, and will not hold ourselves bound by any laws in which we have no voice or representation."[5] Rejected (or at best ignored) in the constitutional framework, women organized through voluntary associations and social movements. Progressive women's organizations founded in the early twentieth century provided a model for the development of the welfare state in the 1930s, and women were integral in the abolition, temperance, and Progressive movements. When modern political campaigns began, women participated by performing duties "consistent with their temperament" (gender roles), by providing food, acting as hostesses and social organizers, and cleaning up afterward. Observers commented that in performing these duties women exhibited a partisan fervor equal to that of men.[6] Alexis de Tocqueville, noting in his essays that Americans were particularly preoccupied with politics, wrote that "even the women often go to public meetings and forget household cares while they listen to political speeches."[7] Although women were often relegated to support roles, they nonetheless participated in politics and acted politically long before they were awarded the franchise.

DISTINGUISHING SEX FROM GENDER

It is important at this juncture to distinguish between *sex* and *gender*. Sex identity as a male or female is a physically defined biological function of chemical hormones. Males and females differ most obviously in their unique contribution to human reproduction. Females alone can give birth and breast-feed. However, assigning women the job of raising children after birth is a socially defined gender role. Gender incorporates society's interpretation of sex-based characteristics and attaches a culturally constructed value to the differences and unique contributions of each sex. In a patriarchal culture, male characteristics are valued more highly than female qualities, and femininity is marginalized. This has significant implications for the ordering of society, the distribution of rights and power, and in the creation of public policy. Although most contemporary scholars, scientists, politicians, and jurists no longer view biology as the sole determinant of human potential, our culture is not entirely free of the view that sex carries an immutable quality linked to social, political, and economic competence. We now prefer to think of human behavior as a combination of nature (biology) and nurture (environment). The relative weight of biology and environment in producing an outcome is complex and subject to robust debate and research in a variety of disciplines. For our purposes, however, it is sufficient to state that simple sex differences do not create the greatest barriers to women's equality. Rather, it is how society interprets differences and values one quality over another that has the greatest impact on women's lives. Gender rather than sex differences will therefore be the focus of our inquiry in this book.

THE FIRST PATH: THE LEGAL EQUALITY DOCTRINE

For as long as women and men have inhabited organized society, three assumptions have governed their relations: men and women have fundamentally different psychological and sexual natures; men are inherently the dominant or superior sex; and male-female difference and male dominance are both natural.[8] Whether understood as a deity's grand plan or as biology's destiny, the presumption that men and women naturally occupy different spheres has dominated political, economic, and cultural thinking for centuries. Aristotle, writing in *The Politics*, ascribed society's rule and command function to men since "women are naturally subordinate to men" and "the male is naturally fitter to command than the female, except when there is some departure from nature."[9] Late nineteenth and early twentieth century psychiatrists and philosophers argued that education might actually be dangerous to a woman's reproductive system. Social Darwinists argued against women's suffrage, warning that because women are by nature the "nurturant and protective class," female voters might interfere with nature's progression by aiding the state in giving help to those who might otherwise not survive on their own (e.g., the poor, the sick, and the disabled).[10] While these theories may sound ludicrous, at their core lies a belief in a natural inevitability of sex and gender differences that enjoys support even today. This belief in the essential differences between women and men, more than any other perspective, separates women from one another and distinguishes between the two paths to equality. Gender equality accomplished through legal doctrine cannot coexist with gender differences if these differences are grounded in essential human nature. Yet equality of rights for women is exactly what many feminists argue is the most basic human right of all.

Although the concept of equality lies at the very heart of a liberal democracy, even politics and constitutions cannot make men and women equal when people believe they are essentially and immutably different. How else could the U.S. founders so eloquently write "We hold these truths to be self-evident: That all men are created equal; that they are endowed by their Creator with certain unalienable rights . . ." in the Declaration of Independence while they ignored the interests of women and slaves? The answer lies in the presumption that a patriarchal society is natural and therefore unalterable through social, economic, or political means. Thus a gendered system—one in which gender is inextricably linked to power, prestige, and fundamental rights—has been a force in American politics since the nation's founding. It is embedded in the very documents that define our institutions and governing practices, if not in the precise language then in the founders' assumptions about human nature. The path toward gender equality pursued by advocates of the legal equality doctrine proposes to alter the assumption of natural differences between men and women by changing the laws that govern human behavior. The presumption is that once behavior is altered, a change in attitude is sure to follow.

Roots of Women's Claims to Legal Equality

Those who argued for women's political equality in the late eighteenth century most often based their claims on the liberal challenge to aristocratic rule and the Enlightenment's legacy of reason and human improvement. Liberalism (or individualism) stresses the importance of rational thought, autonomous action, and choice on the part of each individual. An individual's status is therefore determined by that person's actions rather than by his or her station at birth. Gradually, individualism gained influence to the point that restrictions on the voting rights of free males imposed by property requirements fell by the wayside with the election of Andrew Jackson in 1828. As individuals, free from the barriers to political agency imposed by the requirements of inherited wealth or title, native-born, middle-class white men were able to exercise greater economic and political power. With this emphasis on individualism, education gained a prominent focus. Human beings were not purely subject to the whims of nature, liberals presumed, but open to developing their character through education and training. Individuals on equal footing would enter a social contract with one another to form a society of citizens. Unfortunately for women, early liberal theorists (such as Thomas Hobbes, John Locke, and Jean-Jacques Rousseau) excluded women from full citizenship. Hobbes and Locke were willing to grant women a somewhat ambiguous state of equality in nature, but not in politics. Rousseau assumed from the start that women lacked the natural capacities for full citizenship. All three liberal theorists believed that natural and biological differences between men and women precluded women's full participation in a social contract.[11] In this sense, contemporary political theorist Carole Pateman argues that a *sexual contract* predated a *social contract*.[12] A sexual contract required women to transfer their natural rights to men in exchange for protection, thereby leaving women without any independent rights to exchange with others in forming a social contract. Within this patriarchal arrangement, women could never be men's political equals.

Mary Wollstonecraft, philosopher and author of *A Vindication of the Rights of Men* and *A Vindication of the Rights of Woman*, denied any fundamental difference in character or nature between men and women. She argued that any weaknesses exhibited by women resulted from their faulty education and isolated social position. Wollstonecraft argued that women would gladly trade their lofty, yet isolated, social position in return for their rights. Decades later, another liberal theorist, John Stuart Mill, published *The Subjection of Women* (1869). He too argued that a woman's "disability" in public life did not stem from her sex alone, but rather from her subjugation in marriage:

> [T]he principle which regulates the existing social relations between the two sexes—the legal subordination of one sex to the other—is wrong in itself, and now one of the chief hindrances to human improvement; and that it ought to be replaced by a principle of perfect equality, admitting no power or privilege on the one side, nor disability on the other.[13]

Mill unfavorably compared women's fate in marriage to the institution of slavery (universally discredited among liberals). While slaves were coerced into service, Mill wrote that every aspect of society leads women to willingly enter a state of subjugation and that men's dominion over all and the intimacy men and women share make it impossible for women to cast off their bonds. Suggesting that at one time both slavery and monarchy seemed natural in America, Mill wrote: "So true it is that unnatural generally means only uncustomary, and that everything which is usual appears natural. The subjection of women to men being a universal custom, any departure from it quite naturally appears unnatural."[14] Mill did not propose any solutions to the problem of women's subjection in marriage, but like Wollstonecraft, he believed that the vote could emancipate women's minds and admit them to the public dialogue. As a member of the British parliament, he introduced and supported women's suffrage.

Patriarchy and Limits to Legal Equality

Patriarchal systems are ancient in origin and ubiquitous. Mill captured the pervasiveness of patriarchy's reach in this passage from *The Subjection of Women*:

> Whatever gratification or pride there is in the possession of power, and whatever personal interest in its exercise, is in this case not confined to a limited class, but common to the whole male sex. Instead of being, to most of its supporters, a thing desirable chiefly in the abstract, or, like the political ends usually contended for by factions, of little private importance to any but the leaders; it comes home to the person and hearth of every male head of a family, and every one who looks forward to being so. The clodhopper exercises, or is to exercise, his share of the power equally with the highest nobleman.[15]

Mill rightly recognized that all men were empowered by patriarchy, regardless of their individual ability to exercise their power and privilege wisely. Likewise, all women were disempowered by patriarchy, regardless of their innate abilities for leadership and for the wise exercise of power. Patriarchy assumed that all women, by nature, were incapable of equality and therefore limited women's claims to the natural and political rights flowing from individualism as described by liberal theorists.

Contemporary feminist scholar Adrienne Rich describes the patriarchal tradition's limits on women's opportunities this way:

> Patriarchy . . . does not necessarily imply that no woman has power, or that all women in a given culture may not have certain powers. . . . Under patriarchy, I may live in *purdah* or drive a truck; . . . I may become a hereditary or elected head of state or wash the underwear of a millionaire's wife; I may serve my husband his early-morning coffee within the clay walls of a Berber village or march in an academic procession; whatever my status or situation, my derived economic class, or my sexual preference, I live under the power of the fathers, and I have access only to so much of privilege or influence as the patriarchy is willing to accede to me, and only for so long as I will pay the price for male approval.[16]

Patriarchy, as Rich describes it, leaves room for women to exercise considerable discretion and choice but only within the patriarchal framework in which men control power, resources, and access to both. In other words, even when women believe they are making independent choices and aspiring to and achieving great professional success, they do so within the realm of choices that males allow. So what sorts of choices really exist for women within a patriarchal world? Patriarchy in this context poses serious problems for those who believe gender equality can best be accomplished by the legal equality doctrine. Can truly gender-neutral laws and policies exist when patriarchy is so pervasive?

Posing a slightly different but equally serious challenge for advocates of the legal equality doctrine, sociologist Sandra Bem contrasts patriarchy with the concept of *androcentrism*. Androcentrism is the practice of overvaluing the male experience and undervaluing the female experience. In an androcentric world, "males and the male experience are treated as a neutral standard or norm for the culture or the species as a whole, and females and female experience are treated as a sex-specific deviation from that allegedly universal standard."[17] Thus, feminists who aspire to equality as defined by the legal equality doctrine are faced with the fundamental dilemma: equality measured by whose standard? Can a standard be established apart from the dominance of the male experience? In a patriarchal system, the standard would appear to be whatever constitutes the male norm. Is the male norm an appropriate aspiration for women? Is it the appropriate standard for equality? Do we recognize the gendered character of standards of equality? More specifically, can laws based on the male experience adequately cover circumstances in the female experience? For many, particularly those who advocate the fairness doctrine, the answer is a resounding "no." The male standard can improve women's situation only when women and men are similarly situated. In cases where men and women are differently situated, either because of biology or social norms, the male standard may actually mean additional burdens for women. Thus, while the legal equality doctrine as a path to gender equality has a solid basis in liberal democratic theory, making it an appropriate solution to the problems women face in gaining access to the public sphere, it is not without its theoretical or practical problems. The fairness doctrine addresses some of the problems inherent in the legal equality path but presents a different set of unique challenges for men and women seeking gender equality.

THE SECOND PATH: THE FAIRNESS DOCTRINE

Colonial life in pre-revolutionary America was largely agrarian and home-based. Women worked alongside men, and gender distinctions did not limit women's contribution or workday. However, as the means of production moved from the land to the factory and society was reorganized accordingly, specialization divided human laborers. At the time of the American Revolution, very few women were educated, and literacy rates among women were half those of men.[18] As society's child bearers, women were assigned to the private sphere of home and hearth. Although women had been integral to the maintenance and survival of the agrarian economy, the duties of the home were now defined as distinct from the productive economy and paid labor force outside the home. Opportunities for women to earn money or to control property were severely limited by law and practice. Women constituted the reproductive unpaid labor force and men the productive paid labor force. In this sense, they complemented each other and were said to occupy *separate spheres*.[19]

Separate Spheres Ideology

Women's role in the private sphere was, by definition, incompatible with full participation in society. Separate spheres ideology, although not originally defined by law, clearly identified the activities available for women as consistent with their primary role as child bearers and nurturers. White women's role within the home was raised to new heights of glorification for middle- and upper-class women. The home was her exclusive domain, giving her a certain degree of autonomy. For working-class and lower-class women and for women of color, the separate sphere limited their access to the productive labor pool and depressed the wages paid for their work. Opportunities for work outside the home closely paralleled women's duties within the home. Immigrant women in the 1840s and 1850s, for example, worked in sex-segregated industries like textile, clothing, and shoe manufacturing. Teaching, sewing, and later nursing were also seen as consistent with women's domestic responsibilities, although the pay was almost negligible. Unpaid charitable and welfare activities, particularly those directed at women and children, were encouraged for all white women as appropriate extensions of the private sphere. Slave women in the South were at the bottom of the hierarchy in every respect. They were subject entirely to the white male patriarchal ruling class, and as such, African American women did not enjoy any of the privileges of autonomy that accompanied the separate station enjoyed by white women in the middle and upper classes.

Although separate spheres ideology was ultimately quite constraining for all women, it did provide limited opportunities for middle- and upper-class women to gain experience in forming welfare associations. It afforded them growing access to education and made it possible for women to interact with other women in quasi-public settings. These interactions enabled women to view their condition in a critical light and eventually to organize for a greater role as women and to advocate for more rights in the public sphere. In this sense, the separate sphere was empowering for white middle-class women. However, because power in a capitalist economy flows from those who control valued resources (namely money or goods), men continued to exercise decision-making power both within and outside the home. As separate spheres ideology found its way into court decisions and into the public's understanding of normal daily life, men used the ideology to solidify their control over women's lives and livelihoods.

Separate and Unequal Becomes the Law

Separate spheres ideology was reinforced and given the weight of law through the case of *Bradwell v. Illinois*, decided in 1873. Myra Bradwell, a feminist active in women's suffrage organizations, passed the Illinois bar exam in 1869, but the Supreme Court of Illinois refused to let her practice law. Under Illinois law, females were not permitted to practice law. Bradwell appealed to the U.S. Supreme Court, claiming that the state of Illinois had violated her rights under the Fourteenth Amendment in denying her one of the "privileges of citizenship" (the privilege of practicing law). The U.S. Supreme Court denied her claims and reaffirmed Illinois's power to determine the distinct privileges for men and women under state law. In a concurring opinion, Supreme Court Justice Joseph P. Bradley specifically noted the separate spheres ideology as justification for limiting women's role in the public sphere:

> Civil law, as well as nature herself, has always recognized a wide difference in the respective spheres and destinies of man and woman. Man is, or should be, woman's protector and defender. The natural and proper timidity and delicacy which belongs to the female sex evidently unfits it for many of the occupations of civil life. The constitution of the family organization, which is founded in the Divine ordinance, as well as in the nature of things, indicates the domestic sphere as that which properly belongs to the domain and functions of womanhood. The harmony, not to say identity, of interests and views which belong, or should belong, to the family institution is repugnant to the idea of a woman adopting a distinct and independent career from that of her husband. So firmly fixed was this sentiment in the founders of common law that it became a maxim of that system of jurisprudence that a woman had no legal existence apart from her husband, who was regarded as her head and representative in the social state. (83 U.S. 130, 21 L.Ed. 442)

Note that Justice Bradley relied on a series of assumptions in denying Bradwell's Fourteenth Amendment claim that she was entitled to practice law because she passed the Illinois bar. First, he clearly delineated separate spheres and destinies for men and women, grounded not only in civil and common law, but in nature. Second, Justice Bradley said that the patriarchal family was not only natural but founded in "the Divine ordinance." Finally, he stated that the "law of the Creator" relegated women to the "offices of wife and mother." In other words, what is natural, ordained by the Creator, and made real through civil practice, the U.S. Supreme Court cannot change. Furthermore, all women were captives of nature, the Creator, and common law, since the Court refused to address the privileges and immunities of adult women apart from their marital status:

> It is true that many women are unmarried and not affected by any of the duties, complications, and incapacities arising out of the married state, but these are exceptions to the general rule. The paramount destiny and mission of woman are to fulfil the noble and benign offices of wife and mother. This is the law of the Creator. And the rules of civil society must be adapted to the general constitution of things, and cannot be based upon exceptional cases. (83 U.S. 130, 21 L.Ed. 442)

Like Aristotle in an earlier time, the U.S. Supreme Court treated all women as a group and ruled that even though there may be women whose exceptional abilities fit them for public life, society must be governed by the assumption that a woman's proper role is that of wife and mother. As such, women are dependent on men and cannot be treated as individuals in their own right. Although some women may have abilities that (but for their sex) would entitle them to practice law, society cannot be governed by such exceptions.

Later Court rulings would use the separate spheres ideology as a justification to protect women in the labor force and to accommodate their "special burden" by limiting their civic obligations (e.g., the vote, jury duty, military service). The Court rejected separate spheres ideology only during the last two decades of the twentieth century and then only piecemeal, not entirely. Although most would argue that both sex and race are immutable characteristics not subject to an individual's control, the Supreme Court still assumes that sex bears some relation to one's abilities; it does not, however, make similar assumptions about race. These distinctions and assumptions, embedded in the philosophy of law in the United States, will arise again in later chapters examining education, work, and family issues.

The Basis of Restricted Citizenship for Married Women

Bradwell's status as a *femme covert* (which "covered" women entirely by their husbands' legal identity) also contributed to her being denied the ability to practice law. Coverture, imported to the colonies from the English legal tradition, defined the legal relationship between husband and wife and thus complicated women's claims to equality and their challenges to the constraints of separate spheres ideology. English jurist William Blackstone wrote:

> By marriage, the husband and wife are one person in law: that is, the very being or legal existence of the woman is suspended during the marriage, or at least is incorporated and consolidated into that of the husband; under whose wing, protection and *cover,* she performs every thing. . . . [She] is said to be covert-baron, or under the protection and influence of her husband, her baron, or lord; and her condition upon marriage is called her *coverture.*[20]

As a practical matter, coverture made the husband and wife one person—the husband. A married woman could not execute contracts independently of her husband, nor could she buy or sell property, dispose of personal assets like jewelry and household items, control the destiny of her children, or serve as their guardian apart from her husband's consent. Marital rape was inconceivable because husband and wife were one person. It was not until 1978, when New York included a spouse along with a stranger and an acquaintance in the list of perpetrators of rape, that marital rape was outlawed anywhere in the United States.

In 1805, the U.S. Supreme Court articulated the nation's implicit understanding of a married woman's obligations to the state and her status as a citizen apart from her husband in the case of *Martin v. Massachusetts.* Anna Gordon Martin received approximately 844 acres of land from her father upon his death. As was the custom, her husband, William Martin, controlled the land until his death. The "right of remainder" entitled the land to Anna's heir (her son James) on her husband's death. However, the Massachusetts Confiscation Act of 1779 allowed the state to confiscate properties of individuals who fled with the British during the war, which was considered an act of treason.[21] Anna fled the state with her husband, William. James petitioned for the return of properties confiscated toward the close of the American Revolution, arguing that married women (his mother in this case) were inhabitants, not members, of the state, thereby making the property seizure illegal.

> Upon the strict principles of law, a *femme covert* is not a member; has no *political* relation to the *state* any more than an alien. . . . The legislature intended to exclude femmes-covert and infants from the operation of the act; otherwise the word inhabitant would have been used alone, and not coupled with the word member.[22]

As inhabitants of the state (citizens), all women were subject to its laws, and single women were subject to taxation. The question before the Supreme Court was whether a married woman could have a relationship with the state distinct from that of her husband. There was no question that if William Martin held property, the statute would apply and the state of Massachusetts would have lawfully seized the property. But because Anna Martin owned the property and also met the conditions of the Massachusetts Confiscation Act of 1779, did the state have a right to the property? Attorneys for the Martins argued that Anna, as a femme covert, was incapable of defying her husband by remaining in Massachusetts while he fled. They further argued that the state did not expect married women to act independently and could expect no assistance from them in defending the country: "So far are women from being of service in the defence [sic] of a country against the attacks of an enemy that it is frequently thought expedient to send them out of the way, lest they impede the operations of their own party."[23]

Attorneys for the state crafted their argument based on the principles of natural law, reasoning that a precondition of citizenship was autonomous competence, and because women were considered citizens, they should also be responsible for their own actions even when their actions defied the theory of coverture marriage. They argued that "if patriarchy in politics is rejected, so too must patriarchy in marriage."[24] Despite this line of reasoning, the Court ruled unanimously in favor of the Martins, deciding in effect to abandon patriarchy in politics but maintain patriarchy in the family and in marital relationships. Although women might be citizens in a conceptual sense, marriage took away the privileges of citizenship in a real sense.

This line of reasoning was not merely a post-revolutionary mindset clouded by a tradition of coverture. In 1907, Congress passed a law stating that women who married aliens lost their citizenship even if they remained in the United States. The Supreme Court upheld the law as late as 1915, ruling in *Mackenzie v. Hare* that if a woman voluntarily married an alien, she must give up her citizenship and adopt the nationality of her husband. This law remained in effect until passage of the Cable Act of 1922, which stated, "the right of a person to become a naturalized citizen shall not be denied to a person on account of sex or because she is a married woman." Even then, however, the law covered only marriages to men who were eligible to become naturalized citizens (excluding men from China or Japan, among others). American-born women who married aliens were treated as naturalized citizens, who could lose their citizenship if they lived abroad for two or more years.[25] Thus, well into the twentieth century, a woman's marital status governed her relationship to the state, in terms of both rights and obligations.

This gendered construction of citizenship for women differed from male citizenship in important ways. The same line of reasoning that denied married women property, guardianship of their children, and independent thought and action found its way into debates over suffrage and subsequent Supreme Court rulings that rendered married women both sentimental and legal dependents of their husbands. The American Revolution challenged and abolished political patriarchy, yet even at the height of revolutionary spirit, familial patriarchy was continually reinforced through law, custom, and economic realities. Women remained in the same class as slaves and children when it came to extending the political rights of citizenship. Any attempt to challenge the natural order that kept women entirely in the private sphere was quashed.

Thus the separate spheres ideology, in which women occupy a natural position in the private sphere that is incompatible with public sphere responsibilities, presents the most serious challenge to those who advocate the fairness doctrine as the most appropriate path to gender equality. The logic that recognizes essential differences between men and women that suit them for different roles in society cannot be overcome by law alone. Advocates of the fairness doctrine argue that trying to make men and women alike when they are in fact different is an unproductive approach to improving women's lives. Instead, they urge that women be treated fairly. However, the pervasiveness of a separate spheres ideology makes it difficult to argue that women should participate fully in the public sphere, while believing that women need protection from and accommodation for the burdens of their sex that they bring to the public sphere. Like the legal equality doctrine discussed earlier, the fairness doctrine of gender equality is not without its theoretical and practical problems.

FEMINISM'S DIRECT CHALLENGE TO GENDER RELATIONS

Challenging long-entrenched gender roles and relationships is difficult even for the most committed individuals or groups. Gender exerts a powerful grip on each individual and on the social, political, and economic systems in which we live, study, and work. Without some sensitivity to the power of gendered life, it is easy to miss since gendered life seems so normal. Understanding the world in this way can consequently obscure the workings of an organizing system. The result is a system in which economic, political, social, and cultural forces interact with and reinforce one another in ways that continue to benefit one group and disadvantage the others. As participants in these interlocking systems, humans constantly reproduce the world we know through socialization, education, and role modeling as if we have no other choice. The effect is that the system continues as *normal*, becoming increasingly difficult to challenge as we each take our place within it. Those who suggest the system is corrupt or wrong threaten to upset centuries of tradition and custom that make life predictable and comfortable for the majority.

Feminism provides the most direct challenge to the gendered world, as well as to patriarchy, capitalism, and the sexist assumptions that women's difference from men renders them inherently inferior. Feminism is a complex and somewhat paradoxical ideology that defies a single definition. In fact, feminists are rarely in agreement with one another over the ultimate aims of feminism or the means to achieve them. Although many feminists exhibit a commitment to absolute legal and practical equality, some feminists have argued for separate spheres of influence and an emphasis on difference and complementarity rather than equality.[26] In an oft-quoted passage, Rebecca West wrote in 1913, "I myself have never been able to find out precisely what feminism is. I only know that people call me a feminist whenever I express sentiments that differentiate me from a doormat or a prostitute."[27] The lack of a single, well-articulated definition can lead to confusion, but the rich variety of perspectives accurately reflects the paradox of gender. Feminists of all descriptions wrestle with the same question: How can demands for equality and fairness be reconciled with sex differences?

As a word and concept, feminism is a relatively recent addition to the lexicon, emerging only in the 1910s to express a broader set of goals than the suffrage movement embraced.[28] According to historian Nancy Cott, people in the nineteenth century talked about the "advancement of woman," the cause of woman, or woman's rights and woman suffrage. To our modern ears, the use of the singular "woman" sounds awkward—both grammatically and conceptually. "Nineteenth-century women's consistent usage of the singular *woman* symbolized, in a word, the unity of the female sex. It proposed that all women have one cause, one movement."[29] Now in the twenty-first century, individualism is valued so highly that it would be rare to encounter anyone who believed that all women share a single cause. Modern feminism reflects these sentiments and in doing so, embraces the paradox of gender equality that provides the foundation for the two paths to equality:

> Feminism asks for sexual equality that includes sexual difference. It posits that women recognize their unity while it stands for diversity among women. It requires gender consciousness for its basis yet calls for the elimination of prescribed gender roles. These are paradoxes rooted in the actual situation of women, who are the same as men in a species sense, but different from men in reproductive biology and the construction of gender. Men and women are alike as human beings, and yet categorically different from each other; their sameness and differences derive from nature *and* culture, how inextricably entwined we can hardly know.[30]

So, given this set of paradoxes, how might feminism be defined? Cott offers a very good three-part working definition of feminism:

- a belief in equality, defined not as "sameness" but rather as opposition to ranking one sex superior or inferior to the other, or opposition to one sex's categorical control of the rights and opportunities of the other
- a belief that women's condition is socially constructed and historically shaped, rather than preordained by God or nature
- a belief that women's socially constructed position situates them on shared ground enabling a group identity or gender consciousness sufficient to mobilize women for change[31]

APPROACHES TO FEMINISM

As an ideology, feminism has spawned a number of different "brands," among them liberal feminism, radical feminism, Marxist-socialist feminism, global feminism, black feminism, ecofeminism, gender feminism, and third wave feminism. Scholars differ on how to label and divide the complex terrain of feminist theory, but the preceding list is fairly representative of the major strands of feminist thought today. Philosopher Rosemarie Tong distinguishes among these theories based on the locus of women's oppression in each. For example, liberal, radical, Marxist-socialist, and global feminists (as well as ecofeminists to some extent) attribute women's subordination to macrolevel institutions, such as patriarchy, capitalism, or colonialism. Gender feminists, sometimes also called cultural feminists or maternal feminists, focus on the microcosm of the individual, claiming the roots of women's oppression are embedded deep within a woman's psyche.[32] Third wave feminism developed in the early 1990s among young feminists interested in reclaiming the power of feminism and extending its reach and deepening its impact for women described as the daughters and granddaughters of second wave feminists. A brief critical review of each approach to feminism follows.[33] Distinguishing between the strands of feminism and understanding the variety of feminist perspectives can sometimes seem overwhelming, but to simplify our discussion by examining only one or two feminist perspectives would perilously ignore the diversity among women themselves. Part of understanding why women do not always agree on the best way to advance their individual and collective status in society is grounded in the differing perspectives on what feminism means and how it should operate as an organizing philosophy for the women's movement. This section concludes by exploring the claim that feminism is dead—replaced by a postfeminist reality in the twenty-first century.

Liberal Feminism

Liberal feminism is perhaps the oldest strand of feminism, rooted in the same ferment that promoted individual autonomy over aristocratic privilege in the French Revolution and the U.S. Revolutionary War. Liberalism stresses the importance of rational thought, autonomous action, and choice on the part of each person. Reason is what most clearly distinguishes humans from other forms of animal life. Individual autonomy empowers an individual to make choices in her or his own best interests, thereby elevating individual rights above the common good. Liberal theorists believe that the political and legal systems can be used to promote a liberal agenda for all people. Applied to feminism, early liberal feminists like Mary Wollstonecraft, John Stuart Mill, and Harriet Taylor Mill stressed the importance of educating women, enfranchising women, and providing women equal access to both opportunities and resources in society. Liberal feminists tend to work *within* the existing political system and structures to eradicate all forms of sexual discrimination. Contemporary liberal feminists believe that by reforming the legal and political system to allow women equal access to opportunities and resources, men and women can achieve a state of equality. Liberal feminists target laws that distinguish between men and women based on sex. The Declaration of Sentiments and Resolutions, issued by women at the Seneca Falls Convention in 1848, was a liberal feminist document. It called for the reform of laws restricting women's right to hold property, to control resources, and to vote. The U.S. suffrage movement and suffrage organizations, such as the National American Woman Suffrage Association (NAWSA), extended across three generations women's liberal feminist claims that suffrage was an integral step in achieving political and social equality. The Equal Rights Amendment (ERA) in the United States and the United Nations Convention on the Elimination of All Forms of Discrimination Against Women (CEDAW) are examples of contemporary legal reforms in this tradition.

During the early 1960s, President John F. Kennedy responded to feminists' concerns about equality for women by forming the Commission on the Status

Oppression or Discrimination? Revolution or Reform?

Whether you describe yourself as a radical feminist dedicated to revolutionary change or a liberal feminist dedicated to legal reforms in pursuit of equality most likely depends on whether you see sexism as a form of oppression or discrimination.

Viewing sexism as a form of oppression emphasizes change affecting women collectively—a level of change only possible through a radical reordering of patriarchal society. Women's oppression refers to patriarchy's grip on all women, regardless of class, race, or sexual orientation. As Marilyn Frye notes, "One of the most characteristic and ubiquitous features of the world as experienced by oppressed people is the double bind—situations in which options are reduced to a very few and all of them expose one to penalty, censure or deprivation."[1] Ending oppression requires ending patriarchy, capitalism, and Western dominance. Viewing sexism as a form of discrimination emphasizes the individual. Discrimination refers to "the act of singling out a person for special treatment, not on the basis of individual merit, but on the basis of prejudices about the group to which the person belongs."[2] Ending discrimination against women in employment or education, for example, requires that laws and practices be changed so that women have the same opportunities as men within these institutions.

Feminist scholar bell hooks illustrates the distinction:

> While the contemporary feminist movement has successfully stimulated an awareness of the impact of sexual discrimination on the social status of women in the U.S., it has done little to eliminate sexist oppression. Teaching women how to defend themselves against male rapists is not the same as working to change society so that men will not rape. Establishing houses for battered women does not change the psyches of the men who batter them, nor does it change the culture that promotes and condones their brutality. . . . Demanding an end to institutionalized sexism does not insure an end to sexist oppression.[3]

1. Marilyn Frye, "Oppression," in *The Politics of Reality: Essays in Feminist Theory* (NSW Australia: Crossing Press, 1983).
2. Virginia Sapiro, *Women in American Society,* 4th ed. (Mountain View, Calif.: Mayfield Publishing, 1999), p. 109.
3. bell hooks, *Ain't I a Woman: Black Women and Feminism* (Boston: South End Press, 1981).

of Women. The commission studied various forms of discrimination against women, collected and made public new data on the condition of women, and spawned a number of state-based commissions that had similar missions. As a result of the data presented, the Equal Pay Act was passed in 1963; it promised equal pay for equal work, regardless of sex. Political action groups—the National Organization for Women (NOW), the National Women's Political Caucus (NWPC), and the Women's Equity Action League (WEAL), for example—were formed in the late 1960s to pursue the liberal feminist agenda. This agenda was based largely on a plan to demand enforcement of civil rights laws protecting women from discrimination. NOW and NWPC are still in existence today.

A variety of criticisms have been leveled against liberal feminism. Early and contemporary liberal feminists alike concentrate almost exclusively on the public sphere. Women's unpaid labor in the home, domestic abuse, marital rape, and traditional practices that discriminate against women in many cultures are not addressed within the liberal approach because they occur in the private sphere. These issues are labeled *personal* and therefore are not subject to public scrutiny or redress in the public policy arena. Radical feminists charge that liberal feminism has been co-opted by the male establishment since its goals are to reform the existing system rather than to replace it, as radical feminists demand. Global feminists equate liberal feminists' embrace of individualism with Western values that do not fit well in other cultures where community values are favored over the individual. Additionally, individualism makes sex solidarity and the development of a movement difficult, as liberal feminists have discovered repeatedly throughout history.

Politically conservative critics charge that liberal feminists, with their concentration on ending legal sex discrimination in society, are out of touch with mainstream women who still value marriage, motherhood, and family—all traditionally private sphere concerns. Finally, liberal feminism has been labeled racist, classist, and heterosexist. This last charge suggests that liberal feminism speaks only to concerns of white, middle- and upper-class, heterosexual women. The history of the women's movement to date has offered ample evidence that the concerns of women of color, the working poor, and lesbians have been on the periphery of the agenda.

Radical Feminism

Radical feminism is difficult to define because of the many subgroups within the larger approach. However, there are some common distinguishing features. Unlike liberal feminists who believe that it is possible to produce systemic reforms that would yield women more rights (ultimately leading to equality of rights), radical feminists believe it is the "sex-gender system" itself that is the source of women's oppression.[34] Radical feminists are interested in women's liberation from the bounds of this system and therefore have advocated a total revolution. For this reason, scholars often classify women's organizations as either "reform-minded" or "revolutionary" and link them to liberal or radical feminist theory accordingly.[35] Radical feminist theory spawned a variety of activist groups in the 1960s. Many, although not all, were associated with the political left. Such radical organizations as the Redstockings, Women's International Terrorist Conspiracy from Hell (WITCH), the Feminists, and the New York Radical Feminists were among some of the largest groups formed.

Sexism, as the first form of human oppression, must take precedence over other forms of oppression and must be eradicated first. Beyond agreement on this basic issue, radical feminists differ on the best way to eliminate sexism. Radical-libertarian feminists believe that femininity, women's sex, and reproductive roles limit women's development. They often promote androgyny (eliminating masculine-feminine distinctions) as a way to overcome the limits of femininity and to break the socially constructed link between sex and gender. Radical-cultural feminists, on the other hand, believe that female-feminine qualities are vastly superior to male-masculine characteristics. Women should not try to be like men, but rather they should try to be like women. By this they mean a return to women's essential nature. Therefore, culturally associated feminine traits—interdependence, community, sharing, emotion, nature, peace, and life—should be celebrated over hierarchy, power, war, domination, and death. Androgyny simply clouds the female nature with undesirable male qualities. For these reasons, radical-cultural feminists are often associated with lesbian separatism.

Critics of radical feminism often target the stark choices women have been asked to make. Issues of separatism, lesbianism, and the promotion of reproductive technology over traditional means of conception and biological motherhood draw fire from politically conservative critics who charge that radical feminists are out to eradicate the family. Others criticize radical-cultural feminists' belief in the essential nature of women, charging that it unnecessarily polarizes men and women.

Marxist-Socialist Feminism

In contrast to liberal theory's emphasis on the individual, Marxist-socialist theory stresses the collective aspect of human development. Men and women, through production and reproduction, have collectively created society that in turn shapes them. Capitalism and patriarchy work hand in hand, although Marxist-socialists believe that capitalism, more than sexism, is at the root of women's oppression. Women's economic dependence on men gives them little leverage in other aspects of society. However, rather than singling out women as the oppressed class, Marxist-socialist theories focus on the worker. A woman's situation then can only be understood in terms of her productive work and its relationship to her life. In a capitalist system, women are exploited both in the marketplace (lowest-paying and most menial jobs) and at home (no wages for her domestic labor). Marxist-socialist feminists advocate public policy that aims to redistribute wealth and opportunity. For example, some have argued that women be paid a wage for their housework; others have concentrated their actions on issues of the workplace outside the home and the disparities in pay and position between men and women. The concept of "equal pay for equal work" does not cover women working in traditional occupations that are undervalued. Advocates of equal pay for jobs of comparable worth argue that wage inequities will persist as long as jobs are segregated on the basis of gender.

Critics of Marxist-socialist feminism most often point to the sizable gap between the ideal and the reality in contemporary Marxist-socialist regimes (those remaining and those recently dissolved). Women have filled the majority of low-status and low-paying occupations and, contrary to theory, are still taking primary responsibility for home and child care.

Global Feminism

The forces of colonialism and nationalism have conspired to divide the world into the *haves*, known as the First World, and the *have nots*, known as the Third World. Global feminists seek to expand feminist thought to include issues vital to women in the Third World. They argue that economic and political forms of oppression are every bit as severe as sexual oppression. "For global feminists, the personal and political are one."[36] The ways in which various forms of oppression interconnect and affect women has been the focus of many global feminists. Some charge that First World women are blinded by sexual oppression. As a result, they overlook their own complicity in the oppression of women that multinational corporations and exploitative labor practices cause. Others suggest that color, class, and nationality cannot be separated from sex when addressing the forms of oppression people face. Western feminists, they argue, have been too narrow in their agendas, particularly liberal feminists who were guided by legal reforms in the public sphere. Political participation is a hollow victory for those who cannot feed their families, earn a living wage, control their reproduction, and live free of violence.

Cultural practices that Western feminists and others deem exploitative or damaging to women have presented the most vexing problems for global feminists. Dowry, bride price, female circumcision, and many religious customs are examples of practices that, when taken out of a cultural context, are indefensible in any feminist theory. However, the importance and power of culture, tradition, and religion make passing judgment on these and other issues problematic. Differences among women of various cultures present many challenges to global feminists who attempt to create a feminist theory and set of practices that unite rather than divide women.

Black Feminism

Most feminist anthologies use the term "multicultural feminism" to encompass the diversity of feminist thought among diverse populations. African American feminists in the United States, however, have been among the most vocal critics of the mainstream liberal feminist tradition, and so black feminism is included here as a unique category of feminist thought.

One of the thorniest questions arising in black feminist thought, according to Patricia Hill Collins, is who can be a black feminist.[37] Does authentic voice flow from one's race, one's experiences with the dual oppressions of race and gender, or one's ideas and ideologies regardless of race and gender? The core of the black feminist tradition encompasses several themes: the legacy of struggle, the experience born of multiple oppressions, and the interdependence of thought and action. Black feminists often express frustration that white women seem incapable of understanding the "multiple jeopardy" that black women face on a daily basis. Sexism cannot be separated from racism or classism or any of the other "isms" women must deal with. To pursue a single-minded gender equality strategy is to ignore profound forms of oppression and to exclude women of color from the women's movement. Black women have experienced discrimination in the women's movement (discussed in greater detail in the next chapter) and continue to press feminists to expand the definition of feminism. Alice Walker has offered the term *womanist* as an alternative to feminist, saying "womanist is to feminist as purple is to lavender."[38] A womanist is at heart a humanist pursuing political action as a means to human empowerment—including both men and women of all races, ethnicities, and abilities.

Critics of black feminism are most often African American women themselves. Some critics argue that black feminists have failed to confront sexism strongly enough as it occurs within the black community. Some black women have been reticent to press for stronger laws protecting women's interests, believing that black males are under siege by the dominant white community and would be disproportionately harmed in the process. In 1991, when lawyer Anita Hill charged Clarence Thomas, her former boss at the Equal Employment Opportunity Commission (EEOC), with sexual harassment, the nation was introduced to the divisions within the African American community and among black feminists. Hill's charges became public during Clarence Thomas's Supreme Court confirmation hearings before the Senate Judiciary Committee. Criticism of Hill and her decision to make her charges public came from a variety of quarters, but it was especially strong among blacks. They considered her "disloyal" and criticized her for potentially derailing a black man's chances for a seat on the Supreme Court. Public opinion polls revealed support for Hill among feminists, although 49 percent of American women (black and white) either sided with Thomas or declared the dispute a "draw."[39] Further probing by pollsters found that Hill's Yale law degree and successful law career made her identity as a "black woman" problematic because it did not fit the stereotype many held. This revelation again raised questions about who represents or speaks for black feminists.

Ecofeminism

The term "ecofeminism" was coined by French feminist Françoise d'Eaubonne in 1974. Ecofeminism is a variant of ecological ethics and an emerging branch of feminism that most resembles global feminism in its emphasis on "connectedness." In this case, however, feminists are interested in the connections between all living things—human and nature. "There are important connections between the domination of women and the domination of nature, an understanding of which is crucial to feminism, environmentalism, and environmental philosophy."[40] Ecofeminists charge that patriarchy's hierarchical framework not only damages women but harms nature as well. "Because women have been 'naturalized' and nature has been 'feminized' it is difficult to know where the oppression of one ends and the other begins."[41] Therefore, the liberation of one cannot be effected apart from the liberation of the other. A main goal of ecofeminists is to make visible the "woman-nature" connections and, where they are harmful to women or nature, to dismantle them. Ecofeminists disagree over how closely women should be associated with nature, but all agree that ending women's and nature's oppression should be a joint endeavor. In this sense, the environment is a feminist issue.

Critics of ecofeminism warn that equating women with nature harkens back to essentialist arguments of other feminists. Others charge that feminists should invest their energy in understanding other women and in bridging the divide between nations and cultures before addressing nature.

Gender Feminism

Gender feminism, unlike any of the theories previously described, argues that the root of women's oppression lies somewhere at the intersection of biology, psychology, and culture. Gender feminists believe that the traits culture associates with women and femininity are superior in many respects to masculine traits, and therefore both men and women should strive to develop relational webs. The issues most closely associated with gender feminism include the superiority of women's moral development, women's ways of knowing and thinking, and women's mothering abilities. Because gender feminists argue that men and women are developmentally different, they are sometimes also known as *difference feminists*. However, difference in this case works in favor of women. Among the best-known gender feminists is Carol Gilligan, who challenged psychologist Lawrence Kohlberg's theory of moral development in her book *In a Different Voice*.[42] She argued that Kohlberg's widely accepted model of moral development did not account for differences between male and female moral development. While males resolve moral dilemmas using an ethic of justice, females use an ethic of care. While Gilligan did not at first argue that one was superior to the other, her work has been widely used to promote gender feminism's claim to women's moral superiority.

Maternalism, a subset of gender feminism, celebrates the power of women's reproductive capacity. Mothers in many Latin American nations, for example, have politicized motherhood in opposing dictatorships, raising sensitive political questions, and serving as visible reminders of the repression of immoral regimes. In the United States, mothers' movements are enjoying a contemporary resurgence. On Mother's Day 2000, tens of thousands of mothers marched on Washington, D.C., in the Million Moms' March to protest gun violence against children and to petition the government to take action in the form of tougher gun control legislation.

Critics of gender feminism argue that associating women with caring reinforces the traditional view of women as nurturers, rather than women as autonomous and strong. Particularly in relation to electoral politics, a nurturant posture of care has proven to be a somewhat limited virtue, depending on the domestic political climate in any one election. Others charge that labeling women as the only sex responsible for caring releases men from important social and familial obligations and unnecessarily polarizes men's and women's gender roles. Some also object to the nomenclature of maternal feminism, arguing that not all women are or aspire to be mothers.

Third Wave Feminism

In 1992, in the wake of the William Kennedy Smith rape trial and the Clarence Thomas–Anita Hill hearings, more than 100 young feminists gathered in New York City and organized a network they called "The Third Wave." Rebecca Walker is credited with coining the term in "Becoming the Third Wave," an essay published in *Ms.* magazine in 1992. The vision articulated by organizers was "to become the national network for young feminists, to politicize and organize young women from diverse cultural and economic backgrounds, to strengthen the relationships between young women and older feminists, and to consolidate a strong base of membership that can mobilize for specific issues, political candidates, and events."[43] Even among women who are not associated with an organization, the tendency of third wave feminists is to focus more broadly and integrate women's concerns with larger issues related to justice, including racism, poverty, and environmental issues. Betty Friedan, a founder of the second wave of feminism, said of the third wavers, "Young women are the true daughters of feminism; they take nothing for granted and are advancing the cause with marvelous verve. If they keep doing what they are doing, thirty years from today we may not need a feminist movement. We may have achieved real equality."[44] In addition to newly formed organizations for young feminist's interests, several second wave organizations (such as NOW, the Feminist Majority Foundation, and the National Council of Women's Organizations) have started new campus programs and outreach initiatives targeted at female Millennials, the generation born roughly between 1977 and 1996. Feminist blogs like Femniste and Feministing among others, reach out to women beyond campus and organizational limits. "You cannot overestimate the impact of the Internet on feminism's outreach potential. We reach women who never had a class in women's studies, women in towns with no NOW chapter or any other explicit feminist organization," says Jessica Valenti, founder of Feministing.[45] Blogging has been called the new vehicle for feminist consciousness raising.[46]

However, some veteran feminists of the second wave express concern that third wave feminists are oriented around individual or personal expression rather than sharing the collectivist orientation necessary to agitate for political change. Kalpana Krishnamurthy, codirector of the Third Wave Foundation, says of the conflict, "I think that the impact of the feminist movement was in helping women to achieve a voice. Now we are articulating that voice in a multiplicity of ways."[47] Jennifer Baumgardner and Amy Richards, authors of *Manifesta*, say that young women today do take second wave feminism's gains for granted, that the liberation gained by the second wave infuses their lives like fluoride in water, giving them a certain degree of confidence. They caution, however, that young women also need to develop a political consciousness sufficient to confront today's challenges to equality. This strain of third wave feminism is also echoed in the essays found in *Catching a Wave*.[48] With essays grouped in a way that is designed to mirror the consciousness-raising process developed by second wave feminists to highlight social inequities and then to politicize readers to take action, this collection of essays argues that only by continually confronting the persistent structural inequalities in society, can feminism retain its transformational power.

Postfeminism?

Rather than embrace a third wave of feminism, some (largely in the popular media) have argued that feminism has outlived its usefulness—or to put it more bluntly, that "feminism is dead." In 2004, Professor Mary Hawkesworth addressed the contradiction between the unprecedented growth of feminist activism around the globe and the recurrent pronouncement of feminism's death. She explains the incongruity: "These textual accounts of death serve as allegorical signs for something else, a means of identifying a perceived danger in need of elimination, a way for a community to define itself through those it symbolically chooses to kill."[49] The pronouncement of feminism's demise or failure has been a persistent media theme since the early 1970s, but what would it mean to be in a postfeminist era? Janelle Reinelt describes postfeminism as "a time when the residue of feminism is still with us in terms of its history and some of its commitments, but without the overarching umbrella of an organized social or political movement at either grass roots or national levels."[50] As Deborah Siegel, author of *Sisterhood Interrupted*, puts it, "The dilemma of my generation and those behind me is that we're caught between the hope for a world that no longer degrades women and the reality of a culture that is degrading. We see a few women breaking into the upper echelons of power, and we think things are great. It's confusing to be a daughter of feminism in a culture only half transformed."[51]

For many women, the 2008 presidential primaries and general election campaign opened a new examination of gender matters. Media coverage of the two prominent women candidates in the field, Democratic Senator Hillary Rodham Clinton and Republican Governor Sarah Palin focused new light on sex stereotypes largely thought extinct. In New Hampshire, when two men at a Clinton rally yelled out "Iron my shirts!" the media reacted with amusement, not outrage. Sexism and sexist remarks by journalists and on-air pundits were pervasive throughout the primaries. Mike Barnicle on MSNBC described Senator Clinton as "looking like everyone's first wife standing outside a probate court;" Jack Cafferty on CNN described her as "a scolding mother, talking down to a child." Glenn Beck of CNN observed, "There's something about her vocal range. . . . She's the stereotypical bitch, you know what I mean?"[52] On the Republican side, journalists were obsessed with Sarah Palin's appearance, and in September of 2008, a company called Hero Builders released a highly sexualized Sarah Palin action figure dressed in a red push-up bra and a short schoolgirl tartan plaid skirt. As Kate Zernike observed in the *New York Times*, "A year ago, it all seemed so different. If the nation wasn't quite gender-blind, still, a woman stood poised to become president, didn't she? So unskeptical were women about that possibility that lots of them felt they did not have to vote for 'the woman candidate'; it was the ultimate feminist decision to find Mr. Obama the better candidate—or John Edwards or any of the other men running, although it was Mr. Obama who seemed to transcend the identity politics that many young women in particular found tiresome and anachronistic."[53] *Nation* columnist Katha Pollitt wrote that the 'sulfurous emanations' about Mrs. Clinton made her want to write a check to her campaign, knock on doors, [and] vote for her twice—even though she'd probably choose another candidate on policy grounds. Is anger over sexism in electoral politics enough to advance women's overall agenda? Kate Michelman, a former president of NARAL Pro-Choice America noted, "I do think women are angry, but anger doesn't get us very far. It's a motivator, but it's not enough."[54]

What about a postfeminist world? Can women advance toward equality without an organized political movement sustained and energized by a feminist ideology? As you will see in the chapters ahead, women's pursuit of equality has been slow and progress has come incrementally. The catalyst for major progress has always been the tension created by women's political organizing for and against change.

USING POLITICS TO BRING ABOUT CHANGE

How will we know if and when women realize equality? Most likely the answer to this question depends in part on which path to gender equality you favor. If you favor the legal equality doctrine, you most likely believe that women's equality will resemble a gender-neutral state in which men and women exist as equals. If you favor the fairness doctrine, you probably believe that women are different from men and should remain so, but should not be disadvantaged by those differences. The central question of gender equality is this: Do differences between men and women *require* a sensitivity to sexual difference resulting in special provisions that compensate women for their biological role in child-bearing, or does gender neutrality *require* that no distinctions of any kind be made on the basis of sex? In effect, an affirmative answer to one question or the other delineates the two paths traveled by activists in women's movements—both of which have been traveled in the name of improving women's status. While the two approaches may not be entirely mutually exclusive, their dual existence and favor among women have confounded the ability of women to exhibit sex solidarity around the issues of discrimination and gender inequality. Those who believe men and women are the same, except for their sex-linked contributions to human reproduction, are confident that gender-neutral laws can remedy the discrimination women face by eliminating sex-based barriers to opportunities in the public sphere. However, those who believe that men and women are essentially different are convinced that special legislation is the remedy for the social, economic, and political disadvantages women endure as a result of motherhood and traditional gender roles. Thus women are often most at odds with other women over their common interests.

Where does this leave women and the women's movement? Is feminism still relevant to women today? If so, what kind of feminism should guide women's political and social actions? These are difficult questions to answer. In some respects, this ambivalence is due to the success of the women's movement itself. Women perceive their situation in 2009 as vastly improved over the lives of their mothers, grandmothers, and great-grandmothers. Although the majority of women in 2003 (64 percent) said that more effort is needed to improve women's status, only 43 percent expressed strong agreement that the United States needs a strong women's movement (62 percent agreed overall).[55] Ten issues in particular ranked as top priorities for women in 2003: equal pay; domestic violence and sexual assault; child care; women's health care; family leave; drug and alcohol addiction; electing more women to political office; women in other parts of the world; encouraging more women to pursue careers in math, science, and technology; and sexual harassment. In a study conducted for the National Women's Law Center in 2008, nearly 7 of every 10 (68%) women identified the need for a strong women's movement to push for changes that benefit women. Interestingly, women demonstrate little difference in level of support for a strong women's movement across generations, income levels, political party, and educational attainment. On issues of economic security, equal pay, equal opportunities, health care, child care, and reproductive health, women were substantially more supportive of a strong role for government in doing more to solve problems.[56] All of these issues will be addressed in the chapters that follow. Taken together, these issues make up a robust agenda for the next generation of feminists.

Regardless of their chosen path and strategy, women have worked for nearly two centuries to gain access to the public sphere and to improve the quality of their lives. To effect this change, women have used such conventional forms of political participation as lobbying for constitutional changes, fighting for the right to vote, and pursuing elective office, as well as less conventional methods, including working in organizations outside government and protesting public and private sector inequities. In addition, women have lobbied for policy changes before state legislatures and the U.S. Congress. At various times, the courts have facilitated or hampered their efforts. To quote the National Women's Equality Act (1998), women have "lobbied, litigated, picketed, marched, petitioned, engaged in civil disobedience, and boycotted to win women's rights."[57] However, women have still not gained full political, legal, social, economic, and educational equality. This book examines and analyzes women's political experiences, attitudes, and behaviors, and looks at their successes as well as their failures to understand more clearly where women stand today in their pursuit of gender equality.

Suggested Readings, Web Resources, and Films

Jennifer Baumgardner and Amy Richards, *Manifesta: Young Women, Feminism, and the Future* (New York: Farrar, Straus and Giroux, 2000).

Sandra Lipsitz Bem, *The Lenses of Gender: Transforming the Debate on Sexual Inequality* (New Haven, Conn.: Yale University Press, 1993).

Nancy Cott, *The Grounding of Modern Feminism* (New Haven, Conn.: Yale University Press, 1987).

Rory Dicker and Alison Piepmeier, eds., *Catching a Wave: Reclaiming Feminism for the 21st Century* (Boston: Northeastern University Press, 2003).

Jean Beth Elshtain, *Public Man, Private Woman: Women in Social and Political Thought*, 2nd ed. (Princeton, N.J.: Princeton University Press, 1981).

Mark E. Kahn, *The Gendering of American Politics: Founding Mothers, Founding Fathers, and Political Patriarchy* (Westport, Conn.: Praeger, 1999).

John Stuart Mill, "The Subjection of Women," in *The Feminist Papers*, ed. Alice S. Rossi (Boston: Northeastern University Press, 1972).

Carole Pateman, *The Disorder of Women: Democracy, Feminism and Political Theory* (Stanford, Calif.: Stanford University Press, 1989).

Carole Pateman, *The Sexual Contract* (Stanford, Calif.: Stanford University Press, 1998).

Virginia Sapiro, *A Vindication of Political Virtue: The Political Theory of Mary Wollstonecraft* (Chicago: University of Chicago Press, 1992).

Shira Tarrant, *When Sex Became Gender* (New York: Routledge Press, 2006).

Andi Zeisler, *Feminism and Pop Culture* (Berkeley, Calif.: Seal Press, 2008).

Blog: Feministe: http://www.feministe.us/blog/.

Blog: Feministing: http://feministing.com/.

Blog: The Political Voices of Women: http://politicsanew.com/.

Film: *Ecofeminism Now!* (Institute for Social Ecology, 1996).

Film: *The Way Home* (Harriman, N.Y.: New Day Films, 2002).

Notes

1. Linda Kerber, "The Paradox of Women's Citizenship in the Early Republic: The Case of *Martin v. Massachusetts,* 1805," *American Historical Review* (April 1992).

2. Women's Voices. Women Vote, accessed at http://www.wvwv.org.

3. Maxine Margolis, *Mothers and Such: Views of American Women and Why They Changed* (Berkeley: University of California Press, 1984).

4. Ibid., p. 47.

5. Abigail Adams to John Adams, March 31, 1776.

6. Virginia Sapiro, *The Political Integration of Women: Roles, Socialization, and Politics* (Chicago: University of Chicago Press, 1983), p. 19.

7. Alexis de Tocqueville, *Democracy in America* (1835; reprint, New York: Doubleday, 1969), p. 243.

8. Sandra Lipsitz Bem, *The Lenses of Gender: Transforming the Debate on Sexual Inequality* (New Haven, Conn.: Yale University Press, 1993), p. 1.

9. Aristotle, *The Politics of Aristotle,* trans. Ernest Barker (London: Oxford University Press, 1947), pp. 43–45.

10. Bem, *The Lenses of Gender,* p. 11.

11. Suzanne M. Marilley, *Woman Suffrage and the Origins of Liberal Feminism in the United States, 1820–1920* (Cambridge, Mass.: Harvard University Press, 1996).

12. Carole Pateman, *The Sexual Contract* (Stanford, Calif.: Stanford University Press, 1988).

13. J. S. Mill, "The Subjection of Women," in *The Feminist Papers,* ed. Alice S. Rossi (Boston: Northeastern University Press, 1972).

14. Ibid., p. 201.

15. Ibid., p. 199.

16. Adrienne Rich, *Of Woman Born: Motherhood as Experience and Institution* (New York: Norton, 1976), pp. 40–41.

17. Bem, *The Lenses of Gender,* p. 41.

18. It has been estimated that 70 percent of men in northern cities could read and only 35 percent of women. See Linda K. Kerber and Jane Sherron De Hart, *Women's America: Refocusing the Past,* 4th ed. (New York: Oxford University Press, 1995).

19. Nadine Taub and Elizabeth M. Schneider, "Perspectives on Women's Subordination and the Law," in *The Politics of Law,* ed. D. Kairys (New York: Pantheon, 1982), pp. 125–126.

20. William Blackstone, Chapter 15, in *Commentaries on the Laws of England,* book 1, vol. 4, (1765–1769).

21. Massachusetts Confiscation Act of April 20, 1779.

22. Linda Kerber, "The Paradox of Women's Citizenship in the Early Republic: The Case of *Martin v. Massachusetts*, 1805," 369.

23. Ibid., p. 370.

24. Ibid., p. 375.

25. Ibid.

26. Imelda Whelan, *Modern Feminist Thought: From the Second Wave to "Post Feminism"* (New York: New York University Press, 1995).

27. Nancy Gibbs, "The War against Feminism," *Time*, March 9, 1992, p. 51.

28. Nancy F. Cott, *The Grounding of Modern Feminism* (New Haven, Conn.: Yale University Press, 1987).

29. Ibid., p. 3.

30. Ibid., p. 5.

31. Ibid., pp. 4–5.

32. Rosemarie Putnam Tong, *Feminist Thought: A More Comprehensive Introduction* (Boulder, Colo.: Westview Press, 1998), p. 5.

33. For a more complete description and historical account of each approach to feminism, see Tong, *Feminist Thought*; Whelan, *Modern Feminist Thought*; Allison M. Jagger, *Feminist Politics and Human Nature* (Totowa, N.J.: Roman and Allanheld, 1983); Susan Moller Okin, *Women in Western Political Thought* (Princeton, N.J.: Princeton University Press, 1979); Shulamith Firestone, *The Dialectic of Sex* (New York: Bantam Books, 1970); Mary Daly, *Gyn/Ecology: The Metaethics of Radical Feminism* (Boston: Beacon Press, 1978); Nancy Chodorow, *The Reproduction of Mothering: Psychoanalysis and the Sociology of Gender* (Berkeley: University of California Press, 1978); Carol Gilligan, *In a Different Voice* (Cambridge, Mass.: Harvard University Press, 1982); Patricia Hill Collins, *Black Feminist Thought: Knowledge, Consciousness, and the Politics of Empowerment* (Boston: Unwin Hyman, 1990); Robin Morgan, *Sisterhood Is Global* (Garden City, N.Y.: Anchor, 1984).

34. Tong, *Feminist Thought*, p. 46.

35. There are, however, notable exceptions. Jo Freeman, for example, believed that it was a mistake to label some women's organizations as merely reformist since all groups were breaking away from established gender norms, an act "revolutionary" in itself. She'd prefer to divide branches of the movement into a "younger branch" and an "older branch." Barbara Ryan grouped organizations within the movement into "mass movement" and "small groups."

36. Tong, *Feminist Thought*, p. 227.

37. Collins, *Black Feminist Thought*, p. 19.

38. Ibid., p. 37.

39. Tong, *Feminist Thought*, p. 222.

40. Karen J. Warren, "Feminism and Ecology." *Environmental Review* 9, no. 1 (Spring 1987): 3–20.

41. Tong, *Feminist Thought*, p. 247.

42. Carol Gilligan, *In a Different Voice*.

43. Beth Dulin, "Founding Project Challenges Young Feminists," *New Directions for Women* 21, no. 1 (1993): 33.

44. Joannie M. Schrof, "Feminism's Daughters," *U.S. News & World Report*, September 27, 1993.

45. Linda Hirshman, "Looking to the Future, Feminism Has to Focus," *Washington Post*, Sunday, June 8, 2008; B01.

46. Courtney E. Martin, "Why Feminists Fight with Each Other," posted on June 12, 2007 to AlterNet, accessed at: http://www.alternet.org/story/53844.

47. Jennifer Friedlin, "Second and Third Wave Feminists Clash over the Future," *Women's eNews*, May 26, 2002, accessed at http://www.womensenews.org.

48. Rory Dicker and Alison Piepmeier, eds., *Catching a Wave: Reclaiming Feminism for the 21st Century* (Boston: Northeastern University Press, 2003).

49. Mary Hawkesworth, "The Semiotics of Premature Burial: Feminism in a Post-feminst Age," *Signs: Journal of Women in Culture and Society* 29, no. 4 (2004): 961–985.

50. Janelle Reinelt, "States of Play: Feminism, Gender Studies, and Performance," *The Scholar and Feminist Online* (Summer, 2003), The Barnard Center for Research on Women, accessed at: http://www.barnard.edu/sfonline/ps/reinelt2.htm#section1.

51. Courtney E. Martin, "Why Feminists Fight with Each Other."

52. Susan J. Carroll, "Reflections on Gender and Hillary Clinton's Presidential Campaign: The Good, the Bad, and the Misogynic" *Politics & Gender*, 5 (2009): 1–20.

53. Kate Zernike, "Postfeminism and Other Fairy Tales," *New York Times*, Sunday, March 16, 2008, accessed at http://www.nytimes.com/2008/03/16/weekinreview/16zern.html.

54. Ibid.

55. "Progress and Perils: How Gender Issues Unite and Divide Women: Part Two." Conducted for the Center for Gender Equality by Princeton Survey Research Associates, April 7, 2003. Center for the Advancement of Women, accessed at http://www.advancewomen.org.

56. Peter D. Hart Research Associates, Inc., "Understanding What Women Want in 2008," a poll conducted for The National Women's Law Center, July 17–24, 2008, accessed at http://www.nwlc.org/pdf/2008poll_whatwomenwantmemo.pdf.

57. National Council of Women's Organizations, "National Women's Equality Act for the 21st Century," 1998, p. 3, accessed at http://www.womensorganizations.org.

All Rights Are Not Equal: Suffrage Versus the Equal Rights Amendment

There have been two major points in American history when women have undertaken concerted action in the form of a movement in an attempt to effect a significant change in their public status. The first was the campaign for suffrage, especially between 1910 and 1920, the final phase of women's efforts. The second was during the 1970s, when women mobilized around the Equal Rights Amendment (ERA). In both cases, women eventually organized to achieve a single goal and were willing to make compromises on other important issues to realize that goal. In both cases, women constituted the majority of the proponents for and opponents to the change in their status. In both cases, women's support for or opposition to the vote and the ERA was grounded in their understanding of *equality*, their perspective on women's roles in the private and public spheres, and their concept of *fairness*. Women are not a homogenous political force, and there is no sex solidarity among women regarding gender equality. In the case of suffrage, the campaign was successful, albeit after more than seventy-two years of advocacy. When the Nineteenth Amendment reached the states for ratification, public attitudes had already changed. By then, women were viewed as independent from their husbands and fathers when it came to owning property and earning wages. Additionally, women already had full voting rights in fifteen states and presidential suffrage in another twelve. In effect, the constitutional change that gave women the vote followed a change that had already taken place in social attitudes. This was not so with the Equal Rights Amendment. The Constitution still has no equal rights amendment, even after nearly eighty years of episodic campaigning and an unprecedented thirty-nine-month extension to the ratification deadline granted by Congress in 1978. Why? What can we learn about women's relationship to politics and the controversies of equality in the contrast? This chapter sets out to answer these questions, first by briefly examining the history of both movements, and then by analyzing the arguments for and against each change in light of the paradox of gender equality.

FROM SENECA FALLS TO SUFFRAGE: THREE GENERATIONS OF WOMEN WORK FOR THE VOTE

Although the vote is now considered the most basic act of citizenship, it took women more than seventy-two years of political activism to win the elective franchise. Three generations of women joined the cause, each believing that theirs would be the final effort required to convince enough state and federal legislators that women deserved and required political representation. Initially suffragists argued that admitting women to the political system would result in positive change. Within a generation, they discovered that it was more effective to argue that suffrage for women would not result in any change—positive or negative—but rather was required out of a sense of basic fairness. By the third generation, women were again divided over how to approach the civic gate-keepers. A younger group, led by Alice Paul, who was trained in militant tactics of political resistance, argued that women should not be begging the establishment for the vote; they should be demanding the right to vote. The more established suffragists, led by long-time activist Carrie Chapman Catt, believed that women would win the vote in time, but threatening politicians would only delay their victory. In the end, winning the vote required both approaches and a fundamental shift in public attitudes of legislators and average citizens alike. Women were admitted to the political franchise only after public opinion supported the view that women were capable of rational thought and action independent of their husbands.

Female Social Activists Discover the Suffrage Cause: 1840–1869

Many early advocates of equality and rights for women came to the cause via their dedication to the abolition of slavery or their experiences with other charitable societies.[1] In their drive to help others, women were able to transcend the line between private and public life and, in the process, began to share informally the "problems of their sex" with one another. As they labored for racial equality and political rights for African Americans, they became conscious of their own inequality. Historian Carol Ellen Dubois argues that women working in the abolition movement gained something even more significant than a discovery of their own second-class status: "What American women learned from abolition was less that they were oppressed than what to do with that perception, how to turn it into a political movement."[2] The seed for that political movement germinated with a sex-discrimination incident at the World Anti-Slavery Convention held in London in 1840. Although women were part of the official U.S. delegation, they were not allowed to participate in the proceedings and were relegated to seats in the balcony. Here Elizabeth Cady Stanton and Lucretia Mott began to discuss holding a meeting for the express purpose of discussing women's rights.

In 1848, Stanton and Mott issued a call for participation in a meeting organized to talk about the "social, civil, and religious rights of women."[3] More than 300 people participated in the two-day Seneca Falls Convention and ratified the *Declaration of Sentiments and Resolutions*, as drafted by Stanton. The meeting was odd by contemporary standards. Called to consider the question of women's equality, none of the conveners felt qualified to chair the meeting, and so the task fell to Lucretia Mott's husband, James. The taboo against "public women" fell away slowly, and subsequent conventions often relied on noted male abolitionists as speakers. Education activist Emma Willard, for example, always asked a man to speak on her behalf, or if forced to speak for herself, she did so while seated. Others delivered their remarks from behind a curtain. Historian Glenna Matthews refers to this phenomenon as the social geography of gender.[4] Elizabeth Cady Stanton, after speaking in public for the first time at Seneca Falls, added "access to the public lectern" to the other demands in the *Declaration of Sentiments*. Not until 1850, at a meeting in Salem, Ohio, was the social geography of gender transformed entirely. At that meeting, only women were allowed to speak, whether from the platform or the audience.

The *Declaration of Sentiments* mirrored the Declaration of Independence in form, word, and tone. These similarities suggest that the early advocates for women's rights based their equality claims in the liberal tradition of individualism. The *Declaration of Sentiments* began, "We hold these truths to be self-evident: that all men and women are created equal," and then listed eighteen injuries "on the part of man toward woman," including exclusion from the franchise, coverture in marriage, denial of property rights, blocked access to higher education, and the undermining of "confidence in her own powers . . . and [making] her willing to lead a dependent and abject life." The list was a curious mix of political and personal grievances against men. All of the resolutions passed unanimously at the convention with the exception of suffrage, which passed by a narrow margin (see chapter 9 for the resolutions adopted by the convention). Of all of the demands, the franchise was the most radical and controversial among the conference participants, as well as among women throughout the country. Even Lucretia Mott counseled Stanton against including suffrage in the resolutions, saying, "Thou will make us ridiculous. We must go slowly."[5] Frederick Douglass, former slave and noted abolitionist leader, reassured Stanton and promised to speak in favor of the suffrage resolution. Paula Giddings notes that "although the Black woman's contribution to the women's suffrage movement is rarely written about, Blacks, including women, had a more consistent attitude toward the vote than Whites, as Blacks

Declaration of Sentiments

When in the course of human events, it becomes necessary for one portion of the family of man to assume among the people of the earth a position different from that which they have hitherto occupied, but one to which the laws of nature and of nature's God entitle them, a decent respect to the opinions of mankind requires that they should declare the causes that impel them to such a course.

We hold these truths to be self-evident: that all men and women are created equal; that they are endowed by their Creator with certain inalienable rights; that among these are life, liberty, and the pursuit of happiness; that to secure these rights governments are instituted, deriving their just powers from the consent of the governed. Whenever any form of government becomes destructive of these ends, it is the right of those who suffer from it to refuse allegiance to it, and to insist upon the institution of a new government, laying its foundation on such principles, and organizing its powers in such form, as to them shall seem most likely to effect their safety and happiness. Prudence, indeed, will dictate that governments long established should not be changed for light and transient causes; and accordingly all experience hath shown that mankind are more disposed to suffer, while evils are sufferable, than to right themselves by abolishing the forms to which they were accustomed. But when a long train of abuses and usurpations, pursuing invariably the same object, evinces a design to reduce them under absolute despotism, it is their duty to throw off such government, and to provide new guards for their future security. Such has been the patient sufferance of the women under this government, and such is now the necessity which constrains them to demand the equal station to which they are entitled.

The history of mankind is a history of repeated injuries and usurpations on the part of man toward woman, having in direct object the establishment of an absolute tyranny over her. To prove this, let facts be submitted to a candid world.

He has never permitted her to exercise her inalienable right to the elective franchise.

He has compelled her to submit to laws, in the formation of which she had no voice.

He has withheld from her rights which are given to the most ignorant and degraded men—both natives and foreigners.

Having deprived her of this first right of a citizen, the elective franchise, thereby leaving her without representation in the halls of legislation, he has oppressed her on all sides.

He has made her, if married, in the eye of the law, civilly dead.

He has taken from her all right in property, even to the wages she earns.

He has made her, morally, an irresponsible being, as she can commit many crimes with impunity, provided they be done in the presence of her husband. In the covenant of marriage, she is compelled to promise obedience to her husband, he becoming, to all intents and purposes, her master—the law giving him power to deprive her of her liberty, and to administer chastisement.

He has so framed the laws of divorce, as to what shall be the proper causes, and in case of separation, to whom the guardianship of the children shall be given, as to be wholly regardless of the happiness of women—the law in all cases, going upon a false supposition of the supremacy of man, and giving all power into his hands.

After depriving her of all rights as a married woman, if single and the owner of property, he has taxed her to support a government which recognizes her only when her property can be made profitable to it.

He has monopolized nearly all of the profitable employments, and from those she is permitted to follow, she receives but a scanty remuneration. He closes against her all the avenues to wealth and distinction which he considers most honorable to himself. As a teacher of theology, medicine, or law, she is not known.

He has denied her the facilities for obtaining a thorough education, all colleges being closed against her.

He allows her in Church, as well as State, but a subordinate position, claiming Apostolic authority for her exclusion from the ministry, and, with some exceptions, from any public participation in the affairs of the Church.

He has created a false public sentiment by giving to the world a different code of morals for men and women, by which moral delinquencies which exclude women from society, are not only tolerated, but deemed of little account in man.

He has usurped the prerogative of Jehovah himself, claiming it as his right to assign for her a sphere of action, when that belongs to her conscience and to her God.

He has endeavored, in every way that he could, to destroy her confidence in her own powers, to lessen her self-respect, and to make her willing to lead a dependent and abject life.

Now, in view of this entire disfranchisement of one-half the people of this country, their social and religious degradation—in view of the unjust laws above mentioned, and because women do feel themselves aggrieved, oppressed, and fraudulently deprived of their most sacred rights, we insist that they have immediate admission to all the rights and privileges which belong to them as citizens of the United States.

In entering upon the great work before us, we anticipate no small amount of misconception, misrepresentation, and ridicule; but we shall use every instrumentality within our power to effect our object. We shall employ agents, circulate tracts, petition the State and National legislatures, and endeavor to enlist the pulpit and the press in our behalf. We hope this Convention will be followed by a series of Conventions embracing every part of the country.

Elizabeth Cady Stanton, Susan B. Anthony, and Matilda Joslyn Gage, eds., *History of Woman Suffrage*, vol. 1 (Rochester, N.Y.: Charles Mann, 1881), pp. 67–74.

had fewer conflicts about women voting . . . one would be hard pressed to find any Black woman who did not advocate getting the vote."[6] The reticence among Seneca conventioneers to immediately embrace women's suffrage was a bellwether of the long struggle ahead. Of all those in attendance at Seneca Falls, only one nineteen-year-old woman, Charlotte Woodward, lived long enough to exercise her right to vote.[7]

Within months of the Seneca Falls meeting, women's rights conventions were held in other cities, beginning in Rochester, New York. Susan B. Anthony, a tireless crusader for suffrage later in the movement, was at first slow to join. She heard about the Rochester meeting from her mother and sister, but she was already immersed in the abolition and temperance movements, and felt those causes were more consistent with her Quaker beliefs. In 1851, when men in Akron, Ohio, directly challenged women's ability even to hold such conventions, let alone demand civil and political rights, a former slave named Sojourner Truth responded forthrightly from the floor. Truth's indignant oratory reflects her dual oppression as a black former slave and as a woman:

Sojourner Truth (1797–1883), abolitionist and women's rights activist. *Hulton Archive/Getty Images.*

Well, children, where there is so much racket there must be something out of kilter. I think that 'twixt the Negroes of the South and the women at the North, all talking about rights, the white men will be in a fix pretty soon. But what's all this here talking about?

That man over there says women need to be helped into carriages, and lifted over ditches, and to have the best place everywhere. Nobody ever helps me into carriages, or over mud-puddles, or gives me any best place! And ain't I a woman? Look at me! Look at my arm! I have ploughed, and planted, and gathered into barns, and no man could head me! And ain't I a woman? I could work as much and eat as much as a man—when I could get it—and bear the lash as well! And ain't I a woman? I have borne thirteen children, and seen them most all sold off to slavery, and when I cried out with my mother's grief, none but Jesus heard me! And ain't I a woman?

Then they talk about this thing in the head; what's this they call it? ["Intellect," whispered someone near.] That's it, honey. What's that got to do with women's rights or Negroes rights? If my cup won't hold but a pint, and yours holds a quart, wouldn't you be mean not to let me have my little half-measure full?

Then that little man in black there, he says women can't have as much rights as men, because Christ wasn't a woman! Where did your Christ come from? Where did your Christ come from? From God and a woman! Man had nothing to do with Him. . . .

If the first woman God ever made was strong enough to turn the world upside down all alone, these women together ought to be able to turn it back, and get it right side up again! And now they are asking to do it, the men better let them.[8]

Women's rights and abolition shared a common philosophical claim to equal rights, and the movements were closely linked until divisions surfaced over the Civil War amendments. The start of the war all but suspended the campaign for women's rights. Women in the North and South dedicated themselves to their respective causes, but most suffragists at the time supported the Union effort. In 1863, Stanton and Anthony organized the Women's Loyal National League in the North to promote the emancipation of all slaves through constitutional amendment.[9] The amendment proposed universal suffrage and was intended to include freed slaves *and* women. Many abolitionists objected to women's inclusion in the suffrage clause, fearing that it would cause the amendment to fail. The Republican Party argued that an attempt to enfranchise women would jeopardize efforts to enfranchise black men in the South.[10] The Thirteenth Amendment (1865) was ratified without any mention of the franchise. Then attention turned to the Fourteenth Amendment, which granted citizenship rights to freed slaves.

The American Equal Rights Association (AERA) was formed in 1866 to advance the cause of universal suffrage, and many active in the organization believed that suffrage was already implied in the language of citizenship. Several prominent African American reformers held leadership positions in the AERA, including Harriet Purvis, Sarah Redmond, and Sojourner Truth.[11] Black men and women active in the movement clearly linked women's rights with the vote and focused their efforts on universal suffrage and universal reforms. However, the AERA was embroiled in a battle between those whose first priority was black male suffrage and those who were dedicated first to women's suffrage. The tension found a target in the Fourteenth Amendment. If the Fourteenth Amendment were ratified as proposed, the word "male" would appear in the Constitution for the first time, thereby establishing two categories of citizens: male and female. Suffragists disagreed among themselves as to how they ought to react to the language of the proposed amendment. Anthony and Stanton believed that the amendment should be defeated unless it included women, while others like Lucy Stone argued that it was "the Negroes' hour, and that the women must wait for their rights."[12]

Those who believed in the precedence of women's suffrage could not get past the willingness of others to accept the word "male" in the text of the Fourteenth Amendment and the exclusion of women from the Fifteenth Amendment, which removed race as a disqualifier for the franchise. Having been told to wait their turn during the ratification of the Thirteenth and Fourteenth Amendments, woman suffragists saw the Fifteenth Amendment as their last opportunity to be included in the postwar reconstruction of the nation via constitutional amendment. White female suffragists left the AERA, blaming male abolitionists for sacrificing women in the name of expediency. Black women "remained quiet or divided among the prevailing forces."[13] The disunity resulted in the dissolution of the AERA and the formation of two rival organizations for women's rights in 1869: first, the National Woman Suffrage Association (NWSA), led by Stanton and Anthony, and later the American Woman Suffrage Association (AWSA), led by Lucy Stone and Henry Ward Beecher. The NWSA turned its immediate attention to the fight over women's inclusion in the Fifteenth Amendment and divorced itself entirely from the Republican Party and the "Negro suffrage" question, whereas the AWSA continued to support the Fifteenth Amendment as written, vowing to support a Sixteenth Amendment dedicated to women's suffrage.[14]

Historian Rosalyn Terborg-Penn, writing about African American women's participation in the early suffrage movement, argues that the schism within the movement and black women's reaction to the divide reveals how "they were often torn between identifying with racial priorities or gender priorities."[15] In the process, black women are often left out of accounts of the divisions, and black males are often blamed. The racist overtones of Stanton's and Anthony's woman-first claims have been ignored in many contemporary accounts, according to Terborg-Penn, and worse still, feminists writing historical accounts in the 1970s and 1980s justify white suffragists' racism as expedient, "but often [do] not justify the pro-'Negro suffrage' male behavior as expedient."[16]

The disagreement with abolitionists and the divide among suffragists is significant because it signaled an end to women's quest for universal suffrage and a start to the often ugly nativist and racist rhetoric and action that characterized some claims to the vote for women. Women dove into social activism, dedicated to the universality of natural rights and to full citizenship rights and privileges grounded in the liberal tradition for all adults. However, their negative experiences with allied groups in the formative years of the rights movement pushed women toward exclusivity and self-interest, transforming the women's rights movement into a women's suffrage movement. In a broader sense, it also forced them to give up the philosophical and moral high ground, and to sacrifice forever the most radical notion of all: transforming the social and political structure itself.

Suffragists Disagree over Amending the U.S. Constitution: 1870–1910

Having been divided primarily over strategic disagreements rather than deeper ideological differences, the NWSA and AWSA advanced along similar paths, courted many of the same potential constituents, and advocated many of the same arguments in favor of women's suffrage. There were some differences, however. The NWSA worked for both a federal amendment and state referendums. Of the two organizations, the NWSA was more revolutionary because it at first refused to admit men,[17] attacked the institution of marriage, and published essays on "free love" in its journal, *The Revolution*. Elizabeth Cady Stanton, in particular, targeted the church as a primary source of sexism in society, which led her to reject the Bible.[18] In the 1870s, NWSA used such confrontational tactics as attempting to vote, sponsoring female candidates, and mounting protests at public events.[19] The AWSA maintained its working relationship with abolitionists of both sexes, and its membership reflected a more conservative, middle- and upper-class slice of society. AWSA's publication, the *Woman's Journal*, supported the institutions of family, church, and marriage. For the most part, women's efforts in both organizations to educate the public and legislators involved petitioning legislatures, testifying before legislative committees, giving public speeches, and conducting public referendum campaigns. African American women's voices became more evident in their own right during the period between 1870 and 1890.[20] Never abandoning the cause of universal suffrage, their calls for change incorporated demands for both suffrage and basic civil rights for all black people.

Divisions between the two organizations and the NWSA's embrace of "free love" tarnished the women's suffrage organizations' claims to moral superiority. In the void, the Women's Christian Temperance Union (WCTU) took up the cause of suffrage. Frances Willard, WCTU president from 1879 to 1897, linked suffrage to temperance by arguing that only women could be counted on to cast the votes necessary to prohibit the sale and consumption of alcohol. Alcohol abuse was a leading cause of domestic violence, abandonment, and poverty for women and children. The WCTU was larger than any women's suffrage organization and contributed vast resources to the cause during Willard's presidency.[21]

The combination of efforts yielded success. Two western territories, Wyoming and Utah, granted women the vote, and state legislatures in other regions (except for the South) considered women's suffrage legislation. Political scientist Lee Ann Banaszak calculated that, on average, "in every year between 1870 and 1890, 4.4 states considered legislation giving women the vote."[22]

From 1869 to 1874, NWSA members urged female activists to adopt a more revolutionary strategy. Missouri suffragists Virginia Minor and her husband, Francis, took the lead in developing a reinterpretation of the Fourteenth Amendment and applying its definition of citizenship to enfranchise women.[23] Victoria Woodhull took the same argument to the 1871 NWSA convention in the District of Columbia. Calling the strategy the "new departure," she urged delegates to adopt the tactic in their own communities.[24] African American suffragist Mary Ann Shad Cary, having studied law at Howard University, constructed a legal argument applying the Fourteenth and Fifteenth Amendments to black women as well as black men. In testimony before the House Judiciary Committee, Cary argued that if women were denied the vote, the emancipation amendments would leave women free in name only. She called for an amendment to strike the word "male" from the Constitution.[25] By other accounts, African American women reacted to their personal exclusion from suffrage by working to influence the political decisions of their male kin and friends. Jewel Prestage notes, "According to one [Louisiana] state politician and former state senator, they followed their men from morning to night telling them how to vote, formed a large segment of the audiences at political meetings, and evidenced a deep interest in all that pertained to politics."[26]

In the November election of 1872, several women attempted to vote. Sojourner Truth went to the polls in Battle Creek, Michigan, and attempted to vote, but was turned away. Susan B. Anthony and a small group of women voted in Rochester, New York. Anthony was arrested several weeks later and charged with "illegal voting." Rather than pay her fine and win her release, Anthony instead applied for a *writ of habeas corpus* in an effort to get her case before the Supreme Court. When the judge asked if Anthony had anything to say, she used her trial and conviction to plead the case of women's suffrage before the court of public opinion:

> Yes, your honor, I have many things to say; for in your ordered verdict of guilty, you have trampled underfoot every vital principle of our government. My natural rights, my civil rights, my political rights, are all alike ignored. Robbed of the fundamental privilege of citizenship, I am degraded from the status of citizen to that of a subject; and not only myself individually, but all of my sex, are, by your honor's verdict, doomed to political subjection under this so-called Republican government.[27]

Although the judge at Albany refused to issue the writ and raised her bail to $1,000, Anthony remained steadfast. Unfortunately, her attorney did not. Writing a personal check for her bail, Attorney Henry Seldon scuttled any chances for Anthony to present her case to the Supreme Court. When Anthony asked Seldon if he realized what he had done by paying her bail, he replied,

"Yes, but I could not see a lady I respected put in jail."[28] Misplaced chauvinism denied Anthony the opportunity to make her case to the Supreme Court.

In the same election, Virginia Minor cast her illegal vote in Missouri and was arrested. But unlike Anthony's, Minor's case was eventually heard before the U.S. Supreme Court. She argued that in denying her the vote the state of Missouri had denied her rights under the Fourteenth Amendment guarantee to the privileges and immunities of citizenship. The right to vote, she claimed, is a privilege of citizenship. The Court rejected her claim in *Minor v. Happersett*, 1875. While admitting that women may be citizens, the Court said that not all citizens are voters. The Court based its opinion on the fact that the federal Constitution does not explicitly grant women the right to vote ("if it had been intended to make all citizens of the United States voters, the framers of the Constitution would not have left it to implication") and the fact that no new state added to the Union after ratification had granted suffrage to women.[29] Without constitutional instruction, the states could decide for themselves who had the privilege of voting. In closing, the Court said:

> We have given this case the careful consideration its importance demands. If the law is wrong, it ought to be changed; but the power for that is not with us. The arguments addressed to us bearing upon such a view of the subject may perhaps be sufficient to induce those having the power, to make the alteration, but they ought not to be permitted to influence our judgment in determining the present rights of the parties now litigating before us. No argument as to woman's need of suffrage can be considered.[30]

The ruling in *Minor* led suffragists to the inevitable conclusion that a legal strategy would not advance their cause, and therefore they were left with only two choices: a federal amendment or constitutional amendments in each state. In 1877, the NWSA was once again dedicated to a federal constitutional amendment. This time, however, the goal was not universal suffrage, but rather women's suffrage.

By 1890, old animosities between the NWSA and AWSA had faded sufficiently for a merger to take place. The new organization, the National American Woman Suffrage Association (NAWSA), elected Elizabeth Cady Stanton president. Stanton served only two years before she was forced out after publishing the *Woman's Bible*, a feminist reinterpretation of the Bible. Anthony replaced her, but found herself at the helm of a younger, more moderate membership. The merger did not immediately inject new enthusiasm or success into the movement. In fact, suffrage leaders referred to this period as "the doldrums."[31] After Utah and Idaho enfranchised women in 1896, no other state gave women the vote until 1910, when the state of Washington acted. NAWSA's membership had fallen to fewer than 100,000.[32] Women's rights organizations had been formed in most states by then and were spawning new leaders for the movement. Women formed literary and social organizations as well, eventually leading to the Women's Club Movement.[33] During the same period, African American women organized into clubs, initiating the Black

Women's Club Movement. Most of the early black women's clubs (1880s–1895) were not affiliated with national organizations and formed to deal with local issues facing women of color. In 1896, the largest national black women's clubs merged to form the National Association of Colored Women (NACW), a federation of women's clubs with Mary Church Terrell at the helm as president. The rise of the NACW coincided with the disenfranchisement of black males in the South, and so issues on its agenda included Jim Crow laws and lynchings, as well as women's suffrage.[34] An organization of southern white women came last, was slow to get started, and required the NAWSA to adopt a questionable "states' rights" policy on organizational structure, allowing segregated organizations to flourish in the South. Once again, suffragist leaders sacrificed a basic organizing principle in favor of expediency. This time, women's suffrage gave way to "white women's suffrage" in an effort to bring in southern states. These efforts to exclude African American women did not go unchallenged. The NAACP, formed in 1909, mobilized at the behest of African American suffragists to put pressure on Alice Paul and other white suffrage leaders.[35]

Toward the end of the century, the founding leaders of the movement—Stanton, Stone, and Anthony—were aging and dying. Carrie Chapman Catt briefly replaced Anthony as president of the NAWSA in 1900, before Dr. Anna Howard Shaw assumed the role in 1904. Shaw represented the "intergenerational" leaders of the suffrage movement and provided a bridge between the pioneers and the new younger leadership, including Alice Paul and Lucy Burns. Shaw concentrated the NAWSA's efforts on state referendums and on lobbying state legislatures, forgoing a federal amendment for a time.

The Final Push: 1910–1920

With the new century came new challenges for women's rights organizations. A multitude of clubs and organizations were mobilizing in favor of and in opposition to women's suffrage. Hundreds of African American women's clubs mobilized for the vote during the years 1900 to 1920, both in states that had already granted women the vote and states that still prohibited women from voting. Coordinating efforts and strategies was nearly impossible, and in the end, it was two openly divergent strategies that together delivered women's suffrage.

The NAWSA continued to organize, petition, and lobby in the states. Emmeline Pankhurst had been pioneering direct protest tactics in the English suffrage movement. Harriet Stanton Blatch (Elizabeth Cady Stanton's daughter), Alice Paul, and Lucy Burns traveled to England to participate in this new method of campaigning for women's suffrage. On their return, Paul and Burns lobbied the NAWSA to return to a federal amendment strategy. Although the NAWSA formed a congressional committee in 1912, support for a federal strategy was so meager that the committee was given an annual budget of ten dollars.[36]

Paul and her followers, referred to as the "new suffragists" by some scholars,[37] were different from the "old suffragists." Although the suffrage cause connected both groups, the new suffragists viewed the fight for suffrage as a means to "challenge a social system that attempted to refute their feminist ideology and deny them their identities."[38] Rather than begging for their rights, they intended to demand them. The NAWSA grudgingly agreed to support the congressional committee's proposal (in name only, since they refused to give Paul any funds) to hold a massive parade in Washington, D.C., designed to coincide with Woodrow Wilson's presidential inauguration. Paul was convinced, contrary to the NAWSA leadership, that if suffrage were to become reality, the focus must be on a federal amendment. To Paul that meant that Congress must be convinced to pass legislation and send it on to the states. However, Congress was unlikely to act without some prodding, a task Paul assigned to the president of the United States. The March 3 parade was intended to put both Congress and President Wilson on notice that women would not wait any longer for action on the suffrage question.

Paul and the NAWSA's Congressional Committee devised a strategy by which local suffrage organizations would sponsor (and pay for) their own parade participants. When Howard University women volunteered to march in the college section of the parade, some white marchers threatened to pull out. To Paul's credit, she did not back down. Instead she found sympathetic white male marchers to provide a protective buffer for the Howard women. On the day of the parade, some 8,000 marchers, including twenty-six floats, ten bands, and five squadrons of cavalry with six chariots, participated.[39] More than half a million people watched as the parade headed down Pennsylvania Avenue toward the White House. Although the NAWSA's Congressional Committee had sought additional police protection for the marchers, the superintendent of police refused, saying it was a job for the War Department, not the police department. Trouble started when spectators began insulting participants and pushing the crowd into the parade line. As police stood idle, the situation deteriorated into a near riot. In all, 175 calls for ambulances were sent out, and more than 200 people were treated at local hospitals.[40] A subsequent Senate investigation turned up numerous examples of police ineptitude and complicity with the rioters. The publicity the parade generated and the claims Paul made that the police and top civilian officials had conspired to break up the parade brought unparalleled attention to the suffrage cause. Not all of it was positive. Newspaper editorials chided the female participants for their unruly behavior, and such criticism made the NAWSA's leadership nervous. In the leaders' minds, the Congressional Committee, and not the NAWSA, was pursuing a federal strategy. The NAWSA was still committed to a state-by-state campaign. Conflict between the Congressional Committee and the NAWSA escalated. Allegations and conspiracy theories (none of which were ever proven) began surfacing that Paul and her supporters were working to undermine the state campaign by focusing exclusively on the federal amendment and on financial improprieties.

Frustrated, Paul broke with the NAWSA and established the Congressional Union (CU) as an independent organization in 1914. The CU's first action was to hold Democratic Party elected officials responsible for the failure of federal suffrage legislation. The CU targeted Democratic congressmen in close races and actively campaigned against candidates who did not support enfranchising women. Following the same logic, Paul turned her attention to Woodrow Wilson. She organized pickets in front of the White House and called on Wilson

Encountering the Controversies of Equality

Two Means to the Same End: A Contrast in the Styles of Alice Paul and Carrie Chapman Catt

The leaders of the women's suffrage movement are enjoying renewed public attention in the wake of women's recent electoral gains. The PBS documentary *Not for Ourselves Alone*, written and produced by Geoffrey Ward and Ken Burns, introduced thousands of viewers to Susan B. Anthony and Elizabeth Cady Stanton for the first time. What many people do not realize is that both of these pioneering women were dead long before the Nineteenth Amendment was ratified. Carrie Chapman Catt (1859–1947) and Alice Paul (1885–1977) led the final battle for women's suffrage, but in dramatically different styles.

Catt worked her way through Iowa State University, serving as a school principal and later as one of the nation's first female superintendents. She began her suffrage work with the Iowa Suffrage Association upon the death of her first husband. The prenuptial agreement signed before her second marriage to George Catt in 1890 guaranteed her four months each year to work on suffrage activities. Known for her strong organizational skills, Catt took the helm of the National American Woman Suffrage Association (NAWSA) in 1917 and implemented the "Winning Plan," which combined a careful congressional lobbying strategy for a federal amendment with continued efforts to win suffrage in individual states. Catt believed that Congress would act only when women in enough states had the votes to make them listen. She further believed that rational appeals and careful persuasion would lead Congress and President Wilson to support suffrage in ways that punishing Democrats at the polls would not. She urged NAWSA members to remain nonpartisan in their calls on lawmakers. After the Nineteenth Amendment was ratified, Catt founded the League of Women Voters, a nonpartisan organization dedicated to educating women for full civic participation.

Alice Paul, born to affluent Quaker parents, graduated from Swarthmore College in 1905, and earned a master's degree from the University of Pennsylvania in 1907 to pressure Congress to consider and pass the federal amendment (known by then as the Susan B. Anthony Amendment). On January 10, 1917, the first "Silent Sentinels" appeared.[41] These were women who stood motionless holding banners that read, "Mr. President, What Will You Do for Woman Suffrage?" and "How Long Must Women Wait for Liberty?" These suffragist picketers were the first picketers ever to appear before the White House.

The NAWSA, although not specifically endorsing the pickets, took a wait-and-see attitude under the new leadership of Carrie Chapman Catt. Catt, who

and a Ph.D. in 1912. Her studies combined her overlapping interests in economics, political science, social work, and women's equality. Later in her life she would also earn three law degrees. While pursuing a graduate fellowship in England, Paul met the Pankhurst sisters and was introduced to the militant tactics of the British suffrage movement. When she returned to the United States in 1910, she brought with her an appreciation for the direct and aggressive methods of the English suffragettes. Paul was convinced that suffrage rights needed to be taken and demanded, not begged for. Initially working within the NAWSA as chair of the Congressional Committee, Paul organized a massive suffrage demonstration in Washington, D.C., held the day prior to Woodrow Wilson's inauguration. She believed that the party in power and incumbent politicians should be held accountable for their lack of support for suffrage, and eventually (after being ousted from the NAWSA) organized the National Woman's Party to facilitate women's direct political action. She organized and coordinated the actions of hundreds of women who demonstrated in front of the White House and engaged in hunger strikes while imprisoned. She too had a gift for organizing. As her friend Lucy Burns said of her, "Her great assets, I should say, are her power to make plans on a national scale; and a supplementary power to see that it is done down to the last postage stamp."[1] Paul's methods were viewed as controversial and radical. In an editorial condemning the picketing as such a female thing to do, *The New York Times* wrote, "That the female mind is inferior to the male mind need not be assumed. That there is something about it essentially different, and that this difference is of a kind and degree that with votes for women would constitute a political danger is or ought to be plain to everybody."[2]

What do you think?

Under what circumstances is direct action warranted in pursuit of women's equality? Evaluate Catt's and Paul's respective strategies in light of what you've learned about the history of the suffrage movement and the political climate between 1917 and 1920. Which was more effective in moving the Nineteenth Amendment toward ratification? Would one strategy have been as effective without the other?

1. Christine Lunardini, *From Equal Suffrage to Equal Rights: Alice Paul and the National Woman's Party, 1910–1928* (New York: New York University Press, 1986), p. 10.
2. Ibid., p. 108.

had replaced Shaw as president in 1915, made reforming the organization her first priority. Although Shaw led with great intelligence and moral authority, she did not have Catt's political savvy or her skills in managing the unwieldy NAWSA bureaucracy. Catt's first action was to obtain the allegiance of the national and state association leaders. Her goal was to "enable campaigners in the field and lobbyists in Washington to feel a united organization behind them."[42] Catt did not believe that the NAWSA or the suffrage question should be tied too closely to either of the two major political parties and instead pursued a nonpartisan strategy through ratification and beyond.

At first, the pickets attracted sympathy from the public, and donations poured in from women nationwide. However, in 1917, while other suffragists debated how to respond to the country's war on Germany, Alice Paul transformed the Congressional Union into the National Woman's Party (NWP) and stepped up efforts to call attention to women's disenfranchisement. Ignoring the war, NWP picketers carried signs reading: "Kaiser Wilson, have you forgotten your sympathy with the poor Germans because they were not self-governed? Twenty million American women are not self-governed. Take the beam out of your eye."[43] As the rhetoric heated up, police began arresting picketers, some of whom were physically attacked by daily crowds of onlookers. Each time police arrested a marcher or a woman was felled by attack, another woman was there

March 3, 1913. Suffrage Parade down Pennsylvania Avenue, Washington, D.C. The procession included twenty-six floats, ten bands, five mounted brigades, three heralds, and more than 8,000 marchers. Women from countries that had enfranchised women marched first in the procession, followed by the pioneers in the U.S. struggle. They were followed by sections celebrating working women by occupation, state delegations, and finally, a separate section for male supporters of women's suffrage. *Wisconsin Historical Society, Photo ID #3782.*

to take her place. States sent delegations to the picket lines, and those who couldn't picket sent donations to support those marching in their place. When jailed, women refused to pay their fines and remained in jail. In an attempt to scare off new picketers, prison terms of up to sixty days were imposed. The women engaged in several hunger strikes to protest their unjust incarceration. Prison officials responded by force-feeding them through the nose, a dangerous and terribly painful practice. Public reaction was swift and overwhelmingly sympathetic to the suffragists, prompting early releases. Women released from prison capitalized on the public's sympathy by campaigning for suffrage in their prison garb.

The NWP's militant tactics offended many within and outside of the movement, including many NAWSA members. Under Catt's leadership, the NAWSA was pursuing a state strategy for a federal amendment labeled the "Winning Plan." Under Catt's plan, each state would be accorded resources and attention in proportion to its chances of passing a state constitutional amendment. Members also lobbied Congress to pass the Anthony Amendment. Catt believed that President Wilson could be persuaded to support the federal amendment in time.[44] She feared that the NWP's tactics would only antagonize him and drive him farther from the cause. The "Winning Plan" was carefully orchestrated so that the NAWSA was perceived as "playing by the rules," contrary to the NWP. Catt and others in the NAWSA believed that Paul's tactics were hurting suffrage as a whole. Most scholars, however, attribute the amendment's final passage to a combination of efforts. "Between 1910 and 1920 an average of 15 states considered suffrage legislation each year, and there were more state referenda on women's voting rights than in the previous forty years combined."[45] As women won suffrage rights in increasing numbers of states, pressure mounted on Congress to pass the Nineteenth Amendment and to send it to the states for ratification. In 1918, the federal amendment failed in the Senate by two votes after passing the House of Representatives. Later that year, the NAWSA demonstrated the significance of the women's vote by targeting and defeating two antisuffrage incumbents in the Senate. As a result, the Nineteenth Amendment was sent to the states in 1919. The battle for ratification was waged in the states for fifteen months. The NAWSA state network, built as a part of the "Winning Plan," proved invaluable in mobilizing men and women to pressure state legislatures for timely ratification. On August 26, 1920, by a one-vote margin in Tennessee, the final state to ratify the amendment, the Anthony Amendment was added to the Constitution.

Never Underestimate the Value of One Vote

Tennessee tested women's ability to directly confront opponents and their tactics. It took pressure from President Wilson to convince Tennessee's governor to call the legislature into special session to consider the amendment. Court challenges to the amendment had been dismissed, clearing the way for the summer session called for August 9. Opponents poured into Nashville, and the state suffrage association issued a call for help from the national associations. The NAWSA and NWP worked together to poll for support across the state. At first it looked promising, but support eroded in the face of well-funded and well-organized opposition. "Legislators who had expressed favorable sentiments toward woman suffrage were threatened with the ruin of their business and political careers, some were all but kidnapped, and they were all systematically plied with liquor."[46] The Senate quickly passed the amendment and sent it to the House, where it stayed for ten days. During those ten days, members of the opposition were alleged to have bought votes, tried to break the quorum, appealed to "Negro phobia" and states' rights claims, and threatened legislators that a favorable vote would lead to their political death. Suffrage forces relentlessly counted votes in the House, and when the bill finally reached the floor on August 18, it was two votes short of passage. An attempt to table the bill resulted in a tie and failed when an opponent, Representative Banks Turner, turned proponent. When the final vote was called, it was the youngest member of the chamber, twenty-four-year-old Harry Burns, who cast the surprise "yea." In his pocket was a letter from his mother, an active suffragist:

> Hurrah! And vote for suffrage and don't keep them in doubt. I notice some of the speeches against. They were very bitter. I have been watching to see how you stood, but have noticed nothing yet. Don't forget to be a good boy and help Mrs. Catt put "Rat" in Ratification.[47]

The amendment passed, forty-nine to forty-seven, just in time for twenty-six million women of voting age to participate in the 1920 elections. Writing in 1920, Mary Church Terrell observed: "By a miracle the 19th Amendment has been ratified. We women now have a weapon of defense which we have never possessed before. It will be a shame and reproach to us if we do not use it."[48]

OPPOSITION TO WOMEN'S SUFFRAGE

Traditionally, opponents to suffrage were the liquor industry, big business, and the church. The liquor industry, represented by the U.S. Brewers' Association, the Wholesale Distillers' Association, and the Retail Dealers' Association, held significant power in U.S. politics, particularly in state legislatures. Its direct interest, however, was preventing prohibition rather than preventing women's suffrage. Since many women suffragists were also temperance advocates, the liquor industry believed keeping women away from the voting booth would be in its best long-term economic interests. Businesses, primarily textiles and agriculture, which would be directly affected by women's voting on progressive reform agendas provided a welcome ally for antisuffragists. A relative latecomer to the antisuffrage coalition was the Catholic Church. Suffrage opponents initially shied away from the church because of fears of foreigners and papists. The Catholic Church opposed suffrage primarily on ideological grounds, arguing that the church desired "to prevent a moral deterioration which suffrage could bring and feared the development of a political structure and social climate deleterious to Catholicism."[49] Like other hierarchically organized religions opposed to women's suffrage, the Catholic Church believed that a traditionally constituted society was ordained by God, and any move by either sex on the terrain of the other was viewed as unnatural and a threat to the universal order. The association of the birth control movement with women's rights and suffrage after 1885 only solidified Catholics' official opposition to a more public role for women.

Beginning in about 1880, female suffragists encountered their most vexing opponents to the cause: other women. At first suffragists dismissed the "remonstrants" (as they were called) as inconsequential and misguided. Later these opponents were attacked as fronts for male corporate interests, particularly the interests of their wealthy husbands. To suffragists Carrie Chapman Catt and Nettie Rogers Shuler, the "antis" served to "confuse public thinking by standing conspicuously in the limelight while the potent enemy worked in the darkness."[50] They further dismissed antisuffragists as throwbacks to outdated gender norms. Associating the antis with traditional gender relations spawned a destructive and false dichotomy between "true women" and "new women" that would surface again in the 1970s in relation to the Equal Rights Amendment.

Historian Susan Marshall expresses regret about the simplicity with which antisuffragists have been treated, arguing instead that their very existence is an important element in understanding women as political actors.[51] To suggest that the antis were merely fronts for more powerful males is to rob them of their autonomy and political agency, as well as to undermine the suffragists' own arguments about women's equality. The dichotomy between "modernists" and "traditionalists" or "careerists" and "traditionalists/homemakers" ignores the complex, changing social conditions most women faced at the turn of the century. Opportunities for new roles as well as the increasing economic pressure on families created by periodic recessions meant that women of all classes bridged the divide between private and public life by combining work and family obligations. According to Marshall, antisuffragists had their own gendered class interests that motivated them to undertake political action to "protect their own positions of privilege as elite volunteers, political appointees, and custodians of prosperity." The ideology of separate spheres, so evident in antisuffrage rhetoric, "enhanced their social influence as cultural arbiters, maintaining the exclusivity of elite social networks while simultaneously promoting new standards of domesticity that enhanced class control. . . . From their perspective, the franchise was an inferior form of power to that which they already enjoyed."[52] Antisuffragists' access to money, leisure, and extensive social networks enabled their political action, while "the confines of class mandated a circumspect public image."[53]

Point of Comparison

Women's Voting Rights Around the World

The United States was neither the first nor the last to grant women suffrage. New Zealand, the first nation to introduce universal suffrage did so during "the doldrums" of the U.S. suffrage movement. Katherine Sheppard, a prominent leader in New Zealand's suffrage movement, was also a founding member of the WCTU, an indication of the global character of women's organizations and resources. While there were many similarities in suffrage movements across nations prior to 1945, there were important differences too. Pamela Paxton and Melanie Hughes characterize the U.S. suffrage movement as exceptional in its size, for example, matched only by the mass movement in the United Kingdom. Female suffragists across nations were most similar in their social status—educated and middle to upper class. Their goals and organizing

A woman submits her ballot at a voting station in Rumaithiya May 16, 2009. Kuwaitis are voting in a parliamentary election on Saturday, two months after the ruler of the world's fourth largest oil exporter dissolved the parliament to end a long-running dispute with the government. Voters are casting their ballots in their third election since 2006 with early turnout slow and few confident that the polls will end a tussle between parliament and cabinet that has delayed economic reforms. *Reuters/Stephanie McGehee/Landov.*

ideologies differed however; arguments for universal suffrage were limited by legacies of colonialism, slavery, political authoritarianism, and in many instances by Catholicism.

No matter where women demonstrated for voting rights, they faced opposition. Women in Kuwait only gained suffrage in 2005 after forty years of agitation and struggle. Although the literacy rate for women in Kuwait is 77.5 percent, and women constitute a majority of university graduates, and the country has the highest female labor participation rate in the Middle East region (approximately 33 percent), women were still barred from voting in parliamentary elections and from standing as candidates. Elections were called in 2006, a year earlier than expected, and twenty-eight women declared their candidacy for parliament (making up 11 percent of all candidates). In May 2009 four women won seats in parliament, marking the first time a woman has won a seat in any of the three elections held since 2005. All four women are university professors and will make up 8 percent of the parliament. Saudi Arabia is now the only Gulf state to maintain voting restrictions based on sex.

1893	New Zealand	1924	Kazakhstan		Italy	1950	Haiti
		1928	Ecuador		Japan		India
1902	Australia		Ireland	1946	Guatemala	1951	Nepal
1906	Finland		United Kingdom		Korea, North	1952	Bolivia
1913	Norway				Macedonia	1953	Syria
1915	Denmark	1930	Turkey		Panama	1954	Ghana
1918	Austria	1931	Chile		Romania	1955	Cambodia
	Canada		Spain		Taiwan		Ethiopia
	Georgia		Sri Lanka		Venezuela		Nicaragua
	Poland	1932	Brazil		Vietnam		Peru
	Russia		Thailand	1947	Argentina	1956	Egypt
1919	Belarus	1934	Cuba		Mexico		Mali
	Germany	1935	Puerto Rico		Pakistan		Somalia
	Netherlands	1937	Philippines		Singapore		Tunisia
	Sweden	1939	El Salvador	1948	Belgium	1957	Colombia
	Ukraine	1942	Dominican Republic		Israel		Honduras
1920	Albania				Korea, South		Zimbabwe
	Czech Republic	1943	Yugoslavia		Niger	1958	Chad
	Slovakia	1944	Bulgaria	1949	China		Guinea
	United States		France		Costa Rica	1959	Madagascar
			Jamaica		Greece		Morocco
1921	Armenia	1945	Croatia			1960	Zaire
	Lithuania		Hungary			1961	Rwanda
			Indonesia				Sierra Leone

1962	Paraguay	1963	Kenya	1971	Switzerland	1978	Nigeria
	Uganda	1964	Afghanistan	1974	Jordan	1980	Iraq
	Zambia		Libya	1975	Mozambique	1994	South Africa
1963	Congo	1965	Sudan	1976	Portugal	1999	Qatar
	Iran						

Numerous organizations dedicated themselves to preventing women's suffrage. Many of these were organized at the state level in response to statewide women's suffrage referendum campaigns. These organizations included the Maine Association Opposed to Suffrage for Women and the Massachusetts Association Opposed to Further Extension of Suffrage to Women. The southern states were the last to grant women the vote, and for most, it came only with the federal amendment. Groups like the Southern Woman's League for the Rejection of the Susan B. Anthony Amendment linked the preservation of the southern "way of life" to protecting women's honor from degradation at the polling place. There were also more nationally focused groups like the National Association Opposed to Woman Suffrage and, by extension, *The Woman Patriot*, the organization's national publication that extended the antis' fight beyond ratification in 1920. The Daughters of the American Revolution supported postratification agitation by linking supporters of women's rights with the abolition of family relations.

The majority of those in support of suffrage and those opposed shared important characteristics, first among them being their sex. Like most of the suffragists of this era, women opposed to women's equality tended to be wealthy, well-educated, and well-connected to the political power elite. Historian Susan Marshall argues that it was only after suffragists turned to direct electoral strategies aimed at defeating state legislators and members of Congress opposed to suffrage and stepped up the populist state referendum campaigns that the antis lost their edge. As long as the decision remained in the hands of a few insulated elite male politicians, the antisuffragists were well positioned to exert their brand of influence exercised through kinship and shared class interests, even while maintaining an image of self-sacrificing womanhood.[54] Suffragists, however, were forced to adopt an expedient political strategy that moved them closer to antisuffragists' conservatism. This conservatism is evident in posters proclaiming "Votes for Mothers" and in suffragists' claim that women's unique gender-linked perspective would "clean house" in the political system. Gone were the demands for women's natural rights, and the suffrage movement succumbed to the "cult of domesticity" in the final years before ratification in an effort to expand its base of support—a calculated reaction to the success of the antisuffrage movement.[55]

2001	Bahrain
2003	Oman
2005	Kuwait

Source: Naomi Neft and Ann Levine, *Where Women Stand* (New York: Random House, 1997); Pamela Paxton and Melanie M. Hughes, *Women, Politics, and Power: A Global Perspective* (Thousand Oaks, Calif.: Pine Forge Press, 2007); Hassan M. Fattah, "First Time Out, Kuwaiti Women Become a Political Force," *New York Times*, June 26, 2006; "Kuwaiti Women Elected," *Voice of America News*, May 20, 2009.

POSTSUFFRAGE DIVISIONS: THE EQUAL RIGHTS AMENDMENT OR SPECIAL PROTECTIONS FOR WOMEN?

For the NAWSA and the NWP, the aftermath of suffrage was a time to savor the victory and reevaluate their missions. Much of the scholarly literature chronicles the demise of the organized women's movement in the period immediately following suffrage. Although membership in these two major women's organizations did decline somewhat, that was to be expected since their organizational focal point had been accomplished. Historian Nancy Cott writes that the 1920s, rather than marking the end of feminism, signaled the end of the suffrage movement and the emergence of the early struggle of modern feminism. "That struggle was, and is, to find language, organization, and goals adequate to the paradoxical situation of modern women, diverse individuals and subgroups who 'can't avoid being women whatever they do,' who inhabit the same world as men, not in the same way."[56] The two paths to gender equality clearly emerged during the period immediately following the ratification of the Anthony Amendment.

Women associated with the NAWSA under Catt's leadership had been persuaded to act as nonpartisans in the battle for suffrage, and many remained active in the organization in its new nonpartisan incarnation: the League of Women Voters. Rather than directly entering electoral politics, the League dedicated its efforts to educating newly enfranchised women, studying national legislation and social policy, and participating in local civic matters. Catt's earlier admonition against allegiance to any one party held, and the League separated itself from partisan politics entirely, even refusing to endorse specific candidates or to promote women from within its own ranks as candidates. Ironically, the period immediately following ratification may have yielded the largest "eligibility pool" of potential female candidates with prior political experience, education, and political interest in history, and yet that pool went untapped. The transition from nonpartisan reformers to partisan "insider pols" never took place. Some suffrage activists were offered positions in the administration but turned them down, suspecting tokenism. Other strong leaders who might have been viable candidates for national office turned their attention to suffrage battles in Europe and divorced themselves from American politics almost entirely.

Even Alice Paul, who pushed hardest for the introduction of an Equal Rights Amendment, spent the better part of the 1920s abroad. Like the NAWSA, the National Woman's Party underwent substantial reorganization between 1920 and 1923. It too eschewed a partisan electoral agenda and instead focused on achieving complete legal equality between men and women. For the remainder of the decade, members pursued three avenues toward that objective: the Equal Rights Amendment; its international equivalent, the Equal Rights Treaty; and the Equal Nationality Treaty dealing in a more limited way with citizenship rights.[57]

The history of the Equal Rights Amendment (ERA) is similar to that of the battle for suffrage, with one major exception: The ERA was not ratified. Once women had the vote, disagreements surfaced over how the vote could best be translated into political power so that women could exert influence over issues and legislation. Initially political parties courted women voters by offering reform proposals and including progressive planks designed to appeal to female voters in their party platforms. In 1921, for example, Congress passed the Sheppard-Towner bill for maternity and infant care. However, the *gender gap* that many predicted in 1920 did not actually materialize for another six decades. It wasn't until the election of Ronald Reagan in 1980 that women were significantly more likely than men to support Democratic candidates. When a women's voting bloc failed to materialize after two election cycles, the parties left women to themselves to set a political action agenda for the future.

The Fight for an Equal Rights Amendment: The First Generation

Not all women believed that the vote alone would bring about significant change. After all, the Thirteenth Amendment, which abolished slavery, was not enough to guarantee full citizenship rights to former slaves, thereby requiring the ratification of the Fourteenth and Fifteenth Amendments. Similarly, some suffragists argued that another constitutional amendment was required to guarantee women equal rights under the law. At a 1923 National Woman's Party convention called to identify state laws that discriminated against women, Alice Paul proposed the Equal Rights Amendment. Daniel Anthony, a Kansas representative and nephew of Susan B. Anthony, introduced it into Congress that same year.[58] The language read:

> Men and women shall have equal rights throughout the United States and every place subject to its jurisdiction. Congress shall have the power to enforce this article by appropriate legislation.

The rift between liberal feminists (advocates of the legal equality doctrine) and social reform feminists (advocates of the fairness doctrine) was always present

in the movement, but the single-minded pursuit of suffrage obscured its importance. Historian Nancy Cott argues that the *unity* attributed to the women's rights
movement during the decades preceding ratification was overblown and quite
unrealistic to expect.[59] As noted previously, each generation of women's rights
activists has had divisions over strategy as well as divisions born of race, class,
ethnic, and religious differences among women. It is no more realistic to expect
women to agree with one another than it would be to expect all men to agree with
one another on every issue and political strategy. In fact, some scholars argue that
the Nineteenth Amendment actually freed women to disagree among themselves
and to pursue a wide range of political interests as full citizens and active political
participants.[60] The two paths to gender equality were once again clearly at issue.

Introduction of the ERA brought to the surface the deep divide within both
the women's movement and society as a whole—between those who believed that
equality meant special treatment and enactment of protective legislation that considered the burdens women bore (consistent with the fairness doctrine) and those
who believed that only gender-neutral law and policies could achieve equality
(consistent with the legal equality doctrine). Those favoring the legal equality path
argued that protective legislation, although superficially designed to discriminate
in favor of women, in reality kept women from the best-paying jobs and denied
them the ability to competitively negotiate the terms of their labor as individuals. Women who had worked tirelessly to see fair protective legislation enacted
now accused NWP members of elitism, charging that they had never worked a
twelve-hour factory shift, so they did not, and could not, understand the issues
of working-class women. Labor unions quickly mobilized their membership in
opposition to the ERA and remained opposed to the amendment until 1973.

The rift over the ERA was exacerbated by the ambiguity of feminism as an
organizing ideology. NWP members, themselves arguably the strongest proponents of a legalistic, rights-based form of equality for women, held mixed views
about women's maternal function in society. The NWP focused primarily on
the similarities between men and women, but it also believed that the biological
fact of motherhood led men and women to possess different values. On the one
hand, motherhood was a force for justice in the world and a check on social
and sexual debasement. Yet it also believed "motherhood has been the rod held
over the backs of women to drive them into submission; it has been the chain
to hold them in dependence and to close-rivet them to a condition of slavery."[61]
Women's moral superiority, which flowed directly from maternalism (actual or
anticipatory) in the eyes of some NWP members, required that women be admitted to all quarters of society on an equal basis. Protective legislation proponents
also used this same maternal role to argue for special compensatory measures
for women only—laws that the NWP found inherently discriminatory and economically restrictive. When the NWP approached Alfred E. Smith, governor
of New York, to speak in opposition to protective legislation, he replied, "I
believe in equality, but I cannot nurse a baby."[62] For many, this summed up
the dilemma of equal rights. Women wanted equal opportunities, particularly
in the economic marketplace, but also in education, access to health care, and

marriage and family law. Yet the biological differences that left women with a unique role in perpetuating the species could not be denied. The crux of the debate over equal rights, both then and now, lies in how best to render the two compatible. The NWP and other liberal feminists argued that a blanket constitutional amendment was the only way to guarantee women equal opportunities across the board. Social reform feminists maintained that the only way to "make women equal" was to recognize and compensate women for the burdens they bore relative to childbirth and family responsibilities. To them, gender-neutral laws were inherently unfair to women because such laws would always be blind to women's maternity issues. The ERA provided a foil for the competing visions of women's role in society. In the end, opposition to the ERA from progressive organizations, such as the National Consumer's League, labor unions, and prominent female reformers like Eleanor Roosevelt scuttled any chance the legislation had of a formal hearing before Congress in the 1920s.

Over the next three decades support grew slowly but steadily for the amendment. During the 1930s, the National Association of Women Lawyers and the National Federation of Business and Professional Women's Clubs became sponsors of the ERA. In 1940, the Republican Party supported the ERA in its party platform, and the Democrats followed suit in 1944. In 1950 and 1953, the Senate passed the ERA but attached the Hayden rider, which provided that the amendment "shall not be construed to impair any rights, benefits or exemptions now or hereinafter conferred by law upon persons of the female sex."[63] Women's organizations immediately declared the Hayden rider an unacceptable attempt to have it both ways by allowing states to retain laws providing special benefits for women in employment.

The Second Generation

In the 1960s with the rise of the civil rights movement, the context in which the ERA was debated changed dramatically. When Congress passed the 1964 Civil Rights Act, it effectively removed protective legislation from the controversy over the ERA and paved the way for its eventual consideration. The 1964 act sought, among other things, to alleviate racial discrimination in employment, education, and public accommodations. Title VII of the act dealt with banning discrimination in employment. As the bill moved closer to passage, southern conservatives offered an amendment they thought would surely kill the entire bill. Judge Howard Smith, a Democratic congressman from Virginia, proposed to amend Title VII to include sex in the employment discrimination section. He offered his amendment, he said, "in a spirit of satire and cajolery," and the House promptly designated the day "Ladies Day." Supporters of the Civil Rights Bill feared that adding women to the employment-discrimination section would defeat the entire bill. However, a group of Republican and Democratic women, having planned to offer a similar amendment themselves, joined Smith's coalition of conservative southern Democrats. No committee hearings were ever held on the potential impact of the Smith amendment, nor did anyone pay much attention since it was offered "in jest." The amendment passed the House (and was not touched by the Senate). When the Civil Rights Act was finally passed and signed into law later that summer, liberal feminists gained their most powerful tool yet to combat sex discrimination in the workplace. Since protective employment law designed for women only is inherently discriminatory, such laws quickly fell by the wayside and with them organized labor's opposition to the ERA.

In 1970, two forces brought the ERA to the forefront of Congress's attention. First, the Pittsburgh chapter of the National Organization for Women (NOW) disrupted Senator Birch Bayh's hearings on giving eighteen-year-olds the vote (ultimately the Twenty-sixth Amendment), prompting Bayh to promise to hold hearings on the ERA in the following spring.[64] Second, Congresswomen Martha Griffiths and Edith Green freed the ERA from twenty-two years of captivity in committee without a hearing.[65] Green capitalized on a concurrent campaign to expand the scope of Title VII to include discrimination in education by holding hearings on that topic that eventually became hearings on discrimination against women in all facets of life. The official record from the education subcommittee hearings created a compelling case for equal rights. Representative Griffiths mounted a discharge-petition drive to free the ERA from the House Judiciary Committee, chaired by the very powerful octogenarian Emanuel Celler. A discharge petition is a procedural mechanism for circumventing committee inaction and bringing a resolution directly to the floor of the House of Representatives. It is a bold move and rarely successful. Of the 829 petitions filed prior to Griffiths's, only twenty-four bills were ever successfully discharged, and of those, only twenty passed the House. Of those twenty, only two were enacted into law.[66] Griffiths not only managed to convince 218 House members to sign the discharge petition, but she also got 332 of the 435 members to vote for the discharge resolution on the floor, effectively removing the ERA from the Judiciary Committee's grasp. On the Senate side, however, the resolution was amended to exempt women from the draft, effectively killing the chances for congressional passage in 1970. It was not until 1972, after more than a year of successive hearings, failed amendment attempts, and wording changes, that both houses of Congress successfully passed the bill with the constitutionally required two-thirds, enabling the resolution to be sent to the states.[67] Ironically, Emanuel Celler's congressional career, which began in 1923, the same year the ERA was introduced for the first time, ended in 1972, the year Congress finally passed the ERA. The opponent who defeated him in the Brooklyn district primary was herself an ardent supporter of the amendment.[68]

Unlike suffrage, the ERA enjoyed overwhelming bipartisan congressional favor. Supporters therefore predicted ratification by the states in record time. The experience in the first few months seemed to confirm their optimism. State legislatures competed with one another for the honor of being the first to ratify the ERA. Hawaii ratified the amendment on March 22, 1972—the same day the resolution passed the U.S. Senate. Five additional states ratified the amendment over the next two days, and by early 1973 twenty-four more states were added to the list. By 1977, however, only thirty-five states of the thirty-eight required to add the amendment to the Constitution had ratified it. A rare extension to the ratification deadline was granted in 1978, giving proponents until 1982 to gather the remaining three affirmative state votes. When the extended ratification deadline expired on June 30, 1982, not a single state had been added, and several states were actively working to rescind their prior ratification as the amendment died. The language of the defeated ERA read:

1. Equality of rights under the law shall not be denied or abridged by the United States or any State on account of sex.
2. The Congress shall have the power to enforce, by appropriate legislation, the provisions of this article.
3. This amendment shall take effect two years after the date of ratification.

Two weeks after the extended ratification deadline expired, the amendment was reintroduced in Congress, and it has been introduced in each Congress since that time.

Women Opposed to the Equal Rights Amendment

There is no question that forces opposed to the ERA were better organized and more effectively mobilized within individual states than pro-ERA organizations were immediately after congressional passage. Pro-ERA groups were located primarily in Washington, D.C., enabling them to lobby effectively for congressional passage. Once the resolution went to the states, however, these organizations lacked a network of state-based chapters that could work effectively for ratification. In contrast, opposition groups were founded primarily in the states and worked almost exclusively at the state level to oppose ratification. Two national organizations were formed to oppose the ERA and remain active even today: the Eagle Forum, founded in 1972 by Phyllis Schlafly, and Concerned Women for America (CWA), founded in 1979 by Beverly LaHaye. CWA developed a national network of anti-ERA prayer chains that weekly sought God's direct intervention. Stop-ERA, a Schlafly spinoff from the Eagle Forum, was dedicated specifically to the antiratification campaign in the states and has long been suspected of having direct ties to the John Birch Society. Other John Birch Society ad-hoc groups, such as HOTDOG (Humanitarians Opposed to Degrading Our Girls) in Utah and POW (Protect Our Women) in Wisconsin, formed in the unratified states. Even Stop-ERA spawned ad-hoc groups like AWARE (American Women Already Richly Endowed), Scratch Women's Lib, and the League for the Protection of Women and Children.[69] Most of these spinoff opposition groups were organized on the principle of protecting what were perceived as traditional family values. Operating from their self-appointed position as true defenders of women's interests, Eagle Forum and CWA leaders charged that the feminist agenda "deliberately degrades the homemaker."[70] They warned women that ratification of the ERA would radically alter the balance of power within families and would free men from their traditional economic obligations to their families.

Schlafly and LaHaye are both relatively privileged, well-educated women who head organizations with multimillion-dollar budgets. Yet these women denounce careers for other married women. Both movements claimed the separate spheres ideology as the source of women's fulfillment as well as God's plan for human survival. Married women who worked outside the home did so for selfish, narcissistic reasons and threatened the health and safety of their children and the very stability of the family by doing so. The anti-ERA forces ignored the new economic realities that often drove women into the paid workforce. Schlafly skillfully harkened back to the rhetoric of the antisuffrage campaign by labeling the ERA the "extra responsibilities amendment," a claim reminiscent of the charge that voting constituted an "unfair burden" on women already laden with home and child-care responsibilities. Similar to the antisuffragist leaders of the 1910s, anti-ERA leaders, although elites themselves, successfully portrayed the ERA as harmful to nonprofessional women and the poor. Both the CWA and the Eagle Forum have attracted a base of members from the middle and lower-middle classes and convinced them that ideal womanhood is characterized by the virtue of occupying a distinct and separate private sphere. Influence over men and the power to control men, they argued, flows from this privileged position, not government protection. "True women" are characterized by an attractive femininity that empowers them to speak for women, unlike the "amazons," "feminoids," or feminist "freaks" of the "third sex." By legitimizing an expanded political role for women, historian Susan Marshall concludes, "the feminist movement has bequeathed a much larger legacy to contemporary political culture: the mobilization of conservative women. . . . They serve as ironic testimony to feminist assertions of female equality."[71]

The Failure of the ERA

The debate that prevented the ERA from receiving congressional attention in the 1920s largely centered on economic and workplace issues, particularly special protective legislation that compensated women in the workplace for the additional burdens of caring for children and a family. Equal pay, equal access to educational opportunities, and the right to advance in employment were all tied intimately to the economic debate. Proponents argued that freeing women to act as individuals in the marketplace would empower them to be more effective advocates of their self-interest at home and in politics. They also believed that the ERA would strike down oppressive marriage and divorce laws; provide access to birth-control information; allow women the right to make contracts distinct from their husbands, to control their children, to maintain their names in marriage, and to exercise independent citizenship; equalize moral standards and treatment of sexually transmitted diseases; and even out penalties for sexual offenses.[72] Opponents, however, successfully convinced a majority of men and women that the ERA would radically change the way society was organized along gender lines. Moreover, this reorganization would not only have an impact on the workplace but, more importantly, would also affect the home and potentially the marital bed. This was more change than most citizens at the time were willing to accept. Opponents did not have to invest much in organized opposition because there was never a consensus in favor of the ERA in the 1920s, even among feminists active in major women's organizations. Most women favored fair treatment within the family and society at large. They did not view absolute legal equality as promised by the amendment as fair to women since the law might require that women be treated the same as men were. Any compensatory advantage women gained through progressive employment would be lost, and for many women, this was not the sort of equality they favored.

The climate was quite different in 1972. This time, issues of women's vulnerability in the workplace had largely been settled in the courts. Additionally, protective legislation aimed solely at women had been struck down as incompatible with Title VII of the 1964 Civil Rights Act. The issue of equal pay was broached by the Equal Pay Act of 1963. The debate now, framed largely by the opposition after 1973, centered on home protection and the preservation of traditional family values, including women's *right* to the role of primary caregiver and homemaker. By 1972, a considerable number of women had entered the paid workforce (43.9 percent, comprising 38.5 percent of the total paid workforce[73]), yet women opposed to the ERA voiced fears that full-time homemakers would be *forced* into the paid labor force. They argued that a change in the rules of gender relations would be inherently unfair to women and would lead to a rise in divorce rates, family and child abandonment, and poverty among women and children. They were, in effect, arguing that the separate spheres ideology protected women from the unfair burdens of the paid labor force. By 1982, the year the ERA officially died, more than 50 percent of married women were in the paid workforce. For African Americans, the percentage topped 60 percent.[74] For these women, the glorification of the separate spheres ideology by ERA opponents created a reality gap. They were not free to advocate for the *right* to be a full-time homemaker. Additionally, the Supreme Court acted in 1973 on the issue of abortion. Arguably, abortion was not directly related to the substantive content of the ERA, but opponents nonetheless used the *Roe v. Wade* decision to argue that ratification would inevitably lead to on-demand, government-funded abortions. Conservative groups effectively linked people's unease with the federal government's involvement in the abortion issue, cautioning that the ERA would give the federal government the power to enter private and family life. The conservative movement, organized largely by the fundamentalist Christian Right, gained strength and new members by linking abortion and states' rights issues to the ERA.

Surprisingly few scholarly studies have been published on the failure of the Equal Rights Amendment. Jane Mansbridge's *Why We Lost the ERA* (1986) is probably the best-known book on the subject. She argues that the ERA's failure can be attributed to a variety of causes, among them a backlash against Supreme Court decisions in the 1960s and 1970s (particularly *Roe v. Wade*, 1973), the political mobilization of fundamentalist Christians, the gender imbalance in the state legislatures of nonratifying states, the emergence of new ultraconservative, anti-ERA leadership in the Republican Party (Ronald Reagan, first among them), and a general deceleration in progressive reforms of all types during the 1970s.[75] Mary Frances Berry, in *Why ERA Failed* (1986), compares the ERA to other successful and unsuccessful campaigns to ratify amendments that attempted to make major changes in American life. Berry argues that in order for the ERA to have succeeded, a majority of voters would have had to recognize that a problem existed that had not been remedied by the courts, state legislatures, or the Congress, and which could only be solved by changing the Constitution.[76] She claims that supporters did too little, too late to effect the magnitude of change that was promised (or threatened, depending on one's perspective) by the ERA. Political scientist Janet Boles's book, *The Politics of the Equal Rights Amendment* (1978), examines political decision making under conditions of intense conflict. Her book is unique in that it was published prior to the ERA's final defeat. She argues that legislators in states failing to ratify actually voted against the conflict the ERA created rather than the amendment itself. In *Constitutional Inequality* (1985), Gilbert Steiner claims that between 1971 and 1973 there was a brief window of opportunity during which the ERA could have been ratified. That window was closed forever by three factors: legalization of abortion, the increasing saliency of the draft in the wake of the Soviet invasion of Afghanistan, and the increased prominence of Senator Sam Ervin (a long-time ERA opponent) after Watergate. Finally, *Sex, Gender, and the ERA* (1990) is the most recent book on the demise of the ERA. Authors Donald G. Mathews and Jane Sherron De Hart examine the politicization of women as a result of the ERA fight, and offer a unique state-level perspective.[77] Despite the ERA's defeat, women who became politicized during the ratification fight, regardless of which side they were on, remained active in politics, ushering in the second wave of feminist (and antifeminist) political activity.

The Equal Rights Amendment Reborn?

The Equal Rights Amendment would have become the Twenty-seventh Amendment to the Constitution if three-fourths of the states had ratified it by June 30, 1982. Instead, the "Madison Amendment" governing congressional pay raises, which was sent to the states for ratification in 1789, became the Twenty-seventh Amendment in 1992.[78] ERA supporters argue that acceptance of the Madison Amendment means that Congress has the power to maintain the legal viability of the ERA and the existing thirty-five state ratifications. If so, only three more states need to ratify the amendment to make the ERA a part of the U.S. Constitution. The legal rationale for the "Three-State Strategy" was developed by three law students in an article, "The Equal Rights Amendment: Why the ERA Remains Legally Viable and Properly Before the States," published in the *William & Mary Journal of Women and the Law* in 1997.[79] The Congressional Research Service analyzed this legal argument and concluded that the acceptance of the Madison Amendment does imply that ratification of the ERA by three more states could allow Congress to declare ratification accomplished. Ratification bills have since been introduced into six states (Florida, Illinois, Mississippi, Missouri, Oklahoma, and Virginia) and supporters seek to do the same in the remaining nine nonratifying states (Alabama, Arizona, Arkansas, Georgia, Louisiana, Nevada, North Carolina, South Carolina, and Utah). In 2009, resolutions to ratify have been introduced in Nevada and Arkansas. Similar legislation was introduced in Arkansas in 2007, but failed to advance when a House committee vote resulted in a tie. Phyllis Schlafly, founder of the Eagle Forum and Stop-ERA in the 1970s and now in her mid-80s, testified against the resolution at an Arkansas legislative committee hearing. A poll conducted in 2007 found that 73 percent of the Arkansas public favors the Equal Rights Amendment. The Arkansas legislature meets every two years, so the 2009 legislation is the first to be introduced since the poll was conducted.[79A]

Representative Carol Maloney, Democrat from New York, introduced the Equal Rights Amendment in the House of Representatives in the 108th Congress (2003–2004), 109th (2005–2006), and the 110th (2007–2008). As yet, a similar bill has not been introduced before the 111th Congress (2009–2010) but it is expected soon. The amendment is now also known as the Women's Equality Amendment. The late Senator Edward Kennedy, Democrat from Massachusetts, sponsored the ERA in the Senate each time it was introduced in the House. Both versions reproduce the language passed by Congress in 1972, but do not include ratification deadlines. In addition, Representative Robert Andrews, Democrat from New Jersey, introduced H.R. 38, which would require the House of Representatives to verify the ERA as part of the Constitution if three more states ratify it. All three legislative measures were assigned to committees, but none received floor action. With Democrats in control of both houses of Congress and the White House in 2009, there is potential for renewed federal action on the Women's Equality Amendment. However, even if passed by the requisite two-thirds of both houses of Congress, the proposed amendment would still require ratification by three-fourths of the state legislatures.

Nearly all of the 100 constitutions around the world written since 1980 include either a reference to gender equality rights or a prohibition against discrimination on the grounds of gender.[79B] Although the United States has yet to ratify the international Convention on the Elimination of All Forms of Discrimination Against Women (CEDAW), it did ratify the International Covenant on Civil and Political Rights (ICCPR) in 1992. The ICCPR commits the United States to "ensure the equal right of men and women to the enjoyment of all civil and political rights," including "equal protection" from sex discrimination.[79C] Support for constitutional equality remains high in the United States. A 2001 public opinion poll demonstrated historically high public support for the issue, but also suggested that mobilizing public support in favor of ratification will be difficult. While 96 percent of respondents supported constitutional equality for women and men, and 88 percent want the Constitution to explicitly guarantee equality, 72 percent mistakenly believe that the Constitution already includes this provision.[80]

THREE POLITICAL LESSONS ABOUT GENDER EQUALITY

1. A change in social norms and attitudes about women must precede a legal change, particularly in the case of a constitutional amendment.

The biggest obstacle to enfranchising women was the prevailing social attitude that women were not autonomous beings.[81] For women to be seen as competent in the public sphere, the power of the separate spheres ideology and coverture had to be overcome in the minds of those with the power to change existing law. It is no surprise then that it took so long for women to gain the vote. Centuries of socialization and custom and generations of attitudes had to be significantly altered so that adult women could be viewed as independent actors capable of making informed decisions apart from their fathers, brothers, and husbands. By the time the Nineteenth Amendment was ratified, women already had full voting rights in fifteen states, presidential voting rights in another twelve, and the right to participate in local and school elections in several others.[82] The full effect of the coverture doctrine was diminished when several states passed married women's property acts in the 1840s, giving free married women the right to control property for the first time. This single change—a woman's right to control her own property—was perhaps more democratizing than suffrage itself. Property gave women access to wealth, power, and additional rights that flowed from property ownership, such as the right to enter into and enforce contracts.

Coverture's grip on women's citizenship was, however, more difficult to sever and serves as an example of the principle that rights granted can be taken away. In the 1880s, Congress acted to link a woman's citizenship automatically to that of her husband. If a foreign-born woman married an American, she automatically gained American citizenship. But if an American-born woman married a foreign man, her American citizenship was stripped and she became an alien in her own country. Congress did not equalize citizenship rights until 1934.[83] So, while the ratification of the Nineteenth Amendment was law following a change that had already taken place in attitude and practice, it also offered women constitutional protection for their voting rights and, by extension, the protection of other granted rights since they now had a tool by which to hold legislators accountable.

By the time the Equal Rights Amendment passed both houses of Congress by the required two-thirds majorities in 1972, supporters believed that women's equality had achieved the same "bygone conclusion" status as suffrage had. They were wrong. Unlike the vote, which was a well-defined, single political act, *equality* was a much more ambiguous concept. While suffragists began their fight by arguing that admitting women to the voting population would radically change America for the better, they quickly learned to argue instead that votes for women would actually produce little noticeable change and could point to experience in suffrage states as evidence. Arguing that granting suffrage was really an issue of *fairness* was more palatable and successful than arguing that it would be an agent of change. Advocates of the ERA also tried to argue that fairness required an extension of equal rights to women. Because these rights did not take on a concrete form, it was difficult to persuade people that the radical changes to daily life predicted by Phyllis Schlafly and others opposed to the ERA would not come to pass. The ambiguity of *equal rights* allowed the opposition to suggest that ERA ratification would bring about unisex toilets, wives and daughters in military combat, and homosexual marriages. Despite the lack of evidence that any of their predictions would come true, *proving* otherwise was impossible. Additionally, people who supported women's equality but who were not ERA activists could point to more than a decade of change for the better through legislative action and favorable decisions by the courts. Why clutter the Constitution with rights already granted? Supporters were unable to convey the complexities and vagaries of relying on the courts and legislatures, which were historically unreliable. As long as other federal venues could be pursued, a constitutional change was unlikely.[84] In short, ERA supporters were unsuccessful in convincing the American public that the ERA would simply affirm the country's commitment to women's rights in ways that were consistent with current values. Furthermore, anti-ERA forces were very successful in raising fears about radical social change, the federal government's active intrusion into personal lives, and loss of the traditional family. The ERA was dead.

2. The role that states play in the pursuit of gender equality should not be underestimated.

Another lesson from the contrast has to do with the role that states play in determining women's rights. The United States is organized as a federal system with power shared between the national and fifty state governments. As a result, each state plays a significant role in defining the rights and privileges of its citizens. Although the supremacy clause of the Constitution constrains states to act within the bounds set by the national government, in the absence of national action the states may act alone. Therefore, the laws regarding women's rights differ by state. Two states (Utah and Wyoming) not only gave women the right to vote but also extended equal legal rights when those states first joined the union. Nine other states adopted their own ERAs in the 1970s, while another eight have included language resembling the Fourteenth Amendment's equal protection clause in their state constitutions. This leaves a patchwork of rights for women wholly dependent on their residence. (In chapters 6, 7, and 8, the policy implications of federalism are explored further.) Those working for suffrage were able to convince the public and three-fourths of the state legislatures that the right to vote was so fundamental to a functioning democracy that it could not be left to each state to decide. The wisdom of this strategy came only after decades of working in the states on suffrage referendums and state constitutional amendments. Proponents of the ERA were not successful in making a similar case. ERA supporters were also slow to realize the power each state held in determining the fate of the federal amendment and so delayed in organizing a state-based ratification strategy. Missing from the ERA ratification strategy was a 1970s version of Carrie Chapman Catt's "Winning Plan" that recognized the value of cultivating early allies in the states and state legislatures.

3. All women are not alike. There is no sex solidarity in pursuit of gender equality.

Women do not constitute a homogeneous population. Women proved to be some of the most vociferous opponents of both suffrage and the Equal Rights Amendment, much to the surprise of many female supporters. The same fault lines that divide the social, economic, and political interests of men divide women from one another. Empirical evidence from the 1970s and 1980s suggests that women do not act politically on the basis of shared interests with other women. "On most issues and candidacies that are seemingly relevant to gender, women do not differ materially from men, and both genders show considerable disunity."[85] In other words, gender does not bind women as a group any more than it binds men to one another in constructing and enacting a political agenda. While developing sex solidarity on a limited set of issues may be possible, the pursuit of gender equality is clearly not one of them. Women have developed alliances with African Americans and others similarly disadvantaged by the status quo only to break away when they felt their interests were being subsumed by those of other groups. Because women of different social, racial, or economic groups rarely interact as equals, they have difficulty making gender and common experiences as wives, mothers, and daughters a basis for political solidarity.[86]

The political equality promised women by the Nineteenth Amendment is only now slowly emerging as we enter the twenty-first century. Suffragists argued that the vote could also be used as a tool to extend women's rights and equality in the social and economic spheres; however, that has proven a slow, incremental process. The broad-brush equality in all spheres promised by the ERA threatened too much unpredictable change too quickly for many women. Equality and fairness are sometimes two different, albeit related, concepts. Suffragists started their campaign in 1848 by claiming in the *Declaration of Sentiments* that men and women are created equal and therefore eligible for the same rights and privileges of citizenship. This line of reasoning did not get very far since it said that men and women are the same and therefore should be accorded the same rights. ERA opponents convinced Americans that changing the "rules" (otherwise known as social norms) midway through the game was "unfair" to women who had remained at home to raise their children and support their husbands' careers. To now suggest that men and women be treated equally (the same) meant that women would be responsible for earning a living, paying child support, planning for retirement, and maintaining a mortgage. To many, this was incomprehensible.

The relationship between political, social, and economic equality is complex and illuminates the fault lines in how women's equality is understood and accepted. In order for political equality to be extended, women had to make significant progress in crossing the divide between the public and private spheres and demonstrate their social and economic competence. However, once granted the vote, some women saw an opening to extend equality of rights even further while others viewed the vote as an end in itself. With the death of the ERA in 1982, women in America are once again faced with the prospect of fighting over equality issue by issue. The paradox that characterizes women's equality—the desire to eliminate sex-specific laws and classifications on the one hand, and the desire to recognize women's differences on the other—ensures that the debate will continue for some time. Suffrage for women guarantees that women will be active on all sides of the debates, from inside the political system and as outside activists. Suffrage does not ensure that all women will act on a single agenda or set of interests.

CONCLUSION

It is with some sense of irony that scholars marked women's entrance into the electorate at precisely the moment the power of the vote declined.[87] Women's experience with politics prior to the Nineteenth Amendment (and even after they won the vote) was primarily a nonpartisan model based in voluntary associations. Whether political parties themselves declined in importance, or whether women viewed partisan activity as a "male model" and therefore chose a different strategy, women and partisan politics have been slow to mix. After suffrage was ratified, activists pursued a divided agenda consistent with the two paths to equality: One branch proposed the ERA and pushed for gender-neutral legal reforms; the other remained dedicated to nonpartisan civic participation in pursuit of fairness and inclusion in the existing social, political, and economic system. Although the language of equality remained important to both groups, there was little agreement on the meaning of full equality for women or on a strategy in pursuit of gender equality. Feminism as an ideology provided little guidance or cohesion in this regard.

Women and men are divided over the role women *should* play in politics and in society. In the fight for suffrage and legal equality, the National Woman's

Party adopted the view that women would achieve equality only when they were so fully integrated into politics, society, and the economy that sex no longer served as a useful way to classify citizens. This is consistent with the legal equality doctrine. Other women, some active in the League of Women Voters, viewed eradicating sex classifications as dangerous for women. They viewed women's role in public life as every bit as important as men's but distinctively female in its character. This perspective (which is consistent with the fairness doctrine) sees women as society's caretakers, government's watchdog, and politics' conscience. Some women supported neither path because they viewed any move by women to participate in public affairs as a violation of God's plan and dangerous to the well-being of the traditional family. That these themes dominated the debates over the failed ERA some fifty years after the Nineteenth Amendment was ratified suggests that the controversies of equality have not yet been settled. The next chapter continues the examination of the two paths in pursuit of women's equality by looking at women as voters and participants in the political process.

Suggested Readings, Web Resources, and Films

Beverly Baines and Ruth Rubio-Marin, eds, *The Gender of Constitutional Jurisprudence* (New York: Cambridge University Press, 2005).

Susan D. Becker, *The Origins of the Equal Rights Amendment: American Feminism Between the Wars* (Westport, Conn.: Greenwood Press, 1981).

Martha F. Davis, "The Equal Rights Amendment: Then and Now," *Columbia Journal of Gender and the Law* 17, no. 3 (2008): 419–460.

Carol Ellen Dubois, *Feminism and Suffrage: The Emergence of an Independent Women's Movement in America 1848–1869* (Ithaca, N.Y.: Cornell University Press, 1978).

Eleanor Flexnor and Ellen Fitzpatrick, *Century of Struggle: The Woman's Rights Movement in the United States,* enlarged edition (Cambridge, Mass.: Harvard University Press, 1996).

Helen Irving, *Gender and the Constitution: Equity and Agency in Comparative Constitutional Design* (New York: Cambridge University Press, 2008).

Jane Mansbridge, *Why We Lost the ERA* (Chicago: University of Chicago Press, 1986).

Susan Marshall, *Splintered Sisterhood: Gender and Class in the Campaign Against Woman Suffrage* (Madison: University of Wisconsin Press, 1997).

Nell Irvin Painter, *Sojourner Truth: A Life, A Symbol* (New York: Norton, 1996).

Gilbert Y. Steiner, *Constitutional Inequality: The Political Fortunes of the Equal Rights Amendment* (Washington, D.C.: Brookings Institution, 1985).

Doris Stevens, *Jailed for Freedom: American Women Win the Vote*, ed. Carol O'Hare (1920; reprint, Troutdale, Ore.: New Sage Press, 1995).

Rosalyn Terborg-Penn, *African American Women in the Struggle for the Vote, 1850–1920* (Bloomington: Indiana University Press, 1998).

A History of Women: http://www.roadsfromsenecafalls.org/.

The Equal Rights Amendment: http://www.equalrightsamendment.org/.

The National Women's Hall of Fame: http://www.greatwomen.org.

National Women's History Project: http://www.nwhp.org.

Places Where Women Made History: http://www.cr.nps.gov/nr/travel/pwwmh/.

Women's Rights National Historical Park: http://www.nps.gov/wori/wrnhp.htm.

Film: *Ida B Wells: A Passion for Justice* (Alexandria, Va.: PBS Video, 1990).

Film: *Iron Jawed Angels* (HBO Films, 2004).

Film: *Not for Ourselves Alone* (Alexandria, Va.: PBS Video, 1999).

Film: *One Woman, One Vote* (Alexandria, Va.: PBS Video, 1995).

Notes

1. Glenna Matthews, *The Rise of Public Woman* (New York: Oxford University Press, 1992).

2. Carol Ellen Dubois, *Feminism and Suffrage: The Emergence of an Independent Women's Movement in America 1848–1869* (Ithaca, N.Y.: Cornell University Press, 1978), p. 32.

3. Jeffrey D. Schultz and Laura van Assendelft, eds., *Encyclopedia of Women in American Politics* (Phoenix, Ariz.: Oryx Press, 1999), p. 205.

4. Matthews, *Rise of Public Woman*, p. 117.

5. Eleanor Flexnor and Ellen Fitzpatrick, *Century of Struggle: The Woman's Rights Movement in the United States*, enlarged ed. (Cambridge, Mass.: Harvard University Press, 1996), p. 70.

6. Paula Giddings, *When and Where I Enter: The Impact of Black Women on Race and Sex in America* (New York: Bantam Books, 1984) p. 39.

7. Flexnor and Fitzpartick, *Century of Struggle,* p. 70.

8. Elizabeth Cady Stanton, Susan B. Anthony, and Matilda Joslyn Gage, eds., *History of Woman Suffrage,* vol. 1 (Rochester, N.Y.: Charles Mann, 1881), p. 116. Sojourner Truth could neither read nor write, so Mrs. Frances D. Gage wrote down part of the speech. Mrs. Gage tried to capture Truth's unique dialect and speaking style in her record, but that has been dropped here. Some feminists today have accused white suffragists of recording Truth's words in ways that best served their cause and in the process robbing her of her "authentic voice." See Rosalyn Terborg-Penn, *African American Women in the Struggle for the Vote, 1850–1920* (Bloomington: Indiana University Press, 1998), for more on this debate. The most complete biography of Sojourner Truth is by Nell Irvin Painter, *Sojourner Truth: A Life, A Symbol* (New York: Norton, 1996). Painter has argued that Gage embellished Truth's oratory to create a feminist symbol. In fact, we will never know for sure what Sojourner Truth actually said at the Akron meeting (or at any other time in her life) since she could not write down her own thoughts and words.

9. Barbara Ryan, *Feminism and the Women's Movement: Dynamics of Change in Social Movement, Ideology, and Activism* (New York: Routledge, 1992).

10. Aileen S. Kraditor, *The Ideas of the Woman Suffrage Movement: 1890–1920* (New York: Norton, 1981).

11. Terborg-Penn, *African American Women in the Struggle for the Vote*, p. 24.

12. Kraditor, *Ideas of the Woman Suffrage Movement*, p. 3.

13. Terborg-Penn, *African American Women in the Struggle for the Vote*, p. 26.

14. Lee Ann Banaszak, *Why Movements Succeed or Fail: Opportunity, Culture, and the Struggle for Woman Suffrage* (Princeton, N.J.: Princeton University Press, 1996). See also Ryan, *Feminism and the Women's Movement*, p. 20.

15. Terborg-Penn, *African American Women in the Struggle for the Vote*, p. 27.

16. Ibid.

17. Terborg-Penn wrote (in *African American Women in the Struggle for the Vote*, p. 34) that Stanton and Anthony eventually relented in the face of strong opposition to the antimale stance taken by potential women members. She reported that although males were grudgingly admitted, no male was permitted to hold office in the organization.

18. Banaszak, *Why Movements Succeed or Fail*, p. 7.

19. Ibid., p. 8.

20. Terborg-Penn, *African American Women in the Struggle for the Vote*, p. 36.

21. Barbara Sinclair Deckard, *The Women's Movement: Political, Socioeconomic, and Psychological Issues* (New York: Harper & Row, 1983).

22. Banaszak, *Why Movements Succeed or Fail*, p. 8.

23. Terborg-Penn, *African American Women in the Struggle for the Vote*, p. 37.

24. Ibid., p. 38.

25. Ibid., p. 39.

26. Jewel L. Prestage, "In Quest of African American Political Women," *Annals of the American Academy of Political and Social Science* 515 (May 1991): 92.

27. Stanton, Anthony, and Gage, eds., *History of Woman Suffrage*, vol. 2.

28. Geoffrey C. Ward and Ken Burns, *Not for Ourselves Alone: The Story of Elizabeth Cady Stanton and Susan B. Anthony* (New York: Knopf, 1999), p. 144.

29. *Minor v. Happersett*, 88 U.S. 162 (1875).

30. Ibid.

31. Flexnor and Fitzpatrick, *Century of Struggle*, p. 275.

32. Ryan, *Feminism and the Women's Movement*, p. 28.

33. Ibid., p. 26.

34. Terborg-Penn, *African American Women in the Struggle for the Vote*, p. 91.

35. Prestage, "In Quest of African American Political Women," p. 95.

36. Ryan, *Feminism and the Women's Movement*.

37. Christine A. Lunardini, *From Equal Suffrage to Equal Rights: Alice Paul and the National Woman's Party, 1910–1928* (New York: New York University Press, 1986).

38. Ibid., p. 17.

39. Ibid., p. 29.

40. Ibid., p. 31.

41. Flexnor and Fitzpatrick, *Century of Struggle*, p. 275.

42. Ibid., p. 273.

43. Ibid., p. 277.

44. Ibid., p. 271.

45. Banaszak, *Why Movements Succeed or Fail*, p. 11.

46. Flexnor and Fitzpatrick, *Century of Struggle*, p. 315.

47. Ibid., p. 316.

48. Terborg-Penn, *African American Women in the Struggle for the Vote*, p. 136.

49. Jane Jerome Camhi, *Women Against Women: American Anti-Suffragism, 1880–1920* (Brooklyn, N.Y.: Carlson Publishing, 1994), p. 111.

50. Susan B. Anthony and Ida Husted Harper, eds., *The History of Woman Suffrage*, vol. 4 (Rochester, N.Y.: Charles Mann, 1902), p. xxix.

51. Susan E. Marshall, *Splintered Sisterhood: Gender and Class in the Campaign Against Woman Suffrage* (Madison: University of Wisconsin Press, 1997), p. 529.

52. Ibid., p. 224.

53. Ibid., pp. 12–13.

54. Ibid., pp. 226–227.

55. Ibid., p. 229.

56. Nancy F. Cott, *The Grounding of Modern Feminism* (New Haven, Conn.: Yale University Press, 1987), p. 10.

57. Susan D. Becker, *The Origins of the Equal Rights Amendment: American Feminism Between the Wars* (Westport, Conn.: Greenwood Press, 1981).

58. Doris Stevens, *Jailed for Freedom: American Women Win the Vote*, ed. Carol O'Hare (1920; reprint, Troutdale, Ore.: New Sage Press, 1995).

59. Nancy Cott, "Across the Great Divide: Women in Politics Before and After 1920," in *Women, Politics, and Change*, ed. Louise A. Tilly and Patricia Gurin (New York: Russell Sage Foundation, 1990), pp. 153–176.

60. Marjorie Spruill Wheeler, ed., *One Woman, One Vote: Rediscovering the Woman Suffrage Movement* (Troutdale, Ore.: New Sage Press, 1995), p. 355.

61. Becker, *Origins of the Equal Rights Amendment*, p. 51.

62. Ibid.

63. Jane J. Mansbridge, *Why We Lost the ERA* (Chicago: University of Chicago Press, 1986), p. 9.

64. Ibid., p. 10.

65. Gilbert Y. Steiner, *Constitutional Inequality: The Political Fortunes of the Equal Rights Amendment* (Washington, D.C.: Brookings Institution, 1985), p. 13.

66. Ibid., p. 15.

67. For a more detailed account of the congressional debates over the ERA, see Mansbridge, *Why We Lost the ERA*, pp. 8–19; Steiner, *Constitutional Inequality*, pp. 1–25.

68. Steiner, *Constitutional Inequality,* p. 22.

69. Janet K. Boles, *The Politics of the Equal Rights Amendment: Conflict and the Decision Process* (New York: Longman, 1979).

70. Marshall, *Splintered Sisterhood,* p. 232.

71. Ibid., p. 235.

72. Becker, *Origins of the Equal Rights Amendment,* p. 53.

73. Bureau of Labor Statistics, *Handbook of Labor Statistics,* Table 2; Employment and Earnings, January 1997.

74. Cynthia B. Costello, Shari Miles, and Anne J. Stone, eds., *The American Woman: 1999–2000* (New York: Norton, 1998), p. 294.

75. Mansbridge, *Why We Lost the ERA.* See also Mansbridge, "Organizing for the ERA: Cracks in the Façade of Unity," *in Women, Politics, and Change*, ed. Tilly and Gurin, pp. 323–338.

76. Mary Frances Berry, *Why ERA Failed: Politics, Women's Rights, and the Amending Process of the Constitution* (Bloomington: Indiana University Press, 1986), pp. 2–3.

77. Donald G. Mathews and Jane Sherron DeHart, *Sex, Gender, and the Politics of the ERA: A State and the Nation* (New York: Oxford University Press, 1990).

78. Amendment XXVII: No law, varying the compensation for the services of the Senators and Representatives, shall take effect, until an election of Representatives shall have intervened.

79. Allison Held, Sheryl Herndon, and Danielle Stager, "The Equal Rights Amendment: Why the ERA Remains Legally Viable and Properly Before the States," *William & Mary Journal of Women and the Law* (Spring 1997): 113–136.

80. *The ERA Campaign,* no. 5 (July 2001), accessed at http://eracampaignweb .kishosting.com/newsletter5.html.

81. Ryan, *Feminism and the Women's Movement,* p. 33.

82. Kristi Anderson, *After Suffrage: Women in Partisan and Electoral Politics Before the New Deal* (Chicago: University of Chicago Press, 1996), p. 50.

83. Virginia Sapiro, *Women in American Society,* 4th ed. (Mountain View, Calif.: Mayfield Publishing, 1999).

84. Mansbridge, *Why We Lost the ERA,* p. 35. See also Berry, *Why ERA Failed.*

85. David O. Sears and Leonie Huddy, "On the Origins of Political Disunity Among Women," in *Women, Politics, and Change,* ed. Tilly and Gurin, pp. 252–253.

86. Louise A. Tilly and Patricia Gurin, "Women, Politics, and Change," *in Women, Politics, and Change,* ed. Tilly and Gurin, pp. 24–26.

87. See Suzanne Lebsock, "Women and American Politics, 1880–1920," in *Women, Politics, and Change,* ed. Tilly and Gurin, pp. 35–62.

79A. "ERA Resolutions Filed in Arkansas," January 2009, accessed at: http://www.4era. org/news.html.

79B. Helen Irving, *Gender and the Constitution: Equity and Agency in Comparative Constitution Design* (New York: Cambridge University Press, 2008) p. 166.

79C. Martha F. Davis, "The Equal Rights Amendment: Then and Now," *Columbia Journal of Gender and the Law* 17, no. 3 (2008): p. 439.

Suffrage Accomplished: Women as Political Participants

Once the legal barrier to the ballot was removed, women entered the electorate slowly, although African American women were reported by at least one account to have registered in large numbers in the South.[1] By and large, they voted similarly to men, but initially in smaller numbers. This slow start led one commentator to declare that women's suffrage was a colossal failure. Women's suffrage was not a failure but rather a casualty of unrealistic expectations—both positive and negative. "Men said that woman suffrage had promised almost everything and accomplished almost nothing when neither of these were true."[2] There are some remarkable historical examples of women forming voting coalitions in order to effect social change in their communities. In Nashville, Tennessee, African American and white women formed an alliance to demonstrate their power in expanding government's role and to promote a progressive political agenda.[3] The vote opened the door to the public sphere and a corresponding host of politically relevant activities. Now, more than eighty years after gaining the vote, women are more likely than men to register to vote and to actually vote; they are as likely as men to engage in a whole range of extra-electoral activities. Women are, however, less likely than men to donate large sums of money to campaigns, to express interest in running for elective office, and to be recruited for office by political party elites. Also, the forces that attract women to politics are different from those that attract men. The vote did not, however, make women think alike, act alike, or view issues of gender equality similarly. As we saw in the previous chapter, women differ from one another along roughly the same social, economic, and political lines that divide men. These differences influence women's levels and types of political engagement. This chapter examines women's political participation in the electorate as voters, partisans, and members of political organizations.

In the process we will analyze how women's participation differs from men's and how women differ from one another as they pursue gender equality through political participation.

WOMEN ENTER THE ELECTORATE AS VOTERS

After ratification of the Nineteenth Amendment, procedures had to be clarified before women could actually cast their ballots. For instance, states had to change their laws and practices to allow women to register, and the pace of change varied by region. Women in Mississippi and Georgia, for example, did not vote in the November 1920 election because the state registrars upheld the existing four-month residency requirement.[4] Because counties and states did not always keep records of voting registration rates and hardly ever noted the sex of the voter in their records, little data are available to evaluate women's suffrage during the first decade following ratification. As with other new groups of voters, it took time for women to develop voting habits, including accepting the idea that voting was appropriate behavior for women. Interviews with nonvoting women in Chicago conducted in 1923 found that more than 10 percent still believed it was *wrong* for a woman to vote.[5] In the years that followed ratification, African American women in the North continued to participate in politics, but feeling they had been abandoned by both white feminists in the final hours of the suffrage fight and by the Republican Party, they became disillusioned with national politics.[6]

Although many attribute decreases in overall voter turnout rates during the 1920s to women entering the eligible electorate but not actually casting a ballot, some evidence contradicts that notion. It now seems just as likely that political parties experienced a dealigning period during which partisans of both genders moved away from the existing political parties and were therefore not attracted to vote for a party's candidate.[7] Sophinisba Breckinridge conducted the first empirical study of women's political participation in 1933.[8] In *Women in the Twentieth Century,* Breckinridge examined registration rates of men and women in Illinois, the only state to keep records separated by sex. Between 1914[9] and 1931, women's registration rates in Chicago increased by 10 percent whereas men's decreased by the same percentage. The resulting "male advantage" in registration in 1931 was just 16 percent.[10]

Women Voters Outnumber Men at the Polls

By 1980, the gap in registration rates had narrowed considerably, with 80 percent of men and 77 percent of women registered to vote. Women's registration rates surpassed those of men in the 1984 election and have remained higher in every subsequent national election. The 1965 Voting Rights Act was the catalyst for

African American women's dramatic increase in voter registration, particularly in the South. Although registration figures by gender are not available for the period prior to 1975, later voter participation figures suggest that women were well represented among the newly registered Southern voters.[11] Since 1980, the proportion of female voters has surpassed the proportion of male voters in every presidential election. In 2008, for example, 65.7 percent of eligible female voters cast ballots compared to 61.5 percent of eligible male voters. The absolute number of women voting has also been higher than that of men in every presidential election since 1964. According to the Pew Research Center, 70.4 million women voted in 2008, compared with 60.7 million men.[12] In nonpresidential years, women have outvoted men since 1986. In the midterm election of 1994, labeled the "Year of the Angry White Male," 44.9 percent of women and 44.4 percent of men turned out. In the 1996 presidential election, 55.5 percent of voting-age women cast their vote, compared to 52.8 percent of men. In real numbers, 7.8 million more women than men cast votes in the 2000 presidential contest.[13]

Estimates of men's and women's voting habits are generally based on post-election surveys. This methodology relies on individuals' correctly recalling whether they actually voted on Election Day. While remembering such information seems like a simple task, the considerable social pressure to fulfil one's civic duty to vote causes many people to misreport having voted, thereby slightly inflating the turnout statistics. Evidence from vote validation studies has shown that men are slightly more likely to misreport voting than are women, making the gap between male and female turnout rates potentially even larger than reported.[14]

The gap between men and women at the polls varies depending on a number of sociodemographic characteristics, such as age, race, region of the country, and education. In recent years, women under forty-five years old voted at significantly higher rates than did men in the same age group.[15] However, after fifty-five years of age, the percentage of women voting declined while the percentage of male voters held steady, thus reversing the gender advantage seen in younger age cohorts. For example, among citizens between the ages of sixty-five and seventy-four, 64.8 percent of men reported voting in the 2002 election, compared to only 61.7 percent of women.[16] Researchers are not sure why women's participation tends to decline after age fifty-five when arguably they would have more, not less, resources and time to dedicate to politics. Among African American voters, the gender gap in voter turn-out has been consistently larger than in the population at large. Researchers attribute higher participation rates among African American women than men to a feminist identity developed through experiences with both race and sex discrimination, and strong ties to their community and church.[17] In 2000, for example, 59.7 percent of black women voted, compared to 53 percent of black men. This gap is 4.1 points larger than that of the entire population. In the South, where states were slow to admit women to the voting population even after the federal amendment was ratified, the gender gap was largest prior to the election of 1970. In 1964, the gender gap in the South was nearly double that of the rest of the nation. More recently, regional disparities have largely disappeared. Among those with an elementary-school education, men vote at higher rates than women do. However, a high-school diploma reverses the gap, with women voting at higher rates than similarly educated men. Among those who have some college or a college degree, men and women report voting at roughly the same rates.[18]

Other factors beyond gender influence a person's decision to vote or to abstain. Since voter turnout in the United States is consistently lower than in most other developed nations, researchers have studied the motives and behaviors of voters for several decades to answer: Why *don't* people vote? To cast a ballot, citizens must register to vote, which often means navigating a complex bureaucratic process. The 1993 National Voter Registration Act (NVRA), also known as "Motor Voter," made registering somewhat easier. The NVRA requires states to allow citizens to register to vote at the same time they do other business with the state, such as register a car, renew a driver's license, or apply for some forms of government benefits. Although this program registered more people and created a slightly more diverse voter pool in terms of education, age, and race, the effects of the NVRA on actual voter turnout were not as great as had once been predicted. However, voter registration increased in nearly every demographic group for the 2004 presidential election. The Committee for the Study of the Electorate (CASE) estimates that 72 percent of citizens eligible to vote were registered prior to the 2004 election.[19]

Overall registration rates for the 2008 election were slightly lower than for 2004 at 71 percent of the eligible population registered to vote. A May 2008 survey of state election officials by the Associated Press found that in the six states that collected voter data by gender, comparing 2008 with 2004, the registration rate for new voters was up 89 percent among women, compared with 74 percent among men. Young people between 18–29 and African Americans were also heavily represented among newly registered, first-time voters in 2008.[20]

Political scientists have also investigated why people *do* vote. After years of investigation and countless theories, the answer remains a mystery. Some political scientists posit that citizens undertake a rational calculation of the costs and benefits of voting. If the benefits outweigh the costs, citizens appear at the polls. However, the benefits one person derives are difficult to determine since, according to some calculations, a voter is more likely to be struck by lightning on the way to the polls than to change an election's outcome.[21] So the benefits of voting are more often such intangibles as altruism or a sense of duty fulfilled. The costs vary depending on an individual's circumstances. For women, the costs may be higher than for men since women are still considered the primary caregivers of children and elderly parents, and are more likely to have jobs with less flexible schedules or that pay on an hourly basis, all of which affect the time that women have to go to the polls. And yet women vote at higher rates than men, so other factors must be at work. Most likely, voting is a standing decision or a habit that individuals develop as they join communities and become integrated into the social and political life of their communities. Voting, in this context, is an act of social participation or civic involvement. In general, voters are connected to the larger society and to their communities in ways that nonvoters are not.[22] Women have a history of community-based involvement, and this tradition may help explain why women are more likely to vote than men. In the 2008 presidential election, particularly during the Democratic primaries, there is some evidence that women were drawn to the polls by the prospect of voting for a woman with a strong chance to win the nomination. Likewise, Republican voters had an historic opportunity to vote for a ticket that included a woman vice-presidential candidate for the first time. Candidate Hillary Clinton intentionally targeted

Point of Comparison

Gender and Political Participation: Trends in Voter Turnout

A report issued in 2002 by the International Institute for Democracy and Electoral Assistance (IDEA), dedicated a chapter to women's electoral power. Although the Convention on the Elimination of All Forms of Discrimination Against Women (CEDAW), which was adopted by the United Nations in 1979 and subsequently signed by 165 nations, emphasizes the importance of equal participation of women with men in public life, women remain far from parity worldwide. Laws restricting women's voting rights remain in only a very few states in the Middle East, and although men and women still differ along a number of political dimensions, women's participation as voters has risen to the point that few differences between men and women at the ballot box exist in many advanced industrialized countries. "Long term secular trends in social norms and in structural lifestyles seem to have contributed towards removing many factors that inhibited women's voting participation."[1]

Comparative data on voter turnout that includes a breakdown by sex are difficult to find. Not all nations identify the sex of the voter. Drawing on the Comparative Study of Electoral Systems which is constructed from national election surveys conducted in nineteen countries from 1996–1999, the table below depicts gender difference in turnout in seventeen nations. The percentages in the table represent the proportion of men and women who reported *not voting* in general elections. Note that these data are expressed differently than we are used to seeing them, but the conclusions are the same.

Women reported voting at statistically significantly higher levels than men in only one nation (Norway), in thirteen nations there was no significant gender difference in voting between men and women, and women reported significantly lower levels of turnout in the three newer democracies in Central and Eastern Europe (Poland, Hungary, Romania).

women and called upon all voters to break the "highest and hardest glass ceiling in America." In a May 2008 letter to the Democratic superdelegates, Clinton wrote, "I am in this race for all the women in their nineties who've told me they were born before women could vote and they want to live to see a woman in the White House. For all the women who are energized for the first time, and voting for the first time. For the little girls . . ."[23] Nearly a quarter century earlier, the last time a female held a place on a national presidential ticket, Geraldine Ferraro also reported that "women across the country have told me what a huge personal impact my nomination had on their lives." Exit poll data from the 1984 presidential race found that 23 percent of women agreed that Ferraro's candidacy had made them more interested in politics.[24]

Nation	Men	Women	Difference (W − M)	Sig.
Norway	15.7	12.2	−3.5	.021*
Britain	17.5	17.1	−0.4	.779
Germany	7.3	7.2	−0.1	.919
Spain	10.3	10.5	+0.2	.909
Taiwan	8.3	8.6	+0.3	.860
Israel	16.9	16.5	−0.4	.868
New Zealand	5.0	5.5	+0.5	.438
Japan	15.8	16.8	+1.0	.611
Australia	3.6	5.5	+1.9	.048
Mexico	23.1	25.0	+1.9	.327
Czech Republic	9.3	11.6	+2.3	.192
Ukraine	21.9	24.2	+2.3	.354
USA	21.8	24.7	+2.9	.180
Netherlands	20.1	23.1	+3.0	.092*
Poland	40.4	44.6	+4.2	.056*
Hungary	23.9	28.7	+4.8	.035*
Romania	7.6	15.6	+8.0	.000*
ALL	13.7	15.5	+1.8	

* The significance of the difference between men and women is measured by Gamma and denotes a statistically significant difference in five cases.
1. Pippa Norris, "Women's Power at the Ballot Box," in *Voter Turnout Since 1945: A Global Report* (International IDEA, 2002), pp. 95–102.

Twenty-Something Citizens

Among young men and women between the ages of eighteen and twenty-nine, the female advantage holds in voter-turnout statistics (see Tables 3.1 and 3.2). Yet when first-year college students were asked in 2008 about the importance of influencing the political structure, only 25.1 percent of men and 19.2 percent of women considered it essential or very important (see Table 3.3). This is consistent with other research demonstrating that women tend to be less politically engaged overall than their male counterparts. Yet, 31 percent of female

TABLE 3.1 Percentages of Young Women and Men Voting 1978–2000

	Ages 20–24		Ages 25–29		All Ages	
	Women	Men	Women	Men	Women	Men
2000	37.2	31.3	43.3	37.5	56.2	53.1
1998	19.1	17.7	25.7	23.1	42.4	41.4
1996	36.1	30.7	43.7	36.5	55.5	52.8
1994	23.8	20.3	28.7	27.4	63.2	60.8
1992	47.2	42.1	52.8	46.8	62.3	60.2
1990	22.2	21.1	31.1	27.0	45.4	44.6
1988	39.7	35.8	46.0	41.2	58.3	56.4
1986	24.7	22.6	31.7	29.8	46.1	45.8
1984	44.6	41.0	53.3	48.2	60.8	59.0
1982	26.7	27.8	37.2	35.1	48.4	48.7
1980	43.9	40.4	52.4	50.0	59.4	59.1
1978	26.1	25.3	34.0	33.3	45.3	46.6

Source: Center for American Women and Politics (CAWP), Eagleton Institute of Politics, Rutgers University.

TABLE 3.2 Percentages of Young Women and Men Voting (ages 18–29), 2002–2008

	(%) Women	(%) Men	Female Advantage
2008	54.9	47.2	7.7
2006	27.0	24.0	3.0
2004*	50.0	44.0	6.0
2002	24.0	21.0	3.0

* includes only voters ages 18–24 for this year only.
Source: Mark Hugo Lopez, Emily Kirby, and Jared Sagoff. "Voter Turnout Among Young Women and Men,"CIRCLE (The Center for Information and Research on Civic Learning and Engagement), July 2005 (2004 data); Mark Hugo Lopez, Karlo Barrios Marcelo, and Emily Hoban Kirby, "Youth Voter Turnout Increases in 2006," CIRCLE, June 2007 (2002 and 2006 data); Emily Hoban Kirby and Kei Kawashima-Ginsberg, "The Youth Vote in 2008," CIRCLE, April 2009 (2008 data).

TABLE 3.3 Percentages of First-Year College Students Who Consider It Essential or Very Important That They Influence the Political Structure

	(%) Women	(%) Men	Male Advantage
2008	19.3	25.1	5.8
2006	18.9	25.3	6.4
2004	17.1	22.6	5.5
2002	17.0	22.8	5.8
2000	15.3	20.4	5.1
1998	15.3	20.3	5.0
1996	16.8	21.3	4.5
1994	19.1	22.8	3.7
1992	20.6	24.2	3.6
1990	20.3	24.3	4.0
1988	14.2	19.8	5.6
1986	13.8	19.3	5.5
1984	14.3	20.3	6.0
1982	13.7	20.0	6.3
1980	14.4	22.2	7.8
1978	13.3	20.2	6.9
1976	13.4	20.3	6.9
1974	10.9	16.8	5.9

Source: Center for American Women and Politics (CAWP), Eagleton Institute of Politics, Rutgers University; 2004–2008 data come directly from the Cooperative Institutional Research Program (CIRP); freshman survey conducted annually by the Higher Education Research Institute (HERI) at UCLA (http://www.gseis.ucla.edu/heri/index.php).

first-year students planned to participate in a community action program while only 23 percent of males expressed similar intentions.[25]

A spring 2000 study of young people between the ages of eighteen and twenty-four conducted by The White House Project Education Fund supported the connection between community involvement and voting, particularly among women. Forty-one percent of men and 55 percent of women reported being very or somewhat involved in their communities and with issues important to those communities. Women, however, volunteered at significantly higher rates than men. Twenty-eight percent of young women and only 19 percent of young men reported volunteering at least a couple of times a month. Of the women who frequently volunteered, 43 percent had parents who voted in every election, 34 percent reported that they themselves would probably vote, and 30 percent were registered to vote. For those least involved in their communities, 15 percent of the young women said they were not likely to vote, 21 percent were not registered voters, and 21 percent had parents who did not vote.[26] A study released in 2003 of young people between the ages of eighteen and twenty-five found that more women than men viewed voting as a responsibility (23 percent of women versus 20 percent of men), while more men saw voting as a choice (35 percent of men versus 31 percent of women).[27]

In the 2004 election, an estimated 20.9 million people under thirty voted. Although the proportion of young people in the electorate remained the same as in 2000 (approximately 17 percent), nearly 28 percent more voters under thirty cast ballots, translating into 4.6 million more votes.[28] In the ten most hotly contested battleground states, 64.4 percent of the youth population turned out to vote. This suggests a positive trend for future elections. Because such a large proportion of the 14 million newly eligible voters turned out for their first presidential election, in the next election they will be considered "likely voters" and subject to more attention from politicians. A survey conducted by Rock the Vote found that the issues young voters cared most about differed very little from those important to voters in older age cohorts: jobs and the economy; terrorism and national security; the war in Iraq; education; civil liberties and civil rights; and crime and violence. However, even though the issues were the same, many young voters complained that the presidential campaigns did not frame the issues in a way that spoke directly to young voters. Voters under thirty were more likely than older voters to express concerns about lesbian and gay rights, and keeping abortion legal.

An estimated 44 million 18–29-year-olds were eligible to vote in the 2008 elections, constituting one-fifth (21.4 percent) of the total eligible voting population. Several women's organizations created pre-election summer initiatives designed to register and mobilize young women in November. The Feminist Majority, for example, sponsored "Get Out Her Vote," a voter education and registration drive. Kathy Spillar, executive vice president, noted, "We've seen a huge increase in young people registering and participating in elections. We are going to be educating about what is at stake for young women and abortion rights is a major piece of that, from who constitutes the Supreme Court to what Congress is doing and what is on the ballot." Similarly, the Feminist Majority, which has campus affiliates active on some 120 campuses nationwide, focused on mobilizing participation in states with controversial ballot initiatives. For example, Colorado's Amendment 48, also known as the "Fetal Personhood Initiative," defined life as beginning with fertilization. California's Proposition 4 included a parental notification requirement before a minor could obtain a legal abortion and South Dakota ballots included Measure 11, an attempt to resurrect the abortion ban defeated by a large margin in 2006, but this time with exceptions in the case of rape or incest, or to protect the life and health of the mother. Each of these ballot initiatives was rejected by voters in 2008. Campus groups sponsored panel discussions and education campaigns directed at young and first-time voters. A separate organization, The Younger Women's Task Force, ran a "Voting Vixen" campaign to encourage voter participation under the slogan, "Be pro whatever it is you believe in and get out and vote."[29]

Anticipation of a high turnout for young women and men in November 2008 was based on their record-high participation during the primary season. Youth voter turnout in the 2008 primaries and caucuses was nearly double that in the 2000 primaries. In the 2008 general election, an estimated 22 million voters under 30 participated—an increase of 2 million over 2004. Turnout among young people represented an increase of 11 percent over 2000 rates, and represented the largest single election cycle (2004 to 2008) increase for any age group. The gap between female and male young voters was nearly eight percentage points. Individuals with college experience voted at significantly higher rates than those without (62.1 percent compared with 35.9 percent). Youth turnout was highest in Washington, D.C. (76 percent), Minnesota (68 percent), and Iowa (63 percent). In Washington, D.C., young people voted at a higher rate (by three percentage points) than their adult counterparts for the first time anywhere.

THE GENDER GAP

Pick up a daily newspaper during the months preceding an election and you'll find evidence that journalists and politicians alike perceive the gender gap to be a powerful political phenomenon.[30] The gender gap is said to exist when women as a group vote significantly different from men. The term originated during the 1980 presidential election when the victor, Republican Ronald Reagan, ran a campaign dominated by his opposition to the Equal Rights Amendment and to abortion, and his support of "traditional family values," which many interpreted as a return to traditional roles for women. The Republican Party's continuing affinity for these themes is presumed to have alienated many women voters throughout the 1990s and into the next century.[31]

The gender gap should be calculated by subtracting the percentage of men who voted for a particular candidate from the percentage of women who voted for the same candidate (or vice versa), not by looking at how one candidate did among either women or men alone. Although after 1980 the gender gap referred to the greater likelihood of women's voting for a Democratic Party candidate, a candidate cannot be said to have lost an election because she or he lost the "women's vote." Conceptually, when a single candidate fares well against her opponent among female voters, for example, her opponent fares equally well among male voters. "By definition, the Republicans' 'problem with women' is exactly the same size as the Democrats' 'problem with men.'"[32] Since the size of the gender gap in the 1992 and 1996 presidential contests and in a number of high-profile congressional races was larger than the margin of victory, women have become the target of appeals by both parties. Add to that the fact that more women than men actually cast votes in every election since 1964 and few politicians can afford to ignore the potential of women's electoral power. The Center for American Women and Politics (CAWP) at Rutgers University estimates that the gender gap affected thirteen races in the 1998 midterm elections. Five Democratic victors benefited from women's votes, and eight Republican winners owed their victories to men.[33] In 2000, six women were candidates for the U.S. Senate and sizable gender gaps were evident in three of their races, with women providing the margin of victory for

Hillary Rodham Clinton (D-NY), Debbie Stabenow (D-MI), and Maria Cantwell (D-WA). Similarly, the Feminist Majority Foundation estimates that Al Gore received 54 percent of the female vote, but only 42 percent of the male vote, creating a twelve-point gender gap in the 2000 presidential contest. Working women overwhelmingly preferred Gore to Bush (58 percent for Gore and 39 percent for Bush). The Foundation also estimates that women voters delivered all five of the U.S. Senate races in which Democrats picked up seats in 2000. For example, Debbie Stabenow of Michigan won a close race with an eleven-point gender gap. Similarly, Bill Nelson of Florida enjoyed an eleven-point advantage among women voters; Thomas Carper of Delaware won with a twelve-point gender gap; Mark Dayton won the Minnesota Senate seat with a nine-point gap; and Mel Carnahan posthumously won the Missouri Senate seat with a six-point gender gap. In each of these races, the surplus of women's votes made up for less than a majority of men's votes.[34]

Polling in October prior to the 2008 election found a decided gender gap in five critical presidential battleground states. In Colorado and Florida, for example, Barack Obama benefitted from a 12-point gender gap, while in Nevada, Ohio, and Pennsylvania the gap was single digits (6, 7, and 9 points respectively).[35] Analysis by the Feminist Majority identified a decisive gender gap in four states (Colorado, 7 points; Indiana, 5 points; New Hampshire, 12 points; and North Carolina, 12 points), three of which voted overwhelmingly for George W. Bush in 2004 (Colorado, Indiana, and North Carolina). In these four states, Barack Obama won a majority of women, lost a majority of men, yet won the state overall, leading analysts to conclude that women "delivered" these four states to Obama.[36] Similar analysis attributes New Hampshire Democrat Jean Shaheen's 2008 U.S. Senate victory over Republican incumbent John Sununu to women voters (60 percent of women voted for Shaheen compared to 45 percent of men). Women also accounted for the margin of votes that ousted North Carolina's incumbent U.S. Senator Elizabeth Dole in favor of Democratic challenger Kay Hagan, with an 8-point gender gap in Hagan's favor.[37]

The contemporary gender gap generally ranges from 7 to 12 percentage points in congressional elections, and hovered at about 7.7 percentage points on average in presidential contests from 1980 to 2000. President Clinton enjoyed a significantly larger gender gap in both 1992 and 1996. The gap in 2000 was similarly large. Men and women were clearly divided in their preferences for president, with a majority of women (54 percent versus 42 percent of men) voting for Al Gore and a majority of men (54 percent versus 43 percent of women) voting for George W. Bush. In 2004, the gender gap was only 7 percentage points, with 48 percent of women versus 55 percent of men voting for George W. Bush. The gender gap was largest between women and men who were sixty or over (11 percentage points), unmarried (8 points), or college-educated (9 points).[38] Despite the gender gap in favor of Democratic candidate John Kerry, President Bush increased his overall share of the women's vote in 2004. Kerry's 51 percent share of the women's vote was down from 2000, when Vice President Gore captured 54 percent of the women's vote. President Bush's ability to attract

48 percent of the women's vote (up from 43 percent in 2000) was a major factor contributing to his margin of victory in the popular vote.[39] Democratic pollster Celinda Lake reported that Kerry lost support relative to 2000 levels among white women, working women, and married women. Many political analysts and women's advocates argue that Kerry began to prioritize women's issues too late in the campaign. Susan Carroll, senior scholar at the Center for American Women and Politics, says that Kerry was "so concerned with establishing his commander-in-chief credentials that he failed to address other important issues like job security, retirement benefits and health care." He made women wonder, "Do you really understand the kind of difficulties I'm having?"[40] Alternatively, Marie Wilson of The White House Project argues that security issues drove women more than anyone anticipated. Still others point to the role moral values presumably played in voters' calculus, arguing that Bush conveyed a message that resonated with mainstream voters, including women.

In 2008 women strongly preferred Barack Obama to John McCain (56 percent for Obama, 43 percent for McCain) while men split their votes about evenly between the two candidates (49 percent for Obama, 48 percent for McCain). Thus, the gender gap in 2008 was about 7 percentage points, identical to the gap in 2004. Senator Obama, however, drew more female voters in 2008 than Senator John Kerry did in 2004. Obama enjoyed support from a clear majority of female voters (56 percent), while Kerry attracted only a bare majority of women (51 percent) in 2004. By contrast, Senator John McCain did worse with women voters, attracting only 43 percent of their votes compared to George W. Bush's 48 percent in 2004. Obama's share of white and Latina voters represent gender gaps as well. He pulled 46 percent of white women compared with 41 percent of white men, and among Latino voters, 68 percent of women versus 64 percent of men. There was no gap for African American voters—both sexes overwhelmingly supported Barack Obama (96 percent, women; 95 percent, men).

The impact of the gender gap, therefore, depends wholly on the proportion of men and women voting in any single election. As noted earlier, women have been turning out in both higher proportions and larger numbers than men have in recent elections, making a gender gap favoring women a determining force in the outcome of these elections. The 1996 presidential contest attracted attention in this regard since the gender gap was estimated at 14 percentage points—the largest since World War II—and increased by 40 percent compared to the 1992 vote. Similarly, when it looked like the direction of the gender gap among women had changed in favor of Republican candidate George W. Bush in late September of the 2004 contest, both political parties scrambled to get ahead of the dynamic.[41] Media pundits in 2008 quickly labeled John McCain's choice of Alaska Governor Sarah Palin as his running mate as an overture to women voters—perhaps even women who had supported Hillary Clinton in the Democratic primaries but were slow to transfer their support to Barack Obama. It is important to remember, though, that gender differences do not make up the largest gap within the electorate. The gaps in voting behavior created by race (consistently 50 points between whites and blacks) and economic differences (12 points between the rich and poor in 2004) surpass gender in size, if not in significance. Likewise, gender does not act in a vacuum. We do not yet fully understand, for example, the ways that gender affects political attitudes and behavior across lines of race, class, ethnicity, and country of origin. Thus, a new area of gender research involves "intersectionality."[42] The gender gap attracts media attention because a political "war of the sexes" is more socially acceptable than competition between the races or economic classes.

The Source of the Gender Gap

The definitive source of the gender gap continues to elude scholars, but evidence supports a number of theories. Some attribute the gap to the changing employment circumstances and attitudes of women,[43] while others attribute it to the changing politics of men.[44] More broadly, scholars explain the different candidate preferences of men and women as differences in policy preferences, most especially those regarding government social welfare spending and the importance of a government "safety net." Additionally, "women's issues," such as abortion and women's rights, along with "men's issues," such as the use of force and military expansion, have been investigated as root causes of the gender gap. Perceptions of the economy, either in general (most important to women) or in regard to an individual's personal finances (most salient to men), have been shown to differ by gender.[45] The Feminist Majority Foundation surmises that the gender gap in the 2000 election was fueled by issues such as abortion rights, gun control, military spending, women's rights, and human services.[46] In 2004, although much has been made of the influence of moral values in determining vote choice, careful analysis suggests that jobs and the economy were the top issue for 23 percent, followed by homeland security and terrorism (19 percent), Iraq (13 percent), and moral values (10 percent). These issues did take precedence, however, over issues traditionally defined as "women's concerns." Among voters polled, only 8 percent said that their top concern was health care and prescription drug coverage, and a mere 4 percent reported education as their top issue. Indeed, a majority of women voters believe not enough attention was given to issues such as equal pay for women (60 percent), prevention of violence against women (58 percent), women's equality under the law (61 percent), appointing women to leadership positions in the administration (54 percent), and education (46 percent). Although younger and older women; Democrat, Republican, and independent women; and married and unmarried women varied by degree in their perceptions of candidate attention, all women were more likely than men to believe that not enough attention was paid to these issues.[47]

Similar issues were prominent throughout the 2008 campaign, but by the time people went to the polls in November, the economy and energy were considered the top issue priorities by nearly all voters.[48] Women were significantly more pessimistic than men in their outlook on their economic future. Women were more likely to say they were falling behind economically with a majority (60 percent) reporting that their income was falling behind the cost of living. Fifty-nine percent of women versus 46 percent of men were concerned about "achieving their economic and financial goals over the next five years" as the fall campaign got underway. When asked about equality of opportunity relative to employment and the economy, an overwhelming majority of men believed that they compete with women on a level playing field, with only about half of women saying the same. Not surprisingly then, women supported a larger role for government in solving problems and meeting the needs of people—most especially in providing families with economic security, enforcing equal pay and equal opportunities, ensuring universal access to health care, expanding access to contraceptives and sex education to avoid unintended pregnancies, and ensuring that parents have access to affordable quality child care.[49]

Even when men and women hold the same policy positions, the levels of salience may differ to the extent that a single issue may determine the vote for one gender while being relatively unimportant to the other gender's final decision. This is most evident in the issue of abortion. While men and women do not differ significantly in their relative positions on abortion policy, the salience of the issue acts as a political mobilizing force for women, but not for men.[50] Further, although men and women may encounter the same set of issues in the same political context, they react differently to the political environment. Women and men experience changes in society, politics, and the economy differently and therefore exhibit different political responses to these changes. For example, as the percentage of women who head households increases, the gender gap increases, leading researchers to conclude that economic vulnerability as the result of social and economic changes increases women's Democratic partisanship.[51] Simultaneously, the generality of partisan differences between men and women shapes the political context outside of elections. "They [partisan differences] affect the kinds of issues on the political agenda, the nature of ensuing policy debates and the nomination process, as well as elections themselves."[52] In this respect, the gender gap is both persistent and dynamic. The size of the gender gap likely depends on the behavior of strategic politicians, trends in the nature of families, and economic conditions.

The issue of homeland security and terrorism added a new dimension to the 2004 presidential contest and was immediately interpreted within the context of the gender gap. "Security moms" and "NASCAR dads" joined the "waitress moms" and "soccer moms" of past elections. The media defined "security moms" as married women with children under 18 concerned about security and likely Bush voters as a result. The label's origins have been traced to a Celinda Lake poll reporting that while only 17 percent of men were personally concerned that a member of their family would be the victim of a terrorist attack, 43 percent of women and 53 percent of mothers with children under 18 expressed the same concern. When front-page stories in the *New York Times* and the *Washington Post* (September 22 and 23, respectively), alleging the importance of the "security mom," claimed that women were moving away from Kerry and toward Bush, women's organizations reacted swiftly to debunk the myth of the security mom.[53] Anna Greenberg's memo, "The Security Mom Myth," demonstrates that while Kerry was underperforming among women relative to previous Democratic candidates, this could not be attributed to security issues. Sixty-four percent of women voters in 2004 were married, but only 43 percent had children under eighteen years of age, meaning that only 26 percent of all women voters could be characterized as "security moms." Of these women, only one in four listed terrorism as the top reason to vote for President Bush. Women tend to worry more than men about their personal and economic security largely because they are more likely to be victims of crime at home and they are more likely to live on the economic margins. According to Greenberg, this concern about personal security does not necessarily translate into political preferences in the national security realm.[54] In fact, men were more likely than women to make the war on terrorism and security a part of their voting calculus. The economic downturn in 2008 eclipsed the Iraq war and the "war on terrorism" for both men and women, but women consistently expressed a deeper sense of economic vulnerability that likely translated into greater issue saliency for the economy in their vote choice.

Implicit but often hidden in the labels like "security moms" and "NASCAR dads" is the status of "parent" and the assumption that mothers and fathers have political interests that are distinct from voters without children. Researchers Laurel Elder and Steven Greene have investigated the impact of being a parent on political views.[55] Although in the aftermath of the 2004 election, pundits attributed President Bush's reelection to his improved performance among women and his ability to attract "security moms" to the Republican ticket and the Democrat's failure to win back "NASCAR dads," Elder and Greene find little empirical support for the claims. Both of these labels implied that political forces and parenthood moved voters in a more conservative direction that benefitted Republicans. In fact, data from the 2004 election demonstrate that there was no "mother gap" on issues concerning security—in other words, women with children were no different than women without children. However, there was a gender gap on the majority of defense- and war-related issues. In 2004, women were significantly less likely than men to support increases in defense spending and spending on the "war on terror." Women were also less likely than men to think the Iraq War and the war in Afghanistan were "worth it," and less likely to think that the Bush Administration had made the country more secure. Thus, Elder and Greene conclude, "the 'Security Mom' label was not only inaccurate, but misrepresented the position of mothers to some extent. Mothers, like women overall, were distinctive in being less supportive than men on most defense- and war-related issues in 2004."[56] The only issue on which mothers were substantively distinctive from other women was on issues of social welfare; mothers favored greater access to health care and government support for jobs. The researchers found no evidence in support of a 'NASCAR dad' label. Fathers did not differ on any issue from nonfathers, leading researchers to conclude that "it seems almost pointless to talk about 'dads' as a distinct political entity at all. . . ."[57] Thus, we must approach media frames organized around gender "difference" with some skepticism. While there is indeed evidence of a gender gap in American elections, its source is multifaceted and complex, and its impact is highly contextual in any single election cycle. Rarely can the voting behavior of men and women be so simply labeled and explained.

GENDER DIFFERENCES IN POLITICAL PARTICIPATION BEYOND THE BALLOT

One unique feature of the U.S. political system is the sheer number of opportunities to engage in political activity apart from elections. For our purposes, we can define political participation as "activity that has the intent or effect of influencing government action—either directly by affecting the making or implementation of public policy or indirectly by influencing the selection of people who make those policies."[58] For example, an individual might work on a campaign, contribute funds to candidates or an important cause, serve on a local board or commission, contact public officials, join political or interest-based organizations, or volunteer for a community-based organization. Some forms of participation require resources, whereas others ask for nothing more than interest. Passionate interest sometimes results in protests or other unconventional forms of participation. Women who petitioned for suffrage rights engaged in protests to attract attention in the absence of power and access to other important political resources. Political participation is not equally distributed throughout the population. Ironically, those who stand to benefit the most from working on a cause or for a candidate (e.g., the poor, minorities, women) often participate less frequently than others. Conventional wisdom holds that women participate beyond the ballot box at lower rates than men do. However, a closer examination reveals that if demographic characteristics are held constant, men and women participate at roughly equal levels across many, but not all, forms of political activity.

Do Men and Women Specialize in Forms of Political Participation?

In the largest study of its kind, political scientists Sidney Verba, Kay Schlozman, and Henry Brady surveyed more than fifteen thousand Americans by telephone and then interviewed more than twenty-five hundred in person to understand voluntary civic participation.[59] The researchers used the data to compare men's and women's behavior in traditional political activity and other forms of volunteerism to test the hypothesis that men and women specialize in different types of political engagement. In examining political participation,[60] they found that women engaged in an average of 2.0 political acts, while men undertook 2.3, a minor but statistically significant difference.[61] In other words, men are generally slightly more actively involved than woman in traditional forms of political engagement. More substantively important differences appear in specific acts. The largest differences appear in making a campaign contribution, contacting a government official, and affiliating with a political organization. In each case, men are more likely than women to have engaged in these political activities.[62]

The picture is slightly different for nonpolitical voluntary activities, but perhaps not as different as we might have expected. For nearly two centuries, women have participated at the periphery of politics through community and religious organizations. However, the data here show that men and women engage in about the same number of nonpolitical activities, with a few notable exceptions. Women are more likely than men to attend church and donate their time and money to the church. However, once men and women get involved, the amount of time and money they give is significantly different. Men give more hours to the church than women do, whereas women give more hours to politics than men do. When it comes to money though, men contribute more frequently and are likely to contribute larger sums of money to both the church and to political causes and candidates. This raises the resource question.

Access to Monetary and Political Resources

Do men have access to more monetary resources and do they use those resources to greater political effect than women? Political scientists do not have a complete answer to this question. Research has shown that the propensity to give and the amount contributed depend on both the total family income and the portion of family income derived from the respondent's income. Women's mean family income is lower than men's, and women's personal share of the family income is lower even in cases where both spouses work outside the home. Most often clustered in lower-paying jobs, women have less money to give to the candidates and causes they support. Not only do women give in smaller amounts, they give less consistently and for ideological reasons (to support a cause) rather than for economic reasons.[63] Money is only one type of resource though; others include time and civic skills. Men and women in the Verba, Schlozman, and Brady civic-participation study had roughly the same number of free hours per week, although among full-time workers and full-time workers with preschool children, men had an average of twenty-four more free minutes per week than women did. Essentially, this suggests that life and family circumstances, not gender, determine the time available for civic activity. With respect to skills, the researchers included civic skills acquired on the job, through organizational affiliation, and through church membership. Among those working outside the home and those affiliated with an organization or church, men have significantly more opportunity to practice civic skills on the job than women do. In other settings, there are no differences between men and women. "[M]en's advantage with respect to civic skills exercised on the job results from a process by which men have differential access to jobs that require education and training and not from differential access to skill opportunities in these jobs."[64]

In translating the role that resources play in laying a path to political participation, the researchers found that by and large men and women do not significantly differ in how they engage in politics. Voluntary organizational involvement is an important avenue for women, particularly for women who do not work outside the home. This finding confirms the historical role voluntary associations have played for women in politics. The most striking finding, however, has to do with monetary resources. Women have less money than men do, and less control over the money in their households, disadvantaging them in an increasingly important form of political activity: making political contributions. The wage gap between men and women is well known; but less well known is the way in which the household economic gap exacerbates inequalities in political activity.[65] With respect to campaign contributions, men give more often than women and in substantially larger amounts. Once active in politics, women are more likely than men to give their time, while men are more likely than women to give money. Three-fourths of those who give $200 or more are men.[66] The emergence of women's political action committees (PACs) dedicated to soliciting funds from women in favor of electing women have given women a new and highly instrumental way to channel their campaign contributions. For example, EMILY's List (Early Money Is Like Yeast, it makes the dough rise) was founded in 1985 to recruit, fund, and elect Democratic pro-choice women to federal office. Ninety-four percent of EMILY's List contributors are women. In the 2004 election cycle, EMILY's List ranked tenth on the overall top-contributors list, having contributed over $2,288,619 to the candidates on its list.[67] In 2004, there were forty-five campaign PACs and donor networks that were primarily oriented to women candidates or had a predominantly female donor base. Fourteen were national women's PACs and thirty-one were state or local networks spread throughout nineteen states.[68] These developments suggest that as women gain access to more financial resources, they may choose to dedicate them to supporting women in politics.

The Internet Expands Women's Political Donations and Outreach

The Women's Campaign Fund Forum (WCF) released a report on women's political giving in 2008. Their report, titled "Vote with Your Purse 2.0: Women's Online Giving, Offline Power," focuses on the ways in which women can increase their political engagement and voice through online giving to political candidates.[69] Although women command more than half of U.S. wealth, they accounted for less than one-third (27 percent) of the individual hard-money contributions to federal candidates, party committees, and political action committees—the same share they held in 2006. However, women contributed substantially more in the 2008 presidential contests than in previous races, giving in excess of $109 million as of September 2, 2008, compared with only $37 million during the entire 2000 presidential election cycle. Although the data for 2008 is incomplete, women's giving between 2000 and 2004 nearly tripled, leading analysts to expect a sizable increase when all of the contributions for the 2008 election have been recorded. Data show that women contributed $60 million to Senator Hillary Clinton's primary campaign, accounting for half (49.6 percent) of her total donations. Likewise, the Center for Responsive Politics reports that women represented nearly half of Barack Obama's donors (47 percent) and contributed about $75 million to his campaign (as of September, 2008). The "Vote with Your Purse" study also found that women are more likely to donate to issue-based charitable causes in an effort to produce social change, with single women identified as the "most generous donors." WCF's overall initiative was designed to explore whether female charitable donors could become equally generous political donors in an effort to expand women's political power and voice. They found that the Internet enhances the values that motivate women to give political money (impact, inspiration, information, inclusion, interaction) and that female online donors actively research politics using online sources almost exclusively. Female online donors are heavily engaged in social networking and nearly eighty percent forwarded political information or stories to friends and family along with a request to get engaged with the campaign or to donate money to the campaign. Thus, while women may have been slow to join the online revolution and slow to dedicate their financial resources to politics, the opportunities afforded by online giving may open new doors for women's influence in politics and enhance women's appeal to candidates of both parties.

Do Men and Women Speak in Different Political Voices?

From the same citizen participation data set described above, Verba, Schlozman, and Brady investigated whether men and women speak "in a different voice" when it comes to politics.[70] Do men and women follow their respective *voices* by undertaking particularized political action? The researchers also investigated the type of rewards men and women received from their political participation. This research is significant because it connects attitudes with action. Previous studies have only examined this connection among political elites, such as officeholders or political-party officials. We know, for example, that female legislators' distinctive attitudes are reflected in their choice of legislative priorities and roll-call voting behavior, most notably in sponsoring and promoting legislation dealing with women, children, and the family.[71]

Among the citizenry at large, however, the researchers found that men and women are more similar than dissimilar. Again, conventional generalizations can be misleading in this regard. Gender exercised little direct pressure on defining political voice, rewards gained through participation, or issues that mobilized participation. Rather, race and ethnicity, level of education, and family circumstances—like the presence of school-aged children—were most powerful for both men and women. The differences that exist between men and women are not always predictable. For example, women have historically engaged most directly in grassroots, organizational, and local activities, but researchers were surprised to learn that, at least in 1990 (the year in which this survey was conducted), women were often less locally and organizationally focused than men. Men and women gained similar gratifications from political participation. While voting was motivated by civic gratifications, activities involving campaigns were more likely driven by social motivations. In short, researchers found that the nature of the act rather than the gender of the actor determined the type of gratification experienced. Finally, researchers hypothesized that men and women would be moved by different issues. From a list of eleven issues mentioned by respondents as important in motivating their participation, men and women differed substantially on only two: education and abortion. For women, concern about education motivated 20 percent of their issue-based activity, compared to 13 percent for men. The issue of abortion motivated 14 percent of women's activity, compared to 8 percent of men's activity. Gaps between the advantaged and disadvantaged, and among racial and ethnic groups surpassed gender gaps in almost every case. With regard to children and family issues, previous findings led researchers to hypothesize that women would be moved more directly than men by issues related to children. However, for both men and women action was prompted by having school-aged children in the home rather than by gender. In short, this research cautions that expectations about citizen participation based on gender can best be understood by looking at the complex relational webs that define people's lives. Race, ethnicity, socioeconomic status, and family circumstances are greater predictors of motivation, gratification, and issue interests than gender alone.

Researchers Marc Hooghe and Dietlind Stolle investigated gender differences in anticipated political behavior among fourteen-year-olds.[72] While there is little difference in the level of participation anticipated at this age (girls mention 4.55 political acts, boys mention 4.0), the type of participation varies by gender. Girls intend to participate in various forms of activism, but less so in political parties or in running for office, while boys more often indicated a wish to become party members and/or seek political office. Boys were also nearly twice as likely to mention engaging in some form of radical behavior involving confrontational participation (e.g., spraying slogans, blocking traffic). Explanations for the type of activity indicated included the number of years an individual expected to be in school (correlates positively with conventional political acts and negatively with radical political actions), membership in associations (correlates positively with conventional forms of participation, but bears no relationship to anticipated unconventional actions), and the breadth of formal civics education (corresponds positively with conventional- and social-movement participation and negatively with radical participation). There is no way to tell, of course, whether these findings are predictive of adult behavior. The analysis cannot tell how the political action repertoires of boys and girls will develop over time. This research poses an important reformulation of the basic question "Why do women participate less?" to "Why do adult women fail to do the things they intended to do when they were adolescent girls?"[73]

Levels of Political Interest Among Men and Women

Researchers have long believed that interest motivates political activity.[74] Women in previous generations were conditioned to believe that politics was a "man's world" and therefore beyond the scope of their interest. Perhaps this legacy continues even today. Significant gaps in interest and attentiveness to politics remain between men and women. In analysis based on the 1989 American National Election Study, for example, 61 percent of men, as opposed to only 45 percent of women, reported that they followed politics some or most of the time. In 1996, 74 percent of women, compared to 59 percent of men, said they sometimes did not feel competent to understand public affairs. Interestingly, statistically controlling for differences in level of education between men and women does not eliminate this gap in perceived political competence. Actually, the gap is greatest among college-educated people! Sixty-one percent of college-educated women but only 36 percent of similarly educated men find politics too complicated to understand, according to a March 2000 study conducted by researchers at the University of Pennsylvania's Annenberg Public Policy Center.[75]

At the root of this gender difference may lie a political knowledge gap. Researchers remain puzzled as to why fewer questions on political knowledge are correctly answered by women than men. Using a national sample of adults, researchers at the Annenberg Center asked thirteen questions about the major presidential candidates' backgrounds and their positions on issues to test political knowledge during the 2000 primary campaign. In addition to analyzing the number of correct answers, researchers also paid attention to how often respondents answered incorrectly or stated that they did not know an answer. Previous research on political knowledge found that women were more likely than men to answer that they did not know an answer, while men more often answered questions correctly. In the Annenberg survey, men were more likely to answer correctly, whereas women were more likely to answer incorrectly *and* to state that they did not know an answer. The knowledge deficit for women persisted even when several sociodemographic variables, such as level of education, age, race, income, marital status, party identification, and media exposure, were statistically controlled. Simply being male added one correct answer out of the thirteen knowledge items in the scale.[76]

A recent study tested a slightly different question related to political knowledge, political interest, and political behavior.[77] Rather than test actual knowledge, Mary Christine Banwart analyzed how informed young men and women *perceive* they are about politics. Since previous studies have found that self-assessment of how much one has learned about a candidate predicts knowledge levels, and in turn, knowledge predicts participatory behavior, this study hypothesizes that a person's perceived level of information or knowledge will also influence his or her perspective on politicians and politics, as well as serve as a political motivator for action. A national survey of college students conducted one week prior to the November 2004 elections found that males perceived themselves more informed about the 2004 election, but that interest levels between men and women did not significantly differ and both groups reported a high interest in the upcoming election. However, young women reported higher levels of political cynicism, defined as a "sense of powerless-ness" and as the "feeling that government in general and political leaders in particular do not care about the public's opinions and are not acting in the best interest of the people."[78] Though this skepticism did not impact the vote in 2004 (more young women voted than did men), Banwart notes that it still raises concerns regarding women's confidence in their role in other areas of politics such as running for office and more actively seeking leadership roles. Interest-ingly, when the perceived level of knowledge is held constant between men and women, the difference in political cynicism disappears. Similarly, differences in political cynicism are erased when political interest is held constant between men and women. The study concludes, "Continuing to ask questions about why women and men differ in their perceptions of politics can lead us to a better understanding of the types of messages and information that work to generate an overall more informed, interested, confident, and engaged electorate."[79]

This gap in political knowledge is not a feature unique to American politics. Analyzing election studies in the United States, Great Britain, and Canada, Emily Guyman finds a consistent gap, with men having more political knowl-edge than women.[80] The size of the gap varies by country, ranging between 3 percent and 10 percent. Guyman attributes the gap to a variety of factors, but primarily to the different concerns that men and women face in their daily lives. Women are the primary caregivers of children, and analysis indicates that having children under the age of eighteen has a negative effect on political knowledge. Men and women have different social networks and affiliate with different types of associations. As a result, "political knowledge is not equally distributed."[81]

The consequences of the knowledge gap are varied. Differences in knowl-edge may result in different criteria for choosing candidates. Men may use pocketbook considerations while women may rely on character or social poli-cies as determinants.[82] Other studies find that women discuss politics less often with family and friends and are less likely to try to convince others how to vote.

The ability to discuss politics and persuade others to act is based, to some degree, on political knowledge. If women do not take part in the flow of private and public political dialogue, their opportunity to exert influence over candidates, issues, and agendas will be reduced.[83]

EXPLAINING THE PATTERNS OF PARTICIPATION

The patterns of political participation present us with a puzzle: Women vote at higher rates than men do, but men exhibit more interest in, attentiveness to, and knowledge of politics than women. Among other forms of political participation, gender does not appear to exert a more significant influence than other factors related to a person's life circumstances. There are a variety of plausible explanations for the lingering gender differences in politics, including the power of socialization, real and perceived structural barriers to participation, and cultural counterpressures.

Socialization

The role of socialization is best characterized by Simone de Beauvoir's claim that "Women are made and not born."[84] Socialization is the process by which we, first as children and later as adults, learn and internalize the values, norms, and expectations of the culture and society around us. Gender socialization is the process by which girls and boys learn to differentiate between the sexes and act according to the norms and expectations appropriate to their sex. As early as five years old, most children understand gender differentiation. Along with understanding that boys/men differ from girls/women biologically, children internalize the images of power and the sense of importance that separate the genders. Very quickly they describe the sexual hierarchy they see around them as natural or normal.[85] Thus when boys show a stronger preference for "boys'" toys and same-sex playmates, researchers link their preference to the effects of this gender stratification.[86] Further, girls are more likely to wish that they were boys than the reverse. Researcher Ann Beuf asked sixty-three children, ages three to six, what they would do if they grew up as the opposite sex. More girls had answers, meaning that they had already thought about the possibility. The boys didn't even want to answer the question. "That's a weird question, you know," one replied. When another boy was pressed, he said, "If I were a girl, I'd have to grow up to be nothing."[87] In similar research conducted by Myra Sadker and David Sadker, 42 percent of girls saw positive outcomes in becoming a boy, whereas 95 percent of the boys saw no advantage whatsoever in becoming a girl. In fact, for 16 percent of the boys interviewed, becoming a girl was so unacceptable that they fantasized about committing suicide. In the words of one boy, "I would stab myself in the heart fifty times with a dull butter knife."[88] At a very young age, children have already learned about the gendered world, including which gender is more valued by society. How do they learn the rules of gender hierarchy so quickly?

Gendered norms and expectations are communicated in a variety of ways. According to socialization research, *agents of socialization,* such as the family, school, peers, religion, and the media, play a role in shaping children's attitudes toward, knowledge of, and behavior in both gender and political roles. Early research on children and political learning found that the family transmitted the earliest messages about authority. In two-parent households, more prevalent in the 1950s and early 1960s when this research was conducted, the father was labeled the authority figure, and he was assumed to transmit political information to his children. It was further assumed that if a father was absent, children's political sophistication would suffer. A study of college students in the 1980s, however, examined the impact of family structure and found that it exerted little independent influence on students' political attitudes and voting predilections.[89] Experiences in school reinforce the norms of democratic society. By high school, civics classes transmit specific political information to adolescents. Studies of textbooks have consistently found males depicted as the primary figures in political life, while females are rarely mentioned. When Ann Richards, former governor of Texas, was asked about the historical significance of her governorship, she replied that beyond any policy change she might facilitate, her picture would appear in textbooks and offer a role model for girls to emulate.[90]

Gendered behavior is further encouraged through play with "appropriate" toys. Toy stores are shockingly clear in color-coding "boy" and "girl" aisles (in pink and blue, of course) and choosing displays ("hands-on" versus "look, don't touch"). Social psychologists confirm that children are equally serious about maintaining the separation: "One fourth-grade male reported that if he saw a boy playing with a doll, 'I'd yell at him first, but if he didn't stop, I'd punch him in the nose and call the police.'"[91]

Recent cross-national research involving adolescents in six Indonesian provinces explored gender differences on political attitudes, skills, and engagement. Contrary to other studies, they found that girls were slightly more interested in politics, had participated more, and were more politically tolerant than boys. Most importantly, the researchers found that formal civics instruction increased girls' participation more robustly than boys'. Very few comparative gender studies of political socialization exist, particularly in emerging democracies where the potential gains in girls' and womens' participation are arguably the greatest.[92]

Governments are interested in learning about political socialization because of its power to maintain stable political systems. Socialization processes may also reinforce and maintain patriarchal gender relations. Research done in the 1960s is now criticized for the way in which it interpreted differences between boys and girls on measures of political interest, knowledge, and awareness. Researchers, presumably viewing the data through their own gendered expectations, overestimated the size and significance of differences between primary-school boys and girls.[93] Additionally, the main body of political socialization research suggested that adult political behavior was a direct result of early childhood experiences, overlooking the possibility of change later in life. Only recently have researchers lengthened the time of observation to include adult experiences, such as those in the workplace, as well as the power of social, political, and economic events to reshape attitudes and behaviors.

Since politics in its traditional forms is limited to adults, how might gender socialization translate to political activity? Children learn through imitation, modeling, and apprenticeship opportunities. The previously cited study by The White House Project Education Fund found that the young men and women who are most engaged in politics are also involved and invested in their communities. They come from families in which their parents model civic behavior by voting. These young people are more likely to be registered to vote than those who are least involved in their communities. The men and women in this study who indicate an interest in someday seeking political office themselves are those who have gained leadership experience through school or other apprentice organizations, have been encouraged to run by adults or peers, are the most likely to believe that they can make a positive difference, and the least likely to find politics too complicated.[94] The research suggests that providing girls with role models, mentors, and opportunities to practice politics before they reach adulthood makes a positive difference in women's interest and political ambition. One initiative in this regard that draws ridicule from some quarters and praise from others is the Barbie for President doll, first released in April 2000 and rereleased in 2004 and 2008 by Mattel in conjunction with The White House Project and Girls, Inc.[95] The doll is a part of The White House Project's "Go Vote. Go Run. Go Lead. Go Girl" initiative. Marie Wilson, founder and president of The White House Project, characterizes the Barbie as "a case of invading the culture rather than fighting it, and using the tools of the culture to teach valuable lessons about democracy."[96] The White House Project's "Girl Power" Web page provides girls with a number of activities related to women in politics and leadership. In partnership with the Girl Scouts, girls between the ages of five and eleven can work on projects leading to a White House Project leadership patch, known as the "Ms. President" badge.[97] In anticipation of the 2008 election, The White House Project and the Take our Daughters and Sons to Work Day Foundation launched a national campaign to encourage political participation among girls, entitled "Take our Daughters to the Polls." The campaign encouraged parents, grandparents, and other adults to pledge to take a young girl to the polls on Election Day and released a viral video emphasizing the political power of girls across the country. "Children model their own dreams on what adults and society show them to be possible. By taking girls to the polls on Election Day, we teach them that they are a valuable part of the political process, and that their voice and their vote can make a difference," said Marie Wilson.[98]

Structural Barriers to Women's Participation

Political scientists have long confirmed that certain characteristics make some citizens more likely to participate in politics than others. For example, education, income, and certain occupations are good relative predictors of the frequency and types of citizen participation. Since women lag behind men on several economic indicators and have only recently matched men on years of formal education, lingering barriers to women's full participation remain, reinforcing the gaps found between male and female participation. One additional factor distinguishes women from one another: gender consciousness, or a feminist identity.

A group consciousness that ties an individual woman's interests to those of other women and provides an outlet for her discontent over gender inequities has been found to facilitate women's participation and to set those women apart from others.[99] Feminist consciousness may be shaped by generational forces. Those who come of age during eras of active public feminism—for example, those who turned eighteen during the early 1970s (the start of the second wave of feminism) or during the Clinton administration in the 1990s—are more likely not only to develop feminist consciousness, but also to act on it by supporting collective action advocating feminist policies. Those who come of age in more conservative periods (e.g., the Reagan administration) may also support feminist policies, but are less likely to develop a feminist consciousness leading to support for and engagement in collective action.[100]

Additional research examining the relationship of feminist identity and group consciousness to political attitudes and policy positions finds that feminists differ significantly from nonfeminists. Analysis based on the 1992 National Election Study revealed that women categorized as feminists were more likely than other women to support increased federal spending for child care, unemployment benefits, environmental and welfare programs, and programs to address homelessness, public schools, and urban problems.[101] Nonfeminists were significantly more likely to support additional spending on the military to maintain the United States as a military power. Differences also exist with respect to women's positions on abortion and sexual harassment, with the majority of feminists supporting choice positions and nonfeminists opposing abortion. The 1992 study also found that significantly more feminists than nonfeminists believed that sexual harassment in the workplace is a serious problem for women. A majority of all the women believed that too little was being done to protect women from harassment. Fifty-three percent of nonfeminists and 68 percent of feminists reported that they would be more likely to believe the woman in a case of conflicting stories about sexual harassment.

Feminist consciousness also appears to motivate some types of political participation. For example, feminists are more likely to vote than nonfeminists. During the 1992 presidential election, 41 percent of feminists and only 33 percent of nonfeminists reported that they were very interested in the campaign.

Chip Bok's Editorial Cartoons. *Chip Bok Editorial Cartoon used with the permission of Chip Bok and Creators Syndicate. All rights reserved.*

Interest led feminists to participate in campaigns at higher rates than nonfeminists and to exhibit a higher level of interest in politics overall. The data are not yet available to allow us to explore the relationship between a feminist identity and participation in the 2008 election.[102]

Cultural Messages: Counterpressures to Political Activity

Among the many potential barriers to women's participation are the daily messages present in popular culture and directed at shaping women's identity, expectations, ambitions, and habits. As we learned above, women remain less interested in politics and less knowledgeable about politics than men even today, nearly ninety years since winning the vote. Powerful socialization forces in the nineteenth and early twentieth centuries led women to believe that politics was better left to men.[103] However, contemporary media images of women in politics may be sending the message that women are "damned if they do, and damned if they don't." In October 1992, Deborah Tannen, best known for her work on gender differences in communication styles, wrote an article for the op-ed page of the *New York Times* in which she addressed the "Hillary Factor."

The term was originally coined to refer to the question of whether Hillary Rodham Clinton would help or hurt her husband Bill Clinton's chances to win the presidency. Tannen, however, took the term one step further, saying it represented the double bind that affects accomplished women who do not fit the stereotype of femininity and the expectations of motherhood. When, for example, the Clintons acted to protect their daughter's privacy by shielding her from the press, they were surprised to learn that a majority of Americans thought they were childless and held Hillary Clinton responsible for that misconception. The "Motherhood Bind" has an impact on all women. As Tannen describes it, "If you're not a Mother, you're a Failed Woman. If you are a Mother, you can't have enough attention to pay to serious work. If you are paying attention to serious work, you must be a Bad Mother."[104] She goes on: "By what logic could it be scary rather than comforting for a president's wife, who everyone knows will have his ear, to be unusually intelligent, knowledgeable and accomplished? And to answer: by no logic at all. The hope was to incite emotions—fear and anger—that confront women who do not conform to the old molds." In the 2008 election, Alaska Governor Sarah Palin faced many of the same questions about her suitability for the vice presidency based on her status as a mother of five relatively young children.

Women face a variety of cultural expectations that may vary depending on their physical appearance, race, or ethnicity. In each case, men do not have the same expectations placed on them, and in each case there are significant political implications for women as a result. Ambrose Bierce once wrote, "To men a man is but a mind. Who cares what face he carries or what he wears? But woman's body is the woman."[105] Although Bierce was writing nearly a century ago, consumer-spending statistics suggest his words still ring true. In 1990 alone, women spent well over $1.2 billion on elective cosmetic surgery, and more than $20 billion on cosmetics. The standards of beauty differ across cultures and vary over time, but women are universally expected to aspire to the current standards of beauty in ways that men are not. Men are referred to as *handsome,* connoting achievement and strength. Such terms do not accompany *beautiful,* which is applied only to females, scenes, or objects. This common terminology leads one set of researchers to conclude, "Men are instrumental; women are ornamental."[106] These observations and statistics would be trivial if not for their consequences on how individuals are judged. In a classic 1972 study entitled "What Is Beautiful Is Good," psychologists asked college students to rate photographs of strangers on a variety of personal qualities. Those who were judged attractive were also more likely to be characterized as intelligent, flexible, interesting, confident, assertive, strong, outgoing, friendly, poised, and successful than those considered unattractive. Women were judged more harshly than men.[107] The same attributions are made when considering candidates seeking public office, with important implications for women candidates and voters.

Judging Competence by Appearance: Implications for Women

In a 2005 *Science* article, researchers were able to postdict the outcomes of over 65 percent of the U.S. Senate and House races in 2002 and 2004, using inferences of competence based solely on candidate facial appearance.[108] Faces are a major source of information about other people. From a psychological perspective, researchers have found that rapid automatic inference from the facial appearance of political candidates can influence the way people process subsequent information about the candidates. When naïve study participants were presented with pairs of black-and-white head-shot photographs of the winners and the runners-up from actual U.S. Senate and House races, the candidate who was perceived as more competent won in 71.6 percent of the Senate races and 66.8 percent of the House races (note: if the subject recognized any of the faces, the pair was removed from analysis). To be sure that subjects were identifying competence rather than likeability or some other trait dimension, the researchers conducted a secondary analysis that asked subjects to evaluate candidates across seven traits. They found that the judgments rendered on the basis of a one-second exposure to the pairs of candidate photographs clustered into three distinct factors: competence (competence, intelligence, leadership), trust (honesty, trustworthiness), and likability (charisma, likability). Importantly, only the competence judgments predicted the outcomes of elections.

Further exploring the gender implications arising from this study, researchers at Oklahoma State University reasoned that since candidate facial appearance affects voters' preferences and sex affects facial appearance, perhaps facial appearance and voter inferences have an impact on the electability of women.[109] Previous research has linked the "baby-face/maturity" facial dimension to perceptions of competence. Baby-faced individuals are perceived to be less competent than others because people overgeneralize and attribute other babylike characteristics to them.[110] The study found that male faces are judged more mature, candidates with faces judged mature are perceived as more competent, and the perception of candidate competency affects vote choice. Female candidates are expected, based on gender stereotypes, to possess female traits (compassionate, honest, task-oriented, and focused on issues related to education, poverty, health care, the environment, and social welfare), while men are expected to possess male traits (dominant, tough, decisive, imbued with technical expertise, and focused on issues related to crime and punishment, the economy, trade, taxes, the military, foreign policy, and national security). Voters in national elections prefer candidates they perceive as competent and in possession of masculine traits.[111] Thus, how will voters react when presented with candidates of both sexes, varying appearance along the baby-face/maturity dimension? Subjects were again presented with pairs of candidates to evaluate on the basis of facial appearance. Researchers found that male candidates and mature-faced candidates were perceived as more competent than their counter-parts. Additionally, sex conditions the perceptions—male subjects were more likely to rate mature-faced and male candidates competent than female subjects. Overall, candidates perceived as competent had a higher probability of winning both simulated and real elections. However, even female candidates judged mature-faced were not perceived as more competent than baby-faced men. Researchers attribute this finding to what we know about gender stereotypes—we prefer women, whether they are candidates or not, to appear feminine, but in the national electoral context, masculine traits are preferred. Therefore, a female candidate presenting a mature face may send voters conflicting cues that they cannot process—effectively creating yet another double-bind for women candidates and officeholders.

The media facilitate the public's attention to appearance by focusing on female candidates' hairstyles and the color or design of their clothes, rather than on the content of their messages. Bush campaign operative Mary Matalin described it this way, "Women in politics who look chic are perceived as frivolous. If you're pulled together that means you've been shopping . . . instead of laboring over papers . . . fifteen hours a day. . . . Besides, every woman who looks good gets hit on, and after a while they just don't want to be hassled."[112] Josie Heath, a 1990 and 1992 Democratic senatorial candidate from Colorado, claimed that she could describe her wardrobe during that period by reading her press clippings.[113] Following the 2000 presidential election, Katherine Harris, Florida's secretary of state, who was responsible for several significant deci-sions affecting the state's presidential ballot count, became the object of public ridicule based on her appearance. The *Washington Post* noted that Harris's lipstick was of "the creamy sort that smears all over a coffee cup and leaves smudges on shirt collars" and that she "applied her makeup with a trowel," and compared the texture of her skin to that of a plastered wall.[114] As a can-didate for the Democratic nomination for president, Hillary Clinton was ridi-culed in the press for her "thick ankles" (noted by biographer Carl Bernstein), her laugh ("somewhere between a cackle and a screech," according to Dick Morris), her preference for suits with pants instead of a skirt, and her cleavage (in July 2007, the *Washington Post* noted an outfit in which the "neckline sat low on her chest").[115] In 1996, long before she was a candidate for the U.S. Senate or a national candidate for the presidential party nomination, a Web site dedicated to Hillary Clinton's changing hairstyles received more than forty thousand hits a day.

Michelle Obama presents the media and the American public with an inter-esting set of gender and cultural puzzles. Prior to Hillary Clinton, there had never been a First Lady with a postgraduate degree. Michelle Obama gradu-ated from Princeton and earned her law degree at Harvard. She presents a resume of professional accomplishments that include practicing law at the Chicago firm Sidley Austin (where she mentored a summer associate, Barack Obama); work with the city of Chicago in launching the youth mentorship program, Public Allies; and most recently a community relations position with the University of Chicago. During the campaign, she took a leave of absence from her position as vice president for community and external affairs for the University of Chicago Hospitals. Becoming First Lady has effectively ended Michelle Obama's professional career, raising lots of questions among feminist columnists about what that means for her personally and what it means for women more generally.

Katha Pollitt, writing for the *Nation*, chronicles the media transformation of Michelle Obama from "fist-bumping radical to Mom-in-Chief," references to the two predominant frames used in coverage of Obama.[116] "Her bluntly spoken rejection of a simpleminded, Panglossian vision of America riled conservatives, from high-profile pundits to anonymous bloggers. The *National Review* featured a scowling picture of her on its April cover and characterized her as Mrs. Grievance and a 'peculiar mix of privilege and victimology.' A Fox News commentator famously characterized the Obama's joyful fist tap the night Barack clinched the nomination as a 'terrorist fist jab,' while a satirical *New Yorker* cover depicted her with an Angela Davis 'fro and an AK-47," writes Geraldine Brooks.[117] Rebecca Traister decries the "momification" of Michelle Obama. "The situation is not entirely unique. The battle to conform to wifely expectations was previously fought by Hillary Clinton, a woman who recently made a hell-bent run for exactly the same job her husband held in the years that she was forced to choke on her health plan and write books about the White House cat. . . . But Michelle Obama is in an even tighter bind, in part because of the legacy of left to her by Hillary and her detractors. Powerful couples must now tread as far as possible from the 'two for one' talk, lest the female half get smacked with a nutcracker. But Michelle's power is potentially scarier than Hillary's could ever have been. She is not simply a smart and powerful woman, but a smart and powerful black woman."[118] Yet nothing sparked more blogosphere commentary than David Samuels' March 15, 2009 essay in *New York Magazine*:

> There are clear limits to Michelle's ambition. She went to excellent schools, got decent grades, and stayed away from too much intellectual heavy lifting, and held a series of practical, modestly salaried jobs while accommodating her husband's wilder dreams and raising two lovely daughters. In this she is a more practical role model for young women than Hillary Clinton, blending her calculations about family and career with an expectation of normal personal happiness.

"That Samuels, like a 1950s home ec teacher, advises 'young women' to keep their ambitions 'practical' if they want to be happy shows just how disturbing Hillary Clinton—or rather the nightmare fantasy of Hillary Clinton—has been to certain male psyches," writes Katha Pollitt. The need to "understand" Michelle Obama and to fit her into existing cultural frames of what it means to be a woman in the new century demonstrates again that the issues associated with gender equality are far from over.

Similarly to attractiveness, race and ethnicity modify expectations as well. Scholar Patricia Hill Collins writes that "portraying African American women as stereotypical mammies, matriarchs, welfare recipients, and hot mommas has been essential to the political economy of domination fostering Black women's oppression. Challenging these controlling images has long been a core theme in Black feminist thought."[119] Leaders in the women's movement were relatively silent during the congressional debate over welfare reform even when the tone and content became a thinly veiled racist attack on poor, single mothers. African American women lag behind white women in winning legislative seats at both the state and the federal level.[120] Part of the reason is the lingering belief that black women are not serious and credible candidates.[121] To overcome this hurdle, more women of color need to seek and hold office, but the obstacles to public office are substantial. Money constitutes a barrier for many women, but particularly for women of color. Beyond money, many minority women have little public exposure beyond their immediate communities, yet they face resistance even within their own communities. As Shirley Chisholm said, "Black males feel that the political seats are owed to them because of historical circumstances; therefore, opportunities should redound to them first of all."[122] The Center for American Women and Politics at Rutgers recently partnered with the National Organization of Black Elected Legislative Women (NOBEL) to develop a leadership and training program for African American women interested in pursuing elected and appointive office.[123]

Asian American women, Latina women, and Native American women have also been slow to ascend to public life. Besides having to overcome the previously described barriers, women in these groups (especially Asian and Latina women) face cultural expectations that limit their role to the home and family. Native American women, although historically active in tribal politics and fully integrated in many tribal systems of governance, have only recently explored public life beyond their community of origin. Without role models to give voice to their concerns, women of color are also less likely to be involved in electoral politics as voters.

An Alternative Answer to the Puzzle: Equal Participation, Different Paths

Conventional explanations of voter turnout would lead us to believe that men would consistently vote at higher rates than women because of their greater expressed interest in and knowledge about politics; greater command of resources including time, money, and civic skills; and their current overrepresentation in elective office. Although we have just reviewed a number of plausible explanations for the male advantage in various forms of participation, it may

Encountering the Controversies of Equality

The Newest Motherhood Bind: Can a Pregnant Woman Govern? Can a Mother be Vice President?

"Twin Billing: She's a working mother who is pregnant with twins. Can Jane Swift govern both Massachusetts and her growing family?"—*Newsday*

"To any critics who say a woman can't think and work and carry a baby at the same time, I'd just like to escort that Neanderthal back to the cave."—*Alaska Governor Sarah Palin*

Women candidates or women in elective office may also find that they are victims of another sort of motherhood bind. Jane Swift became the Commonwealth of Massachusetts' first female governor (interim) on April 10, 2001, when Governor Paul Cellucci resigned to serve as U.S. ambassador to Canada. Also the youngest governor in the country at age thirty-six, she was pregnant with twins when she took office. Pregnant with her first daughter while campaigning for the job of lieutenant governor in 1998, Swift campaigned on her ability to combine motherhood and the statehouse. As *Washington Post* columnist Jennifer Frey wrote, "She volunteered for the Supermom mantle." As promised, upon her victory her husband left his job as a contractor to stay at home full-time with their daughter.

Things started to go sour for Swift when she was forced to pay an ethics fine for creating the appearance of impropriety when she asked aides to watch her daughter in her office and for using a state helicopter to fly to her home in Williamstown, Massachusetts, when her then fourteen-month-old daughter became ill. (Massachusetts is one of six states in the country that does not have a governor's mansion, meaning a more than two-hour commute for her to the statehouse.) According to Swift, "You just don't see that many women being involved in politics at a high level at the same time that they're giving birth and having children. I think I am the first of hopefully many, and I think it's true that the desire to eventually get women to the very highest levels of office in our country is going to necessitate that women enter politics at an earlier age."

Wendy Kaminer, in an article for *The American Prospect,* wrote:

Today it's difficult to suggest that bearing children may even temporarily disqualify a woman from high office, or any extremely demanding and stressful full-time job. It's hard to ask the question "Is Jane Swift fit to serve?" without calling up more than 100 years of crippling stereotypes about the emotional, moral, and physical attributes of normal women. Still, it's a question that ought to be asked. . . . If she intended to assume the office of governor when Cellucci moved on, Swift could have postponed her pregnancy.[1]

Governor Swift gave birth to twin girls on May 15, 2001. Her spokesman reported, "She is resting, she has her feet up, but as she would tell you, her brain is still working." Swift did not seek reelection in large part because elites in her own party recruited Mitt Romney to challenge her in the Republican primary.

Fast-forward to 2008 and Sarah Palin's nomination as Republican John McCain's vice presidential running mate. Reactions varied to Palin's dual status as national candidate and mother of five children—the last child a four-month-old infant with Down's Syndrome and her second child an unmarried and pregnant seventeen-year-old daughter. Like Swift, Palin did not down play her status as a mother in the campaign, repeatedly identifying herself as "just a hockey mom." Author and columnist Emma Gilbey Keller notes, "Her hockey mom personal narrative is used to demonstrate that she gets the concerns and shares the values of ordinary (non-elite) Americans. Her ability to juggle a BlackBerry and a breast pump, to dismiss the chef and chauffeur, to be governor and the CEO of the Palin family, is all put forth as evidence of impressive managerial skills. . . . Yet the McCain/Palin campaign has tried to have it both ways: She's the family-values candidate, but you're a sexist if you examine her family values."[2] Palin's candidacy also generated divergent reactions among conservative women. Staunch ERA opponent and mother of six Phyllis Schlafly commented to the *New York Times,* "People who don't have children or who have only one or two are kind of overwhelmed at the notion of five children. I think a hard-working, well-organized C.E.O. type can handle it very well." However, conservative talk-radio host, Dr Laura Schlesinger blogged:

> Couldn't the Republican Party find one competent female with adult children to run for Vice President with McCain? I realize his advisors probably didn't want a "mature" woman, as the Democrats keep harping on his age. But really, what kind of role model is a woman whose fifth child was recently born with a serious issue, Down Syndrome, and then goes back to the job of Governor within days of the birth?. . . Certainly, if a child becomes ill and is rushed to the hospital, and you're on the hotline with both Israel and Iran as nuclear tempers are flaring, where's your attention going to be? Where *should* your attention be? Well, once you put your hand on the Bible and make that oath, your attention has to be with the government of the United States of America.[3]

What do you think?

Is a pregnant woman or a new mother "unfit" for high public office? The law treats pregnancy as a "temporary disability"; would a male governor have been subject to the same speculation about his ability to do the job if he had been hospitalized for prostate cancer or a broken leg? Swift was twenty-five years old when she was first elected to the state senate. Is she right that unless women get started early they will never achieve the highest political offices? How does this square with Kaminer's claim that women should time their pregnancies so as not to interfere with demanding jobs or the responsibilities of high office? Should Sarah Palin have declined the vice presidency because of her responsibilities as a mother? The Obamas had two children under ten when elected in 2008. What if Michelle Obama had been the candidate instead of Barack Obama? Would she have faced motherhood questions that he did not face as a father? On what do we base this question? On what do you base your answer?

1. Wendy Kaminer, "Mama's Delicate Condition." *American Prospect* 12, no. 7 (April 23, 2001), accessed at http://www.prospect.org/print/V12/7/kaminer-w.html.
2. Emma Gilbey Keller, "Motherhood, Careers and Sarah Palin." *Women on the Web,* September 12, 2008, accessed at http://www.wowowow.com/books/emma-gilbey-keller-comeback-motherhood-careers-and-sarah-palin-102787.
3. Dr. Laura, "Sarah Palin and Motherhood," accessed at http://www.drlaurablog.com/2008/09/02/sarah-palin-and-motherhood/.

also be that researchers have overlooked an important ingredient in predicting the key political act of voting. New research by Allison Harell identifies the distinct importance of social capital in explaining female voter turnout.[124] Social capital has been defined as "social networks and the norms of reciprocity and trust that facilitate collective action . . . social capital is embedded in all sorts of formal and informal social networks from rotary clubs and parent-teacher association (PTA) meetings to bowling leagues, card parties, and socializing with neighbors."[125] In this sense then, social networks become resources that individuals can access. This is particularly important in considering women's participation since too often the variety of ways that women engage with others in their community has been rendered invisible in the private sphere while "politics" takes place in the public sphere. Harell argues that women's informal and formal networks tend to be nonhierarchically organized, located at the local community level, and centered on care work, making them harder to recognize and measure in political participation studies. Using data from the Canadian National Survey of Giving, Volunteering, and Participating (NSGVP), Harell is able to demonstrate that membership in an association (social or political) and informal volunteering (care work done on one's own) increase the odds of voting among women but not men. When all of the other traditional predictors of voting are held constant, and only the interaction between sex and informal volunteering is examined, women's likelihood of voting increases by 4 percentage points while men's likelihood of voting remains unchanged. This study is important because of what it says about the way in which political acts and the resources assumed to predict or explain those political acts are studied. First, social capital has been treated as a gender-neutral variable, when in fact this research demonstrates important gender differences in both the source of social capital and the ways in which it is linked to explicit acts of political participation. Second, in overlooking social capital as a unique resource for women, standard voting models are also not gender neutral and need to be reexamined. Finally, viewing social capital as acquired by women as a resource directly related to women's political participation effectively incorporates private sphere activities into explanations of political activity in ways previously ignored.

MOBILIZING WOMEN'S POLITICAL PARTICIPATION

As this chapter has shown, men and women approach politics similarly and from different perspectives depending on the activity and on life circumstances. While women vote at higher rates than men do, women remain less likely to donate money to a candidate, participate in political organizations, or seek elective office themselves. This chapter concludes by examining four factors that may increase women's political participation: events and issues, high-profile female candidates, organizations that target women, and the role of political parties.

Political Events and Issues Stimulate Interest and Raise Gender Consciousness

Although many factors combined to make 1992 an especially good year for women in politics, two distinctly mobilizing events stand out: the Clarence Thomas Supreme Court confirmation hearings and the Tailhook scandal. In 2002, CODEPINK emerged as a woman-initiated grassroots peace and social justice movement in reaction to the Bush administration's intention to invade Iraq. The organization's name is a play on the color-coded homeland security alerts designed to indicate the danger of a terrorist threat. CODEPINK is known for its creative protest tactics and nonviolent direct action campaigns. Preceding the 2004 election, several women's organizations tried to create an event to mobilize women voters in November by calling attention to the Bush administration's record on reproductive choice, justice, and women's health. On April 25, 2004, the March for Women's Lives attracted an estimated 1.15 million people to Washington, D.C., for what organizers called the largest public demonstration in U.S. history. We will examine how spontaneous and staged events serve to mobilize women's political action apart from the activity directed at women as voters during electoral campaigns.

On July 1, 1991, President Bush nominated Clarence Thomas to fill a vacancy on the U.S. Supreme Court. By October 6, 1991, the Senate Judiciary Committee had already voted to forward Thomas's nomination to the full Senate for a vote. On that date, however, Nina Totenberg of National Public Radio alleged that the committee had suppressed allegations of sexual harassment against Thomas brought by a University of Oklahoma law professor, Anita Hill. Hill had worked for Thomas at the Equal Employment Opportunity Commission (EEOC), the federal agency that enforces antidiscrimination policy. On October 8, Democratic congresswomen marched from the House to the Senate to demand an investigation. The Senate relented, and new hearings were called with Anita Hill as the primary witness. Her testimony before the Senate Judiciary Committee was televised, giving many voters, particularly female voters, their first glimpse at the all-male, all-white committee. Interest in the hearings was incredibly intense. Senator Paul Simon reported receiving nearly twenty thousand letters on the subject, compared to fewer than sixteen thousand on the Gulf War. Millions watched the televised hearings, which had a larger audience than the NFL games that were on at the same time.[126] Women were outraged at what they saw and what many perceived as the unfair and condescending treatment of Hill. T-shirts proclaiming "I Believe Anita Hill," "He did it," and "She Lied" sprang up across the country. A full episode of a prime-time sitcom, *Designing Women,* was dedicated to the controversy. After the show's airing, CBS received more than fifteen hundred mostly positive phone calls—the largest number in the network's history in response to a single show.[127]

Sexual harassment as an issue separated men from women in many ways. Women, regardless of race or class, shared experiences similar in nature, if not in severity, to those described by Anita Hill. It appeared clear to even those most uneducated in fair-trial norms that the deck was stacked against Hill. Senator Arlen Specter stated that Professor Hill's testimony "was flat-out perjury,"[128] and senators speculated openly on national television about various psychological disorders Hill might be suffering. The phrase "men just don't get it" was born.

One of the first political victims of the Hill-Thomas hearings was Senator Alan Dixon, who lost his seat in the Illinois primary to political newcomer Carol Mosely Braun. Ms. Braun went on to win Dixon's Senate seat and ultimately a seat on the Judiciary Committee. Braun was one of several women moved by the Hill-Thomas debacle to seek public office themselves. An unusually large number of seats opened up in Congress as a result of retirements and reapportionment, which further encouraged women to announce their candidacies. In all, twenty-two women sought Senate seats in 1992, compared to just eight in the previous election. A record four new women entered the Senate, raising the total to six in 1992,[129] including Braun, who was the first African American woman to be elected to the Senate. In the House of Representatives, forty-eight women were elected, nearly doubling the number of female members. Facilitating this increase were a number of grassroots women's organizations whose membership also rose after the Hill-Thomas event. Membership in EMILY's (Early Money Is Like Yeast) List, an organization supporting prochoice, Democratic female candidates, went from 3,000 to 23,000 in just one year. EMILY's List contributed more than $6 million to candidates in the 1992 elections, a fourfold increase over the elections of 1990.[130] The National Organization for Women (NOW) reported that anger over the Senate's handling of Hill's charges "has translated into 13,000 new members in the final months of 1991," and the Feminist Majority reported receiving an unsolicited contribution of $10,000 after the hearings and a 30 percent rise in contributions overall.[131] Clearly, a single event can have powerful organizational implications in mobilizing women to attend to and participate in politics.

In September 1991, naval aviators belonging to the Tailhook Association held their annual convention in Las Vegas. The revelry became assaultive, alleged Lt. Paula Coughlin, as male aviators "formed a gauntlet down a narrow hallway and tore at her clothes, grabbed at her breasts, and seized her buttocks with such force she was hoisted airborne."[132] Other women reported that they were thrown to the ground, had their clothes torn off, and were molested by drunken airmen. In all, 119 Navy and 21 Marine Corps officers were referred by Pentagon investigators for possible disciplinary actions. None of these 140 cases ever went to trial, however, and nearly half were dropped for lack of evidence. Twenty-eight junior officers were eventually disciplined for "indecent exposure" and "conduct unbecoming an officer." None of the aviators were charged with sexual assault, and Coughlin's charges against a specific Marine captain for sexual molestation were dropped for lack of evidence. The investigation and disciplinary hearings stretched on for more than three years, culminating in the resignation of Secretary of the Navy Lawrence Garrett III and the early retirement of Admiral Frank Kelso, the navy's top officer, who was found to have witnessed several incidents, but failed to intervene. Women following the progress of the investigation were introduced to the dark side of military culture. Outraged that sexual assault charges were dismissed as "high jinks" and dismayed to learn that the "gauntlet" had been a fixture at every Tailhook Convention since 1986 without any intervention by navy officials, civilian women's groups rallied to Coughlin's cause. The fallout resulted in new sexual harassment policies and training for personnel, along with the slogan "Not in Our Navy."[133] Women in and outside the military service are more aware of policies and procedures designed to ensure a safe and productive workplace as a result of this incident. Congress now regularly monitors sexual harassment and incidents of assault reported by students in the service academies, and provides oversight of the Department of Defense's intiatives to enforce sexual harassment policies and prosecute assault cases (see chapter 7 for more information on women in the military).

On April 25, 2004, an estimated 1.15 million people converged on Washington, D.C., for the March for Women's Lives. Seven groups collaborated in organizing the march: American Civil Liberties Union, Black Women's Health Imperative, Feminist Majority, NARAL Pro-Choice America, National Latina Institute for Reproductive Health, National Organization for Women, and Planned Parenthood Federation of America. The demonstration was in protest of the Bush administration's actions limiting women's rights, particularly in the area of reproductive choice. Upon taking office in 2001, President Bush issued an executive memorandum reinstating the global gag rule on international family planning assistance. Bush timed his action to coincide with the twenty-eighth anniversary of the *Roe v. Wade* decision. Under the global gag rule, foreign family planning agencies may not receive U.S. assistance if they provide abortion services, including counseling on abortion or referrals to other clinics, or lobby to make or keep abortion legal in their own country.[134] On November 5, 2003, Bush signed the Partial-Birth Abortion Ban Act into law. This federal law is the first to ban a specific kind of abortion procedure known as dilation and extraction. The very rare procedure is almost always performed only when the mother's life or health is endangered by the pregnancy, and no alternative methods are considered safer. Similar state legislation in Nebraska has already been ruled unconstitutional (*Stenberg v. Carhart*, 2000; see chapter 8 for more information). Three separate constitutional challenges were filed almost immediately. More broadly, on April 8, 2004, the National Women's Law Center released the report *Slip-Sliding Away: The Erosion of Hard-Won Gains for Women Under the Bush Administration and an Agenda for Moving Forward.*[135] The report focuses on ten key areas: women at work; girls at school; child care and other supports women need to work; tax and budget policies; retirement security; health and reproductive rights; violence against women; women in the military; judicial nominations; and government offices charged with safeguarding women's interests. The NWLC charged that the Bush

CodePink Women's Peace Vigil has several thousand marching down 16th Street near Scott Circle Saturday, March 8, 2003 in Washington to protest the Bush administration's war plan on Iraq. © *Lisa Nipp/ AP Photo.*

administration rolled back women's progress by closing key offices and ending initiatives designed to promote it (e.g., the administration ended the Equal Pay Initiative and removed all materials on narrowing the wage gap from the Department of Labor's website), by refusing to enforce existing law (e.g., the Department of Justice dropped cases challenging sex discrimination in employment), and by advancing economic policies that will disproportionately harm women (e.g., the plan to restructure Medicaid will result in more women without health insurance).

March organizers believed that by calling attention to the Bush administrations' actions, particularly the strong measures undertaken to criminalize abortion and restrict access to information and women's health services, they could motivate women to channel their anger through electoral politics in November and vote Bush out of office. They also hoped that the march would energize young women to fight to protect rights won by previous generations of feminists. Senator Clinton told the crowd, "All the people are here today not only to march on behalf of women's lives but to take that energy into the election in November."[136] Although the march organizers labeled the event an overwhelming success, and the sheer size of the turnout sent a powerful message about women's political potential, it is difficult to identify the event an effective mobilizing tool for women in the November election since President Bush was reelected to office contrary to the organizer's hopes. More research on the connections between women's experience at the march and their political activities throughout the campaign will be critical to evaluating whether organized events can mobilize women as effectively as naturally occurring political events.

Do Female Candidates Bring Women to the Voting Booth?

Was the election of 2008 in itself a mobilizing force for women in politics? As more female candidates appear on ballots for local, state, and national elections, will it stimulate higher rates of participation from women across the multiple dimensions of political engagement? The data on the 2008 election are not complete at this time, but we have more than anecdotal evidence with which to consider the question. Female candidates send signals or cues to the electorate on a number of important factors related to symbolic representation. For example, the presence of women candidates can signal a greater openness in the system and more political opportunities for all. Likewise, women on the ballot send the signal that politics is no longer an exclusively male domain and that female participation is important and valued. Finally, women candidates are more likely to include issues of interest to women in their campaigns, thereby attracting their attention.[137] A study of gender and political participation in the U.K. found that women are significantly more likely to turn out and vote if they are represented by a woman, and are more likely to become involved in an electoral campaign on behalf of a female candidate. The study, conducted in 2004 by academics at Harvard and Birkbeck College in London, also found that women are more likely to agree with the statement that "government benefits me," if represented by a woman (49 percent compared to 8 percent in constituencies with a male representative).[138]

Finding that much of the previous research investigated the impact of women on the ballot in 1992 (labelled the Year of the Woman), Kathleen Dolan examined national election data from 1990 to 2004 to examine whether the attitudes and behaviors of those of people living in states and districts with a woman candidate for the U.S. Senate or House differ from those voting in elections where there are no women candidates. This analysis covers different levels of office, differing conditions of competitiveness, different political party conditions, and a longer time frame of elections than previous research and yet, "the results show, overall, that there is little empirical analysis to support the assumption that symbolic representation is provided by women candidates or at least there is little support for the idea that their symbolic presence translates into any widespread increase in political attitudes and behaviors . . . we are left to conclude that the influence of women candidates is, at some level, a function of idiosyncratic circumstances of particular elections—such things as the mix of candidates, their positions, the issues of the day, media coverage, and public awareness."[139] If the influence of female candidates on the ballot is contextual, the presidential election of 2008 offers an entirely new context to investigate. Further, it may be the case that the power of female candidates is much like the power of more women visible in public office in that the symbolic benefits are derived not from the one-on-one relationship of constituent or voter to officeholder or candidate, but something more generalized.[140] The presence of Clinton as a viable candidate for the Democratic nomination for president and Palin's spot on the Republican ticket in the general election increased the media's focus on the overall lack of women in politics and shed light on the fact that the United States lags behind other nations in electing a woman head of state/government, as well as in the overall representation of women at the legislative level. The gap between representative ideals and the gendered reality may have drawn women's attention to politics in a new way. Whether the presence of viable female candidates affects women's political participation specifically or more generally will therefore remain a rich area for new research.

Organizations

In both the Hill-Thomas hearings and the Tailhook incident, women's organizations rallied to the cause. Groups such as NOW and the National Women's Political Caucus (NWPC), as well as conservative organizations such as the Independent Women's Forum and Second Amendment Sisters, enjoy membership surges when highly publicized events remind women that the controversies of equality are not yet settled. A "women's organization" should not be construed to mean a "feminist organization," although many explicitly political organizations dedicated to women share some feminist aims. NOW, for example, is an organization in the liberal feminist tradition. It was founded in 1966 in response to concern that the discrimination provisions of the 1964 Civil Rights Act and Title VII were not being properly enforced. NOW focuses on eliminating sexism in American society through legislation and court action. The NWPC, founded in 1971, is a bipartisan organization with the explicit goal of bringing more women, Republicans and Democrats alike, into office. Both organizations' activities are most consistent with the goals of the legal equality doctrine.

There is tremendous variety in organizations for women, and groups have been organized around every point along the ideological spectrum. Organizational involvement is intimately tied to participation in larger political arenas.[141] Organizations do this in a number of ways. First, a member's contact with the organization extends her social network to include political activists and introduces political newcomers to the efficacy of political action in solving public problems. Further, in local chapters, members gain valuable political and leadership skills that allow them to access politics at all levels. In this way, associations may act as a feeder network to political-party activity. Organizations may also facilitate citizen contact with public officials by encouraging letter-writing campaigns, visits to elected officials, or participation in organized demonstrations.[142] Beginning with the 2004 presidential election, women's organizations used the Internet to reach out to young women and urge them to get involved and to vote. For example, "Women's Voices. Women Vote" was a dedicated effort to register the 22 million single women who did not vote in 2000. Exit poll data suggest that an estimated 7.5 million more unmarried women voted in 2004 than in 2000, and that unmarried women constituted 23 percent of the electorate (up from 19 percent of the electorate in 2000).[143] Seventy percent of unmarried female voters supported Barack Obama in the 2008 election, an increase in support for the Democratic candidate of 16 percentage points over 2004. Buoyed by their electoral success, WVWV is now collaborating with organized labor and others to create an unmarried woman's policy agenda and train women as political activists and lobbyists. They intend to play an active role in the legislative health care reform debate as well as other income-related issues.

Apart from mobilizing participation, women's organizations provide a wide range of services to members and nonmembers alike. The Internet provides women's groups even greater visibility and allows women around the world to access political information and resources twenty-four hours a day. Candidates and women who are thinking of seeking office can use the Internet to access training seminars, consultants, and networks of volunteers. A majority of women serving in state legislatures today list a women's organization as an important source of support. Women's organizations can mobilize women to vote and to participate in politics by drawing attention to important issues at stake in an election or to a contest between two evenly matched candidates. Women's organizations have, at times, joined forces to propose policy agendas and to lobby for congressional action on women's issues. The National Council of Women's Organizations (NCWO) is a bipartisan network of leaders from more than 200 organizations representing more than 11 million women in the United States. Member organizations collaborate through substantive policy work and grassroots activism to address issues of concern to women, including family and work, economic equity, education, affirmative action, older women, corporate accountability, women and technology, reproductive freedom, women's health, younger women, and global progress for women's equality. The council proposes a "National Women's Agenda" every two years, which corresponds to a new session of Congress. One of their newest projects is called "The Church Ladies Project," a collaborative effort between NCWO and the National Congress of Black Women (NCBW), designed as a strategic program of African American women in religious auxiliaries and professional organizations to conduct electoral engagement including voter registration, turnout, and education linking issues to the vote. The Church Ladies Project will reach approximately 2.4 million African American women.[144]

Throughout history, women have been actively involved in peace activism. Julia Ward Howe organized a Mother's Peace Day in 1873 and appealed to mothers of the world to "unite across national boundaries to prevent the war of human life which they alone know and bear the cost."[145] In opposition to the Iraq War and hostilities in Afghanistan, several women organized CODEPINK in 2002. "Bush Says Code Red, We Say Code Pink!" was their rallying cry as they initiated a series of nonviolent protests directed at the Bush administration and other political leaders they believed were responsible for the wars. The group started with a White House vigil on November 17, 2002, that lasted four months, culminating on March 8 (International Women's Day) with a ten-thousand-person march on Washington. The organization has sent delegations to Iraq on several occasions to meet with Iraqi women and children, and they have published research reports on the impact of the U.S. occupation on the status of Iraqi women. Known for their political street theater and creative protests, CODEPINK has become one of the most visible antiwar groups in the United States. CODEPINK organizes annual rallies on Mother's Day in Washington, D.C., and in many of the states. Although organized by women and largely supported by women, the group welcomes men as members and activists.[146]

The Role of Political Parties

Although political parties made early overtures to female voters in anticipation of the immediate postsuffrage elections, they largely abandoned the "women's vote" when no such voting bloc materialized. Many women continued their activities with political parties, but, as political scientist Jo Freeman said, they entered mainstream parties "one room at a time":

> Party women had their own style of action. Whereas feminists had assaulted the citadel, and reformers had banged on the door, party women had infiltrated the basement of politics. But while their actions were incremental and only occasionally attracted notice, their numbers expanded and they helped bring about significant changes to the parties. They also built a base of well-informed women with years of party service who were quick to take advantage of the opportunities created by the new feminist movement that arose in the late 1960s.[147]

Both national political parties, as well as many state party organizations, created special women's auxiliaries designed to educate and mobilize female voters. Women's divisions proved both a facilitator and a ghetto for women interested in ascending to political power. At the same time that parties recruited women to organize other women, they denounced "sex solidarity" and encouraged their female organizers to do the same. Party loyalty was the first priority for parties. For party women, inclusion was the first priority. Party women, according to Freeman, were not interested in promoting a "women first" agenda, but rather in receiving "equal rewards for equal service."[148] The odd waltz between parties and feminists continued with women and parties alike trying to argue both sides: Parties tried to appeal to women by identifying women's issues in their platforms but appealing to their partisan loyalty first. Women worked tirelessly for the party, but always held out the possibility of a women's bloc vote to motivate the party to listen to women.

Both political parties now have programs for developing women's leadership. For example, *Winning Women: Leadership for a New Century* is the Republican National Committee's program to turn women into leaders through its "Excellence in Public Service" Series. The series originated in Indiana in 1989 and selects women to participate in a year-long series of eight monthly training sessions and a three-day leadership seminar in Washington, D.C. "Classes are meant to encourage, prepare and inspire women leaders to seek new levels of involvement in government and politics."[149] Twelve states currently have programs, with three more in the process of developing similar programs. The Democratic Party sponsors the Women's Vote Center and the Women's Leadership Forum (WLF). The Democratic National Committee's Women's Vote Center, founded in 2001, is dedicated to educating, engaging, and mobilizing women voters in order to "elect more Democrats to office at all levels of government." The WLF, established in 1993, is a membership organization intended to bring women into the political process and serves primarily as a way to target women in fundraising efforts.[150]

Attachment to political parties in general is on the decline, making it essential that new groups of voters be recruited into the ranks of the faithful. For example, in 1998 both parties targeted "waitress moms." Their profile (older than fifty, white, working multiple hourly wage jobs to support children) fit the Democratic Party best, and yet their votes were in play largely because of the Clinton-Lewinsky scandal. "They're values oriented," said pollster Celinda Lake, who coined the term. "They've been swung back and forth by events, so they're a question mark."[151] Republicans appealed to women fitting the waitress-mom profile because of their promise to lower taxes. At a fundraising dinner, former Vice President Quayle said, "Think of the waitress that works extra hours at night so she can buy a book for her child. She might want to be at her son or daughter's soccer game, but she has to work because of high taxes."[152] In the 2004 election, the Kerry campaign dramatized their candidate's contention that the war was going badly with "military moms." Eight mothers and wives of servicemen and guardsmen traveled across seven battleground states in minivans to share their personal stories and concerns about the war in Iraq with voters.[153] In 2008, with women prominent in the national presidential campaigns of both parties, the Republicans and Democrats made a variety of appeals to attract female voters. There were women-focused events at both parties' summer conventions.

In May 2009, the Pew Research Center for the People and the Press released a report on trends in political values and core attitudes for the years 1987–2009.[154] In 2002, the country was evenly divided along partisan lines, with 43 percent identifying with or leaning toward the Republican Party and an identical percentage aligned with the Democratic Party. In 2009, half of the public (50 percent) identifies with or leans toward the Democratic Party, compared with 35 percent who align with Republicans. As Republican identification has dropped, the tendency of men to call themselves independents has increased substantially. In 2009, just 24 percent of men call themselves

Republican, compared with 31 percent in 2004. Meanwhile, the share of men calling themselves independents has moved from 34 percent to 42 percent, a record high. There has been virtually no change in the proportion of men calling themselves Democrats. The trend among women is different. While there has been a similar decline in Republican identification (from 28 percent in 2004 to 22 percent in 2009), the share of women who identify themselves as Democrats has risen three points to 41 percent, and the share of women identifying themselves as independents has risen from 27 percent to 31 percent over the same time period. These shifts in how men and women identify themselves with political parties has meant that the gender differences among Republican identifiers has nearly disappeared (24 percent men, 22 percent women), while the 13-point gender difference among Democratic identifiers (28 percent men, 41 percent women) is the largest in twenty years. These shifts pose tremendous challenges and opportunities for the political parities and we can expect both parties to continue to court women as candidates, voters, and party activists.

CONCLUSION

Women constitute a substantial political force in the abstract. However, a variety of historical and contemporary forces work to minimize the chances that women will act together as a unified group in politics. Despite the gender gap, a "women's bloc" did not materialize immediately following ratification of the Nineteenth Amendment nor has it since materialized in American politics. Most likely, even the possibility of a women's voting bloc was the stuff of political mythmaking or propaganda, depending on one's perspective. The evidence suggests that men and women, for the most part, participate in politics at about the same rates and in about the same ways, with some variation on issue priorities. Women are divided by race, class, family status, and education in the same ways that men are politically stratified. Where men and women differ in their rates or modes of participation, resources are most likely at issue rather than gender. Women still lag behind men in their wages. As a result, women lag behind men in their ability to spend precious capital on politics. It remains to be seen whether political organizations, high visibility female candidates, parties, or episodic events and issues can help women overcome the remaining barriers to full political participation and mobilize women's involvement. Achieving gender equality, even if merely political equality, depends not only on women's ability to vote but also on their ability to express their collective will and interests effectively through other forms of political participation. So far, women have been unable to coordinate their goals in a way that easily translates into a unified women's agenda and perhaps that remains an unrealistic expectation. Gender equality does not easily translate into policy platforms or campaign promises, particularly considering the complexities introduced by the paradox and the two different paths to the realization of gender equality. The 2004 presidential election was unique because of the unprecedented effort to mobilize women voters. Advocacy groups of all political and ideological persuasions worked to get women registered and to the polls. As a result, sixty-two million women voted, a marked increase over the fifty-nine million who voted in 2000. The 2008 presidential election was unique due to the historic presence and success of Hillary Clinton's candidacy for the Democratic nomination for president and Sarah Palin's nomination as vice president on the Republican presidential ticket. As a candidate, Hillary Clinton attracted over 18 million votes in the primaries from both men and women. There is some preliminary evidence that having female high-profile viable national candidates mobilized women's political engagement in new ways, but it is far from definitive. Similarly the Internet has made access to political information on issues and candidates more available, and evidence suggests that women are heavy consumers of political websites and social networking tools. Access to the Internet may also increase the likelihood that women donate money to political candidates, parties, and PACs, thereby raising the volume of their collective political voice. Although women did not all vote for the same candidates or even in completely predictable patterns, the interest shown in attracting women voters is an important indication that women matter in politics. That so many of the registration and mobilization efforts were undertaken by women's advocacy organizations suggests that the women's movement is enjoying a resurgence as well.

The fact remains that women make up 53 percent of the U.S. population, women constitute the majority of registered voters, and consistently vote at higher rates than men. In this sense, women's votes are key to winning elections for both male and female candidates. Empirical studies caution that female candidates and Democratic candidates should not take women's votes for granted, any more than male candidates or Republican candidates should write them off. The next chapter examines another form of political participation that could translate into the power to more directly set the political agenda: women as candidates for public office.

Suggested Readings, Web Resources, and Films

Lonna Rae Atkeson, "Not All Cues are Created Equal: The Conditional Impact of Female Candidates on Political Engagement," *Journal of Politics* 65, no. 4 (November 2003): 1040–1061.

Jo Freeman, *A Room at a Time: How Women Entered Party Politics* (Lanham, Md.: Rowman & Littlefield, 2000).

Robert Johns and Mark Shephard, "Gender, Candidate Image and Electoral Preference," *British Journal of Politics and International Relations* 9, no. 3 (2007): 434–460.

Karen M. Kauffman and John R. Petrocik, "The Changing Politics of American Men: Understanding the Sources of the Gender Gap," *American Journal of Political Science* 43, no. 3 (July 1999): 864–887.

Catherine E. Rymph, *Republican Women: Feminism and Conservatism from Suffrage Through the Rise of the New Right* (Chapel Hill: University of North Carolina Press, 2006).

Richard Seltzer, Jody Newman, and Melissa Vorhees Leighton, *Sex as a Political Variable: Women as Candidates and Voters in U.S. Elections* (Boulder, Colo.: Lynne Rienner Publishers, 1997).

Virginia Sapiro, *The Political Integration of Women* (Urbana: University of Illinois Press, 1983).

Sidney Verba, Kay Lehman Schlozman, and Henry E. Brady, *Voice and Equality: Civic Voluntarism in American Politics* (Cambridge, Mass.: Harvard University Press, 1995).

Lois Duke Whitaker, ed., *Voting the Gender Gap* (Urbana: University of Illinois Press, 2008).

Center for American Women and Politics, Eagleton Institute of Politics, Rutgers University, http://www.rci.rutgers.edu/~cawp.

Feminist Majority: http://www.feminist.org.

League of Women Voters: http://www.lwv.org/index.html.

National Women's Political Caucus: http://www.nwpc.org.

Women's Campaign Fund Forum: http://wcfonline.org/sites/wcf/.

Women Leaders Online: http://www.wlo.org.

Women's Voices. Women Vote: http://wvwv.org/.

Blog: Women and Politics-Women's Campaign Forum: http://womenandpolitics.org/.

Blog: BlogHer: http://www.blogher.com/.

Blog: The Political Voices of Women: http://politicsanew.com/.

Film: *The Speeches of Famous Women* (Overland Park, Ill.: MPI Home Video, 1995).

Notes

1. Jewel L. Prestage, "In Quest of African American Political Women," *Annals of the American Academy of Political and Social Science* 515 (May 1991): 95.

2. Jo Freeman, *A Room at a Time: How Women Entered Party Politics* (Lanham, Md.: Rowman & Littlefield, 2000), p. 3.

3. Anita Shafer Goodstein. "A Rare Alliance: African American and White Women in the Tennessee Elections of 1919 and 1920," *Journal of Southern History* 64, no. 2 (May 1998): 219–246.

4. Kristi Anderson, *After Suffrage: Women in Partisan and Electoral Politics Before the New Deal* (Chicago: University of Chicago Press, 1996), p. 50.

5. Charles Merriam and Harold Gosnell, *Non-Voting: Causes and Methods of Control* (Chicago: University of Chicago Press, 1924), pp. 36–37.

6. Rosalyn Terborg-Penn, *African American Women in the Struggle for the Vote, 1850–1920* (Bloomington: Indiana University Press, 1998), p. 137.

7. Anderson, *After Suffrage.*

8. Sophinisba Breckinridge, *Women in the Twentieth Century: A Study of Their Political, Social, and Economic Activities* (New York: McGraw-Hill, 1933).

9. Illinois granted women presidential suffrage in 1914.

10. Virginia Sapiro, *The Political Integration of Women* (Urbana: University of Illinois Press, 1983), p. 22.

11. Prestage, "In Quest of African American Political Women," p. 97.

12. Mark Hugo Lopez and Paul Taylor, "Dissecting the 2008 Electorate: Most Diverse in U.S. History," report from the Pew Research Center, April 30, 2009, accessed at http://pewresearch.org/assets/pdf/dissecting-2008-electorate.pdf.

13. Turnout and registration statistics from "Sex Differences in Voter Turnout," fact sheet compiled by the Center for American Women and Politics, Eagleton Institute of Politics (New Brunswick, N.J.: Rutgers University, 2004).

14. Sidney Verba, Kay Lehman Schlozman, and Henry E. Brady, *Voice and Equality: Civic Voluntarism in American Politics* (Cambridge, Mass.: Harvard University Press, 1995), p. 254n.

15. Richard A. Seltzer, Jody Newman, and Melissa Vorhees Leighton, *Sex as a Political Variable: Women as Candidates and Voters in U.S. Elections* (Boulder, Colo.: Lynne Rienner Publishers, 1997), p. 68.

16. Center for American Women and Politics, "Sex Differences in Voter Turnout," 2004.

17. Sandra Baxter and Marjorie Lansing, *Women and Politics: The Invisible Majority* (Ann Arbor: University of Michigan Press, 1980), pp. 107–110.

18. Ibid., pp. 68–69.

19. Committee for the Study of the American Electorate, "President Bush, Mobilization Drives Propel Turnout to Post-1968 High," November 4, 2004, accessed at http://www.fairvote.org/reports/CSAE2004electionreport.pdf.

20. "Women's Vote Watch: Women's Votes Could Determine Election Outcome," Center for American Women and Politics, Eagleton Institute of Politics, Rutgers University, October 10, 2008.

21. Nelson W. Polsby and Aaron Wildavsky, *Presidential Elections: Strategies and Structures of American Politics* (New York: Chatham House, 2000), p. 8.

22. Ibid., p. 9.

23. Michael Nelson, "The Setting: Diversifying the Presidential Talent Pool," in Michael Nelson, ed., *The Elections of 2008* (Washington, D.C.: CQ Press, 2009).

24. Lonna Rae Atkeson, "Not All Cutes Are Created Equal: The Conditional Impact of Female Candidates on Political Engagement," *Journal of Politics* 65, no. 4 (November 2004): 1040–1061.

25. 2008 data come directly from the Cooperative Institutional Research Program (CIRP). Freshman survey conducted annually by the Higher Education Research Institute (HERI) at UCLA (http://www.gseis.ucla.edu/heri/index.php).

26. Kathleen Hall Jamieson, Richard Johnston, and Michael Hagen, "The Primary Campaign: What Did the Candidates Say, What Did the Public Learn, and What Did It Matter?" (Philadelphia: Annenberg Public Policy Center, University of Pennsylvania, March 27, 2000), accessed at http://www.appcpenn.org.

27. The Center for Information and Research on Civic Learning and Engagement, *Voter Turnout Among Young Men and Women* (Baltimore: School of Public Affairs, University of Maryland, May 2003).

28. Kourtney Stamps, "Don't Believe Everything You Hear—The Youth Vote Was Up in 2004!" accessed at http://www.now.org/issues/election/elections2004.

29. Besa Luci, "Summer Voter Drives Target Younger Women" *Women's eNews,* August 19, 2008, accessed at http://www.womensenews.org.

30. Kathleen A. Frankovic, "Why the Gender Gap Became News in 1996," *PS: Political Science and Politics* 32, no. 1 (March 1999): 20–23.

31. Jeff Manza and Clem Brooks, "The Gender Gap in U.S. Presidential Elections: When? Why? Implications?" *American Journal of Sociology* 103, no. 5 (March 1998): 1235–1266.

32. Seltzer, Newman, and Leighton, *Sex as a Political Variable,* p. 4.

33. "Gender Gap Evident in Numerous 1998 Races," fact sheet compiled by the Center for American Women and Politics, Eagleton Institute of Politics (New Brunswick, N.J.: Rutgers University, 1999).

34. Feminist Majority Foundation, "Gender Gap Decisive in Election 2000," accessed November 8, 2000, at http://www.feminist.org.

35. "Gender Gap a Factor in Battleground States," Women's Vote Watch, a project of the Center for American Women and Politics, Eagleton Institute, Rutgers University, October 3, 2008, accessed at http://www.cawp.rutgers.edu/press_room/news/documents/PressRelease_10-03-08_womensvote.pdf.

36. Jennifer Jackman, "2008 Election Gender Gap," Feminist Majority, November 2008, accessed at http://www.feministmajority.org/elections/2008gendergap.asp.

37. "2008 Election Analysis: Gender Gap Delivers," *Feminist Daily News Wire,* Feminist Majority, November 10, 2008, accessed at http://feminist.org/news/newsbyte/uswirestory.asp?id=11374.

38. "Gender Gap in 2004 Presidential Race Is Widespread," Center for American Women and Politics, Eagleton Institute of Politics (New Brunswick, N.J.: Rutgers University, 2004), accessed at http://www.cawp.rutgers.edu/Facts/Elections/GG2004widespread.pdf.

39. Votes for Women 2004, "Gender Gap Persists in the 2004 Election," http://www.votesforwomen2004.org.

40. Robin Hindery, "Tighter U.S. Gender Gap Tied to Fewer Issues," *Women's eNews,* November 7, 2004.

41. Katherine Q. Seelye, "Kerry in a Struggle for a Democratic Base: Women," *New York Times,* September 22, 2004, p. A1.

42. Lisa Garcia Bedolla, Jessica L. Lavariega Monforti, Adrian D. Pantoja, "A Second Look: Is There a Latina/o Gender Gap?" *Journal of Women, Politics & Policy* 28, no. 3/4 (2006): 147–171.

43. Manza and Brooks, "The Gender Gap in U.S. Presidential Elections."

44. Karen M. Kaufmann and John R. Petrocik, "The Changing Politics of American Men: Understanding the Sources of the Gender Gap," *American Journal of Political Science* 43, no. 3 (July 1999): 864–887.

45. Susan Welch and John Hibbing, "Financial Conditions, Gender and Voting in American National Elections," *Journal of Politics* 54 (1992): 343–359.

46. Feminist Majority Foundation, "Gender Gap Decisive in Election 2000," accessed at http://www.feminist.org/news/newsbyte/uswirestory.asp?id=4507.

47. Lake Snell Perry and Associates, "The Gender Gap and Women's Agenda for Moving Forward," accessed November 9, 2004, at http://www.votesforwomen2004.org/ Election%20 Poll%20Analysis%2011-04.pdf.

48. "Issues and the 2008 Election," PEW Forum, August 1, 2008, accessed at http://pewforum.org/docs/?DocID=339.

49. "Poll Findings: Understanding What Women Want in 2008," National Women's Law Center and Peter D. Hart Research Associates, Inc., August 5, 2008.

50. Kay Lehman Schlozman, Nancy Burns, Sidney Verba, and Jesse Donahue, "Gender and Citizen Participation: Is There a Different Voice?" *American Journal of Political Science* 39 (1995): 267–293.

51. Janet M. Box Steffensmeier, Suzanna DeBoef, and Tse-Min Lin, "The Dynamics of the Partisan Gender Gap," *American Political Science Review* 98, no. 3 (August 2004): 515–528.

52. Ibid., p. 527.

53. Greenberg Quinlan Rosner Research, "Re: The Security Mom Myth," accessed October 2004 at http://www.GreenbergResearch.com; Dan DeLuce, "Pollsters Call 'Security Moms' a Myth," *WeNews,* accessed October 2004 at http://www.womensnews.com; Kim Gandy, "The Perils of Polling," accessed October 2004 at http://www.now.org/news/note/100104.html.

54. Greenberg, "Re: The Security Mom Myth," p. 8.

55. Laurel Elder and Steven Green, "The Myth of 'Security Moms' and 'NASCAR Dads': Parenthood, Political Stereotypes, and the 2004 Election," *Social Science Quarterly* 88, no. 1 (March 2007): 1–19.

56. Ibid., p. 11.

57. Ibid., p. 16.

58. Verba, Schlozman, and Brady, *Voice and Equality,* p. 38.

59. For information on the sample and methodology, see Verba, Schlozman, and Brady, *Voice and Equality,* Appendix A.

60. Defined in this study as whether the respondent voted, worked on a campaign, made a campaign contribution, worked informally or in the community, served on a local governing board, contacted a government official, attended a protest, or was affiliated with a political organization.

61. Kay Schlozman, Nancy Burns, and Sidney Verba, "Gender and the Pathways to Participation: The Role of Resources," *Journal of Politics* 56, no. 4 (November 1994): 969.

62. Ibid., pp. 968–969. In each case, the gender differences were statistically significant.

63. Wendy Kaminer, "Crashing the Locker Room," *Atlantic* 270, no. 1 (July 1992): 58–70.

64. Scholzman, Burns, and Verba, "Gender and the Pathways to Participation," p. 977.

65. Ibid., p. 987.

66. Christine L. Day and Charles D. Hadley, *Women's PACs: Abortion and Elections* (Upper Saddle River, N.J.: Pearson Prentice Hall, 2005).

67. Open Secrets, "2004 Election Overview: Top Overall Donors," accessed at http://www.opensecrets.org.

68. "Women's PACs and Donor Networks: A Contact List," fact sheet compiled by the Center for American Women and Politics, Eagleton Institute of Politics (New Brunswick, N.J.: Rutgers University, 2004).

69. "Vote with Your Purse 2.0: Women's Online Giving, Offline Power," Women's Campaign Fund Foundation, September 2008, accessed at http://wcf.bluestatedigital.com/sites/wcf/index.php/Found/vote_with_your_purse.

70. Schlozman, Burns, Verba, and Donahue, "Gender and Citizen Participation." The phrase "in a different voice" is from Carol Gilligan's 1982 book of the same title.

71. See, for example, Susan Welch and Sue Thomas, "Do Women in Public Office Make a Difference?" in *Gender and Policymaking,* eds. Susan J. Carroll, Debra Dodson, and Ruth B. Mandel (New Brunswick, N.J.: Center for American Women and Politics, Eagleton Institute of Politics, Rutgers University, 1991).

72. Marc Hooghe and Dietlind Stolle, "Good Girls Go to the Polling Booth, Bad Boys Go Everywhere: Gender Differences in Anticipated Political Participation Among American Fourteen-Year-Olds," *Women and Politics* 23, no. 3/4 (2004).

73. Ibid., p. 19.

74. Sidney Verba and Norman Nie, *Participation in America: Political Democracy and Social Equality* (New York: Harper & Row, 1972).

75. Jamieson, Johnston, and Hagen, "The Primary Campaign."

76. Ibid.

77. Mary Christine Banwart, "Gender and Young Voters in 2004," *American Behavioral Scientist* 50, no. 9 (May 2007): 1152–1168.

78. Ibid., p. 1155.

79. Ibid., p. 1166.

80. Emily Marie Guyman, "The Gender Gap in Political Knowledge: A Comparison of Political Knowledge Levels in the United States, Canada, and Great Britain," unpublished master's thesis, Louisiana State University, May 2004.

81. Ibid, p. 52.

82. Michael R. Alvarez and Edward J. McCaffery, "Is There a Gender Gap in Fiscal Political Preferences?" Unpublished paper presented at the American Political Science Association meeting, September 2000.

83. Susan B. Hansen, "Talking About Politics: Gender and Contextual Effects in Political Proselytizing," *Journal of Politics* 59, no. 1 (February 1997): 73–103.

84. Simone de Beauvoir, *The Second Sex* (New York: Knopf, 1952).

85. Sapiro, Political Integration of Women, p. 40.

86. Paul H. Mussen, "Early Sex Role Development," in *Handbook of Socialization Theory and Research*, ed. David Goslin (New York: Rand McNally, 1969).

87. Katherine Blick Hoyenga and Kermit T. Hoyenga, *Gender-Related Differences: Origins and Outcomes* (Boston: Allyn and Bacon, 1993), p. 265.

88. David Sadker and Myra Sadker, *Failing at Fairness: How America's Schools Cheat Girls* (New York: Scribner, 1994), pp. 84–85.

89. Kathleen Dolan, "Political Development and the Family: An Examination of Alternative Family Structures," dissertation, University of Maryland, 1991.

90. Sue Thomas, *How Women Legislate* (New York: Oxford University Press, 1994), p. 56.

91. Hoyenga and Hoyenga, Gender-Related Differences, p. 266.

92. Suzanne Soule and Jennifer Nairne, "Are Girls Checking Out? Gender and Political Socialization in Transitioning Democracies," paper presented at the annual meeting of the Midwest Political Science Association, Chicago, April 20, 2006.

93. See Roberta S. Sigel, *Ambition and Accommodation: How Women View Gender Relations* (Chicago: University of Chicago Press, 1996), pp. 9–17; Sue Tolleson Rinehart, *Gender Consciousness and Politics* (New York: Routledge, 1992), pp. 21–27.

94. "Pipeline to the Future: Young Women and Political Leadership," findings on mobilizing young women, from a survey and focus groups conducted by Lake Snell Perry and Associates for The White House Project Education Fund, April 12, 2000, p. 22, accessed at http://www.thewhitehouseproject.org/.

95. The White House Project Education Fund, "Barbie Is Running for President!" press release April 19, 2000, accessed at http://www.whitehouseproject.org.

96. http://voterunlead.org/. Vote, Run, Lead is an initiative of The White House Project.

97. http://www.thewhitehouseproject.org/old_site/GirlZone/home_page.html.

98. "National Take Our Daughters to the Polls Campaign Launched in Historic Year for Women's Political Leadership," The White House Project press release, October 16, 2008, accessed at http://www.whitehouseproject.org.

99. M. Margaret Conway, Gertrude A. Steuernagel, and David Ahern, *Women and Political Participation: Cultural Change in the Political Arena* (Washington, D.C.: Congressional Quarterly Press, 1997).

100. Elizabeth Adell Cook, "The Generations of Feminism," in *Women in Politics: Insiders or Outsiders,* ed. Lois Duke Whitaker, 3rd ed. (Upper Saddle River, N.J.: Prentice Hall, 1999), pp. 45–55.

101. Conway, Steuernagel, and Ahern, *Women and Political Participation,* pp. 66–68.

102. Ibid., pp. 87–91.

103. Gerhard Falk, *Sex, Gender and Social Change: The Great Revolution* (Lanham, Md.: University Press of America, 1998), p. 175.

104. Deborah Tannen, "The Real Hillary Factor," *New York Times,* October 12, 1992, op-ed section.

105. Estelle Disch, *Reconstructing Gender: A Multicultural Anthology,* 2nd ed. (Mountain View, Calif.: Mayfield Publishing, 2000), p. 308.

106. Ibid., p. 306.

107. Kenneth Dion, Ellen Berscheid, and Elain Walster, "What Is Beautiful Is Good," *Journal of Personality and Social Psychology* 24 (1972): 285–290.

108. Asexander Todorov, Anesu N. Mandisodza, Amir Goren, and Crystal C. Hall, "Inferences of Competence from Faces Predict Election Outcomes," *Science* 308 (June 10, 2005): 1623–1626.

109. Rebekah Herrick, Jeanette Mendez, Sue Thomas, and Amanda Wilkerson, "Gender Affects on Competence Inferences Based on Facial Appearances," paper presented at the annual meeting of the American Political Science Association, Boston, August 2008.

110. Leslie A. Zebrowitz and Joann M. Montpare, "Appearance DOES Matter," *Science* 308 (June 10, 2005): 1565–1566.

111. Lonie Huddy and Nayda Terkildsen, "The Consequences of Gender Stereotypes for Women Candidates at Different Levels and Types of Office," *Political Research Quarterly* 46, no. 3 (September 1993): 503–525.

112. Linda Witt, Karen M. Paget, and Glenna Mathews, *Running as a Woman: Gender and Power in American Politics* (New York: Free Press, 1993), pp. 59–60.

113. Kaminer, "Crashing the Locker Room," pp. 58–70.

114. For more on this story, see Caryl Rivers, "Commentary: Mockery of Katherine Harris Shows Double Standard," November 29, 2000, accessed at http://www.womensenews.org.

115. For an interactive review of Hillary Clinton's "Body Politic," see *New York Magazine,* October 3, 2007, accessed at http://nymag.com/daily/intel/2007/10/a_brief_history_of_hillary_cli.html.

116. Katha Pollitt, "Media's Whiplash on Michelle Obama: From Fist-Bumping Radical to Mom-in-Chief," *Nation,* April 3, 2009, accessed at http://www.alternet.org.

117. Geraldine Brooks, "Michelle Obama and the Roots of Reinvention." *More Magazine,* October 2008, accessed at http://www.more.com.

118. Rebecca Traister, "The Mommification of Michelle Obama," *Salon.com,* November 12, 2008, accessed at: http://www.salon.com/mwt/feature/2008/11/12/michelle_obama/index.html.

119. Patricia Hill Collins, *Black Feminist Thought* (London: Routledge Press, 1991), p. 67.

120. R. Darcy, Charles D. Hadley, and Jason F. Kirksey, "Electoral Systems and the Representation of Black Women in American State Legislatures," *Women and Politics* 13 (1993): 73–76.

121. Irene Natividad, "Women of Color on the Campaign Trail," in *The American Woman: 1992–1993,* eds. Paula Ries and Anne J. Stone (New York: Norton, 1992).

122. Ibid., p. 136.

123. Center for American Women and Politics, "CAWP in Partnership with NOBEL Women," *CAWP News* (Fall 2000): 4.

124. Allison Harell, "Equal Participation but Separate Paths? Women's Social Capital and Turnout," *Journal of Women, Politics & Policy* 30, no. 1 (January–March, 2009): 1–22.

125. The term "social capital" is attributed to the work of Robert Putnam in *Making Democracy Work: Civic Traditions in Modern Italy* (Princeton, N.J.: Princeton University Press, 1993); quoting from Harell, "Equal Participation but Separate Paths?" p. 5.

126. Charles J. Olgetree, Jr., "The People vs. Anita Hill: A Case for Client Centered Advocacy," in *Race, Gender, and Power in America*, eds. Anita Faye Hill and Emma Coleman Jordan (New York: Oxford University Press, 1995), pp. 142–176.

127. Anna Deavere Smith, "Anita Hill and the Year of the Woman," in *Race, Gender, and Power in America*, eds. Hill and Jordan, pp. 248–270.

128. Ibid., p. 250.

129. A seventh female senator, Kay Bailey Hutchison, Republican from Texas, was seated after winning a special election to replace Senator Lloyd Bentsen after he was appointed secretary of the treasury.

130. Cynthia B. Costello, Shari Miles, and Anne J. Stone, eds., *The American Woman: 1999–2000* (New York: Norton, 1998), p. 97.

131. Toni Cabrillo et al., *The Feminist Chronicles* (Los Angeles: Women's Graphics, 1994), p. 143.

132. Susan Faludi, "Going Wild," 1994, in *Debating Tailhook, Frontline* program resource accessed at http://www.pbs.org/wgbh/frontline/shows/navy/tailhook/debate.html.

133. Katherine Boo, "Universal Soldier: What Paula Coughlin Can Teach American Women," *Washington Monthly,* September 1992.

134. http://www.plannedparenthood.org/gag/.

135. http://www.nwlc.org/pdf/AdminRecordOnWomen2004.pdf.

136. The Kaiser Daily Reproductive Health Report, "More Than 500,000 Abortion Rights Advocates March on National Mall," April 29, 2004, accessed at http://www.planned.org/site/News2?JServSessionIdr003=vqtv2ypgo1.app7b&page=NewsArticle&id=6054&security=1&news.

137. Kathleen Dolan, "Symbolic Mobilization?: The Impact of Candidate Sex in American Elections," *American Politics Research* 34, no. 6 (November 2006): 687–704.

138. The Electoral Commission, *Gender and Political Participation,* research report, April 2004; referenced in Sarah Hall, "Political Gender Gap Deters Women Voters," *Guardian,* April 28, 2004, accessed at http://www.guardian.co.uk/politics/2004/apr/28/uk.gender1.

139. Kathleen Dolan, "Symbolic Mobilization?: The Impact of Candidate Sex in American Elections," p. 699.

140. Jennifer L. Lawless, "Politics of Presence? Congresswomen and Symbolic Representation," *Political Research Quarterly* 57, no. 1 (2004): 81–99.

141. David Knoke, "The Mobilization of Members of Women's Associations," in *Women, Politics, and Change,* eds. Louise A. Tilly and Patricia Gurin (New York: Russell Sage Foundation, 1990), pp. 383–409.

142. Ibid.

143. Women's Voices. Women Vote, accessed at http:wvwv.org/docs/WVWV_novmemo .pdf.

144. "The Church Ladies Project – Women of Faith," accessed at http://www.womens organizations.org/index.php?option=com_content&task=view&id=21&Itemid =125.

145. Barbara C. Burrell, *Women and Political Participation: A Reference Handbook* (Santa Barbara, Calif.: ABC-CLIO, 2005).

146. CODEPINK maintains an active web presence at http://www.codepink4peace. org/.

147. Freeman, *A Room at a Time,* p. 6.

148. Ibid.

149. http://www.winningwomen.com/eps.html.

150. http://www.democrats.org/wvc/about/index.html.

151. Melinda Henneberger, "Want Votes with That? Get the 'Waitress Moms,'" *New York Times,* October 25, 1998, p. 3.

152. Ibid.

153. http://www.johnkerry.com/communities/military_families/mommymission.html; http://www.tampabays10.com/news/news.aspx?storyid=10376.

154. "Trends in Political Values and Core Attitudes: 1987–2009. Independents Take Center Stage in Obama Era," Pew Research Center for the People and the Press, May 21, 2009, accessed at http://people-press.org/reports/pdf/312.pdf.

Women Seeking Office: The Next Phase of Political Integration

As of 2009, a total of 263 women have served in the U.S. Congress since Jeanette Rankin was first elected in 1916; 225 of those in the U.S. House of Representatives. If all 225 women served together, they would make up slightly more than half of the total 435 seats in the House.[1]

Eighty-nine years after suffrage, what is the status of women in office? In 2009, women occupy 90 (16.8 percent) of the 535 seats available in the U.S. Congress. A record seventy-three women serve in the House of Representatives in 2009, with an additional three women serving as nonvoting delegates. Congresswoman Nancy Pelosi, a Democrat from California, is Speaker of the House and second in the presidential line of succession. She is the first woman to hold the Speaker's position. In the Senate, women hold 17 of the 100 available seats. Three states (California, Maine, and Washington) are represented by two female senators. Maine is the first state with more women than men in the congressional delegation, but nineteen states are not represented by a woman in either house (an increase of three over 2008). Although the number of congresswomen has tripled over the last twenty years, at the current rate of progress, it will be 2076 before women achieve equal representation.[2] By winning the New York Senate seat in 2000, Hillary Rodham Clinton became the first First Lady to hold elective office. Her victory also marked the first time a woman had represented New York in the Senate and the first time a New York woman had been elected to a statewide office in her own right. Following the 2008 election, Senator Clinton was nominated by President Obama to serve as Secretary of State. Upon her confirmation, New York Governor David Paterson appointed Congresswoman Kirsten Gillibrand as her replacement.

In addition, women were elected to fill 24.2 percent of the available seats in state legislatures in 2009, and 75 (23.9 percent) of the 314 statewide elective offices available. Following the 2008 elections, eight women serve as governor of a state, eight women serve as lieutenant governor, four women serve as attorney general, thirteen as secretary of state, and ten as state treasurer. Thirteen women were elected to the New Hampshire state senate in 2008, making it the country's first legislative body with more women than men (holding thirteen of 24 seats). The election of Christine Gregoire as governor of Washington (after two recounts and by a margin of 129 votes in 2004, and with 53 percent of the vote against the same opponent in 2008) produced the first state where women hold the top three political offices. President Obama drew heavily from the ranks of female governors in appointing his cabinet. Arizona Governor Janet Napolitano now serves as Secretary of Homeland Security (she was succeeded as governor by Arizona Secretary of State Jan Brewer, a Republican). Kathleen Sebelius, Governor of Kansas, was picked as Secretary of Health and Human Services and confirmed in April 2009.

Local offices have been much harder to track, but as of April 2009, eleven of the nation's 100 largest cities have female mayors (three are African American).

TABLE 4.1 Women's Representation in Elective Office Over Time, 1977–2009

Year	U.S. Congress	Statewide Elective	State Legislature
1977	4%	10%	9%
1979	3%	11%	10%
1981	4%	11%	12%
1983	4%	11%	13%
1985	5%	14%	15%
1987	5%	14%	16%
1989	5%	14%	17%
1991	6%	18%	18%
1993	10%	22%	21%
1995	10%	26%	21%
1997	11%	26%	22%
1999	12%	28%	22.5%
2001	13%	27.5%	22.4%
2003	13.6%	26%	22.4%
2004	13.8%	26%	22.5%
2005	14.9%	25.1%	22.5%
2006	13.8%	24.8%	22.8%
2007	15.3%	24.1%	23.5%
2008	16.4%	23.2%	23.7%
2009	16.8%	23.9%	24.2%

Source: Center for American Women and Politics (CAWP), National Information Bank on Women in Public Office, Eagleton Institute of Politics, Rutgers University.

In cities with populations of 30,000, 17 percent (or 193) of mayors were women.[3] At the highest levels of government, 2008 was a good year for women. Hillary Clinton attracted over eighteen million primary votes in her quest for the Democratic presidential nomination. Republican nominee John McCain's selection of Alaska Governor Sarah Palin as his vice-presidential running mate was the first time a woman had shared the top of a Republican Party ticket. Geraldine Ferraro's nomination, in 1984, was the only other time a woman has run in the second spot on a major party ticket. Prior to Hillary Clinton's 2008 campaign, only three women had sought the presidential nomination of a major party, while a fourth got as far as an exploratory committee before bowing out. A total of thirty-nine women have held posts in presidential cabinets since Frances Perkins first assumed her position as secretary of labor in 1933. Twenty-two of these women were appointed by a Democratic president while seventeen were appointed by a Republican president. Patricia Harris, appointed to two cabinet posts by President Jimmy Carter, was the first African American woman appointed to a presidential cabinet. Aida Alvarez, appointed by President Clinton, was the first Latina to serve at the cabinet level. President George W. Bush appointed Elaine Chao secretary of labor in 2001, making

TABLE 4.2 Women's Representation in National Legislatures Around the World: Sixteen Countries Ranking Highest for Women's Representation in National Legislature, Lower House (2009)

Country	Proportion of Women Members
Rwanda*	56.3%
Sweden**	47.0%
Cuba	43.2%
Finland**	41.5%
Netherlands**	41.3%
Argentina*	40.0%
Denmark**	38.0%
Angola*	37.3%
Costa Rica*	36.8%
Spain*	36.3%
Norway**	36.1%
Belgium*	35.3%
Mozambique**	34.8%
New Zealand	33.6%
Iceland**	33.3%
Nepal*	33.2%

* Legal gender quotas in place.
** Party gender quotas in place.
Source: Inter-Parliamentary Union, "Women in Parliaments: World Classification," as of February 28, 2009, accessed at http://www.ipu.org/wmn-e/world.htm.

her the first Asian-American woman to hold a cabinet position. Madeleine Albright, appointed by President Clinton, was the first woman to serve as secretary of state. She was followed by Condoleezza Rice during the George W. Bush administration. To date, no woman has served as secretary of the Treasury or as secretary of defense. President Obama's first cabinet will be the most diverse in history with seven women and nine racial and ethnic minorities among the twenty-one members.

When the United States is compared to other developed nations in terms of the number of women in political office, the United States clearly lags behind (see Table 4.2). Of 188 countries, the United States places seventy-first based on the percentage of women serving in the lower (or single) house of the national legislature.[4] Following the 2008 elections, women hold 16.8 percent of the seats in the U.S. House of Representatives. A UN Development Report stated, "While it is true that no definite relationship has been established between the

Point of Comparison

The Power of Positive Discrimination: Electoral Quotas to Advance Women in Office

Throughout the book, we have used the term "discrimination" in a negative context to refer to the ways in which women are treated unequally because of their sex or gender, usually resulting in some identifiable harm. But, in some countries, positive discrimination in the form of electoral gender quotas has resulted in a greater share of political representation for women. See Table 4.2 for data on women's representation in the sixteen countries with the highest proportion of women serving in the lower house of the national legislature. Of the sixteen, only two (Cuba and New Zealand) do not have some type of electoral gender quotas in place.

All electoral systems employ some kind of quotas; most are designed to reflect population density and geographic diversity. Gender quotas are designed to enhance women's participation and representation. "Gender quotas ensure that women constitute a specific number or percentage of the members of a body, be it a candidate list, a parliamentary assembly, a committee or the government."[1] The quota system places the burden of recruitment not on the individual woman, but on those who control the recruitment process. When quotas are effectively implemented, the proportion of women in politics increases rapidly. Even when quotas are temporary measures, women are elected at higher rates following their removal.[2]

There are different types of quotas. The primary distinction is between constitutional (e.g., Nepal, the Philippines, and Uganda) and legislative (e.g., Belgium, extent of women's participation in political institutions and their contribution to the advancement of women, a 30 percent membership in political institutions is considered the critical mass that enables women to exert meaningful influence on politics."[5] The Women's Environment and Development Organization (WEDO) established the "50/50 Campaign: Get the Balance Right" in 2000 in pursuit of gender parity in legislatures worldwide. By the end of 2008, twenty countries had achieved a critical mass of 30 percent women in national parliaments. Over the decade following the 1995 Beijing World Conference on Women, where the goal of gender parity was embraced by 189 governments, the percentage of women legislators has increased by only 0.5 percent each year.[6] The international average stands at 18.4 percent for both houses combined, but an average hides considerable variation.[7] Notably, among the democracies ranking highest for women's representation, nearly all employ proportionally based electoral systems. In countries with the greatest success

Bosnia-Herzegovina, Serbia, Sudan, and in many parts of Latin America) quotas officially mandating that all political entities participating in elections apply them equally versus voluntary political party quotas (e.g., Argentina, Bolivia, Ecuador, Germany, Italy, Norway, and Sweden) that are designed to guarantee the nomination of a certain number or proportion of women. A "zipper-style" system alternates an equal number of women and men on a party list. "Double quotas" ensure that women are not relegated to the bottom of party lists (used in Belgium and Argentina). Quotas can be introduced at any level of the political system—federal, national, regional, or local. Quotas can also be "gender-neutral" in the sense that they merely specify that neither gender should occupy more than 60 percent and no less than 40 percent of the seats, for example.

Gender quotas may apply to the number of female candidates proposed by a party for election, or they may take the form of reserved seats in the legislature. In 2009, 100 countries have adopted some form of electoral gender quotas, with an average level of representation of women at 20 percent (the world average for upper and lower houses combined is 18 percent). Although electoral gender quotas have been very effective in rapidly increasing the share of representative seats held by women in diverse settings, they are controversial for a variety of reasons. Quotas represent a shift from one kind of equality to another—from "equal opportunity" or "competitive equality" to "equality of result." Thus the idea of quotas is in conflict with other values such as fairness, competence, and individualism. Gender quotas are most easily introduced in proportional representation (PR) electoral systems, but they have been successfully introduced in some mixed systems or even majority systems.

1. Drude Dahlerup, "Comparative Studies of Gender Quotas," paper presented at International IDEA workshop, February 2003, accessed at http://www.quotaproject.org/CS/CS_Dahlerup_25-11-2003.pdf.
2. Rikhil R. Bhavnani, "Do Electoral Quotas Work After They Are Withdrawn? Evidence from a Natural Experiment in India," *American Political Science Review* 103, no. 1 (February 2009): 23–35.

in promoting women's representation, there is generally some form of quota system for candidacy by which women are guaranteed a minimum proportion of winnable positions available on candidate lists (see Point of Comparison). Among countries with a substantially lower proportion of women, plurality or majoritarian systems are almost exclusively in place, and none have any formal system to encourage women's candidacies.

In the United States, a full explanation for women's low representation is not clear. Conventional wisdom used to explain women's political under-representation by saying that the country was not ready for women in high office; voters, particularly women voters, would not support a woman candidate; women could not raise sufficient funds to mount successful campaigns; or political-party elites conspired to keep women from being nominated to winnable seats.[8] The reality today is that women candidates are as likely to win elections as men. "The reason there aren't more women in public office is not that women don't win, but that not enough women have been candidates in general elections."[9] So why aren't there more women candidates? The answer is multifaceted and constitutes a major portion of this chapter. Also included is a detailed examination of women's experiences as candidates for elective office and an analysis of how their experiences differ from those of their male counterparts. Finally, this chapter looks at potential electoral reforms and current initiatives designed to increase the number of women running for public office.

WOMEN CANDIDATES ARE AS LIKELY TO WIN ELECTIONS AS MEN

The long-held conventional wisdom that a woman has a poor chance of electoral victory is empirically unsubstantiated. That does not mean, however, that the myth does not continue to scare women away from running for office. "If women think the system is biased against them, then the empirical reality of a playing field on which women can succeed is almost meaningless." Women and men with equivalent professional and political credentials view the electoral system quite differently even today. Women, for example, view local and congressional elections in their area as more competitive than men do; anticipate that they will have a harder time raising money; and perceive that it is more difficult for a woman to be elected than for a man. Likewise, more women (29 percent) than men (17 percent) rate the odds of winning their first race as "very unlikely."[10]

A study, conducted by Richard A. Seltzer, Jody Newman, and Melissa Vorhees Leighton, comparing the actual success rates of male and female candidates for general elections for state legislature, U.S. House and Senate, and governor during comparable time periods found that "a candidate's sex does not affect his or her chances of winning an election."[11] Researchers in this study were careful to compare like candidates in like situations. In other words, they compared challengers with challengers and incumbents with incumbents in both open-seat races and those with incumbents running for reelection. This is a crucial point of distinction. Previous studies looked only at the electoral landscape as a whole and simply compared winners to losers on the basis of sex. Since more men have run for office overall and more men have been incumbents, men seemed to have won more often than women. These findings were in fact inaccurate, the result of an error in the methodology used in the earlier studies. Incumbency, not sex, is the main determinant of victory in general elections in the United States.

Seltzer, Newman, and Leighton found that in state house races, female incumbents won 93.6 percent of their elections, compared to 93.8 percent for male incumbents. Women vying for open seats won 52.2 percent of their contests, compared to men, who won 53 percent of the time. What's more, women challengers won 10.9 percent of their elections, compared to 9.7 percent for men. In state senate races, incumbent women won 90.1 percent of their elections, compared with 92.2 percent for men; women running for open seats won 55.8 percent of their races, compared with 54.9 percent for men; and women challengers won 15.2 percent of their elections, compared with 11.6 percent for men.[12] Interestingly, men's and women's chances of victory are similar across the country except in the New England and East North Central regions, where female incumbents and challengers did slightly better than males. Southern women, who have been the most politically disadvantaged by their sex, suffered no disability.

Because state legislative seats have historically been most accessible to women, a better test of the influence of a candidate's sex might be found at the national level. Here, too, researchers found that women fare as well as men in general elections. Incumbent women in U.S. House races won 93.6 percent of their elections, compared to 94.8 percent for incumbent men. Women running for open seats won 47.9 percent of the time, compared to 51.2 percent for men, and women challengers won 4 percent of their contests, compared to 6.2 percent for men. Analysis by party found that in the Republican Party women did better than men, whereas in the Democratic Party men were more successful. Researchers were unable to calculate similar statistics for gubernatorial and U.S. Senate races because of the small number of women running for these offices.[13]

Success rates for women compared to men did not vary significantly, even in 1992. The media attention surrounding the "Year of the Woman" in politics should really have been a celebration of the number of women who *sought* office rather than the number of women who *won* their races. A number of factors expanded women's opportunities to run, including a record number of open seats in the U.S. House resulting from retirements, resignations, and reapportionment. Women fare much better in open-seat contests than as challengers to incumbents, as evidenced in the statistics above. Recall that incumbent women in U.S. House races won 93.6 percent of their races, female candidates for open seats won 47.9 percent, and challengers to incumbents won only 4 percent. As Jody Newman of the National Women's Political Caucus (NWPC) notes:

> Consider what would happen if women made up half of all open seat candidates and challengers in the general elections for the U.S. House starting in 1994. Assuming 50 open seats per election cycle and the same success rates as those found in this study, then women would hold a third of the seats in the U.S. House by the year 2000.[14]

But, in fact, women held only 13 percent of the house seats (59 of 435 seats) in 2000; increasing the number of women candidates matters!

Whether spurred by the Anita Hill–Clarence Thomas spectacle or by a rational assessment of their chances for victory, by April 30, 1992, more than 213 women had announced they would seek their party's nomination for the U.S. House or Senate. The most striking increase was in the number of women who announced their bids for the Senate, which historically has been the hardest legislative office for women to win. By early spring 1992, twenty-two women had announced candidacies, compared to only eight in 1990.[15] Ultimately twenty-nine women filed, and eleven won their primaries in 1992.[16] From 1972 to 1994, only 7.9 percent of the candidates for the Senate were women. Likewise, only 7.8 percent of the candidates for the House and 6.6 percent of gubernatorial candidates were women. From 1986 to 1994, just 21.3 percent of state house and 17.3 percent of state senate candidates were women.[17] But in open-seat races for higher office in 1994, only one candidate in ten was a woman. Despite the big surge in 1992, fewer than one candidate in four was a woman in open-seat contests for state legislatures in 1994. By contrast, twenty women ran in thirty-five open House races in the 2000 election. In all, 122 women won their 2000 primary elections while only 46 women lost them, resulting in a record 12 woman-to-woman races for the U.S. House.[18] In the 2004 cycle, 141 women were candidates for House seats (57 incumbents, 20 women running in open-seat contests in 18 districts, and 64 running as challengers), establishing a new record. In eleven House districts, both candidates were women.[19]

Despite these advances, without a substantial increase in the number of women candidates in each election cycle, the rate of gain in the proportion of women in office is likely to remain very small. In 2004, there were 131 House races in which at least one candidate was female. If a female candidate had won each one of those races, women would still hold only 30 percent of the seats in the U.S. House of Representatives. In fact, women held only 14.9 percent of the available seats following the 2004 election. In 2008, 33 states had U.S. Senate races and of those, five were open seats. Women were candidates in only six of the thirty-three states. Of the 435 House races in 2008, 132 women won their primary (67 incumbents, 11 women in 10 districts with open seats, and 54 women ran as challengers). Overall, the number of candidates has not significantly increased from records set in 1992.[20] Women will not achieve substantial gains in representation, let alone reach parity with men, until the

Women of the NH State Senate women. The New Hampshire State Senate is the first legislative body in the United States in which women hold the majority of seats (13 of 24). *Courtesy of the New Hampshire State Senate.*

proportion of women seeking seats reaches or exceeds the number of male candidates.

WOMEN ARE *NOT* AS LIKELY TO BE CANDIDATES

The decision to seek political office is not one that can be empirically tested or objectively quantified. The decision is intensely personal, and studies show that family, friends, and confidants have usually had more of an impact on potential candidates than national parties or other organizational appeals.[21] There are, however, some factors that all candidates take into consideration when deciding whether to seek public office. Many of these factors play differently for men and women. The first and foremost calculation has to be the chance of winning the election.

Perception of Electability

A 1994 study conducted by pollster Celinda Lake for the National Women's Political Caucus found that two-thirds of voters believed that women have a tougher time winning elections than men do.[22] This belief was based on assumptions that women face discrimination from the gatekeepers in elections—the party elites responsible for recruitment of new candidates. Those surveyed also felt that voters would not support a woman and that women would have a tougher time raising money. Although these perceptions may or may not be true in any single contest, their power lies in the fact that women may not see themselves as viable candidates and party leaders may not see women as viable candidates purely as a result. Studies find that women are more likely than men to carefully consider their qualifications for office and often to undervalue their credentials. On the other hand, similarly situated men tend to overestimate their qualifications. These factors combine to produce the *pipeline* thesis, which argues that there are fewer women candidates and office holders because not enough women possess the qualifications or have met the requirements to hold elective office. The pipeline refers to the group of vetted potential candidates that have met the formal and informal requirements and have been deemed electable. Although age, citizenship, and residence are the only formal qualifications for most offices, the informal requirements might include experience and name recognition, which may be more difficult for women to meet. Education, previous experience holding political office, occupational prestige, and even marital status combine to create the *eligibility pool* from which viable candidates are drawn. In many cases, previous experience in political office is a crucial characteristic of those in the eligibility pool. Political scientist Sue Carroll notes the importance of experience in constructing the pipeline for women candidates:

> The importance of this women's political base—of the development of a sizable pool of potential candidates with experience at state and local levels—is evident from an examination of the 24 women elected to the U.S. House of Representatives for the first time in 1992. Of these 24 women, 11 had served in state legislatures. Of the 13 who had not been state legislators, two had been county commissioners, four had served on city councils, one had been municipal court judge, one had been a state party chair, and one had held a cabinet position in state government.[23]

The characteristics of electable candidates depend in part on the level of the office in question (national, state, or local). The higher the office, the more experience, education, and professional prestige are expected. Candidates for the U.S. Senate are drawn from a select pool of individuals, many of whom come from corporate boardrooms, the ranks of senior management, prestigious law firms, or the U.S. House. Women have only recently broken into this select group, and their numbers are still very small: fifteen women act as CEOs of Fortune 500 companies, women constitute roughly 14.7 percent of board members of Fortune 500 companies and only 16 percent of the partners of large law firms, and women make up only 19 percent of full professors at doctorate-granting institutions nationwide. For many, this suggests that the reason for women's lack of representation in politics rests with their small numbers in the pipeline to office. In other words, there are simply not enough qualified female candidates. Advocates for more women in office are advised to be patient. As more women enter the public sphere overall, there will be more female candidates and therefore more women elected officials. Chapter 7 explores the validity of the pipeline thesis as it relates to occupational choices and wages.

There is no doubt that levels of preparation for the eligibility pool are already changing among young men and women. In 2008, the educational attainment levels of women between the ages of twenty-five and twenty-nine exceeded those of men in the same age group—29.4 million women and 28.4 million men held a bachelor's degree or higher. Women had a larger share of high school diplomas, as well as associate's, bachelor's, and master's degrees. More men than women held a professional or doctoral degree.[24] Women are approaching parity in law schools (46.9 percent in 2007), but there is a considerable drop-off in the number of women who are actually practicing law. Beyond education, the progress into other avenues of power has proceeded more slowly. One path to higher office has traditionally been to work in local or state politics to gain experience as well as visibility within a political party. Women's numbers at this level are increasing, but at a very slow rate. The proportion of women holding state legislative seats has remained static since 1993, increasing by only 4 percentage points in the sixteen years since the "Year of the Woman."

Women face additional obstacles in entering the pipeline for higher office. While women's numbers have been growing at the local and state legislative levels, the average age when first elected to office remains significantly higher for women than for men. Women often wait to seek office until their children are grown,[25] which limits their ability to climb the ladder to progressively higher positions. In a study released in 1991, only 15 percent of women office-holders were forty years old or younger, compared to 28 percent of men. Men in office were twice as likely as women to have pre-teenage children at home.[26] While fatherhood is seen as compatible with a professional career and political office, motherhood is seen as a full-time job.[27] Women with small children face tough questioning as candidates about how they expect to handle both jobs. Men, however, are rarely asked whether their political responsibilities will take them away from their children. Congresswoman Connie Morella of Maryland recalls a party slating meeting in 1976, the year in which she first sought office: "One of the men who hoped he would get the nomination . . . asked, 'Well, Ms. Morella, in light of your extended family do you think you'll really have time to run for Congress, much less serve?'"[28] In 1972, Patricia Schroeder, former Democratic congresswoman from Colorado, had a two-year-old daughter when she was first elected to the House. She spent the first few days in office answering queries from constituents, as well as from her new congressional colleagues, about how she was going to "do it."[29] On the other hand, unmarried women without children are likely to face questions about their sexuality. "A single woman politician, without family to provide the paternalistic equivalent of coverture, will be gay-baited, or lusted after, or pestered with questions about why she can't get a man."[30] Demonstrating that women in leadership posts matter, Speaker of the House Nancy Pelosi announced the creation of a special room for nursing mothers in the Cannon House Office Building in 2007. "Many women face great challenges in managing both motherhood and career. In order for the House to continue to attract and maintain the brightest and most committed public servants, we must ensure that it becomes a family-friendly place to work," Pelosi said. "This is a step in the right direction."[31] When congresswoman Linda Sanchez gave birth to a son in May 2009, she became only the eighth member of the House of Representatives to give birth while serving in office.

Men and women may also seek political office for different reasons. Historically, women have sought local office to solve a particular problem rather than to start a career in politics. Once the community problem is solved, many women choose to leave public service rather than seek higher office, limiting their numbers in the pipeline. Women are less likely than men to see themselves as politicians, let alone career politicians. For a long time, women's primary path to elective office was in the wake of a male relative, usually a father or a husband. The *widow tradition* has a long history in the United States and accounts for many of the "first" women in Congress, state legislatures, and governors' offices. Women who ran for national office in their own right as recently as the early 1970s were likely to have come from a political family and carry the legacy of a political name. Now-retired Senator Nancy Kassebaum Baker, for example, is the daughter of one-time presidential contender Alf Landon. As Marion Saunders, a defeated 1954 congressional candidate said, "Those who take to politics like ducks to water have generally grown up in the pond."[32] Women today are not limited by family legacy or the widow's tradition. Instead they can aspire to public service based on their own motivations and undertake the preparation necessary to be successfully elected.

In a study conducted in the spring of 2000 for The White House Project Education Fund, researchers interviewed young women and men to learn more about the pipeline of the future. The study found that young people, particularly women, are extraordinarily dedicated to their communities and to solving problems within them. Although they hold negative attitudes about politics and politicians in general, more than four in ten young adults would consider running for office themselves. Young women are more inclined to get involved in politics if they believe they will be able to accomplish their goals and address issues they care about through political involvement. Young women who have held leadership positions in their school or community and who have been encouraged to seek office are far more likely than other women to express a desire to seek political office. Encouragement has twice the power of any other factor in predicting whether a young woman will consider running for office. Therefore, young women can be cultivated to seek elective office.[33]

An obvious place to gain leadership experience, as well as experience with elections, for many women is in university student government. Many of the explanations for why women are underrepresented in local, state, and national politics have to do with barriers to candidacy including family responsibilities, interest in politics, and a failure to accurately perceive their qualifications for public office. These theories, especially the first regarding family responsibilities, should have less relevance for student government elections since male and female college students are more similarly situated in terms of resources so that educational attainment and occupational prestige are not factors. A 2004 study, however, found that while women were elected as representatives to student government, they were underrepresented in presidential or vice-presidential positions. Surveys sent to thirty-four Midwestern universities in seven states found that while women held nearly half (47.9 percent) of the student government positions, 71.4 percent of the student government presidents and vice presidents were male. Looking back over a five-year period, the findings were similar. Out of 105 chances for a student to be elected over 5 years, a woman was elected 25 times (or in 24 percent of the instances). Females were elected vice president more frequently (47 out of 105 chances). Although this research is largely descriptive, investigators found some evidence that having a female as student government faculty advisor was positively correlated with females in leadership positions in student government. Interestingly, the ratio of female to male students enrolled on campus was not positively correlated with female student leadership. Because there is no multivariate analysis included, the researchers can only describe the phenomenon but they cannot explore the reasons behind women's underrepresentation in student government leadership. The positive correlation between a female adult advisor and female leadership suggests that role models might be one area to explore further.[34]

The Power of Role Models

Christina Wolbrecht and David Campbell examined the influence of women in elected office on adolescent girls' anticipated involvement—their intention to be politically active in adulthood.[35] They hypothesized that the presence of visible female role models makes young women more likely to express an intention to engage in political activity as adults. The data for the study come from the Civic Education Study (CES), a survey administered in twenty-seven countries to adolescents (target age: fourteen years old) enrolled in a civics-related course. Respondents were asked, "When you are an adult, what do you expect that you will do?" and offered a list of political activities including: join a political party, write letters to a newspaper about social or political concerns, and be a candidate for local or city office. Voting was not included because in some of the nations in the sample, voting is mandatory. Obviously, anticipatory intention is different than actual activity, but this particular measure does provide insight into adolescents' state of mind—do they envision themselves as politically active in the future? Socialization research supports the connection between identifying as potential political participants and actual adult political engagement. When Wolbrecht and Campbell examined anticipated political involvement by gender, they found that in seventeen of twenty-seven nations, boys have a statistically higher rate of anticipated involvement, while in another eight there are no statistically significant differences between boys and girls, and in two nations (Finland and the United States) girls have a higher level of anticipated involvement than boys. Moving on to the hypothesized relationship between women in office as role models and anticipated political engagement, they find that more women in office positively correspond to a smaller gap in anticipated involvement even when the Scandinavian nations are removed. In explaining the role model effect, however, they are only able to isolate one potential explanation:

> Specifically, our analysis leads us to suspect that the presence of female role models changes how adolescent girls perceive not gender roles in general or the system as a whole, but simply their own relationship to the political system. Having seen women successfully pursue elective office they are able to envision themselves as active participants in the political process. . . . the presence of role models hel ps girls make the leap from psychological political engagement to an intention for actual political activity.[36]

In a subsequent study that included adults as well as adolescents, Wolbrecht and Campbell found that the presence of women as members of parliament (MPs) had an impact on the aspirations of women and girls, although the influence was strongest on adolescent girls. This study found that where there are more female MPs, adolescent girls are more likely to discuss politics with friends and to say that they will participate in politics as adults. Adult women are more likely to actually participate and to discuss politics.[37] Finally, the same pair of scholars examined the role-model effect in the United States where the proportion of women in the national legislature is very small. In this case, they test the hypothesis that girls are more likely to express an intention to be active in politics when they see women running for high profile offices; visibility is a critical component in the relationship. Visibility takes several forms in the analysis—visibility associated with a high-profile office (president, for example), the viability of the candidate, and the extent to which gender is salient in the election. Similar to the other research, they find that the more women politicians are made visible (usually by the national media), the more likely adolescent girls are to indicate an intention to be politically active. The role-model effect here leads to greater likelihood for political discussion within girls' homes, enriching the overall political socialization environment.[38]

The results of these studies pose a kind of "chicken-and-egg" problem. More women officeholders and more visible and viable female candidates provide role models that in turn make it more likely that young women will discuss politics in the present and plan for a political life of engagement in the future. The role-model effect persists across nations. Therefore, we would expect that over time, the remaining gap in various forms of political engagement beyond voting that still persist between males and females would close. However, to get girls involved there have to be more women political role models. As we have noted throughout this chapter and the previous chapter, increasing the number of women politicians in the United States has been a long, slow, incremental process. There are institutional mechanisms such as electoral gender quotas that would more rapidly increase the number of visible female role models, but they have not been seriously considered in the United States. Thus, the factors that influence a woman's decision to stand for election become all the more crucial.

Candidate Emergence: Gender Differences in Making the Initial Decision to Run

Women, even in the highest tiers of professional accomplishment, are substantially less likely than men to demonstrate ambition to seek office. These results hold regardless of age, partisan affiliation, income and profession.[39]

Some of the most significant new research in the area of women candidates challenges both the eligibility pool and the pipeline theses in explaining why so few women seek office in each election cycle. Recall that the theories we discussed above predicted that as more women met the formal and informal eligibility requirements, there would be more women in the political pipeline; and as more women filled the pipeline, the number of women candidates would increase, thereby increasing the number of women in public office. Research by Richard Fox and Jennifer Lawless suggests that these theories may rest on a fundamentally flawed assumption: that women will respond to political opportunities in the same ways that men traditionally have.[40] As the authors point out, little attention has been paid to the process by which gender affects men's and women's emergence as candidates for public office. To rectify this, Fox and Lawless conducted a national survey of 3,700 potential candidates in the "eligibility pool" (men and women with the same personal characteristics and professional credentials in business, law, education, and political activism) for all levels of office. They found that women overall are less likely than their male colleagues to consider running for office, even though they share the eligibility pool credentials for success and surpass men in their interest in politics.[41] Similar to the findings in other studies, among respondents within their sample who actually ran for office, 63 percent of the women and 59 percent of the men were successful. Although statistically significant gender differences characterized even the consideration of running for office, the major differences appeared at the next stage of the process. Men were

50 percent more likely to have actually undertaken any one of a number of steps necessary to mount a campaign (e.g., investigated how to place their name on the ballot, or discussed running with potential donors, party or community leaders, or family and friends). "Despite starting out with relatively equal proportions of similarly situated and equally credentialed women and men as potential candidates, and regardless of the fact that women are just as likely as men to win elections, men are nearly twice as likely as women to hold office: 7 percent of the men, compared to less than 4 percent of the women, from the initial pool of potential candidates hold an elective position."[42] Lawless and Fox resurveyed more than 2,000 of the original respondents in 2008 and found that "despite the historic events of the last seven years—such as the war in Iraq, frustration with the political process, and the emergence of a more diverse group of political candidates and leaders—overall ambition for women and men have remained fairly constant."[43]

So what explains women's lack of ambition for political office? Fox and Lawless investigated a number of factors related to traditional gender socialization, political culture, family responsibilities, and self-perceived qualifications, based on the original survey and interviews conducted in 2001. They did not find any empirical support for the traditional barriers to women's entry into politics; women's ambition is not depressed by political culture, family structure, or primary caretaking responsibilities, or by ideological motivations. Rather women's self-perceptions of their qualifications for office and the degree to which they receive encouragement to run are central to predicting whether women will seek political office. When women perceive themselves as "very qualified" for holding an elected position, they are significantly more likely to consider running. For women, the impact of self-perceived qualifications on the decision to seek office is nearly double that for men. Other researchers have found that women's lack of political confidence relative to their male counterparts emerges as early as high school and college, even among women with substantially more actual political experience in student government. Senator Susan Collins (R-ME) says, "Far too often, smart, capable women simply talk themselves out of running for office . . . a woman will think that in order to discuss trade policy, she needs a PhD in economics; a man who sells Hondas considers himself an expert."[44]

Both men's and women's ambition for office increases when they receive encouragement, particularly when it comes from political *and* nonpolitical sources. In some cases, being asked may be important even to the most initial decision to seek office. Gary Moncrief and Peverill Squire found that 37 percent of women, compared to 18 percent of men, had never thought of running for office before someone asked them.[45] Despite the impact encouragement has on the decision to run, 43 percent of men, compared to 32 percent of women, had been encouraged to run by a party leader, an elected official, or a political activist. In this respect, "vestiges of patterns of traditional gender socialization in candidate recruitment hinder the selection of women candidates."[46] Laurel Elder also found evidence that role models play an important role in moving women from being potential to actual candidates.[47] Women were far more conscious than men were of women politicians, and as we discussed earlier, there is evidence that female role models have a unique and positive impact on women's political interest, knowledge, and engagement.

Fox and Lawless concluded that although women who run for office are just as likely as men to emerge as winners, the winnowing process in candidate emergence yields a smaller number of female candidates. The pool of candidates who *actually* run, therefore, looks very different from the eligibility pool of potential candidates. Women are significantly less likely than men to receive political encouragement to run and to self-assess themselves as qualified to run for office, but at the same time they are more likely to rely on their own assessment when considering whether to enter the political arena. There are a number of interesting implications for these findings. First, looking only at the end of the electoral process is not a very good gauge of the ways in which gender operates in candidate recruitment and elections. The women who ultimately decide to run have already overcome a number of barriers and may, as a result, actually be more qualified candidates than the males they compete against. In this respect, the electoral contest may be less gender-neutral than first imagined. Second, relying on the inevitable advance of women in the professions will not be sufficient by itself to produce more women candidates or elected officials. Both the eligibility pool and pipeline theses must be reexamined relative to advancing women from being qualified candidates to actually running for office.

The research emerging from the 2008 follow-up survey conducted by Lawless and Fox provide a more nuanced look at the ways in which women's perceptions of a biased and competitive electoral arena, as well as their self-assessments that they are less qualified to seek and hold elective office, limit their political ambition. Most importantly, the gender gap in political ambition persists in 2008 even though the political environment might appear more hospitable to a woman's candidacy. In the overall sample, 51 percent of the respondents say that they have thought about running for elective office. Of those, 56 percent are male and 42 percent are female. This means that men are 35 percent more likely than women to think of themselves as political candidates—a political ambition gender gap that crosses political party, income, age, race, profession, and region. Further, in thinking about seeking office, men are significantly more likely than women to have undertaken the steps necessary to actually run for office (discussed running with family, friends, community leaders, and/or party leaders; investigated how to place their name on the ballot; and discussed financial contributions with potential supporters). Consistent with women's entrance into politics in general, women are most likely to have considered a candidacy at the local level and least likely at the federal level. In fact, men are twice as likely as women to express an interest in seeking elected office at the federal level

(U.S. House, Senate, president) and 30 percent more likely to be interested in a state-level office. The only position for which women express significantly more interest than men is the local school board. In exploring the reasons behind the persistent gender gap in political ambition, the 2008 study looked specifically at men's and women's attitudes about engaging in a campaign, the role of political recruitment, the impact of family obligations, the role of self-assessment of electoral qualifications and viability, and their perceptions about bias in the political system. These factors, as examined in the 2008 follow-up study by Lawless and Fox, are examined further in the sections below.

Political Parties: A Help or a Hindrance?

Political parties serve a unique role in recruiting potential candidates to run in primary elections, where voters select one candidate to represent their party in the general election. Scholars have long suspected that party leaders are biased against women, but conclusive research to back up those suspicions has been mixed. Denise Baer calls political parties the missing variable in women and politics research.[48] Research using party financial contributions to candidates as a proxy measure of party support for women candidates has found no evidence of bias.[49] Bias, however, was detected in a 1998 study conducted by David Niven in which both county-level party chairs and potential women candidates were interviewed about their experiences and preferences.[50] Niven hypothesized that because as many as 97 percent of county-level party chairs are male in some states, male attitudes toward potential women candidates may take on the form of assumptions about women as a group. This phenomenon is known as the *outgroup effect*. A prior study of male and female state legislators found some evidence of the outgroup effect. Younger, less-experienced males were encouraged by the party to run for office, while only those women who had extensive party experience and a strong background were considered acceptable candidates. In other words, party elites judged males on their potential, but not females. In interviewing potential women candidates, Niven discovered that 64 percent of those who ran for state legislative or congressional seats had experienced some form of discrimination at the hands of party leaders. Niven found support that this perception of bias was real and attributed its cause to the outgroup effect. Party elites consistently recruited and preferred potential candidates they judged most similar to themselves. This is significant because 85 percent of the same women reported that they would not seek higher office if their party were unsupportive.

Other studies have found that in recruiting candidates for office, party elites tend to look for candidates similar to themselves in order to ensure shared values.[51] Since women are seen as part of the other group, they do not pass the similarity test during the initial screening. Another phenomenon explored in this research is the *distribution effect*. In this case, men's and women's distribution in productive roles (jobs and occupations) results in abstractions of the sexes in general. As a result, men are judged more likely to succeed based on the prevalence of men in occupations viewed as feeders for political office.

Women experience this bias in a number of different contexts, such as being chosen as candidates only for unwinnable contests while being overlooked for races in which the party has a good chance of winning the seat.

> In 1974, when Barbara Mikulski first ran, unsuccessfully, for the U.S. Senate, she told a television audience that Maryland's Democratic Party appeared "very happy to support a woman against someone who they thought couldn't be beat . . . [It was] Okay, good old Barb. . . . Let her take the nosedive for the party. When the race was winnable, like most women candidates, I was not considered a good investment."[52]

Harriett Woods, former lieutenant governor of Missouri and former president of the National Women's Political Caucus, experienced a similar slight when she first ran for the Missouri state senate in 1974:

> I had been in the city council eight years, a television producer for ten years, two years on the state highway commission . . . Well, it was the shock of my life when the party said, "We have to have a man for the job."[53]

Woods ran anyway and won the race. In a 2006 study of negative recruitment at the state legislative level, researcher David Niven found additional evidence that political elites continue to value men's political leadership more than women's. In this case, although both men and women received encouragement, women were significantly more likely than men to receive a negative response to their prospective candidacies. In particular, men receive encouragement from political elites to run in favorable districts (races their party is likely to win) and discouragement from political elites to run in unfavorable districts (races their party is unlikely to win). Women receive the opposite message. Unfortunately, Niven also found that women were more apt to value the input they received from party elites.[54]

Using data from 1971–1999, Kira Sanbonmatsu analyzed how party affiliation affects the recruitment of women to run for the lower houses of state legislatures.[55] She found that the incentive structure for women candidates differs for Democrats and Republicans, suggesting that there is not a single path to office, but rather one that varies by party. Political parties therefore play a differential role in recruiting women to office, based on distinctly different eligibility pools and opportunity structures. Sanbonmatsu found that traditional party organization serves as a barrier for both Republican and Democratic women; however, when there is a Democratic majority in the lower house, Democratic women candidates are negatively affected while Republican women are not. Democratic women are less likely to enjoy party support during a primary, regardless of region, turnover, and legislative professionalism. This study suggests that in situations where it is difficult for the party to find candidates, they may actively seek women to run. However, when seats are competitive, "the party role may be to referee political ambition rather than cultivate it, and the party may be less likely to seek out women candidates."[56] Thus, not only do men and women approach the decision to run differently, as Fox and Lawless found, but also women's experiences with party gatekeepers may differ from one another depending on their party.

In U.S. congressional elections, the political primary contests require that candidates act as entrepreneurs, building a following among likely voters, raising money, creating a campaign organization, and designing a winning strategy. Even though primaries are designed to winnow the field to one candidate in each party competing in the general election, political party organizations play a very small role in contemporary primary contests. Political parties tend not to provide resources in primary campaigns, creating a "candidate-centered" model that may pose additional challenges for women. A recent study of primaries for the U.S. House of Representatives from 1958 to 2004 found no evidence of widespread, aggregate bias against women candidates.[57] However, that does not mean party primaries are gender neutral. Women comprised only 8 percent of the total House candidates during that time period (2,648 women). Eighty-seven percent of all primary races were exclusively male; while 12 percent included one woman (1 percent included more than one woman). Women running in congressional primaries are disproportionately Democratic—Democrats make up 60 percent of the total pool of female candidates. The study's authors attribute this party imbalance to several factors, chief among them that voters perceive all female candidates as more liberal than male candidates (regardless of party), giving Democratic primary contestants an edge with partisan Democrats but disadvantaging Republican women among primary partisans who tend to come from the party's more conservative base. There is some evidence that Democratic party activists are more active in identifying and recruiting women to run, in addition to the direct participation of Democratic national political action committees and political organizations (EMILY's List, for example) that are more active than their Republican counterparts.

Overall, women win primaries at rates comparable to men (57 percent of the time for women, 59 percent of the time for men). Republican men tend to win more often than Republican women (63 percent win rate for men, 60 percent for women). Women face more crowded primaries and draw more challengers when they compete for reelection as incumbents. In all Republican primaries with a woman, the mean number of candidates is 3.9, while in Republican contests without a woman candidate, the mean number of candidates is only 2.2 (a statistically significant difference). The same pattern holds for Democrats—the mean number of candidates in a primary contest in which a woman competes is 4.3, compared to a mean of 2.5 for contests without a woman candidate. Female incumbent House members draw more competition from within their own party and in the other party's primary, and a female incumbent is more likely to draw a female challenger into the other party's primary contest. This finding, in particular, may have some negative consequences over time. If female candidates replace women officeholders, there is no progress toward increasing women's overall representation. Finally, this research demonstrates that the overall number of women entering congressional primaries has decreased over time. "Taken together, our results suggest that primary elections are not gender neutral. And it is likely that these primary election dynamics affect the initial decision to run for office."[58]

The Pressure to Raise Money

When asked what would prevent them from seeking political office, young men and women interviewed for The White House Project Education Fund study listed as the number one barrier raising large sums of money for the campaign.[59] Likewise, in the Lawless and Fox 2008 sample, "soliciting campaign contributions" ranked second only to "potentially having to engage in a negative campaign" as a campaign activity so negative that it would deter the respondents from running for office (29 percent of women versus 21 percent of men, a statistically significant gender difference). Conventional wisdom suggests that women have had a harder time than men in raising and spending money to get themselves elected to public office. Women are not equally represented in prestigious companies that have access to large single donations, nor have they traditionally attracted equal amounts of political action committee (PAC) money. But, similar to the perceptions of other forms of bias in the electoral system, this conventional wisdom is no longer borne out by empirical fact. After all, Hillary Clinton raised more than $233 million during the Democratic primaries! The 1990s appear to mark the turning point in women's prowess as fund-raisers. Political scientist Barbara Burrell studied major party nominees for the U.S. House over a number of years, and found that as early as 1972, female candidates for the House began raising and spending nearly as much money as male candidates. In House races between 1974 and 1980, a period that saw the number of women candidates increase dramatically, women raised and spent about 75 percent of what men raised and spent. In 1988, women raised 119 percent of what men raised, and in 1992, they raised 111 percent and spent 108 percent of what men raised and spent.[60] A study of the 1994 U.S. House and Senate elections showed no disadvantage for women candidates.[61] Likewise, women's parity with men in fundraising persisted through the 2006 election cycle. Decades of experience and research now indicate that "women have become prodigious fund-raisers in their own right and on their own behalf, that they have organized as women to become formidable players in national politics, and that they have become major actors in their party organizations' efforts to acquire financial resources for their candidates."[62] In the 2006 cycle, women major party nominees facing major party challengers raised more money on average than their male counterparts did. Burrell examined six electoral conditions for each of the two major parties by sex (e.g. challenger, open seat, incumbent). Only among Republican open-seat nominees did women, on average, raise less than men did, even as female Republican incumbents outraised nominees in all conditions. A candidate's ability to raise money is critical in attracting the support of national party leaders and interest from political action committees and other affinity organizations. Women's interest organizations have been quick to recognize the value of early money to the success of women's candidacies.

The Women's Campaign Fund, founded in 1974, and the Political Action Committee (PAC) associated with the NWPC were among the first to dedicate money specifically to electing women. EMILY's List (Early Money Is Like Yeast—it makes the dough rise), founded by Ellen Malcom in 1985, was one of the first partisan PACs. EMILY's List supports prochoice, Democratic women who have been carefully screened and judged to be strong candidates. Women have traditionally had the hardest time raising early money that in turn allows them to purchase television airtime for advertisements and increase their name recognition as well as ultimately their donor base. The List pioneered the practice of *bundling,* an effective and creative way to circumvent the Federal Election Campaign Act's $5,000 limit on PAC contributions to a single candidate. Members of EMILY's List join the organization with a membership fee and then agree to write three checks in the amount of at least $100 to each of three candidates selected from the List. These candidates have been interviewed and their contests thoroughly analyzed by Malcom and her staff. Through bundling, candidates receive an envelope full of checks written directly to them, rather than to the organization, that can total far more than the $5,000 limit.

The first high-profile test for a women's PAC came in 1986 when Congresswoman Barbara Mikulski of Maryland decided to seek a vacant Senate seat by challenging a popular congressman and an incumbent governor in the Democratic primary. Donations from EMILY's List have been credited with allowing her to purchase an early poll that provided solid evidence of her support throughout the state. This evidence made it possible for her to raise additional funds and eventually win the primary and the Senate seat. Since that race, EMILY's List has become one of the largest and most powerful PACs in the nation. In 1994, EMILY's List distributed $8.7 million to prochoice Democratic women candidates, which made it the third-highest PAC money raiser in the 1994 election cycle.[63] Republican women quickly formed WISH (Women in the Senate and House) to support prochoice Republican candidates. WISH was then countered by an establishment group (formed by wives whose husbands were serving in the Bush administration) called the Republican Women's Leadership Network (WLN). The WLN's philosophy is more in keeping with the Republican Party's stand on abortion.[64] Another recent prolife addition is the Susan B. Anthony List, which reportedly distributed $34,000 to prolife female candidates in 1994. These national PACs have now spawned local and statewide affiliates dedicated to raising money for women who seek all levels of office. For example, the Los Angeles African American Women PAC (LAAAWPAC) was organized in 1990 as the first African American women's PAC in California. The organization supports women running for office, sponsors community forums, provides information on complicated ballot propositions, and awards the "Power PAC Pioneer Award" to women who make a difference in their community.[65] Efforts of such magnitude, largely made by women on behalf of women, illustrate the importance of electoral politics to the larger movement for women's equality.[66]

Ann Telneas cartoon titled, "Hillary Tears". *Ann Telnaes and Women's eNews in conjunction with the Cartoonist Group. All rights reserved*

In 2009, the Center for American Women and Politics (CAWP) identified forty-eight PACs and donor networks that either give money predominantly to women candidates or have a predominantly female donor base (not including issue PACs). Fifteen are national, with the remaining thirty-three at the state or local level. Twenty-one states now have women's PACs or donor networks and four states host more than one.[67] In addition to raising and contributing money, many of these groups also engage in recruiting, training, and providing other forms of aid to female candidates. In 1978, the National Organization for Women formed NOW-PAC, which is the only PAC that contributes to both men and women based on their "feminist credentials."[68]

Gender Stereotypes and the Campaign Experience

Gender stereotypes affect campaigns in a number of ways. Although such stereotyping is difficult to isolate as *the* cause of women's reticence to run for office, researchers have demonstrated how gender stereotypes have caused voters and the media to view men differently from women and therefore to judge them differently within a political context. Political scientists Leonie Huddy and Nayda Terkildsen found that voters' gender stereotypes have had potentially negative implications for women candidates, particularly those running for higher national office. Voters prefer male characteristics in candidates seeking higher office. Policy areas in which males are typically judged more competent, including the military and economics, are given greater importance the higher the level of office. Competence in female policy areas, such as poverty, education, children, and health care, is viewed less favorably the higher the level of office. This may explain, in part, why voters are less willing to back women for president or vice president but are overwhelmingly likely to vote for women at the state and local levels.[69] These findings also suggest that women interested in seeking top national elective office must convince voters of their atypicality by emphasizing their "male traits." Many scholars think this is particularly true after the September 11, 2001, terrorist attacks. This is not easy to do, nor are candidates in total control of the images and message presented to voters. In some cases, women may want to emphasize stereotypically "feminine" traits in differentiating themselves from other candidates. They seek to become what Shauna Shames, research director for The White House Project, terms "un-candidates."[70] Analysis of campaign commercials from 1964 to 1998 suggests a number of circumstances where both men and women might seek "outsider status" by focusing on femininity. These include an anti-incumbent mood among voters, an electoral context dominated by political scandal, and economic conditions favorable for government expansion in education and health care. Under these circumstances, women can turn gender and gender stereotypes to their electoral advantage by running "as women."[71]

However, think about how the research findings might be applied to the political climate women faced leading up to the elections in November 2008—wars in Iraq and Afghanistan, a "war on terror," and a shaky economy. When the 2008 presidential nomination contest began (early in 2007), it looked like war and national security concerns would dominate the debate and shape voter choice. Hillary Clinton, the only woman in the presidential race for either party, had to anticipate how gender and voter gender stereotypes might work relative to these issues. Since we know from social-psychological research that women are perceived as "communal" (warm and selfless), but not very "agentic" (assertive, instrumental, capable of decision making), and men are assumed to possess these qualities in reverse, any woman seeking the presidency must convince voters of their competence and leadership abilities without appearing so "agentic" that they are labeled insufficiently feminine.

The "Goldberg paradigm" refers to bias in perceptions of men's and women's behavior relative to stereotypical expectations. When women occupy a male-dominated role (like politics) and behave "like men" within that domain, they are rated lower than their male counterparts, particularly when males are doing the rating.[72] The presidency, as the highest national office, is presumed to require agentic leadership. Thus, a woman seeking that position must walk a very fine line lest voters punish her for appearing "too masculine" at the very same time she is auditioning for the most masculine job in politics. Political scientist Susan Carroll notes that while Hillary Clinton's campaign strategy emphasizing experience, strength, mastery of policy details, and a readiness to "lead on day one" was the only choice open to her, given what we know about voter gender stereotypes, it left her vulnerable to critics who labeled her cold and not sufficiently "human." In a further irony, although women's candidacies are usually associated with "outsider status" or "change" and female candidates in general tend to do well in political environments ripe for change (e.g., conditions of corruption, voter mistrust or dissatisfaction), Hillary Clinton lost the nomination to another candidate who "embodied change in his physical appearance and also embraced the mantle of change."[73] Marie Wilson of The White House Project put it this way, "He's the girl in the race. Clinton came out tough; she voted for the war. Obama came out as the person bringing people together and offering messages of hope and reconciliation."[74]

Gender stereotypes further constrained Clinton in her ability to directly address her vote to authorize the Iraq War. By the time the first caucus was held in Iowa in January 2008, voters had transformed their fear of another terrorist attack into anger over the mounting human and material costs of the Iraq War and they were starting to feel the effects of the declining economy. "A number of feminists and progressives felt that they could not support Hillary Clinton in the 2008 election because of her vote to authorize the Iraq War; so long as gender stereotypes persist, those feminists and progressives are likely to find it very difficult to support not only Hillary Clinton but also any woman who has a serious chance of winning the presidency," observed Carroll.[75] Thus, while there are no doubt multiple reasons that Barack Obama clinched the Democratic nomination over Hillary Clinton, it would be hard to say, as commentator Al Hunt did, that "gender no longer is a big deal in American elections."

Press coverage of candidates is a crucial component of elections. "Because a small proportion of the electorate has the opportunity to meet candidates in person, voters rely on news coverage—and other forms of mass media, such as paid advertising—in forming their opinions of those running for office."[76] The use of stereotyping to render a decision increases within three contexts. Stereotyping will be more common when a voter must make a decision but lacks information and has neither the time nor the motivation to get that information. Because many women are newcomers to politics and more likely to be challengers, voters are more likely to have information about male candidates and to rely on gender as a relevant cue. Second, stereotyping is more likely to occur when individual characteristics, such as gender, are especially salient. If, for example, a pool of candidates includes only one woman, gender stereotypes will be more prevalent and will exert more influence on a voter's ultimate decision. Finally, the act of stereotyping itself encourages the confirmation of preexisting stereotypes. When voters are exposed to stereotyping in media accounts of a campaign, they are more likely to pay attention to gender characteristics and to interpret new information about the candidate in ways that are consistent with their preexisting gender stereotypes.[77]

In a similar study, Monika McDermott used a quasi-experimental design to examine voters' stereotypes of women and African Americans.[78] She found that race and gender signal voters in two ways: on ideology and on issues. Women and black candidates are stereotyped as more liberal than the average

Encountering the Controversies of Equality

Madam President After Hillary: Still the Ultimate Glass Ceiling in American Politics?

> In 1995 Wal-Mart advertised a t-shirt with a cartoon of Dennis the Menace's pal Margaret saying, "Someday a Woman will be President." When customers objected—too political for children—Wal-Mart executives pulled the item off the shelves explaining that Margaret's message went against the corporation's philosophy of "family values."[1]

> "Although we weren't able to shatter that highest, hardest glass ceiling this time, thanks to you, it's got about 18 million cracks in it and the light is shining through like never before, filling us all with the hope and the sure knowledge that the path will be a little easier next time." Hillary Clinton, June 2008.[2]

Just what are the prospects for a woman to be elected president and to move into the White House? The first woman ever to serve as prime minister was Sirimavo Bandaranaike of Sri Lanka (then Ceylon), chosen in 1960, and the first woman president was Isabel Peron of Argentina in 1975. Between 1960 and 2002, forty-four different women have served as prime minister or president in thirty-six countries around the world, twenty-four of them in the 1990s.[3] Geraldine Ferraro was the first woman in the United States nominated for a spot on a national major party ticket (vice president, 1984) and twenty-four years later in 2008, Sarah Palin became the second woman nominated for vice president on a national major party ticket.

Seventy-three percent of the world's female executives have entered into office in parliamentary systems, while only 10 percent are from presidential systems. Because presidential systems rely on the popular vote for selection, they serve as an obstacle. In parliamentary systems, the party rather than the person is selected. Women are able to earn promotion by working within the party structure. Another path to executive office, particularly in South and Southeast Asia and Latin American countries, is through familial ties to husbands or fathers.

Women in the United States face the prospect of having to earn a chance for the presidency by first campaigning for a party's nomination. A 2003 analysis of where presidential candidates come from is sobering. "Taking into account all of the women who have ever had the same experience as our recent presidents (been governor, served in the House and Senate, served as vice president, or held the rank of five-star general), there have only been twenty-six, and one of them (Margaret Chase Smith) did run for president."[4] Thus one of the most significant barriers to women's presidential candidacy has been that so few occupy the positions in the pipeline that serve as traditional gateways to the White House.

However, even if the pipeline were flush with women, female candidates would still run headlong into attitudes like those expressed by Wal-Mart management—a woman president isn't consistent with our cultural expectations of women as mothers and domestics. Women candidates need to *earn* the voters' judgment of competence, whereas for males a certain threshold of competence is implied by their very presence in the race. For example, Morry Taylor, president of Titan Wheel International, Inc. shared the debate stage with the eventual 1996 Republican nominee, Senator Robert Dole. By contrast, when the National Organization for Women (NOW) endorsed Carol Moseley Braun, an editorial in the *New York Times* chastised the "feminist outpost" for its "silly" choice of a "vanity" candidate.

The Gallup Organization has polled attitudes on electing a woman to the presidency since 1937, when only 33 percent of respondents said they would vote for a woman if she qualified "in every other respect" (assuming, of course, that her sex was the most serious disqualifier). The question now asks if respondents would vote for a qualified woman if she were nominated, and in 1999, 92 percent answered "yes," but that support dropped to just 87 percent in May 2004, rose only to 88 percent in 2007 (while 94 percent said they would support a African American candidate for president—presumably a male African American candidate). Most observers identify the decline as a consequence of the September 11 terrorist attacks and the continuing focus on national security.[5]

Finland's Vigdis Finnbogadottir served as president for sixteen years. During her tenure, she reports, little boys would ask if a man could be president too. Perceptions of "normal" can change very quickly—but it takes a "first." A CBS News poll conducted in June 2008 found that 69 percent of Americans believed that Hillary Clinton's candidacy has made it easier for other women to run (60 percent of men, 76 percent of women). Eighty-eight percent agreed with the statement, "I am glad to see a woman as a serious contender for president." Seventy-nine percent of those under age 45 said they think a woman president is likely in their lifetime (69 percent overall, 44 percent among those 65 years of age and older).[6] When Shirley Chisholm sought the nomination in 1972, she explained, "I ran because somebody had to do it first. I ran because most people thought the country was not ready for a black candidate, not ready for a woman candidate. Someday —it was time in 1972 to make that someday come."[7]

What do you think?

When do you think the first woman will be elected president of the United States? What will it take for a woman candidate to overcome the barriers identified in this box and those discussed elsewhere in this chapter? Make a list of the top ten women you judge qualified to seek the presidency. Evaluate each candidate's background, political experience, and skill at fundraising and campaigning. Compare lists. Will one of these be the first? If you need help making the list, see American Women Presidents, a PAC dedicated to identifying and recruiting female candidates for the presidency at *http://www.americanwomen presidents.org*. If you cannot identify ten women to consider, ask yourself why.

1. Judith Nies, "Ms. President," *Woman's Review of Books: A Feminist Guide to Good Reading* (November 2003), accessed at http://www.wellesley.edu/womensreview/.
2. Hillary Clinton, quote from speech delivered on June 7, 2008, when she ended her campaign for the Democratic nomination for president.
3. Farida Jalalzai, "Women Political Leaders: Past and Present," *Women and Politics* 26, no. 3–4 (2004): 85–108.
4. Erika Falk and Kathleen Hall Jamieson, "Changing the Climate of Expectations," in *Anticipating Madam President*, eds. Robert P. Watson and Ann Gordon (Boulder, Colo.: Lynn Rienner, 2003), p. 45.
5. Jennifer Lawless, "Women, War, and Winning Elections: Gender Stereotyping in the Post-September 11th Era," *Political Research Quarterly* 57, no. 3 (September 2004): 479–490.
6. CBS News Poll, "Breaking the Glass Ceiling: A Woman Presidential Candidate" June 3, 2008, accessed at: http://www.cbsnews.com/htdocs/pdf/May08b-Woman.pdf.
7. Film Synopsis, "Shirley Chisholm '72: Unbought and Unbossed," POV (February 7, 2005), accessed at http://www.pbs.org/pov/pov2005/chisholm/about.html.

white male. While African American candidates are more closely associated with minority rights than whites, women are viewed as more dedicated to honest government. McDermott found that voters decide on which candidate to support by considering how much the candidate agrees or disagrees with the ideologies and issues attributed to the stereotype of that candidate, rather than on a candidate's actual ideology and position on an issue. This leaves women candidates in a quandary about how to craft a campaign message and establish credibility as a viable candidate.

Voters may also approach an electoral contest with a distinct preference for male or female candidates.[79] This "baseline gender preference" is a standing predisposition built on gender stereotypes about candidate traits, beliefs, issue competencies, and voter gender. "Individuals who think men are more emotionally suited for politics, who think that men are more likely to take their position on government spending, and prefer men to handle stereotypically male issues are more likely to prefer male candidates."[80] One of the strongest predictors for a female candidate is voter gender: women prefer female candidates. In addition, individuals who think women are more likely to take their position on abortion are more likely to prefer the female candidate, as are those who think women are better able to handle the issue of Social Security. Political scientist Kira Sanbonmatsu investigated the link between a general preference for a male or female candidate and vote choice in male-female contests. Using an experimental condition in which respondents were presented with biographies of two candidates running in a hypothetical primary race for the U.S. House of Representatives, Sanbonmatsu asked voters to indicate which candidate they would support. Sanbonmatsu varied the sex of the first candidate to analyze the use of gender stereotypes expressed through the voters' baseline gender preference. When given the chance, voters with a female baseline preference were much more likely to vote for the female candidate than the identical male candidate. When presented with a male-male race, voters with a female baseline preference opted for a "change-oriented" male candidate (arguably a female characteristic). However when the change-oriented male candidate was running against a female candidate, these voters chose the woman. "When given a chance to vote for a woman, these voters responded."

Kathleen Dolan examined how voters evaluated women candidates for Congress between 1990 and 2000.[81] In contrast to most studies testing the relevance of candidate gender to vote choice, which generally employ hypotheticals under experimental conditions, Dolan used data from the American National Election Study (ANES) to examine voter candidate evaluations in real elections. Under these conditions, gender is less central to the evaluations of congressional candidates over time. "[C]andidate sex, by itself, is not necessarily the primary influence on evaluations but instead may be interacting with other influences in the electoral environment." As we have seen in earlier sections of this chapter, political parties play an important role in how voters evaluate candidates. Dolan found that Democratic and Republican women are evaluated differently by voters. While Democratic women are seen as more liberal than Democratic men, voters do not make such stark ideological distinctions between Republican women and men. Furthermore, people employ female issue stereotypes when evaluating Democratic women but do not use issue stereotypes when evaluating Republican women.[82] Over the ten years and six election cycles Dolan studied, the ways in which voters evaluated women candidates and the patterns of who voted for them and why were not consistent. In some elections, women voters were more likely to support women candidates, but not in others; in some years, issues such as abortion or defense were related to choosing women, but not in all. Dolan concludes that the impact of a candidate's gender is, in part, conditioned by external forces. Two of the most important forces in shaping evaluations of women candidates proved to be political-party correspondence and incumbency status—the two main influences in any congressional election, regardless of the gender of one or both candidates. The effects of issues, voter demographics, and the amount of gender information in the electoral context are limited when compared to the more traditional political influences.[83]

Women who decide to seek public office know that they will face tough opposition in a primary or a general election, or maybe both. And yet women candidates are often unprepared for the level of combat a campaign entails. Nancy Pelosi, representative from California, warns women, "Don't think of this as some League of Women Voters type of thing to do. It's brutal. It's tough. You are going for power. It's never been just given away. It's highly competitive trying to take power, and as long as you understand that and are ready to take a punch square in the face, then you'll love it."[84]

Women candidates face a number of dilemmas associated with their gender when they try to craft a campaign message. They want to appear tough, but not so tough or aggressive that voters will be scared away. Harriett Woods learned this lesson from her "crying farmer" ad when she ran for the Senate in 1986 on the Democratic ticket against Republican Kit Bond. Woods thought that she had found *the* issue to counter the effects of President Reagan's high approval ratings when she came out in strong support of farmers who were facing the worst agricultural crisis since the 1930s. Bob Squier, a noted Democratic consultant who was working on her campaign, came up with an ad that showed Woods firmly denouncing farm foreclosures. In the ad, Woods talked to a farmer who was crying about the foreclosure of his farm by an insurance company on whose board Kit Bond served as director. Woods later said, "When Squier previewed it, I told him he might win an award, but I would lose the election."[85] When the commercial finally aired, it backfired terribly when Bond's campaign learned that Squier had not informed the farmer that the footage would be used as part of a "political attack." The farmer's wife was quoted as saying, "I kinda felt like we had been used." Although Woods fired Squier, the damage was never repaired in the minds of Missouri voters. Bond's ratings fell, but Woods's fell too. "All the years of building a reputation as the high-minded campaigner for truth and good government, of asserting my identity as not just another politician, were going down the drain," Woods said. In her recent book, *Stepping Up to Power,* she reflects:

> Voters often see women candidates as different, more honest and not playing the usual political games. We're seen as outsiders who are less likely to be corrupted or get caught in any shenanigans. This generalized image is part of the advantage that balances the automatic no votes against us as too weak and unassertive. If anything happens to puncture that image, it can mean a disproportionate loss in support.[86]

Here again, the paradox of gender equality is evident. Woods eloquently captures the delicate balancing act a female candidate must master in seeking public office. If she decides to use the argument that women are different from men and says (or implies) that women are also *better* than men, she runs the risk of being held to a higher standard—perhaps one that is too high for any mortal to meet. Alternatively, if she decides to pursue political office by arguing that she is the same as a man, voters might rebel against what they view as a challenge to appropriate gender roles. As Barbara Curran, former New Jersey Assembly member, said, "The biggest asset for a woman candidate is being a woman, and the biggest liability is not being a man."[87]

Negative campaign ads are now an accepted strategy for many candidates, but can still be treacherous territory for women candidates. In narrow circumstances, however, women may stand to benefit with voters by using negative ads. When a female candidate uses a "male" issue as the basis of an attack on her male opponent, she is judged more competent on the issue.[88] This suggests that negative advertising could be an effective tool to neutralize the disadvantages caused by stereotypes. Research suggests that women are more constrained than men in deciding whether to use negative advertising. "Women may adjust their strategy in response to citizens' stereotypes about preferred feminine behavior."[89] A gender gap appears in relation to a number of other campaign tactics. In a study of 4,000 candidates at the local, state, and federal level, candidates were asked whether they believed it was acceptable, unethical, or questionable to engage in a range of campaign strategies including making factually true statements out of context, attacking an opponent in an attempt to discourage that candidate's supporters from turning out to vote, and engaging in push polling (calling voters pretending to take a survey, but attacking the opponent instead). The gender gap widens the higher the office a candidate seeks, but in all cases women were significantly more likely to oppose each of the activities.

As the number of women in competitive races has increased, so has the likelihood that women are the target of negative campaigning. Using an experimental design, researchers explored whether negative commercials aimed at women candidates had the same effect as negative commercials attacking males. Subjects were presented with a television commercial for a U.S. Senate candidate, based on an authentic 2006 race in North Dakota but with the candidate names and state changed so that respondents could not hold any preexisting attitudes about the candidates. Subjects were randomly assigned to various conditions displayed in the advertisement and then asked to assess the candidates' traits, competence, and ultimately asked to make a vote choice. Overall, they found that negative commercials are far less effective at depressing evaluations of female candidates compared to male candidates. "When exposed to identical attacks on a candidate, citizens are more receptive to critical comments made about a male candidate compared to the exact same criticisms leveled at a female candidate. In other words, the gender of the candidate conditions peoples' reactions to negative messages about political candidates. . . . the presence of gender stereotypes appears to soften the blow of negative attacks, leading people to discount attacks on women candidates, compared to identical attacks on male candidates."[90]

CAN WOMEN CANDIDATES EXPECT SUPPORT FROM WOMEN VOTERS?

When women step forward as candidates, can they count on the support of women voters? While all candidates can count on some women's support, is there any evidence that women actually prefer a woman candidate? We've already learned that women are more likely to support a Democratic candidate—the gender-gap phenomenon. We also know that the majority of women candidates are Democrats. However, to accurately test whether women voters prefer women candidates, apart from their running on the Democratic ticket, we need to look at the size of the gender gap in races where one candidate was a woman. Researchers Seltzer, Newman, and Leighton analyzed 167 statewide races: 90 for U.S. Senate and 77 for governor in 1990, 1992, and 1994. One-fourth (42) of those races were contests between a man and a woman. The researchers found a gender gap in almost all of the 167 races, with the percentage of women who voted for the Democratic candidate sometimes being as much as 15 points higher than the percentage of men who voted for the Democrat. The gender gap grew by several points on average when the Democratic candidate was a woman, and it shrank by several points when the Republican candidate was a woman.

> In ninety U.S. Senate races, the gender gap averaged 5.4 points in races between two men, 8.6 points in races between a Democratic woman and a Republican man, and 1.2 points in races between a Republican woman and a Democratic man. In the seventy-seven gubernatorial races, the gender gap averaged 4.8 points in races between two men, 8.2 points in races between a Democratic woman and a Republican man, and 1.4 points in races between a Republican woman and a Democratic man.[91]

In several cases, a reverse gender gap occurred when the Republican candidate was a woman and more women voted Republican than men did. This reveals that the sex of the candidate affects the gender gap and confirms that women have given an edge to women candidates in the races studied. However, we cannot say that women make the difference for women candidates in all cases. In 130 of the 167 elections studied, the outcome of the race would have been the same if only one sex had voted. On average, though, women supported women candidates slightly more often than men did.[92] As we learned in chapter 3, women do not constitute a monolithic voting bloc. They do, however, constitute over half the voting population, and as such should be carefully analyzed and courted in the same way that serious candidates have treated male voters. Women candidates should not assume that the female electorate is a naturalally.

Some women candidates have learned this lesson the hard way. Author Amy Handlin includes a story about Carol, a founder and director of a women's shelter, in her book *Whatever Happened to the Year of the Woman*.[93] After running the shelter for five years, Carol decided to seek election to the all-male city council. She had been active in party politics for years, networking and organizing fund-raisers for other candidates, so she felt she had valuable personal connections to politicians in "high places." She was confident that she could count on a base of support from women in her party and from women in the community she had met in the process of developing the shelter.

> I learned that there's this invisible line you cross when you decide to run for office . . . all of a sudden you're competing for this position that's very desirable, and some people look at you differently. . . . Before you were like them; now you seem very threatening. . . . What really bothered me, though, was when I learned that several key women officials in my party were working against me. They said that I didn't deserve a council seat because I hadn't worked hard enough for the party—in other words, I hadn't done the same things they did. Some told me that I had to "wait my turn," because I was younger than the men who also wanted the seat.[94]

The NWPC commissioned a study in 1987 to learn more about voters' attitudes toward women candidates. Voters who said they would be most supportive of a woman candidate were "younger voters, minorities, voters [who] never married, Catholics, urban residents, and higher educated, white-collar workers— and especially women in these groups." Voters who said they were least likely to support a woman candidate tended to be "over 60, live in small towns or rural areas, . . . [have] lower levels of formal education, . . . [work] in lower-white-collar and blue-collar jobs, [be] homemakers [or] . . . retired, and . . . [from] the South."[95] Consistent with other studies, the female voters who were least supportive of women candidates were older women and homemakers. In 1990, a survey of 7,000 women commissioned by *McCalls* magazine found that 35 percent of the respondents preferred voting for a woman, though 25 percent still said they preferred voting for a man.[96] Research among college undergraduates suggests that women are more supportive of female candidates than are men. In a study conducted in 1989, political scientist Kathleen Dolan found that while men and women were about equally likely to support female candidates at the local level, as the level of office increased, the gap between men and women also increased. When asked if they would support a woman candidate for local office, 92 percent of the men and 96 percent of the women responded affirmatively. When similar questions were asked about a woman running for office at the state level, 87 percent of males and 96 percent of females were supportive. The gap widened to 14 points when the students were asked about candidates for national office in general (82 percent of the men were supportive versus 96 percent of the women), and increased to a full 26 points when asked if they would support a woman for president (54 percent of the men and 80 percent of the women).[97] Note the sizable drop-off for both men and women when they were asked about supporting a woman for president of the United States. Extensive polling prior to the 2008 election probed likely voters' willingness to vote for a variety of nontraditional candidates, including a woman. Voters across generations, race and ethnic categories, and sex report the following: America is ready for a woman president; they believe a majority of people would support a qualified woman for president, and by an even larger margin they themselves would vote for a woman. Eighty-four percent said it was likely that a woman would be elected president within the next ten years.[98]

More evidence comes from focus groups in Sherrye Henry's *The Deep Divide*. About seven out of ten women (69 percent) said that the country would be different if more women held powerful positions. Forty-four percent believe this because they think women in power will improve the quality of life, 14 percent believe women will formulate a better economic policy, and 31 percent think women will do a better job with social policy. Seventy-four percent of the women, including 67 percent of the nonfeminists, said that they think more women in powerful positions will lead to greater equality. However, when asked if they plan to vote for a woman "because another woman understands the problems women face, or does sex not make a difference," 74 percent said that sex does not make any difference! While the majority of these women believed that women in power would make some positive difference, they were unwilling to give women the advantage at the polls.[99] These findings reflect the power of the paradox of gender equality. Although voters in a variety of studies discussed in this section clearly feel that female officeholders can offer something different from males, they are hesitant to act on that belief at the polls. Women candidates are caught within the paradox. Voters say that they believe women in office might result in substantively different policies, which suggests that candidates might effectively appeal to this belief during the campaign. However, women voters also say that gender does not make any difference in their decision at the polls, so female candidates might be encouraged to campaign on the basis of no difference from male candidates.

SYSTEMIC SOURCES OF ELECTORAL BIAS AGAINST WOMEN CANDIDATES

Aside from voter perceptions of women candidates, some sources of bias remain within the electoral system itself. Incumbency is a powerful force in American politics that limits access to political office for both male and female challengers, but it appears to be a more powerful deterrent for women candidates. Over time, the number of open seats in Congress has diminished. For example, only 28 members vacated U.S. House seats in 2006 and there were only 13 open-seat House races in 2008. Since incumbents are reelected at a rate of more than 90 percent, it is very difficult for challengers to gain legislative seats.[100] Likewise, research suggests that women fare better as candidates in multimember districts than in the single-seat districts that characterize most state legislatures as well as the U.S. Congress. Popular initiatives to limit politicians' terms in office have been approved in a number of states to remedy the power of incumbency, but it is not clear whether these changes will result in more women being elected to office.

Incumbency and the Potential of Term Limits

We have already discussed the negative effects that incumbency exerts on women challengers. Term limits, if enacted, may remedy this problem. Term limits enforced at the state level (term limits enacted by states and intended to apply to congressional seats were ruled unconstitutional) would require an officeholder to give up his or her seat after having served a preset number of terms in office. While term limits are a relatively recent reform, the effects are already being felt in some state legislatures as long-time incumbents are forced to leave office. As of February 1996, twenty-one states had passed ballot initiatives limiting terms of office. Obviously, term-limit-induced retirements increase the number of open-seat contests, thereby potentially improving the climate for female candidates.[101] Additionally, one study found that 93 percent of state legislators initially affected by term limits were male.[102] Speculative research and research based on simulations and forecasting suggest that term limits would benefit groups that serve for a limited time anyway (male incumbents serve for an average of 13.8 years, compared to female incumbents' 11.9 years of service), and would have the greatest impact in opening leadership positions to women. Assemblywoman Carol Migden of California, chair of the Appropriations Committee, states it this way: "Most people don't get Appropriations in six years . . . but I got it in six months. Who says term limits aren't working?"[103] Similar successes in Maine have been reported in the *Wall Street Journal*: "As part of the increased turnover—40 percent of the legislators are freshmen—Maine has its first female House speaker and half of the legislature's leaders are women, the most ever."[104]

Research beyond speculation and modeling has only recently become available as the first states (California, Colorado, and Oklahoma) have implemented term limits. With the 1996 election, California became the first state to "retire" an entire assembly of incumbent members. In evaluating the impact of term limits on women's progress in the California assembly, Stanley Caress cautions that term limits in themselves will not be sufficient to increase the number of women in office. More than term limits, it is the political climate—reflected in improved prospects for women candidates nationwide between 1990 and 1992—combined with reapportionment's opening up a number of open-seat races, that accounts for more women being elected to office. Caress concludes that "initially, term limits may provide an advantage for women if there is not already a large number of women incumbents. But as the 1994 and 1996 elections suggest, term limits do not provide women candidates with an advantage if they already are well represented in a legislature's membership."[105]

Preliminary analysis of state legislatures affected by term limits in the 1998 elections, conducted by CAWP, shows mixed results. The number of women serving in seats vacated by term-limited incumbents increased in the state senates, but decreased in the state houses. The number of minority women serving in term-limited state house seats decreased slightly following the 1998 elections.[106] CAWP also found that a large proportion of women were replaced by men when term limits forced them to vacate their seats. In many cases, no women even sought to replace them. CAWP found that in both the 1998 and 2000 elections there were no women candidates running in primary elections for the majority of seats opened by term limits or for a very large proportion of seats vacated by women incumbents forced out by term limits.[107] Women in state house seats have taken advantage of the opportunities afforded them to move up to state senate seats opened as a result of term limits.[108] Women were most successful in term-limited states in 1998, when there were organized efforts to recruit, support, and fund women candidates for state legislative seats; however, researchers found that neither the Democratic Party nor the Republican Party made a major effort to identify women candidates, encourage women to run for open seats, or support women candidates in primary and general elections in term-limited states.[109] The Center for American Women and Politics initiated the Political Opportunity Program (POP) training seminars in an effort to increase the number of women in the candidate pool for seats open as a result of term limits. As you recall from our previous discussion on the emergence of women candidates, significant effort is required to recruit women to run for public office. Term limits alone, therefore, are not likely to yield large increases in women or minority legislators. Says Gary Moncrief, a political scientist studying legislators, "The logic [of term limits] was impeccable, the empirical evidence not at all. The problem is there aren't as many women running as we expected."[110] Term limits are in effect in fifteen states, while in six others term limits have been repealed. Overall, the increase in female representation has been smaller than in states without limits.

Single-Member Versus Multimember Districts

The electoral system itself is another source of potential bias or discouragement for women candidates. Most people take it for granted that elections are neutral contests, at least as far as the formal rules are concerned. However, political arrangements are not neutral.[111] African Americans and other minority groups have challenged electoral systems, though women have not. Research comparing electoral contests in which representation was chosen through single-member districts versus multimember districts has found that more women ran and more women were elected through multimember systems. Researchers have identified four main reasons why women have done better in multimember districts. First, party and community leaders who are under some pressure to respond to interests in a district are more sensitive to including and supporting women candidates. Second, voters may be more comfortable voting for a woman if she is among a slate of candidates than if she is their only representative. Third, running as a woman among a group of candidates may produce some novelty value and attract more publicity and ultimately more votes. Finally, women are more willing to run for office in multimember districts since there is no specific opponent and women would therefore be running on their own qualifications and program ideas.[112]

Political scientists R. Darcy, Susan Welch, and Janet Clark examined state legislatures in the United States in an effort to empirically test the theory that women fare better under some electoral systems than others. Since states are constitutionally free to adopt any election method, there are a variety of experiences to examine. The findings are clear. In states that use both single-member and multimember district systems, women ran in greater proportions in multimember districts, and in seventeen out of twenty-one cases the proportion of women running and winning in multimember districts was about double the proportion of those running and winning in single-member districts. Further, in states with all single-member districts, the proportion of women elected was less than in states with multimember or mixed systems.[113]

The Political Geography of Women's Election

Even a cursory examination of the map in Figure 4.1 will demonstrate that female members of Congress are not evenly distributed across the United States. While there are currently seventeen women serving in the U.S. Senate, one-third come from just three states where both senators are female (California, Maine, and Washington). Likewise, of the seventy-three women serving in the U.S. House in the 111th Congress, half come from just four states (19 from California, 5 from Ohio, and 6 from New York and from 6 Florida).[114] Two states have never sent a female to Congress (Iowa and Mississippi) and nineteen states have no women among their congressional delegation in the 111th session of Congress. Of the 90 women currently serving, 69 are Democrats and 21

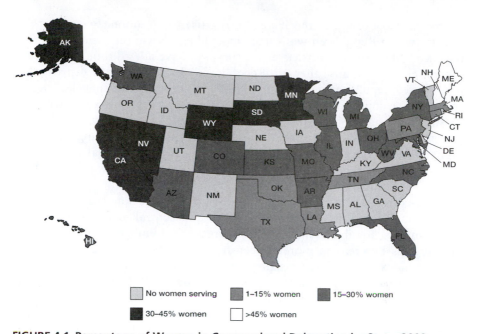

FIGURE 4.1 Percentage of Women in Congressional Delegation by State, 2009

Source: 50–50 by 2020: Equal Representation in Government, accessed online at http://www.ergd.org/Congressional Profile.htm

are Republicans. These demographics suggest that district characteristics must play some role in electing women to office in addition to political party and gender.

Political scientists Barbara Palmer and Dennis Simon have identified "women-friendly" districts and created an index of "women-friendliness" that takes into account partisanship and ideology, geographic factors, race and ethnicity, and socioeconomic factors to explain and predict where women are most likely to seek and win congressional office. While we noted earlier in this chapter that women have an easier time winning in open-seat contests (races without an incumbent), Palmer and Simon discovered that even some open-seat races are more women-friendly than others.[115] "Female Democratic House members tend to win election in districts that are more liberal, more urban, more diverse, more educated, and much wealthier than those won by male Democratic members of the House; they come from much more compact, 'tonier,' upscale districts than their male counterparts. Female Republican House members tend to win election in districts that are less conservative, more urban, and more diverse than those electing male Republicans; they come from districts that are 'less Republican.'"[116] These results are true for white women only; the African American women in Congress (all of whom have been Democrats) come from districts that are similar to those electing African American men. This analysis is particularly useful in explaining the small number of Republican women elected to Congress and the increasing partisan gap among women. "The districts where Republican women are most likely to win the primary because they are female are the districts where they will have a hard time winning the general election because they are Republican." In other words, districts that have elected Republican women are very similar to the districts that elect Democratic men. Congressional districts are re-created every ten years following the census. Palmer and Simon found that the number of women-friendly districts have increased substantially over time largely as a result of the changing demography of the electorate; as constituencies have grown more racially and ethnically diverse and the proportion of voters with college degrees rises, political opportunities for women have increased.

The next redistricting will follow the 2010 census. We noted earlier that it is highly unlikely that the United States will adopt electoral gender quotas; however, it may be possible to more rapidly increase the number of women serving in Congress by creating more women-friendly districts. Using the women-friendly index as a guide, legislators or commissions charged with drawing district lines could engage in "gender gerrymandering." Alternatively, political parties and organizations interested in electing more women to office could strategically recruit women to run in districts identified as most likely to produce a win for either a Republican woman or a Democratic woman. Palmer and Simon, for example, were able to identify twenty congressional districts that offer two potential opportunities for women—should the male incumbent retire, the district is likely to be highly receptive to a female candidate and even if the incumbent seeks reelection, he may be particularly vulnerable to a woman challenger in districts high on the index of women-friendliness. In either case, strategic recruitment of female candidates is part of both the short- and long-term solution to increasing women's share of the political representation.

INITIATIVES DESIGNED TO INCREASE THE NUMBER OF WOMEN CANDIDATES

In addition to the structural reforms we've discussed, a number of organizations have undertaken special initiatives to identify, recruit, and support women candidates. Here are samples of these initiatives (you will find more on the Web site associated with this text):

- *The White House Project* is a nonprofit, nonpartisan public-awareness campaign to change the political climate so that women can launch successful campaigns for the U.S. presidency and other key positions. The project is committed to raising awareness of women's leadership in U.S. politics and mobilizing Americans of all ages to participate in civic life. The White House Project recently launched the "Go Vote. Go Run. Go Lead. Go Girl!"

campaign,[117] aimed at mobilizing and engaging young women between the ages of eighteen and thirty-four as voters, as political activists, and as candidates for political office.[118]

- *National Federation of Republican Women Campaign Management School* trains Republican women through a series of two-day courses held throughout the country. The training focuses on developing a strategy and message, raising money, targeting voters, managing volunteers and communications. Similar training for Republican women is offered through state-based *Excellence in Public Service* programs typically sponsored by a prominent Republican in the state. For example, the program in New Jersey is sponsored and named for Christine Todd Whitman. A message from the former governor articulates the mission of the program, "I firmly believe that government can best serve the interests of its citizens when they are fully represented. The more diversity in the process, the more likely the process will work. Women bring a very different perspective to issues because our life experiences are different, along with our priorities. By expanding the pool of talent, we are able to draw upon more of those experiences to make good policy."[119]

- *EMILY's List Political Opportunity Program (POP)*, established in 2001, is EMILY's List's training program for female candidates. Reacting in part to the loss of women's representation in legislatures altered by term limits and redistricting, POP is a series of state and local candidate training seminars designed to help women develop a strong fundraising base, pursue critical issue priorities, develop strong communication strategies, and form key alliances with local advocacy groups, and to build a grassroots network of support that will help women win progressively higher offices. Since its inception in 2001, POP has trained more than 5,550 women interested in running for the state legislature and local office. In 2008, EMILY's List helped 175 prochoice Democratic women in 32 states run and win; eighty-six of these women are new to their positions. The rationale for POP is tied directly to Fox and Lawless's study that found women less likely than men to view themselves as qualified to run for office and less likely than men to receive encouragement to run for office.[120]

- *The Women's Campaign School at Yale University* is cosponsored by Yale Law School and the Gender Studies Program. Each year the school offers a four-day training session designed to teach a wide range of campaign skills and introduce participants to professionals in the campaign and political arena. The school also offers a series of regular one-day workshops that cover such topics as "Secrets of Successful Fundraising," "Campaign Message and Strategy," and "Politics: The Uncommon Career Choice," among others.[121]

- *Women Under Forty Political Action Committee* is a multipartisan political action committee that supports women under the age of forty who run for state and federal office. Discouraged by the low number of young women in political office, a group of interested women gathered in Washington, D.C., in January 1999 and organized WUFPAC. During the 2000 election cycle, WUFPAC focused on raising money and making contributions to women under forty running for Congress. Of the seven women candidates who were under forty in the 2002 election cycle, most were substantially outspent in the general election: their opponents raised between five times and ninety-two times as much money as the young women candidates did. WUFPAC now supports women seeking seats in their state legislatures. "We're trying to do everything we can to encourage young women to become more interested in politics, take politics more seriously and understand the impact of politics in their lives," says Susannah Shakow, president of WUFPAC. "We need to have more women in the pipeline in order to end up with more women who want to run for Congress."[122]

- *Invite a Woman to Run* is an e-mail campaign sponsored by The White House Project. Recognizing that women are more likely than men to require someone to approach them before they will consider seeking political office, this initiative makes it easy to do so (and compiles a list of potential candidates in the process!). By typing in your e-mail address and that of the person you would like to recruit, you can send a letter directing them to The White House Project Web site for information on how to run for office.[123]

- *Running Start*'s mission is to empower young women to run for political office. A nonprofit, nonpartisan organization, Running Start educates young women about the importance of politics in their lives and provides leadership training. "Our goal is to give young women a running start in politics so that they will run for elected office earlier, climb higher on the leadership ladder, and share more in the decision-making power of this country." Running Start works with high school, college, and young professional women through four programs: the Young Women's Political Leadership Program, Campaign College, Running Start/Wal-Mart Star Fellowship Program, and Path to Politics Seminars.[124]

- *Women Building for the Future PAC (The Future PAC)* is dedicated to building the national network of support and funding that progressive African American women candidates need to launch effective campaigns and win elections. "The Future PAC aims to put in office African American women who will develop policies and programs that will improve the lives of African American people," explains Gwen Moore, a former California assemblywoman who serves as president of the organization. The organization includes several high-profile black women leaders, such as Donna Brazile, chairwoman of the Democratic National Committee's Voting Rights Institute and campaign manager for Clinton-Gore; Joy Atkinson, founder of Los Angeles African American Women PAC; Dr. Dorothy I. Height, president emerita of the National Council of Negro Women; Marianne Spraggins, president and CEO of Atlanta Life Insurance Company Investment Advisors; Eddie Bernice Johnson of the Congressional Black Caucus; and Susan Taylor, editorial director of *Essence*. "Black women cannot get elected without money and, collectively, we control a lot of it, so we have to channel our energy and resources into our candidates," says founder Marianne Spraggins. Recognizing that African American women are a consistently strong voting presence, this group hopes to leverage that power into recruiting and funding African American women to seek office.[125]

POLITICAL APPOINTMENTS: AN ALTERNATIVE PATH TO POLITICAL OFFICE

In addition to elective office, women also gain political power through appointments to governmental positions. Frances Perkins, appointed by President Franklin D. Roosevelt in 1933 as secretary of labor, was the first woman to serve in a presidential cabinet. Since the cabinet was established in 1789, thirty-two female cabinet members have served (roughly 5 percent of the whole). In December 1996, President Bill Clinton named Madeleine K. Albright secretary of state, making her the highest-ranking woman ever to serve in the U.S. government.[126]

When Clinton was elected in 1992, he pledged to appoint a first-term cabinet that "looked like America." In keeping that promise, he appointed four women to cabinet positions, including Janet Reno, the first woman ever appointed attorney general. In 2001, George W. Bush appointed Dr. Condoleezza Rice national security advisor. Rice joined four other women in Bush's cabinet during the first administration and was appointed secretary of state in the administration's second term. Women, when they have held executive appointments, have traditionally served as secretary of labor, health and human services, housing and urban development, or education—offices consistent with women's traditional points of intersection between the private and public spheres. In order to expand women's sphere of influence by diversifying women's appointments, the NWPC established the Coalition for Women's Appointments, made up of about sixty women's professional and issue groups. The Coalition identified qualified women candidates for appointed positions and provided the new administration with "seven hundred resumes of highly qualified, individually vetted women, including many who filled break-through positions in the military, economic, and scientific areas, such as chief scientist at the National Aeronautics and Space Administration."[127] Similarly, The National Political Congress of Black Women (NPCBW), through its Commission for the Presidential Appointment of African American Women, has created a talent bank of highly qualified African American women for top political appointments.[128] Ultimately, more than 40 percent of Clinton's appointments were women, including six women in cabinet-level positions and a record 46 percent of all Senate-confirmed positions. More African American women were appointed to high-level positions in the Clinton administration than in any other administration. The previous administration under President George Bush had appointed women to 22 percent of Senate-confirmed positions. In the first year of George W. Bush's first administration, 26 percent of jobs requiring Senate confirmation went to women. President Obama has to-date appointed seven women to cabinet-level appointments, including Hillary Clinton as secretary of state.

President Ronald Reagan appointed Sandra Day O'Connor, the first woman on the U.S. Supreme Court, early in his first term. While his record of appointing women and minorities to his administration had been poor, O'Connor's appointment was met with overwhelming enthusiasm.[129] The Senate unanimously confirmed her appointment. President Clinton added the second woman, Ruth

TABLE 4.3 Women Appointed to Presidential Cabinets

Appointee	Position	Appointed By	Dates
Frances Perkins	Secretary of Labor	F. D. Roosevelt	1933–1945
Oveta Culp Hobby	Secretary of Health, Education, and Welfare	Eisenhower	1953–1955
Carla Anderson Hills	Secretary of Housing and Urban Development	Ford	1975–1977
Juanita A. Kreps	Secretary of Commerce	Carter	1977–1979
Patricia R. Harris	Secretary of Housing and Urban Development	Carter	1977–1979
Patricia R. Harris	Secretary of Health and Human Services	Carter	1979–1981
Shirley M. Hufstedler	Secretary of Education	Reagan	1981–1985
Jeane J. Kirkpatrick	U.N. Ambassador*	Reagan	1981–1985
Margaret M. Heckler	Secretary of Health and Human Services	Reagan	1983–1985
Elizabeth H. Dole	Secretary of Transportation	Reagan	1983–1987
Anne McLaughlin	Secretary of Labor	Reagan	1987–1989
Elizabeth H. Dole	Secretary of Labor	Bush	1989–1991
Carla Anderson Hills	Special Trade Representative*	Bush	1989–1993
Lynn Morley Martin	Secretary of Labor	Bush	1991–1993
Barbara H. Franklin	Secretary of Commerce	Bush	1992–1993
Madeleine K. Albright	U.N. Ambassador*	Clinton	1993–1997
Hazel R. O'Leary	Secretary of Energy	Clinton	1993–1997
Carol M. Browner	Environmental Protection Agency*	Clinton	1993–2001
Janet Reno	Attorney General	Clinton	1993–2001

TABLE 4.3 Continued

Appointee	Position	Appointed By	Dates
Donna E. Shalala	Secretary of Health and Human Services	Clinton	1993–2001
Alice M. Rivlin	Director, Office of Management and Budget*	Clinton	1994–1996
Laura D'Andrea Tyson	Chair, National Economic Council*	Clinton	1995–1997
Janet L. Yellen	Chair, Council of Economic Advisors*	Clinton	1997–1999
Madeleine K. Albright	Secretary of State	Clinton	1997–2001
Aida Alvarez	Administrator, Small Business Administration*	Clinton	1997–2001
Charlene Barshefsky	U.S. Trade Representative*	Clinton	1997–2001
Alexis Herman	Secretary of Labor	Clinton	1997–2001
Janice R. Lachance	Director, Office of Personnel Management*	Clinton	1997–2001
Christine Todd Whitman	Environmental Protection Agency*	G. W. Bush	2001–2003
Elaine Chao	Secretary of Labor	G. W. Bush	2001–2009
Gale Norton	Secretary of Interior	G. W. Bush	2001–2006
Condoleezza Rice	National Security Advisor	G. W. Bush	2001–2005
Ann Veneman	Secretary of Agriculture	G. W. Bush	2001–2005
Margaret Spellings	Secretary of Education	G. W. Bush	2005–2009
Condoleezza Rice	Secretary of State	G. W. Bush	2005–2009
Mary Peters	Secretary of Transportation	G. W. Bush	2006–2009
Susan Schwab	U.S. Trade Representative*	G. W. Bush	2006–2009
Hillary Rodham Clinton	Secretary of State	Obama	2009–present
Janet A. Napolitano	Secretary of Homeland Security	Obama	2009–present
Christina Romer	Chair, Council of Economic Advisors*	Obama	2009–present
Lisa P. Jackson	Environmental Protection Agency*	Obama	2009–present
Susan Rice	U.N. Ambassador*	Obama	2009–present
Hilda Solis	Secretary of Labor	Obama	2009–present
Kathleen Sebelius	Secretary of Health and Human Services	Obama	2009–present

* Position considered cabinet level during this administration.
Source: "Women in the Presidential Cabinet," 50-50 by 2020: Equal Representation in Government, 2009, accessed at http://www.ergd.org/Women.Cabinet.Members.htm.

Bader Ginsburg, to the Court in 1993. On May 26, 2009, President Obama nominated Federal Appeals Court Judge Sonia Sotomayor to replace retiring Justice David Souter. Justice Sotomayor was confirmed by the U.S. Senate on August 6, 2009 making her only the third woman and the first Latina to serve on the Supreme Court.

In addition to providing role models for other women, according to some evidence, women in appointed positions govern differently from men. President Jimmy Carter's female appointees were more feminist than his male appointees, while the women in the Clinton administration selected more women to serve under them than the men did.[130] Alternatively, analysis of women in the executive branch over several administrations since the 1960s suggests that women had difficulty overcoming the status of token or "other" in providing substantive governance on the basis of their gender.[131] In a contrary example, Secretary of State Madeleine Albright was an active participant and leader in international conferences dedicated to improving women's rights and exhibited a greater sensitivity to women's concerns in shaping U.S. policy toward refugees. Secretary of State Hillary Clinton is expected to continue that work.

CONCLUSION

There is a wonderful story from the turn of the century about a Member of Parliament in Britain who welcomed Lady Astor as she took her seat there, the first woman ever to be elected to that body. "Welcome to the most exclusive men's club in Europe," he said with a grin. "It won't be exclusive for long," Lady Astor replied, with an even larger smile. "When I came in, I left the door wide open!"[132]

The assumption underlying this chapter has been, of course, that it is desirable to increase the number of women in office and that this goal could best be accomplished by increasing the number of women candidates who seek office. This assumption may be challenged by those who are happy with the status quo and so should be addressed. Women should participate fully as citizens and rulers within government for a variety of important reasons. The quality of representation suffers when women are excluded from elective office or the political opportunity structure is such that only a particular type of woman is elected. Men and women hold different views on issues and exhibit different policy preferences for dealing with public problems. When women are absent from legislative bodies or executive administrations, their perspective is also absent, robbing the country of valuable insight. As long as society is gendered, women will live a different life from men. Compared to men, women are more likely to earn less money, to work in hourly wage jobs and in part-time rather than full-time positions, and to rely on government assistance to feed, house, and educate their children. They are less likely than men to carry health insurance for themselves or their children. Priorities born of these experiences play an important part in establishing the priorities for a nation. The next chapter discusses in greater detail how women govern once they are elected or appointed to office and how women have continued to work for change outside the bounds of formal power.

Suggested Readings, Web Resources, and Films

Maria Braden, *Women Politicians and the Media* (Lexington: University of Kentucky Press, 1996).

Barbara Burrell, *A Woman's Place Is in the House: Campaigning for Congress in the Feminist Era* (Ann Arbor: University of Michigan Press, 1994).

Susan J. Carroll and Richard L. Fox, eds., *Gender and Elections: Shaping the Future of American Politics* (New York: Cambridge University Press, 2006).

Erika Falk, *Women for President: Media Bias in Eight Campaigns* (Urbana: University of Illinois Press, 2008).

Amy Handlin, *Whatever Happened to the Year of the Woman: Why Women Still Aren't Making It to the Top in Politics* (Denver, Colo.: Arden Press, 1998).

Kathleen Hall Jamieson, *The Double Bind: Women and Leadership* (New York: Oxford University Press, 1995).

Kim Fridkin Kahn, *The Political Consequences of Being a Woman* (New York: Columbia University Press, 1996).

Lia Larson, *Skirting Tradition: Women in Politics Speak to the Next Generation* (Hollis, N.H.: Hollis Publishing Company, 2004).

Jennifer L. Lawless and Richard L. Fox, *It Takes a Candidate: Why Women Don't Run for Office* (New York: Cambridge University Press, 2005).

Jennifer L. Lawless and Richard L. Fox, "Why Are Women Still Not Running for Public Office?" *Issues in Governance Studies* no. 14 (May 2008).

Susan Morrison, *Thirty Ways of Looking at Hillary: Women Writers Reflect on the Candidate and What Her Campaign Meant* (New York: Harper Perennial, 2008).

Barbara Palmer and Dennis Simon, *Breaking the Glass Ceiling: Women and Congressional Elections*, 2nd ed. (New York: Routledge, 2008).

Kira Sanbonmatsu, *Where Women Run: Gender and Party in the American States* (Ann Arbor: University of Michigan Press, 2006).

Amy Sewell and Heather Ogilvie, *She's Out There: Essays by 35 Young Women Who Aspire to Lead the Nation: The Next Generation of Presidential Candidates* (New York: Lifetime Media, 2009).

Harriet Woods, *Stepping Up to Power: The Political Journey of American Women* (Boulder, Colo.: Westview Press, 2000).

Democratic Women's Vote Center: http://www.democrats.org/a/communities/women.

Elect Women Magazine: http://www.electwomen.com.

EMILY's List: http://www.emilyslist.org.

League of Women Voters: http://www.lwv.org.

National Federation of Republican Women: http://www.nfrw.org.

The National Congress of Black Women: http://www.ncbw.org.

National Hispana Leadership Institute: http://www.nhli.org.

National Women's Political Caucus: http://www.nwpc.org.

National Political Congress of Black Women: http://www.npcbw.org.

The White House Project: http://www.thewhitehouseproject.org.

The Wish List: http://www.thewishlist.org.

Women's Voices. Women Vote: http://www.wvwv.org.

Women Count: http://www.womencount.org.

The Women's Campaign School: http://www.wcsyale.org/contents.html.

Women's National Democratic Club: http://www.democraticwoman.org.

Women Under Forty PAC: http://wufpac.org.

Film: *The Best Campaign Commercials: The Year of the Woman* (Washington, D.C.: Campaign Magazine, 1993).

Film: *Running in High Heels* (52 Women Films, 2005).

Film: *Killing Us Softly III: Advertising's Image of Women* (Media Education Foundation, 2000).

Notes

1. 50-50 by 2020: Equal Representation in Government, accessed at http://www.ergd .org/index.html.

2. "Congressional Profile," 50-50 by 2020: Equal Representation in Government, accessed at: http://www.ergd.org/CongressionalProfile.htm.

3. "Women in Elective Office 2009: Fact Sheet," compiled by the Center for American Women and Politics, Eagleton Institute of Politics (New Brunswick, N.J.: Rutgers University, 2009).

4. Inter-Parliamentary Union, "Women in Parliaments: World Classification," as of February 28, 2009, accessed at http://www.ipu.org/wmn-e/world.htm.

5. International Foundation for Election Systems, "Representation of Women in National Elected Institutions: Differences in International Performance and Factors Affecting This," paper prepared for seminar on *Women's Political Representation in the Coming 2004 Election* (June 2001), p. 3.

6. Women's Environment and Development Organization (WEDO), "Women in Government: 50/50 in 2005," accessed at http://www.wedo.org/balance.htm.

7. Inter-Parliamentary Union, "Women in National Parliaments," 2005, accessed at http://www.ipu.org.

8. Richard A. Seltzer, Jody Newman, and Melissa Vorhees Leighton, *Sex as a Political Variable: Women as Candidates and Voters in U.S. Elections* (Boulder, Colo.: Lynne Rienner Publishers, 1997), p. 76.

9. Jody Newman, *Perception and Reality: A Study Comparing the Success of Men and Women Candidates* (Washington, D.C.: National Women's Political Caucus, 1994).

10. Jennifer L. Lawless and Richard L. Fox, "Why Are Women Still Not Running for Office?" *Issues in Governance Studies* no. 14 (May 2008): 1–20.

11. Seltzer, Newman, and Leighton, *Sex as a Political Variable,* p. 79.

12. Ibid., p. 80.

13. Ibid., pp. 82–83.

14. Newman, *Perception and Reality,* p. 35.

15. Linda Witt, Karen M. Paget, and Glenna Mathews, *Running as a Woman: Gender and Power in American Politics* (New York: Free Press, 1993), p. 4.

16. "Women Candidates in 2000: An Early Glimpse," fact sheet compiled by the Center for American Women and Politics, Eagleton Institute of Politics (New Brunswick, N.J.: Rutgers University, February 28, 2000), accessed at http://www.rci.rutgers. edu/~cawp/facts/CandLook2000.html.

17. Seltzer, Newman, and Leighton, *Sex as a Political Variable,* p. 85.

18. "Women Candidates in 2000."

19. "Women Candidates in 2004," accessed at http://rci.rutgers.edu/~cawp/facts/Cand Look2004.html.

20. "Summary of Women Candidates 2008," Center for American Women and Politics, Eagleton Institute of Politics, Rutgers University.

21. Paul Herrnson, *Party Campaigning in the 1980s* (Cambridge, Mass.: Harvard University Press, 1988).

22. Georgia Duerst-Lahti, "The Bottleneck: Women Becoming Candidates," in *Women and Elective Office: Past, Present, and Future,* eds. Sue Thomas and Clyde Wilcox (New York: Oxford University Press, 1998), pp. 15–25.

23. Susan J. Carroll, *Women as Candidates in American Politics,* 2nd ed. (Bloomington: Indiana University Press, 1994), p. 161.

24. U.S. Department of Commerce, Bureau of the Census, "Educational Attainment in the United States: 2008" (Washington, D.C., 2009), accessed at http://www.census .gov/Press-Release/www/releases/archives/education/013618.html.

25. Susan Carroll and Wendy Strimling, *Women's Routes to Elective Office* (New Brunswick, N.J.: Center for American Women and Politics, Rutgers University, 1983).

26. Witt, Paget, and Mathews, *Running as a Woman,* p. 95.

27. R. Darcy, Susan Welch, and Janet Clark, *Women, Elections and Representation,* 2nd ed. (Lincoln: University of Nebraska Press, 1994), p. 106.

28. Witt, Paget, and Mathews, *Running as a Woman,* p. 97.

29. Ibid.

30. Ibid., p. 62.

31. Nancy Pelosi, "We Are Making the House Family-Friendly for New Mothers," press release, July 9, 2007, accessed at http://www.house.gov/pelosi/press/releases/ July07/mothers.html.

32. Witt, Paget, and Mathews, *Running as a Woman,* p. 105.

33. "Pipeline to the Future: Young Women and Political Leadership," findings on mobilizing young women from a survey and focus groups conducted by

Lake Snell Perry and Associates for The White House Project Education Fund, April 12, 2000, accessed at http://www.womensleadershipfund.org/programs/research.html#content.

34. Carol D. Miller, "Participating but not Leading: Women's Under-representation in Student Government Leadership Positions," *College Student Journal,* September 2004.

35. Christina Wolbrecht and David E. Campbell, "Do Women Politicians Lead Adolescent Girls to be More Politically Engaged? A Cross-National Study of Political Role Models," paper delivered at the annual meeting of the American Political Science Association, September 2005.

36. Ibid., p. 24.

37. Christina Wolbrecht and David E. Campbell, "Leading by Example: Female Members of Parliament as Political Role Models," *American Journal of Political Science* 51, no. 4 (2007): 921–939.

38. David E. Campbell and Christina Wolbrecht, "See Jane Run: Women Politicians as Role Models for Adolescents," *Journal of Politics* 68, no. 2 (2006): 233–245.

39. Lawless and Fox, "Why Are Women Still Not Running for Office?" pp. 1.

40. Richard L. Fox and Jennifer L. Lawless, "Entering the Arena? Gender and the Decision to Run for Office," *American Journal of Political Science* 48, no. 2 (April 2004): 264–280.

41. Ibid., pp. 268–269.

42. Ibid., p. 269.

43. Lawless and Fox, "Why Are Women Still Not Running for Office?" p. 1.

44. Laurel Elder, "Why Women Don't Run: Explaining Women's Underrepresentation in America's Political Institutions," *Women and Politics* 26, no. 2 (2004): 27–56; Susan Collins, "Through the Glass Ceiling," in *Skirting Tradition,* ed. Lia Larson (Hollis, N.H.: Hollis Publishing Company, 2004), p. 96.

45. Kathleen Murphy, "See Jane Stop Running," *Stateline: Politics & Policy News,* June 18, 2004, accessed at http://www.stateline.org.

46. Fox and Lawless, "Entering the Arena," p. 273.

47. Elder, "Why Women Don't Run," pp. 43–44.

48. Denise Baer, "Political Parties: The Missing Variable in Women and Politics Research," *Political Research Quarterly* 46 (1993): 547–576.

49. See, for example, Barbara Burrell, *A Woman's Place Is in the House: Campaigning for Congress in the Feminist Era* (Ann Arbor: University of Michigan Press, 1994).

50. David Niven, "Party Elites and Women Candidates: The Shape of Bias," *Women and Politics* 19, no. 2 (1998): 57–80.

51. Kenneth Prewitt, *The Recruitment of Political Leaders* (Indianapolis: Bobbs-Merrill, 1970).

52. Witt, Paget, and Mathews, *Running as a Woman,* p. 217.

53. Ibid., p. 218.

54. David Niven, "Throwing Your Hat Out of the Ring: Negative Recruitment and the Gender Imbalance in State Legislative Candidacy," *Politics & Gender* 2, no. 4 (December 2006): 473–489.

55. Kira Sanbonmatsu, "Political Parties and the Recruitment of Women to State Legislatures," *Journal of Politics* 64, no. 3 (August, 2002): 791–809.

56. Ibid., p. 805.

57. Jennifer L. Lawless and Kathryn Pearson, "Competing in Congressional Primaries," in *Legislative Women: Getting Elected, Getting Ahead,* ed. Beth Reingold (Boulder, Colo.: Lynne Rienner Publishers, 2008).

58. Ibid., p. 32.

59. "Pipeline to the Future," p. 16.

60. Barbara Burrell, "Campaign Finance: Women's Experience in the Modern Era," in *Women and Elective Office: Past, Present, and Future,* eds. Sue Thomas and Clyde Wilcox (New York: Oxford University Press, 1998), pp. 26–37.

61. Barbara C. Burrell, "Money and Women's Candidacies for Public Office," in *Women and American Politics: New Questions, New Directions,* ed. Susan J. Carroll (Oxford: Oxford University Press, 2003), p. 79.

62. Barbara Burrell, "Political Parties, Fund-raising, and Sex," in *Legislative Women: Getting Elected, Getting Ahead,* ed. Beth Reingold (Boulder, Colo.: Lynne Rienner Publishers, 2008), p. 49.

63. Burrell, "Money and Women's Candidacies for Public Office," p. 36.

64. Witt, Paget, and Mathews, *Running as a Woman,* p. 139.

65. Los Angeles African American Women Political Action Committee, accessed at http://www.laaawpac.org.

66. Christine L. Day and Charles D. Hadley, *Women's PACs: Abortion and Elections* (Upper Saddle River, N.J.: Pearson Prentice Hall, 2005), p. 7.

67. "Women's PACs and Donor Networks: A Contact List," Center for American Women and Politics, Eagleton Institute of Politics, Rutgers University, May 2009, accessed at http://www.cawp.rutgers.edu/education_training/resources_for_candidate_campaign/documents/pacs.pdf.

68. Burrell, "Campaign Finance," p. 128.

69. Leonie Huddy and Nayda Terkildsen, "The Consequences of Gender Stereotypes for Women Candidates at Different Levels of Office," *Political Research Quarterly* 43, no. 3 (1993): 503–525.

70. Shauna Shames, "The 'Un-Candidates': Gender and Outsider Signals in Women's Political Advertisements," *Women and Politics* 25, no. 1–2 (2003): 115–147.

71. Paul S. Herrnson, J. Celeste Lay, and Atiya Kai Stokes, "Women Running 'as Women': Candidate Gender, Campaign Issues, and Voter-Targeting Strategies," *Journal of Politics* 65, no. 1 (February 2003): 244–255.

72. Susan J. Carroll, "Reflections on Gender and Hillary Clinton's Presidential Campaign: The Good, the Bad, and the Misogynic," *Politics & Gender* 5 no. 1 (March 2009): 1–20.

73. Ibid.

74. Amy Sullivan, "Why Didn't More Women Vote for Hillary?" *Time,* June 5, 2008, accessed at http://www.time.com/time/magazine/article/0,9171,1812050,00.html.

75. Ibid., p. 11.

76. James Devitt, *Framing Gender on the Campaign Trail: Women's Executive Leadership and the Press* (Philadelphia: Annenberg Public Policy Center, University of Pennsylvania, 2000).

77. Kim Fridkin Kahn, *The Political Consequences of Being a Woman* (New York: Columbia University Press, 1996).

78. Monika McDermott, "Race and Gender Cues in Low-Information Elections," *Political Research Quarterly* 51, no. 4 (1998): 895–918.

79. Kira Sanbonmatsu, "Gender Stereotypes and Vote Choice," *American Journal of Political Science* 46, no. 1 (January 2002): 20–34.

80. Ibid., p. 26.

81. Kathleen A. Dolan, "Gender Differences in Support for Women Candidates: Is There a Glass Ceiling in American Politics?" *Women and Politics* 17, no. 2 (1997): 27–41.

82. Ibid., p. 84.

83. Ibid., p. 160.

84. Witt, Paget, and Mathews, *Running as a Woman,* p. 214.

85. Harriett Woods, *Stepping Up to Power: The Political Journey of American Women* (Boulder, Colo.: Westview Press, 2000), pp. 117–119.

86. Ibid., p. 118.

87. Quoted in Shames, "The 'Un-Candidates,'" p. 139.

88. Ann Gordon, David M. Shafie, and Ann N. Crigler, "Is Negative Advertising Effective for Female Candidates? An Experiment in Voters' Uses of Gender Stereotypes," *Press/Politics* 8, no. 1: (2003): 35–53.

89. Paul S. Herrnson and Jennifer Lucas, "The Fairer Sex? Gender and Negative Campaigning in the U.S. Elections," unpublished manuscript; the quote cited is from Peter L. Francia, Paul S. Herrnson, and Jennifer Lucas, "Campaign Ethics and Reform: What Candidates Say," *Campaigns and Elections* (June 2002): 45–47.

90. Kim L. Fridkin, Patrick J. Kenney, and Gina Serignese Woodall, "Bad for Men, Better for Women: The Impact of Stereotypes During Negative Campaigns," *Political Behavior* 31, no. 1 (March 2009): 53–77.

91. Seltzer, Newman, and Leighton, *Sex as a Political Variable,* p. 100.

92. Ibid., p. 102.

93. Amy Handlin, *Whatever Happened to the Year of the Woman: Why Women Still Aren't Making It to the Top in Politics* (Denver, Colo.: Arden Press, 1998).

94. Ibid., pp. 41–42.

95. "The New Political Woman Survey," in Witt, Paget, and Mathews, *Running as a Woman,* p. 172.

96. Handlin, *Whatever Happened to the Year of the Woman,* p. 62.

97. Kathleen Dolan, "Gender Differences in Support for Women Candidates: Is There a Glass Ceiling in American Politics?" *Women and Politics* 17, no. 2 (1997): 27–41.

98. Rasmussen Reports, "Woman President," September 3, 2008, accessed at http://www.rasmussenreports.com/.

99. Sherrye Henry, *The Deep Divide: Why American Women Resist Equality* (New York: Macmillan, 1994), pp. 320–322.

100. Michelle Swers, "Research on Women in Legislatures: What Have We Learned, Where Are We Going?" *Women and Politics* 23, no. 1–2 (2001): 167–185.

101. See Joel A. Thompson and Gary F. Moncrief, "The Implications of Term Limits for Women and Minorities: Some Evidence from the States," *Social Science Quarterly* 74, no. 2 (1993): 300–309.

102. Darcy, Welch, and Clark, *Women, Elections and Representation,* p. 165.

103. Handlin, *Whatever Happened to the Year of the Woman,* p. 158.

104. Ibid.

105. Stanley M. Caress, "The Influence of Term Limits on the Electoral Success of Women," *Women and Politics* 20, no. 3 (1999): 45–63.

106. Susan J. Carroll and Krista Jenkins, "Term Limits and the Representation of Women, Minorities, and Minority Women: Evidence from the State Legislative Elections of 1998" (New Brunswick, N.J.: Center for American Women and Politics, Rutgers University, 1999), accessed at http://www.rci.rutgers.edu/~cawp.

107. Mary Hawkesworth and Katherine E. Kleeman, "Term Limits and the Representation of Women" (New Brunswick, N.J.: Center for American Women and Politics, Rutgers University, May 2001), accessed at http://www.rci.rutgers.edu/~cawp.

108. Susan J. Carroll and Krista Jenkins, "Unrealized Opportunity? Term Limits and the Representation of Women in State Legislatures," *Women and Politics* 23, no. 4 (2001): 1–30.

109. Susan J. Carroll and Krista Jenkins, "The Effect of Term Limits on the Representation of Women: An Analysis of the 1998 Elections" (New Brunswick, N.J.: Center for American Women and Politics, Rutgers University, 1999), accessed at http://www.rci.rutgers.edu/~cawp.

110. Peter Slevin, "After Adopting Term Limits, States Lose Female Legislators," *Washington Post,* Sunday, April 22, 2007; A04.

111. Darcy, Welch, and Clark, *Women, Elections and Representation,* p. 140.

112. Ibid., p. 158.

113. Ibid., p. 163.

114. Center for American Women and Politics, "Fast Facts: Women Serving in the 111th Congress, 2009–2011," accessed at http://www.cawp.rutgers.edu/fast_facts/levels_of_office/Congress-Current.php.

115. Barbara Palmer and Dennis Simon, *Breaking the Glass Ceiling: Women and Congressional Elections,* 2nd ed. (New York: Routledge, 2008).

116. Ibid., p. 178.

117. White House Project, accessed at http://www.thewhitehouseproject.org; Vote, Run, Lead, accessed at http://www.voterunlead.org.

118. "Pipeline to the Future," p. 27.

119. National Federation of Republican Women Campaign Management School, accessed at: http://www.nfrw.org/programs/political_education.htm; Excellence in Public Service, Whitman Series, accessed at http://www.whitmanseries.org/.

120. Political Opportunity Program (POP), accessed at http://www.emilyslist.org/do/pop.

121. The Women's Campaign School, accessed at http://www.yale.edu/wcsyale.

122. Women Under Forty Political Action Committee, accessed at http://www. wufpac .org.

123. http://www.thewhitehouseproject.org/invite_woman/index.html.

124. Running Start, http://www.runningstartonline.org/home/.

125. Lonnae O'Neal Parker, "The Black Woman's Vote Can Often Determine the Outcome of an Election, Yet When It Comes to Political Power, We Aren't Getting Our Due . . . ," *Essence* (February 2003); Shara D. Taylor, "Future PAC Empowers Women in Politics," *Hilltop: The Student Voice of Howard University* (September 30, 2003).

126. "Gender Gap in Government," accessed at http://www.gendergap.com.

127. Woods, *Stepping Up to Power,* p. 2.

128. National Political Congress of Black Women, profile, accessed at http://www .npcbw.org.profile.html.

129. Tanya Melich, *The Republican War Against Women,* (New York: Bantam Publishing, 1996) pp. 155–157.

130. Susan J. Carroll and Barbara J. Geiger-Parker. *Women Appointed to the Carter Administration,* Center for American Women and Politics, 1983, accessed at http://www.cawp.rutgers.edu/research/reports/carter_admin.pdf.

131. MaryAnne Borrelli and Janet M. Martin, eds., *The Other Elites: Women, Politics, and Power in the Executive Branch* (Boulder, Colo.: Lynne Rienner Publishers, 1997).

132. Olympia Snowe, "Too Often Met with Silence," in *Skirting Tradition,* ed. Lia Larson (Hollis, N.H.: Hollis Publishing Company, 2004) p. 63.

Women as Political Actors: Representation and Advocacy

Despite steady progress over the last twenty years and even more rapid gains in recent elections, the number of women in political office in the United States is still significantly smaller than the number of men. Does it matter if more men than women are in politics? Are we concerned about this issue from a purely numerical standpoint, or is it that women in office govern differently from men and are therefore better able to represent women's interests? The paradox of gender equality again provides a useful way to evaluate our expectations about the number of women in office as well as how we think women will (or should) behave once in office. Those who believe that equality stems from the similarities between men and women view parity (equal numbers of men and women) as the standard for equality of representation in political office. Therefore, equal numbers of women serving is paramount for *descriptive representation*. Women in this regard provide role models, and a diverse, descriptively representative government lends legitimacy to its decisions and actions. A political institution like Congress or a presidential administration appears to be more representative of the people when its membership reflects the characteristics of the population it serves. Alternatively, for those who believe that equality requires a recognition of the differences between men and women, women's involvement in politics is important because of their unique perspective as women. Therefore, having women in public office is important for what they bring to the job and the ways they *substantively represent* women and their interests. Of course, as we've seen repeatedly, these perspectives are not mutually exclusive and, in the case of political representation, are quite complimentary. Both paths in pursuit of equality embrace the goal of bringing more women into politics.

This chapter examines women as political actors, defined broadly to include women working within the formal channels of government as insiders, as well as women working as outsiders, pressuring government from beyond the boundaries of formal office. The previous chapter reviewed a number of initiatives designed to increase the number of women candidates and, by extension, the number of women elected officials. Here we examine women's experience and behavior as legislators and appointed public officials working as political insiders. We also look at the ways in which men and women are similar and different in their actions as political insiders. We will also examine the ways women differ from one another as political actors. Women have had a long-standing tradition of working as advocates and political outsiders, initially because they were legally excluded from participating as insiders. Now, women have both strategies at their disposal. How do they differ in their means and ends? As political activists and advocates, women work with nongovernmental organizations and within a variety of social movements to influence politics and promote policies favorable to the interests of gender equality. Often their goals include trying to change the system itself as well as its outputs. We will look at how women's advocacy and activism shapes the political agenda and evaluate whether the issues women address as insiders vary from those women address as outsiders. In both cases, women are engaged in political representation through their actions.

POLITICAL REPRESENTATION

On October 25, 1991, the National Women's Political Caucus ran a full-page ad in the New York Times. Under a pen and ink drawing of a diverse hearing panel made up entirely of women, the heading read: "What If . . ." "What if fourteen women, instead of fourteen men had sat on the Senate Judiciary Committee during the confirmation hearings of Clarence Thomas? . . . Sound unfair? Just as unfair as fourteen men and no women."[1]

As this advertisement illustrates, feminists believe that more women in office will translate into a more woman-friendly political system, which in turn will generate government actions responsive to women's unique concerns. The ad further implies that it is "unfair" when one group in society dominates political representation so completely and that women, if elected, will act differently than men once in office. This is a complicated set of expectations born of our conceptual understanding of political representation.

Contemporary political theorist Hannah Fenichel Pitkin describes four types of political representation: formal, descriptive, symbolic, and substantive.[2] Formal representation refers to mechanisms in a political system that ensure representation exists and allows citizens to hold representatives accountable for their actions. In the U.S. political system, elections are the mechanisms of formal representation. This explains why women were so anxious to participate in elections as voters and ultimately as elected representatives.

WHAT IF?

What if 14 women, instead of 14 men, had sat on the Senate Judiciary Committee during the confirmation hearings of Clarence Thomas?

Sound unfair? Just as unfair as fourteen men and no women.

What if even **half** the Senators had been women? Women are, after all, more than half the population. Maybe, just maybe, women's voices would have been heard. Maybe the experiences and concerns of women would not have been so quickly dismissed or ridiculed. And maybe all of America would have benefited.

The behavior and performance of the United States Senate during the Clarence Thomas confirmation hearings demonstrated a stark truth: women are tragically under-represented politically. As long as men make up 98% of the U.S. Senate and 93% of the U.S. House of Representatives, women's voices can be ignored, their experiences and concerns trivialized.

The need for women in public office has never been more obvious. Or essential.

Men control the White House, the Congress, the courthouse and the statehouse. Men have political power over women's lives. It's time that women help make the rules, create the policies, and pass the laws about sexual harassment, day care, affordable health care, and hundreds of decisions that affect American families every day.

The National Women's Political Caucus is determined to even

the odds. To hear the voices of women echo in the halls of power.

If you're angry about what you've witnessed in the United States Senate, don't just raise your fist, raise your pen. Join us. The goal of the National Women's Political Caucus is to increase the number of women elected and appointed to public office. We're the only national bi-partisan grassroots organization working across this country to recruit, train and elect women into office at all levels of government.

Turn your anger into action. Join us.

NWPC

Count me in. I want to help the National Women's Political Caucus increase the number of women elected and appointed to public office.

Enclosed is my check payable to NWPC Inc. for:
( )$250 ( )$100 ( )$50 ( )$35 OTHER $____

Name _____

Address _____

City/State/Zip _____

Please bill my ( ) Mastercard ( ) Visa   Amount $____

Account Number _____ Expiration Date _____

Signature _____ Date _____

Contributions to NWPC are not tax deductible.

National Women's Political Caucus
1275 K Street, N.W., Suite 750, Washington, D.C. 20005

Paid for by the National Women's Political Caucus

The next three types of representation refer to how a person is represented. When demands for more women in office stem from claims of justice and equity, descriptive and symbolic representation are in play. When women represent other women simply by their presence in government, women are descriptively represented. We assume that if someone shares our descriptive characteristics such as sex, race, or other defining features, they will also share and protect our interests. Our image and interests are mirrored by the representative who is "like us." Symbolic representation adds an emotional or affective component to representation in that it occurs when we feel represented by another. When women looked at the all-male, all-white Senate Judiciary Committee, it neither mirrored their image nor made them feel as if their interests were being represented, and the palpable disconnect produced a strong negative reaction in many. Thus, women's numeric representation in Congress, state legislatures, or other halls of power is important for symbolic reasons in the sense that women *stand for* other women. Women standing for women act as important role models in that they challenge the mental image of political leadership as male in its embodiment. "When we don't see women as leaders, we continue to think of leaders as men. . . . In a circular fashion, the absence of women as political leaders contributes to the continued absence of women as political leaders."[3] Recall from the previous chapter the important function female role models play for young women in motivating them to think about running for office themselves.[4] Substantive representation occurs when women *act for* other women by pursuing distinctive interests and policy preferences unique to women. This is perhaps the most important form of representation, although it is also the most problematic to implement. As we have seen repeatedly throughout this volume, women do not constitute a homogeneous group. As such, defining "women's interests" along a single dimension is nearly impossible. Therefore women acting for other women will reflect the diversity of ideological perspectives and issue positions among the women elected representatives. Rarely will all women adopt the same substantive position simply because they are women. In fact, many women in public office do not view themselves as acting for other women. Descriptive representation, therefore, may not have any predictable relation to support for women's substantive interests.

Another way of conceptualizing women's representation of other women is through surrogate representation.[5] Given the small number of women elected representatives, most female citizens are not represented by a woman in Congress. However, surrogate representation suggests that a representational relationship can exist outside the boundaries of an electoral district. In this sense, the relationship between the citizen and representative is based on a shared ideological perspective or group identity. "This concept of surrogate representation is potentially of great significance in considering how women representatives may be helping to transform the institution of Congress and its policy agenda. To the extent that women members of Congress see themselves and act as surrogate representatives for women outside the geographic boundaries of their districts, they bring something distinctive to their roles as representatives, something that most men do not bring."[6]

Arguably, substantive representation could exist without descriptive or symbolic representation. In other words, men could act for women, but do they? In 1970, a CBS News poll found that more than 78 percent of women favored federally established daycare centers. In 1970, women held fewer than

4 percent of the seats in Congress, and no action was taken. For that matter, no action has been taken in the more than thirty-five years since.[7] Is this because women are not present in large enough numbers or because female representatives share no solidarity on this issue? Alternatively, a lack of action could exist because this particular issue does not have the popular support needed to pressure Congress to act, regardless of how many of its members are women. Representative Leslie Byrne (D-VA), elected in 1992, observes: "Most of us didn't come in as women's issues people, but what we have found when we got there is that if we didn't step in, those issues weren't addressed. I have always said that all issues are women's issues. But there are particular issues that affect women in greater proportions than others that don't seem to get the attention, and those are the ones you find yourself looking at just out of an issue of fairness."[8] Following the 2008 election, women hold just under 17 percent of the seats in Congress and 24 percent of the seats in state legislatures, and as this chapter shows, that small percentage often makes it difficult to get particular issues on the official agenda. It is impossible to tell for certain whether gender parity in representation would alter the public agenda, but some evidence suggests that it would.

Does the public desire gender parity and might their preference for or against it be a factor in explaining the relatively slow progress toward parity in descriptive political representation in the United States? New research by Kathleen Dolan and Kira Sanbonmatsu explores the public's view of the ideal gender composition of government.[9] When asked, "In your opinion, in the best government the U.S. could have, what percentage of elected officials would be men?" the most common response was parity (50 percent men, 50 percent women). The mean response was 60 percent men, leaving 40 percent of the seats for women (keep in mind that even this imbalance is far from the reality of the 82–17 proportion in Congress and 76–24 imbalance in the state legislatures). Indeed, 45 percent of the respondents gave a figure for their ideal level of men's representation of 60 percent or higher (11 percent of those questioned wanted a government that was 75 percent male; 8 percent preferred it be 80 percent male).[10] Less than 10 percent of the sample preferred a government made up of a majority of women. More women (12 percent) than men (7 percent) preferred a majority female "ideal government," but both women (44 percent) and men (47 percent) prefer government that is majority male. Thus, while the public prefers a government with more women than currently serve in office, there is no evidence of an overwhelming desire to work toward a female-majority government. In exploring the reasons for the public's preferences, Dolan and Sanbonmatsu found that gender stereotypes about male and female suitability for politics and issue competency shape the public's perception of ideal descriptive representation. "Respondents who believe that women are better suited emotionally for politics and who believe that women are better able to handle crime are more likely to believe that men should be half of elected officials." Further, the experience of being represented by a woman did not affect support for higher levels of representation among men or women. This research raises interesting questions about whether the public is truly interested in advancing women's share of descriptive representation in legislatures. What we cannot tell, however, from this research is to what extent a desire for or against a more gender-balanced ideal government impacts voting behavior in elections. When faced with a single contest in which they have the opportunity to vote for a female and thereby potentially add to the overall numbers of women in office, will the abstract desire for gender parity outweigh the traditional predictors of vote choice? Part of the answer may lie in the extent to which people believe female representation is unique.

Are Women Unique as Representatives?

Descriptive, symbolic, and substantive representation, although conceptually distinct, are in reality interwoven in complex ways that form the assumptions we make and the expectations we hold for women in political office. For example, because of the power of sex role socialization, we believe women are different from men and possess different traits and characteristics that are stereotypically feminine (e.g., compassionate, conciliatory, compromising). Some feminists see this difference as empowering and therefore expect women to behave differently from men within political institutions, to pursue different policy solutions, to hold different attitudes, and to act to shape the political processes and institutions into being more responsive to women's particular concerns. In recent elections, female candidates have been able to capitalize on voters' desires for change by promising that if elected, women would be different—whatever that means. The meaning of "different" is left to the voters' (and the media's) imagination, but the invitation to rely on positive stereotypes in evaluating women candidates and their promises is clear. Implicit in the message is also the suggestion that women will not only be different, but they will also be *better* than men. Some of these expectations have been confirmed by research studies, while others have not. Simply electing more women to office will not directly translate into the adoption of feminist policies. There is considerable diversity among women as a whole, as well as among women officeholders—particularly since the late 1990s.[11] Assuming that all women share some essential quality that can be translated into a single political voice ignores the diversity among women and, in effect, silences the interests of some women in favor of more dominant women's interests.[12]

An alternative perspective among feminists considers women's claim of difference as somewhat dangerous in the sense that it recalls the theory of separate spheres that relegated women to second-class status and confined them largely to the private sphere purely on the basis of their perceived difference from men. If women encourage voters to rely on stereotypes and place an emphasis on difference, it may backfire when the electoral context or public mood changes. Supreme Court Justice Sandra Day O'Connor, for one, is skeptical of the wisdom of women's claims to virtue and difference:

The gender differences cited currently are surprisingly similar to stereotypes from years past. They recall the old myths we have struggled to put behind us. For example, asking whether women attorneys speak in a "different voice" than men do is a question that is both dangerous and unanswerable. . . . It threatens, indeed, to establish new categories of 'women's work' to which women are confined and from which men are excluded.[13]

Others worry that women will be held to a higher standard and be judged ineffective in short order if they cannot alter the political system after taking office. Madeline Kunin, former governor of Vermont, said, "We cannot expect the few women in political life to change the values and the rules of the game alone, although that is sometimes precisely the expectation."[14] Key in her warning is "the few." Even today, women still constitute the minority in Congress and in all fifty state legislatures. Some research suggests that until women make up a critical mass (defined as 30 percent), they cannot be expected to exert much influence over the institution in which they serve.[15] Whether women are in fact different from men may be unanswerable, as Justice O'Connor claims. Nonetheless, the perception of difference is a powerful force in American politics.

POLITICAL INSIDERS: HOW DO MEN AND WOMEN DIFFER?

The research on differences between male and female political actors offers some direction in analyzing women as insiders and evaluating the type of representation they provide. Later in this chapter we will evaluate whether men and women differ in their ideological outlooks on politics and whether women pursue policies that are distinctly different from the policy priorities of male legislators.[16] We will then examine the results of research on gender and policymaking, and investigate whether women adopt a particularized style as political actors that differs from that of their male colleagues.[17]

Ideology and Attitudes

A number of studies have found that women officeholders at both the state and the federal levels are more liberal than their male counterparts, regardless of their political party. In an early study of women in Congress, political scientist Freda Gehlen found that female representatives were more likely than males to support such liberal initiatives as the 1964 Civil Rights Act and the Equal Rights Amendment.[18] Women during that period, which also corresponded to the early years of the second wave of the feminist movement, supported a tentative feminist coalition (or at least a coalition of female members) in the House of Representatives.[19] Longitudinal analysis of women in office from 1972 to

1980 found that the nature of the issue and the influence of a representative's constituency were as important or more important than gender in explaining male and female representatives' voting behavior. Although women voted more liberally than men in the early 1970s, the size of the difference in voting records decreased over time and did not exist in some regions of the country. Researchers thus concluded that legislative districts that supported liberal policies were more likely to elect women legislators during the 1970s and 1980s.[20] What initially appeared to be gender differences in voting behavior was actually a result of unique characteristics of the relatively few women elected to Congress at the time.

Political scientist Barbara Burrell replicated the early longitudinal analysis of House voting patterns in three sessions of Congress between 1987 and 1992 to see whether gender differences between male and female legislators' voting records remained even after accounting for the fact that women may disproportionately represent more liberal districts.[21] She found, similar to research from prior decades, that liberal ideology is strongest among Democratic women who represent northern urban districts. However, even when controlling for political party and constituent factors, gender remained a significant point of departure in predicting a legislator's liberal voting record across social, economic, and foreign-policy issues. Political party is a slightly greater determinant than gender. Democratic women make the Democratic Party more liberal, whereas Republican women moderate the Republican Party. "In terms of general political ideology, female representatives as a group continue to influence the policy preferences of Congress from what they would be if only men served."[22] Burrell concluded that after taking into account all of the external factors that might make women appear more liberal than men (e.g., district characteristics, political party), women in Congress, as a group, do indeed vote differently from men on issues.

In state legislatures, the trend is similar. A study sponsored by the Center for American Women and Politics (CAWP) found a gender gap on a variety of issues, from the death penalty to construction of nuclear power plants; however, the gap was largest on issues of abortion policy. For example, only 26 percent of women agreed that abortion should be prohibited in almost all circumstances, compared to 39 percent of men. Fifty-seven percent of women opposed mandatory parental consent for minors wanting abortions, whereas only 33 percent of men opposed the restriction.[23] A 1995 study found that women were more ideologically liberal than men on almost all issues, although they were somewhat less so on fiscal matters. Women are far more likely to oppose the death penalty, mandatory prayer in schools, and tax cuts that also require a cut in government spending, and to support abortion rights.[24] Relative to their constituents, women are consistently more liberal than men in either party. These ideological and attitudinal differences are also reflected in the interest groups that legislators associate with. For example, the Christian Coalition, as well as groups that support term limits and oppose abortion rights and gun control, are all more likely to support Republican men than

Republican women and Democratic men and women. As it turns out, groups that support Republican men were more active in the 2000 election than were labor unions, feminist groups, environmentalists, and abortion-rights and gun-control groups—all of which most often favor women and Democrats. The authors conclude that these data "suggest that the electoral tides of the early 1990s may be shifting to the disadvantage of women state legislative candidates."[25] Indeed, although women made substantial one-time gains at the state legislative level in 1992, subsequent gains have been minimal and relatively flat. Women's percentage of state legislative seats rose from 17 percent in 1989 to 21 percent in 1993, but increased only to 22.5 percent in 1999; it dropped slightly to 22.4 percent in 2001 and appears to be holding steady at 24.3 percent through 2009.[26]

Male and female state legislators also have different perceptions of their political roles and the impact their gender has on career and effectiveness in office.[27] Public opinion surveys suggest that voters view women legislators as "more nurturant than men, more compassionate, more accessible, more honest, and more moral, the flip side of the perception that women are less swayed by 'politics as usual.'"[28] Women state representatives view themselves differently as well. For example, they see themselves as more hardworking, more patient, more attentive to detail, better prepared in their daily tasks, and better equipped to deal with female constituents' concerns than their male colleagues. As for their work, they think of themselves as more interested in long-term implications of policy and as driven more by the common good than by personal gain. In short, most female legislators see themselves as distinct "outsiders" even within the confines of their respective legislatures. Only about a quarter of the women interviewed did not see any connection between their sex and their role as a legislator, believing that women are no different from men. The author of the study concludes that such stark differences among women in how they view the intersection of gender and their legislative role leave women officeholders with a need for more complete models of how best to combine gender and political roles.

Susan Carroll's recent study on women in Congress provides interesting insights into how congresswomen view their representational roles and work styles.[29] Of particular note is how women bridge ideological or party differences in order to work together. Carroll says, "The obligation most congresswomen feel to act as surrogate representatives for women seems to be rooted in their beliefs that there are underlying commonalities. . . . Most women in Congress, regardless of party or ideology or race or ethnicity, believe that there are ties that bind women together across divisions." Representative Elizabeth Furse (D-OR) described women's commonality as a "not-male experience."[30] Senator Olympia Snowe (R-ME) said, "Women are focused on outcomes, results, and getting the job done. Basically women don't spend a lot of time on the periphery of a problem. They generally like to delve into it and achieve the results and figure out what's the best way to achieve that outcome." Senator Blanche Lincoln (D-AR) noted women's interest and success at developing compromises:

"Women are good at compromising . . . realizing that sometimes it's better to get a step ahead than just stay in the same place for 14 years."[31]

"Styles" of Political Behavior

Several studies have found that, in carrying out their role as legislators, women spend considerably more time "keeping in touch" with constituents and helping constituents solve problems than men do. Within the legislature itself, women tend to be "team players" more often than men, spending more time

---

Point of Comparison

Current Female World Leadership, 2009

Country	Female Leader (Year Elected/Appointed)	Percentage of Women in Lower House
Ireland	President Mary McAleese (1997)	13.3%
Finland	President Tarja Halonen (2000)	41.5%
Philippines	President Gloria Macapagal-Arroyo (2001)	20.5%
Mozambique	Prime Minister Luisa Diogo (2004)	34.8%
Germany	Chancellor Angela Merkel (2005)	32.2%
Liberia	President Ellen Johnson-Sirleaf (2006)	12.5%
Chile	President Michelle Bachelet (2006)	15.0%
Bosnia-Herzegovina	President Borjana Kirsto (2007)	11.9%
India	President Pratibha Patil (2007)	10.9%
Ukraine	Prime Minister Yuliya Tymoshenko (2007)	8.2%
Haiti	Prime Minister Michele Pierre-Louis (2008)	4.1%
Moldova	Prime Minister Zinaida Grecianii (2008)	23.8%
Argentina	President Christina Fernandez de Kirchner (2008)	40.0%
Bangladesh	Prime Minister Shikh Hasina Wajed (2009)	18.6%
Iceland	Prime Minister Johanna Sigurdardsottir (2009)	42.9%

Source: "Guide to Women Leaders," http://www.guide2womenleaders.com; Inter-Parliamentary Union http://www.ipu.org/wmn-e/classif.htm.

building coalitions within and across political parties.[32] Women's interest in building bridges also extends to their leadership styles. Researchers developed a typology of leadership along two major dimensions: leadership styles (command, coordinating, and consensus) and leadership goals (power, policy, and process). Along each dimension qualities range from a narrow focus on the self to a broader focus on others and the system as a whole. Previous evidence suggests that women would be more likely to be found among the consensus- and process-oriented leaders. Interviews with ninety legislative leaders in twenty-two states found that women more often considered their leadership styles to be based on cooperation and consensus-building qualities, while men usually described their styles as strong, directive, and oriented toward power and control.[33] Significantly, the trend toward professionalized legislatures (higher salaries, more days in session, larger staffs) is also producing a trend toward the feminization of leadership. As legislatures have become more professional, their members have become more resistant to autocratic leadership styles. Thus, women have benefited in two distinct ways: First, the number of women in leadership positions has increased almost in proportion to the number of women serving in state legislative institutions. Second, both male and female leaders are more prone to adopt a "female" style of leadership that emphasizes consensus building and broader concerns about the political system as a whole in response to underlying changes in the institutions themselves.[34] By contrast, a study of female committee chairs found that legislative professionalization produced a negative effect on the collaborative style favored by women.[35]

One of the most important leadership positions within legislative institutions is the committee chair. Legislatures divide the work of detailed policy development and scrutiny among committees that are charged with drafting legislation, holding hearings, reaching compromises on competing interests, and ultimately with presenting the draft legislation to the full body for consideration. This makes committees a central force of power and influence within the institution. Two important studies of chairwomen's performance were done in the 1990s. The first, conducted by political scientist Lyn Kathlene, examined the gendered dynamics of verbal exchanges within committee hearings that were chaired by a man or a woman.[36] When women chaired committees, they spoke less, took fewer turns at speaking, and interrupted less frequently than chairmen. Male chairs influenced committee hearings by engaging in substantive comments more than females did and, in the process, interjected their opinions more often. In one out of six turns, men "interjected personal opinions or guided the committee members and witnesses to a topic of their interest."[37] Chairwomen used their position of power to facilitate discussion among participants and only rarely interjected personal opinions. Among committee members, the gendered patterns of participation persisted as well. Male members spoke up earlier in the hearing than women (halfway versus two-thirds of the way through) and spoke longer, took more turns, and encountered more interruptions than women did. As the proportion of women on a committee increased, men became significantly more vocal. When a sponsor of a bill before the committee was female, men both spoke earlier and began questioning her or female witnesses as soon as the bill was introduced. Men did not engage in this same type of eager scrutiny when a male sponsored a bill or was a supporting witness.[38] To increase women's effectiveness as chairs and members of committees, Kathlene observes, each woman should either be seated beside a woman or be within the line of sight of other women. This is consistent with the findings of a 1985 study of county supervisors in Santa Clara, California. Political scientist Janet Flamang found that the presence of supportive female colleagues allowed women to speak out and participate in the legislative process where they might otherwise exhibit reticence.[39]

In the second study of female committee chairs, conducted in 1994, political scientist Cindy Simon Rosenthal found important demographic differences between male and female chairs. Because leadership positions have most often been awarded to those with the greatest seniority, Rosenthal found that chairwomen were significantly older than chairmen and were less likely to hold advanced degrees. They were also less likely to have worked outside the home and more likely to have developed their leadership skills in community or volunteer settings rather than in political office.[40] In many ways, the profile of female chairs in this 1994 study more closely resembles the majority of women serving in the 1970s and early 1980s than the women elected after 1988.[41] Chairwomen in this study viewed themselves as task and team oriented, managerial, assertive, skilled at interpersonal dealings, and frank and direct. Males, on the other hand, viewed themselves as more competitive, willing to intimidate, and opportunistic.[42] Ironically, Rosenthal concludes that women's task-oriented style of leadership, rather than facilitating their rise to power, may actually act as a barrier. Women feel obligated to finish a task or to "get things done," even if it means passing up an opportunity to seek higher office or pursue progressively higher leadership positions.

In an interesting study of women's leadership styles and organizational structures in women's membership associations, Maryann Barakso concludes "while men and women may exhibit different leadership styles when they work together, these differences are not reflected in the institutions created by women."[43] Noting that much of the existing research pointing to differences in women's and men's behavior—specifically that women prefer democratic decision-making processes—is based in organizations or institutions that were not only formed by men but are dominated by men, Barakso analyzed associations created by women. Will women's allegedly more participatory and democratic style persist in female-founded organizations? She examined the electoral and policymaking rules of 37 membership-based women's associations and found a good deal of variation in bylaws and decision-making processes, leading her to observe that women "appear no more likely to emphasize democratic practices than mixed-gender organizations." Factors such as the year the organization was founded and the extent to which the organization relies on membership dues influenced the degree of democratic structure. Does this mean that gender does not influence behavior? Not exactly—Barakso concludes that men and women bring their expectations of gender roles into the

It's not about one...

Jim Borgman, Cincinnati Enquirer, Universal Press Syndicate.

This 2007 cartoon by Jim Borgman inspired the title for filmmakers Amy Sewell's and Susan Toffler's 2008 feminist documentary, *What's Your Point, Honey?*, exploring the pipeline for future female presidential candidates. In addition to interviews with preteens, prominent women leaders, and citizens, the film features seven college-age women participating in Project 2024, a collaboration between *CosmoGIRL!* and The White House Project to train a new generation of women leaders and, ideally, elect a woman to the White House by 2024. Women selected to participate complete a summer internship with women who are leaders in their fields. This model draws on the research literature about the power of role models to stimulate political interest and activity. The tagline for the film is "it's not about one...," alluding to the need to combat the backlash from Hillary Clinton's presidential campaign and make sure that women are a reliable presence in national campaigns and in public office. The film has not been widely distributed. When Sewell and Toffler approached a powerful female decision maker in Hollywood about distributing the film, the first words out of her mouth were, "You have to understand, I'm one woman in a room with ten men." You may download the film or purchase a DVD directly from the Web site http://www.whatsyourpointhoney.com/front/.

institutional spaces they inhabit, thus "it may be that in mixed-sex workplaces, legislatures and other organizations, women opt for more participatory leadership styles because they are expected to behave this way, not necessarily because they prefer to do so."[44]

Leadership Roles

If we are to conclude that women make a substantial difference in politics, we must move past style and even policy outcomes to examine their impact on the institution itself. Do women, by their very presence, change the way Congress works? It is a difficult question to answer. One way to go about it is to investigate whether women change their male colleagues' behavior or significantly impact the way male legislators "see" politics. Another way to leave a lasting impact is for women to fully integrate the leadership structure from committee chair to formal power positions such as Speaker of the House. Representatives in these positions play a central role in defining the legislative agenda and may serve either as facilitators or gatekeepers for other members with leadership ambitions.

"Simply put, men continue to represent the face of the United States' political institutions."[45] Representative Patricia Schroeder was the first woman ever appointed to the House Armed Services Committee (93rd Congress, 1973–74), and recalls that her appointment was not met with enthusiasm by the chair, Edward Hebert of Louisiana:

> He didn't appreciate the idea of a girl and a black forced on him. He was out-raged that for the first time a chairman's veto of potential members was ignored. He announced that while he might not be able to control the makeup of the committee, he could damn well control the number of chairs in his hearing room. . . . He said that women and blacks were worth only half of one "regular" member, so he added only one seat to the committee room and made Ron [Dellums] and me share it.[46]

In the 111th Congress (2009–2011), women still occupy a limited set of leadership positions. Representative Nancy Pelosi (California) was reelected to a second term as Speaker of the House of Representatives. Her election to the Speaker's post in the 110th Congress represented a first for women and shattered, Pelosi said, "not a glass ceiling but a marble ceiling" in the halls of Congress.[47] Five other women serve in majority leadership positions in the 111th Congress: Representatives Diana DeGette (Colorado), Jan Schakowsky (Illinois), Debbie Wasserman Schultz (Florida), and Maxine Waters (California) serve as Democratic chief deputy whips. Representative Rosa DeLauro (Connecticut) serves as the chair of the Democratic Steering Committee. On the minority side, Representative Cathy McMorris Rodgers (Washington) serves as the vice chair of the Republican Conference. In the U.S. Senate, Senator Barbara Boxer (California) acts as the Democratic chief deputy whip. Senator Patty Murray (D-WA) is the Democratic Conference secretary and Senator Debbie Stabenow (Michigan) chairs the Democratic Steering Committee. Serving as chair of Democratic Rural Outreach is Senator Blanche Lincoln (Arkansas).[48]

There have been no significant gains in women's representation among the highest echelons of committee power in either house. Women have never chaired more than three committees in a single Congress. More significantly, no woman has ever chaired one of the "power/prestige committees," which include the Appropriations and the Ways and Means committees in the House

and the Appropriations, Armed Services, Finance, and Foreign Policy committees in the Senate. In the 110th Congress (2007–2009), Representative Louise
Slaughter, a Democrat from New York, became the first woman ever to chair
the Rules Committee of the House, a position she still holds in the 111th Congress. Women in the Senate currently chair the Committee on Environment and
Public Works (Senator Barbara Boxer) and the Small Business and Entrepre-
neurship Committee (Senator Mary L. Landrieu, Louisiana). In addition to the
Rules Committee, Democratic women in the House currently chair the Committee on Ethics (Representative Zoe Lofgren, California) and the Committee
on Small Business (Representative Nydia Velezquez, New York).

In 2001, Representative Marge Roukema, a Republican member from New
Jersey, was publicly passed over for the position of chair of the Financial Services Committee despite her status as the most senior Republican on the panel in
favor of Mike Oxley although he had no previous service on the committee.[49]
Worth far more than symbolism, women's ascension to leadership positions,
particularly policy committee chairs, puts them in a position to shape the legislative agenda and exert substantive policy influence. After twenty-four years
in the House of Representatives, Colorado Representative Patricia Schroeder
had risen sufficiently in seniority to chair a *subcommittee* of the House Armed
Services Committee. Among the limited number of women who have chaired
committees, most have now retired (including Schroeder). Researchers Jennifer
Lawless and Sean Theriault conclude that women's early retirements may work
against their accumulating sufficient seniority to achieve powerful committee
positions. Members of the House who have served for a long time without
attaining powerful positions were more likely to retire than both long-serving,
powerful members and newly elected members.[50] In this sense, some members
encounter "career ceilings." Furthermore, the more satisfied members are with
their careers, the longer they are likely to stay. Positional considerations played
a more central role in women's decision to leave. Whereas men seem more or
less satisfied by service in the House, women appear to need policy influence
to satisfy their career goals. When their initial goals have been met and no new
challenges in the form of substantive leadership positions present themselves,
women are likely to leave the House, thereby foreclosing the additional power
and influence that accrues with seniority. Thus, women's numeric underrepresentation is exacerbated by the fact that women are less likely to hold leadership positions in the institutional power hierarchies in Congress. If men and
women did not differ in their policy priorities, perhaps it wouldn't matter.
However, there is clear evidence that women and men in public office pursue
distinctly different agendas.

Policy Priorities

The contemporary focus on women as "different" is in part fueled by psychologist Carol Gilligan's work on the moral reasoning of men and women.

Her book, *In a Different Voice*, provides theoretical fuel for political scientists to empirically test whether men's and women's approaches to policymaking differ in substantive ways. Lyn Kathlene's research shows that men tend to be more instrumental in their attitudes and behavior as policymakers, while women approach the world from a more contextual viewpoint.[51] As instrumentalists, men view individuals as situated within a hierarchical and competitive world, value the protection of individual rights, and are more likely to solve problems using an "ethic of justice." Alternatively, women view the world as a series of interdependent, connected relationships. Because Gilligan believes that women are more likely to see individuals in terms of their "symbiotic relationships" to others, she argues that women will approach problem solving from an "ethic of care." Using this framework, Kathlene interviewed state legislators in Colorado, analyzed transcripts of committee hearings, and conducted content analyses of 360 proposed bills in an effort to understand how men and women conceptualize problems and formulate policy solutions.[52] She found that on average women consulted more sources and used more resources to define problems and explore solutions. Men were more likely to rely on a few experts or to rely more heavily on information from lobbyists. These differences persisted regardless of party, age, or number of terms in the legislature.

Applying this research to a specific policy area, Kathlene interviewed forty-seven Colorado legislators about the problem of crime.[53] Again she found differences between the way men and women conceptualized the problem and the type of solutions they proposed as bills. Men tended to see criminals as individuals who had chosen a life of crime, whereas women most often viewed criminals within the broad context of social opportunities or, more accurately, the inequalities of social opportunities (e.g., disintegrating families, poverty, educational inequities). These differences persisted even across political party lines. In proposing policy solutions to stop crime, men focused on the crime itself and proposed bills with a short-term legal focus (increasing penalties; addressing criminal justice, prison administrative issues, and legal proceedings; or expanding existing laws to include new crimes). Women, however, adopted a long-term perspective, focused on crime prevention, and proposed bills that focused on intervention or rehabilitation. Some woman-sponsored bills also had a legal focus, but these constituted only 37 percent of the total crime-related bills sponsored by women. Eighty-three percent of the bills proposed by men became law in the year of Kathlene's study, while only 37 percent of the women's bills were passed. More specifically, all of the prevention and intervention bills sponsored by women were indefinitely postponed. Kathlene concludes, "Women's policy approaches are not understood or appreciated, but seen at best as tangential to the problem at hand."[54] At least in this narrow case, women did not substantively change the nature of the legislative discourse or policy outcomes regarding crime.

Sociologist Rosabeth Moss Kanter found that when members of a minority group made up 15 percent or less of the total membership of a group, the larger group perceived them as tokens. This token status changed their behavior, and these minority-group members tended to respond to their differential status in "unnatural" ways. As minorities in organizations reached "tilted" status (between 15 and 40 percent of the whole) or approached a "balanced" status (defined as a 60–40 split), they were able to respond in an unrestrained fashion. Building on a theoretical framework first proposed by Kanter,[55] political scientist Sue Thomas hypothesized that as the percentage of women in a legislative body increases, so too does the likelihood that women legislators will sponsor more bills relating to women, children, and the family. Likewise, in states with more women legislators, the passage rates for bills on women, children, and the family will be higher.[56] Thomas's study of women in twelve state legislatures found that in states with more than 20 percent women legislators, women gave priority to bills related to women, children, and the family more often than men did. In states that had the lowest percentages of women in their legislatures, no bills related to women, children, and the family were introduced by either men or women.[57] Although women's presence alone did not alter the ethic of the legislature, in states with higher percentages of women or in legislatures with organized women's caucuses both women and men were more attentive to "women's issues."

In more recent research, however, the picture emerges slightly differently. Kathleen Bratton examined legislative behavior (agenda setting, bill sponsorship, number of women's interest bills passed) in three states over thirty years (1969–1999) and found little support for the expectation that women serving in legislative bodies where their status is that of "token" (institutions with less than 15 percent women) differed from their male colleagues; "indeed, gender differences in agenda-setting behavior in some states narrow as the percentage of women in the legislature increases."[58] She also found that women were at least as likely as men to pass legislation even present in very small numbers, and in two of the three states (California and Illinois), "token women" were actually more successful relative to men than their counterparts in more equitable settings. In exploring explanations for these findings that appear contrary to what Kanter's theory would predict, Bratton suggests women may respond to their token status with overachievement. More likely, the legislative and political contexts are substantively different than the corporate world Kanter used to develop her theory. Women elected officials are interested in "women's issues," they may have campaigned based on a women's agenda, and they are less likely to object to being singled out as a woman than females in the corporate world where identity has less relevance to the substantive work. Finally, Bratton is careful to point out that her findings do not mean that women do not encounter discrimination in the legislative body or process. "However, the likely *response* of women to discriminatory treatment is different from that of sales personnel in Kanter's study. Women serving as tokens in a political setting are quite likely to emphasize gender differences and successfully bring a different perspective to lawmaking." Overall, the aggregate results indicate that as the number of women in a legislature grows, the potential for changes in the lived experiences of female citizens improves.[59]

Although women have constituted greater numbers in local political office than at the state or national level, little research has been done on gender differences in style, priorities, or policy outcomes. This is in part because there are so many local officials and the contexts in which they function differ so dramatically (e.g., size of city, type of government, resources, etc.). However, in a study of mayors in cities with populations over 30,000, researchers found more similarities than differences between women and men on policy issues and the use of power. Significant differences were identified, however, in the budgetary process. Female mayors were more willing than male mayors to change the budget process and to admit fiscal problems existed. In describing how they would change the budgetary process, women were more inclusive and sought broader participation in the process. Men, if they were interested in change, sought more control over the budgetary process.[60]

Other research suggests that by their very presence women can alter the way male legislators talk about some issues.[61] Representative Steny Hoyer (D-MD) offers one perspective on women's influence: "The fact that we have appreciably increased the number of women has heightened issues of historical concern to women: women's health issues, reproductive rights issues, issues of the working family. Also because you have more women in Congress, there is greater attention to women's issues by men. Just by virtue of their presence, it serves as a reminder and raises the consciousness level on issues of concern to women."[62] Studies of women at the local legislative level have also found that their presence can lead to a new kind of politics. Janet Boles, for example, claimed that women legislators in Milwaukee, Wisconsin "sensitized" male legislators to women's issues.[63] Analysis of congressional debate on the Hyde Amendment offers empirical evidence of women's influence within the national legislative chamber. The Hyde Amendment, first passed by Congress in 1976 as a rider on the Health, Education, and Welfare Appropriations bill, prohibits the use of federal funds to pay for or promote abortion. The Hyde Amendment has been debated and altered numerous times, but is still in effect. A study based on content analysis of the Hyde Amendment debates for each year that it was considered between 1974 and 1997 (eight debates spanning twenty-four years) suggests that women made a difference on three distinct levels.[64] First, the language women used when discussing the Hyde Amendment differed considerably from that of men. Men were much more likely to characterize their support of the Hyde Amendment in terms of "the morality of killing an unborn child," to question the appropriateness of using public money to fund abortions, and to express no concern about the inequity of allowing wealthy women to fund abortions privately while in effect preventing poor women from receiving them. By contrast, women expressed concern about the impact of an abortion on a woman's health, argued that all women should have the same access to abortion regardless of income, and pointed to the constitutionality of abortion under *Roe v. Wade*. Second, men and women differed in their level of support for the Hyde Amendment. Looking only at men and women who spoke from the floor in debate, researchers found that, regardless of party, women were more likely than men to oppose the restrictions imposed by the Hyde Amendment. Finally, the participation of women in floor debates on the Hyde Amendment seems to have altered the way men talked about the issue over time. While women talked consistently about women's health issues across all eight debates, men talked more about health issues and less about the fetus over time, suggesting that women effectively reshaped the debate over the twenty-four-year time span. The more women in Congress and the more women participating in the floor debates, the more alike men's and women's rhetoric became. The study's authors conclude, "Our findings suggest that the presence of women in Congress does make a difference. The difference women make is not only in the fact that they vote differently and speak differently than men about abortion, but that their differences may be *changing* how men speak about abortion."[65]

HOW EFFECTIVELY DO WOMEN STAND FOR WOMEN'S INTERESTS?

Thomas's research, to some extent, tested the assumption that more women in office led to better representation of women's interests and showed that women officeholders render substantive representation, or stand for women and their interests. A study linking women's representation and women-friendly policy demonstrates a strong positive relationship between the proportion of women in legislative seats and executive positions across the fifty states and the adoption of policy favorable to women.[66] There is also some evidence that women officeholders provide an important form of symbolic representation in the form of political empowerment. Women represented by other women are more interested in politics, participate more, and have a greater sense of efficacy and political competence.[67] A study of men and women living in congressional districts served by female legislators found that women exhibited a sense of political empowerment, a sort of psychic benefit derived from being represented by a woman in Congress. Men, however, did not derive the same benefit. The statistical differences noted between men's empowerment when represented by a woman and alternatively by a man suggest that the effect on women is derived from a type of symbolic representation and not district-specific characteristics that could also explain the election of a woman. Interestingly, women do not appear to expect more in the way of tangible benefits when they are represented by a woman.[68] Whether women's satisfaction with mere symbolic representation will decline over time as female officeholders become a more integral part of governing remains to be seen. Presumably, tangible benefits could combine with symbolic empowerment to produce an even stronger relationship between the gender of constituents and their representatives.

Very little research has been done to investigate how partisanship shapes women's representation of women's issues. Since there are more Democratic women in office and Democrats are more likely to publicly advance a women-friendly policy agenda, we might assume that Republican women are silent on women's issues or that they speak in a more ideologically conservative voice. A study by Colleen Shogan demonstrates, however, that Republican and Democratic female House members invoke women in their public statements with the same frequency.[69] By moving beyond roll-call voting, Shogan was able to explore how women take positions on issues and how women profess to represent women in their rhetoric captured in *Congressional Record* entries of the 105th Congress (1997). Republican and Democratic women differed very little in the frequency of woman-invoked rhetoric (the overall amount of rhetoric is higher for Democrats because there are more of them), but the content of their remarks differed in interesting ways. One issue was salient to both groups of women: abortion. Nearly one-third of all speeches invoking women were arguments about abortion policy (either prochoice or pro-life). Beyond abortion, Democratic women tended to dedicate more of their rhetoric to paying tribute to female achievements (20 percent of the total, compared to 11 percent for Republican women). Republican women discussed the effects of personal economics on women at a higher frequency than Democratic women (18 percent versus 8.6 percent for Democrats). Health issues also ranked higher for Republican women (24.5 percent, compared to 15.4 percent for Democrats). Foreign policy received little attention from either group of female representatives (3 percent overall). Most surprisingly, speeches referring to gender equity or civil rights consumed only 3 percent of the rhetoric overall (4.5 percent for Democrats and less than 1 percent for Republicans)! Democratic women of color devoted less time than white women to speaking about women and addressed different concerns than did white Democratic women. Shogan attributes this difference to their need to address the concerns of multiple constituencies, consistent with other studies in which black legislators define their constituencies more broadly than whites to include "all blacks and disadvantaged people within the United States."[70]

African American women in Congress constitute a rather small but highly visible group. They face additional expectations about their behavior as legislators, and feel pressure to represent the interests of both women and African Americans. Their dilemma again stems from difficulty in defining a constituency based on some essential characteristic that may or may not unite members of the minority group around a common agenda. "We're expected to be representatives on economic issues, health issues, housing issues, the issue of incarceration of black males and drugs," says Maxine Waters, a Democratic congresswoman from California. "But at the same time, because of the nature of this job and the nature of our work, it creates the need to be assertive. And sometimes [women lawmakers] are criticized for being too aggressive. Somehow, there is a desire for [women] to be tough, but not to show it, or to be aggressive, but to mask it in ways that men are not asked to do."[71] Eleanor Holmes Norton, the nonvoting delegate from the District of Columbia, says that her preparation to represent dual interests stems from a lifetime's experience with both racism and sexism:

> Much of my view of women comes out of the life I've lived and the commitments I've made long before even thinking about running for Congress. Growing up in a segregated city and going to segregated schools raised my consciousness very early about [racial] discrimination. . . . The transfer of that from blacks to women was almost automatic. . . . By the time I got to Congress, my view on women and my feeling of responsibility for pressing forward their demands was very well formed. . . . This was just another place, another forum, to act on them.[72]

Very few studies have been conducted on minority women's behavior as public officials, maybe because of the relatively small sample of minority officials to study. In 2009, twenty of the ninety women in Congress are women of color (twelve African American, six Latina, two Asian Pacific Islander). Seven statewide elected executives (9.5 percent) and 349 state legislators (19.5 percent) were women of color. Among mayors in the nation's 100 largest cities, there are currently three women of color serving (in Atlanta, Baltimore, and Greensboro, NC).[73] African American women serving in southern state legislatures report that the biggest impediments to securing elective office have been structural (e.g., inability of black voters to register and vote, white gerrymandering plans that fragmented black voting power, and white vote-dilution tactics).[74] Interviews conducted with African American state legislators revealed that, once elected, women seek influence on issues that directly benefit their communities. "Specific issues included social benefits to families, especially poor women and their children; women's reproductive rights; issues of concern to African American women, including forced sterilization; reform of the criminal justice system; and educational and job opportunities." African American women pursue these issue priorities through assignment to committees with appropriate jurisdiction. Women reported that although they felt relatively confident that they could effectively pursue their policy agenda through committee work, their ability to expand their agenda was constrained by the attitudes of African American male colleagues, who viewed black women as merely supporters of their own political objectives and agendas. They also reported difficulties working productively with white female colleagues at times. "Long accustomed to exercising white-skin privilege, some white female legislators refrain from working with African American female legislators as equals in addressing and seeking solutions to problems. Some respondents charged that conflicting loyalties meant that some white women legislators 'sell out' African American women if the issue is constructed in such a way that assistance and resources can be racially determined."[75] More research in this area beyond the experiences of women in the South would enrich our understanding of the diversity among women and of the way individual politicians deal with the dual identities of race and gender when representing their constituents and acting within the legislative arena.

Institutional constraints may also prove to be powerful limitations on the ways in which women of color exercise power once elected to office. Mary Hawkesworth argues that "racing-gendering" within institutions like Congress creates a political process that "silences, stereotypes, enforces invisibility, excludes and challenges the epistemic authority of Congresswomen of color."[76] Hawkesworth analyzed qualitative data based on interviews with eighty-one congresswomen, including fifteen women of color who served in the 103rd and 104th Congresses. She found the narratives of congresswomen of color to be markedly different from those of white congresswomen, containing tales of insult, humiliation, frustration, and anger. The case of welfare reform best illuminated the intersection of race and gender for women in Congress. Although largely shut out of the legislative process surrounding the debate and formation of new welfare policy, the women of color did not shy away. Instead, their response could be characterized as "resistance and the political mobilization of anger that racing-gendering engenders."[77] To confront racialized stereotypes of welfare recipients, congresswomen of color tried to inject social science research into the debate. A 1993 conference on "Women and Welfare Reform: Women's Opportunities and Women's Welfare," sponsored by the Institute for Women's Policy Research, Inc. and cochaired by Representatives Patsy Mink (D-HI), Maxine Waters (D-CA), Ed Pastor (D-AZ), and Lynn Woolsey (D-CA, and the only person in Congress to have ever received welfare), resulted in an alternative welfare reform bill that included a proposal for a living wage, education and training opportunities, job creation, and child-care and transportation allowances. When the 104th Congress convened, the Republicans were in the majority and Republican welfare reform proposals framed poverty as a matter of "personal responsibility" rather than as structural in nature. Although all congresswomen of color actively worked to get measures from their alternative bill incorporated into the majority's proposal, they were spectacularly unsuccessful. Empirical arguments were overwhelmed by myths about welfare, race, and gender. Hawkesworth concludes that although their "opposition was intense and consistent across two Congresses . . . their stories of marginalization and thwarted effort, of the silencing of reason and evidence, and of the pervasive racing-gendering of welfare recipients and Congresswomen of color provide a resounding indictment of this form of majority rule."[78] Women's ability to speak for and act for women is clearly constrained in a number of ways by the culture and norms of the institution in which they operate.

The Role of a Women's Caucus in Facilitating Legislation for Women

Several studies note that an organized caucus for women's interests facilitates favorable legislation for women. Sue Thomas found that without gender balance or a critical mass of women in state legislatures, women's caucuses were instrumental in bringing attention to issues related to women, children, and families.[79] "When a caucus bands together, the result is political clout—a weapon with the potential to overcome skewed groups."[80] The percentage of women in the U.S. Congress has increased more slowly than that of women in state legislatures. In 1977, when only eighteen women (a little more than 3 percent) sat in Congress, fifteen of those eighteen women founded the Congresswomen's Caucus, later renamed the Congressional Caucus for Women's Issues (CCWI). Since its inception, the women's caucus has been a bipartisan organization cochaired by a Democrat and a Republican. To extend the caucus's influence, the Women's Research and Education Institute (WREI) was also founded in 1977 and remained organizationally linked to the caucus until 1985.[81] The caucus had two early policy successes in the 95th Congress: a bill preventing employer discrimination against pregnant women and attention to gender disparities in federal employment and Social Security benefits.[82] Beyond these, women had little success convincing the overwhelmingly male Congress that women's issues were not only linked to one another, but were also embedded in programs that initially seemed unrelated to "women's issues." That changed in 1978 when the caucus mobilized colleagues to extend the life of the Equal Rights Amendment. Besides the extension, which few thought possible, its members put Congress on notice that they were capable of moving legislation and setting policy priorities favorable to women's interests.

The CCWI provided two functions: to advocate for women and families, and to serve as an information clearinghouse on women's issues in Congress. During the 1980s and early 1990s, the CCWI introduced and sponsored several omnibus legislative packages, including the Economic Equity Act (1981), the Family and Medical Leave Act (1985), the Women's Health Equity Act (1990), and the Violence Against Women Act (1993). Portions of each of these packages have now been adopted into law. In addition, the caucus brought new attention to the issue of breast cancer and won approval to earmark more than $500 million for breast cancer research. The caucus's most successful legislative session was the 103rd Congress (1993–1994), during which sixty-six measures of direct benefit to women and families were passed and signed into law. The caucus also endorsed reproductive rights, ending a fifteen-year self-imposed silence on the divisive issue. Patricia Schroeder remarked that the 103rd Congress "should finally put to rest the question, 'What difference does having more women in Congress make?'"[83] Although there were victories, how successful was the CCWI in establishing a legislative agenda that was compatible with women's interests?

The CCWI suffered organizational difficulties during the early 1980s as founding members either retired, were defeated, or passed away. Attracting new members proved difficult in the 1980s, particularly among newly elected Republican women. For a variety of reasons (unwillingness to pay membership dues, wariness of affiliation with "women's issues," or a fear of alienating the conservative Reagan administration), membership lagged, and the caucus's ability to influence the legislative agenda diminished substantially. In 1981, the CCWI took dramatic steps to extend its influence and opened its membership to men. Over time, the caucus grew from one of the smallest legislative service organizations to one of the largest. New bylaws restricted membership on its executive committee to women only but retained the bipartisan cochair arrangement, as well as its tradition of focusing on issues that united women. During the 103rd Congress, the caucus's membership included forty-two of the forty-eight women in the House as well as the speaker of the House, the majority leader, the majority whip, and a number of powerful committee and subcommittee chairs.[84] This resurgence was short lived. When the Republicans took over Congress after the 1994 elections, rule changes stripped legislative service organizations of their budgets, staff, and office space. As a result, the CCWI reorganized as a congressional member organization, and three former staff members established a nonprofit organization called Women's Policy, Inc. (WPI) to carry on the caucus's weekly newsletter and information services.[85]

As a member organization, the CCWI welcomes all members of the House of Representatives and continues to be cochaired by a Democratic and a Republican member. In the 111th Congress (2009–2011), Representatives Jan Schakowsky (D-IL) and Mary Fallin (R-OK) will serve as cochairs. With membership now totaling 78 (including the three delegates from U.S. territories), it is one of the largest in Congress, outnumbered only by the party caucuses in each chamber. The U.S. Senate does not have a caucus of women or for women's issues, nor are they included in the House caucus membership. However, the seventeen women in the Senate (thirteen Democrats, four Republicans) meet regularly and are hosted by the most senior female member of the Senate, Barbara Mikulski (D-MD). Mikulski quipped, "We're not a caucus, we're a force. We believe every issue is a women's issue."[86] Women are expected to play a key leadership role in other congressional caucuses. Representative Barbara Lee (D-CA) will chair the Congressional Black Caucus, Representative Nydia Valazquez (D-NY) will chair the Congressional Hispanic Caucus, and Delegate Madeleine A. Ordallo (D-GU) will serve as secretary of the Asian Pacific American Caucus.

Research on the CCWI's effectiveness prior to its change in status showed that the organization was moderately successful in shaping the agenda of the 103rd Congress on issues of women's health, abortion rights, and health-care reform.[87] Women in the CCWI were able to transform the area of women's health from an invisible issue to one that is politically highly charged. As one Capitol Hill lobbyist explained, "If the women had not been there, there would be no women's health agenda. There never would have been. I think they are wholly and completely responsible."[88] The caucus began work on women's health in the 101st Congress by introducing the Women's Health Equity Act (WHEA), an eighteen-item omnibus bill designed to address inequities in the treatment of women's health issues. By using the WHEA as the cornerstone of future initiatives on women's health, legislators increased the number of bills on women's health to thirty-two by the 103rd Congress. What's more, women had sponsored twenty-three of those thirty-two bills. Women's health is a good example of an issue that brings women together regardless of party or political ideology. The bills on women's health came from women on both sides of the partisan aisle. Researcher Debra Dodson attributes three factors to women's success in getting Congress to focus on women's health: First, allocating more federal dollars for health research allowed women to avoid partisan or ideological divides that often derailed other initiatives. Second, the rise of a grassroots movement to fight breast cancer put pressure from their constituents on members of Congress to support women's health issues and to take women's health more seriously overall. Finally, there was no organized opposition to women's health. Of all the issues the CCWI pursued, it was most successful in shaping the overall congressional agenda and in seeing legislation enacted in the area of women's health.

Abortion rights was a more divisive issue than women's health, both within and outside the caucus. Although the caucus had voted to take a pro-choice stance on abortion rights, not every member agreed, and the internal divisions limited the organization's ability to promote bipartisan solidarity on the issue. Unlike women's health, abortion rights had a well-developed opposition to overcome. African American women were instrumental in setting the CCWI's priorities on reproductive rights. Until then, the focus on reproductive rights had been the Freedom of Choice Act (FOCA). FOCA attempted to protect a woman's access to abortion and to limit the restrictions states could impose on abortion services. Rather than support FOCA, African American members argued that the CCWI should push for funding and the removal of barriers to funding for poor women covered under Medicaid. The differences in priorities reflected the differences among the women members themselves and among the constituencies they were elected to represent. Ultimately the caucus agreed to push for funding as their top priority. In the same session, Congressman Don Edwards reintroduced FOCA without consulting either the senior congresswomen or the CCWI. The caucus's dedication to pursuing funding for poor women eventually robbed Edwards of the energy he needed to push FOCA, which died before reaching the floor for debate. Although women were ultimately unsuccessful in procuring funding guarantees, House members clearly understood that neither senior women nor the caucus could be ignored in setting the reproductive-rights agenda in the future. The caucus's success in the area of reproductive rights was limited to demonstrating their power to grant or to withhold its support for particular legislation consistent with its own priorities as an organization. To many, the caucus's decision to forgo support for FOCA in favor of pursuing Medicaid funding seemed shortsighted since in the end they lost both bills. In the long term though, the caucus strengthened its position within the institution as an integral player in setting the congressional agenda.

Finally, in the area of healthcare reform, women were able to insert into the Clinton healthcare package a number of narrow provisions on services for women. Women were less successful in shaping healthcare reform than in either of the previous two issue areas because of the breadth of the overall initiative and the level of organized opposition that quickly developed to the Clinton plan. Women were successful in highlighting women's health concerns within the larger debate. Members of the caucus met with Hillary Rodham Clinton, chair of the Health Care Task Force, early in the process to talk about women's health priorities. The caucus urged the task force to improve the coverage for mammograms, pap smears, and pelvic exams in the basic benefits package.

Researcher Debra Dodson concluded that although women and the CCWI were successful in bringing significant new attention to women's health, reproductive rights, and healthcare reform, successfully passing legislation still largely depends on women's positions within the traditional institutional power structure—serving on relevant committees, chairing committees and subcommittees, and earning seniority as legislative leaders. "Until women are chairs of powerful and key committees, hold half the leadership positions, and have the expertise that comes through years of experience, they will have to continue to build the strong ties to male colleagues that enable them to accomplish goals they could not otherwise accomplish."[89] This also implies that until more women are elected, rise to power, and become a more visible presence in the institution, their power to set and to enact legislation that is favorable to women's interests will be limited.

The Congressional Caucus for Women's Issues agenda for the 111th Congress includes expanded funding and support for research and treatment in women's health matters, in particularly, heart disease. Heart disease is the leading cause of death for women in the United States. The CCWI has supported a bill that would require extensive research on heart disease in women; implementation of a nationwide education campaign; and development of a national heart disease screening program for women. Similar legislation passed the House in the previous Congress, but was not acted upon by the Senate. In addition, the CCWI agenda for 2009–2011 includes the bipartisan issues of equal pay, human trafficking, sexual and domestic violence, and women in the military. The Military Domestic and Sexual Violence Response Act, supported by the CCWI, aims to prevent, prosecute, and treat sexual assault in the military. The Caucus was a strong advocate for the expansion of family and medical leave to allow a family member up to 26 weeks a year of unpaid leave from their job to care for a service member with a serious duty-related injury. Previously, the standard 12 weeks of unpaid leave applied and parents and siblings of the affected service member were not eligible for the leave. The CCWI is also expected to be active in the debates over health-care reform, elevated on the nation's agenda by the election of President Barack Obama. This issue, unlike others specifically adopted by the CCWI, is likely to expose the partisan differences among female members. For that reason, the organization has chosen to stay out of issues like universal health insurance and abortion, even though such issues are uniquely significant to women and the organization's absence from the debates limits women's collective voice.[90]

On Saturday, November 7, 2009, as the U.S. House of Representatives neared a final vote on health care reform (America's Affordable Health Choices Act of 2009), Representative Bart Stupak (D-MI) offered an amendment barring any insurance plan that is purchased with government subsidies from covering abortions except in cases of life-threatening situations. The amendment passed (240–19) and subsequently the healthcare bill passed by a narrow margin, 220–215. Representative Diana DeGette, cochair of the Pro-Choice Caucus, claims that the bill violates the principle of "abortion neutrality" urged by President Obama—meaning access to abortion should not be enhanced or restricted under any new health care law. Under the new legislation, individuals could not purchase private insurance that covers abortion if they receive a government subsidy to make health coverage affordable. Currently, some 85 percent of private insurance plans in the U.S. cover abortion services. In a letter to the president signed by forty other Democrats, congresswoman DeGette warned: "We will not vote for a final bill that contains language that restricts women's right to choose any further than current law." This bill will eventually have to be resolved with any bill passed by the Senate prior to a vote on final passage. The controversy illustrates again the divergent views of women and the difficulty in identifying a single women's agenda.[91]

The Difficulty in Defining "Women's Interests"

Although the CCWI was a bipartisan organization, members often differ along partisan lines in defining "women's interests." Historically, if feminists have felt comfortable with either of the two parties, it has been with the Democrats. As women officeholders become more diverse in terms of their ideology, partisanship, and interests, it produces interesting controversies as to who is actually "standing for" women. Additionally, women officeholders must make decisions and take actions "inside" that appear to "outsiders" as if they are compromising their feminist principles and selling out women's interests. Three cases illustrate this point: the debates leading up the Persian Gulf War and the welfare reform vote in the 104th Congress, and the inclusion of Medicaid funding for family planning in the 2008 economic stimulus package.

In 1991, Congress spent three days debating resolutions authorizing the use of force in Iraq. The debate was prompted by the news that Saddam Hussein and his Iraqi military force had invaded Kuwait, removed the ruling family, and taken over the oil production facilities. The Persian Gulf War ensued in an attempt to drive Hussein from Kuwait, restore the previous government and ruling family to power, and maintain the stability of the Middle East. The terms of the debate were largely framed around world power, the importance of stability in the Middle East, and the United States' strategic interests in maintaining the flow of oil from the region. Only one woman, Barbara Boxer, raised issues related to women and war during the congressional debates. More than 32,000 women soldiers served in the Persian Gulf War, the highest number of women ever to serve in an armed conflict. Some in the media dubbed the operation a "mommy's war" because of the large number of women with children in the U.S. forces. The footage of women in fatigues kissing their children good-bye again raised questions among some about the appropriateness of women in the armed forces. However, others believed that women's presence in both the military forces and Congress should have influenced the decision to go to war in the first place. Arguing that "power-over" politics silenced congresswomen during the debates over the war, author Adrienne Elizabeth Christiansen suggests that women nevertheless should have spoken out in defense of women and war issues. Power-over politics is defined as the use of force to get one's way. In her essay, Christiansen argues that even though women were present in Congress for the debate, they were effectively silenced since they lacked the military experience that lends legitimacy to participants in such a debate. Without legitimacy, the issues they might have raised about women, children, and the environment went unaddressed. In short, "until women and men are able to directly challenge the underlying assumptions of power-over politics and this conceptual framework, wars will continue to be fought and the effect on women and the environment will continue to seem irrelevant."[92] This argument assumes that women's perspective on issues related to war differs substantively from men's and it again raises the question of "essential" characteristics related to gender. Are men by nature more aggressive and prone to violence than women?[93] Is a government run by men more likely to engage in wars than a government run by women? These remain hypothetical questions since we do not have any empirical observations on which to base an answer. However, these questions and others about the Persian Gulf War, as well as those about women in the military and women's role in Congress as it debates the use of force, again raise the paradox of gender equality as it relates to women's ability to define and stand for women's interests. Are women's interests the same as men's or do women have a unique set of concerns that only women representatives in government can adequately address?

The same questions have been raised about women's interests and welfare reform. As the Republican leadership and the Clinton administration worked to "end welfare as we know it," women members were openly chastised in several quarters for failing to influence the content and character of the legislation. Republicans, in control of both houses of Congress by 1995, proposed to replace the welfare system known as Aid to Families with Dependent Children (AFDC) with a much smaller program administered largely by the states through block grants. The biggest change in the proposal was to eliminate entitlement to welfare benefits. Under AFDC, single women with children who met the income qualifications were entitled to receive support for their children. The new legislation proposed a five-year lifetime benefit cap with some leeway for states to enact their own restrictions. Welfare-rights advocates cited studies that predicted the new legislation would force 1.1 million more children into poverty. When the final vote came, only Senator Carol Mosely Braun joined ten male Democratic senators to vote against the bill. The sharp rhetoric surrounding the welfare debate and its particular focus on blaming poor women for the ills of the welfare system prompted few public objections from women in Congress. This silence led columnist and feminist critic Katha Pollitt to condemn the congresswomen's inaction as more "business as usual." "The truth is," Pollitt wrote, "except on a few high-profile issues—abortion rights, sexual harassment, violence against women—electoral feminism is a pretty pallid affair: a little money for breast cancer research here, a boost for women business owners there. The main job of the women is the same as that of the men: playing toward the center, amassing campaign funds, keeping business and big donors happy, and currying favor with the leadership in hopes of receiving plums."[94] One Washington-based activist summed up her disappointment, characterizing the conflict women officeholders face in trying to become effective insiders, "They [congresswomen] didn't want to be marginalized, they wanted to be at the table, and they wanted Bill Clinton to like them."[95]

The National Organization for Women, while it committed considerable resources to fighting the welfare changes, still felt compelled to write an op-ed piece defending the women who voted in favor of the bill that NOW labeled anti-woman:

> When the Senate voted recently for the harsh Republican welfare repeal bill, Senator Carol Mosely Braun stood alone among the women senators in opposing it. This did not go unnoticed by reporters. Despite their invitations, we resisted the temptation to lash out at the other women senators and renounce our strategy of electing more feminist women. We are convinced that real, lasting change can only come from having women's rights supporters both outside and inside the system—in much larger numbers. While activists must hold insiders accountable, even when they are operating in an ugly, hostile climate, we must also recognize the valuable roles each of us plays. . . . It took more than 70 years to get women the vote in this country. We know it will take years longer before we build the critical mass to wield a fair share of power on Capitol Hill.[96]

In January 2009, the new Obama administration presented Congress with a package of bills designed to stimulate the economy. Included in the $825 billion dollar package was a $200 million dollar provision that would have allowed states to cover family planning services and supplies (contraceptives) to low-income women who are not eligible for Medicaid *without* the state seeking a federal waiver. States could continue, under the provision, to use the existing waiver authority if they preferred. At the time of the debate, twenty-seven states were already funding such services with a waiver, but many had asked for relief from the waiver requirement due to excessive administrative delays. House Minority Leader John Boehner (R-OH) claimed that the package would "spend hundreds of millions on contraceptives" igniting a political and ideological firestorm. House Speaker Nancy Pelosi defended the inclusion of the provision by saying, "Family planning services reduce cost. They reduce cost. The states are in terrible fiscal budget crises now and part of what we do for children's health, education and some of those elements are to help the states meet their financial

"It Was a Vote of Conscience"

O N SEPTEMBER 15, 2001, the U.S. Congress approved a resolution authorizing President Bush to use "all necessary and appropriate force" against anyone associated with the terrorist attacks of September 11. The measure passed on a vote of 98–0 in the Senate and 420–1 in the House of Representatives. Representative Barbara Lee, a Democrat from California, cast the lone dissenting vote. Unlike Jeannette Rankin, the first woman to be elected to the U.S. House of Representatives in 1916, Lee does not consider herself a pacifist. Rankin voted against America's entry into World Wars I and II, and she was the only member of Congress to oppose the declaration of war on Japan. Only four days after taking office, Rankin broke with chamber protocol by speaking during the roll call before casting her vote, declaring "I want to stand by my country, but I cannot vote for war. I vote no."

Representative Lee, the daughter of a retired lieutenant colonel in the U.S. Army, said on the House floor, "I am convinced that military action will not prevent further acts of international terrorism against the United States. There must be some who say, 'Let's step back for a moment and think through the implications of our actions today—let's more fully understand the consequences.'"[1] The price for Lee's vote of conscience has been twenty-four-hour police protection in the face of numerous death threats. In her office the phone lines shut down under the weight of thousands of phone calls from all over the country—many irate, some of them threatening.

> Some people are calling me un-American and all that. I know that I'm unified with our country. . . . I know that my actions are as American as anyone else's. I'm trying to preserve the people's right to have some kind of oversight and some say in the cycle of violence that could occur if we go into war without an end in sight. The Congress has a responsibility to provide the checks and balances and to exercise some oversight. I don't believe we should disenfranchise the people of America in

needs. One of those—one of the initiatives you mentioned, the contraception, will reduce costs to the states and to the federal government." The political debate soon escalated to include charges that the stimulus bill would federally "fund the abortion industry." When the Congressional Budget Office (CBO) assessed a virtually identical provision in 2007, it found that it would save the federal government $200 million over five years by helping women voluntarily avoid pregnancies that otherwise would result in Medicaid-funded births. Feminist and women's reproductive health organizations argued that as women lost their jobs, they also lost their health insurance and would be less likely to be able to afford contraception leading to unintended pregnancies. "The Medicaid Family Planning State Option fully belonged in the economic recovery package," said Marcia D. Greenberger, co-president of the National Women's Law Center. "The Republican leadership opposition to the provision shows how out of touch they are with what it takes to ensure the economic survival of the war-making decision making process. At least minimally, we should be able to know which nation we're planning to attack and have some input into that. . . . I try to explain my position, but there are some people who are just angry, and that's understandable. But I believe that many people in our country . . . are beginning to understand what the use of restraint means . . . . they understand when you explain that this resolution gives up a congressional role in declaring war against a sovereign nation. And that does not mean that you don't want these terrorists to come to justice, that you don't want to stamp out terrorism. That's not even a question.[2]

Consider the following:

- Unlike Jeannette Rankin, Representative Barbara Lee did not lose her seat because of her vote. In exercising a "different voice," Barbara Lee stood alone. Do you believe that women are likely to exercise a "vote of conscience" more often than men? On what basis might women's experiences prompt them to vote differently on questions of war?
- Rankin was very active in the suffrage movement, serving as the field secretary of the National American Woman Suffrage Association (NAWSA) from 1912 until she returned to Montana to organize for suffrage and to seek her seat in Congress in 1916. Some of her NAWSA colleagues, including Carrie Chapman Catt, decried her antiwar vote, believing it opened the suffrage cause to criticism as "impractical and sentimental." Thinking back to the arguments for and against suffrage in chapter 2, how is Catt's concern related to the paradox of gender equality?

1. Peter Carlson, "The Solitary Vote of Barbara Lee," *Washington Post*, September 19, 2001, p. C01.
2. Bill Hogan, "Alone on the Hill," *Mother Jones.com*, September 20, 2001, accessed at http://www.motherjones.com/news/feature/2001/09/lee.html.

working women and their families." Ultimately, at President Obama's request, congressional Democrats removed the provision from the bill. With a female Speaker of the House, Democratic Party majorities in the House and Senate, and a Democrat in the White House, reproductive rights advocates viewed this move as an unnecessary capitulation to the ideological Right and a bad sign for women's reproductive health interests in the future.[97]

What is women's role in defining and promoting women's interests? To argue that women alone are responsible for protecting women, children, and the vulnerable in society suggests again that women have some quality in their nature that men lack. Does this line of reasoning promote women's equality or relegate women to the sidelines of institutional politics? As we've seen repeatedly, not all women think alike or act alike. The conflicting expectations for women in public office, born of the paradox of gender equality, create a complex environment for women insiders.

Women in the Executive Branch

The Office of Personnel Management is the human resources arm of the federal government. The Pendleton Civil Service Act of 1883 established a nonpartisan federal workforce. The Pendleton Act classified certain jobs, removed them from the patronage ranks, and set up the Civil Service Commission to administer a system based on merit rather than political connections. As the classified list was expanded over the years, it provided the American people with a competent and permanent government bureaucracy. By 1897, almost half of all federal employees were in classified positions. Today, with the exception of a few thousand policy-level appointments, nearly all federal jobs are handled within the civil service system. Although hiring is presumably based on merit, women still occupy a smaller percentage of the federal civil service workforce, have historically been overrepresented in the lower grades (meaning they are paid less), and are less likely than men to qualify for the preferences granted to veterans. Between 1992 and 2002, the percentage of women executive branch employees (excluding postal service employees) rose from 43.5 percent to 44.6 percent.[98] The percentage of women in white-collar occupations has remained fairly steady in the decade between 1992 and 2002, averaging 49.6 percent of the total. In 2002, women held 35.8 percent of all jobs in the General Schedule and Related grades 12–15, compared to 25.2 percent in 1992. Between 1998 and 2006, women's share of the jobs in the lowest grades decreased by 30 percent while their share of the jobs in the highest grades increased by 42.6 percent. Women's share of all executive branch jobs in 2006 was 44.2 percent. They are most heavily represented in the Department of Health and Human Services (62.1 percent of all employees) and constitute the lowest percentage of employees at the Department of Labor (just 2 percent of 15,324 employees). The General Schedule grade determines salary, and GS grade 12–13 is considered the gateway to professional/supervisory positions. In 1999, women's average GS grade was 8.4, while men's was 10.4. Correspondingly, women's salaries averaged $39,593 to men's $49,114. Women are less evident in the highest-paying Senior Executive Service positions, making up just 26 percent in 2004. Upon the release of the 1999 report "Women in the Federal Government: A Statistical Profile," Office of Personnel Management Director Janice R. Lachance remarked, "The report shows that while the glass ceiling hasn't completely shattered, women are lifting it to new heights. I am confident that this will continue."[99] The Office of Personnel Management has developed resources designed to improve recruitment, retention, and career development for women. Overall, the rate of female employment in the federal workforce (44.2 percent) does not differ much from that of the civilian labor force (45.6 percent) in 2008. African American women (10.9 percent versus 5.3 percent) and Native American (1 percent versus 0.3 percent) women are more heavily represented among federal workers than in the civilian labor force.[100]

Women in the Federal Judiciary

To date, 110 justices have served on the U.S. Supreme Court, and two have been women. Justice Sandra Day O'Connor was the first woman appointed to the Court in 1981 and was later joined by Justice Ruth Bader Ginsburg in 1993. Justice O'Connor announced her retirement on July 1, 2005, leaving Justice Ginsburg as the only woman on the Court. On May 1, 2009, Justice David Souter announced his retirement giving President Barack Obama his first opportunity for a judicial nomination. On May 26, 2009, President Obama nominated sitting Federal Appeals Court Judge Sonia Maria Sotomayor to fill the vacancy and upon her confirmation, she became the third woman and the first Hispanic to serve on the U.S. Supreme Court. Justice Ginsburg openly advocated for a woman to join her on the Court: "Women belong in all places where decisions are being made. I don't say [the split] should be 50–50. It could be 60% men, 40% women, or the other way around. It shouldn't be that women are the exception." Following Justice O'Connor's retirement, Ginsburg has been more vocal about her belief that her eight male colleagues may not understand the discrimination women face. In a recent case involving a 13-year-old girl who was strip-searched by Arizona school officials looking for drugs, Ginsburg said, "They have never been a 13-year-old girl. It's a very sensitive age for a girl. I didn't think that my colleagues, some of them, quite understood." She was perturbed enough by her colleagues' lack of understanding in the Lilly Ledbetter pay discrimination case that she took the unusual step of reading her dissenting opinion from the bench and called upon Congress to reverse the Court (which they did at the start of the 111th Congress—see chapter 7). The court ruled in Ledbetter that women could not sue for pay inequities resulting from sex discrimination that had occurred years earlier. Ginsburg claimed that her male colleagues showed "a certain lack of understanding" of the bias women can face on the job. Similarly, in a case over awarding credit toward pension benefits during maternity leave, Ginsburg claimed, "Discrimination on the basis of pregnancy is surely discrimination on the basis of sex."[101]

In 1970, women made up only 5.4 percent of law school students and only 4.7 percent of all attorneys. Candidates for federal judgeships are generally twenty years out of law school, thus the pipeline for judicial appointments has only recently begun to fill with highly qualified women eligible for appointment to the federal bench. Title IX, discussed at length in the next chapter, is largely responsible for eliminating the "quotas" on the number of women admitted to law programs. In 2009, about half of all law degrees were awarded to women and about one-third of attorneys are women.

Only eight women had served as federal judges before 1977, when President Jimmy Carter unveiled his plan to diversify the federal courts. Carter added forty-one women to the judiciary, amounting to 16 percent of his judicial appointments. By comparison, the Kennedy and Johnson administrations were together responsible for appointing just four women to lifetime appointments;

Nixon and Ford combined to add just two more women to the bench.[102] The high point for women's appointment to the judiciary came in the Clinton administration. During his first term in office, 30 percent of his judicial nominees were women; in his second term, 28.7 percent of his nominees were women. In 2008, 47 of the 163 active judges sitting on the federal courts of appeal were female (29 percent) and around twenty-five percent of U.S. district court judges were women.[103] Although there are more women attorneys and judges in the justice system today, research is somewhat mixed on whether gender matters in this context. While no one could disagree that increasing women's representation in the judiciary is a significant form of descriptive representation, whether women jurists substantively represent women through their decisions is less clear. Some feminists argue that the presence of women in the legal system will have a profound impact because female lawyers and judges "bring a different perspective to the law, employ different methods, and reach different conclusions."[104] When presented with an opportunity to make a nomination to the U.S. Supreme Court, President Obama acknowledged the importance of "life experience" in judicial decision-making:

> The process of selecting someone to replace Justice Souter is among my most serious responsibilities as President. So I will seek somebody with a sharp and independent mind and a record of excellence and integrity. I will seek someone who understands that justice isn't about some abstract legal theory or footnote in a casebook. It is also about how our laws affect the daily realities of people's lives—whether they can make a living and care for their families; whether they feel safe in their homes and welcome in their own nation.
>
> I view that quality of empathy, of understanding and identifying with people's hopes and struggles, as an essential ingredient for arriving as just decisions and outcomes. I will seek somebody who is dedicated to the rule of law, who honors our constitutional traditions, who respects the integrity of the judicial process and the appropriate limits of the judicial role. I will seek somebody who shares my respect for constitutional values on which this nation was founded, and who brings a thoughtful understanding of how to apply them in our time.[105]

Judge Sonia Sotomayor, a daughter of Puerto Rican parents who was raised in a Bronx public housing project and later went on to graduate *summa cum laude* from Princeton University and earn her law degree from Yale Law School, was his choice. In announcing her nomination he said, "When Sonia Sotomayor ascends those marble steps to assume her seat on the highest court in the land, America will have taken another important step towards realizing the ideal that is etched above its entrance: Equal justice under the law."[106] Instantly, conservative opponents claimed that she would not only be a "judicial activist" on the Court, but some in the movement latched onto a line from a 2001 lecture delivered at the University of California, Berkeley, School of Law as evidence of Sotomayor's "racism." She noted, "I would hope that a wise Latina woman with the richness of her experiences would more often than not reach a better conclusion than a white male who hasn't lived that life." Within the full context of the speech, Judge Sotomayor was exploring the role that life experience plays in all judicial decisions and she had been asked to speak directly to her life as a Latina jurist.[107]

Theories of feminist jurisprudence have been instrumental in reconceptualizing the way laws affecting employment, divorce, domestic violence, rape, reproductive rights, and sexual harassment are understood and interpreted. While researchers hypothesized that women judges would be more liberal than their male counterparts, studies comparing sentencing patterns of trial court judges, voting behavior on the U.S. Courts of Appeals, and decisions in cases involving criminal procedure found no significant differences between men and women.[108] Arguably, difference is most important in areas directly affecting women's rights and claims to equality. Particularly because issues like gender equality and reproductive rights are judicially created rights, representation by women in all aspects of the legal system is important. "The constitutional and statutory bases of women's rights are limited, which leaves the protection of such rights to the federal courts."[109] Similar to the research on women in Congress, a study of appellate court judges found that the presence of one or more females on an appeals court panel tended to alter the behavior of their male colleagues, particularly on issues of most concern to women.[110] Reviewing the existing scholarship on gender influence, Boyd, Epstein, and Martin found that in about one-third of approximately thirty previous studies, differences in the votes of male and female judges or differences in the votes of a panel of judges when one member is a woman could be identified. Their own study found that the probability of a judge ruling in favor of a plaintiff in a discrimination case decreases by 10 percent when the judge is a man. When a woman is on the panel, the likelihood that a male colleague will rule in favor of the plaintiff increases 12 to 16 percent. Law Professor Deborah Rhode urges caution in drawing conclusions from such research, "Even if such research cumulatively suggests that the sex of a judge does influence the outcome of certain cases, sex is by no means a reliable predictor of the voting behavior of any particular nominee. Much depends on other aspects of a judge's background and how they influence his or her world view. . . . In short, the importance of diversity in judicial appointments should neither be overlooked nor overstated."[111]

As the number of women in Congress, the executive branch, and the judiciary grows, women will increasingly face the contradictions inherent in the pursuit of equality. Even while promising a "different voice," women have found themselves quickly confronted with the practicalities of functioning within political institutions that may require behavior that is antithetical to their idea of "different." It will be important to watch this dynamic unfold as women's presence continues to grow in legislatures at the state and national levels. If women in government continue to be perceived as ineffective or no more effective than men in "standing for" the interests of women, then one of the primary arguments for women's election to positions of power will be undermined. The warnings of those wary of the "difference" argument's power to promote

Encountering the Controversies of Equality

If Women Don't Run the World, Maybe They Should

A 2001 World Bank report, *Engendering Development through Gender Equality in Rights, Resources, and Voice*,[1] explored the relationship between more equal rights for women and corruption in government. Citing a number of studies, the report poses two reasonable hypotheses to explain the negative relationship between gender equality and corruption in government. First, "if egalitarian and participatory societies are more likely to eschew gender discrimination and more likely to institute social checks and balances that make corrupt practices less profitable, then gender equality and corruption would appear to be negatively correlated." Alternatively, "there may be intrinsic differences in the behaviors of women and men that lead to cleaner government when more women are in key government positions."[2] Perhaps women are more "community oriented" and "selfless" than men and more likely to "exhibit generosity and altruism" than men? Analysis based on the World Values Survey in two decades (1981 and 1991) shows that women are "less accepting of dishonest or illegal behaviors" than men. The report draws several conclusions:

- While statistically significant gender differences are not found in all countries, gender-differentiated attitudes toward corruption seem to be more or less a worldwide phenomenon;
- Governments are less corrupt the more active women are in the labor force or politics; and
- Corruption falls as the proportion of parliamentary seats held by women rises.[3]

Yet, is there an alternative explanation? A 2003 study found evidence contrary to the "fairer sex" hypothesis and instead attributed the apparent relationship to indicators of a liberal democracy (i.e., rule of law, freedom of the press, frequent and free elections). Even though both women in government and liberal democracy are negatively related to political corruption, when both are included in the same statistical model, the effects of women in government disappear and liberal democratic institutions remained very powerful. Freedom of the press proved to be the strongest predictor of low corruption in government. Sifting through these various and conflicting studies, UNIFEM concluded, "more women in politics are not the cause of low corruption, but rather, democratic and transparent politics is correlated with low corruption, and the two create an enabling environment for more women to participate in politics."[4]

In the United States, the economic collapse of 2008–2009 prompted a number of surveys, commentaries by scholars, and speculation about whether Wall Street would have collapsed if women had been running corporate America. Marty Linksy, cofounder of Cambridge Leadership Associates, wrote, "There is little doubt that with more women in top positions in Wall Street and government, the economic crisis would have been less severe."[5] He and others make this claim based on research that find women are more risk averse than men. Deborah Kolb, Deloitte Ellen Gabriel Professor for Women and

Leadership at the Simmons School of Management, argues that reality is more nuanced, "Women tend to take the broader context into account in making decisions that entail risk to them and their organizations . . . so it is possible that having women in leadership roles might have lessened the severity of the crisis. . . ."[6]

Pew Research Center recently announced, "Americans believe women have the right stuff to be political leaders."[7] Based on a sample of 2,225 adults, women were rated more highly on five out of eight traits important to leadership. The public rated women as more honest (50% to 20% for men), intelligent (38% to 14%), compassionate (80% to 5%), outgoing (47% to 28%) and creative (62% to 11%). Women and men tied on "hardworking" and "ambitious" while men were perceived as more decisive than women by a ten-point margin (44% to 33%). Given that the public rated women higher on the traits of leadership, you might conclude that they would then say that, overall, women make better political leaders than men. No! Only 6 percent of the sample said that women make better leaders, compared with 21 percent who say men make the better leaders, while the majority (69%) says that men and women make equally good leaders. Probing more deeply into performance in office, Pew researchers found that women were rated higher than men on four public-office performance skills (working out a compromise, keeping government honest, representing your interests, and standing up for what they believe) and were perceived to be better at dealing with social policy, while men were believed to be better suited to deal with issues of crime and public safety, and national security and defense. Pew identifies this as a paradox—the public rates women's leadership ability and political skills highly, but few are elected to office or hold the highest positions in corporations.

What do you think?

This book is organized around the paradox of gender equality—how can men and women be equal if they are different? Throughout the chapters we have been exploring the concept of "equality" as well as "difference." The gender differences presented here imply that women are or would be *better* political leaders and that various political, economic, and social outcomes would be *better* if women were present in greater numbers; what do you think? Is the evidence definitive? Will we ever know whether men or women make better leaders? Is there anything about the claim that women are "better" than men that concerns you? Do you, like Supreme Court Justice Sandra Day O'Connor (quoted earlier in this chapter), see claims of gender difference as "dangerous"? How will perceptions of gender difference influence the reality you face when you look for a job or run for public office? Are women advantaged or disadvantaged?

1. World Bank, *Engendering Development Through Gender Equality in Rights, Resources, and Voice* (New York: Oxford University Press, 2001), accessed at http://www-wds.worldbank.org/.
2. Ibid., p. 93.
3. Ibid., p. 93 and p. 95.
4. Anne Marie Goetz, *Who Answers to Women? Gender and Accountability*, Progress of the World's Women 2008/2009 (New York: United Nations Development Fund for Women, 2008), accessed at http://www.unifem.org/progress/2008.
5. Marty Linsky, "Imagining 'Ellen' Greenspan," *Washington Post*, March 2009, *On Leadership*, accessed at http://views.washingtonpost.com/leadership/.
6. Deborah Kolb, "Are Women Really Risk Averse?" *Washington Post*, March 2009, *On Leadership*, accessed at http://views.washingtonpost.com/leadership/.
7. "Men or Women: Who's the Better Leader? A Paradox in Public Attitudes," Pew Research Center, August 25, 2008, accessed at http://pewresearch.org/pubs/932/men-or-women-whos-the-better-leader.

stereotypes and unreasonable expectations of women will resonate. Columnist Ellen Goodman, writing after the 1992 elections, asked, "How long before we read the first story asking why six women in the Senate haven't changed the institution?"[112] If anything, as the number of women in Congress has increased, the rich diversity among women has become more evident, which contributes to the mixed expectations for women's concerted behavior as a group. Working together across party and ideological lines, women have been able to add important issues to the public agenda. However, analysis presented in this chapter suggests that women's power beyond the agenda-setting stage of policy formation may still be limited by their lack of significant numbers and the influence that comes with leadership positions within institutions of government. The limits to women's power from within are seen in examples such as the 1996 welfare reform legislation and in the U.S. Senate's failure to ratify the Convention on the Elimination of All Forms of Discrimination Against Women (CEDAW) despite its adoption by 177 other countries.

Women's rights organizations can sometimes put pressure on legislators, members of the administration, and even the judiciary to act in women's interests. When government institutions are reticent to act, women's organizations can "go public" by issuing report cards on progress (or lack thereof) relative to well-known benchmarks or in comparison to other nations, launching investigations, or simply renewing the public's interest in the differential status of women on any number of important issues. When there are not enough female voices inside government and politics or when their voices are muted, women can agitate and lobby for policy changes from the outside. During the eight years of the conservative George W. Bush administration, a number of research institutes issued report cards that assessed women's status and attracted media and public attention. Research organizations or think tanks can shape public policy in this way by using data and information.

ADVOCACY THROUGH INFORMATION: RESEARCH AND POLICY CENTERS

The National Council for Research on Women (NCRW) is an alliance of 100 leading U.S. and international research and policy centers.[113] The National Women's Law Center is dedicated to using law to advance the progress of women and girls at work, in school, and in virtually every aspect of their lives.[114] The Institute for Women's Policy Research (IWPR) is a scientific research organization dedicated to informing and stimulating the debate on public policy issues of critical importance to women and their families.[115] Each of these three organizations, and many others with similar missions, use information and research as a form of advocacy. By disseminating research results, advocates educate citizens as well as mobilize men and women to pressure government to take action on policy issues relevant to women. In most cases, this information has been readily accessible and free via the Internet. Ironically, the first example, discussed in the next paragraph, is a report on information removed from the public domain. In anticipation of a new administration, each of these organizations produced agendas focusing on issues important to women.

In March 2004, the National Council for Research on Women issued its report "Missing: Information About Women's Lives." The report identifies a "disturbing pattern of decisions by federal agencies to close down, delay, alter, or spin data about what is happening to American women." Accurate gender-disaggregated data is crucial to solving problems and achieving equality. The report focuses on the areas of health, employment, and violence against women. In the area of health, for example, NCRW found that a central health information Web site (http://www.4women.gov) presented misleading information linking abortion to breast cancer. In 1997, a National Cancer Institute fact sheet cited broad medical consensus that no such link existed. However, in 2002, the fact sheet was changed to state that studies on the subject were inconclusive. "After an outcry by members of Congress forced the convening of a panel of experts, the NCI posted the panel's finding: abortion is not associated with an increased breast cancer risk." Economic information has disappeared as well. Twenty-five key publications of the Department of Labor are no longer available on its Web site, including information about pay equity and child care. "Accurate, trustworthy, science-based information and data matter, and we should be able to count on government to provide it." The National Council for Research on Women urged people to call on their elected representatives to confront the issue, arguing that "without specific attention to gender differences in information collection and publication—gender disaggregation of data—the effects of gender differences are hidden in a box. With such information, researchers can find which policies are working, and which need attention."[116] Most recently, the NCRW has been collaborating with a variety of research and policy organizations in "The Big Five" campaign. Five issues provide focus to the coalition's research and dissemination efforts: economic security, health, violence, immigration, and education. The coalition includes 115 research, policy, and advocacy centers.[117]

In April 2004, the National Women's Law Center released "Slip-Sliding Away: The Erosion of Hard-Won Gains for Women Under the Bush Administration and an Agenda for Moving Forward." The seventy-five-page report details actions taken during the first term of the Bush administration that NWLC argues erode or threaten to erode the progress that women have fought hard to win. The report evaluates the administration's record across ten areas: work, education, child-care and other work supports, tax and budget policies, retirement security, health and reproductive rights, violence against women, women in the military, judicial nominations, and government offices and advisory bodies charged with safeguarding women's interests. In each area, the report documents instances where the Bush administration has taken constructive actions on issues important to women as well as actions and positions that cause harm to women. For example, the administration ended the Equal Pay Matters Initiative and removed all materials on narrowing the wage gap from the Department of Labor's Web site. The Department of Education reduced Title IX enforcement while it established a commission to find ways to weaken athletics policies that open opportunities for female students. The Defense Department limited the role of the fifty-five-year-old Defense Advisory Committee on Women in the Services (DACOWITS), designed to promote recruitment and retention of women in the military. The size of the committee has been cut by two-thirds and serves at the direction of the secretary of defense rather than setting an independent agenda. The report concludes with an "Agenda for the Future" that calls on the administration to restore policies that advance equality for women and girls. The National Women's Law Center urges advocates for women's rights inside government and throughout the nation to use the agenda to advance positive change in the lives of women. In 2008, the NWLC released *Nowhere to Turn: How the Individual Health Insurance Market Fails Women* and *A Platform for Progress: Building a Better Future for Women and their Families*. Although the majority of women in the U.S. have health insurance through an employer (two-thirds of women aged 18 to 64) or through a public program such as Medicaid (16 percent), those that must purchase heath coverage directly from an insurance company find that individually purchased plans are not covered by federal and state nondiscrimination laws. Women find that coverage varies dramatically across plans and regions of the country on vital services like maternity care and they face higher premiums than men purchasing the same coverage. The NWLC's report identifies the problem through their research and then recommends ways that these inequities can be addressed through reform initiatives.[118] The *Platform for Progress* is an agenda-setting document produced in anticipation of a new president and Congress. The comprehensive report details issues facing women and their families in the areas of health, education, economic security, support for families, and the workplace, and makes specific recommendations to the new Congress, the judiciary, and the new administration in taking steps to guarantee equal rights.[119]

Finally, the Institute for Women's Policy Research (IWPR) is a scientific research organization dedicated to informing and stimulating the debate on public policy issues. IWPR focuses on issues of poverty and welfare, employment and earnings, work and family, health and safety, and women's civic and political participation. Each year, the institute publishes "The Status of Women in the States" reports. For ten years, these reports have profiled individual states (a subset each year) and have addressed trends in women's status across the states. The reports are produced to "inform citizens about the progress of women in their state relative to women in other states, to men, and to the nation as a whole. . . . Data on status of women give citizens the information they need to address the key issues facing women and their families."[120] Identification as one of the "best states" or the "worst states" for women is useful in focusing statewide elected officials' and state legislators' attention on women's issues.

The rankings are based on composite indices within each issue area. States are assigned a score, a rank, and a grade in each area.[121] The media, interest groups and lobbyists, and public officials often quote the information provided by research organizations. Attention generated by information can serve as a catalyst for women inside government to focus their attention on specific issues related to women's status and equality. Like the other organizations discussed in this section, IWPR's work focuses on the issues central to women's quality of life: child care and family leave, poverty, welfare and economic security, health, and women's democratic engagement.

The White House Council on Women and Girls

On March 11, 2009, President Obama signed an executive order creating the White House Council on Women and Girls. The council is made up of cabinet secretaries and top White House staff. Senior Advisor Valerie Jarrett is chair of the council and the White House director of public liaison, Tina Tchen, serves as executive director. During its first year, the council will focus on formulating comprehensive, coordinated policies in the areas of economic security, work-family balance, violence against women, and women's health care, including reproductive choice. "The purpose of this council," said President Obama, "is to ensure that American women and girls are treated fairly in all matters of public policy." The council is charged with ensuring that all of the federal agencies, not just the few offices dedicated to "women's issues" will take into account the particular needs and concerns of women and girls. The first step was to ask each agency to examine their current status to be certain they are adequately focusing, both internally and externally, on women and girls. In his remarks, the President referred to the women in his own life:

> I sign this order not just as a president, but as a son, a grandson, a husband, and a father, because growing up, I saw my mother put herself through school and follow her passion for helping others. But I also saw how she struggled to raise me and my sister on her own, worrying about how she'd pay the bills and educate herself and provide for us.

> I saw my grandmother work her way up to become one of the first women bank vice presidents in the state of Hawaii, but I also saw how she hit a glass ceiling—how men no more qualified than she was kept moving up the corporate ladder ahead of her.

> I've seen Michelle, the rock of the Obama family—(laughter)—juggling work and parenting with more skill and grace than anybody that I know. But I also saw how it tore at her at times, how sometimes when she was with the girls she was worrying about work, and when she was at work she was worrying about the girls. It's a feeling that I share every day.

> So now it's up to us to carry that work forward, to ensure that our daughters and granddaughters have no limits on their dreams, no obstacles to their achievements—and that they have opportunities their mothers and grandmothers and great grand-

mothers never dreamed of. That's the purpose of this council. Those are the priorities of my presidency.[122]

Not all women were happy with the council's creation. "I think it falls short of what's needed," said Martha Burk, former chairwoman of the National Council of Women's Organizations. Burk and others in the women's movement had been pushing for a cabinet-level office or a Presidential Commission on Women and were not satisfied with the interagency task force—in part because it did not come with a full-time staff or a cabinet-level leader.[123] A more general objection to the White House Council on Women and Girls was articulated by conservative columnist Kathleen Parker when she asked, "Where's the White House Council on Men and Boys?" The renewed focus on the status of women and girls comes in stark contrast to the near invisibility of programs directed at improving the status of women and girls in the United States during the George W. Bush administration.[124] The last executive initiative for women, the White House Office on Women, was created in 1995 by President Bill Clinton but disbanded by George W. Bush.

Maria Shriver, in partnership with the Center for American Progress and the University of Southern California's Annenberg Center of Communication Leadership and Policy, launched "A Woman's Nation" in April of 2009 and *The Shriver Report* was released in November of 2009. The project includes an empirical study of American women as workers and breadwinners, as well as the role women play in government, business, faith, education, and health. A Woman's Nation is modeled after the Commission on the Status of Women created in 1961 by President John F. Kennedy and chaired by Eleanor Roosevelt. A Woman's Nation will report their findings to the Congress and President Obama. *Time* magazine has agreed to disseminate the results of the study and to report on the various discussions, hearings, and roundtables.[125]

CONCLUSION

Historically, women have been forced to act as outsiders in politics because of the legal and customary barriers to their direct participation as insiders. Contemporary female political actors, however, have a wide range of activities and strategies available in the pursuit of equality. Women elected to office who promise a different approach to governing do so in the hope of capitalizing on voters' positive gender stereotypes of women as moral, civic minded, and dedicated to the interests of families, children, women, and those traditionally excluded from power. Outside the bounds of formal power, women continue to agitate for change here in the United States and globally. Women are more involved in politics, the political process, and governing than at any other time in our history. However, women still encounter obstacles to their pursuit of equality. As a nation, the United States perceives itself as a leader in securing women's rights. The Senate's refusal to ratify CEDAW and its slow progress in addressing other areas of critical concern suggest, however, that there is still work to be done. Advocacy for women's equality has taken on new significance for women elected officials and for those who serve as watchdogs and information lobbyists. Women inside and outside the formal structures of power continue to shape policies that affect women and to pursue gender equality.

To this point, we have largely focused on how women have utilized politics to enter politics themselves, first as voters and later as public officials. The next three chapters of the book examine several broad policy areas to better understand how women shape and are shaped by public policies. The paradox of gender equality is integral to explaining both processes. Women shape public policy in a number of ways. In some cases, women's presence in legislative bodies makes it more likely that issues previously defined as private are transformed into public issues that can be addressed through the public policy process. Issues as diverse as domestic violence and quality child care have only recently been understood as problems that warrant attention in the public sphere. As activists and as officeholders, women can bring issues to the government's attention and influence the content of legislation. As administrators, they can influence how policy is implemented, enforced, and evaluated. The paradox of gender equality can be found squarely at the center of most debates over policy affecting women. Three broad policy areas at the heart of the paradox of gender equality are addressed: education, work, and family.

Suggested Readings, Web Resources, and Films

Mary Anne Borrelli and Janet M. Martin, eds., *The Other Elites: Women, Politics, Power in the Executive Branch* (Boulder, Colo.: Lynne Rienner Publishers, 1997).

Karen Foerstel and Herbert N. Foerstel, *Climbing the Hill: Gender Conflict in Congress* (Westport, Conn.: Praeger, 1996).

Ruth Bader Ginsburg and Laura W. Brill, "Women in the Federal Judiciary: Three Way Pavers and the Exhilarating Change President Carter Wrought," *Fordham Law Review* 64, no. 2 (1995): 281–290.

Georgia Duerst-Lahti and Rita Mae Kelly, eds., *Gender Power, Leadership, and Governance* (Ann Arbor: University of Michigan Press, 1995).

Sonia R. Garcia, Valerie Martinez-Ebers, Irasema Coronado, Sharon A. Navarro, and Patricia A. Jaramillo, *Politicas: Latina Public Officials in Texas* (Austin: University of Texas Press, 2008).

Barbara Lee, *Renegade for Peace & Justice* (Lanham, Md.: Rowman and Littlefield Publishers, Inc., 2008).

Jane Mansbridge, "Should Blacks Represent Blacks, and Women Represent Women? A Contingent 'Yes'," Politics Research Group (Cambridge, Mass.: John F. Kennedy

School of Government, Harvard University, 2000), http://www.ksg.harvard.edu/prg/mansb/should.htm.

Cindy Simon Rosenthal, *When Women Lead: Integrative Leadership in State Legislatures* (New York: Oxford University Press, 1998).

Michele L. Swers, *The Difference Women Make: The Policy Impact of Women in Congress* (Chicago: University of Chicago Press, 2002).

Sue Thomas, *How Women Legislate* (New York: Oxford University Press, 1994).

Center for American Women and Politics: http://www.cawp.rutgers.edu/.

Executive Women in Government: http://www.execwomeningov.org/.

Girls, Inc.: http://www.girlsinc.org/girls-inc.html.

Institute for Women's Policy Research: http://www.iwpr.org/index.cfm.

Ms. Foundation for Women: http://www.ms.foundation.org/.

National Women's Law Center: http://www.nwlc.org/.

National Council for Research on Women: http://www.ncrw.org/.

WomenCount: http://www.womencount.org/.

Women in Government: http://www.womeningovernment.org/home/.

Women's Policy, Inc.: http://www.womenspolicy.org/welcome/.

Women, Power and Politics: http://www.imow.org/wpp/index.

Blog: Feminist Law Professors: http://feministlawprofessors.com/.

Blog: The Real Deal Blog: http://www.ncrw.org/ncrwbigfive/?page_id=20.

Blog: Women's Stake—Our Take on What's at Stake: http://www.womenstake.org/.

Film: *The Legacy of Barbara Jordan: Four Speeches* (Greenwood, Ind.: The Educational Video Group, 1996).

Film: *Sexual Harassment Hearing Compilation* [videorecording]. Senate Judiciary Committee, Public Affairs Archives (W. Lafayette, Ind.: Purdue University, 1991).

Film: *Shirley Chisholm '72: Unbought and Unbossed* (PBS POV film, February 7, 2005).

Film: *What's Your Point, Honey?* (250 Pick Up Productions, 2008, http://www.whatsyourpointhoney.com/front/).

Film: *Women World Leaders* (Washington, D.C.: Council of Women World Leaders, 1996).

Notes

1. Harriet Woods, *Stepping Up to Power: The Political Journey of American Women* (Boulder, Colo.: Westview Press, 2000), p. 163.

2. Hannah Fenichel Pitkin, *The Concept of Representation* (Berkeley: University of California Press, 1967).

3. Georgia Deurst-Lahti and Dayna Verstegen, "Making Something of Absence: The 'Year of the Woman' and Women's Political Representation," in *Gender Power, Leadership, and Governance*, eds. Georgia Deurst-Lahti and Rita Mae Kelly (Ann Arbor: University of Michigan Press, 1998), pp. 213–238.

4. Laurel Elder, "Why Women Don't Run: Explaining Women's Underrepresentation in America's Political Institutions," *Women and Politics* 26, no. 2 (2004): 27–56.

5. Jane Mansbridge, "Should Blacks Represent Blacks, and Women Represent Women? A Contingent 'Yes'," Politics Research Group (Cambridge, Mass.: John F. Kennedy School of Government, Harvard University, 2000), accessed at http://www.ksg.harvard.edu/prg/mansb/should.htm.

6. Susan J. Carroll, "Representing Women: Congresswomen's Perceptions of Their Representational Roles," paper presented at Women Transforming Congress: Gender Analyses of Institutional Life, Carl Albert Congressional Research and Studies Center, University of Oklahoma, April 13–15, 2000.

7. Kim Fridkin Kahn, *The Political Consequences of Being a Woman* (New York: Columbia University Press, 1996), p. 137.

8. Carroll, "Representing Women," p. 4.

9. Kathleen Dolan and Kira Sanbonmatsu, "Gender Stereotypes and Attitudes Toward Gender Balance in Government," *American Politics Research* 37, no. 3 (May 2009): 409–428.

10. The data come from the 2006 American National Election Study (ANES) Pilot Study, see pp. 414–415 for initial frequency results.

11. Jean Reith Schroedel and Nicola Nazumdar, "Into the Twenty-first Century: Will Women Break the Political Glass Ceiling?" in *Women and Elective Office: Past, Present, and Future*, eds. Sue Thomas and Clyde Wilcox (New York: Oxford University Press, 1998), pp. 203–219.

12. Mansbridge, "Should Blacks Represent Blacks?"

13. Linda Witt, Karen M. Paget, and Glenna Matthews, *Running as a Woman: Gender and Power in American Politics* (New York: Free Press, 1993), p. 268.

14. Ibid.

15. Sue Thomas, "The Impact of Women on State Legislative Policies," *Journal of Politics* 53, no. 4 (1991): 958–975.

16. Barbara Burrell, "The Political Leadership of Women and Public Policymaking," *Policy Studies Journal* 25, no. 4 (1997): 565–568.

17. Debra Dodson, ed., *Gender and Policymaking: Studies of Women in Office* (New Brunswick, N.J.: Center for American Women and Politics, Rutgers University, 1991).

18. Freda Gehlen, "Women Members of Congress: A Distinctive Role," in *A Portrait of Marginality*, eds. Marianne Githens and Jewel Prestage (New York: David McKay, 1977).

19. Kathleen Frankovic, "Sex and Voting in the U.S. House of Representatives: 1961–1975," *American Politics Quarterly* 5 (July 1977): 515–530.

20. Susan Welch, "Are Women More Liberal Than Men in the U.S. Congress?" *Legislative Studies Quarterly* 10 (February 1985): 125–134.

21. Barbara Burrell, *A Woman's Place is in the House: Campaigning for Congress in a Feminist Era* (Ann Arbor: University of Michigan Press, 1997). See, in particular, chapter 8.

22. Ibid., p. 158.

23. Debra L. Dodson and Susan J. Carroll, "Reshaping the Agenda: Women in State Legislatures," (New Brunswick, N.J.: Center for American Women and Politics, Rutgers University, 1991).

24. John M. Carey, Richard G. Niemi, and Lynda W. Powell, "Are Women State Legislators Different?" in *Women and Elective Office*, eds. Thomas and Wilcox, pp. 87–102.

25. Ibid., p. 99.

26. Fact sheet compiled by the Center for American Women and Politics, Eagleton Institute of Politics (New Brunswick, N.J.: Rutgers University, 2004).

27. Sue Thomas, "Why Gender Matters: The Perceptions of Women Officeholders," *Women and Politics* 17, no. 1 (1997): 27–53.

28. Ibid., p. 29.

29. Carroll, "Representing Women," pp. 6–7.

30. Ibid., p. 7.

31. Ibid.

32. Carey, Niemi, and Powell, "Are Women State Legislators Different?" p. 91.

33. Marcia Lynn Whicker and Malcom Jewell, "The Feminization of Leadership in State Legislatures," in *Women and Elective Office*, eds. Thomas and Wilcox, pp. 163–174.

34. Ibid., p. 174.

35. Cindy Simon Rosenthal, "Determinants of Collaborative Leadership: Civic Engagement, Gender, or Organizational Norms?" *Political Research Quarterly* 51, no. 4 (1998): 847–868.

36. Lyn Kathlene, "Power and Influence in State Legislative Policy Making: The Interaction of Gender and Position in Committee Hearing Debates," *American Political Science Review* 88 (1994): 560–575.

37. Lyn Kathlene, "In a Different Voice: Women and the Public Policy Process," in *Women and Elective Office*, eds. Thomas and Wilcox, p. 198.

38. Ibid., p. 199.

39. Janet Flamang, "Female Officials in the Feminist Capital: The Case of Santa Clara County," *Western Political Quarterly* 38 (1985): 94–118.

40. Cindy Simon Rosenthal, "Getting Things Done: Women Committee Chairpersons in State Legislatures," in *Women and Elective Office*, eds. Thomas and Wilcox, pp. 175–187.

41. For a discussion of the professionalization of women in the 1990s state legislatures, see Carey, Niemi, and Powell, "Are Women State Legislators Different?" For a discussion of the lingering gender differences in the compatibility of legislative service and private roles related to children and family, see also Debra Dodson, "Change and Continuity in the Relationship Between Private Responsibilities and Public Officeholding: The More Things Change, the More They Stay the Same," *Policy Studies Journal* 25, no. 4 (1997): 569–584.

42. Rosenthal, "Determinants of Collaborative Leadership," p. 184.

43. Maryann Barakso, "Is there a 'Woman's Way' of Governing? Assessing the Organizational Structures of Women's Membership Associations," *Politics & Gender* 3, no. 2 (June 2007): 201–227.

44. Ibid., p. 222.

45. Jennifer L. Lawless and Sean M. Theriault, "Women in the U.S. Congress: From Entry to Exit," in *Women in Politics: Outsiders or Insiders?* 4th ed., ed. Lois Duke Whitaker (Upper Saddle River, N.J.: Prentice Hall, forthcoming).

46. Eleanor Clift and Tom Brazaitis, *Madam President: Shattering the Last Glass Ceiling* (New York: Scribner, 2000), p. 239.

47. Juliet Eilperin, "Nancy Pelosi Set to be First Female Speaker," *Washington Post*, Wednesday, November 8, 2006; A32.

48. "Women in Congress: Leadership Roles and Committee Chairs," Center for American Women and Politics, Eagleton Institute of Politics, Rutgers University, accessed at http://www.cawp.rutgers.edu/fast_facts/levels_of_office/documents/conglead.pdf.

49. Alexander Bolton, "Roukema Wants HHS Job After Losing Chair," *The Hill* (Washington, D.C.: Capitol Hill Publishing Corp., 2001).

50. Lawless and Theriault, "Women in the U.S. Congress," p. 17.

51. Kathlene, "In a Different Voice," p. 190.

52. Ibid., pp. 190–193.

53. Lyn Kathlene, "Alternative Views of Crime: Legislative Policy Making in Gendered Terms," *Journal of Politics* 57 (1995): 696–723.

54. Kathlene, "In a Different Voice," p. 196.

55. Rosabeth Moss Kanter, "Some Effects of Proportion on Group Life: Skewed Sex Ratios and Response to Token Women," *American Journal of Sociology* 82 (1977): 965–990.

56. Sue Thomas, "The Impact of Women on State Legislative Policies," *Journal of Politics* 53, no. 4 (1991): 958–976.

57. Ibid., p. 967.

58. Kathleen A. Bratton, "Critical Mass Theory Revisited: The Behavior and Success of Token Women in State Legislatures," *Politics & Gender* 1, no. 1 (March 2005): 97–125.

59. Ibid., p. 122.

60. Lynne A. Weikart, Greg Chen, Daniel W. Williams, and Haris Hromic, "The Democratic Sex: Gender Differences and the Exercise of Power," *Journal of Women, Politics & Policy* 28, no.1 (2006): 119–140. 61.

61. Dana Levy, Charles Tien, and Rachelle Aved, "Do Differences Matter? Women Members of Congress and the Hyde Amendment," *Women and Politics* 23, no. 1–2 (2001): 105–127.

62. Ibid., p. 108.

63. Janet K. Boles, "Local Elected Women and Policy-Making: Movement Delegates or Feminist Trustees," in *The Impact of Women in Public Office*, ed. Susan Carroll (Bloomington: University of Indiana Press, 2001).

64. Dana Levy, Charles Tien, and Rachelle Aved, "Do Differences Matter? Women Members of Congress and the Hyde Amendment," p. 110.

65. Ibid., p. 124.

66. Amy Caizza, "Does Women's Representation in Elected Office Lead to Women-Friendly Policy? Analysis of State-Level Data," *Women and Politics* 26, no. 1 (2004): 35–70.

67. Angela High-Pippert and John Comer, "Female Empowerment: The Influence of Women Representing Women," *Women and Politics* 19, no. 4 (1998): 53–65.

68. Ibid., p. 62.

69. Colleen J. Shogan, "Speaking Out: An Analysis of Democratic and Republican Woman-Invoked Rhetoric of the 105th Congress," *Women and Politics* 23, no. 1–2 (2001): 129–146.

70. Carol Swain, *Black Faces, Black Interests* (Cambridge, Mass.: Harvard University Press, 1998).

71. Lisa Jones Townsel, "Sisters in Congress Prove They Have What It Takes to Bring About Change," *Ebony*, March 1997, pp. 36–39.

72. Debra Dodson, "Representing Women's Interests in the U.S. House of Representatives," in *Women and Elective Office*, eds. Thomas and Wilcox, pp. 130–149.

73. "Women of Color in Elective Office 2009," fact sheet compiled by the Center for American Women and Politics, Eagleton Institute of Politics (New Brunswick, N.J.: Rutgers University, 2009), accessed at http://www.cawp.rutgers.edu/.

74. Marsha J. Darling, "African American Women in State Elective Office in the South," in *Women and Elective Office*, eds. Thomas and Wilcox, pp. 158–159.

75. Ibid, pp. 160–161.

76. Mary Hawkesworth, "Congressional Enactments of Race-Gender: Toward a Theory of Raced-Gendered Institutions," *American Political Science Review* 97, no. 4 (November 2003): 529–550.

77. Ibid., p. 532.

78. Ibid., p. 546.

79. Sue Thomas, *How Women Legislate* (New York: Oxford University Press, 1994).

80. Thomas, "The Impact of Women on State Legislative Policies," p. 973.

81. Lesley Primmer, "The Congressional Caucus for Women's Issues: Twenty Years of Bipartisan Advocacy for Women," in *The American Woman, 1999–2000*, eds. Cynthia B. Costello, Sheri Miles, and Anne J. Stone (New York: Norton, 1998), pp. 365–375.

82. Irwin Gertzog, *Congressional Women: Their Recruitment, Integration, and Behavior*, 2nd ed. (Westport, Conn.: Praeger, 1995), p. 188.

83. Ibid., p. 371.

84. Primmer, "The Congressional Caucus for Women's Issues," p. 367.

85. See Women's Policy, Inc. Web site: http://www.womenspolicy.org.

86. Rich Daly, "Women's Caucus Puts Health at Top of its '09 List," *Women's eNews*, January 5, 2009, accessed at http://www.womensenews.org/article.cfm?aid=3877.

87. Dodson, "Representing Women's Interests in the U.S. House of Representatives," pp. 134–143.

88. Ibid., p. 134.

89. Ibid., p. 149.

90. Daly, "Women's Caucus Puts Health at Top of its '09 List."

91. David M. Herszenhorn and Jackie Calmes, "Abortion was at the heart of Wrangling," *New York Times*, November 8, 2009, accessed at http://www.nytimes.com/2009/11/08/health/policy/08scene.html.

92. Adrienne Elizabeth Christiansen, "Women and War: How 'Power-Over' Politics Silenced U.S. Congresswomen in the Persian Gulf War," *Humanist* 58, no. 1 (Jan.–Feb. 1998): 12–20.

93. For an interesting perspective on biological differences and aggression related to politics, see Francis Fukuyama, "Women and the Evolution of World Politics," *Foreign Affairs* 77, no. 5 (Sept.–Oct. 1998): 24–31.

94. Katha Pollitt, "Subject to Debate: Most Women in Congress Support Harsh Welfare Reform," *Nation* 261, no. 19 (December 4, 1995): 697.

95. Ibid.

96. National Organization for Women, "'Insider' Women Are Still Making a Difference," March 1996, press release, accessed at http://www.now.org/nnt/03-96/oped.html.

97. "How Contraceptives Factored into the Economic Stimulus Plan," Our Bodies Ourselves, January 27, 2009, accessed at http://www.ourbodiesourblog.org/blog/2009/01/how-contraceptives-factored-into-the-economic-stimulus-plan.

98. U.S. Office of Personnel Management, Central Personnel Data File (CPDF), "Executive Branch (Non-Postal) Employment by Gender, Race/National Origin, Disability Status, Veterans Status, Disabled Veterans," accessed at http://www.opm.gov/feddata/demograp/02demo.pdf.

99. "OPM Director Janice R. Lachance Announces Key Employment Gains for Women in the Federal Government," July 21, 1999, Office of Personnel Management press release.

100. Office of Personnel Management, "Women in the Federal Government: A Guide to Recruiting and Retaining," accessed at http://www.opm.gov/employ/women/; 2008 statistics come from the FY 2008 annual Federal Equal Opportunity Recruitment Program report, accessed at http://www.opm.gov/About_opm?reports/FEORP/2008/feorp2008.pdf.

101. Joan Biskupic, "Ginsburg: Court Needs Another Woman," *USA Today,* May 5, 2009, accessed at http://www.usatoday.com/news/washington/judicial/2009-05-05-ruthginsburg_N.htm.

102. Ruth Bader Ginsburg and Laura W. Brill, "Women in the Federal Judiciary: Three Way Pavers and the Exhilarating Change President Carter Wrought," *Fordham Law Review* 64, no. 2 (1995): 281–290.

103. National Women's Law Center, "Women in the Federal Judiciary: Still a Long Way to Go," (2009), accessed at http://www.nwlc.org/pdf/numberofwomeninjudiciary09.pdf.

104. Richard L. Pacelle Jr., "A President's Legacy: Gender and Appointment to the Federal Courts," in *The Other Elites: Women, Politics, and Power in the Executive Branch*, eds. MaryAnne Borrelli and Janet M. Martin (Boulder, Colo.: Lynne Rienner Publishers, 1997).

105. "Obama's Remarks on the Resignation of Justice Souter," *New York Times*, May 1, 2009, accessed at http://www.nytimes.com/2009/05/01/us/politics/01souter.text.html.

106. Peter Baker and Jeff Zeleny, "Obama Hails Judge as 'Inspiring'," *New York Times*, May 27, 2009, accessed at http://www.nytimes.com/2009/05/27/us/politics/27court.html.

107. See the full text of Judge Sotomayor's lecture here: http://www.nytimes.com/2009/05/15/us/politics/15judge.text.html?pagewanted=1&_r=2.

108. Sue Davis, Susan Haire, and Donald Songer, "Voting Behavior and Gender on the U.S. Courts of Appeals," *Judicature* no. 77 (1993): 129–133.

109. Pacelle, "A President's Legacy," p. 149.

110. Tajuana Massie, Susan W. Johnson, and Sara Margaret Gubala, "The Impact of Gender and Race in the Decisions of Judges on the United States Courts of Appeals," paper presented at the Midwest Political Science Association meeting (April 2002).

111. Deborah Rhode, "In a 'Different' Voice: The Real Effect of Women on the Bench," *DoubleX*, June 10, 2009, accessed at http://www.doublex.com; Christine L. Boyd, Lee Epstein, and Andrew D. Martin, "Untangling the Causal Effects of Sex on Judging," paper presented at the annual meeting of the Midwest Political Science Association, April 2007.

112. Witt, Paget, and Mathews, *Running as a Woman*, p. 269.

113. National Council for Research on Women, http://www.ncrw.org.

114. National Women's Law Center, http://www.nwlc.org.

115. Institute for Women's Policy Research, http://www.iwpr.org.

116. National Council for Research on Women, http://www.ncrw.org.

117. The National Council for Research on Women, "The Big Five," accessed at http://www.ncrw.org/ncrwbigfive/index.php.

118. National Women's Law Center, "Nowhere to Turn: How the Individual Health Insurance Market Fails Women," (September 2008), accessed at http://action.nwlc.org/site/DocServer/NowhereToTurn.pdf?docID=601.

119. National Women's Law Center, *A Platform for Progress: Building a Better Future for Women and Their Families* (2008), accessed at http://www.nwlc.org/pdf/PlatformforProgress2008.pdf.

120. Institute for Women's Policy Research, http://www.iwpr.org.

121. Institute for Women's Policy Research, "The Status of Women in the States, Introduction," accessed at http://www.iwpr.org/States2004/PDFs/National.pdf.

122. The White House, Blog Post, "Opportunities their mothers and grandmothers and great grandmothers never dreamed of," March 11, 2009, accessed at http://www.whitehouse.gov/blog/09/03/11/Opportunities-their-mothers-and-grandmothers-and-great-grandmothers-never-dreamed-of/.

123. Josh Gerstein, "Some Women Wanted More from White House," *POLITICO*, March 12, 2009, accessed at http://www.politico.com/news/stories/0309/19936. html.

124. Kathleen Parker, "Bring the Boys Along: The White House Council Obama Forgot," *Washington Post*, Wednesday, March 18, 2009; A13.

125. A Woman's Nation: A Project of Maria Shriver and the Center for American Progress, April 15, 2009, accessed at http://www.americanprogress.org/ issues/2009/04/womans_nation.html. *The Shriver Report* can be accessed at http://www.awomansnation.com/index.php.

Education and the Pursuit of Equality

Education is a critical resource for human advancement at the individual and the societal levels. Education occupies a critical nexus for women between the private and public spheres. It isn't an accident that women won the right to be educated nearly 100 years before they embarked on the campaign for suffrage. Education empowers individuals to act on the basis of their self-interest, which is why it has been treated as a restricted commodity. Early nineteenth century Enlightenment theorists believed that education was crucial to developing the ability to reason and for attaining full citizenship. Therefore, only those who could become citizens needed to be educated, and that did not include women. Withholding education is a form of social control and a way of maintaining the status quo by ensuring that those at the bottom of the social hierarchy raise few objections.

We begin our discussion with the question, Why educate women? Although this may sound rhetorical today, in many countries and in some subcultures of the United States, education is still reserved almost exclusively for males, or after a certain level is limited to males. In 2009, for example, girls in Afghanistan are the target of acid attacks and other forms of physical intimidation to dissuade them from going to school. Women's access to education in professional programs and in some institutions had been limited until Title IX, which was passed in 1972 as an amendment to the 1964 Civil Rights Act. Designed to address questions of gender equity in education by banning discrimination based on sex, Title IX receives the most public attention for what it has meant to girls' and women's athletics. In 1992, the American Association of University Women (AAUW) put the issue of gender equity in the classroom squarely before the public by issuing *How Schools Shortchange Girls*, a major research study that documented how girls were being unfairly disadvantaged by common classroom practices that gave preference to boys and valued boys over girls. More recently, critics have charged that the situation is quite the opposite: Rather than schools cheating girls, as the AAUW report charged, boys are now at a disadvantage and are suffering from discrimination in education.[1] We will evaluate both arguments. Finally, education is such a fundamental resource that its long-term influence is felt throughout a person's lifetime. We will examine the effect of education or the lack of education on women's status in the United States. The chapter concludes with an examination of issues in education facing future generations of citizens and policymakers.

A BRIEF HISTORY OF THE EDUCATION OF WOMEN

Education by its very nature empowers individuals, cultures, and nations to survive. From the beginning of human existence, informal education provided essential information about how to find and prepare food, build shelter, heal the sick, give birth to new life, and mourn the dead.[2] Access to formal education throughout time and regardless of place has been a restricted privilege. In Ancient Greece, for example, athletics, music, and reading were the formal educational requirements for young males destined for full membership in the citizen class. By the Middle Ages, daughters of royalty were sometimes tutored, but it was not until the nineteenth century that even a few men beyond royalty received a formal education. "Formal education was considered irrelevant for most free citizens, dangerous for men of lower status and for women, and even illegal for enslaved black people."[3] With very few exceptions, education for elite women was restricted to music, foreign languages, and literature—all taught at home and for the express purpose of training women for their station in life.

The public debate over the character of women's education began in the seventeenth century in Europe and extended to the colonies. The dominant philosophy regarding women's education did not seek to enlighten and empower women, but rather to ensure that women remained confined to their "fortune and condition." Women's training focused on building moral character and developing the necessary submissive nature and skills to maintain a marriage, run a household, and supervise children. Women in the colonies taught religion, but only to other women. Women were permitted to preach only to other women and then only the words and thoughts derived from their husband's or minister's minds.[4] Women who demonstrated independence in thought or word were often declared insane and a threat to social order. The most famous example is the prosecution of Anne Hutchinson by the conservative religious authorities of the Massachusetts Bay Colony. Her banishment was a direct result of Hutchinson's overstepping the bounds of women's proper role.

Although Enlightenment theorists were a powerful influence on the expansion of education as a social good, women's education was still relegated to "patient submissiveness to male authority." Jean-Jacques Rousseau, who argued for the importance of education in reason to liberal theory's promise of human emancipation through government by consent, did not extend those same views to women's education. In *Émile* (1762), his treatise on the ideal education for a young man, Rousseau argued that the proper object of education for women was men. Anything beyond that was counterproductive since women's role and purpose was to marry and support their husbands, raise children, and manage the household. Educating women in reason and independence would not only be a waste, but it would also be a dangerous challenge to nature's designation of women as the object of men's pleasure.[5] Catherine MacCaulay and later Mary Wollstonecraft offered feminist critiques of Rousseau. In *Letters on Education*, published in 1790, MacCaulay asserted that men and women needed to understand each other better. Through coeducation, both men and women would develop the physical and intellectual powers required to accept the political responsibilities of the liberal state. If educated similarly to men, women could shoulder their share of these responsibilities. Likewise, Wollstonecraft, in *Thoughts on the Education of Daughters* and later *A Vindication of the Rights of Woman*, advocated coeducation, insisting that women also needed to develop independence, rationality, and competence. While she recognized that most women would become wives and mothers, she argued that women could best fulfill those roles if they first respected themselves as individuals.[6]

While Wollstonecraft herself was labeled a radical, her ideas nonetheless suffused the philosophy of republican motherhood that emerged in post-Revolutionary America. Women should be good "republican mothers" able to educate the sons of liberty, argued leading educational theorists of the time. Judith Sargent Murray, writing as "Constantina," provided the first American feminist voice regarding the education of women, and was one of the first to challenge the prevailing notion that men and women were different by nature. Murray claimed that men and women were taught to be different:

> Will it be said that the judgment of a male of two years old is more sage than that of a female's of the same age? I believe the reverse is generally observed to be true. But from that period on what partiality! How is the one exalted and the other depressed, by the contrary modes of education which are adopted! The one is taught to aspire, the other is early confined and limited![7]

Access to education expanded in the United States throughout the 1800s. In the 1830s and 1840s, girls were admitted to free public elementary schools, particularly in the Northeast. Emma Willard opened the first "college" for women in 1821, the Troy Female Seminary. Prudence Crandall opened a similar academy for black women in 1833, only to be jailed and see her school burned to the ground.[8] Coeducational colleges developed in the 1830s, with Oberlin College in Ohio the first to admit both men and women, regardless of race. Women made up nearly one-third to one-half of the student body, and although allowed to mix freely with men in classrooms and during meals, were primarily admitted to the "Ladies' Department." The women's course of study omitted Latin, Greek, and higher mathematics. Women students were expected to wash and repair the clothing of the male students, as well as take charge of the dining hall tasks. When Lucy Stone, a future leader in the suffrage movement, was admitted to Oberlin, she was permitted to take the regular four-year collegiate course only after first completing the program of equal length in the Ladies' Department.[9]

Wheaton College was founded as the first real women's college in 1834, followed by Mount Holyoke in 1837. Iowa was the first state university to admit women, beginning in 1855. In 1904, Mary McCleod Bethune opened a small school for black women in Daytona Beach, Florida, which later became Bethune-Cookman College. By 1873, 60 percent of all American secondary schools had mixed-sex classes, and by the late 1880s, the majority of teachers were women.[10] Women's progress in education provoked some to issue dire warnings about the consequences of "too much" education. In 1872, Dr. Edward Clarke of the Harvard Medical School was invited to address The New England Women's Club in Boston. Several prominent women were in attendance, including Julia Ward Howe, Louisa May Alcott, and Lucy Stone. Dr. Clarke warned that education for women, and the mental exertion involved, could result in deadly physical consequences: "monstrous brains and puny bodies; abnormally active cerebration and abnormally weak digestion; flowing thought and constipated bowels."[11] The womb was especially at risk since it was already "housed in frail bodies 'diseased' by monthly bleeding." As historian Louise Bernikow notes, "Myths about the frailties of bodies that bled monthly assumed the form of restrictions on female athletics in our time, but they were rooted in 19th century desires to shut down that most dangerous organ, the female brain."[12]

As women joined the ranks of teachers in increasing numbers, the profession's prestige and salary began to fall. Kathryn Kish Sklar argues that the growth of mass education in the United States was accomplished cheaply as a result of low salaries for women. Low salaries were justified by three arguments: Women did not have to support families as men did. Women deserved less pay since they would quit their jobs when they married. Women's salaries were determined by the market, and since women had few options beyond teaching, they accepted whatever salary was offered, no matter how low.[13] Most schools *required* that women leave the teaching profession once they married, but women's entrance into paid teaching positions opened avenues to other "suitable" occupations over time and accorded some women new public stature within their communities. As more women were educated, the number of women's clubs and organizations dedicated to improving and expanding education increased dramatically throughout the 1870s.

In the twentieth century, the science of homemaking was introduced to the curriculum through courses in home economics, nutrition, psychology, sociology, and even biology and chemistry. Educators reasoned that women also needed mathematics in addition to courses in the natural sciences to "help their children with their homework." The assumption that women's primary function was to marry and raise children remained dominant even as women entered higher education in greater numbers. Women's enrollment in college programs continued to ebb and flow throughout the century, dependent largely on the country's economic condition and men's needs. After World War II, for example, the percentage of women in higher education dropped substantially, reflecting the return of men to the classroom with federal assistance through the GI Bill. Women were encouraged to "return to normalcy," meaning that they were actively discouraged from seeking either education or employment beyond providing for the immediate needs of their family and home. By the early 1990s, women had surpassed men in enrollments in four-year colleges and universities in the United States and the gap has continued to widen (Figure 6.1).

LEGISLATING GENDER EQUITY IN EDUCATION: TITLE IX AND THE WEEA

The first major piece of legislation to address gender equality in education was not passed until 1972, the same year that the Equal Rights Amendment was sent to the states for ratification. Although discriminatory educational practices based on race had been addressed in Title VI of the 1964 Civil Rights Act,

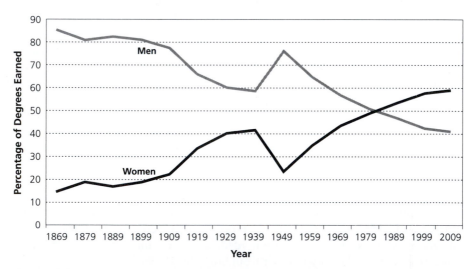

FIGURE 6.1 Earned Bachelor's Degrees by Sex, 1869–1999

Source: U.S. Department of Education, National Center for Education Statistics, "Earned degrees conferred by degree-granting institutions, by level of degree and sex of student: 1869–2011," Table 246: prepared 2002.

sex was not included anywhere in the Civil Rights Act except in Title VII, which dealt with employment. For many in the women's movement, issues of pay equity and employment discrimination were more overt and immediate barriers to women's equal status. While education plays an obvious and important role in preparing women for full employment, most schools were coeducational, thereby masking the many covert forms of educational discrimination against women. In 1970, President Nixon's Task Force on Women's Rights and Responsibilities called discrimination in education "one of the most damaging injustices women suffer."[14]

Title IX, also known as the Educational Amendments of 1972, banned sex discrimination in education at all levels of formal education. The language of this legislation mirrored other equal-protection legislation:

> No person in the United States shall, on the basis of sex, be excluded from participation in, be denied the benefits of, or be subjected to discrimination under any education program or activity receiving federal financial assistance.

Cosponsored by Congresswoman Edith Green and Senator Birch Bayh, the bill met little opposition from within Congress or from lobbyists when it was introduced. In fact, Green specifically asked women's organizations *not* to testify on behalf of the legislation, fearing the publicity would attract opponents and endanger the legislation's chances for passage.[15] While the legislation was designed to eliminate the crippling barriers in all sorts of educational programs, institutions, and curriculum, the law is now almost exclusively described in relation to increasing women's access to sports programs—even in accounts of the women's movement or women's history.[16] The legislation specified that no federal funds could go to educational institutions that were already receiving federal dollars and practiced sex discrimination in any of their programs, including admissions, athletics, financial aid, counseling, facilities, and employment.

Today, Title IX extends to issues of sexual harassment, pregnancy, parental status, and marital status. In 1992, the U.S. Supreme Court ruled that a student could bring a Title IX claim for damages for a sexually hostile environment created by a teacher (*Franklin v. Gwinnett County Public Schools*). In 1999, in *Davis v. Monroe County Board of Education*, the Court ruled that schools may also be liable if one student harasses another student at school. Schools are obligated to take reasonable steps under Title IX to prevent and eliminate sexual harassment. A 2001 study by the American Association of University Women (AAUW) found that 81 percent of students in public schools in grades eight through eleven had experienced some form of sexual harassment. Although girls were more likely to have experienced sexual harassment at some point in high school, boys reported experiencing sexual harassment "occasionally" or "often."[17] Sexual harassment, even noncontact encounters, is different from bullying and schools must deal with them as two separate problems. Susan Fineran, coauthor of a recent study on sexual harassment in grades 5–12, says, "Title IX protects everybody in school against this kind of behavior, but as soon as you call something 'bullying,' then it's just viewed as ill behavior that one student does to another student. Sexual harassment is really an environmental problem for the school. The school needs to do something about stopping sexual harassment because they are legally bound to." Her study found that although girls and boys were equally likely to report having been a victim of sexual harassment, girls and sexual minorities were far more upset by it and more likely to suffer low self-esteem, poorer mental and physical health, and more trauma symptoms as a result.[18]

The most recent AAUW study (2006) found that a majority of college students experience sexual harassment; one-third reported an encounter in their first year. A majority of encounters are noncontact in nature (sexual remarks or electronic messages). Male and female students are almost equally likely to be the target of sexual jokes, comments, gestures, or looks. Male students are more likely to be called gay or a homophobic name. Both male and female students are more likely to be harassed by a man than a woman. More than one-third of college students do not tell anyone about their experiences; those who do confide in someone usually tell a friend. Less than 10 percent of all students report incidents of sexual harassment to a college or university employee. Sexual harassment on college campuses is serious and can lead to emotional damage and academic disruption for the victim, and contributes to a hostile learning environment for all students. For the university, sexual harassment and the failure to act when incidents of harassment are brought to their attention can be costly and harm their reputation.[19]

Sexual harassment complaints make up 63 percent of non-sports-related Title IX complaints filed with the Office of Civil Rights (OCR). Seventy percent of elementary and secondary school and 59 percent of college and university complaints involve sexual harassment. While only 26 percent of high school students in the 1993 AAUW study said their school had a policy to deal with sexual harassment and complaints, by 2001, 69 percent of students reported knowledge of such a policy.[20]

Prior to Title IX, pregnant students were almost always forced to leave school. Under Title IX, schools are prohibited from discriminating against pregnant and parenting students. Schools may not exclude a student from any educational program or activity, including extracurricular activity, on the basis of pregnancy. This also means that pregnant students may not be forced into separate schools. Schools must accommodate pregnant students to the same degree they would extend allowances for any other temporary disability, including granting a temporary leave from school. Pregnant student-athletes are permitted a one-year extension of the five-year period of eligibility. While there have not been many court cases involving Title IX coverage of pregnant or parenting students, a number of pregnant students have brought suit after being denied admission to, or being dismissed from, the National Honor Society (NHS). The NHS invites students for membership based on a combination of academic achievement and moral character. In each of the NHS cases, the school claims that the student's exclusion was based not on her pregnancy but rather on the fact that the student had engaged in premarital sex, a moral character issue. Pregnant students may not be excluded on this basis unless male students are similarly screened for sexual activity. Title IX is a gender-neutral law, thus it may permit discrimination on the basis of premarital sexual activity, but not against pregnant girls alone.[21]

In a 2003 case involving a pregnant student-athlete, Tara Brady filed suit under Title IX, alleging that her basketball scholarship was revoked after she became pregnant and decided to carry her pregnancy to term. A student-athlete and star basketball player at Sacred Heart University in Connecticut, she claimed that her coach told her that she would be a "distraction" and should leave the school. Brady alleges that she requested "medical redshirt" status (a temporary leave that would not negatively impact her five-year eligibility), but that the coach never registered her for it and her scholarship was subsequently revoked when she did not report for practice. The following fall however, she discovered that she had been listed as a "medical redshirt" and contacted the University to request that her scholarship be reinstated. It was and she rejoined the team, but her coach refused to speak to her unless it was through an intermediary. Ultimately she left the institution and filed suit, becoming the first pregnant athlete to file suit under Title IX.[22] Under Title IX, institutions are not permitted to single out pregnant students or to treat them any worse because of their pregnancy. Pregnancy must be treated like any other temporary disability and students must be allowed to take a one-year leave without penalty and to have their prepregnancy status reinstated in full upon their return. In 2001, Eric Butler put off his plans to play college football when his girlfriend became pregnant. He played one season in 2003 and another in 2005, but by July 2006 his eligibility had expired. Butler petitioned the NCAA for a waiver and then filed suit under Title IX. He argued that under NCAA bylaws, an institution can grant a one-year extension to the five-year eligibility "for a female student-athlete for reasons of pregnancy." The district court sided with the NCAA which had interpreted "for reasons of pregnancy" to refer to the biological inconvenience of pregnancy rather than the work of parenting. In 2008 the NCAA responded to a growing number of issues related to pregnant and parenting collegiate athletes, and produced the NCAA Model Pregnancy and Parenting Policy toolkit to assist schools in complying with Title IX gender equity provisions. A survey found that 85 percent of Division I schools, 94 percent of Division II schools, and over 98 percent of Division III schools lacked any written policy covering student-athlete pregnancy and parenting issues. The NCAA's Model Pregnancy Policy is gender neutral.

Provisions for enforcement of Title IX have been weak from the start. Women's rights organizations expended more energy protecting the legislation during its implementation than during its passage through Congress. The Department of Health, Education, and Welfare (HEW) was charged with writing the specific implementation and administrative regulations. Enforcement rested with the Office of Civil Rights in the Department of Justice, where it remains today. Few objections have been raised over the provisions for equity in admissions policies or curriculum. Some conservative women's organizations have charged that efforts to promote gender equity in education, particularly through a non-sexist curriculum and textbooks, are detrimental to women's traditional role in society. As a result of Title IX regulations, schools dropped admissions quotas that limited the number of women enrolled in some professional programs (e.g., engineering, medicine, and law) and were required to evaluate men and women under the same set of admission standards. Congress did not, however, end single-sex education. Private, single-sex institutions were not required to change the character of their mission or their admissions process. The legislation merely prohibited public coeducational institutions from becoming single sex in composition, and required that men and women, once admitted, had to be treated equally and have equal access to all aspects of the educational experience. This meant that girls could not be "advised" to pursue a traditional course of study, such as home economics, nor could boys be relegated to vocational courses, such as shop. Title IX, however, also required gender-neutral counseling, meaning that special efforts to redirect girls into nontraditional courses in higher mathematics, sciences, or vocational training were not permitted. Segregation by sex was still allowed in sex-education classes or in ability-grouped physical education classes, and school-affiliated organizations could maintain their traditional sex segregation if they were purely social rather than academic or professional in character. This meant that social fraternities and sororities on college campuses could remain single sex.

Title IX and Equity in Athletics

The most immediate and vociferous opposition to Title IX came from college and high school athletic directors and coaches. The National Collegiate Athletic Association (NCAA) initially tried to lobby HEW and Congress to exclude athletics from Title IX coverage. When total exclusion was unsuccessful, the NCAA argued, again unsuccessfully, that only the programs within an institution that actually received federal dollars should be subject to the equity provisions. Since few athletics programs at either the college or the high school level are direct recipients of federal dollars, this interpretation would mean a de facto Title IX exemption for athletics. The Office of Civil Rights, the primary enforcement agency, refused the NCAA's efforts, maintaining that if any program took federal money, the entire institution was subject to Title IX compliance. In 1974, the NCAA supported the Tower Amendment, which would have exempted men's intercollegiate football and basketball (the revenue-generating sports). A House-Senate conference committee rejected the amendment, leaving the NCAA to challenge the constitutionality of the gender-equity provision in the courts. Although initially unsuccessful, a 1984 Supreme Court case, *Grove City College v. Bell*, temporarily gave Title IX opponents what they sought. The Court ruled that only those programs receiving federal funds must comply with the statute. Congress acted (over President Ronald

Reagan's veto) in 1988 to reinstate the original intent of Title IX by passing the Civil Rights Restoration Act. Four years later, in *Cohen v. Brown University*, a federal court ruled that Brown University had violated Title IX's provisions when it cut two women's teams and two men's teams. Although the university cut the same number of varsity teams for men and women, several women on the gymnastics team filed suit, claiming that the effect of Brown's action violated Title IX. Cutting the two women's programs had saved the university more than $62,000, while eliminating the two men's programs saved only $16,000. In other words, female athletes were disproportionately affected by the cuts.

The regulations under Title IX provide three ways an institution can show that it is providing equitable opportunities for women athletes. First, a school can show that the percentage of its female athletes is substantially proportionate to the percentage of women in its student body. Second, if there is not proportionality, schools are required to show that they are actively engaged in a meaningful process that will provide equity for women. In 2003, for example, the University of Maryland promoted its cheerleading squad and women's water polo team to varsity status to create more scholarships and playing opportunities for female athletes on campus. By moving into compliance, the University of Maryland was able to return some scholarships to eight underfunded men's programs.[23] And last, a school is in compliance if it is meeting the actual level of athletic interest among women. It is this third provision that has energized opponents to Title IX. In Brown University's case, the institution argued that while 51 percent of its student body was female, only 38 percent of its intercollegiate athletes were women, suggesting that it was more than meeting the "interest test" required for compliance. It is difficult, however, to ignore the circuitousness of the interest argument. Girls and women are interested in sports when they have the opportunity to play sports. "The fact that 2.8 million girls play sports in high school refutes any claim that there is insufficient interest to fill the approximately 170,000 slots now available to participate in intercollegiate athletics or the additional opportunities to which they are entitled under the law."[24] In 2005, without any notice or opportunity for comment, the Department of Education issued an "Additional Clarification of Intercollegiate Athletics Policy Guidance: Three-Part Test—Part Three," allowing colleges to use a single e-mail survey to show that they have met women's interest in playing sports.[25] Title IX's impact on women's interest and participation in sports was almost immediate and has been overwhelmingly successful. For example, in 1961, nine states actually prohibited interscholastic sports for females, presumably because of the stereotype that females were too delicate for physical activity and not suited for competitive sports. In 1971, only 7.5 percent of the nearly 4 million high school athletes were female. By 1997, the twenty-fifth anniversary of Title IX, girls made up more than 40 percent of the 6-million-plus high school athletes. By 2007, the thirty-fifth anniversary of Title IX, girls held steady at 40 percent of nearly 7.1 million high school athletes, representing a 904 percent increase over participation levels in 1972. However, in 2007, girls made up 49 percent of the high school population, but received 41 percent of the participation opportunities. The laws in support of Title IX do not require high schools to publicly report gender breakdowns by sport, resources, and funding. Two bills are before the 111th Congress (2009–2011), the High School Athletics Accountability Act (House) and the High School Sports Information Collection Act (Senate), but both have been introduced since 2004 without receiving any action. The purpose of both bills would be to require high schools to collect and report information on male and female sports, including participation opportunities, funding, and other resource allocation decisions. This would be particularly helpful in identifying problems in urban schools. Research by the Women's Sports Foundation found that urban girls of color have some of the lowest rates of sports participation among all U.S. adolescents. By the eleventh and twelfth grades, 84 percent of urban girls reported no physical education classes during the previous week. A 2007 Harris Survey found that although 54 percent of boys and 50 percent of girls in the suburbs described themselves as "moderately involved" in athletics, only 36 percent of urban girls described themselves as "moderately involved" (compared to 56 percent of the urban boys).[26] To counter urban girls' lack of physical activity, the New York City public high schools established double-dutch jump rope as a competitive sport in 2008–2009.[27]

Prior to Title IX, women made up 15 percent of college athletes, but received 2 percent of the total athletic budget. In 2007, women accounted for 44 percent of the student-athletes at Division I institutions and received 45 percent of the athletic scholarships (up from 26 percent in 1996–1997) and 37 percent of the overall dollars spent on athletics. While more than 57 percent of the undergraduates at Division I schools are female, they receive only 43 percent of the opportunities to play sports, and women's programs accounted for only 37 percent of overall university athletic budgets, 32 percent of recruiting funds, and 28 percent of coaches' salaries.[28] In 2000–2001, the average college in Division I spent more than $3 million on women's sports and $5.8 million on men's sports. In June 2002, the National Women's Law Center released a list of thirty colleges that it said fail to give female athletes a fair share of athletic scholarship dollars. The report estimated the difference between male and female scholarship money at the thirty schools came to nearly $6.5 million for the 2000–2001 academic year. Those at the top of the list of thirty included the University of Miami, Kansas State, and Notre Dame.[29] Challenges persist in the allocation of coaching jobs. Women make up only 18 percent of the head coaches of both women's and men's teams across all divisions, 35 percent of athletic administrators, and 19 percent of athletic directors. Since Title IX was passed in 1972, the number of females coaching women's teams at the college level has actually dropped. In 1971, 90 percent of head coaches of women's teams were women, compared to only 42 percent in 2006.[30]

The impact of Title IX on women's participation beyond collegiate athletics is also clear. On July 9, 1999, 90,185 people (including President Clinton) crowded into the Rose Bowl in Pasadena, California, to see the U.S. women's soccer team defeat China to win the World Cup. Not only was that the largest crowd ever, across all sports, to watch a women's sporting event, it was also the most watched soccer event in U.S. history. An estimated 40 million viewers watched the game on television.[31] A record 44 percent of athletes at the Athens Olympics (summer 2004) were women, with no more than five all-male delegations. The IOC predicts gender parity within a decade.

Title IX has long been labeled "unfair" to males because, in the interest of equity, some institutions have chosen to cut male sports programs to move toward compliance. From the perspective of coaches and athletes whose budgets or prestige are likely to be reduced in the name of gender equity, Title IX promotes discrimination, a highly charged accusation. As John Weistart commented, "The particular rhetorical flourish that rallies these groups is the declaration that present policies under Title IX are 'affirmative action'—a not-so-subtle attempt to push the claims of women for recognition of their athletic aspirations into the swirl of anger that makes racial preferences such a political hot spot."[32] In 1995, J. Dennis Hastert, a former high school wrestling coach and a Republican congressman from Illinois, attempted and failed on two successive occasions to cut funding for the enforcement of Title IX. In a 1998 speech he said, "The story is, the people who have gained are women's sports, and that is great. The sports that have lost are men's sports . . . What we really want to do is treat kids fairly." Following Newt Gingrich's resignation as Speaker in 1998, Hastert became Speaker of the House, which put him in a much better position to continue his fight against Title IX enforcement. Empirically, the claims of drastic cuts to men's programs are not supported. A 2003 study conducted by *The Chronicle of Higher Education* found that, although individual schools may have cut back on men's sports programs to bring about gender equity, nationwide only thirty-eight schools have reduced the number of male athletes by more than 10 percent since 1996–1997. Over the same period, 165 schools have added more than 10 percent. "If you look at it from an overall standpoint, the number of male athletes participating in Division I sports has actually increased over the past 20 years."[33] Seventy-two percent of colleges and universities that have added women's teams have done so without cutting any teams for men.[34] In an ironic twist on the "fairness" claim, the U.S. Olympic Committee was concerned enough about the decline in U.S. medals in men's swimming and gymnastics to pledge $8 million from 1997 to the 2000 Olympic Games to help college conferences strengthen and restore their programs. Additionally, the Olympic Committee spent $4.4 million on men's gymnastics programs and built training centers in San Antonio, Minneapolis, and Salt Lake City for the men's sports that some colleges no longer offer.[35]

Title IX opponents claim that "studies consistently find higher rates of interest in athletic participation among males, be they eighth-graders or college students."[36] As law professor Robert C. Farrell counters, "It is hard to have a high level of interest in a sports program that doesn't exist." The U.S. Court of Appeals agreed. In rejecting Brown University's "level of interest" argument, it stated, "To assert that Title IX permits institutions to provide fewer athletic participation opportunities for women than men, based upon the premise that women are less interested in sports than are men, is among other things to ignore the fact that Title IX was created to remedy discrimination that results from stereotyped notions of women's interests and abilities."[37] In 1997, the Supreme Court refused to review the appeals court decision. The *Brown* decision should not be viewed too enthusiastically, however; after twenty-five years of Title IX enforcement, only 36 of the top 300 colleges and universities are in compliance.[38] In celebrating the twenty-fifth anniversary of Title IX, President Clinton extended the law's protections and announced more vigorous enforcement actions, prompting one administration official to say, "We are not stepping up our enforcement of Title IX, we are beginning it."[39]

The public is behind efforts to provide equity in sports. A 1999 CBS News poll found that more than 77 percent of adults supported gender parity in college sports, even if it meant cutting some men's teams.[40] A 2007 poll by the Mellman Group found strong support for Title IX—82 percent of Americans support the legislation while only 15 percent oppose it; an even higher percentage of respondents supports taking action under Title IX when evidence of discrimination is identified.[41] Attendance at Women's World Cup Soccer matches, as well as enthusiastic crowds at Women's National Basketball Association games and Olympic competitions featuring female athletes and team sports, suggests that Title IX's impact on collegiate opportunities for women athletes extends beyond intercollegiate competition.

Challenges to Title IX

The most recent assaults on Title IX came in conjunction with its thirtieth anniversary. In February 2002, the National Wrestling Coaches Association filed a lawsuit against the Department of Education alleging that the interpretation of Title IX embodied in the three-prong test for compliance is unlawful and authorizes intentional discrimination against male athletes amounting to *reverse discrimination* and *quotas*.[42] On June 11, 2003, U.S. District Court Judge Emmet Sullivan dismissed the lawsuit, *National Wrestling Coaches' Association v. United States Department of Education*. The court ruled that Title IX cannot be blamed for cuts to men's teams because educational institutions make decisions based on multiple unrelated factors. The court took further pains to recognize the importance of Title IX as a "landmark civil rights statute" with significant flexibility built into its implementing policies, negating the allegation of "quotas."

In June 2002, President Bush appointed a fifteen-person Commission on Opportunity in Athletics to examine Title IX on eight specific questions. The first question asked if Title IX standards for assessing equal opportunity in athletics are working to promote opportunities for men and women, suggesting that the impetus for forming the commission in the first place is to determine whether implementation of Title IX is "unfair" to men.[43] The commission held town meetings throughout the country to gather information before submitting a report to Secretary of Education Rod Paige. Several of the report's proposals threatened to dismantle Title IX protections and current interpretations of compliance requirements, including, for example, replacing the proportionality standard with a 50-50 standard (disregarding the actual proportion of males and females in the undergraduate population); developing an interest survey and tying the percentage of opportunities that must be offered for women to the results of that survey (in lieu of proportionality as the basic standard); eliminating nontraditional students (students older than eighteen through twenty-four and any student with children) when determining the percentage of males and females in the student body for purposes of calculating proportionality; and repealing the Equity in Disclosure Act, which requires public disclosure of financial and participation information by colleges and universities.[44]

Two female commission members, Donna de Varona (a two-time Olympic gold medal swimmer and chairperson of the U.S. Olympic Committee's government relations committee) and Julie Foudy (former member of the U.S. women's soccer team and president of the Women's Sports Foundation) issued a minority report:

> Our decision is based on (1) our fundamental disagreement with the tenor, structure and significant portions of the content of the Commission's report, which fails to present a full and fair consideration of the issues or a clear statement of the discrimination women and girls still face in obtaining equal opportunity in athletics; (2) our belief that many of the recommendations made by the majority would seriously weaken Title IX's protections and substantially reduce the opportunities to which women and girls are entitled under current law; and (3) our belief that only one of the proposals would address the budgetary causes underlying the discontinuation of some men's teams, and that others would not restore opportunities that have been lost.[45]

The three-part minority report begins by presenting findings and recommendations that de Varona and Foudy believe the commission should have included, offers an evaluation of the commission's recommendations and an explanation for why they cannot support the majority recommendations, and, finally, addresses the commission's process, which they believe was flawed. The minority report is quite detailed in estimating the potential impact the commission's recommendations would have on women's participation in athletics. In every instance, women would be substantially disadvantaged and would lose ground relative to the status quo.

On July 11, 2003, the Bush administration announced that there will be no changes to the mechanisms currently in place to measure compliance, and in fact, none of the recommendations from the Commission on Opportunity in Athletics will be adopted. Largely in response to the orchestrated efforts on the part of women's organizations to block any changes to Title IX, the Bush administration was forced to back down. "One year, one stacked commission, and the outrage of women's groups all over the country, and finally the Bush administration realizes the vast support for Title IX," said Eleanor Smeal, president of the Feminist Majority. "Too bad it made us lose vital time and money that could be better spent enforcing Title IX."[46] Gerald Reynolds, assistant secretary for civil rights for the Department of Education, sent a letter to educational institutions across the country announcing the decision and the commitment of resources to an educational campaign on Title IX compliance and aggressive enforcement of Title IX standards. Women's organizations interpreted the Bush administration's actions as a recognition of the power of women's votes.

The U.S. Supreme Court heard arguments in *Jackson v. Birmingham Board of Education* in December 2004. The case involves a high school girls' basketball coach who was fired after complaining that his team did not have equal access to facilities and equipment and that its resources were inequitable in violation of Title IX. The lower court dismissed Mr. Jackson's suit, finding that Title IX does not prohibit retaliation. The Bush administration supported Mr. Jackson's claim that without the ability to protect individuals who bring discrimination charges, enforcement of Title IX and other civil rights laws will be nearly impossible. On March 29, 2005, the U.S. Supreme Court held that Title IX authorizes suits to challenge retaliation for protesting sex discrimination. In doing so, the Court reaffirmed the broad coverage that Congress intended to give the law and recognized that it would be nearly impossible to protect against discrimination without also protecting those who report unlawful practices.[47]

Title IX's Broad Impact on Access to Education

More women than ever before are enrolled in colleges and universities (see Table 6.1). In 1979, the number of women surpassed the number of men enrolled in college for the first time, and the upward trend has continued ever since. Most demographers expect that increase to continue, even as the proportion of male enrollees continues to decline.[48] One negative trend in women's college enrollment, however, has been tied to the Personal Responsibility and Work Opportunity Reconciliation Act of 1996 (welfare reform). States were given leeway to define "work" to include full-time enrollment in school or training programs. In states that do not allow time in school to count as work, the law has resulted in a 20–25 percent reduction in the college attendance by high-school-educated unmarried mothers, aged 24 to 29.[49]

Among African Americans the gap between men and women is even more substantial. In 2001, women earned 66 percent of all bachelor's degrees, 70 percent of all master's degrees, and 64 percent of all doctorates awarded to African Americans.[50] Women earned 61 percent of all of the professional degrees awarded to African Americans in 2001. This represents a threefold increase over the rate of degree attainment in 1980. Only in business schools do men continue to outnumber women among African Americans. In 1976,

TABLE 6.1 College Enrollment Rates of High School Graduates, by Sex: 1960–2008

Year	Total	Males	Females
1960	45.1%	54.0%	37.9%
1962	49.0%	55.0%	43.5%
1964	48.3%	57.2%	40.7%
1966	50.1%	58.7%	42.7%
1968	55.4%	63.2%	48.9%
1970	51.8%	55.2%	48.5%
1972	49.2%	52.7%	45.9%
1974	47.5%	49.4%	45.8%
1976	48.8%	47.2%	50.3%
1978	50.1%	51.0%	49.3%
1980	49.3%	46.7%	51.8%
1982	50.6%	49.0%	52.1%
1984	55.2%	56.0%	54.5%
1986	53.8%	55.9%	51.9%
1988	58.9%	57.0%	60.8%
1990	59.9%	57.8%	62.0%
1992	61.7%	59.6%	63.8%
1994	61.9%	60.6%	63.2%
1996	65.0%	60.1%	69.7%
1998	65.6%	62.4%	69.1%
2000	63.3%	59.9%	66.2%
2002	65.2%	62.1%	68.4%
2004	66.7%	61.4%	71.5%
2006	65.8%	65.5%	66.0%
2008	68.6%	65.9%	71.5%

Source: U.S. Department of Labor, "College Enrollment and Work Activity, High School Graduates: 1960–2008," (Washington, D.C.: Bureau of Labor Statistics, various years through 2009). Data can be found at http://www.bls.gov/hsgec.pdf.

women earned 11 percent of all MBAs, but today they receive more than 40 percent of all MBA degrees awarded to African Americans.

Although the trends are clear, the reason for the decline in male enrollments is not. The trend is also not limited to the United States. Over the last decade, more than 70 percent of the increase in full-time undergraduates in the United Kingdom has been female. Sixty percent of University of Ottawa students are women. In the 1990s, women accounted for 100 percent of the enrollment growth at German universities and more than 60 percent in France and Australia.[51] Part of the change can be attributed to an increase in academic and professional opportunities for women that require a bachelor's degree. Some attribute the decline in male enrollments to a transitional economy and more non-college-related options for men. "Men have more options than women when they graduate from high school. There's the military, trade unions, and jobs that require physical strength," said one director of admissions. "A young woman who wants to have a career may think she has to go to college, whereas men see other alternatives."[52] Historical trends in educational expectations of young men and women reveal significant gender differences in expectations of college graduation over the past two decades. As the 1970s came to a close, the National Longitudinal Survey of Youth showed that fifteen- to sixteen-year-old males and females had statistically identical expectations of completing a four-year degree. In 1997, however, females were significantly more likely than males (ten points higher) to report that they expected to complete four years of college.[53] Given that educational expectations are highly correlated with ultimate educational attainment, we should expect the gender gap in enrollments to continue.

Colleges and universities must admit the best students in the applicant pool, regardless of gender, and the majority of those applicants are now female. Women tend to perform better than men in high school and in college. Admissions officials at some institutions have started modifying their promotional material to appeal to male applicants, in an attempt to attract more men to campus. The University of Dallas in Irving, Texas, brought back varsity baseball after a sixteen-year hiatus and added twenty-six men to the campus as a result. Other universities are also using athletics, both varsity and intramural, to broaden the appeal of their campuses to male applicants. Dickinson College in Pennsylvania started their campaign to attract more males by including more pictures of male students and athletics in their admissions materials and highlighting their new physics, computer science, and math building. Dickinson also started a program in international business, in part to attract and retain more male students. Between 1999 and 2006, Dickinson went from 36 percent males in the incoming class to 44 percent male. The biggest factor in increasing the number of men on campus, according to Robert Massa, vice president for enrollment, was accepting a higher percentage of males that applied. "The secret of getting some gender balance is that once men apply, you've got to admit them. So did we bend a little bit? Yeah, at the margin we did, but not to the point that we would admit guys who couldn't do the work," he said.[54] Morgan State University has implemented mentoring and tutoring programs aimed at men and yet women's "graduation rates are higher, achievement rates are higher and leadership roles are ten times greater."[55] At the 2000 annual meeting of the National Association for College Admissions Counselors, two panel discussions addressed the absence of men in the college applicant pool.[56] During these panels, titled "Where Have All the Men Gone?" and "Are Our Boys at Risk?," participants confirmed the trend in declining male enrollments but offered few solutions beyond giving preferential treatment to men in the admissions process. The idea of preferential treatment for male applicants was met with interest, rather than scorn, by other admissions counselors in the audience. For the past two years, 2007 and 2008, the University of Pennsylvania has held a student affairs and admissions "Conference on College Men." In the late 1990s, the University of Georgia began giving an edge in admissions to male applicants, but stopped in the face of a federal lawsuit.[57] In 2005 Towson experimented with a program called Academic Special Admissions. The Towson program was designed to admit more male students with poor high school grades but satisfactory SAT scores (high school grades are known to be a better predictor of college success than are SAT scores). In its first year Towson enrolled 190 students under the program, 85 percent of them male. By 2007, Towson had dropped the program because of poor retention rates. Only 70 percent of the students enrolled under the special program remained enrolled for more than a year—a 15 percentage point differential from regularly admitted students.[58] A report on the potential economic and social consequences of the gender gap in college enrollments, prepared by researchers at Northeastern University for The Business Roundtable, warned that "marginalization of men on the educational front will jeopardize the ability of men to perform vital economic and social functions that are key to strengthened family life and safe, stable and prosperous communities." From an economic perspective, they argue:

> Weaker educational attainment among men results in a reduction of the size of the skilled labor force—a resource that is vital to keep the nation's economic engine humming—and in labor productivity and economic growth. In the social arena, men play numerous roles: as husbands, fathers, breadwinners, and role models for young men.[59]

Educational choices have economic consequences for both men and women. On average, male college graduates earn at least $23,000 a year more than men with only a high school diploma, and the gap gets larger every year. And yet men account for 57 percent of the sixteen- to twenty-four-year-olds in the labor force who hold only a high school diploma. With an edge in education, women could presumably quickly close the salary gap and move into positions of power as heads of corporations and political leaders. That is, if and only if a college degree remains highly prized in the economic marketplace, and if and only if the economic disadvantage that comes purely from being a female is somehow reduced. At a time when universities are competing with glitz and sports to attract male applicants and giving males a slight break on the admission standards, college-educated women in the full-time workforce still make only $12,334 more a year on average than high school–educated men.[60] Why then are women choosing college and men choosing work? One reason may be that men have a clear edge in their interest in advanced technology and computer skills. Career Training Foundation, a nonprofit organization that supports U.S. trade and vocational schools, estimates that more than two-thirds of the people entering technology fields are male.[61] Girls still make up almost 90 percent of the students enrolled in classes leading to traditionally female occupations and only 15 percent of those in classes in traditionally male fields (see Table 6.2 below). After Congress eliminated the funding for school guidance and equity counselors to eliminate sex bias and stereotyping in educational tracking, little has been done to assist individual boys and girls in choosing career paths. As the salaries for high-technology workers escalate and women lag behind men

TABLE 6.2 Percentage of Bachelor's Degrees Conferred to Women by Field of Study

Field of Study	1969–70	1979–80	1989–90	1999–2000	2005–06
Total*	43.1	49.0	53.2	57.2	57.5
Agriculture and Natural Resources	4.1	29.6	31.6	42.9	47.7
Accounting	8.7	36.1	53.3	60.4	N/A**
Biological and Life Sciences	29.7	42.1	50.8	58.3	61.5
Business Management	9.0	33.1	46.5	49.5	N/A**
Computer and Information Sciences	12.9	30.2	29.9	28.1	20.6
Education	75.3	73.8	78.1	75.8	79.1
Engineering	0.7	9.3	13.8	20.4	17.9
Health Professions	68.8	82.2	84.4	83.8	86.0
Mathematics	37.4	41.5	45.7	47.1	45.1
Physical Sciences and Science Technologies	13.6	23.7	31.3	40.3	41.8
Psychology	43.4	63.3	71.5	76.5	77.5
Social Sciences and History	35.9	43.6	44.2	51.2	50.0
Business					49.8

*Total percentage of bachelor's degrees awarded to women regardless of field of study; includes fields not listed in the table.
**The categories for fields of study changed such that Accounting and Management were no longer recorded as separate fields. Business now takes their place.
Source: U.S. Department of Education, National Center for Education Statistics, Higher Education General Information Survey (HEGIS), Table 27-1, "Number and Percentage of Bachelor's, Master's, and Doctoral Degrees Women Earned," 2008, accessed at http://nces.ed.gov/pubs2008/2008031_3.pdf.

in choosing engineering, mathematics, and science as their major programs of study, the salary gap is ironically likely to increase even as women's edge in enrolling and earning bachelor's degrees continues to grow.

There is some evidence that women are making choices at the high school level that will give them a wider variety of choices in college. In content-specific courses at the high school level, girls continue to lag behind boys in entering science and higher mathematics courses in general. However, among college-bound males and females, girls caught up in the late 1990s and in some cases have exceeded boys in years of study in science and math. In 2000, the most recent year for which statistics are available, 65.7 percent of girls took chemistry in high school, versus only 58 percent of the boys. Girls also outnumbered the boys in math courses through precalculus, but boys continued to outnumber girls in calculus courses, but only by a small margin (11.1 percent of girls, 12.2 percent of boys). In the last ten years, the number of girls taking the AP Calculus AB exam has increased by nearly 60 percent, and the number of girls taking the AP Physics B exam has more than doubled. Girls now make up 48 percent of AP test takers in calculus, 47 percent in chemistry, and 58 percent in biology. In 2007, half of the 40 finalists in the Intel Science Talent Search were girls.[62]

Science, technology, engineering, and math are collectively known as the STEM disciplines. At the college level, the proportion of women studying science and engineering increased from 16 percent in 1960 to more than 40 percent in 1990. The proportion of women earning doctoral degrees in science and engineering rose from 6.3 percent in 1960 to 44 percent in 2004.[63] In 2004, women earned 60 percent of the PhD's and the majority of bachelor's degrees in fields other than science and engineering. Men still earn most of the degrees in computer sciences; earth, atmospheric, and ocean sciences; mathematics and statistics; physical sciences; and engineering. "In engineering and computer sciences—the fastest-growing STEM fields with the greatest workforce demand—the percentages of women have reached a plateau or dropped over the last decade." Attrition of female faculty in STEM fields is also higher than in other disciplines, leaving very few female professors to take on leadership roles or serve as mentors to undergraduates in the STEM pipeline. In 2003, although 41 percent of all assistant professors in science and engineering were women, only 17.6 percent of professors were women. At elite institutions the proportion of women at the rank of professor has remained roughly 10 percent for the past five decades.

Why are women leaving? Researcher Sue Rosser found, contrary to conventional wisdom, it is not because women lack interest or mental aptitude; if that were the case, women in STEM disciplines would consistently underperform relative to male students in college and graduate school. "The data show the contrary: women outperform men academically; receive more awards; have higher graduation rates and better attitudes toward education." According to Rosser, two factors stand out in explaining why women exit from STEM careers: the need to balance career and family, and a lack of professional networks. Other researchers found that single men and single women participate about equally in the STEM workforce. By contrast, a married female PhD is thirteen times less likely to be employed than a married male PhD. If the married female PhD has young children, she is 30 percent less likely than a single male PhD to be employed.[64] The lack of federal or institutional supports for childbearing and family care in the United States disadvantage women here relative to female research scientists in other countries who enjoy more generous supports, such as paid family leave and on-site day care.[65] "Male faculty members who start families within five years of receiving their PhDs are 38 percent more likely to earn tenure than women who do the same." Put somewhat differently, "for every three women who take a fast-track (elite or research university) job before having a child, only one ever becomes a mother." The other deterrent for women comes from the lack of career networks and mentors. As we have noted in previous chapters, mentors play a unique role in encouraging young women to pursue nontraditional paths in politics and employment; STEM careers are

Socialization or Discrimination: Larry Summers vs. Women in Science

Slowpoke © 2005 Jen Sorensen, http://www.slowpokecomics.com/strips/womenscience.html.

The president of Harvard University, Lawrence H. Summers, sparked controversy with comments he made at a January 2005 conference on Diversifying the Science and Engineering Workforce. In remarks, intended to "synthesize the scholarship" as conference organizers asked him to do, Dr. Summers offered three possible explanations for the small number of women in high-level positions in science and engineering: first, the reluctance or inability of women with children to work 80-hour weeks; second, that women are subject to discrimination and different socialization, but discrimination was economically unlikely since institutions that discriminated against women would lose them to those who did not; and third, fewer girls than boys have top scores on science and math tests in late high school years. Dismissing the impact of socialization and elaborating on the third point, Summers said, "No one really understands why this is, and it's an area of ferment in social sciences. Research in behavioral genetics is showing that things people previously attributed to socialization weren't due to socialization after all." Summers went on to say that women do not have the same "innate ability" or "natural ability" as men in some fields, particularly at the highest levels.

Although not all of the participants were offended by Summers's remarks, several prominent women in science walked out. Nancy Hopkins, a Harvard graduate and one of the women who left, is a biologist at MIT and the driving force behind an influential study documenting inequalities for women at MIT. Hopkins doesn't argue that there *can't* be any differences between the abilities of women and men, but noted that there is ample research that demonstrates social and environmental factors affect women's performance. Detractors also pointed to the drop in the percentage of tenured job offers made to women by the University's Faculty of Arts and Sciences during Summers's tenure as president (only four of thirty-two tenured jobs went to women in the 2004 hiring cycle). In defense of his comments, Summers repeatedly stated that he was trying to provoke his audience. In that he was successful! This controversy and several others led to a vote of no confidence by the faculty and ultimately to his resignation as president of Harvard in June 2006. His permanent successor is Dr. Drew Gilpin Faust, Harvard's first female president.

What do you think?

What are the implications of Dr. Summers's claim about "innate ability" differences between men and women in science for "equality" as you now understand it? This is an excellent example of the ways in which sex and gender differ. Dr. Summers is making a claim based on sex differences and discounting the social context that produces gender and gender differences. Can these two positions be reconciled? Some critics refer to the basis for Dr. Summers claim as "junk science" since there has not yet been any empirical proof of a correlation between the physical differences in men's and women's brains and differences in their intellectual abilities. Why is society so quick to latch onto the potential for intellectual differences? Can you imagine it working the other way, they ask? For example, given that there is a higher incidence of learning disabilities, autism, and mental retardation among boys, where are the corresponding assertions that males must have inferior brains?

no different. Women scientists have fewer graduate and postdoctoral students to support their work than men and less diverse networks. Women faculty report fewer referrals from collegial networks to work as paid consultants, serve on science advisory boards, and interact with industry. In finding solutions to these problems, some novel approaches have been tried. For example, Clare Booth Luce Professorships, funded by the Henry Luce Foundation and designed to advance the careers of women in science, engineering, and mathematics, provide funding to cover professional expenses—defined to include child care as well as conference travel and publishing expenses. Although efforts to attract and retain women in STEM fields have been underway for decades, comments made in 2005 by Harvard President Lawrence Summers reignited the debate about low numbers of women in STEM fields, and led several institutions (including Harvard) to redouble their efforts to improve the overall climate for women in science.

WEEA: Women's Educational Equity Act

Title IX requires gender-neutral treatment of men and women in education. The results have been more opportunities for women and fewer overt barriers to college admission and career choices. However, without proactive counseling and intervention strategies designed to increase the numbers of girls in nontraditional courses of study, the opportunities created by Title IX are likely to go unrealized. In 1974, Congress passed the Women's Educational Equity Act (WEEA), which authorized funds to promote bias-free textbooks and curriculum, support research on gender equity, and revamp teacher training programs. The effort was significantly underfunded by Congress and ignored by Republican administrations through Reagan and George H. W. Bush. It was not until the American Association of University Women (AAUW) published its report, *How Schools Shortchange Girls*, in 1992 that a credible effort to support WEEA materialized. Fiscal year 1996 had no appropriation for WEEA; however, between 1997 and 1999, funding remained constant at $3 million a year. As part of the original legislation, a national Equity Resource Center was established. It remains active as a clearinghouse for teacher training, developing equity curriculum materials, and conducting research related to gender equity in education. The center's definition of gender equity in education addresses the chances for both females and males to learn in an environment free of limits:

> Gender equity is a set of actions, attitudes and assumptions that provide opportunities and create expectations about individuals, regardless of gender. Gender equity is a chance for females and males at learning regardless of the subject; preparing for future education, jobs, and careers; high expectations; developing, achieving and learning; equitable treatment and outcomes in school and beyond. Gender equity is linked to and supports race, ethnic, economic, disability, and other equity concerns.[66]

In September 2004, Congress passed the Maloney-Woolsey-Sanchez Amendment, which provided $3 million to fund the WEEA for 2005. The Heritage Foundation, a conservative Washington-based think tank, lobbied to end program funding, arguing that WEEA is outdated:

> "On nearly every indicator of academic success girls outperform boys. The gender gap in reading and writing achievement, Advanced Placement participation, honors course participation, high school and college graduation rates, and other indicators favors girls. Boys, however, are more likely to be in Special Education, to repeat a grade, to be suspended, or to be involved with crime, drugs, and alcohol."[67]

The Heritage Foundation issued a report in 2001 titled "Wasting Dollars: The Women's Educational Equity Act," in which it argued that "focusing on

TABLE 6.3 First Professional Degrees Awarded, by Sex and Race: 2004–2005

	Total*	Men	Women
Dentistry (DDS or DMD)	5.1%		
White		37.8%	24.3%
African American		1.7%	2.6%
Hispanic		2.5%	2.6%
Medicine (MD)	17.7%		
White		36.1%	30.2%
African American		2.4%	4.6%
Hispanic		2.7%	2.2%
Pharmacy (PharmD)	10.1%		
White		21.3%	41.7%
African American		2.4%	6.5%
Hispanic		1.3%	2.7%
Veterinary Medicine (DVM)	2.6%		
White		21.6%	68.6%
African American		0.89%	.93%
Hispanic		0.93%	2.4%
Law (LLB or JD)	49.7%		
White		41.7%	35.4%
African American		2.4%	5.3%
Hispanic		2.9%	3.0%

* The "Total" column represents the number of degrees in that field as a percentage of all professional degrees awarded.
Source: National Center for Education Statistics, "First Professional Degrees Conferred by Degree-Granting Institutions, by Sex, by Racial/Ethnic Group and Major Field of Study: 2004–2005," (Washington, D.C.: U.S. Department of Education, 2009). This table can be accessed at http://www.nces.ed.gov (Table 277).

What About Men?

Women's studies courses have proliferated on college and university campuses since they were first introduced in the 1960s. By some estimates, there are more than 700 organized programs in women's studies at all levels of education, from an undergraduate minor to a doctoral-degree program. Women's studies, by definition, focuses on transforming the "study of women," in which women are objects, into "women's studies," in which women are subjects. But what about men?

Michael Kimmel is a professor of sociology who studies men and masculinity. He argues that understanding gender requires an examination of masculinity. "To fully integrate gender . . . we have to see both men and women as gendered . . . . As gender inequality is reduced, the real differences among people—based on race, class, ethnicity, age, sexuality, as well as gender—will emerge in a context in which each of us can be appreciated for our uniqueness as well as our commonality."[1] Kimmel credits feminist scholars for focusing our attention on gender, but he challenges all scholars to examine the impact of gender on the experiences of both men and women and to make gender visible to men. Masculinity is a socially constructed manifestation of gender that warrants attention in classrooms and in scholarship. Just as there is not only one female experience, there is not only one male experience. "[M]aking masculinity visible is the first step towards de-centering it as the unexamined norm."[2]

non-existent problems like gender inequity diverts funds and attention from the real—and critical—problems in America's educational system."[68] The National Coalition for Women and Girls in Education (NCWGE), however, lobbied hard for the amendment and funding. WEEA is the only remaining program solely focused on advancing gender equity and it is one of the smallest programs in the Department of Education. Equity advocates remain concerned about the way in which funds have been allocated. Previously, over one-third of the appropriation was used to fund the WEEA Equity Resource Center.[69] Although the resource and information Web site is no longer active, WEEA continues as a federal program and continued to invite grant applications as recently as January 2009.

EQUITY IN ACTION: HOW GIRLS AND BOYS EXPERIENCE SCHOOL

The AAUW's 1992 report called immediate attention to a long-standing gender-equity problem. Although girls and boys attended the same classes within the same schools, their experiences differed dramatically. *How Schools Shortchange Girls* became a rallying cry for feminists to reexamine sexist

Courses on men and masculinity first emerged in the 1980s, and now there are hundreds of such courses at colleges and universities. In a controversial move, a group of University of Chicago students formed "Men in Power," a student organization that promises to help men get ahead professionally. The group, formed in 2009, would be the first male advocacy group on a campus with approximately nine women's advocacy groups. The name of the group has led to charges of misogyny from some critics and led others to question the need for such a group since males still dominate the corridors of power in U.S. business, law, and politics. Others applaud the group's formation as a way to explore what it means to be a man in today's society, particularly at a time when the recession is hitting male-dominated occupations particularly hard.[3]

In what ways is the study of gender enhanced by focusing on both women and men? In what ways might women's lives be improved by examining a masculine ideology? Are there reasons not to include men in the study of gender? Are there any courses on men and masculinity at your institution? If not, should there be such a course?

1. Michael Kimmel, "Educating Men and Women Equally," *AAC&U on Campus with Women* 28, no. 3 (1999): 3.
2. Ibid., p. 15.
3. Sara Olkon, "'Power' Move by Male Students Ruffles University of Chicago," *Chicago Tribune*, May 27, 2009, accessible at http://www.chicagotribune.com.

attitudes in the classroom. As a result of the report, parents started paying more attention to their children's experiences in school.[70]

In 1982, the Project on the Status of Education of Women, a research effort commissioned by the Association of American Colleges (AAC), reported on the "chilly climate" for women in college classrooms. The research detailed the often subtle ways faculty treated male and female students differently. It found, for example, that female and male faculty alike were more likely to ask questions of male students, to focus more intently on the answers of male students, and to ask "higher order" critical questions of men, but not of women. In examples offered in class, males occupied the role of "professional," while women were more often the "client" or "patient," thereby making it difficult for women to view themselves in professional roles. Project researchers found more blatant examples of male faculty sexualizing female students and denigrating their future aspirations by treating them as less serious than those of male students. Similarly, they found the *attribution error* at work among faculty. A male's success was more often attributed to skill or ability, while a female's success was attributed to luck or a lack of difficulty with a task. The chilly climate has harmed both men and women. Women, over time, may grow to view their presence in a class or program of study as peripheral, have little expectation of participating in class discussions, and learn that their capacity for full intellectual development or career aspirations is limited. Male students

Doonesbury

BY GARRY TRUDEAU

are disadvantaged by not being challenged by all of their peers. Also, reinforcing any negative views of women may make their transition to the workplace more difficult and limit their ability to work with and view women as equals.[71]

Two years later, in 1984, the same project released a study of the chilly climate facing women outside the classroom on college campuses. The study concluded that "even though men and women are presumably exposed to a common liberal arts curriculum and other educational programs during the undergraduate years, it would seem that these programs serve more to pre-serve, rather than to reduce, stereotypic differences between men and women in behavior, personality, aspirations and achievement."[72] The report went on to document experiences in support services, campus employment, admissions and financial-aid counseling, health care offered on campus, campus safety, and a lax attitude about harassment or degradation of women on campus that disadvantaged female students.

Both the AAC and AAUW reports peg the roots of the chilly climate to early educational disparities in elementary school classrooms. In 1973, Myra Sadker published *Sexism in School and Society*. In many respects it was the first such book, written for teachers but released to a wider audience, that documented sex-segregated classes, gender bias in required textbooks, and sexist teach-ing and counseling practices. Myra Sadker, with her husband and intellectual partner, David, continued to research bias in the classroom and, in particu-lar, teachers' treatment of students. They published their results in *Failing at Fairness: How Our Schools Cheat Girls*, which was released in 1994. Coupled with the AAUW report, educators and parents could not ignore the findings on the treatment of girls in the primary-school classroom. The basic findings were these: Primary-school teachers tended to talk more to boys than to girls, asked boys more "higher order" questions, and worked with them to derive the answers rather than dismissing the first answer as wrong and moving on as they did with the girls. Teachers were also more likely to give boys specific instructions on how to complete an assignment but showed girls how to do it or did it for them. Additionally, teachers were more likely to praise boys for the content of their thinking as it was reflected in their work, whereas they praised girls for their neatness. The Sadkers' work was based on thousands of hours of classroom observations, many of which were videotaped. In the tapes, viewers could see teachers encouraging boys to work harder to answer a question while silencing girls by quickly moving on after their answer was offered. The teachers were not acting maliciously; they were simply not aware of their actions or of the detrimental consequences of their actions for girls.

The Backlash: How Schools Cheat Boys

Concurrent with the release of the previously mentioned studies on girls' educational experiences were several popular books on the psychological and intellectual development of girls in adolescence. Mary Pipher's *Reviving Ophelia* and Peggy Orenstein's *Schoolgirls: Young Women, Self-Esteem, and the Confidence Gap* appeared in bookstores in 1994, and detailed the precipitous decline in intellectual confidence, voice, self-worth, and ambition in girls after about eleven years of age. Wildly popular with parents, educators, and women's groups, the books served to intensify the focus on girls. Congress responded by passing the Gender Equity in Education Act in 1994, which authorized additional research on girls' development, gender-equity issues in education, and strategies to counter bias where it exists.

Quietly at first, and then more stridently, boys' advocates began to object to all the attention showered on girls, presumably at the expense of boys. They cited U.S. Department of Education statistics showing that girls get better grades than boys, have higher educational aspirations, participate in advanced-placement classes at higher rates, and surpass boys in reading and writing skills. Studies of fourth, eighth, and twelfth graders show that girls are more "engaged" in school in almost all aspects. They are more likely to come to school prepared (with paper, pencils, books, and the like), and they are more likely to do assigned homework. By the time boys are seniors in high school, they were four times as likely as girls not to do their homework. Boys are more likely than girls to be suspended from school, to be held back a grade, and to ultimately drop out of school altogether. Boys are three times as likely as girls to be diagnosed with some form of learning disorder and more likely to be involved with crime, alcohol, and drugs. Although girls attempt suicide more often than boys, boys are more often successful.[73]

In 1997, the Public Education Network (PEN) released a new teacher-student survey administered in grades seven through twelve that seemed to directly contradict the findings of the AAUW-sponsored research: Contrary to girls' suffering neglect in the nation's classrooms, the PEN study found that boys consistently underperformed on a number of indicators. "Contrary to the commonly held view that boys are at an advantage over girls in school, girls appear to have an advantage over boys in terms of their future plans, teachers' expectations, everyday experiences at school and interactions in the classroom."[74] Most striking is the boys' perception, expressed by more than 31 percent of the boys in the study, that teachers do not listen to what they have to say. In contrast, only 19 percent of the girls shared this perception. Other studies released in the late 1990s offered similar findings relative to boys' current state of affairs. In almost all cases, girls outperformed boys, particularly on indicators related to school and aspirations for a college education.

The cover story of the May 2000 issue of the *Atlantic Monthly* was an article by Christina Hoff Sommers titled "The War Against Boys." The article charged that the "crisis" in girls' education of the early 1990s was generated on false assumptions, based on "bad science," and concocted by "girls' partisans" for political purposes. The article prompted an outcry from many feminist quarters, particularly from those such as Carol Gilligan and David Sadker, who were the objects of Sommers's critique. The response from readers was "swift and substantial."[75] Both the article and exchange of letters offer an extraordinary glimpse at the power of gender and the intensity with which gender operates in shaping our perceptions of important social questions, the facts gathered in order to answer those questions, and how the "facts" are interpreted in order to make public policy. In May 2008, AAUW released a report reviewing 40 years of data on achievement from the fourth grade through college. For the first time, the report analyzed gender differences within economic and ethnic categories. The headline-grabbing aspect of the report was that "there is no crisis for boys" in schools. Rather, "If there is a crisis, it is with African American and Hispanic students and low-income students, girls and boys," said co-author Christianne Corbett. The report found a literacy gap in favor of girls, but that it had not changed substantially in nearly thirty years. Similarly, the math gap favoring boys persists but has not increased. Students, boys and girls, from families with a combined income of $37,000 or less are less likely to be proficient in math and reading. Gender differences vary significantly by race and ethnicity. Catherine Hill, director of research a the AAUW Educational Foundation, said that the study was undertaken to dispel myths about a "boy crisis" and so that educational policy can be guided by fact.[76] The report states:

> Girls' educational successes have not—and should not—come at the expense of boys. If girls' achievements come at the expense of boys, one would expect to see boys' scores decline as girls' scores rise, but boys' average test scores have improved alongside girls' scores in recent decades. For example, girls' average scores on the NAEP mathematics test have risen during the past three decades—as have boys' scores (indeed, older boys retain a small lead in math). Girls tend to earn higher average scores on the NAEP reading assessments, but this lead has narrowed or remained the same during the past three decades.[77]

There may well be another explanation for the mixed evidence on girls' and women's school experiences. Title IX was made into law in 1972, the AAUW report was based on schools in the mid to late 1980s, and the statistics offered to counter its findings are from the late 1990s. Rather than "bad science," perhaps the new statistics on women's performance in education reflect an outcome of gender-equity policy some thirty years later. Reports based on more recent data confirm that although girls and women have made substantial gains since Title IX was passed in 1972, they are still underrepresented in mathematics, science, and technology fields; men still earn the majority of advanced degrees; and men still occupy the majority of decision-making positions within universities and continue to earn higher salaries. Women account for 36 percent of college faculty, but only 7 percent of full professors. The earnings gap between men and women is largest at the rank of full professor. Most scholars agree that gender equity in education is a pressing problem for both boys and girls. The odd mix of gender-neutral and gender-specific education policy currently on the books ensures that this debate will continue with each "side" armed with gendered facts to support its pursuit of equality in education.

EDUCATION'S LONG-TERM IMPACT ON WOMEN'S PURSUIT OF EQUALITY

In previous chapters we've addressed the question of women's agency; in other words, their ability to act by themselves and for themselves. Education serves as a vital resource in enabling women to exercise their agency as it relates to participation in politics, fertility issues, health decisions for themselves and their children, and the assurance of economic stability within their families. A tremendous body of research literature links women's education, employment, and empowerment.[78] In the United States, women's median income has increased both in real terms and relative to men's income, largely as a function of the increase in women's level of education.[79] In 2006, based on median annual earnings, women with a college degree earned 82 percent of what similarly educated men earned, while women with a high school diploma or the equivalent earned 80 percent of what similarly situated men earned (see Table 6.4). Better-educated workers (both male and female) tend to raise the productivity levels of firms in most industries, and are more likely than their less educated peers to be employed and to work more weeks and hours during the year.[80] In 2002, 80.7 percent of women with a bachelor's degree or higher but only 46 percent of those with less than a high school degree and 66.3 percent of those with a high school diploma or GED were employed full time.[81]

Where once there was a "success gap" referring to the trade-off many women made between advanced education and marriage, the gap has narrowed considerably and is projected to disappear altogether by 2010. In 1980, a woman with three years of graduate school education was 13 percent less likely to be married than a woman with only a high school education. By 2000, that gap was less than 5 percent.[82] Although the media continue to perpetuate the stereotype that advanced education somehow disadvantages women in their ability to marry if they choose to (e.g., *Newsweek*'s erroneous statistic that "a 40-year

TABLE 6.4 The Wage Gap by Education: 2006

	Total	High School	Bachelor's	Master's
All Men	$40,836	$33,074	$55,425	$67,992
White	$50,606	$40,636	$62,446	$76,079
Black	$36,070	$31,569	$49,171	$60,588
Hispanic	$30,754	$30,844	$45,917	$68,157
All Women	$35,090	$26,737	$45,408	$52,438
White	$36,735	$27,848	$46,165	$52,202
Black	$30,823	$24,894	$41,765	$52,298
Hispanic	$25,990	$24,273	$40,377	$51,170

These figures represent the median earnings in 2006 for full-time, year-round workers, twenty-five years and older.

Source: U.S. Census Bureau, "Current Population Survey, Annual Social and Economic Supplement, Table PINC-03," last revised August 28, 2007, accessed at http://pubdb3.census.gov/macro/032007/perinc/new03_000.htm.

old woman had a statistically higher chance of being killed by a terrorist than getting married"; *New York Times* columnist Maureen Dowd's assertion that "men don't like to date successful women"; and Sylvia Ann Hewlett's 2002 book *Creating a Life: Professional Women and the Quest for Children*, in which she erroneously asserts that more successful women were less likely to have children), empirical research demonstrates that while marriage rates for all women fell in the last decade, the marriage rate for women with three years of graduate school increased by 3 percentage points.

Comparative research documents that increases in nutritional intake in households are a result of women's independent income. Research in India and elsewhere has shown a correlation between women's education, economic independence, and child survival rates.[83] Analysis by the UN Family Planning Agency has illustrated over the years that increases in educational attainment by women directly correlate with lower fertility rates, thereby easing the negative impact of population growth. Education also empowers women to use new communication technology to access information and to make their specific needs known to policymakers. As more women become policymakers themselves, there is evidence of a reciprocal impact on education for girls and women. In Bhopal, India, for example, the last four women rulers introduced compulsory education for girls that creates a standard for universal education for girls.

There remain challenges. Illiteracy among women remains an international problem, although in the last decade the gap between men and women has closed somewhat. UNESCO estimates that nearly two-thirds of the world's 876 million illiterates are women, and that number is expected to decline by only about 10 million by 2007.[84] Throughout the world, girls are more likely to leave school early because of family obligations. Boys too leave school early but more often because of economic reasons, rather than to care for siblings or to perform unpaid household duties. Illiteracy rates among the young (ages fifteen through twenty-four) remain very high in countries where children are involved in economic activity. Census data collected in 2000 by the United Nations reported that more than one in four women between fifteen and twenty-four years old are illiterate.[85] Africa has one of the highest female illiteracy rates among young women (40 percent). In southern Asia, the UN estimates that 22 million girls and 13 million boys are not in school. Despite progress made during the past 10 years, around 218 million children between the ages of 5 and 17 work, with around 74 million children under the age of 14 engaged in hazardous employment. Girls often fare worst as they are forced to work inside and outside the home, and are vulnerable to special risks in hidden work situations. Where poor families have to choose which children will be educated, it is often girls who lose out. "There is no better investment for a society than education, in particular girls' education," said the director-general of UNESCO, Mr. Koïchiro Matsuura. "Educating girls today has a lifelong impact on health, nutrition, employment and growth. Most fundamentally, education is a basic human right that is currently denied to 75 million children, 55 percent of whom are girls."[86] The future impact on women, their families, and the world's economy will be severe. Girls denied an education are more vulnerable to poverty, hunger, violence, abuse, exploitation, and trafficking. The positive impact of education, in the United States and around the world, is evident in women's health, earning potential and long-term economic stability, family stability, and an increase in the likelihood that women will ensure that their own children are educated. Finally, a better-educated and more-literate female population should also increase civic engagement and voting rates and strengthen democracy.[87]

EDUCATION ISSUES FACING FUTURE GENERATIONS IN THE UNITED STATES

Although women today enjoy unprecedented access to education and high achievement within educational programs, their success has not gone unnoticed and is not universally celebrated. When education is viewed as a zero-sum game, improvements in educational opportunities and performance for women are interpreted by some as discrimination against men. Title IX's requirement that institutions receiving federal dollars treat men and women equally in all aspects of educational programming, including athletics, does not specifically tell institutions *how* to accomplish gender equity. When universities choose to cut men's nonrevenue sports such as wrestling, swimming, or gymnastics in order to add women's programs in a move toward equity, it is an institutional decision, not one required by the policy. The perception is, however, that women's progress comes at men's expense. The controversy over how girls and boys are treated in the classroom has at its core the belief that when one sex is advantaged, the other must be disadvantaged.

The Unique Nature of Education as a Public Good

Education is unique in the sense that it is a commodity that has direct benefits for both society and the individual.[88] It is also a divisible or competitive good, meaning that it can be given to some and withheld from others. As we discussed earlier in this chapter, women and African Americans were barred from schools and even from privately acquiring the knowledge and skills an education provides. Laws now guarantee access to education for all. However, education is also a good that can be consumed differently by each individual even when everyone has access to the same presentation of the good. Sometimes this is an individual's choice, but in other cases, either through the socialization process or through subtle or not-so-subtle messages, individuals are directed to consume the good differently. Course-taking patterns suggest that men and women have consumed and may still consume education differently. The consequences of policy and individual choices are exhibited in the demographic characteristics of our population. Education plays a direct role in health, life expectancy, occupation and income, family size, and the quality of life citizens enjoy. Because of the importance of education, it remains a top policy priority in presidential campaigns and in successive sessions of Congress.

In the coming years, policymakers will be faced with making decisions about education policy that will have direct gender implications even if they are not at first evident. For example, school vouchers offer one way to give parents more say in their children's education. Vouchers would allow parents to enroll their children in the school of their choice, and the federal dollars dedicated to education would follow that child. In practice, this would mean that parents could choose to enroll their children in parochial schools with assistance from the government. It remains unclear how this might impact existing policy that requires gender equity in all aspects of an institution that receives federal funds. How might gender issues be treated in a Catholic school's curriculum or in a school that adheres to fundamentalist Christian tenets? If school vouchers are adopted, will there be Title IX issues? How strictly will the provisions of Title IX be enforced when they conflict with other educational goals? As we have seen in the discussion above, Title IX has come under heightened scrutiny because it is perceived as aiding women and girls at the expense of men and boys, even though the legislation itself is gender neutral.

Single-Sex Schools

Another area facing policymakers in the future will be same-sex education. Title IX prohibits sex segregation in education only in vocational, professional, and graduate schools, and in public undergraduate programs that have not limited admission to one sex from their founding. Unlike race equity and education, sex equity does not require integration in all schools and programs. In 1954, the Supreme Court reasoned in *Brown v. Board of Education* that separate can never be equal because of the perception of inferiority that race segregation entails. Neither the Supreme Court nor most feminists and policymakers, for that matter, have ever applied the same reasoning to sex-segregated schools. Because of the difference in how boys and girls experience education (which was described earlier in this chapter), many feminists actually advocate separate education for girls. Others argue that same-sex institutions are detrimental to females' development since they deny women the opportunity to compete with and interact with males as they will be required to do in the workforce and in society. Largely because of this difference of opinion, the federal courts and policymakers have not adopted a view of educational equity that requires integrating males and females.

Although same-sex schools are not forbidden under Title IX or, in most cases, other federal laws, their popularity waned throughout the 1970s and 1980s, leaving very few, mostly private, single-sex institutions by the 1990s. Legal challenges to single-sex institutions in the 1970s established that single-sex institutions were not inherently unconstitutional. The Supreme Court has allowed single-sex programs to remain as long as an individual denied admission could reasonably seek the same educational opportunity elsewhere or the practice of limiting admission to one sex was not arbitrary. For example, in the 1970 case of *Williams v. McNair*, men sought admission to then all-female Winthrop College in South Carolina. At the time, a U.S. District Court maintained Winthrop as a women's college, arguing that there were other coeducational colleges in South Carolina that offered similar liberal-arts programs to those offered at Winthrop. The plaintiffs in this case could not argue that the women-only admissions practice was arbitrary since South Carolina maintained separate state-supported institutions for men and for women (Winthrop for women, the Citadel for men). In that same year, however, a district court ruled that the University of Virginia[89] had to admit women because it offered a quality of education not available at other public institutions in the state. The first case the Supreme Court heard on this question came in 1982 in *Mississippi University for Women v. Hogan*. In this case, a male applicant to that school's nursing program was denied purely on the basis of his sex. The Supreme Court ruled that the gender discrimination was subject to scrutiny under the equal protection clause of the Fourteenth Amendment. This required the state of Mississippi to show that the admissions policy served an "important governmental objective" and that the single-sex admissions policy was "substantially related to the achievement of those objectives" (referred to as middle-level scrutiny). In this case, Mississippi failed to meet the test and males were admitted. The Court did not, however, directly address the constitutionality of state-supported single-sex schools.

Point of Comparison

Global Educational Attainment

The most fundamental prerequisite for empowering women in all spheres of society is educational attainment. Without education of comparable quality and content to that given to boys and men, and education "relevant to existing knowledge and real needs, women are unable to access well-paid, formal sector jobs, advance within them, participate in, and be represented in government and gain political influence."[1] In many industrialized countries, women now represent a slight majority of all university students. "Ironically, as this trend has been identified it has immediately been labeled as worrisome: social analysts are starting to warn against the 'feminization of education' and the apparent alienation of men from schooling."[2]

Global Gender Gap in Education

Country	World Economic Forum Educational Attainment Ranking	Adult Literacy W	Adult Literacy M	Girl's Share Primary Enrl.	Women's Share Tertiary Enrl.[3]
TOP TEN					
Sweden	1	99%	99%	48.7%	59.6%
Uruguay	2	98%	98%	48.3%	61.9%
Argentina	3	98%	98%	48.8%	58.7%
United Kingdom	4	99%	99%	48.9%	57.3%
Denmark	5	99%	99%	48.7%	57.4%

In 1996, the Court addressed this very question in *U.S. v. Virginia*. The case was brought by the U.S. government in an attempt to force the state of Virginia to admit women to the Virginia Military Institute (VMI). The case first entered the federal courts in 1992. At issue was the character of the program and whether a military-style program required VMI to retain its male-only admissions policy (the same set of questions applied to the Citadel in Charleston, South Carolina). The lower courts initially agreed that the single-gender character of VMI's adversative training program was essential; however, they also ruled that Virginia had indeed violated the Constitution in denying women

Norway	6	100%	100%	48.8%	59.8%
Iceland	7	99%	99%	48.6%	64.4%
United States	8	99%	99%	49.0%	57.4%
Ireland	9	99%	99%	48.5%	55.1%
Finland	10	100%	100%	48.9%	53.9%

. . . .

BOTTOM TEN

Switzerland	49	99%	99%	48.5%	47.0%
Bulgaria	50	98%	99%	48.0%	53.5%
Romania	51	97%	98%	48.4%	55.4%
Zimbabwe	52	88%	94%	49.6%	38.8%
Indonesia	53	88%	95%	48.3%	43.7%
Thailand	54	93%	96%	48.0%	54.5%
Turkey	55	81%	96%	47.9%	42.4%
Egypt	56	61%	84%	47.0%	N/A
India	57	54%	77%	46.6%	39.9%
Pakistan	58	40%	69%	41.0%	44.5%

Sources: UN Statistics Division, "Statistics and Indicators on Women and Men," accessed at http://unstats.un.org/unsd/demographic/products/indwm/statistics/htm; Augusto Lopez-Claros and Saadia Zahidi, *Women's Empowerment: Measuring the Global Gender Gap* (Switzerland: World Economic Forum, 2005).

[1] Augusto Lopez-Claros and Saadia Zahidi, *Women's Empowerment: Measuring the Global Gender Gap* (Switzerland: World Economic Forum, 2005), p. 5.
[2] Joni Seager, *The Penguin Atlas of Women in the World*, 4th ed. (New York: Penguin Books, 2009), p. 30.
[3] Tertiary refers to "third level" and is equivalent to "university level."

the opportunity for the same training. Virginia was given three options: admit women, establish a separate but equal program for women in the state, or convert VMI to a private institution. Virginia chose the second option and established the all-female Virginia Military Institute for Leadership (VMIL) at Mary Baldwin College. In 1996, the Supreme Court ruled that VMIL did not provide a substantially equal opportunity for women since VMI and VMIL were not of equal quality or stature in the state. Justice Ruth Bader Ginsburg issued the Court's majority opinion and came as close as the Court ever has to applying the same level of equal protection scrutiny to sex discrimination as it applies to race discrimination (called strict scrutiny). In a test now referred to as the "skeptical scrutiny" test, Ginsburg ruled that in discriminating on the basis of sex, the state must demonstrate an "exceedingly persuasive" justification for the action that bears a substantial relationship to important governmental objectives. The state also must describe "actual purposes," not rationalizations for differential treatment of the sexes. In other words, the state may not use stereotypic or traditional views of gender differences as its justification for different policies for men and women.[90] Immediately after the Supreme Court's decision, the Citadel announced that it too would admit women. VMI included women in its incoming class in 1997. By 2000, a woman had been chosen as a battalion commander. Erin Nicole Claunch ranked fifteenth in her class of 298 with a 4.0 grade average and beat the average score for physical fitness among all cadets. The appointment to battalion commander is based on academic performance, leadership ability, and physical fitness and is one of the highest honors at VMI.[91] Women made up 8.5 percent of the Citadel's applications in 2003–2004, and represented 8.5 percent of the positive admissions decisions. Of the 2,000 members of the Corps of Cadets, 39 were women in 2009 (down from a high of 53 in 2007).[92]

Although largely settled in higher education, professional, and vocational programs, the issue of sex-segregated schools remains viable at the primary and secondary levels of public education. In 1996, the California legislature passed legislation authorizing $500,000 to districts that agreed to create all-boy or all-girl academies with equal facilities and agreed to evaluate the results of their pilot programs.[93] Several school districts have experimented with girls-only science and higher-mathematics classes in an attempt to encourage more girls to continue with science and math. In 1998, Intel Corporation, as part of its "Women in Science" program, awarded several $75,000 grants to high schools and middle schools to mount a three-year pilot sex-segregated science class. Females make up about 29 percent of Intel's high-technology workforce, and Intel designed the program to increase the number of women entering science.[94] In other areas, high schools have been experimenting with all-male English classes. In both cases the programs are designed to use a learning style that best suits the constituency and the subject matter in an area where students have traditionally shown weaknesses. There is little doubt that initiatives like these will continue—and will continue to spark controversy since they introduce gender-specific educational practices in a field dominated by gender-neutral policies. There has not been a definitive legal ruling on whether separate-but-equal is acceptable for gender under these circumstances. The Office of Civil Rights, however, has said that single-sex schools are an acceptable way to diversify educational choices as long as a district offers boys and girls the same classes and the same resources, as in the California example. When New York City established the Young Women's Leadership School in East Harlem, it prompted a warning from the Civil Rights Office. That warning cited a potential violation of Title IX unless New York developed an equal program and facility for boys. Many feminists remain wary of returning to the days of separate educations for boys and girls, even when they believe theoretically that girls may benefit from a single-sex education. Peggy Orenstein, author of *Schoolgirls: Young Women, Self-Esteem, and the Confidence Gap*, who has documented the problems of girls in schools, expressed concern for the Young Women's Leadership School in New York. "Beyond the legal issues, the creation of public girls' schools is risky," Orenstein said. "The United States has been down the separate-but-equal road before, and it was not a happy trip. Once institutionalized, who can guarantee that educational resources will be divided fairly?"[95] On March 9, 2004, the U.S. Department of Education issued proposed regulations that would allow public schools to provide separate programs for boys and girls that would not have to meet equal education standards as required under Title IX, civil rights laws, and the U.S. Constitution. The current law allows single-sex classes and programs when appropriate, but prohibits such efforts from perpetuating harmful stereotypes or limiting opportunities. Under proposed regulations, parent or student preference is enough to meet the "appropriateness" standard, contrary to the central tenets of civil rights law. The Bush administration issued a similar version as the final regulation in 2006, even though nearly all of the 6,000 public comments submitted were against the changes. The new regulations require coeducational public schools to provide rationale for creating a single-gender classroom and there must be accessible, co-ed classes in the same subject. However, enforcement of these provisions is weak. Feminist and gender organizations mobilized immediately to challenge the new regulations, but over 500 public schools implemented some form of single-sex education as a result of this window. There are currently 392 public schools in the United States offering single-sex educational opportunities in the 2008–2009 school year. Ninety-seven of these schools are exclusively single-gender schools.[96]

CONCLUSION

Women were granted access to formal education nearly 100 years before they were granted access to the vote. Both of these rights have become powerful tools in the pursuit of equality. Because of the unique character of education as a "public good," one that benefits society and the individual, and because education is such a fundamental resource that is linked to myriad quality-of-life indicators, education policy is by its very nature contested ground. This chapter looked at the way public policy can lead society toward a more equitable distribution of educational access and content. Title IX has proven to be a powerful tool for changing the nature of education in the United States. Its detractors charge that gender-equity laws are unfair to males because they require that limited resources be redistributed among both males and females. This does, in many cases, require that exclusive privileges once granted to males alone be shared. Gender equity in education, at its most basic level, requires that boys and girls share equally in consuming the resources required to develop skills and acquire knowledge. It also requires careful attention to the process of education to ensure that boys and girls are learning in a bias-free atmosphere. Finally, gender equity in education requires that society present both boys and girls with the full complement of life's opportunities beyond formal education. The next chapter examines how education is linked to work and wages. Education has permitted women to move from the private sphere to the public sphere, although as the next chapter shows, the move is far from complete.

Suggested Readings, Web Resources, and Films

American Association of University Women, *How Schools Shortchange Girls: A Study of Major Findings on Girls and Education* (Wellesley, Mass.: Wellesley College Center for Research on Women, 1992).

Roberta M. Hall and Bernice R. Sandler, "The Classroom Climate: A Chilly One for Women," Project on the Status and Education of Women (Washington, D.C.: Association of American Colleges, 1982).

Roberta M. Hall and Bernice R. Sandler, "Outside the Classroom: A Chilly Campus Climate for Women?" Project on the Status and Education of Women (Washington, D.C.: Association of American Colleges, 1984).

Christina Hoff Sommers, "The War Against Boys," *Atlantic*, no. 5 (May 2000), accessed at http://www.theatlantic.com/issues/2000/05/sommers.htm.

John Weistart, "Equal Opportunity? Title IX and Intercollegiate Sports," *Brookings Review* 16, no. 4 (Fall 1998): 39–43.

American Association of University Women: http://www.aauw.org.

Fair Play Now: http://www.fairplaynow.org.

Girls, Inc.: http://www.girlsinc.com.

International Federation of University Women: http://www.ifuw.org.

Jeanette Rankin Foundation: Women Succeeding Through Education: http://www.rankinfoundation.org/.

National Women's Studies Association: http://www.nwsa.org.

Women's College Coalition: http://www.academic.org.

The Women's Educational Equity Act Equity Resource Center: http://www.edc.org/womensequity.

Working Groups on Girls: http://www.girlsrights.org.

Blog: Title IX Blog: http://title-ix.blogspot.com/.

Film: *Fair Play* (Digital Divide: Teachers, Technology, and the Classroom series).

Film: *Minerva's Machine: Women and Computing* (New York: Association for Computing Machinery, 1995).

Film: *The Need to Know* (Women: A True Story series, Films for the Humanities, 1997).

Notes

1. See, for example, Christina Hoff Sommers, "The War Against Boys," *Atlantic,* no. 5 (May 2000), accessed at http://www.theatlantic.com/issues/2000/05/sommers.htm.

2. Hunter College Women's Studies Collective, *Women's Realities, Women's Choices,* 2nd ed. (New York: Oxford University Press, 1995).

3. Virginia Sapiro, *Women in American Society: An Introduction to Women's Studies,* 4th ed. (Mountain View, Calif.: Mayfield Press, 1999), p. 146.

4. Ibid.

5. Nannerl O. Keohane, "'But for Her Sex…': The Domestication of Sophie," *University of Ottawa Quarterly* 49 (1980): 390–400.

6. Hunter College, *Women's Realities,* p. 374.

7. Judith Sargent Murray, "On the Equality of the Sexes," in *The Feminist Papers,* ed. Alice S. Rossi (Boston: Northeastern University Press, 1988), p. 18.

8. Sapiro, *Women in American Society,* p. 148.

9. Hunter College, *Women's Realities,* p. 382.

10. Kathryn Kish Sklar, "Catherine Beecher: Transforming the Teaching Profession," in *Women's America*, eds. Linda K. Kerber and Jane de Hart Mathews (New York: Oxford University Press, 1982), pp. 140–148.

11. Louise Bernikow, "December 16, 1872: Dr. Edward Clarke Tells Women to Take It Easy," *Women's eNews*, November 30, 2004, accessed at http://www.womens enews.org.

12. Ibid.

13. Sklar, "Catherine Beecher."

14. President's Task Force on Women's Rights and Responsibilities, *Task Force Report: A Matter of Simple Justice* (Washington, D.C.: GPO, April 1970), p. 7.

15. Joyce Gelb and Marian Lief Palley, *Women and Public Policies: Reassessing Gender Politics* (Charlottesville: University of Virginia Press, 1996), p. 99.

16. See Ruth Rosen, *The World Split Open: How the Modern Women's Movement Changed America* (New York: Viking Press, 2000).

17. National Coalition for Women and Girls in Education (NCWGE), "Title IX at 30: Report Card on Gender Equity," p. 41, June 2002, accessed at http://www.ncwge. org/title9at30-6-11.pdf.

18. Tara Parker-Pope, "Sexual Harassment at School," *New York Times,* May 1, 2008.

19. Catherine Hill and Elena Silva, *Drawing the Line: Sexual Harassment on Campus* (Washington, D.C.: AAUW Educational Foundation, 2006).

20. National Coalition for Women and Girls in Education (NCWGE), "Title IX at 30: Report Card on Gender Equity," pp. 42–43.

21. NCAA Model Pregnancy and Parenting Policy, available at http://www.ncaa.org/ wps/ncaa?ContentID=39941.

22. Joanna Grossman, "A New Lawsuit by a Female Athlete Tests Title IX's Protection Against Pregnancy Discrimination," *FindLaw Commentary,* May 6, 2003; "Pregnant

Student Athlete Files Title IX Suit Claiming Discrimination," *Ms. Magazine Online*, May 27, 2003, accessed online at http://www.msmagazine.com/news/uswirestory.asp?id=7814; NCWGE, "Title IX at 30," pp. 55–58.

23. Emily Badger, "In the Spirit of Title IX: U-Md. Makes Cheerleading a Sport," *Washington Post*, September 27, 2003, p. A01.

24. Donna de Varona and Julie Foudy, "Minority Views on the Report of the Commission on Opportunity in Athletics," submitted to Secretary of Education Rod Paige, February 2003, p. 3, accessed at http://www.savetitleix.com/minorityreport.pdf.

25. NCWGE, "Title IX at 35: Beyond the Headlines," (Washington, D.C.: 2008), accessed at http://www.ncwge.org.

26. Katie Thomas, "A Team's Struggle Shows Disparity in Girls' Sports," *New York Times*, June 14, 2009.

27. Carla Murphy, "Girls' Sports Opportunities MIA in City Schools," *Women's eNews*, March 18, 2009, accessed at http://www.womensenews.org.

28. George J. Bryjak, "The Ongoing Controversy Over Title IX," *USA Today* (Magazine), July 1, 2000: 62.

29. Jack Carey, "Women's Group Puts 30 Schools on Title IX Notice," *USA Today*, June 19, 2002, accessed at http://www.usatoday.com/sports/college/stories/2002-06-19-title-ix-notice.htm.

30. NCWGE, "Title IX at 35," p. 11.

31. "Attendance Numbers for USA 1999 Set New Marks," July 11, 1999, accessed at http://www.soccertimes.net/worldcup/1999/jul11.htm.

32. John Weistart, "Equal Opportunity? Title IX and Intercollegiate Sports," *Brookings Review* 16, no. 4 (Fall 1998): 39–43.

33. Associated Press, "Analysis Finds a Gap in College Sports Spending," July 22, 2003, accessed at http://www.cnn.com.

34. de Varona and Foudy, "Minority Views," p. 8.

35. Karen Goldberg Goff, "Does Athletic Equity Give Men a Sporting Chance?" *Insight on the News* 15, no. 2 (January 11, 1999): 38.

36. Bryjak, "Ongoing Controversy Over Title IX."

37. *Cohen v. Brown University*, 991 F. 2d. 888. 1993; F. Supp. 185 (D.R.I. 1995).

38. Weistart, "Equal Opportunity?" p. 39.

39. Joe Leo, "Gender Police: 'Pull Over!'" *U.S. News & World Report*, March 23, 1998, p. 11.

40. The Mellman Group, Inc. "Title IX," June 14, 2007.

41. Bryjak, "Ongoing Controversy Over Title IX."

42. Joanna Grossman, "On the Thirtieth Anniversary of Title IX, We Need to Preserve, Not Reverse, Its Guarantee of Equity for Women in College Athletics," *FindLaw Commentary*, June 18, 2002.

43. Department of Education, "Secretary's Commission on Athletic Opportunity," accessed at http://www.ed.gov/about/bdscomm/list/athletics/qsandas.html.

44. Christine Grant, "Briefing Paper No. 3," NCWGE, accessed at http://www.ncwge.org/pressbriefing3.pdf.

45. de Varona and Foudy, "Minority Views."

46. "Women's Rights Groups Win Title IX Victory," *Ms. Magazine Online*, July 14, 2003, accessed at http://www.msmagazine.com/news/uswirestory.asp?id=7924.

47. *Jackson v. Birmingham Board of Education*, No. 02-1672 (March 29, 2005).

48. Shannon Dortch, "Hey Guys: Hit the Books," *American Demographics* 19, no. 9 (September 1997): 4–10.

49. Doug Lederman, "Welfare Reform and Women's College Enrollment," *Inside Higher Education*, November 14, 2008.

50. "Black Women Now Hold a Large Lead Over Black Men in Enrollments at Most of the Nation's Highest-Ranked Professional Schools," *Journal of Blacks in Higher Education* (2004), "News and Views," accessed at http://www.jbhe.com.

51. Wendy Berliner, "Where Have All the Young Men Gone?" *Guardian*, May 18, 2004.

52. Ibid., p. 6.

53. John R. Reynolds and Jennifer Pemberton, "Rising College Expectations Among Youth in the United States: A Comparison of the 1979 and 1997 NLSY," *Journal of Human Resources* 36, no. 4 (Fall 2001): 703–726.

54. Tamar Lewin, "At Colleges, Women are Leaving Men in the Dust," *New York Times*, July 9, 2006.

55. Michael A. Fletcher, "Degrees of Separation: Gender Gap Among College Graduates Has Educators Wondering Where the Men Are," *Washington Post*, June 25, 2002, p. A01.

56. "Notebook," *Chronicle of Higher Education* (October 20, 2000): A29.

57. Fletcher, "Degrees of Separation."

58. "Towson University Drops Admissions Program with Laxer Standards for Men," *Chronicle of Higher Education*, October 25, 2007.

59. Andrew Sum, Neeta Fogg, Paul Harrington, et al., "The Growing Gender Gaps in College Enrollment and Degree Attainment in the U.S. and Their Potential Economic and Social Consequences," paper prepared for The Business Roundtable (Boston: Center for Labor Market Studies, Northeastern University, 2003), pp. 5–6.

60. U.S. Census Bureau, Current Population Survey, Annual Social and Economic Supplement, Tabale PINC-03, last revised August 28, 2007, accessed at http://pubdb3.census.gov/macro/032007/perinc/new03_000.htm.

61. Ibid.

62. NCWGE, "Title IX at 35," p. 15.

63. Leslie A. Barber, "U.S. Women in Science and Engineering, 1960–1990: Progress Toward Equity?" *Journal of Higher Education* 66, no. 2 (March–April 1995): 213–235; Sue V. Rosser and Mark Zachary Taylor, "Why Are We Still Worried About Women in Science?" *Academe*, May – June, 2009, pp. 7–15.

64. J. Scott Long, *From Scarcity to Visibility: Gender Differences in the Careers of Doctoral Scientists and Engineers* (Washington, D.C.: National Academies Press, 2001).

65. Yu Xe and Kimberlee Shauman, *Women in Science: Career Processes and Outcomes* (Boston: Harvard University Press, 2005).

66. Information can be accessed at http://www.edc.org/Women'sEquity.

67. Krista Kafer, "Girl Power: Why Girls Don't Need the Women's Educational Equity Act," WebMemo #536, Heritage Foundation, September 8, 2004, accessed at http://www.heritage.org/research/education/wm563.cfm.

68. Krista Kafer, "Wasting Dollars: The Women's Educational Equity Act," Heritage Foundation Backgrounder Report #1490, October 11, 2001, accessed at http://www.heritage.org/Research/Education/bg1490.cfm.

69. "House Passes Amendment to Continue Funding Small Educational Equity Act," Feminist Daily News Wire, September 10, 2004, accessed at http://www.feminist.org.

70. American Association of University Women, *How Schools Shortchange Girls: A Study of Major Findings on Girls and Education* (Wellesley, Mass.: Wellesley College Center for Research on Women, 1992).

71. Roberta M. Hall and Bernice R. Sandler, "The Classroom Climate: A Chilly One for Women," Project on the Status and Education of Women (Washington, D.C.: Association of American Colleges, 1982).

72. Roberta M. Hall and Bernice R. Sandler, "Outside the Classroom: A Chilly Campus Climate for Women?" Project on the Status and Education of Women (Washington, D.C.: Association of American Colleges, 1984).

73. Sommers, "The War Against Boys."

74. Public Education Network, "The American Teacher 1997: Examining Gender Issues in Public Schools," (Rochester, N.Y.: Louis Harris and Associates, 1997).

75. See both the article and the reader letters, accessed at http://theatlantic.com/issues/2000/05/sommers.htm.

76. Christine Corbett, Catherine Hill, and Andresse St. Rose, "Where the Girls Are: The Facts About Gender Equity in Education (Washington, D.C.: American Association of University Women, 2008), accessed at http://www.aauw.org/research/upload/whereGirlsAre.pdf.

77. Ibid., p. 22.

78. United Nations Development Programme, *Women's Political Participation and Good Governance: 21st Century Challenges* (New York: United Nations Development Programme, 2000), accessed at http://magnet.undp.org.

79. Cynthia Costello and Barbara Kivimae Krimgold, eds., *The American Woman 1996–1997: Women and Work* (New York: Norton, 1996), p. 23.

80. Sum, Fogg, and Harrington, et al., "The Growing Gender Gaps."

81. U.S. Department of Commerce, Bureau of the Census, "Percent of 25- to 35-Year-Olds Who Were Employed, by Sex and Level of Educational Attainment," (March 2002).

82. Kelly DiNardo, "Marriage Rates Rise for Educated Women," *Women's eNews*, April 6, 2004, accessed at http://www.womensenews.org.

83. Amartya Sen, *Development as Freedom* (New York: Knopf, 1999).

84. United Nations, *The World's Women 2000: Trends and Statistics* (New York: United Nations, 2000), pp. 86–87.

85. Ibid., p. 88.

86. UNESCO, "Girls Are the Focus of World Day Against Child Labor," June 10, 2009, accessed at http://portal.unesco.org/education/en/ev.php-URL_ID=59240&URL_DO=DO_TOPIC&URL_SECTION=201.html.

87. UNICEF, *The State of the World's Children 2004*, accessed at http://www.unicef.org.

88. Margaret M. Conway, David W. Ahern, and Gertrude A. Steuernagel, *Women and Public Policy: A Revolution in Progress*, 2nd ed. (Washington, D.C.: Congressional Quarterly Press, 1999), p. 19.

89. *Kirstein v. University of Virginia*, 309 F. Supp. 184 (1970).

90. *U.S. v. Virginia*, 976 F.2d 890 (1992); 52 F.3d 90 (1995); 116 S Ct 2264 (1996).

91. American Association of University Women, "Breaking Barriers at VMI," *Outlook* 94, no. 2 (2000): 52.

92. The Citadel, The Military College of South Carolina. "Quick Facts," accessed at http://www.citadel.edu/main/about.html.

93. Tamar Lewin, "Experimentation with Single-Sex Education Is on the Rise," *New York Times*, October 9, 1997.

94. Information can be accessed at *Mountain Democrat,* http://www.mtdemocrat.com/news/intel60598.shtm.

95. Peggy Orenstein, "All-Girl Schools Duck the Issue," *New York Times*, July 20, 1996, p. 19.

96. Kristen Pearson, "Research Divided on Same-Sex Classrooms," *News Record*, October 5, 2008.

Women and Work: In Pursuit of Economic Equality

Even more than education, work exemplifies the contradictions of the paradox of gender equality. Although separate spheres ideology may have faded over time as the primary organizing principle of gender relations, its legacy is very much alive today in how women and men experience work. Title VII makes it illegal to restrict jobs to one sex or the other based purely on sex or stereotypical assumptions about gender-linked abilities, but gender segregation is pervasive throughout the labor force. Three-quarters of all women who work do so in just twenty occupations, each of which is nearly 80 percent female.[1] The economy is organized into "men's jobs" and "women's jobs" that are eerily consistent with the public-sphere/private-sphere division of labor. For example, 2003 Bureau of Labor statistics reported that women made up 98 percent of the nation's kindergarten and preschool teachers, 80.9 percent of its elementary school teachers, 96 percent of its secretaries and administrative assistants, and 90 percent of its registered nurses. Alternatively, men made up 96 percent of the nation's firefighters, 74 percent of its physicians, 97 percent of its construction workers, and 99 percent of its auto mechanics.[2] If all occupations enjoyed the same level of prestige and pay, gender segregation in the labor force would not disadvantage women; however, that is not the case.

The median income for all full-time male workers in 2007 was $44,255, compared with $34,278 for all full-time female workers; women's income constituted 78 percent of men's, putting the wage gap at roughly 22 percent.[3] Moreover, even when men and women were similarly educated and working in the same profession, women were more likely to be at the bottom of the wage and prestige scales. Women's median earnings in 2007 in the legal occupation were estimated at \$53,800, compared with an estimated \$108,400 for men. For example, women constitute 30 percent of all lawyers in the United States, yet only 15 percent of the partners in the 250 largest law firms and only 5 percent of managing partners in large firms. Women represent 15 percent of the senior executives in Fortune 500 companies (up from 8 percent in 1995) and earn roughly two-thirds the salaries of their male counterparts. Women's concentration in low-paying, service-sector jobs also contributes to their high poverty rates. Are the disparities between men and women in employment a result of socialization and education, employment discrimination, and negative public attitudes about women's work, or a result of women's choices?

This chapter examines women's entrance into the labor force and assesses the power of the paradox of gender equality in shaping their experiences. Employment policies consistent with the legal equality doctrine have been very effective in expanding occupational choices for women and in regulating the workplace to limit forms of discrimination such as sexual harassment. Gender-neutral policies in employment are designed to guarantee women equal pay for substantially equal work, equal access to Social Security and other employment-related benefits, and equal access to opportunities for advancement within their careers. The Equal Pay Act of 1963 guarantees that men and women will be paid equally for doing the same job. Title VII of the 1964 Civil Rights Act prohibits discrimination on the basis of sex in hiring and employment. Affirmative-action policies in force until recently have ensured that women could not be ignored in hiring and promotions. The reality of women's experiences, however, suggests that gender-neutral policies do not aid in balancing the responsibilities of work and family, nor do they credit women for the impact of their family responsibilities throughout their lifetimes, particularly in retirement.

Gender-neutral policies work best for women who most resemble the male model of employment, but since 77 percent of women with children between the ages of 6 and 17 are in the workforce and nearly 90 percent of all women will bear a child in their lifetimes, few women fit that male model.[4] Gender-specific policies in employment that would grant women accommodations for childbirth, family obligations, and frequent interruptions in their participation in the labor force are nearly impossible to design without violating the prohibitions of sex discrimination so central to Title VII. As a result, policies such as the Family and Medical Leave Act (FMLA) were consciously designed to benefit both men and women in balancing family obligations with employment and do not specifically deal with women's experience. Likewise, although child care is theoretically a family issue relevant for both male and female employees, the reality is that women are more often responsible for finding quality child care and dealing with the daily logistics of children. The absence of federal child-care policy is felt more acutely by women than by men in the workforce. When policies are gender neutral but affect men and women differently, women are almost always disadvantaged. Most often the root of the policy's disparate impact is in the persistence of separate spheres ideology and in the attitudes that place women in the private sphere and men in the public sphere. When women are active in both spheres (home and work), they retain full responsibilities in both and face what sociologists have labeled the "double day." In this light, we will examine the impact of the wage gap, the status of child-care policy, Social Security, and the proposals to privatize or substantially reform Social Security. Ambivalent public attitudes about women's participation in the public sphere and paid labor force are apparent in the expectation that most women are supposed to handle their responsibilities at home as well as at work as an individual, as if the dual role is entirely a personal choice. Attitudes about women and work intersect with attitudes about race and class in shaping economic policies aimed at poor women and their children. In this light, we will examine the 1996 welfare reform legislation and evaluate its impact on women's poverty rates more than a decade after the legislation was passed. The 2008 recession, the deepest since the Great Depression, has not been gender neutral in its impact. We will examine the differential impact of job loss on men and women, as well as the pernicious impact the gender wage gap has on families when women become the sole wage earners.

WOMEN ENTER THE WORKFORCE: A BRIEF HISTORY

Men and women have always worked. The industrial revolution moved the means of production from the homestead to the factory. As a result, the value of labor was assessed in the currency of money rather than the sustainability of one's family. In preindustrial society, although men and women performed different tasks, both men's and women's work were necessary for survival.[5] There was little distinction between home and the workplace because they were often one and the same. In Colonial America, the home was the center of production, with men working in the fields and women tending to the home by cooking, cleaning, bearing and caring for the children, and manufacturing the goods the family needed to survive. Women did spinning and weaving, and made soap, candles, and shoes, among other things. What their families did not consume, women offered for sale, which brought in additional income for the family.[6] However, industrialization changed the means of production and the division of labor between men and women. The value attached to gendered work became more starkly differentiated. So much so that participants in the Seneca Falls Convention in 1848 included among their demands issued in the *Declaration of Sentiments* women's ability to work and be fairly compensated.

Early in our nation's history, women entered the paid labor force in large numbers as teachers, seamstresses, domestics, or mill operators—occupations clearly consistent with their private sphere roles. In 1860, women comprised

10.2 percent of the free labor force. Almost one out of every ten free women over the age of ten were wage earners. That women *could* work in other, less traditional venues was clearly demonstrated in the labor patterns of female slaves. Not only did African female slaves work side-by-side with men in the fields, they tended to domestic chores for the master as well as for their own families. Prior to the Civil War, the slave labor force included nearly 2 million women. Their entry into the paid labor force is reflected in the proportion of women working after the next census. In 1870, 13.7 percent of women worked for pay, making up 14.8 percent of the nation's total workforce. By 1910, one out of every five workers was a woman, representing three times the number of female wage earners in 1870.[7] Since 1870, the proportionate increase in the number of employed women has exceeded the proportionate increase of employed men in every decade.[8]

Domestic work dominated women's choices for paid labor during the first phases of economic assimilation. In 1870, seven out of every ten women workers were servants. As new jobs opened in factories, retail stores, offices, and classrooms, the proportion of women working as domestic servants fell.[9] Employment patterns were still sex segregated. In industry, women were concentrated in the manufacture of cloth, clothing, food, or tobacco products. In the expanding white-collar sector, women were also relegated to a limited range of low-level jobs, such as teachers, nurses, office workers, salesclerks, and switchboard operators.[10] Women employed in these capacities were likely to be young, urban, unmarried, and the daughters of recent immigrants. The sole exception was the African American woman worker, who might have been of any age and was more likely to have been married while employed.

White women's youth was evidence of work's temporary nature for women of this period. The average white woman worker viewed employment as a temporary phase that would come to an end once she married. This attitude perpetuated from the start of women's wage-earning employment the expectation that women worked to contribute to the family but not to independently provide for their own support. Women's short time in the labor force limited their earning potential since, by definition, they were perpetual newcomers to the workforce, viewed as temporary and therefore not worth training for higher-paying skilled jobs. Women were, therefore, relegated to the lowest-level jobs with little or no possibility of economic security or advancement.

Cultural pressure on women to adhere to the "domestic ideal" of hearth and home directly collided with increasing opportunities for women in the economy.[11] Even if employers were willing to accept women as full workforce participants, eligible for any job at any salary, the majority of the public was not. As Theodore Roosevelt wrote at the turn of the century, "If the women do not recognize that the greatest thing for any woman is to be a good wife and mother, why, that nation has cause to be alarmed about its future."[12] Thus the history of women and work is characterized by the often conflicting forces of economy and culture. In times of crisis, the nation accepts and in fact relies on women's labor. Although more often than not, once the crisis passes, women are expected to return to the domestic ideal. After recruiting women into the workforce in unprecedented numbers during World War II, the government implemented a "return to normalcy" campaign to convince women to leave the workforce to men and return to their responsibilities at home. By that time, however, most of the social prohibitions against married women working had fallen by the wayside, a direct result of women's wartime experiences. Women had learned to accommodate the dual burdens of work and family. Women's participation in the post–World War II labor force continued to increase, and by the late 1960s, nearly 40 percent of all women were employed outside the home.[13]

Women's labor history is also replete with contradictions about race and class. While middle- and upper-class white women aspired to and were in fact pressured to adhere to the domestic ideal, poor working-class women, along with women of color and recent immigrants, were not included in the ideal. The economic realities of low salaries meant that most working-class men could not be their families' sole wage earner. That was particularly true for recently emancipated slaves. Survival often required that women and their children entered the paid labor force and accepted whatever low-paying, high-risk jobs were available. As white women moved from domestic labor to clerical and sales positions, African American women took their place. The percentage of African American women domestic workers increased from 38.5 percent in 1910 to 59.9 percent in 1940. Over the next two decades, African American women diversified their labor participation to include manufacturing and clerical work. By the late 1960s, only 20 percent of working African American women were employed in private households.

Women's working conditions were also hampered by their exclusion from organized labor movements. During the first half of the nineteenth century, unions did not accept female members. By 1920, only 7 percent of women belonged to unions, compared with 25 percent of men.[14] Women in some industries attempted to form their own labor organizations (e.g., the Working Girl's Societies, the Women's Trade Union League). Women's unions tried unsuccessfully to alter the beliefs that women were temporary workers who were motivated only by the opportunity to earn "pocket money" to supplement their husband's income, or alternatively, that working women were selfishly pursuing a career at the expense of their family responsibilities at home. These attitudes about women's motivations for work persisted well into the twentieth century.[15]

By the mid-nineteenth century, approval of working women was conditional at best. Employment was only acceptable for women at opposite ends of the age spectrum, for those without children or whose children were grown, and for those who were willing to settle for part-time, low-wage positions. But by the 1960s, pressures of inflation collided with the rebirth of the feminist movement to produce an "awakening" among women as a group and within the larger public's consciousness. As a result, the proportion of all types of women in the workforce rose. The job prestige gap between white and African American women continued to close. In 1996, two-thirds of African American women and three-fourths of white women held white-collar jobs. Two-income families are now the norm across class and race, but the ambivalence over women's dual roles in the private and public spheres persists. The proportion of men and women in the wage and salaried workforce is nearly even (51 percent male, 49 percent female), and yet two in five men still think women's place is in the home. In 2008, 79 percent of all families (both with children and childless) were characterized as "dual-earner families." In 2008, employed women in dual-earner couples contributed an average of 44 percent of annual family income. Combined work hours for dual-earner couples with children rose from 81 hours per week in 1977 to 91 hours a week.[16]

Gender Socialization and Attitudes About Work

Gender specialization in work and the expectations for work relative to gender may develop in early childhood, built on a foundation of separate spheres ideology. Studies show that girls over five years old not only spend more time on household chores than boys do, they also begin doing chores at an earlier age.[17] Girls specialize in cooking and cleaning (jobs that are performed regularly), while boys were more likely to take out the garbage and help with yard work (jobs that are performed less frequently). Because parents view regularly performed chores, such as washing dishes, as contributing to the good of the family, they are usually done without pay (allowance), while such infrequent tasks as washing the car are likely to be compensated. Boys are more likely to find a neighborhood "market" for outdoor chores like shoveling snow or raking leaves, but girls are less likely to earn money cleaning a neighbor's house (although girls may earn money by babysitting and are more likely to perform that task than their brothers). Children have reason to conclude that the tasks males occasionally perform have monetary value, but the tasks females frequently perform do not. "Children have reason to think that boys labor for payment, while girls 'labor for love'. . . . The sexual division of children's play and labor induces both boys and girls to see housework and child care as women's responsibility, a responsibility that, ideally, is performed with love and pleasure. If housework, especially child care, is a woman's labor of love, equity does not come into the picture."[18]

In studies of the division of household labor between adults, women consistently perform more hours of labor in the home, regardless of race, class, education, and occupational status. In 2008, for example, women performed 31 hours of housework a week compared to an average of 14 hours for men. When women do not work in the labor force, they perform an average 38 hours of housework a week compared to men's 12 hours. The inequities are even greater among couples with children, although the most recent data suggest that the Millennial generation (individuals born roughly between 1980 and 2000) is seeking more balance in caring for their children. Fathers with children under 13 spend an average of three hours per workday caring for their children, while women spend slightly more, at 3.8 hours per workday. Women's time on child care has remained steady at 3.8 hours between 1977 and 2008, while men's has increased by a full hour.[19] Somewhat surprisingly, men and women accept inequities at home and see them as "fair." When married women who work outside the home are doing 66 percent of the housework, they judge the division fair. It is only when their portion of housework approaches 75 percent that they judge the distribution as unfair to themselves. Men, on the other hand, view their doing about equal hours of housework (48 percent) as unfair to themselves and see the division as fair when they perform about 36 percent of the labor.[20]

Why have women willingly accepted this "double burden" of carrying the majority of the housework and child care on top of a full-time job outside the home? Again the answer can be found in the separate spheres ideology. Virginia Valian, author of *Why So Slow? The Advancement of Women*, suggests three reasons. First, both men and women see equity as a relevant concept in the workplace, but neither sees home as the workplace. Because taking care of the family is a labor of love for women, demanding equity makes her appear heartless. "Women have learned to help others directly, by caring for them, even if that help comes at their own expense. Men, on the other hand, have learned to help others indirectly, by earning money to provide material well-being and educational opportunities."[21] Second, because of years of socialization in nonoverlapping roles, men and women define certain jobs as feminine and others as masculine, making it particularly difficult for a man to retain his masculinity when performing "feminine" jobs in the home. Finally, men tend to compare themselves with other men and women compare themselves with other women. Particularly if men and women compare their own division of labor within their marriage with that of their parents, both husband and wife view themselves as "better off" than either of their parents. Both men and women believe (correctly in most cases) that contemporary men are doing substantially more than their fathers ever did, particularly in the area of child care. This relieves men of the responsibility for equal housework and denies women grounds (or so she perceives) for demanding a more equitable division of labor in the home.[22] This leaves women to figure out ways to combine a professional career or full-time job with the demands of the home and children, and defines resolving work and family pressures as a female problem rather than a human one. Thus, the need for higher-quality, more-affordable child care; family-leave policies; and more-flexible work hours are all defined within the policy process as "women's issues." The burden of finding solutions in the absence of government action is squarely placed on women in most cases. Placing these issues on the public policy agenda is crucial for women's continued advancement within the economy.

LEGAL PATHS TO EQUALITY: EQUAL PAY, TITLE VII, AND AFFIRMATIVE ACTION

Women's work, as we saw earlier, is largely a function of the interplay of the economy and cultural sex-role expectations. As the need for more workers put more women in the workforce, women themselves sought opportunities beyond those prescribed by traditional gender roles. In this sense, they were aided by government. As the need for skilled workers surpassed the available male labor pool, the National Manpower Council, the Department of Labor, and the Women's Bureau joined forces to explore ways to develop women's labor potential. In 1957, these organizations issued a report affirming that the principles of equality of opportunity and pay should apply to women as well as men.[23] The women's movement, largely dormant at this point anyway, did not immediately seize on this report as an opening because it was experiencing internal divisions over the pursuit of equal opportunities at the expense of protections for women workers. In this sense, the first equal-employment laws were not a direct result of actions by the women's movement, but rather they happened despite inaction and division within the movement.

The two paths to equality that stemmed from the paradox of gender equality were both evident as the government struggled with how to extend women equal-employment rights. On the one hand, a strictly gender-neutral approach guaranteed legal equality for men and women in the workplace, assuming that men and women experienced the workplace in similar ways. In passing the Equal Pay Act of 1963, Congress guaranteed women equal pay for work equal to that of male employees. Title VII of the 1964 Civil Rights Act prohibits discrimination against both men and women in employment on the basis of sex. Alternatively, gender-specific policies recognize differences between men and women. In enacting protective legislation, popular with progressives and social-reform feminists in the early twentieth century, the government attempted to protect women from long hours or dangerous working conditions and to accommodate their "special burden" related to bearing (and raising) children. Liberal feminists argue that protective legislation, regardless of its intent to favor women, will in the end disadvantage and stigmatize women. The passage of Title VII essentially ended the debate over which path the government would pursue, but it is not clear that this path has been most advantageous for women or that it will facilitate full equality. In addition, women have directly benefited from affirmative-action policies that were set in motion by executive orders 11246 and 11375. While affirmative action initially appears to contradict the equality doctrine and the ideology of individualism, women nonetheless advocated the inclusion of sex in affirmative-action policy. With the exception of affirmative action, the history of gender antidiscrimination employment law in the United States is one that has been based on the legal equality doctrine. While this approach appears to promise women equal employment conditions through strictly gender-neutral policy, the results have been mixed particularly

Point of Comparison

The Global Wage Gap

According to a report issued by the International Trade Union Confederation, the global gender wage gap calculated by Incomes Data Services using publicly available data sources (Eurostat and the International Labour Organization statistics) is 16.5 percent, meaning that on average women around the world earn roughly 83 percent of men's pay. The 2006 data include incomes from 63 countries; 30 European countries and 33 countries in the rest of the world. However, when the global gender gap is recalculated using Internet surveys of trade union organizations in addition to publicly available data, the gap increases to roughly 22 percent.[1] Women fare better in Europe, Oceania, and Latin America, and tend to fare worse in Asia and Africa. As in the United States, the global wage gap tends to be higher in female-dominated work environments (health, education, and social work). Trade union membership decreases the wage gap.

World Economic Forum	Empowerment Ranking Economic Opportunity[2]	Percentage of Women Working for Pay[3]	ITUC Report Gender Wage Gap
	TOP TEN		
Denmark	1	59%	17%
Norway	2	63%	16%
Hungary	3	42%	11%
Czech Republic	4	55%	18%
Estonia	5	52%	25%
Latvia	6	49%	16%

with the passage of time and as a greater percentage of women enter the permanent full-time, year-round workforce.

The Equal Pay Act of 1963

The Equal Pay Act of 1963 was not the government's first foray into regulating pay equity. Largely as a way to prevent employers from dampening wages by hiring women, the government required that women and men be paid

Iceland	7	71%	10%
Luxembourg	8	45%	14%
France	9	48%	11%
Russian Federation	10	54%	14%
United States (ranked 46)		**59%**	**22.4%**
BOTTOM TEN			
Italy	49	37%	12%
Egypt	50	20%	12%
Ireland	51	53%	9%
Japan	52	48%	33%
Bangladesh	53	53%	21%
Pakistan	54	33%	29%
South Korea	55	50%	31%
South Africa	56	46%	33%
Zimbabwe	57	64%	17%
Turkey	58	28%	22%

[1] "The Global Gender Pay Gap," International Trade Union Confederation Report, 2008, accessed in English at: http://www.ituc-csi.org.

[2] The economic opportunity indicator includes: duration of maternity leave, percentage of wages paid during leave period, number of women in managerial positions, availability of government-provided child care, impact of maternity laws on hiring women, and wage inequalities between men and women in the private sector.

[3] Joni Seager, *Women of the World*, 4th ed. (New York: Penguin Books, 2009). Data is from 2005.

Source: "The Global Gender Pay Gap" International Trade Union Confederation Report, 2008. Accessed in English, online at: *http://www.itcu-csi.org*.

equally at several points prior to 1963. The Fair Labor Standards Act of 1938 prohibited classifying jobs and wages according to age or sex, provided a minimum wage for some job classifications, and required fair treatment for wage and hourly workers. When women flooded the workforce during both world wars, government took action to alleviate the fear that women in men's jobs would depress wages. Policy dictated that women holding "men's jobs" be paid "men's wages." Hardly a statement on gender equality, the policy was designed to protect men's jobs and wage rates. Since attitudes about women working were still largely ambivalent, policy directed at equalizing wages based on a doctrine of equality did not surface until the Kennedy administration sent an equal pay bill to Congress. The Women's Bureau, led by Esther Peterson, argued that "fairness" dictated equal pay for men and women. Initially, the Women's Bureau pursued "equal pay for comparable work" but relented under pressure from employers who argued that defining comparable work would invite excessive government intrusion. Given the persistence of the "dual labor force," both Congress and the law's detractors in industry were confident that an equal pay law within the context of a sex-segregated workplace would not jeopardize men's jobs or wages. By the time Congress took action, twenty-three states already had equal pay laws on the books.

The federal law requires that when men and women perform the same (or substantially same) job in the same place and under the same conditions, they must receive equal pay.[24] However, seniority, merit, and measures related to the quantity and quality of the work provide a legal basis for pay differentials, as do "any other factor other than sex." Initially, the law, which was an amendment to the Fair Labor Standards Act, covered only wage and hourly employees and exempted employers with fewer than twenty-five employees. In 1972, the law's protections were extended to workers in small firms not covered by minimum-wage laws, professionals including teachers, and state and local government employees. Enforcement moved from the Department of Labor exclusively to the Equal Employment Opportunity Commission (EEOC) in 1978, but that move did not result in more stringent application of the law. Primarily, enforcement is the result of an individual or group of workers filing a claim with the EEOC. The prevailing 22 percent wage gap in 2009, nearly fifty years after the law was passed, suggests that both the law and its enforcement have not rectified the problem of wage discrimination (see Figure 7.1). Out of the nineteen Organization for Economic Co-operation and Development (OECD) countries, the United States has the largest gender earnings gap, save for Austria and Switzerland.[25]

Title VII of the 1964 Civil Rights Act

Now singularly powerful in combating gender discrimination in employment, Title VII of the 1964 Civil Rights Act resulted from an amendment offered by Congressman Howard Smith, a conservative southern Democrat from Virginia. Smith was determined to undermine the prohibitions against race discrimination at the core of the act by suggesting that men and women should be treated equally in the workplace. He was sure that the inclusion of sex along with race, color, religion, or national origin would derail the bill in the Senate, if not in the House. Without the amendment, many argued that white women would have been the only workers unprotected from employment discrimination under federal law. While accounts of his precise motivations vary, the Smith amendment did, in fact, survive to become one of the most powerful federal antidiscrimination employment laws. The inclusion of sex along with the other protected

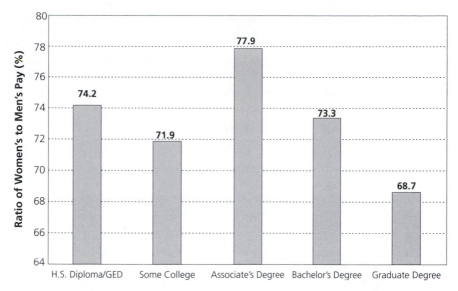

FIGURE 7.1 Pay Ratios of Women to Men by Level of Education, 2007

Source: U.S. Bureau of the Census, 2008. Data is for full-time workers age twenty-five and older.

categories was opposed by several prominent women's organizations, including the President's Commission on the Status of Women, the Women's Bureau, and the American Association of University Women. Their opposition arose mainly in response to the issue of "protective" legislation for women and the recognition that special accommodations for women would no longer be permitted under Title VII.[26] The law has since been amended three times. The first change extended the authority of the EEOC and expanded coverage to include public employers and educational institutions. The second amendment, known as the Pregnancy Discrimination Act (1978), declared that classifications based on pregnancy and pregnancy-related disabilities fall within the meaning of "sex" under Title VII. Third, the Civil Rights Act (1991) amended Title VII to reverse the effects of several Supreme Court rulings in the late 1980s that made job discrimination suits harder to win.

The EEOC, now responsible for administering all of the nation's equal protection provisions, was created under the 1964 Civil Rights Act and charged from the start with developing guidelines for Title VII's implementation. It was clear that the EEOC was not going to be very ambitious in writing guidelines on sex discrimination, and women's organizations like the newly formed National Organization for Women (NOW) rallied to pressure the agency to act more diligently. The specific provisions in Title VII most relevant to sex discrimination are found in section 703(a):

It shall be an unlawful employment practice for an employer (1) to fail or refuse to hire or to discharge any individual, or otherwise to discriminate against any individual with respect to his compensation, terms, conditions, or privileges of employment, because of such individual's race, color, religion, sex, or national origin; or (2) to limit, segregate, or classify his employees or applicants for employment in any way which would deprive or tend to deprive any individual of employment opportunities or otherwise adversely affect his status as an employee, because of such individual's race, color, religion, sex, or national origin.[27]

An important exception to Title VII's coverage arises from what is called a bona fide occupational qualification (BFOQ):

Notwithstanding any other provision of this subchapter (1) it shall not be an unlawful employment practice for an employer to hire and employ employees . . . on the basis of his religion, sex, or national origin in those certain instances where religion, sex, or national origin is a bona fide occupational qualification reasonably necessary to the normal operation of that particular business enterprise.[28]

Like many policies passed by Congress, the basic provisions and language of Title VII have been subject to interpretation by the Supreme Court. Two of the statute's critical phrases have provided the basis for such cases. Title VII prohibits discrimination practices "because of sex." Congress did not specify exactly what it intended in choosing this particular language, so the courts decided what it means through a succession of cases. In 1912, Justice Holmes best articulated for the Court the basic principle of the equal-protection clause that allows some sex-based laws to stand, even today in the face of Title VII's prohibition of sex discrimination: "The Fourteenth Amendment does not interfere [with state legislation] by erecting fictitious equality where there is real difference."[29] Unlike race, which the Court views as an immutable characteristic that bears no relationship to job performance, sex is assumed to create real and meaningful differences in a man's or a woman's ability to get and hold some jobs. However, the determination of the relevance of sex differences to employment cannot, the Court ruled, be based on assumptions of women as a group or any stereotypical characteristics as a group and must be based in fact.

One of the first Title VII cases brought on the basis of sex, *Phillips v. Martin Marietta*, was decided in 1971. In this case, Ida Phillips challenged the Martin Marietta Corporation's policy against hiring women with preschool children, although it had no such policy against hiring men with preschool children. Two lower courts ruled that the employment policy did not violate Title VII since it did not rely solely on sex, but also relied on a criterion "other than sex" (preschool children). The Supreme Court rejected the "sex plus" criterion as a violation of Title VII's intent.

Several cases have been brought before the courts on the basis of the BFOQ exception to Title VII. One of the earliest, *Weeks v. Southern Bell Telephone and Telegraph* (1969), challenged a rule that prevented women, but not men, from holding positions that required lifting more than thirty pounds. Lower courts ruled that the company had based its decision to limit women's employment on stereotypes rather than on real abilities of its employees or applicants. Similarly, in *Rosenfeld v. Southern Pacific Company* (1971), the Ninth Circuit

Court of Appeals ruled against Southern Pacific's policy of excluding women from certain jobs that were deemed "unsuitable" for women because (1) they involved irregular hours and lifting weights of up to twenty-five pounds; and (2) state laws limited working conditions for women under a variety of protective statutes. The court ruled that neither reason constituted a BFOQ exception to Title VII because both relied on stereotypes of women's abilities rather than on a finding of fact.[30]

BFOQ defenses constitute a large number of employment discrimination cases. Some of the most important rulings defining permissible BFOQ defenses have involved a male plaintiff bringing suit to open occupations previously limited to women. In *Diaz v. Pan American World Airways, Inc.* (1971), Celio Diaz applied for a job as a flight attendant, but was refused employment because of his sex. Pan Am's policy of hiring only women as cabin attendants raised the question of whether an employee's sex in situations where the public expected to find one sex or the other (customer preferences) constituted a legitimate BFOQ. The Supreme Court reversed a lower court's support for the policy, ruling that Title VII only permits sex to operate as a BFOQ when it is reasonably necessary to the operation of a business. The Court left open the possibility that there might be some instances when "the essence of the business operation would be undermined by not hiring members of one sex exclusively," but ruled that Pan American had not argued that female flight attendants were essential to their business success.

Ten years after the Pan Am ruling, another case involving an airline's hiring policy refined the Court's test for business necessity. In *Wilson v. Southwest Airlines Company* (1981), Southwest Airlines argued that female flight attendants were necessary to the financial success of its business in the highly competitive aviation industry. Southwest Airlines had adopted a public relations campaign based on an image of female sexuality that catered to the almost exclusively male business travelers. Using the slogan "We're Spreading Love All Over Texas," Southwest gained on its competitors throughout the 1970s. When sued for its refusal to hire male flight attendants, Southwest Airlines argued that in this case, sex operated as a BFOQ since their financial success depended on the appeal of their female flight attendants. In its decision, the Supreme Court created a two-pronged test based on two questions: (1) does the job under consideration require that the worker be of one sex only, *and* if so, (2) is that requirement reasonably necessary to the essence of the employer's business? In requiring affirmative answers to both questions, the Court sought to retain Title VII's intent. Since Southwest Airline's primary business was providing safe air transportation, requiring flight attendants to be female was not reasonably necessary to the essence of safe travel. The Court concluded, "Sex does not become a BFOQ merely because an employer chooses to exploit female sexuality as a marketing tool or to better insure profitability."[31]

Under some conditions, however, sex does serve as a legitimate BFOQ, but they are few. For example, conditions of privacy warrant one sex exclusively (restroom attendant or undergarment fitter), as do jobs that require authenticity, such as an actor or actress playing a particular role in a movie or play. A 1977 Supreme Court ruling in *Dothard v. Rawlinson*, however, disappointed most feminists. In rejecting a woman's bid to become a prison guard in an Alabama state penitentiary, the Court allowed Alabama to discriminate against qualified women applicants because of the dangerous conditions in Alabama's prison system. While allowing that unconstitutional overcrowding creates a danger to men as well as women, the Court nonetheless held that "a woman's ability to maintain order . . . could be directly reduced by her womanhood. . . . There would also be a real risk that other inmates deprived of a normal heterosexual environment would assault women guards because they were women."[32] This ruling was very narrowly written and did not even extend to most other state prisons that attempted to prohibit female guards. However, as Justice Thurgood Marshall pointed out in his dissenting opinion, the majority opinion "regrettably perpetuates one of the most insidious of the old myths about women—that women, wittingly or not, are seductive sexual objects." Most jobs now have been ruled open to both sexes. Proving gender discrimination at all stages of employment, however, is difficult.

In most cases, enforcement of Title VII occurs in reaction to a complaint filed by an individual or group with the EEOC. There are primarily three types of proof of discrimination. The first is proof of *prior intent to discriminate*, requiring written or sworn oral testimony that there was intent on the employer's part to discriminate against one sex in hiring, promoting, paying, or providing benefits. While there were blatant cases of intent throughout the 1970s, more recent cases have not presented such clear proof and have mostly fallen under either *disparate treatment* or *disparate impact*.

Disparate treatment refers to an employer deliberately favoring or disadvantaging one group protected under Title VII over another. In these cases, the burden of proof falls on the plaintiff, who must demonstrate that the disparate treatment is due to sex rather than some legitimate reason unrelated to sex. In short, the person making the charge is required to counter the employer's defense with hard evidence to the contrary. When a group files suit, evidence may take the form of statistics showing a pattern of discrimination in hiring over time or that women are underrepresented in the company's employee or applicant pool relative to those qualified to hold the position in the population at large. Alternatively, if an individual files suit, evidence is often difficult to obtain. Disparate impact cases arise where an employer's policies appear to be gender neutral, but have the effect of treating men and women differently, for example, minimum-height requirements or the ability to lift a certain weight or the need to travel for extended periods of time. A defense in this case requires the employer to prove that the requirements are related to the job and that they constitute a business necessity. In other words, if the qualifications for a position list the ability to lift more than seventy-five pounds, but in performing the job, the employee is never asked to lift heavy loads, the business-necessity defense is not legitimate and instead the qualifications constitute Title VII discrimination. The burden of proof in demonstrating a "business necessity" in these cases lies with the defendant (the employer), and the plaintiff is not required to prove that the company intended to discriminate through its hiring practices.[33] As a result of the Civil Rights Act of 1991, the courts are now bound by legislation to hold employers responsible for demonstrating that their employment practices that may result in a disparate effect are related to a legitimate business necessity.

Pregnancy Discrimination Act

A 1978 amendment to Title VII of the Civil Rights Act of 1964, the Pregnancy Discrimination Act (PDA) prohibits workplace discrimination on the basis of pregnancy. The impetus for the legislation was the 1976 U.S. Supreme Court ruling in *General Electric v. Gilbert*, in which the Court ruled that a policy that distinguishes between pregnant and nonpregnant persons does not constitute sex discrimination against women.[34] The PDA effectively overturns the *Gilbert* decision. The law prohibits discrimination against pregnant women in all areas of employment including: hiring, firing, seniority rights, job security, and fringe benefits. If the employer offers health insurance to employees, they must include coverage for pregnancy, childbirth, and related conditions. Employers who do not provide insurance for health or temporary disabilities are not required by the act to provide coverage for pregnant women. The Pregnancy Discrimination Act is consistent with the legal equality approach, even though only women can get pregnant. The act specifically says that employers cannot treat pregnancy "more or less" favorably than other temporary disabilities. Therefore, pregnant women are not eligible for pregnancy-specific special accommodations. Prior to passage of the Family and Medical Leave Act (1993) that meant that the PDA did not require an employer to provide paid or unpaid maternity leave or guarantee that a job would be protected following childbirth, even though the Supreme Court ruled that the PDA does not specifically prohibit employment practices that might favor pregnant women. California and Washington are the only two states in the country to mandate paid family leave.[35]

Although the Pregnancy Discrimination Act has been in place for over thirty years, reports of pregnancy discrimination hit an all-time high in 2007. In that year, the EEOC received 5,587 complaints of pregnancy-related discrimination (an increase of 14 percent over 2006; up 40 percent since 1987). According to a study by the U.S. Census Bureau, women are working longer into their pregnancies and taking shorter maternity leaves. In 2000, 67 percent of women worked during a pregnancy. Combined with more women working, experts believe the increase in pregnancy discrimination complaints can, in part, be attributed to more pregnant women in the workplace. Several advocacy groups support pregnant working women. The organization 9-to-5, for example, maintains a pregnancy bias hotline. Other organizations have mounted campaigns against "maternal profiling," a term recently named one of the new buzzwords of

2007 in the *New York Times*. Maternal profiling is defined as employment discrimination against a woman who has, or will have, children. The term has been popularized by members of MomsRising, an advocacy group promoting the rights of mothers in the workplace.[36]

In May 2009, the U.S. Supreme Court issued a 7–2 ruling in *AT&T Corporation v. Noreen Hulteen, et al.*, saying that an employer does not violate the PDA by paying pension benefits calculated using prior standards that are no longer acceptable under current law. The plaintiffs in this case are four current or former female AT&T employees who took unpaid, uncredited maternity leave prior to the Pregnancy Discrimination Act's implementation in 1979. As a result, their pension benefits today are smaller. Justice David Souter, for the majority, wrote "Although adopting a service credit rule unfavorable to those out on pregnancy leave would violate Title VII today, a seniority system does not necessarily violate the statute when it gives current effect to such rules that operated before the PDA." Justice Ruth Bader Ginsburg said in dissent, "I would hold that AT&T committed a current violation of Title VII when, post-PDA, it did not totally discontinue reliance upon a pension calculation premised on the notion that pregnancy-based classifications display no gender bias." The majority's opinion in this case mirrors the reasoning in the 2007 *Lilly Ledbetter v. Goodyear Tire & Rubber Co.* (discussed at length below), in that both deal with correcting employment discrimination retroactively to address current inequalities that arise from the past discriminatory act.[37]

Affirmative Action Policies: Executive Orders 11246 and 11375

In 1965, President Lyndon Johnson signed executive order 11246, which required companies that do business with the federal government to take "affirmative action to ensure that applicants are employed, and that employees are treated during employment without regard to their race, color, religion or national origin."[38] The Office of Federal Contract Compliance was established within the Department of Labor to enforce the order. Unlike Title VII, sex was not included in the original affirmative action order. However, pressure from women's organizations and others convinced the Johnson administration to sign executive order 11375 (1967), which included sex among the protected categories in affirmative action policies. Unlike Title VII or the Equal Pay Act, both of which require employers to treat similarly situated men and women in a similar manner, affirmative action has gone a large step further. Recognizing that today's inequalities are rooted in past discrimination, affirmative action requires that employers consciously monitor their employment practices and take action if women are underrepresented or have been underrepresented in the past. Affirmative action takes the form of a proactive remedy to past discrimination. As such, critics of the policy have long referred to affirmative action as "reverse discrimination." The Supreme Court, however, has made it

very clear that a lawful affirmative action program "must apply only to quali-fied candidates, have a strong reason for being developed, and be narrowly crafted to minimize negative effects."[39] This means that a program cannot legally promote unqualified candidates at the expense of qualified individuals, nor can an affirmative action program use quotas, contrary to popular antiaf-firmative action political rhetoric.

Studies consistently document the persistence of discriminatory treatment based on race and gender. Tests conducted by the Fair Employment Council of Greater Washington continue to find that white applicants are favored over minority applicants who have identical credentials. The Fair Employment Coun-cil sends paired "testers," one white and one black, to apply for the same job. Although each person has identical work experiences, backgrounds, demeanor, interviewing skills, and physical builds, a 1992 study found that almost half of the white testers received job offers, compared with only 11 percent of the African American applicants.[40]

Although many of the most vehement attacks on affirmative action policies have come at the expense of racial minorities, women of all races stand to lose a considerable tool in the pursuit of equality if the principles of affirmative action are undermined or ruled unconstitutional. Studies show that African American women, long relegated to the bottom of the ladder in hiring, salary, and promotion, have gained in both employment opportunities and wages as a result of affirmative action laws.[41] All women seem to have gained as a result of an increase in the public's consciousness of equal opportunity and diversity in the workplace and in admissions to professional schools. The rise in the number of women entering law and medical programs, while not directly due to affirmative action policies per se, can be positively linked to greater aware-ness of gender balance in admissions.

During the 1980s and the Reagan administration, a conservative Supreme Court did significant damage in both practice and concept to affirmative action principles. While the Civil Rights Restoration Act of 1988 and the Civil Rights Act of 1991 reversed many of the Court's more damaging rulings on federal equal employment opportunity law, it would, nevertheless, be fair to say that the cli-mate in the United States toward affirmative action remained hostile throughout the 1990s. In November 1996, 54 percent of California's electorate voted for Proposition 209, labeled the California Civil Rights Initiative by its proponents. The proposition prohibited the implementation of race and gender affirmative action programs and resulted in dramatic changes in admission practices in the state's extensive college and university system. While the country remains divided over the politics of affirmative action policy, the principle of distributing opportunities evenly across the sexes and across racial lines retains support.

On June 23, 2003, the U.S. Supreme Court issued two decisions involving class-action lawsuits filed on behalf of white students denied admission to the University of Michigan's undergraduate (*Gratz v. Regents of the University of Michigan*) and law school (*Grutter v. Regents of the University of Michigan*) programs. In the case involving undergraduate admissions, the Supreme Court ruled (6 to 3) Michigan's award of 20 of 150 points to all minority applicants purely because of race to be insufficiently "narrowly tailored to achieve the interest and educational diversity that respondents claim justifies their program." However, the majority opinion affirmed the concept of affirmative action and diversity as a compelling interest. In *Grutter*, a 5-to-4 decision written by Justice Sandra Day O'Connor, the majority opinion identified diversity in higher education as a compelling state interest and upheld the law school admission program. "Effective participation by members of all racial and ethnic groups in the civic life of our Nation is essential if the dream of one Nation, indivisible, is to be realized." The difference between the two cases is in the role race played in the admissions decision relative to the consideration of other individualized factors. In *Gratz*, the automatic award of points toward a positive admission decision purely on the basis of race was ruled unconstitutional because it was not sufficiently individualized. The Court provided a clear statement about the appropriate use of race in admissions, holding that the individualized consideration of race must be the hallmark of a carefully designed admissions policy that promotes educational diversity. The ruling also effectively overruled major portions of a 1996 U.S. Court of Appeals ruling in *Hopwood v. Texas* and allowed institutions in Texas, Louisiana, and Missouri to use race-conscious admissions policies designed to advance educational diversity. State universities in Florida, Washington, and California are still prohibited by state law from considering race in the admissions process. However, many scholars cite the Court's rulings in these two cases as evidence that assaults on the very concept of affirmative action to promote diversity will not get a friendly hearing. A joint statement of constitutional law scholars at Harvard said, "Although the Supreme Court has yet to address the constitutionality of diversity-based affirmative action programs outside of higher education admissions, language in the *Grutter* decision reveals the Court's support for the importance of diversity in other contexts, including K-12 education, as well as employment and business."[42]

Although women are the major beneficiaries of affirmative action policies, a recent study found that only 2 percent of news media coverage is devoted to affirmative action's impact on women.[43] Only 15 percent of media coverage makes any reference to bias or inequality, while 23 percent of coverage uses "preferences" and "affirmative action" interchangeably, suggesting that the status quo is free of preferences. Affirmative action continues to be an important tool for women and minorities in pursuit of equality. A Department of Labor study estimated that 5 million minority workers and 6 million women are in higher occupational classifications today than they would have been without the affirmative action policies of the 1960s and 1970s.[44]

The new frontiers of affirmative action policies for women and girls are closely related to expanding access to and interest in traditionally male-dominated fields where salaries are often higher. By 2010, one in four new jobs will be "technically oriented" or involve computers. However, high school girls represent only 17 percent of those taking the computer science AP test in 2006 (representing a slight decrease from the period 1996–2002), only 12 percent of the girls taking the SAT exam in preparation for college applications expressed an interest in majoring in computer science. Overall, women comprise 20 percent of information technology (IT) professionals in 2006, a marked decrease from 38 percent in 1984.[45] Affirmative action policies also mitigate the impact of the "glass ceiling." Although women as a group have made significant gains over the last decade in combating sex discrimination in employment, the rates of progress differ considerably by age, race, ethnicity, and disability. For example, sex discrimination charges filed with the EEOC increased by 12 percent overall between 1992 and 2003, yet claims filed by African American women increased by 20 percent and those filed by Hispanic women increased by 68 percent. The study found similar variations by group on sexual harassment claims, pregnancy discrimination suits, retaliation claims, and age discrimination charges.[46]

THE IMPACT OF FEDERAL POLICIES ON WOMEN'S WORK EXPERIENCES

There is ample evidence that the three major federal policies previously described have not entirely eliminated discrimination in employment for women, nor have they fundamentally altered the ways in which men and women experience the workplace. The "dual labor force" is still intact even in the face of advances that women have made in the professions. Women are still more heavily concentrated in "women's jobs" at the low end of the pay and prestige scales and less likely to carry the benefits that provide health care for themselves and their families. The wage gap remains real, even accounting for occupational differences and education. Economist Evelyn Murphy, president of the WAGE Project (Women Are Getting Even), estimates that over a lifetime (roughly 47 years of full-time work) the wage gap amounts to a $700,000 loss for a high school–educated woman, a $1.2 million loss for a college-educated woman, and a financial penalty of over $2.0 million for women with graduate or professional degrees.[47] Workplace climate issues were raised in a very public way in both Clarence Thomas's Senate confirmation hearings and in President Clinton's impeachment hearings in the House of Representatives and trial in the Senate. Sexual harassment remains a very real threat to many women's security and advancement, even though stricter laws have been established to punish offenders. In this section, we will examine how contemporary women enter and experience the workplace three decades after the major federal equal employment laws were passed.

Women in the Professions

The combination of Title IX (discussed in the previous chapter) and federal affirmative action goals has motivated professional programs to examine their admissions policies and the gender balance in their classrooms. Title IX eliminated quotas for women in specific programs, allowing women to compete for admission on their merits. The result was a steady increase in the number of women enrolled in law, medicine, engineering, science, and dentistry postgraduate programs. Between 1974 and 1994, overall job growth was the fastest for managers and other professionals; in 1994, 7 million women held managerial and professional positions, almost double the number in 1974.[48] In 1990, the typical employed woman was more likely to be in an administrative support job than in a managerial or professional job. In 2000, just a decade later, the reverse was true.[49]

Using both aggregate data (all men and women) to examine trends and cohort data (men and women born in the same year) to compare men and women with identical education and backgrounds, Virginia Valian examined men's and women's advancement in the professions. She made sure to note similarities in "human capital," a variable that represents education, experience, and other qualifications and is often used to dismiss the size of the wage gap. Valian nevertheless found that men in business, medicine, government, and the law advanced more easily than women in the same professions.[50] In 1978, two women were heads of Fortune 1,000 companies in the United States; in 1994 that number remained unchanged. In 1996, four women headed up Fortune 1,000 companies; in 2009 there were thirteen women CEOs of Fortune 500 companies.

In 1990, women made up less than one-half of 1 percent of the most highly paid officers and directors of 799 major companies. A 1996 review of the 1,000 largest firms in the United States found that women held only 1 percent of the top five jobs in those corporations; more than a decade later, that proportion has climbed to 6 percent. The lack of women in positions of corporate power extends beyond the United States. In the fifty largest publicly traded corporations in each nation in the European Union, women make up on average 11 percent of the top executives and 4 percent of the CEOs and heads of boards. Just 1 percent of *Fortune* magazine's Global 500 have female CEOs. Why so few? When Valian examined the relative progress made by men and women in the same cohort and with college degrees and MBAs, she found that men were promoted more quickly and advanced to higher salary grades more quickly than women were. The situation was similar for engineers.

Women were overrepresented in lower-prestige ranks, and men were overrepresented in higher-prestige ranks, even though both the men and the women had identical training, education, and experience. She concluded, "In engineering, as elsewhere, men accumulate advantage more easily than women do."[51]

In an attempt to explain why a few women reach the highest leadership positions, but the majority do not, Alice H. Eagly and Linda L. Carlie employ a labyrinth metaphor (for another explanation, see The Glass Ceiling section below).[52] "For women who aspire to top leadership, routes exist but are full of twists and turns, both unexpected and expected." Among the barriers creating walls in the labyrinth, Eagly and Carli include vestiges of sex discrimination, particularly related to marriage and parenthood, which promote men's careers and stymie women's. There remains a resistance to women's leadership born of the clash between communal and agentic qualities that put women in a bind (see chapter 4 for an application of this theory to female political candidates). Personal qualities and dominant behavior that is attributed to effective leadership or leadership potential in men often leads to women being vilified or labeled negatively. If women are too communal, they don't "have what it takes"; if they are too agentic, they aren't likeable and warm (self-promotion is not rewarded in women; since being modest and considerate is socially expected of women, they do not receive any additional points in leadership potential if they display this behavior, while in men it is viewed as "impressive"). Women in leadership are acutely aware of these contradictions. A Catalyst study of Fortune 1000 female executives found that 96 percent of them rated as critical or fairly important that they develop "a style with which male managers are comfortable."[53]

The demands of family add another wall to the labyrinth. Although the fact that women devote more hours per week to household chores and child care than men is well known, Eagly and Carli note that contemporary mothers spend more time than did earlier generations. Married mothers increased the time they spent on primary child care (not combined with other household duties) from 10.6 hours in 1965 to 12.9 hours in 2000. Men increased their time with their children as well—from 2.6 to 6.5 hours per week. "Thus, though husbands have taken on more domestic work, the work-family conflict has not eased for women; the gain has been offset by escalating pressures for intensive parenting and the increasing time demands of most high-level careers." Finally, the authors link the work-family tension to an "underinvestment in social capital," meaning that women have less time to socialize with colleagues and build professional networks. Studies demonstrate that managers who invest more time in socializing, politicking, and interacting with colleagues and those outside the business are more successful than those who simply concentrated on internal tasks (management activities). Even if women find the time to informally network, they too often find themselves nearly exclusively in the company of men and participating in traditionally masculine activities (sports, strip-club outings, hunting, or fishing). The article concludes with a number of interventions that enable women to rise in the leadership ranks, but nearly all of them have to do with changing people's attitudes about women, gender roles, or work norms or changing the way corporate work is organized and rewarded.[54]

Women in business have enjoyed increased visibility and success in the last decade. In 2003, eight Fortune 500 companies with women CEOs outperformed the broader market by a substantial margin. This news was greeted by a flurry of rationalizations: "2003 was a fluke; the glass ceiling has been so difficult to crack that women who reach the top are, on average, better executives than their male counterparts; many recently promoted women were at companies that were on life support at the time. Those companies might have been too desperate to attract men of quality and ambition."[55] That market observers felt the need to "explain" women's success speaks to the power of the paradox of gender equality. Although the percentage of female corporate officers nearly doubled from 1995 to 2002, 90 percent of line jobs (heads of divisions measured by their profits and losses, and the position from which most CEOs rise) are still held by men. Among the five highest-paid corporate officers at each Fortune 500 company, 5.2 percent were women in 2002, up from 1.2 percent in 1995.[56] Women accounted for 50.8 percent of all workers in the high-paying management, professional, and related occupations in 2008. Women outnumbered men in such occupations as insurance underwriters (80.3 percent), medical and health services managers (69.4 percent), human resource managers (66.3 percent), advertising and promotion managers (62 percent), accountants and auditors (61.1 percent), budget analysts (57.1 percent), and financial managers (54.8 percent).[57] Women are more advantageously distributed across the management fields as well. The largest proportion of employed women worked in management in 2008 (39.5 percent); 20.6 percent in service occupations; 5.9 percent in production, transportation, and material-moving occupations; and 0.9 percent in natural resources, construction, and maintenance occupations.

A recent study by Catalyst found men and women equally ambitious for top corporate leadership positions. Fifty-five percent of female and 57 percent of male respondents aspired to their organization's top position. Similarly, roughly equal numbers of men and women reported that they did not want the top job (26 percent of female executives, 29 percent of the males). Having children made no difference to the level of ambition expressed by women or men. Ambition was particularly strong among individuals in line positions (82 percent of women and 77 percent of men). The survey also found that men and women shared similar advancement strategies (consistently exceeding performance expectations, successfully managing others, seeking high-visibility assignments, and demonstrating expertise), and have experienced similar barriers to advancement (displaying a behavioral style that is different than an organization's norm, lack of significant general management or line experience, and lack of awareness of organizational politics).[58] There were also differences uncovered between men's and women's experiences. Women reported encountering gender-based stereotypes, exclusion from informal networks, lack of role models, and an inhospitable corporate culture. The study also addressed the problem of balancing work and personal life, a problem that will be discussed later in this chapter and one that has recently attracted attention as the media have focused on a relatively small group of professional women who have "opted out" of the workplace. Both men and women in Catalyst's study reported difficulty achieving a desirable work-life balance, and men and women expressed equal desires to explore more flexible work arrangements. However, women reported making more "trade-offs" than men, particularly when it came to deciding not to have children (27 percent of women, compared with 3 percent of men) or to postpone having children (20 percent of women vs. 10 percent of men). "Despite the trade-offs they have made, a large majority of both women and men report comfort with their choices."[59]

Women currently earn 48.5 percent of all the law degrees in the U.S. and make up 32 percent of American attorneys. Women comprise 27 percent of federal circuit court of appeals judges and 25 percent of federal district court judges, but only two women have ever served as Justice in the history of the U.S. Supreme Court. Minority women are further underrepresented, making up less than 3 percent of the profession and less than 1 percent of law firm partners. Women attorneys in 2007 earned a median income of $93,600, compared to men's median earnings of $120,400.[60] Exacerbating the slow progress for women in the legal field is the perception, particularly among men, that "full equality is upon us or just around the corner. Only 3 percent of male lawyers think that prospects for advancement in the legal profession are greater for men than for women."[61] A 2001 study by the American Bar Association (ABA) suggests that most attorneys equate gender bias with intentional discrimination; however, the major barriers to women's advancement uncovered by the study include unconscious stereotypes, inadequate access to support networks, inflexible workplace structures, sexual harassment, and bias in the justice system.[62] The problem is as much a sticky floor as it is a glass ceiling. The income gap between male and female lawyers begins during the first year of practice and widens from there.[63] According to the National Association for Law Placement, a trade group that provides career counseling to lawyers and law students, only about 17 percent of the partners at major law firms nationwide were women in 2005, a figure that has risen only slightly since 1995, when about 13 percent of partners were women. The attrition rate for women attorneys is more than double that of men within the first two years and thereafter. Deborah Rhode, author of the ABA's report, "The Unfinished Agenda," and a professor at Stanford School of Law, argues that women who aspire to leadership roles in firms face "double standards and double binds." Women are rated lower, particularly by male evaluators, when they adopt a typically "masculine" style of authority. Women attorneys suffer from a presumption of incompetence and are therefore held to higher standards than their male counterparts, especially if they are mothers. "Those who want extended leaves or reduced schedules appear to be lacking as professionals. Those who seem willing to sacrifice family needs to workplace schedules appear to be lacking as mothers." Workplace structures, according to the ABA report, fail to accommodate family commitments. Even though over 90 percent of firms report allowing associates part-time schedules, only 3 to 4 percent of lawyers actually use them. Finally, women in law (as in business and elective politics) lack access to mentors and supportive networks.[64]

In medicine, women fared better salary-wise when pay was based on hourly wages, with female doctors earning nearly 87 percent of male doctors' earnings. However, 55 percent of women, compared with 42 percent of men, practiced in the three lowest-paying specialties—pediatrics, general practice, and general internal medicine. Conversely, only 14 percent of women worked in the four highest-paying fields (radiology, general surgery, anesthesiology, and subspecialty surgery), compared with 27 percent of men.[65] Valian found that men and women choose specialties that are congruent with gender expectations and that senior medical staff encouraged young medical students to choose specialties that conformed to gender roles. Like their counterparts in law, women in medical school find a predominantly male faculty. Only 14 percent of the tenured faculty at medical schools is female, with 12 percent of those achieving the rank of full professor.[66] According to the Association of American Medical Colleges (AAMC), women made up more than 50 percent of the applicants in 2007 and constituted slightly less than 50 percent of the entering class, 47 percent of residents, and 33 percent of medical school faculty. The AAMC's report concludes, "The number of women entering medical school has led to the premature conclusion that gender equality has been achieved."[67]

In computer science and technology, gains made by women in the 1980s and early 1990s have actually eroded. In 1984, women received 37 percent of the undergraduate degrees in computer science. In 1999, women constituted only 20 percent of those earning computer science degrees, but over the past ten years women's share of computer science bachelor's degrees has only risen to 25 percent. Although women constitute nearly half of the workforce, they hold just 12 percent of the science and engineering jobs.[68] At the same time, the National Council for Research on Women has reported that women have made substantial gains in biology and mathematics. In 2004, women earned 62 percent of all biological sciences undergraduate degrees and 45.9 percent of the undergraduate degrees in mathematics. Women have enjoyed similar gains in graduate degrees in the same fields: women earned 58.6 percent of the master's and 46.3 percent of the doctoral degrees in biological sciences and 45.4 percent of the master's and 28.4 percent of the doctoral degrees in mathematics. The study attributes women's increasing participation in these fields (over information technology and engineering, for example) to "more flexibility in those workplaces, increased numbers of women in positions of power and in the classroom," and a greater interest in science professions that appear to have a direct impact on the quality of people's lives.[69]

Women in the Military

Prior to 1967, there was a 2 percent cap limiting women's service in the military.[70] By 2008, the proportion of active-duty enlisted women had risen to 14.2 percent.

The Air Force has the highest proportion of women on active duty (19.6 percent) and the Marine Corps has the lowest (6.2 percent). The Army reports 13.6 percent women and the Navy 15 percent women among enlisted personnel. The Office of the Assistant Secretary of Defense identifies four factors that affect the proportion of enlisted female members: women tend to have a lower inclination to enlist than men do; combat exclusions restrict the positions in which women may serve; the military personnel system is "closed," meaning that growth comes from the bottom up and from within—the proportion of women depends primarily on the proportion of women recruited; and finally, women leave the services at a higher rate than men.[71] The increase in the proportion of women in the military has resulted in changes in nearly all aspects of military life: training programs and physical fitness regimens, assignments, living arrangements, and medical services. New policies had to be created to address pregnancy, single parents in the military, child care during peacetime and deployment, and dual-service marriages, sexual harassment and sexual assault.

In 1994, Congress repealed the "risk rule" barring women from all combat situations and allowed each branch of the service to determine which positions would be open to women. Secretary of Defense Les Aspin advised, "Women should be excluded from assignment to units below brigade level whose primary mission is to engage in direct combat on the ground." Combat was defined as "engaging an enemy on the ground with individual or crew-served weapons, while being exposed to hostile fire and to a high probability of direct physical

Lioness Marines in Iraq search female Iraqi women in support of counterinsurgency operations. —Image by © Ed Darack/Science Faction/Corbis. *Ed Darack/Corbis*

contact with the hostile force's personnel." As a result, thousands of previously restricted positions are now open to women: 91 percent of positions in the Army, 96 percent in the Navy, 93 percent in the Marine Corps, and 99 percent in the Air Force. Although women are still prohibited from certain assignments in each branch of the service, most experts think it is only a matter of time until there is full gender integration. Department of Defense evidence suggests that mixed crews perform as well as or better than all male units. A RAND Research Brief from 1997 reported that the integration of women has not adversely affected military readiness. Using interviews, surveys, and focus groups, the researchers probed issues of unit cohesiveness, readiness, and morale. While gender played some role in unit cohesiveness, this typically occurred only in units where conflict was already a problem. The presence of women was also cited as raising the level of professional standards. Morale was affected by gender in two areas: sexual harassment and a perception of double standards related to physical standards.[72]

Female recruits tend to have more education and better test scores than men. As technology continues to advance, women will gain more opportunities. "U.S. military superiority is in our intelligence and technology. People who remain skeptical of having women fight for their country act like we're still attacking with fixed bayonets," says Linda DePaw of the Minerva Center (a military think tank). Although pregnancy rates, sexual harassment, and sexual assault remain problems, the public's reaction to women in combat and female casualties has proved milder than predicted. According to Carolyn Becraft, a deputy assistant secretary of defense under President Clinton, "It's been a nonissue."[73]

The first Gulf War (Desert Storm) marked the largest deployment of women to a combat zone in U.S. history. More than 41,000 women served in the Gulf, comprising 7 percent of the deployed force during Desert Storm. Their roles included flying helicopters on reconnaissance and search-and-rescue missions, driving convoys, staffing Patriot missile placements, piloting planes, and guarding POWs, among others.[74] Thirteen women were killed in the line of duty, and two were taken as prisoners of war. Deployment of women in the current war in Iraq is even larger, estimated now at 11 percent of the total forces. "Iraq has advanced the cause of full integration for women in the Army by leaps and bounds. They have earned the confidence and respect of male colleagues," says Peter, R. Mansoor, a retired Army colonel who served as executive officer to General David H. Petraeus while he was top American commander in Iraq. As of August 2009, over 356,000 women are serving throughout the armed forces (roughly 16 percent of the total) including the Reserves and National Guard. This deployment has also stretched the limits of the law on women in combat roles. When commanders need more soldiers for crucial jobs, like bomb disposal and intelligence, they often resort to "bureaucratic trickery" to "attach" women to a combat unit rather than "assign" them. According to retired Air Force Brigadier General Wilma L. Vaught, "You've got more women carrying weapons with the possibility that they'll use them to fight or defend themselves. That's one of the big differences between this war and others. Women haven't done this type of war before."[75] Blurred lines between front-line positions and combat support have resulted in higher female casualties. As of August 2009, 121 military women have been killed, 66 have been killed in combat. An additional 620 women have been wounded.[76]

There are currently over 1.8 million female veterans (roughly 8 percent of the veteran population) living in the United States. Female veterans suffer the same difficulties as many male veterans upon returning from a war zone. In addition to combat-related injuries and mental trauma, women often report being victims of sexual assault while deployed or in training. Estimates of sexual assault rates vary widely from 30 to 70 percent, but the Pentagon admits that sexual assault is an underreported crime and estimates that only 10 and 20 percent of cases ever get reported. Because women are officially barred from combat, those suffering from posttraumatic stress disorder (PTSD) face a higher burden of proof. Swords to Plowshares, a veteran's service organization, says that female Iraq War veterans are among the fastest-growing population of homeless. Women returning from war face challenges in accessing appropriate medical care since a majority of the Veterans hospitals and medical facilities are organized to care for male vets.

The public is largely unaware of the number of women currently serving in war zones and the issues they face. *Lioness*, a 2008 documentary directed by Meg McLagan and Daria Sommers, tells the gripping story of a group of female Army support soldiers who were among the first group of women to engage in direct ground combat with insurgents in Iraq.[77] Events related to the wars in Iraq and Afghanistan have stimulated the public debate over women's roles in military combat. As CBS News reported in October 2004, "The unexpected realities of the war in Iraq are forcing the Pentagon to reexamine its long-standing ban on women in combat in a guerrilla war fought mainly in cities and without front lines." A July 2009 New York Times/CBS News poll found that a majority of the public supports allowing women to do more on the battlefield. Fifty-three percent of the respondents would favor permitting women to "join combat units, where they would be directly involved in the ground fighting." More than a dozen countries allow women to serve in some or all ground combat operations.[78] Those opposed to women in the military, particularly in positions likely to face hostilities, often ground their opposition in the essential natures of men and women. Allan Carlson of the Family Research Council, a conservative Washington think tank, says, "Having mothers on or near the front lines violates the most basic human instincts." Phyllis Schlafly of the Eagle Forum writes, "The men in our government and in the U.S. military lack the courage to stand up to feminists and repudiate their assault on family and motherhood."[79] Conservative commentator Linda Chavez writes, "No matter how much we modernists pretend otherwise, women are different from men, and their roles are not interchangeable. Females are not just smaller versions of males; they are also, on average, far less aggressive and more nurturing, qualities that suit them to be good mothers but not warriors."[80] In an ironic twist, Pfc. Monica Brown was presented with the Silver Star, the nation's third-highest combat medal, for repeatedly risking her life to aid fellow soldiers trapped in a fire fight with Taliban fighters in eastern

Afghanistan. Brown, a medic assigned to a cavalry unit, is the second woman since World War II to receive the Silver Star. Within days of her heroic acts, the Army pulled her out of her unit and reassigned her because "Army restrictions on women in combat barred her from such missions."[81]

In a 2007 study, the RAND Corporation declared the current policy unworkable. "Crafted for a linear battlefield, the policy does not conform to the nature of warfare today." The study found that noncombat units where women were serving in Iraq and Afghanistan faced many of the same threats that all-male combat units face and they performed equally well in the face of those dangers. The Rand study recommended that the policy against women in combat be revoked or substantially revised. The wars in Iraq and Afghanistan have placed strains on the military, including longer deployments (on average 15 months in the war zone) followed by shorter periods at home. For women who want to continue a career in the military and begin a family, longer deployments mean increased tension between work and family. The Army grants six weeks of maternity leave and four months before sending a new mother back into a war zone. The Marine Corps and Navy allow anywhere from six months to a year before a new mother must deploy. Surveys show that for both men and women, time away from families due to long and frequent deployments is the top reason for leaving the Army. Officials believe this also accounts for a decrease in women's "propensity to serve." The willingness of women to serve in the military has dropped faster than that of men in recent years, from a high of 10 percent of 16- to 21-year-olds surveyed in November 2003 to just 4 percent in July 2007. Nearly 40 percent of women on active duty in 2008 have children and about 10 percent of women in the military become pregnant each year. An estimated 75,000 children of active military personnel are younger than one year old. Major General Gale Pollock, deputy surgeon general for Army force management, characterizes the dilemma for military recruiters, "Without women we would not make our volunteer numbers, so if we destroy the interest of women to volunteer it puts us in a particularly bad place, because the nation does not want a draft."[82] Deployments in the other branches have been shorter than the Army's 15 months—an average of seven months for both the Navy and Marine Corps.

Women today make up 6 percent of the military's top ranks. Fifty-seven women were serving as generals and admirals in the active-duty military in 2008. Ann E. Dunwoody became the first four-star Army general in 2008 and many more women lead all-male combat troops into battle. President Obama appointed Tammy Duckworth, a former Army Black Hawk helicopter pilot, as assistant secretary of the Department of Veterans Affairs. Duckworth was shot down while serving in Iraq and lost both legs as a result of the crash. Part of her job within the VA is to connect older veterans with younger ones, regardless of gender. Although progress must seem slow at times, military women have, for the most part, resisted any focus on their gender. After battling for decades to open opportunities in the military and change a culture that accepted sexual harassment and assault, they "abhor anything that smacks of special treatment."[83]

The issue of women in combat presents the paradox of gender equality in its starkest terms. Congress may well be forced to confront gender in any future debates over military conscription. When President Jimmy Carter reactivated the draft registration process, Congress did not act on his recommendation and amend the act to include females. In *Rostker v. Goldberg* (1981), the U.S. Supreme Court ruled that Congress's decision to exempt women from registration "was not the 'accidental by-product' of a traditional way of thinking about females" and did not violate the due process clause. The Court reasoned that because of the combat restrictions on females at the time, men and women were not "similarly situated" for the purposes of draft registration. With combat restrictions relaxed and women's strong performance in the 1991 Gulf War, the most recent Iraq War and hostilities in Afghanistan, it is hard to see how the Court could use the same reasoning in upholding women's exclusion today.

Sexual Harassment

Sexual harassment is a form of gender discrimination in employment and educational institutions that is covered under Title VII and Title IX, respectively. In 1980, the EEOC defined sexual harassment as a form of discrimination:

> Unwelcome sexual advances, requests for sexual favors, and other verbal or physical conduct of a sexual nature constitute sexual harassment when (1) submission to such conduct is made either explicitly or implicitly a term or condition of an individual's employment; (2) submission to or rejection of such conduct by an individual is used as a basis for employment decisions affecting such individual; or (3) such conduct has the purpose or effect of unreasonably interfering with an individual's work performance or creating an intimidating, hostile, or offensive working environment.[84]

The EEOC's regulation encompasses the two most common types of harassment: quid pro quo (an exchange of favors) and creating a hostile environment. The standards for applying Title VII to allegations of sexual harassment in the workplace were developed by a series of federal circuit court decisions and the EEOC before a case ever reached the Supreme Court. In 1986, ruling in *Meritor Savings Bank v. Vinson*, the Court outlined a pattern of proof of hostile environment cases, in which the plaintiff must show that

> (1) she was subjected to unwelcome sexual conduct; (2) these were based on her sex; (3) they were sufficiently pervasive or severe to create an abusive or hostile work environment; and (4) the employer knew or should have known of the harassment and failed to take prompt and appropriate remedial action.[85]

The Court specifically took note of the EEOC guidelines in deciding the *Meritor* case, which prompted the lower courts to do the same. In determining the character of "unwelcome" sexual advances and the severity of an abusive or hostile work environment, the courts have tended to use a "reasonableness standard." This means that, under similar circumstances, would a "reasonable person" in the harasser's position have known the behavior was unwelcome.

Feminists objected to this standard, arguing that harassers are usually men and that men do not have a good track record on understanding the seriousness of sexual harassment or the difference between "teasing" and "harassment." The Court later adopted a "reasonableness" standard related to the victim's perspective, noting that the previous standard ran the risk of reinforcing the prevailing level of discrimination. In *Ellison v. Brady*, the Ninth Circuit Court of Appeals adopted the perspective of a "reasonable woman." In ruling, the court was careful not to establish a higher level of protection for women (a fear expressed by some liberal feminists), noting, "A gender-conscious examination of sexual harassment enables women to participate in the workplace on an equal footing with men. By acknowledging and not trivializing the effects of sexual harassment on reasonable women, courts can work toward ensuring that neither men nor women will have to 'run a gauntlet of sexual abuse in return for the privilege of being allowed to work and make a living.'" Thus, when a male plaintiff alleges a hostile environment, the standard would be that of a "reasonable man."

The courts' willingness to hold an employer accountable for the behavior of its managerial and supervisory employees has prompted most businesses and schools to develop policies on sexual harassment. These policies include guidelines on how to report incidents of harassment and procedures for an internal resolution of the complaint. A victim of sexual harassment may always file a sex-discrimination claim with the EEOC. In the wake of the Anita Hill–Clarence Thomas hearings in 1991, the EEOC reported a 60 percent increase in the number of complaints in the nine months following the televised hearings. Included in the Civil Rights Act of 1991 are provisions allowing victims of sexual harassment to sue for monetary damages (up to $300,000). In 1993, the Supreme Court ruled in the case of *Harris v. Forklift Systems* that the victim of sexual harassment need only demonstrate impairment of work or education to prove that an environment is hostile. Lower courts had been heading toward requiring evidence of severe psychological harm.

In 1998, the Court announced its decision in *Oncale v. Sundowner Offshore Services*, the first case to consider whether Title VII applies to sexual harassment between persons of the same sex. Joseph Oncale worked for a Louisiana offshore oil company. Oncale claimed that other male employees, including two with supervisory authority over him, had psychologically and physically abused him. All of the men involved were heterosexual. The company defended the behavior of its employees and attributed the content and intensity of the behavior as "simply hazing" and the product of an all-male environment. Ultimately, Oncale quit and filed suit. The lower federal courts dismissed the case, saying that Title VII does not apply to claims of same-sex harassment. In a unanimous ruling for the Supreme Court, Justice Antonin Scalia wrote that Title VII protected men from discrimination and that its protection against sexual harassment extended to same-sex conduct. Illegal conduct is not limited to that associated with sexual desire and could well arise from hostility. The Court applied the "reasonable person" standard in determining the behavior was so severe that it could be classified as sex discrimination.[86] Thus sexual harassment results from gender-based hostility manifested as sexualized conduct, normally between a woman and a male employer or authority figure, but not exclusively so. *Oncale* suggests that it is the hostility and the severity of the behavior, even if directed at a member of one's own sex, that makes sexual harassment illegal under Title VII. Two cases decided after *Oncale* indicate that the courts will continue to apply the protections of Title VII to cases in which individuals are harassed for not exemplifying the social gender norms expected of their sex. In other words, illegal sexual harassment can also include victimization of males for not being "manly" enough.[87]

The Pay Gap

Ironically, while Title IX and Title VII opened doors to education and employment in well-paying professions previously limited to men, the Equal Pay Act, the first among the major federal equality initiatives, has not effectively guaranteed women equal pay for equal work. Regardless of occupation, level of experience, skills, or education, the pay gap remains. Women lawyers make on average $366 a week less than their male colleagues, women secretaries earn about $122 a week less than male clerical workers, female physicians' and surgeons' median weekly income is nearly $681 less than that of their male colleagues, and female nurses earn $90 a week less than male nurses. Male college faculty earn nearly $244 a week more than women in the same rank, and male elementary school teachers take home about $60 more a week than female teachers.[88] On average, women working full-time, year-round earn 78–80 percent of median weekly earnings for men working full-time, year-round. That means that if you are "an average woman accountant in the United States, you work Monday through Friday to earn what the man at the next desk has earned by noon on Wednesday." Nationwide, working families lose over $200 billion of income annually to the wage gap. Female workers have an average career wage gap of $434,000—ranging from $270,000 for a woman with less than a high school education to $713,000 for a woman with a bachelor's degree or higher. Women also earn less from benefits that are tied to salary. The size of raises and the percentage of retirement savings matched by their employer will be smaller due to a lower wage base. The gap is much larger for women of color. On average, African American women earn 66 percent of the pay of white men, Hispanic women earn 59 percent, and Asian women 87 percent. Thus women of color earn less than men of color and also less than white women (see figure 7.2).[89]

The wage gap varies by state. Women who work full-time in Utah, Michigan, Arkansas, Iowa, New Hampshire, and Oklahoma fare the worst relative to men, receiving, on average, 68 percent of men's wages. Women fare best (on average, 81 percent of men's wages) in the District of Columbia, Vermont, Hawaii, Delaware, New York, Montana, and Maryland. Men working in

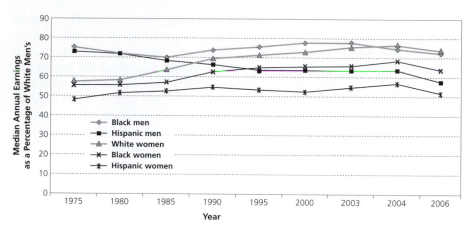

FIGURE 7.2 Wage Gap by Gender and Race, 1975–2006

Source: U.S. Department of Labor, Bureau of Labor Statistics, Women's Bureau, "Highlights of Women's Earnings," Statistics and Data, 2006.

predominantly female occupations across all states lost an average of $6,259 a year as a result of depressed wages in those occupations.[90] At the current rate, it will take more than fifty years before women's paychecks will equal men's.

In marking the thirty-fifth anniversary of the Equal Pay Act in 1998, the Clinton administration called on Congress to strengthen the enforcement of the law in recognition of the wage gap. Clinton included a call for tougher enforcement of the EPA in his State of the Union Address, and included more than $14 million in the FY 2000 budget to close the wage gap. The Department of Labor and the Equal Employment Opportunity Commission (EEOC), both charged with enforcing provisions in the law, stepped up their efforts accordingly. Texaco agreed to pay a record $3.1 million to female employees who had consistently been paid less than male employees. The 1999 settlement included more than $900,000 in salary increases and more than $2.2 million in back pay.[91] In the largest employment discrimination suit ever filed, female employees have sued Wal-Mart for paying women less than men for similar work and for denying women promotions (*Dukes v. Wal-Mart Stores, Inc.*). In June 2004, a federal judge in San Francisco granted class-action status to the suit and the ruling was appealed by Wal-Mart. Merits of the class-action status were argued before a Ninth Circuit eleven-member *en banc* panel in March 2009 but no ruling has yet been issued. The case now covers nearly 1.6 million current and former female Wal-Mart employees. U.S. District Judge Martin Jenkins found that attorneys for the plaintiffs "present largely uncontested, descriptive statistics which show that women working in Wal-Mart stores are paid less than men in every region, that pay disparities exist in most job categories, that the salary gap widens over time even for men and women hired into the same jobs at the same time, that women take longer to enter into management positions, and that the higher one looks in the organization, the lower the percentage of women."[92] Women make up more than 70 percent of Wal-Mart's hourly employees, but less than one-third of its store management. As of June 2009, there are at least 80 class-action lawsuits in 41 states (including *Dukes*) pending against Wal-Mart; 76 percent of the suits involve wage discrimination. Although the majority of the cases are still pending, the allegations themselves have focused consumer and stockholder attention on Wal-Mart's employment practices as well of their retail competitors. Wal-Mart has already made changes. For example, 15 percent of a manager's bonus is now tied to meeting diversity goals (to have the sex and race of those promoted more closely reflect the percentages of those who apply), and Wal-Mart now requires that new hires with the same experience receive the same rate of pay regardless of their pay history.

Unlike the Clinton administration, President George W. Bush did not encourage the EEOC to move aggressively to close the wage and pay gap. To the contrary, his 2002 budget underfunded the activities of the EEOC by nearly $9 million. In 2008, more than 95,400 charges of employment discrimination in the private sector were filed, up 15.2 percent from the previous year and up 26 percent from the previous year. The size of the staff, however, decreased during the Bush administration from approximately 2,850 in 2000 to around 2,000 in 2008. The result is a tremendous backlog and very few lawsuits actually filed against employers. Diana Furchtgott-Roth, a member of Bush's Council of Economic Advisers, has previously testified before the Equal Employment Opportunity Commission that "the average wage gap is not proof of widespread discrimination, but of women making choices about their educational and professional careers in a society where the law has granted them equality of opportunity to do so." President Bush opposed the Paycheck Fairness Act, and did not support increasing the minimum wage during his two terms (Congress acted to increase the minimum wage in 2006 immediately after the Democrats regained the majority in the House of Representatives). Media reports in the summer of 2004 uncovered a pay gap within the Bush White House itself. According to White House salary figures leaked to the *Washington Post*, men in the Bush White House earned an average of $76,624, while women earned $59,917 on average. Women in the White House earned 78 percent of men's pay, roughly equivalent to the national pay gap for all women. However, the pay disparities in the Bush White House may more accurately be described as evidence of the "glass ceiling" than the wage gap. Of the seventeen Bush staff who earned $157,000, twelve were men.[93] President Barack Obama campaigned for president on the issue of pay equity, supported the Lilly Ledbetter Fair Pay Act and signed it into law, and has spoken of the need to more vigorously enforce the Equal Pay Act. While a U.S. senator, he cosponsored the Fair Pay Act introduced by Senator Tom Harkin (D-IA). Closing the wage gap is also on the agenda of the newly created White House Council on Women and Girls.

Equal Pay Day, celebrated each year in April, marks the day each year on which women "catch up" to men in terms of wages. It is an occasion to call attention to the wage gap and to examine progress toward closing the wage gap between women and men. It also sparks a barrage of criticism about the focus on the wage gap by many who say that the gap is an artifact of women's choices and not a result of gender discrimination in hiring, promotions, or pay. Labeling the wage gap a product of the popular media culture's "women as victims" theory, Diana Furchtgott-Roth and Christine Solba of the ideologically conservative American Enterprise Institute and the Independent Women's Forum argue that self-selected statistics and anecdotal evidence have led women and policymakers to believe a myth.[94] The myth of the pay gap stems, they argue, from faulty methodology and an unwillingness to admit that women have made progress in the last three decades. They also argue that the "glass ceiling," for example, reflects the lack of qualified women in the pipeline for top corporate positions and not systematic discrimination as reported by the Glass Ceiling Commission (created as a result of the Civil Rights Act of 1991). The Glass Ceiling Commission reported that women held only 5 percent of the top management posts in Fortune 1,000 industrial and in Fortune 500 service companies. Furchtgott-Roth and Solba argue that since women were not well represented in professional schools in the 1950s and 1960s, few would have the requisite qualifications (an MBA and twenty-five years of experience) to hold industry's top positions and therefore would not be among those at the top of their professions today.[95] This is partially true since many professional programs did not admit women until required to do so by Title IX, passed in 1972. While Furchtgott-Roth and Solba may label the delay in women's "earning" the experience necessary to be CEO of Fortune 500 companies a "pipeline" problem, it also represents the effects of systematic discrimination. Attrition of women from the ranks of CEOs, top scientists, lawyers, and other professions results in what some have labeled a "leaky pipeline."

With regard to the pay gap, Furchtgott-Roth and Solba focus on the "choices" women make. For women and men with similar education, continuous years in the workforce, age, and occupation, the "adjusted wage gap" is much smaller (though it still exists). Numerous studies support the persistence of gender bias in hiring, promotion, and pay-setting in explaining a portion of the wage gap. For example, Claudia Goldin and Cecelia Rouse found that if women auditioned for symphony orchestras from behind a screen so that their sex was not evident, they were more likely to be hired.[96] Examining the workplace experiences of transgender people, researchers documented that while transgender people have the same human capital after their transitions, their workplace outcomes often change radically. Average earnings for female-to-male transgender workers increase slightly following their gender transitions, while average earnings for male-to-female transgender workers fall by one-third. A loss of earnings is often accompanied by a loss of authority and harassment. Alternatively, becoming a man often brings an increase in respect and authority.[97]

A 2008 study of the federal workforce by the Government Accountability Office (GAO) found that although the decline in the pay gap over the last twenty years is due mostly to changes in the makeup of the workforce (women have more education, experience, and are more likely to work in professional and managerial jobs than in previous years), there is a 7 percent gap that cannot be explained by shifting demographics (including race and regional location). In a separate report to Congress, the GAO found that oversight agencies such as the Equal Opportunity Commission and the Office of Federal Contract Compliance Programs needed to do more to monitor antidiscrimination efforts.[98] A 2007 study by the American Association of University Women (AAUW) examined the gender pay gap for college graduates. One year out of college, women working full-time earn only 80 percent as much as their male colleagues. To be sure, the choice of major in college and occupational field plays a role in the size of the gap; however, even between men and women with the same major and in the same occupation a pay gap remains. In education, a female-dominated major, women earn 95 percent as much as their male colleagues just one year after graduation. In biological sciences, a mixed-gender major, women earn only 75 percent as much as men. In mathematics, still largely a male-dominated field, women earn 76 percent as much as their male colleagues.[99]

Another intriguing explanation for the persistent 7 to 11 percent pay gap, once other explanations are held constant, comes from new research on women's willingness to negotiate salary. Linda Babcock and Sara Laschever used experimental conditions to test whether an individual's sex was correlated with his or her willingness to bargain. For example, volunteers in a laboratory setting were asked to play the word game Boggle and were told that they would be paid anywhere from $3 to $10 for their time. After playing the game, each subject was given $3 and asked if the sum was acceptable. Male subjects were eight times more likely than female subjects to ask for more money. When the conditions of the experiment were changed slightly so that all of the subjects were explicitly told that their payment was negotiable (thus giving them tacit permission to bargain), the gender gap remained. Only 58 percent of the women compared to 83 percent of the men asked for more money. Finally, in a survey of master's degree graduates about their actual first job offers, Babcock and Laschever found that four times as many men as women had negotiated for a higher salary rather than simply accepting the first offer (51 percent of the men, compared to 12.5 percent of the women). Those who negotiated were rewarded with an average salary 7.4 percent higher than those who had not bargained.[100]

This remarkable finding is tempered somewhat by research that identified perceptual bias against women who tried to negotiate.[101] Both men and women in this study were likely to subtly penalize women who asked for a higher salary. In this study, respondents were randomly assigned to groups and provided with identical descriptions of highly qualified male or female job applicants who tried to negotiate a higher starting salary, as well as descriptions of applicants who simply accepted the initial salary offer. Volunteer subjects were asked to decide whether they would hire each of the candidates. Although both men and women were negatively affected by bargaining, the size of the negative impact for women was twice that for men. Likewise, when asked to rate whether they would be willing to work with each of the candidates, male volunteers tended to rate negatively women who had negotiated but were less likely to similarly penalize men; women rated negatively both males and females who bargained and preferred those who accepted the salary offered. Overall, women who negotiated were perceived as "less nice." Similar studies found that male and female job applicant behavior was modified by the sex of the employer making the job offer—women were more likely to negotiate if the offer came from another woman. Thus, "there is an economic rationale to negotiate, but you have to weigh that against the social risks of negotiating. Those risks are higher for women than for men."[102]

One of the biggest salary penalties appears to stem from women's "choice" to have children. Citing a study of women who received their college degrees around 1972, Furchtgott-Roth and Solba note that "among those who have had a successful career, as indicated by income level, nearly 50 percent were childless."[103] Denise Venable of the National Center for Policy Analysis wrote under the subheading *The Good News*: "When women behave in the workplace as men do, the wage gap between them is small. . . . Among people 27 to 33 who have never had a child, women's earnings approach 98 percent of men's. Women who hold positions and have skills and experience similar to those of men face wage disparities of less than 10 percent. . . . Claims of unequal pay almost always involve comparing apples and oranges."[104] Comparing men and women with the same experience and education in 1991, women without children averaged 95 percent of men's wages, while women with children made just 75 percent of men's wages. The presence of children accounted for women's but not men's lower wages, according to two other studies. This, Furchtgott-Roth and Solba argue, is due to a woman's choice to spend time with her children, accept more flexible, lower-paying jobs to do so, or to aspire to less demanding occupations in anticipation of having children. In this sense, the "pink ghetto" of lower-paying jobs represents an "oasis" to women who plan to have children. Unless women forgo children entirely, adopting a male career pattern is nearly impossible. Venable labels care responsibilities "lifestyle choices," noting that women place more importance on their relationships— caring for children, parents, spouses, etc.—than on careers. But what is the alternative? As we'll see below, support for caregiving responsibilities is negligible for most families, and work is not currently structured to allow women or men the time necessary to coordinate work and family responsibilities. As Furchtgott-Roth and Solba conclude:

> The choices women make *outside* the workplace have significant consequences for their achievement *within* the workplace and . . . women, like men, can make it to the top—but not without sacrifice. What appears to be happening (and what those who cite discrimination ignore) is that women in many professions are making decisions to balance work and family priorities and that those decisions can result in fewer women reaching the top of their fields. . . . A preference for more time at home with less pay and less job advancement over more time at work with more pay and advancement is a legitimate choice for women.[105]

Of course, what this argument fails to address is the persistent dominance of the separate spheres ideology that places almost exclusive responsibility on women for both bearing and raising children. Presumably, having children is a choice made jointly and shared by a man and woman; however, the cost in this case for what is falsely labeled an "individual choice" falls solely on women in the form of lower wages, forgone promotions, and lost economic opportunities.

Lisa Belkin set off a firestorm with "The Opt-Out Revolution," an article published in the *New York Times Magazine* (October 26, 2003). Based on interviews with eight fellow Princeton alumni, Belkin fired this shot: "Why don't women run the world? Maybe it's because they don't want to."[106] As supporting "evidence," she offers a number of anecdotal experiences in which women encounter structural and institutional problems in combining work and family. Belkin's article is filled with women exercising their right of "choice" and deciding to leave their jobs. Tellingly, not a single one of the women's spouses is interviewed, and the perspective of the sole remaining breadwinner is conspicuous by its absence. A 2000 Harris poll reported that more than four-fifths of men in their twenties and thirties said a work schedule that allowed for family time was more important to them than a high-paying job.[107] A new census report based on 2007 data runs counter to the prevailing cultural myth that high-achieving professional mothers are leaving careers to return home and care for their families. The first of its kind, the new report found that stay-at-home mothers tended to be younger, less educated, with lower family incomes. They are also more likely than other mothers to be Hispanic or foreign born. In an essay that followed the release of the census report, Judith Warner wrote: "These findings really ought to lead us to reframe our public conversations about who mothers are and why they do what they do." But to date, they have not. Sociologist Paula England explains it this way: "The reason we keep getting this [choice] narrative is that there is deep cultural ambivalence about mothers' employment. On the one hand, people believe women should have equal opportunities, but on the other hand, we don't envision men taking on more child care and housework and, unlike Europe, we do not seem to be able to envision family-friendly work policies."[108]

In another recent article in the *New York Times Magazine*, "Look Who's Parenting," Ann Hulbert contrasts the parenting values of the baby boom generation with those of the post-boomer Generation X.[109] According to data collected by Reach Advisors, half of the Gen-X fathers devoted three to six hours a day to domesticity and complained of too little time with their kids. Restructuring the workplace in favor of a balanced life and greater long-term economic security requires men and women to act as agents of change. Women and men seek more balance in their lives and more support in juggling the full-time responsibilities of family and work. To suggest that it is only women who can or must make choices in this regard breathes new life into the separate spheres ideology in ways directly contrary to the pursuit of equality.

The Underside of Globalization—Are Immigrant Women Becoming the New "Wife" at Home?

According to the United Nations Population Fund, the number of people living outside their country of birth has almost doubled during the last fifty years. By 2006 nearly half of all international migrants, roughly 94.5 million individuals, were women.[1]

Millions of women from poor countries in the south migrate north to do "women's work." Barbara Ehrenreich and Arlie Hochschild label this pattern a worldwide gender revolution.[2] As male wages and overall earning power have fallen, women have increased their share of market participation to "make up the gap" in both rich and poor countries. "The lifestyles of the First World are made possible by a global transfer of the services associated with a wife's traditional role—child care, homemaking, and sex." As women in the United States and other developed nations have increased their roles in the public sphere by increasing their hours and commitment to paid labor, there is a gap in caregiving in the private sphere created by their absence. "The 'care deficit' that has emerged in wealthier countries as women enter the workforce *pulls* migrants from the Third World and post communist nations; poverty *pushes* them."[3]

Only 19 of 65 countries surveyed by the International Labour Organization (ILO) had specific laws or regulations governing domestic work, leaving migrant women vulnerable to a wide range of abuses. Women who are desperate to find work are easy prey for traffickers. Trafficked women are forced into sex work, domestic roles, or sweatshop labor. Human trafficking is the third most profitable criminal enterprise in the world (after arms and drugs). An estimated 800,000 humans are trafficked across international borders each year—up to 80 percent are women, half are children.

Lest one believe that the global transfer of female labor is exclusively pulled by women, Ehrenreich and Hochschild note that although American women took on more hours of paid work outside the home, they maintained (and

LIMITS OF THE LEGAL EQUALITY DOCTRINE IN PROMOTING ECONOMIC EQUALITY

Policies designed on the legal equality doctrine are gender neutral in their intent yet not always in their impact. Title VII and the Equal Pay Act have neither substantially changed the demographics of the labor force by ending sex slightly increased) the hours dedicated to child care and household chores, while men only slightly increased their share of the domestic burden. "So, strictly speaking, the presence of immigrant nannies does not enable affluent women to enter the workforce; it enables affluent *men* to continue avoiding the second shift."[4]

As we noted earlier in this chapter, low wages paid to workers in the private sector increase pressure on the public sector to provide increased public assistance to fill the gap. Just like California's charge that Wal-Mart was "essentially shifting part of its labor costs onto the public" (see The Consequences of a Gendered Economy section in this chapter), the lack of paid family leave, public child care, and universal access to health care in the United States shifts the communal responsibility for caregiving to the private sector. With nobody home and no public support, caregiving in the United States has increasingly been outsourced to female migrant laborers.

"This trend toward re-division of women's traditional work throws new light on the entire process of globalization."[5]

What do you think?

In what ways is the global transfer of female labor an issue of gender equality? When women migrate, their children rarely accompany them, making it highly likely that a poor woman will raise the children of an affluent woman even as her own children are raised by relatives or in orphanages in her home country. A 1995 documentary titled *When Mother Comes Home for Christmas*, produced by Nilita Vachani, explores the complexities of transnational migration. In what ways does this disjuncture demonstrate the impossibility of entirely reconciling the separate spheres for women? In some ways, the reality of women's labor migration is decidedly antifeminist in its character—what supports one woman's social advancement involves the sacrifice of another woman's labor—or is it? Discuss what feminism has to contribute to this debate and elaborate the limits of feminist ideology in alleviating the issues giving rise to women's transnational migration.

1. United Nations Population Fund, "General Fact Sheet on Women Migrants" (2006), accessed at http://www.unfpa.org.
2. Barbara Ehrenreich and Arlie Russell Hochschild, *Global Woman: Nannies, Maids, and Sex Workers in the New Economy* (New York: Henry Holt, 2002).
3. Ibid., p. 8.
4. Ibid., p. 9.
5. Ibid., p. 11.

segregation and eliminating the pay gap nor made it legally possible for women to ascend to the highest positions in proportion to their presence in the work-force. The limits to women's promotions once a company has hired them have been labeled the *glass ceiling*. Further, some issues go unaddressed by gender-neutral policies. Fetal protection policies, developed in the 1980s and 1990s, limit women's access to some of the best paying jobs in hazardous industry.

The character of the workplace has not changed significantly in response to the likelihood that both a husband and a wife will be full-time wage earners for the length of their working lives. This leaves issues of child care and family responsibilities to individuals to handle as best they can, and since women still carry the primary responsibility for home and children even when working full-time, these private decisions have fallen to women more often than not. As a result, women's work lives are interrupted to bear and care for children in ways that men's are not. In addition to the pay differential, women are also disadvantaged in retirement. Social Security benefits are calculated based on lifetime earnings, and women consistently draw lower benefits than men. These issues are discussed below.

The Glass Ceiling

The barrier that prevents otherwise qualified women from attaining the highest positions, along with their corresponding prestige and pay, has been labeled the *glass ceiling*.[110] Titles IX and VII allowed women to make tremendous gains in education and in the workplace. There are few overt barriers to jobs for women today. However, by June 2009, there were only thirteen women CEOs of Fortune 500 companies and women comprised less than 5 percent of top corporate earners. When Carly Fiorina was appointed president and CEO of Hewlett-Packard, she proclaimed that there was no glass ceiling for women (only to later characterize it as a "dumb thing to say"). After her firing in 2005, she published her memoir *Tough Choices* in which she details the ways in which the corporate world is still a difficult place to be a woman. In an interview with *Salon*, she noted, "I thought when I went to HP that we had come further than we had. I hoped I was advancing women in business by putting women in positions of responsibility. But it's clear that we don't yet play by the same rules and it's clear that there aren't enough women in business, and the stereotypes will exist as long as there aren't enough of us."[111] The glass ceiling has barely been cracked in boardrooms. In 2005, "women held 14.7 percent of the board seats at S&P 500 firms and 10 percent at S&P 1500 firms." Catalyst, a nonprofit organization that tracks women in business, describes the advances of women in corporate leadership since 2000 as "stagnant." In part the reason may again lie in a lack of role models and mentors. Analysis of 2005 data found that the average number of women on a board was less than 1.67, meaning that in most cases there was only one woman serving. The likelihood of appointing women to boards when vacancies occurred depended on the presence of a woman on the board at the time. When there were already one or more women serving on the board of directors, the likelihood of appointing another female board member decreased significantly. Research shows that women placed in groups highly dominated by males are generally viewed as tokens, subject to increased scrutiny, and less likely to succeed. Token status and the negative relationship between a woman on the board and the appointment of more women explain why overall progress has been so slow. While white women face a glass ceiling, women of color have characterized it as a "concrete ceiling." Minorities held just 8.8 percent of 7,500 board seats at S&P 1500 companies.[112] Surveys of women of color in management reveal that a lack of networking opportunities is perceived as the number one barrier to advancement. A vast amount of research literature documents the power of the old-boy network in excluding women's participation in the types of informal informational exchanges that result in client referrals and overall advancement in an organization.[113] The largest sex discrimination settlement won by the EEOC for women on Wall Street resulted in an award of $54 million to 340 women in a class-action suit against Morgan Stanley. Allison Schieffelin, the lead plaintiff, charged that Morgan Stanley's work environment constituted sex discrimination. The case was settled prior to trial and the consent decree requires Morgan Stanley to conduct management training sessions covering performance reviews, compensation, promotion, assignment of accounts, pregnancy, maternity leave, and maternal status. Morgan Stanley is also required to conduct a comparative analysis of promotion and compensation of women in a unit with men who hold the same positions. A 2003 survey by the Securities Industry Association showed a gradual decrease in the number of women in the securities industry workforce. Women comprised 37 percent of the industry in 2003, down from 43 percent in 2001.[114]

A new but related phenomenon has been labeled the "glass cliff." A study cited by BBC News found that women are often promoted to leadership positions once a company is doing badly. Given a choice between a male and a female candidate, companies were much more likely to choose the female candidate. The author of the study labels the trend a "new form of subtle discrimination."[115] A recent report by Catalyst suggests that women at the top benefit the company financially: "On average, companies with the highest percentage of women in top management outperform companies with the lowest percentage."[116]

Rather than employment policies that are obviously discriminatory, organizational culture and practices have created the glass ceiling. Ingrained in these cultures are traditional assumptions about gender stereotypes that can influence women's ability to reach the highest levels in a profession. Research suggests that both men and women perceive successful managers as those with more male characteristics than female characteristics. Women managers are perceived as less aggressive and independent than their male colleagues, although women are thought to have better interpersonal skills.[117] The characteristics that are valued and encouraged in an organization can often be gleaned from its mission statement and official publications. Companies that use motivational metaphors that draw on male-associated sports or military references and that make little positive mention of women in presentations of their corporate image are unlikely to have many women in top positions.[118]

The reasons for the persistence of the glass ceiling bear a striking resemblance to the reasons for so few women in politics. The pipeline thesis draws upon the proportion of women earning degrees in business and professional fields to suggest that it is really only a matter of time until women work their

"Aha! Just as I suspected!"

way up to corporate leadership positions. Qualifications for a senior leadership post include a graduate degree and twenty-five years of continuous work experience.[119] Although in the 1970s women made up only 5 percent of law and MBA degrees, today women earn over 40 percent of all law degrees and 35 percent of MBAs. However, as demonstrated elsewhere, a degree in the field does not guarantee that a woman will remain in the profession long enough to attain a leadership position. Motherhood, whether or not a woman leaves the full-time workforce, serves as one kink in the pipeline since the presence of children may limit a woman's ability to work long hours, travel extensively, and alter her schedule at a moment's notice. A lack of role models and female colleagues may create a work environment perceived as hostile to women's persistence. When women are tokens, their successes and failures are scrutinized more closely. A 2006 study found that among upper-level employees, women were less likely to be promoted than men, and if they were promoted they had significantly stronger performance ratings than males, suggesting that only exceptional women are promoted while men are held to a more moderate standard.

Fetal Protection Policies

In previous chapters we have reviewed the debate in the women's movement over protectionist legislation designed to insulate women from dangers in the workplace. Those who favor equality characterized by the legal equality doctrine view protectionist legislation as detrimental to women's cause since it limits a woman's ability to independently set the terms for her labor and to choose where, when, and for how long she works. Alternatively, those who favor equality characterized by fairness argue that a woman's reproductive role requires that she be accommodated differently from men in the workplace. Both sides agree that protectionist legislation is theoretically designed to favor women; however, the two sides differ on whether the implementation of protectionist policies works to the advantage or disadvantage of women. The debate effectively ended with the adoption of Title VII of the Civil Rights Act of 1964. Title VII requires equal treatment of men and women and prohibits employment discrimination on the basis of sex, with a few narrowly defined exceptions described earlier.

The protectionist debate was renewed when several private-sector employers adopted fetal protection policies in the 1980s and 1990s, raising new questions about gender equality and occupational health and safety. Fetal protection policies are designed to restrict women from specific jobs deemed by employers to be potentially hazardous to women and to fetuses. As many as 20 million women may have already been excluded from certain jobs, usually the highest-paying jobs, as a result of these exclusionary policies. In *United Auto Workers v. Johnson Controls, Inc.* (1991), the U.S. Supreme Court held that the fetal protection policies adopted by the company violated Title VII because they constituted disparate treatment on the basis of sex, since employees were classified by gender and reproductive capacity rather than by individual circumstances. In addition, the Court found that the policy was not justified under the bona fide occupational qualification (BFOQ) defense to sex discrimination. Johnson Controls argued that it was permitted to bar fertile women to protect their potential offspring and that a BFOQ of "sterility" was justified. The company further claimed that the BFOQ was closely related to job skills and aptitudes because it was necessary to ensure the safe and efficient production of batteries. The Court disagreed, saying in essence that an employer was not permitted to discriminate against women based on their *potential* for pregnancy unless it prevented them from doing their jobs. Treating all female employees as potentially pregnant constitutes discrimination on the basis of sex. The Court did not directly address questions of an employer's responsibility to provide a safe workplace for all employees regardless of sex, the argument about potential tort liability and business solvency, or the existence of fetal rights.

In subsequent years, states have attempted to develop "fetal rights" policies that subordinate women's interests to the prospective rights of a fetus (see chapter 8 for more on this general topic). Fetal rights applied to women's employment conditions pit the interests of an individual woman against prenatal societal interests. As Suzanne Uttaro Samuels, author of *Fetal Rights Women's Rights: Gender Equality in the Workplace*, notes, "Like the dystopia in Atwood's *The Handmaid's Tale*, a society that allows employers to adopt fetal protection policies reifies women's procreative role while denigrating their other contributions. In such a society, women can never be the equals of men."[120]

Comparable Worth and Pay Equity

The Equal Pay Act of 1963 was written to enforce equal pay for the same work but has done little to address the effects of employment patterns that show many women doing "women's work" and therefore receiving "women's wages." Advocates of the original EPA gave up the words "equal pay" for "comparable work" in order to get the bill passed. In recent years, however, the concept of comparable worth has returned as a public-policy issue. Comparable-worth legislation would ensure that women who work as *prison matrons*, for example, would be paid the same as men who work as *prison guards*. Similarly, 911 dispatchers would receive the same pay as emergency operators at the fire department, a social worker's wages would equal those of a probation officer, and a nursery worker who tends children would not be paid less than a nursery worker who tends plants.[121] In an attempt to garner public support, advocates of comparable worth have adopted the rhetoric of "paycheck fairness." As we have seen repeatedly, a change in the status or conditions women face is much more likely to be accomplished in the name of "fairness" than in the pursuit of "sameness." Some opponents of comparable worth still worry that men's wages will be depressed under comparable worth. Others recognize the large redistribution of income that would be required to eliminate the dual labor market.

For more than a decade, the Fair Pay Act (promoting comparable worth) and the Paycheck Fairness Act (providing additional remedies for discrimination) have remained stalled in Congress. Labor unions and many women's organizations have supported a pay equity or comparable-worth approach to reducing the pay gap. Businesses and manufactures are strongly opposed because of the inherent costs in setting pay scales to equalizing wages and the salary disclosure requirements included in the legislation. But in 2007, when the U.S. Supreme Court ruled 5 to 4 that Lilly Ledbetter, the lone female supervisor at a tire plant in Gadsden, Alabama, did not file her lawsuit against Goodyear Tire and Rubber Company within the time frame specified by Title VII of the Civil Rights Act of 1964, the issue of pay equity immediately found a new face and new champions.

When Lilly Ledbetter retired from Goodyear in 1998, she received an anonymous note revealing the salaries of her fifteen colleagues (all male and some with less seniority). Only then did she realize that she was the victim of pay discrimination and attributed her pay inequity to her sex. At first her salary was similar to her male supervisor colleagues, but over time she received smaller raises even though her performance ratings were positive. Because subsequent raises are often a percentage of the last base rate of pay, the cumulative effect was substantial. Quoting Justice Ruth Bader Ginsburg's dissent, "Ledbetter was paid $3,727 per month; the lowest paid male area manager received $4,286 per month, the highest paid $5,236." Ledbetter filed a complaint with the EEOC. A jury found that Goodyear had violated her rights under Title VII. Goodyear argued that she filed her complaint too late, and the majority of the Court agreed. The majority opinion written by Justice Samuel Alito applied a very narrow interpretation of the statute's requirement that a suit be filed within 180 days of the alleged unlawful employment practice. The Court claimed that it was incumbent on Ledbetter to file charges year-by-year, each time Goodyear failed to increase her salary commensurate with the salaries of male peers. Justice Ginsburg, in her dissenting opinion which she read aloud from the bench, took the majority to task for its failure to understand the nature of pay discrimination and women's experiences in the workplace. "Pay disparities often occur, as they did in Ledbetter's case, in small increments; cause to suspect that discrimination is at work develops only over time. Comparative pay information, moreover, is often hidden from the employees view. Employers may keep under wraps the pay differentials maintained among supervisors, no less the reasons for those differentials. Small initial discrepancies may not be seen as meet for a federal case, particularly when the employee, trying to succeed in a non-traditional environment, is averse to making waves."[122] Citing precedent she claimed the majority ignored, Ginsburg argued that the "unlawful practice" is the current payment of salaries "infected by gender-based (or race-based) discrimination," a practice that occurs whenever a paycheck delivers less to a woman than to a similarly situated man. In other words, gender-based wage disparities are most often the "cumulative effect of individual acts." The majority identified only the "pay-setting decision," discrete from prior and subsequent decisions, as the "unlawful practice." Lilly Ledbetter's salary fell 15 to 40 percent behind her male co-workers as a result of the repetition of pay decisions undervaluing her work. Under the Court's ruling, "Each and every pay decision she did not immediately challenge wiped the slate clean. Consideration may not be given to the cumulative effect of a series of decisions that, together, set her pay well below that of every male area manager. Knowingly carrying past pay discrimination forward must be treated as lawful conduct."[123] Ginsburg argued that the majority issued a "cramped interpretation of Title VII" at odds with the statute's broad and robust protection against workplace discrimination and concluded her dissent by urging Congress to "correct this Court's parsimonious reading of Title VII."

The reaction to the *Ledbetter* decision was swift. Women's advocates decried the decision as a setback for women and a setback for civil rights. Business groups applauded what they called a "fair decision," one that the U.S. Chamber of Commerce said "eliminates a potential wind-fall against employers by employees trying to dredge up stale pay claims."[124] Lilly Ledbetter was

President Barack Obama signs the Lilly Ledbetter Bill as a bipartisan group of Congress persons and Lilly Ledbetter (third from left) stands behind, in the East Room of the White House in Washington, D.C., on January 29, 2009. *KATIE FALKENBERG/The Washington Times /Landov.*

invited to speak to the delegates at the Democratic National Convention held in Denver, Colorado, on August 26, 2008 (Women's Equality Day). She said:

> Many of you are probably asking: Who is that grandmother from Alabama at the podium? I can assure you, nobody is more surprised, or humbled, than I am. I'm here to talk about America's commitment to fairness and equality, and how people like me—and like you—suffer when that commitment is betrayed.
>
> How fitting that I speak to you on Women's Equality Day, when we celebrate ratification of the amendment that gave women the right to vote. Even as we celebrate, let's also remind ourselves: the fight for equality is not over. I know that from personal experience. I was a trailblazer when I went to work as a female supervisor at a Goodyear tire plant in Gadsden, Alabama.
>
> My job demanded a lot, and I gave it 100 percent. I kept up with every one of my male co-workers. But toward the end of my 19 years at Goodyear, I began to suspect that I wasn't getting paid as much as men doing the same job. An anonymous note in my mailbox confirmed that I was right. Despite praising me for my work, Goodyear gave me smaller raises than my male co-managers, over and over. . . . Those differences affected my family's quality of life then, and they affect my retirement now. When I discovered the injustice, I thought about moving on. But in the end, I couldn't ignore the discrimination. So I went to court.[125]

Democrats in the House of Representatives filed the first version of the Lilly Ledbetter Fair Pay Act immediately after the Supreme Court's ruling and subsequently passed the bill, but it was defeated in the Senate by Republicans who claimed it would lead to frivolous lawsuits. The House and Senate versions were reintroduced at the start of the 111th Congress in January 2009 and with expanded Democratic majorities in both houses, passed before the month was over. President Barack Obama signed the bill into law, the first of his presidency, on January 29, 2009, effectively nullifying the Supreme Courts decision. The law amends the Civil Rights Act of 1964 by stating that the 180-day statute of limitations for filing an equal pay lawsuit regarding pay discrimination resets with each new discriminatory paycheck. In signing the bill into law, President Obama said, "I sign this bill for my daughters, and all those who will come after us, because I want them to grow up in a nation that values their contributions, where there are no limits to their dreams and they have opportunities their mothers and grandmothers never could have imagined."

While certainly an important tool for pursuing wage discrimination litigation in the courts, the new law does little to enhance the effectiveness of the Equal Pay Act or to redress any of the issues Justice Ginsburg raised in her dissent. The Paycheck Fairness Act (passed by the House in January 2009 as a companion to Ledbetter, but stalled in the Senate) would strengthen the penalties that courts may impose for equal pay violations and provide compensatory as well as punitive damages, in addition to back pay, to individuals denied equal pay for equal work. In addition, this bill would authorize class-action lawsuits and would direct the Department of Labor to provide public information about strategies for eliminating wage discrimination and to issue guidelines for evaluating comparable jobs. Employees would be able to share pay information without employer retaliation (grounds for dismissal in many workplaces). The bill also establishes a competitive grant program to develop salary negotiation training for women and girls. Lisa Maatz of AAUW distinguishes between the Ledbetter Equal Pay Act and the Paycheck Fairness Act this way: "Ledbetter provides the legal basis for the ability to seek redress for discriminatory pay practices; the Paycheck Fairness Act gives individuals the tools to find out that they're being discriminated against in the first place." Opponents to the Paycheck Fairness Act claim that revealing salary information violates privacy, that the wage gap (if it exists) is a product of women's choices, and that the legislation would encourage employers to hire only men in order to avoid lawsuits.[126] The Paycheck Fairness Act has been introduced in ten previous sessions of Congress without a positive vote.

Child Care

The issue of child care was politicized seemingly overnight as two women were forced to withdraw their nominations for attorney general of the United States under the newly elected Clinton administration in 1993. Zoe Baird, the first female nominee for attorney general, was forced to withdraw her nomination because of allegations related to employment and payroll taxes for her nanny. Kimba Wood, President Clinton's second choice for the post, was also forced to step down over similar issues related to her child-care arrangements. Clinton's third choice, also a woman, was not subject to this line of inquiry since Janet Reno was unmarried and without children. No previous nominee had ever been questioned about his child-care arrangements during Senate confirmation hearings. Then, on February 4, 1997, the country and the world learned of the death of eight-month-old Matthew Eappen, allegedly at the hands of his eighteen-year-old British au pair, Louise Woodward. In all three of these cases, public reaction centered on choices that women with full-time jobs made about child care. Deborah Eappen, Matthew's mother, was publicly vilified for leaving her son with an au pair when she returned to work part-time as an ophthalmologist. Baird and Wood were painted as "yuppie moms," abusing the tax code by paying for child care under the table instead of paying payroll taxes as required by law. The fact is that child care is largely an underground industry in the United States, only loosely regulated, largely unsupported by federal or state dollars, and subject to market forces that make child-care workers some of the lowest-paid members of the workforce.

The demographics of the full-time workforce have changed dramatically over the last thirty years, but the social support structures to help families care for children, the elderly, or the ill have not changed substantially. For families with children between the ages of three and five, child care is the third-greatest expense after housing and food.[127] Finding adequate child care is a widespread problem that cuts across all demographic boundaries. Sixty-three percent of women with children under age six work, and 78 percent of women with children between the ages of six and seventeen have jobs. One-quarter of all households with children under the age of eighteen are headed by a single female.

Policy solutions to families' changing needs have been slow to materialize. Unlike equalizing pay or opening educational programs to women, a single policy on or government program for child care is not likely to fit every family's needs. Even more central to the problem is the public's ambivalence over women's dual role as both a mother and a full-time employee. This is not a new problem and individuals left on their own to find solutions to the dilemma of raising children and working full-time are also not a new phenomenon. In 1993, President Clinton signed the Family and Medical Leave Act (FMLA), allowing individuals to take up to twelve weeks of unpaid leave to care for a newborn, a sick child, or a sick family member, or to deal with their own illness. However, FMLA covers only a small percentage of the workforce, and two-thirds of employees who needed and were eligible for FMLA did not take it because they could not forgo the income.[128] Infants and toddlers demand time and constant attention, while older elementary-school children demand less time, but their parents need more flexible schedules to meet with teachers and attend school-related events during traditional work hours. The parents of teenagers report that they need the ability to leave work on a moment's notice to deal with emergencies. Thus, families with children of various ages continue to seek solutions that best accommodate the stresses of combining work and raising children. Often one parent (most often the mother) will drop out of the workforce to care for very young children until they enter kindergarten at the age of five. In doing so, those parents severely limit their long-term wage-earning capacity, risk the erosion of job-related skills and knowledge, and reduce the size or security of their pension. Alternatives to parent-centered child care come in many forms, ranging from part-time or full-time in-home care to group day care outside the home. There are advocates for each form of care, but government subsidies are only available to poor families with children in group daycare programs. Tax credits and deductions for child-care expenses benefit mainly the middle and upper classes, but do nothing to address the accessibility and quality of child care. Both President Barack Obama and First Lady Michelle Obama have indicated that they will make support for working families a top priority.

Women's full-time employment is not an assumption but rather it is still treated as an anomaly or a "social problem." Although the United States professes to care deeply about its children, the culture of limited government, individualism, and familial autonomy and privacy claims conspire to worsen an old problem: Who will care for the children? As we said earlier, the assumption that women will not only bear children but also take primary responsibility for their care stems from the separate spheres ideology and therefore eliminates men from the very definition of the problem. The question of "who will care for the children" does not include fathers in its implicit or explicit assumptions. *Working father* is not a part of our modern lexicon—in fact, it seems redundant in ways that *working mother* does not. This dichotomy negatively affects both men and women, but for women the consequences are likely to be economic. Why isn't child care viewed as a "public good," like education (see previous chapter)? In the same way that education benefits both the individual and larger society, doesn't society have an interest in ensuring that generations of children become competent adults? If there is a social contract to educate all citizens, why isn't there one to care for the nation's infants? The answer is in the pervasive influence of gender-specific expectations that stem from the separate spheres ideology. Furthermore, the question of child care, like that of education, cannot be understood without recognizing the power of class in defining the problem. While middle-class women are being pressured to stay home with their children, *in the interests of their children*, poor women are being told to join the workforce, *in the interests of their children*. In other words, for professional women, no child care is good enough to justify leaving their children to go off to work, but for poor women, no child care is bad enough to justify providing public support for them to stay home with their children.[129]

Government initiatives on child care have been spotty at best. In times of national crisis (an economic depression or a war), when women were *needed* to work, the government has taken a more active role in providing assistance with child care. However, once the crisis passed, government's involvement virtually vanished. During World War II, government needed women in heavy industry and in white-collar jobs to replace the men sent off to war. To meet this critical national emergency, government actively recruited women into wage work and *facilitated* women's entrance into the labor force by providing comprehensive child-care centers. Not only did World War II nurseries tend children, women were also able to drop off mending and the week's shopping list and collect a ready-made dinner from the center's take-away counter. Infirmaries cared for sick children and a medical staff tended to immunizations and regular check-ups. Facilities created under the Lanham Act of 1941 were in a sense accidental. The act allocated funds for the exigencies of wartime production, and the mobilization of the female labor force created a dire need for child-care facilities. When the war ended, so did the national commitment to women's role in the paid labor force and to the support structures that made it possible. Not only did the financial support disappear, the national rhetoric about the positive benefits of nursery education for children took a dark cold-war turn. In the postwar effort to "return to normalcy," individualized care at home was celebrated over state daycare centers characterized as providing "highly regimented, one-size-fits-all care that stifled the individuality of the child."[130] State-sponsored day care was successfully co-opted by the ideological right and became "sovietized" in the national mindset. Between the mid-1950s and the 1970s, as women's full-time participation in the workforce became more the norm than the exception, government tax deductions or tax credits encouraged private solutions to a very public problem. Public child care was provided in the 1960s concurrent with the growth in public housing to combat poverty. Thus the link between public child care and public assistance for the poor precluded a national discussion about the public's responsibility for universal child care that other developed, primarily European, nations provide.[131]

Congress attempted to address the need for universal child care in 1971 in the Child Development Act, which would have created a network of child-care facilities with fees based on a family's income. The public's negative reaction to out-of-home care as the standard prompted a presidential veto and shelved the discussion for nearly twenty years. In the 1990s, when it was evident that women's participation in the full-time workforce not only included the majority of women and women with small children, but that women would work throughout the course of their lifetime rather than for a short time before marriage and children, government began to re-examine the issue. In 1990, Congress passed the Child Care and Development Act. Consistent with other "new federalism" programs of the decade, Congress authorized funding in the form of block grants to states, which allowed each state to decide how the money would best serve its needs. On the one hand, this allowed states to experiment with child-care strategies that were tailored to their unique constituencies and needs. Alternatively, by not providing uniform standards for quality, training, and services, the Child Care and Development Act did not do anything to standardize the accessibility or quality of child care nationally. Further, 75 percent of the block-grant funding was targeted for low-income families, which perpetuated the myth that child care was a class issue. In the fall of 1997, the Clinton administration convened a White House Conference on Child Care. The result was a proposal to increase tax credits for child care and improve the quality and accessibility of child-care centers.

For two-paycheck families, reliable, high-quality child care is scarce and exorbitantly expensive. The failure to move child-care policy beyond an adjunct to public assistance means that most parents are on their own in locating and paying for a provider. Nearly 50 percent rely on extended family or neighbors to care for their children. An estimated 5 million children are left unsupervised after the school day ends. It is a patchwork system at best, and for most families it constitutes a significant expenditure. For low- and middle-income families with children between the ages of three and five, child care represents the third-greatest expense, after housing and food. For families with higher incomes (annual income above $66,900), it represents the second-greatest expense after housing.[132] The price of child care can easily run between $4,000 and $10,000 annually. In forty-eight states, the cost of center-based child care for a four-year-old is greater than tuition at a four-year public college.[133] Subsidies for the cost of child care are very limited. In a number of states, the income eligibility cutoffs for child-care assistance are so restrictive that the working poor do not qualify. For example, a family of three in Missouri earning above $17,784 cannot qualify for child-care assistance. Inadequate funds at the state level mean long waiting lists. There are 48,800 children on the waiting list in Florida, 26,500 in Texas, and over 20,000 in Tennessee. Despite research demonstrating the importance of early learning to a child's development, public investments in education and development are more than seven times greater during school-age years than during the early learning years. Business has not stepped in to fill the gap. A survey of over 1,000 American companies found that only 9 percent of businesses with 100 or more employees offer on-site child care even though extant studies and statistics confirm that the benefits of on-site day care are vast: It aids in recruiting and retaining high-quality workers, particularly women; enhances productivity and heightens employee morale; and provides employers with a competitive edge in a changing labor market.[134] Privatizing child care—arguably a public good—leaves parents to bear the bulk of early child-care costs without any public accountability for adequate provision and quality of child-care services.

Without a consensus that child care is a public good that should be subject to shared costs and responsibilities across all citizens, the government, employers, and parents will continue to wrestle with the vagaries of the private market in finding suitable child-care arrangements. Employers, while excused from any government-mandated responsibility for providing child care as an employment benefit, are left to deal with the consequences of the incompatibility of family and work responsibilities of both male and female employees.[135] Men, although not usually the primary caregiver in the family, are increasingly partnered with women who work full-time, which leaves men without anyone at home to organize the affairs of the family. Sociologist Arlie Hochschild contends that men and women have actually increased their time at work, contrary to their claims of wanting to spend more time with their children and families. The reason, she explains, is that the work environment is less stressful, more orderly, and one in which they feel more competent.[136]

Attempts to create family-responsive workplaces have been met with mixed success. Companies that invest in child care, family-benefit packages that include flextime, or other work arrangements have benefited by increased profits, less turnover, and lower rates of absenteeism among employees.[137] However, policies vary considerably, and the policies on paper may not reflect the reality of the practice. Most human-resource scholars admit that the financial incentive is probably not large enough to get companies to invest heavily in family benefits. In fact, employers might have more of an incentive to steer clear of employees who plan to have or already have children (most of whom are young women).[138] This leaves government to take a larger role in providing a policy that supports families. Optimally, the solution would allow parents to make choices about the form and duration of the care their children receive from others. While disincentives for parents who choose to stay at home with their children should be minimized, the assumption that only women can care for children should be actively challenged by policy alternatives that grant men and women equal opportunities to care for their families.

Strengthening Family and Medical Leave

The United States remains one of only three countries (along with Australia and Libya) without paid family leave. Regulations implementing the Family and Medical Leave Act (FMLA) are limited to companies with over fifty employees and merely guarantee that an employee's job or a similar job will be available upon their return from up to twelve weeks of unpaid leave. When Representative Patricia Schroeder of Colorado first introduced the bill in 1985, no one would join her as a sponsor. After eight years of legislative debate and two George H.W. Bush presidential vetoes, the 1993 FMLA signed by President Clinton applies to barely half the workforce in the United States and has not amounted to undue interference in the private market as business once feared. Policies like FMLA that mandate job-guaranteed leave but do not require wage replacement are of limited value to most workers, particularly the working poor. The FMLA did, however, assert a public interest in family care and opened an important door.

Proposals introduced in the 106th Congress attempted to extend FMLA coverage to employers with twenty-five or more employees, to eliminate the hours-of-service requirement (currently an employee has to have worked for 1,250 hours in the last year to qualify for coverage), to allow employees to take FMLA leave to address domestic-violence situations, and to extend FMLA to allow parents to attend and participate in school events, teacher-parent conferences, and field trips.[139] Under the Clinton administration, the Department of Labor granted a waiver to states in order to allow voluntary experimentation with funding paid leave through unemployment insurance. In 2002, sixteen states were actively considering proposals to use the so-called "Baby UI" regulation. Before any state could adopt and implement new regulations, the Bush administration rescinded the UI regulation. Skirting the objections to using unemployment insurance funds for otherwise able-bodied workers with emergent family responsibilities, California pursued a paid-leave policy using temporary disability insurance. In September 2002, California became the first state to adopt legislation to provide up to twelve weeks of partial wage replacement to workers who take leave for approved family situations. The California Family Temporary Disability Insurance program, funded entirely by employee contributions, will provide 55 percent (up to $728 per week) of eligible workers' pay. The cost to workers is minimal—estimated to average $27 a year for most. California remains the only state to have adopted a wage replacement policy for family leave.

Results of the National Study of the Changing Workforce suggest that women's decision to work part-time in order to care for children or family limits their ability to access FMLA leave. Although 86 percent of fathers covered under FMLA had worked the required 1,250 hours, only 73 percent of mothers met that requirement. As a result, the study estimated that only 41 percent of employed women were covered by FMLA, compared to 49 percent of men.[140] Even when employees are covered by FMLA, the likelihood is that their leave must be unpaid. Two-thirds of workers who are eligible for leave opt not to take it because of financial reasons, and one in eleven who used FMLA was actually forced onto public assistance to make ends meet. Americans strongly support providing paid family leave. In a Center for Policy Alternatives survey, 68 percent of women and 56 percent of men would be more likely to vote for a candidate who favors expanding the FMLA. A 2000 survey found that 80 percent of adults and 88 percent of parents with children six or younger support "paid parental leave that allows working parents of very young babies to stay home from work for their children."[141] The same survey found that 85 percent of adults support expanding "disability or unemployment insurance to help families afford to take time off from work to care for a newborn, a newly adopted child, or a seriously ill family member." Only 14 percent of those surveyed said that they opposed such measures. Both business and government get mediocre marks from survey participants on their efforts to make changes in the workplace that would help workers meet the needs of their young children. Fifty-nine percent of those surveyed said that employers are doing a fair or poor job, whereas 63 percent said that government is doing a fair or poor job in assisting workers.

Opponents of the regulations to allow states to use unemployment insurance funds to pay for family leave argue that the practice will be too expensive and will bankrupt states' unemployment insurance funds, particularly in times of economic recession when unemployment rates are high.[142] The Employment Policy Foundation (EPF) characterizes the policy change as "pitting the 'haves' (those with jobs) versus the 'have-nots' (the unemployed)."[143] EPF cautions that notification and reporting requirements can limit personal freedom and privacy rights. In response to unfavorable comparisons of the current FMLA with more generous European family leave policies, the EPF argues that the U.S. economy benefits from a free-market approach that allows workers to negotiate benefits privately with their employers.

In the first changes to FMLA since its adoption fifteen years ago, the U.S. Department of Labor published new rules that took effect on January 16, 2009. The most significant change is an expansion of FMLA coverage to individuals providing assistance to members of the military, especially to wounded veterans. Under the new military coverage, eligible employees are entitled to take up to 12 weeks of unpaid leave to help manage the affairs of a soldier or the soldier's family before, during, and after deployment. Employees would be eligible for up to 26 weeks of unpaid leave to care for a family member who was wounded while serving in the military. This entitlement extends beyond a parent, child, or spouse to include "next-of-kin."

The Federal Employees Paid Parental Leave Act, introduced in the 111th Congress (2009–2011) would give federal workers four weeks of paid family leave to care for a newborn or adopted child. The bill also would let federal workers use up to eight weeks of accrued paid sick time or annual leave immediately following the first four weeks of parental leave. This policy could potentially cover 2.7 million federal employees and pave the way for legislation providing the same benefit for private-sector employees.

One of the biggest objections to paid family leave is the cost. Heather Boushey, senior economist at the Center for American Progress, has proposed funding and administering family-leave insurance through the existing Social Security system.[144] "Social Security Cares" would cover any worker currently covered by Social Security insurance, including low-wage, young, and part-time workers who are not currently eligible for unpaid family leave. Workers would be able to access Social Security benefits for income to cover events spelled out in FMLA (i.e., childbirth, adoption, illness, or family care). The bureaucracy is already in place to finance the system and to deliver the checks. Because Social Security covers a variety of life circumstances apart from retirement, there is already a structure in place to establish eligibility requirements. This approach is also supported by Workplace Flexibility 2010, a policy initiative based at Georgetown University School of Law Center, as well as several academics and policy advocates in the field of work-life balance. One obvious sign that FMLA needs to be expanded and updated is the rise in family-leave lawsuits. Although no antidiscrimination statute exists that explicitly protects family caregivers in the workplace, more than 1,150 lawsuits have been filed in federal and state courts, representing a 300 percent increase since the mid-1990s. More than half of the plaintiffs have won in court—a success rate considerably higher than for conventional employment discrimination cases (20 percent success rate).[145] "The flood of cases reflects not just the increased presence of women in the workplace but also the growing difficulty Americans of all social backgrounds seem to be having in balancing the demands of work and family." Most cases are brought under Title VII arguing that even seemingly gender-neutral employment policies and decisions can have a disparate and negative effect on women. Joan Williams, author of *Unbending Gender*, argues that the tension between work and family that so many women (and men) feel stems from the fact that work is organized around an "ideal worker" model whereby the employee can be fully dedicated to the employer because there is someone at home providing full-time care. Dual-earner families are the norm rather than the exception, but the structure of paid employment has not changed to accommodate the new reality of no caregiving adult in the home full-time. Although roughly four-fifths of the plaintiffs in family-leave lawsuits are female, males can suffer family discrimination when employers deny them time to care for family, under the assumption that men should not have any family-care duties. Women, on the other hand, encounter a powerful set of negative assumptions about motherhood.

Researchers with Cornell University's Cognitive Bias Working Group, published a study in 2007 that confirmed this bias against mothers.[146] Subjects were asked to evaluate a group of equally qualified male and female job applicants on the basis of a resume and resumes were sent to a sample of real employers. On some of the resumes there was a cue about parenthood. The bias against mothers but not fathers was striking among both the volunteer subjects and the actual employers. Mothers were consistently rated as less competent, less committed, and they were held to higher performance and punctuality standards. Mothers were 79 percent less likely to be hired and if hired, received a starting salary offer $11,000 lower than nonmothers. This pattern was mirrored among actual employers as well. Women without children were more than twice as likely as equally qualified mothers to be called for interviews. Fathers fared the best and were offered the highest starting salaries of any group (including men who were not fathers) by the volunteer respondents.

Some businesses are making changes to practices by offering flexible work schedules and the opportunity to work from home; however both the lawsuits and reliance on the private sector to "do the right thing" by caregivers are unlikely to create real and lasting social change. By contrast with the United States, British employees with children under six now have the right to request schedule flexibility. Employers have the right to refuse a request for legitimate business reasons, but they must explain their refusal in writing. In Sweden, parents have the right to work a six-hour day at an adjusted salary until their children turn eight years old. Similar federal policy in the United States seems unlikely; however, the EEOC has issued new guidelines to clarify existing anti-discrimination law as it applies to employees with caregiving responsibilities.

Paid Sick Leave

Approximately 160 countries provide mandatory paid sick days, with 127 nations providing a week or more each year. In the United States there is no such policy; effectively leaving 60 million workers, or 43 percent of the private industry labor force, without any paid sick days. Business owners have been among the staunchest opponents of paid sick leave, arguing that it would amount to a costly government mandate, particularly during an economic recession. However, a May 2009 Gallup Poll reported that one in four, or 23 percent of Americans, are "very worried" about keeping up with their monthly bills, up from 19 percent one year earlier. One of the consequences of not having paid sick leave is that employees feel compelled to go to work even when contagious or risk losing their job. A survey conducted by the Center on Work Life Law, found that one in six workers said that they or a family member had been fired, suspended, punished, or threatened by an employer for taking time off to care for themselves or a family member. The National Partnership for Women and Families (NPWF) found that paid sick days actually reduce the business costs of employee turnover, absenteeism, and lack of productivity when an employee is sick on the job. The NPWF study estimates that seven days of annual paid sick leave would yield a net savings of more than $8 billion to the national economy.

San Francisco and the District of Columbia already have laws guaranteeing paid sick days, and voters in Milwaukee, Wisconsin, approved a similar guarantee through a ballot initiative in November 2008 (it was subsequently ruled unconstitutional by a Milwaukee County judge in June 2009). In another 15 states, there are active paid sick leave campaigns underway. Pending in Congress, the Healthy Families Act would be binding on employers that had 15 or more workers and guarantee employees one paid hour off for every 30 hours worked, up to seven days each year. Paid sick days could be used to care for a child, parent, spouse or one's self. The bill, sponsored in the House by Representative Rosa DeLauro (D-CT) and in the Senate by Edward Kennedy (D-MA) was introduced in May 2009. Although it might be expected to encounter greater resistance in a poor economic climate, President Obama campaigned on the issue of paid sick leave, and during the H1N1 (swine flu) pandemic urged workers who experienced flulike symptoms to stay at home. Dr. Jody Heyman, founder of the Project on Global Working Families, argues that the United States is harming its economy by not adopting worker protections. Advocates from a variety of perspectives urge the adoption of paid sick leave as an employment standard just like the federal minimum wage.[147] At least 145 countries provide paid sick leave for short- or long-term illnesses, with 136 providing a week or more annually.[148]

Women in Retirement: Social Security and Private Pensions

The current Social Security system was established under the Social Security Act in 1935. Numerous changes have been made since its inception, but the basic philosophy has remained intact. The Social Security system is an example of a gender-neutral law because it does not treat men and women differently in the law itself, though men and women experience the system quite differently as a result of differences in employment and wage patterns. Social

Security is particularly important for women because women are 60 percent less likely than men to have a private pension, and when they do, the average size is about half that of men's.[149] They also live an average of five years longer than men, and because of pay inequities and time spent away from work to raise children, women have lower lifetime earnings than men. Women make up 57 percent of Social Security beneficiaries age 62 and older and approximately 69 percent of beneficiaries age 85 and older.[150] Half of the women aged 65 and older would be poor if not for Social Security benefits, and for 25 percent of elderly women who live alone, Social Security is their only source of income. Without Social Security, the poverty rate for women over 65 would be nearly double its current rate.[151] As it is, nearly 70 percent of all poor old people are female. However, there is tremendous variation by race and ethnicity. The poverty rate for white women was 10 percent (nearly double that for white men). Among elderly African American women, the poverty rate in 2003 was 27.4 percent (compared with 17.7 percent for African American men), and it was 21.7 percent for Hispanic women aged 65 and above (compared with 16.6 percent for Hispanic men).[152] Social Security contributes 60 percent of retirement income for the average woman and 100 percent for one in five. Despite this greater reliance, older women's benefits are lower than older men's benefits. The average monthly Social Security benefit for older women in 2007 was $909 while for men it was $1,183.[153] Although some adjustments to the laws have been made to recognize women's increased participation in the labor force, the Social Security system is premised on the 1930s traditional gender roles in families, which today characterize a tiny fraction of modern families. Social Security was intended to be a supplement to private pension plans and savings accumulated over the course of a lifetime, but only about half of men and a quarter of retired women earn additional income from private pensions.

Social Security is a pay-as-you-go system, meaning that current payroll taxes are used to pay benefits to current retirees. In 1983, Congress increased the payroll tax rate to ensure that Social Security took in more than it paid out in anticipation of a bulge in retirees when the baby boomers started to retire. As a result, there is a surplus of funds, but still nearly 90 percent of that money is required to cover the costs of current retirees. Without changes to the system, Social Security will remain solvent and able to pay 100 percent of promised benefits until 2041, according to the latest estimates.[154] Social Security benefits are protected from erosion by inflation because the annual cost-of-living adjustment is indexed to inflation.

Under the current Social Security system, workers are eligible to retire with full benefits at age sixty-five and to receive partial benefits at age sixty-two. However, for workers born after 1937, eligibility for retirement with full benefits is age sixty-seven. Social Security benefits are based on the thirty-five years of highest taxable earnings of at least $520 each quarter of the year. The benefit formula is a progressive calculation, and the five lowest earning years (including years with zero earnings) in an individual's working life are dropped. A married person is eligible for the larger of either 100 percent of his or her own retired-worker benefit or 50 percent of his or her spouse's retired-worker benefit. A woman whose benefit, based on her own work record, is less than or equal to the spousal benefit she could claim is said to be "dually entitled" and does not gain additional benefit from having worked. A man is similarly entitled to benefits from his wife's accounts, but in reality nearly all who use the spouse's benefit are women. This may change if more men opt to help raise children by either reducing the number of hours they work or by leaving the paid labor force entirely for a period of time. For women currently working, this provision raises some interesting equity questions. Leanne Abdnor, author of the Cato Institute's report "Social Security Choices for the 21st Century Woman," argues that social Security has an outdated benefit structure that has failed to keep pace with the changing nature of U.S. families.[155] Abdnor contends that single women and women in dual-earner couples are unfairly being asked to subsidize the benefits of stay-at-home married women who do not pay Social Security taxes. Abdnor advocates giving women, particularly young women in the workforce, more control over their retirement savings through personal retirement accounts similar to a plan advocated by the Bush administration. By doing so, some portion of a working woman's retirement income would be hers alone and would not go toward subsidizing women who do not work outside the home.

Other women's organizations oppose privatizing Social Security, even though they admit that the system is perhaps "unfair" to working women and should be updated to account for changes in work patterns and family structure. The Institute for Women's Policy Research report on women and Social Security recommends adopting minimum benefits and child-care credits as a way of treating all women more equitably. Minimum benefits would give credit for time spent in the labor force rather than the amount contributed through Social Security taxes, thereby benefiting low-wage workers, many of whom are women. Child-care credits would give women who stay home to raise their children "credit" within the retirement system for the "unpaid" work of caregiving.[156] Because Social Security provides women with far more than simple retirement benefits, most women's organizations argue against anything that will siphon money out of the current system, although most advocate some type of reform to maintain solvency. Eighty percent of adult male recipients are retired workers, compared to only 33 percent of female beneficiaries. "Women are more than ten times as likely as men (34 percent compared to 0.3 percent) to receive benefits as the spouses, dependent parents, or disabled children of a worker." Stated differently, "95 percent of adults who receive benefits as the relative of a disabled, deceased, or retired worker are women."[157] While more women in the future will receive benefits calculated on the basis of their independent earnings, women's lifetime earnings are considerably lower than men's. The National Women's Law Center projects that in 2070 40 percent of women will still receive higher benefits based on their spouse's earning record.[158] For this reason, the system itself needs to be reexamined in light of changing workforce demographics and the disproportionate wage penalties women experience in the workforce, particularly if they have children.

Several reform proposals are being actively considered in Congress. The most common type of reform, and the one former President Bush made a priority early in his second term, includes some aspect of privatization of the current system by diverting some or all of the current payroll tax dollars to an individually held private investment account. The plans differ in how much would be diverted (all or only a percentage) and in what type of private account the money would be invested. Some people would like to see individual reform initiatives that will invest primarily or solely in equities (stocks), whereas others would prefer a more conservative investment strategy in bonds or in some split between the two that could change over the course of one's lifetime, becoming more conservative as retirement nears. Some plans call for collective investment of the trust fund assets or the collective investment of only some of the assets to try to increase the size of the trust fund itself. The economic recession and the recent decline in the value of the stock market have all but ended talk of privatization strategies for now.

The Task Force on Women and Social Security, a joint project of the National Council of Women's Organizations and the Institute for Women's Policy Research, has made several proposals that would strengthen Social Security for women.[159] Among its many recommendations is the provision of a "family service credit," which could include an earnings credit and a provision for a number of "drop-out years" in calculating benefits. Social Security, and social retirement welfare in general, raises the question of whether women fare better under a gender-neutral equality approach or a gender-accommodative approach that aims to be fair to women. Mona Harrington Meyer and Pamela Herd note, "The American welfare system is based on an outdated male breadwinner-female homemaker model in which men make claims as paid workers or rights bearers, and many women make claims as dependents or clients. The former tend to receive more generous and stable benefits that are considered social rights and the latter smaller and more precarious benefits that are considered social favors."[160] Advocates of the equality doctrine favor re-defining women's roles so that they claim benefits equivalent to men's. They worry that policies that acknowledge and accommodate women's persistent and disproportionate share of unpaid care work (e.g., the family service credit noted above) or time outside of the paid labor force will simply perpetuate traditional gender roles by linking new benefits to old duties. Advocates of the fairness doctrine argue that any social retirement system must take into account the unequal amounts of unpaid work that women perform outside the formal economy and claim that the basis for retirement rewards needs to be reexamined. Both groups agree that the current Social Security system, although somewhat antiquated in its assumptions about gender and work, continues to be an effective antipoverty program for women in their twilight years. Social Security absorbs over 40 percent of the social welfare budget, making it larger

Is Social Security Reform Good for Women?

In assessing the various reform proposals, the National Council of Women's Organizations has developed a "Women's Checklist to Strengthening Social Security."[1] Use this checklist to evaluate current and future reform proposals under consideration. In each case, does the proposal:

- *Continue to help those with lower lifetime earnings, who are disproportionately women?* The current benefits formula compensates women and other low-wage earners for lower lifetime earnings. Any reform proposal should adopt a similar progressive benefit formula that replaces a larger share of low-income workers' past earnings as a protection against poverty.
- *Maintain full cost-of-living adjustments?* The current Social Security system protects against inflation, a crucial protection against the erosion of benefits. This feature is particularly important to women because they live, on average, seven years longer than men. Women also rely more on Social Security for their total retirement income since they often lack private savings or pension funds.
- *Protect and strengthen benefits for wives, widows, and divorced women?* Social Security's family protection provisions help women the most by providing guaranteed, inflation-protected, lifetime benefits for widows, divorced women, and the wives of retired workers. While theoretically spousal benefits accrue to both men and women, figures show that 63 percent of female beneficiaries aged 65 and older receive benefits based on their husbands' earning records, while only 1.2 percent of males receive benefits based on their wives' earning records. These benefits go some way toward offsetting the wage disparity between men and women.
- *Preserve disability and survivor benefits?* Social Security now provides benefits to 3 million children and the remaining parent in the event of a premature death or disability of a working parent. Two out of five of today's twenty-year-olds will face premature death or disability before reaching retirement age. Spouses

than any other single program, but it remains very popular even among those that decry "big government" programs.[161]

THE CONSEQUENCES OF A GENDERED ECONOMY: THE DEMOGRAPHICS OF POVERTY

The single best predictor of poverty in America is gender. Add to that the presence of children and the absence of marriage, and you have the "feminization of poverty" in the United States. The phrase "feminization of poverty" was of disabled workers and widows and widowers of workers who die prematurely receive guaranteed lifetime benefits.

- *Ensure that women's guaranteed benefits are not subject to the uncertainties of the stock market?* Proposals that divert payments from the Social Security system into individually held private stock accounts, whose returns would be dependent on volatile investment markets, would not be guaranteed to keep pace with inflation nor provide spousal benefits and could reduce the retirement income of many women. Without the guarantees of a shared insurance pool, cost-of-living increases, and spousal and lifetime benefits, many women could outlive their assets.

- *Address the caregiving and labor-force experience of women?* The current system is based on marriage and work patterns that have changed dramatically. The benefit formula, which generally helps those with low lifetime earnings, also favors those with thirty-five years of workforce participation. Many women fall short of this mark because they drop out of the labor market to care for children or the elderly. The effects of sex-based wage discrimination during their working years are not fully offset by more generous benefits to low earners. Therefore, at the same time the fiscal integrity of the system itself is under consideration, issues such as divorce, absence from the workforce for caregiving responsibilities, and the difference in current benefits between one- and two-income families need to be considered as well.

- *Further reduce the number of elderly women living in poverty?* Social Security has helped to reduce the poverty rate among women older than sixty-five from 35 percent in 1959 to less than 11 percent in 1996. Without Social Security, the poverty rate among elderly women would be greater than 50 percent. Yet, unmarried women still suffer disproportionately: Single, divorced, and widowed women over sixty-five have a poverty rate of 22 percent, compared to 15 percent for unmarried men and 5 percent for married couples.

1. National Council of Women's Organizations, "Women and Social Security Project," accessed at http://www.women4socialsecurity.org.

coined to characterize the growing numbers over the last three or more decades of single-parent, female-headed households living in poverty.[162] The reasons for single-parent households headed by women vary. Fewer women are getting and staying married. From 1970 to 2005, the percentage of women married dropped from 60 percent to 52 percent, but the number of women divorced more than doubled from 6 percent to 13 percent. In 2005, women comprised 84 percent of single parents and as a group were equally divided between those never married and those divorced or separated. About two-thirds of all first marriages end in separation or divorce. Additionally, half of all females over sixteen years old have custody of a minor child, and of these women, one out of every three is not married. This means that one woman out of every six is a single mother.[163] Two out of every three mothers have a job outside the home, although because women work on average fewer hours per week than men and earn less than men, women's average annual earnings stand at about half those of men. Because of the changes in the marketplace, there are fewer high-paying, low-skill jobs available for men and women. The "deindustriali-zation" of America has reduced the number of manufacturing jobs to one-sixth of all jobs available.[164] Conversely, service and retail jobs now make up more than half of the jobs available, and that proportion is expected to increase in the coming years. Sixty-two percent of the employees in the service sector are female, compared to just 32 percent in manufacturing.[165] Wages paid in manu-facturing jobs outpaced those paid in the service sector by nearly 85 percent in 1995. In this sense, both men's and women's earning power has declined, so even among married couples, both husband and wife are likely to work full-time to support the family.

In sum, there are a variety of contradictory trends that contribute to the disproportionate number of women who live below the poverty line. Fewer women are married, although nearly half of all women have children and nearly 90 percent of women in the United States will have children at some point in their lives. A single head of household with minor children, regard-less of sex, is at a severe disadvantage since he or she will be required to do both the unpaid labor of the household as well as to work for a living outside the home. When a woman is the single head of a household, this problem is made worse because women's wages are lower than men's. Households with children must either contract for child care or work only part-time and provide some measure of care themselves. With either option, the household income is diminished. Add to this the contradictory messages men and women receive about the importance of "family." We value children in theory, but we do not value the care of children enough to pay professional child-care workers adequately or to set up social support systems (e.g., Social Security) based on life choices to care for children. Individuals are largely on their own to figure out how to care for their children and work full-time to support their families. Communal support structures are largely absent, even though there is much talk about communal responsibility. Additionally, we lack consensus on the very definition of a family (see more on this topic in the next chapter). Finally, although we believe that having a job is crucial to supporting one's family and serving as a contributing member of the community, there is a shortage of jobs and jobs that that provide a "living wage." The growth in low-wage service-sector jobs and the decline of high-wage manufacturing jobs have resulted in a situation where, in 1995, 12 percent of adults under age sixty-five were living below the poverty line yet holding a full-time, year-round job.[166] In 2001, a U.S. Conference of Mayors survey found that 37 percent of adults seeking emer-gency food aid were employed. Of the adults in households seeking emergency food aid through America's Second Harvest, 17 percent (or 2.5 million adults) worked full-time.[167] A major reason for such poverty among the working poor is the erosion of the minimum wage. During the 1960s and 1970s, the poverty level for a family of three was roughly equal to the yearly earnings of a full-time, year-round worker earning the minimum wage. However, the minimum wage remained unchanged from 1981 until April 1990, and the increase did not restore all of the lost value. For a family of three to reach the poverty level in 2001 ($14,129), a full-time, year-round worker would have needed to earn $6.80 per hour, or $1.65 more than the minimum wage at that time.[168] A Ms. Foundation for Women study found that a two-parent family with two children would have to work a combined 3.5 full-time minimum-wage jobs (roughly 140 hours per week) just to make ends meet.[169] The economic recession, home foreclosures, and the dramatic spike in unemployment between 2007 and 2009 only exacerbated this situation.

Several municipalities have adopted a "living wage" ordinance. A living wage ordinance requires employers who have contracts with the city or county to pay wages that are above minimum wage levels. The living wage is typically set at the wage a full-time worker would need to earn to support a family above the federal poverty line.[170] In 2009, the living wage for the nation is estimated to be $10.31 for employees with health benefits and $11.57 for those without. The actual minimum wage as of July 2009 is $7.25 per hour. Opponents of living wage ordinances claim that the living wage will create a hostile climate for business and pose an undue burden on taxpayers since most existing laws apply to public employees or employees of companies that do business with the city or county where the ordinance is in effect. However, low wages paid in the private sector have implications for state budgets as well. In 2001, the state of California estimated that it paid $86 million in public assistance because workers at Wal-Mart, now the nation's largest private employer, earn such low wages.[171] The report concludes that Wal-Mart is "essentially shifting part of its labor costs onto the public." Changes in the economy in the mid- to late-1990s and cultural contradictions have resulted in increasingly shrill rhetoric about poor people and their "responsibility" for their circumstances. Within this context, Congress and the Clinton administration negotiated major changes to the welfare system in the United States in 1996.

The Gender Implications of Welfare Policy and Welfare Reform

Welfare policy in the United States began more than eighty-five years ago with state-level mothers' pension policies, which were designed to reduce the poverty of mothers without husbands. The New Deal nationalized mothers' pensions with the Aid to Dependent Children (ADC) program. The ADC program was based on a number of assumptions about gender, poverty, and the need to lift single women "toward the norms of Anglo-American, middle-class culture," argues historian Gwendolyn Mink.[172]

Aid to single mothers went from being a program that was designed to supervise and educate women to enable them to make choices that more closely approximated the dominant cultural norm in the 1930s to one that focused on the choices and behaviors of welfare mothers and disputed women's entitlement to support in the 1960s. ADC was modified to include a grant to mothers as well as children in 1950, and then it became Aid to Families with Dependent Children (AFDC) in 1962. During that time, the program's goals and focus shifted from ensuring that children did not grow up in poverty for lack of a male breadwinner to those that enforced gender ideology and racial and cultural control.[173] As barriers to eligibility and moral supervision were lowered, more women of color joined the program and the public's perception that women on welfare "don't deserve it" increased.

Pressure throughout the 1980s and 1990s to "end welfare as we know it" was rooted in a variety of myths about welfare recipients and cultural stereotypes about women in general—specifically African American women. Prior to national work requirements and time limits imposed by the 1996 legislation, 43 percent of AFDC recipients either combined work with welfare or cycled between the two, and 56 percent of AFDC recipients were enrolled on welfare continuously for fewer than two years.[174] Furthermore, welfare payments alone never enabled a woman and her children to escape poverty. In 1996, the maximum AFDC benefit for a family of three in New York, the most generous state, was $703 a month, while the maximum payment in Mississippi, the least generous state, was $120 a month. In 1996, a family of three was below the poverty line when its annual income was $12,980 ($1,082 a month) or less. Even with food stamps, the combined benefit in the most generous state was only $935 a month—well below the poverty standard. The median combined payment per month was only 65 percent of the poverty line.[175] AFDC families were allowed to own a car as long as its value did not exceed $1,500. They were allowed to have no more than $1,000 in cash, checking, savings, or other assets, and once on welfare, families could keep only $50 of any child-support payments, with the balance going back to the state. Welfare, although designated as an antipoverty program, did not "pay" women enough to escape poverty, did not provide incentives to get the education and training that would allow women to seek jobs above poverty-level wages, and did not address the fact that a single woman did not have a "wife" at home to care for her children when she did enter the workforce to support her children.

The Heritage Foundation, a conservative think tank, promoted another dominant myth—that welfare was "breaking the national bank." In a 1994 report, it stated, "In 1992, federal, state, and local governments spent $305 billion on means-tested welfare programs for low-income Americans. Welfare now absorbs 5 percent of the GNP, up from 1.5 percent in 1965 when the War on Poverty began."[176] In fact, spending on both welfare and Medicaid declined between 1980 and 1993, when the two programs combined, to make up 0.7 percent of the gross domestic product and 2.4 percent of the federal budget. Contrary to Heritage's assertion that welfare cost the nation $305 billion, total government spending (state and federal) on women and their children in 1992 (for AFDC, food stamps, and Medicaid for AFDC families) was $70.5 billion. By comparison, the value of the tax exemption for employer-sponsored health insurance in the same year was $47 billion, and the mortgage deduction from income taxes was $49 billion. Relative to other government "welfare" programs, spending for AFDC and its companion support programs was not disproportionately high.[177]

The reform package passed by Congress and signed by President Clinton in 1996, called the Personal Responsibility and Work Opportunity Reconciliation Act (PRWORA), had as its centerpiece a replacement for AFDC known as Temporary Assistance to Needy Families (TANF). The basic goal of the new program is to replace government assistance with earnings. In addition, funding is accomplished through block grants to the states, which are given the authority to design and administer welfare programs within their boundaries. The entitlement to public assistance was ended with the 1996 legislation. States have designed programs around work requirements, allowing recipients to keep a larger percentage of the wages they earn and to still be eligible for assistance, education, and training programs to develop job skills. These programs offer support that is limited to two to five years (over a person's lifetime in most cases), have increased efforts to collect child support from biological fathers, and have given more attention to child-care demands. Since TANF was passed, the number of families receiving public assistance in most states has decreased, but the reasons for the decline are not clear. Community-based nonprofit service providers report that more families are seeking assistance in soup kitchens and shelters. Beyond the effects within individual communities, researchers at the Economic Policy Institute estimate that an influx of low-skilled workers into the workforce will increase the competition for already underpaid occupations and will most likely drive down wages. They concluded that the work requirements under the 1996 reforms would drive down the average hourly wage for the bottom third of the workforce by 12 percent—from $5.47 an hour to $4.82 an hour.[178] Even working forty-hour weeks, a single, hourly wage earner cannot support a family. In *Nickel and Dimed: On (Not) Getting By in America*, author Barbara Ehrenreich went "undercover" as a low-wage worker to test the proposition that women leaving welfare will be able to achieve self-sufficiency through work. Even in the best-case scenario, with all the advantages of education, health, a car, and money for first month's rent, Ehrenreich had to work two jobs, seven days a week, and still almost wound up in a shelter. In all three communities she explored (in Florida, Maine, and Minnesota), the rental housing markets, because supply was tight and rents were high, made it nearly impossible for her to live on one low-wage job even though each position paid more than the federal minimum wage.[179]

A more systematic study of the same issues commissioned by Wider Opportunities for Women confirmed the need for higher wages and more support services for families struggling for self-sufficiency.[180] The study examined three scenarios in ten communities: the adequacy of wages alone at four different wage levels (minimum wage, average welfare leavers' monthly earnings, $10 per hour, and $12 per hour), the impact of work supports at each wage level, and policies and programs designed to bridge the gap between low-wage work and self-sufficiency. Self-sufficiency is a measure of how much income it takes for working families to meet their basic needs without public or private subsidies. This measure does not include anything beyond the basics—no entertainment, fast food, savings, credit card debt, or emergency expenses. For example, in Boston, the self-sufficiency standard for a single parent with an infant and a preschool-age child is $28.19 per hour, or $59,544 per year. In Orleans Parish, Louisiana, where the standard is lowest, it would still take an hourly wage of $13.10 and an annual wage of $27,660 to support the same family (the federal minimum wage rate in 2004 was $5.15). Researchers found that across all ten communities, low-wage work alone is not enough. In fact, on average, wages cover only 34 percent of basic costs of living. At $12 per hour, a working parent can meet roughly 72 percent of basic needs. Even combining a $10-per-hour full-time job with the welfare-to-work package covers only 92 percent of a family's basic needs. Child-care assistance makes the most significant impact on a family's ability to meet basic needs, reducing expenses by as much as 35 percent. This is significant in light of the number of children currently on waiting lists in the states. The Children's Defense Fund estimates that only one out of seven children are receiving the subsidized child care they are eligible for under federal guidelines. The study recommended that state and the federal government adopt an objective standard similar to the self-sufficiency standard to assess the impact of policy on progress toward self-sufficiency; increase the minimum wage; expand education and job-training opportunities; make work supports available to families; and develop incentives to encourage states to move welfare clients into "opportunity" jobs that promote economic security.[181] As Congress begins the process of review and reauthorization of key provisions of the welfare reform legislation, this information is essential.

A new study on trends in women's employment (1970–2007) conducted by the Carsey Institute at the University of New Hampshire examines the economic condition of rural women in comparison to women living in urban areas and elsewhere. In particular, this study analyzes the decline in women's employment, most evident between 2000–2004, and its impact on women and their families.[182] Although the media's focus has been on privileged, college-educated women leaving elite jobs for a role as full-time homemaker (effectively a 4 percent reduction since 2000), the largest decline has been among mothers with less than a high school diploma. "That all women are leaving the workforce suggests something other than choice is influencing the trends. Those with less education typically make less money and can least afford to stay home with their children, particularly since welfare reform now mandates work and imposes time limits. Therefore, they are more likely leaving the workforce not by choice but because they have been pushed out by economic downturn."[183] When women lose well-paid jobs in today's economy, they are unlikely to find an equally well-paying job. When welfare reform was first passed, work mandates for women focused on promoting self-sufficiency among single mothers. In concert with the 1996 legislation, Congress also increased work support programs like the Earned Income Tax Credit (EITC), raised the minimum wage, extended Medicaid for all children, and increased child-care subsidies.[184] A robust and expanding economy in the late 1990s increased the availability of low-wage jobs and employment rates among poor women increased and welfare rolls decreased. "However, low wages and unstable work continues to dominate for these women, resulting in the replacement of the welfare poor with the working poor." Median hourly wages for employed poor women are substantially lower than wages earned by all women ($6.58 compared with $13.85 in 2006). In 1970, 10 percent of women aged 16 to 64 years lived in poverty. In 2007, 12 percent of women live in poverty, with rates for rural women closer to 15 percent. One in every five rural mothers lives in poverty today.

Education is a strong predictor of wages and job type, but as we noted in the previous chapter, the number of high school–educated unmarried mothers enrolled in college fell by 25 percent as a result of welfare reform. "The more heavily the women are working, and the more women are living in states that require a lot of work and don't count education as work, the less likely they are to be in school. They can't seem to do both, so 'work first' comes at the expense of education."[185] Thus, there is some question whether the 1996 Personal Responsibility and Work Opportunity Reconciliation Act will benefit poor women over time. Although the number of people on welfare has declined, the poverty rate has not. Peter Edelman, a staunch critic of the 1996 reforms, characterized the policy's impact this way:

> The number of Americans on welfare [in 2008] is one and a third percent, while poverty is at 12.3 percent. Less than a third of poor children are part of families receiving welfare assistance. That percentage has been cut in half over the past dozen years. . . . Welfare is no longer an entitlement. That means that it is basically a matter of local discretion. It is now very difficult to get on welfare. The welfare rolls are up a little now, given the current recession, but compare what has happened to food stamps, which are still a legal entitlement. The food stamp rolls were down to 17 million people in 2000, but are now back up to 28 million people. Did the need for welfare assistance go down during this same time period? I don't think so.[186]

The implications of the 1996 welfare reforms are only now becoming evident. States will no doubt make changes as programmatic evaluations are completed. However, the character of the reforms adopted in 1996 are so dramatically different from those of any of the other federal benefit programs that one wonders whether single mothers will remain the country's best scapegoat. Positive incentives are few and far between in the current policy, and the expectation that single mothers will be able to move off public assistance on the basis of an hourly wage job that does not provide health, pension, or child-care benefits is unrealistic at best, particularly in a global recession. TANF eliminated a welfare mother's ability to choose education over an hourly wage job in order for her to continue to receive benefits, thereby further limiting her long-term earning power.

A 2003 study conducted by the Institute for Women's Policy Research, titled "Before and After Welfare Reform," examined the income sources and employment patterns of low-income families just before and approximately three years after the implementation of the 1996 welfare reforms.[187] Although more low-income women were working, well over three-quarters of them were concentrated in four typically low-wage occupations, there was no increase in the proportion of women who receive health insurance through employment, and there was evidence of a pay gap between male and female welfare leavers. Since 2001, even as the number of welfare recipients declined, the poverty rate has increased. In 2008, 37 million people lived below the poverty line and 12.9 million of those were children. The percentage of single-mother families living in poverty rose from 25.4 percent in 2000 to 28 percent in 2007. Even though a higher percentage of women are working, they are working longer hours and earning less than their male counterparts. Finally, the educational attainment of single parents declined significantly under the work-first requirements of TANF. Single-parent welfare recipients who have "some college" declined from 24.1 to 16.8 percent.

Poverty rates remain high among welfare leavers in part because wages are so low and the same gender-based forms of discrimination that plague women in general are relevant to poor women. Occupational segregation (38 percent of welfare recipients are employed in the service sector), longer hours for lower wages than similarly situated male beneficiaries, limited access to health and other forms of employment-based benefits, and scarce and inadequate child care are common employment barriers for all working women.

The Pursuit of Economic Equality in a Recession

Can women make progress toward gender equality even in the midst of the worst economy since the depression of the 1930s? It depends. The recession is not gender neutral. Old challenges like occupational segregation in part-time and low-wage jobs typically without health benefits means that although women have been more likely than men to keep their jobs, they are not getting ahead financially. Heavy layoffs and rising unemployment in manufacturing and construction—sectors heavily dominated by men—have resulted in an increase in women's share of the overall workforce (now estimated at 49.1 percent) and have increased the likelihood that a woman is the new breadwinner in her family. However, the persistence of the wage gap and sluggish job growth in the sectors most likely to be occupied by women (education, health care, and the service sector) have meant that women's earnings have not increased to match their new role as their family's sole wage earner. In the typical dual-earner family, a woman contributed roughly 35.6 percent of the total family income in 2008. Therefore, women may be safer in their jobs but find it nearly impossible to support their family on their wages alone.

Beyond employment, women are one-third more likely than men to have subprime mortgages, nearly 60 percent of impoverished children are living in female-headed households, and the poverty rate is higher among women than it is among men of any race. In nearly 44 percent of African American families with children, a woman is the primary breadwinner (including families headed by working single mothers and married-couple families in which the husband is unemployed).[188] Women workers still bear the burdens of the "double shift" even though they are more likely to have an unemployed male partner at home. According to economists Alan B. Krueger and Andreas Mueller, "unemployed men's child care duties are virtually identical to those of their working counterparts, and they instead spend more time sleeping, watching TV and looking for a job, along with other domestic duties."[189] Historically, the gendered division of labor in households has been resistant to change. While men have increased their share of domestic labor and child care over the last twenty years, they have not done so in direct proportion to a decrease in employed women's time on household tasks. The gap has been outsourced—dining out, cleaning services, and paid child care. "As declining incomes force families to cut back on these outlays," says Heidi Hartmann, chief economist at the Institute for Women's Policy Research, "women will most likely pick up the slack."

The 2009 economic stimulus package, known as the American Recovery and Reinvestment Act, focused on job creation related to "shovel ready" infrastructure projects and secondarily in support for state and local governments, education, and health. Although it is too early to measure the results, early critics charged that women were largely excluded from the jobs creation aspect of the President's stimulus proposal. Linda Hirshman, for example, asked in a December 2008 New York Times op-ed, "Where Are the New Jobs for Women?"[190] The White House estimated that 42 percent of the jobs created by the stimulus package would go to women, especially those in fields such as education and health care, where federal spending would bridge state and local budget gaps. Yet, this particular approach does nothing to ameliorate the impact of low-wage occupational segregation and the lifetime effects of the wage gap. Led by freshman Representative Jared Polis (D-CO), advocates urged Congress and the White House to use the recession as an opportunity to invest in training women for high-paid nontraditional employment and to provide incentives for government contractors that fill a portion of newly created jobs with women and minorities. In addition, existing hiring goals could be updated and oversight enforced. "Currently, contractors are supposed to be working toward a 6.9 percent hiring rate for women, a goal articulated in 1981 and never revised." Under the George W. Bush administration, the Department of Labor's Office of Federal Contract Compliance lost a quarter of its field monitors charged with enforcing hiring guidelines. "The economic crisis has the potential to radically change how certain employers conceive of women workers, but government must provide the leadership and incentives."[191]

CONCLUSION

In this chapter we have covered a lot of topics related to work, the economy, wages, retirement, and the different ways men and women experience the labor market over the course of their lifetimes. It is clear that society has not resolved its ambivalence over women in the full-time workforce, even though the majority of women and the majority of women with small children are full-time year-round participants in the economy. Antiquated notions of why women work reinforce "pink ghettos" of low-wage occupations primarily held by women and also depress women's wages overall. The wage gap not only deprives women and their families of income now and cumulatively over a 47-year work life, but it also reduces retirement benefits. While Title VII and Title IX have opened doors to women's employment and educational opportunities, the Equal Pay Act has been largely ineffective in equalizing wage rates for men and women. The Lilly Ledbetter Fair Pay Act, the first piece of legislation signed by President Obama in January 2009, does not guarantee equal pay; it merely provides women a longer time period in which to seek a legal remedy once pay discrimination is discovered. The Paycheck Fairness Act would provide more transparency in pay scales and more powerful legal remedies, but it does not fully adopt a theory of comparable worth. Women and their partners are left alone to negotiate child care and other caregiving arrangements when both are working full-time. If one partner stops working for any length of time to care for children or an ailing family member, he or she risks erosion of employment skills and a reduction in overall earnings, as well as a loss in pension and other retirement benefits. The United States has yet to develop a universal system of child care that is integrated with the educational system to provide families with a single stream of child development assistance. Unless the government takes seriously the need to provide policy solutions to these persistent challenges, the next generation of men and women entering the workforce will also face wage inequities and the struggle to reconcile work with family issues.

Is a gender-neutral approach to employment policy effective for women or does gender neutrality merely increase the burden on women who work full-time in both the paid and unpaid labor sectors? Our analysis in this chapter suggests that the policies adopted in the 1960s and still subject to interpretation by the courts today have not been sufficient to change the character and existence of the dual labor market, the wage gap, or the "glass ceiling" and "sticky floor" problems. A majority of women entering the workforce today will hold a wage-earning job until retirement. Some women may still opt to drop out of the workforce entirely to bear and raise children, but most will either stay in the workforce or return once their children have started school. Some women will work because they find it fulfilling. Most women, however, will work for their lifetime out of economic necessity. As we have noted in previous chapters, until public attitudes catch up with the realities of women in the workforce, public policy is unlikely to address the most pervasive problems women face.

It remains to be seen whether the current recession will serve as a catalyst for change or an additional drag on women's earnings and employment.

Suggested Readings, Web Resources, and Films

Linda Babcock and Sara Laschever, *Women Don't Ask: Negotiation and the Gender Divide* (Princeton, N.J.: Princeton University Press, 2003).

Lisa Bowden and Shannon Cain, eds., *Powder: Writing by Women in the Ranks from Vietnam to Iraq* (Tuscon, Ariz.: Kore Press, 2008).

Barbara Ehrenreich and Arlie Russell Hochschild, *Global Woman: Nannies, Maids, and Sex Workers in the New Economy* (New York: Henry Holt, 2002).

Diana Furchtgott-Roth and Christine Solba, *Women's Figures: An Illustrated Guide to the Economic Progress of Women in America* (Washington, D.C.: AEI Press and the Independent Women's Forum, 1999).

Janet C. Gornick, Marcia K. Myers, and Katerin E. Ross, "Supporting Employment of Mothers: Policy Variations Across Fourteen Welfare States," *Journal of European Social Policy* 7 (1997): 45–70.

Sharlene Hesse-Biber and Gregg Lee Carter, *Working Women in America: Split Dreams* (New York: Oxford University Press, 2000).

Arlie Russell Hochschild, *The Time Bind: How Work Becomes Home and Home Becomes Work* (New York: Henry Holt, 1997).

Augusto Lopez-Claros and Saadia Zahidi, *Women's Empowerment: Measuring the Global Gender Gap* (Geneva, Switzerland: World Economic Forum, 2005).

Pamela Stone, *Opting Out? Why Women Really Quit Careers and Head Home* (Berkeley: University of California Press, 2007).

Virginia Valian, *Why So Slow? The Advancement of Women* (Cambridge, Mass.: MIT Press, 1998).

Joan Williams, *Unbending Gender: Why Family and Work Conflict and What to Do About It* (New York: Oxford University Press, 2000).

Kayla Williams, *Love My Rifle More Than You: Young and Female in the U.S. Army* (New York: Norton, 2006).

Novel: Allison Pearson, *I Don't Know How She Does It: The Life of Kate Reddy, Working Mother* (New York: Alfred A. Knopf, 2002).

Novel: Meg Wolitzer, *The Ten Year Nap: A Novel* (New York: Riverhead Books, 2008).

AFL-CIO: http://www.aflcio.org/women.

Catalyst: http://www.catalystwomen.org.

Center for WorkLife Law: http://www.worklifelaw.org/.

Institute for Women's Policy Research: http://www.iwpr.org/index.cfm.

The Glass Hammer: http://www.theglasshammer.com/.

National Committee on Pay Equity: http://www.feminist.com/fairpay/.

National Partnership for Women and Families: http://www.nationalpartnership.org.

NEW: Nontraditional Employment for Women: http://www.abanet.org/legalservices/dialogue/downloads/dialsu08.pdf.

Service Women's Action Network (SWAN): http://www.servicewomen.org.

U.S. Equal Employment Opportunity Commission: http://www.eeoc.gov/.

Blog: Feminist Law Professors: http://feministlawprofessors.com/.

Blog: Feminist Majority Foundation Choices Campus Blog: http://feministcampus.blogspot.com/.

Blog: Women in Media and News: http://www.wimnonline.org/WIMNsVoicesBlog/.

Film: *The Fairer Sex?* (segment of *Prime Time Live* television series, 1994).

Film: *Fast Food Women* (Appalshop Film Catalog, 1991).

Film: *The Life and Times of Rosie the Riveter* (Los Angeles: Direct Cinema, 1987).

Film: *Lioness* (Room 11 Productions, 2008).

Film: *With Babies and Banners: Story of the Women's Emergency Brigade* (Franklin Lakes, N.H.: New Day Films, 1978).

Notes

1. Sharlene Hesse-Biber and Gregg Lee Carter, *Working Women in America: Split Dreams* (New York: Oxford University Press, 2000), p. 54.

2. Bureau of Labor Statistics: Women's Bureau, "20 Leading Occupations of Employed Women Full-Time Wage and Salary Workers: 2003 Annual Averages," June 22, 2004.

3. U.S. Census Bureau, "Median Earnings in the Past 12 Months of Full-Time, Year-Round Workers 16 and Older by Sex and Women's Earnings as a Percentage of Men's Earnings by State: 2007," 2007 American Community Survey, issued August 2008, accessed at http://www.census.gov/prod/2008pubs/acs-09.pdf.

4. Hesse-Biber and Carter, *Working Women in America*, pp. 167–168.

5. Eleanor Flexnor and Ellen Fitzpatrick, *Century of Struggle: The Women's Rights Movement in the United States* (Cambridge, Mass.: Harvard University Press, 1996).

6. Hesse-Biber and Carter, *Working Women in America*, p. 18.

7. Nancy Woloch, *Women and the American Experience* (New York: Alfred A. Knopf, 1984), p. 220.

8. Julie A. Matthaei, *An Economic History of Women in America: Women's Work, the Sexual Division of Labor, and the Development of Capitalism* (New York: Schocken Books, 1982).

9. Woloch, *Women and the American Experience*, p. 221.

10. Ibid., p. 220.

11. Ibid., p. 221.

12. Maxine L. Margolis, *Mothers and Such: Views of American Women and Why They Changed* (Berkeley: University of California Press, 1984), p. 195.

13. Hesse-Biber and Carter, *Working Women in America*, p. 37.

14. Rosalyn Baxandall, Linda Gordon, and Susan Reverby, *America's Working Women: A Documentary History—1600 to the Present* (New York: Vintage Books, 1976), pp. 255–256.

15. Ann Gordon, Mari-Jo Buhle, and Nancy Schrom, "Women in American Society: An Historical Contribution," *Radical America 5*, no. 4 (1971): 3–66.

16. J. Ellen Galinsky, Kerstin Aumann, and James T. Bond, "Times are Changing: Gender and Generation at Work and Home," Families and Work Institute: 2008 National Study of the Changing Workforce, accessed at http://familiesandwork.org/site/research/reports/Times_Are_Changing.pdf.

17. J. J. Goodnow, "Children's Household Work: Its Nature and Functions," *Psychological Bulletin* 103 (1988): 5–26.

18. Virginia Valian, *Why So Slow? The Advancement of Women* (Cambridge, Mass.: MIT Press, 1998), p. 33.

19. Ellen Galinsky, Kerstin Aumann, and James T. Bond, "Times are Changing: Gender and Generation at Work and Home," p. 14.

20. Ibid., p. 40.

21. Ibid., p. 44.

22. Ibid.

23. National Manpower Council, *Womanpower* (New York: Columbia University Press, 1957).

24. *Equal Pay Act of 1963*, 77 Stat. 56 (1963).

25. Department for Professional Employees, AFL-CIO, "Fact Sheet 2008 Professional Women: Vital Statistics," June 2008, accessed at http://www.ala-apa.org/salaries/Professional%20women%202008.pdf.

26. J. Ralph Lindgren and Nadine Taub, *The Law of Sex Discrimination*, 2nd ed. (Minneapolis, Minn.: West Publishing, 1993), pp. 145–146.

27. Ibid., pp. 146–147.

28. Ibid., p. 174.

29. *Quong Wing v. Kirkendall*, 233 U.S. 59, 63 (1912).

30. Lindgren and Taub, *Law of Sex Discrimination*, p. 177.

31. *Wilson v. Southwest Airlines Company*. 517 F. Supp. 292, 301, 302 (N.D. Tex. 1981).

32. *Dothard v. Rawlinson*, 433 U.S. 321 (1977).

33. *Griggs v. Duke Power Company*, 401 U.S. 424 (1971).

34. *General Electric v. Gilbert*, 429 U.S. 125 (1976).

35. *California Federal Savings and Loan Association v. Guerra*, 479 U.S. 272 (1987).

36. MomsRising, accessed at http://www.momsrising.org/.

37. Joanna Grossman, "*AT&T v. Hulteen*: The Supreme Court Deals a Blow to Once-Pregnant Retirees," FindLaw Commentary, May 26, 2009, accessed at http://writ.news.findlaw.com/grossman/20090526.html.

United Auto Workers v. Johnson Controls, Inc. 499 U.S. 187 (1991).

38. *Executive Order 11246*, 30 F.R. 12319, 1965.

39. Jocelyn C. Frye, "Affirmative Action: Understanding the Past and Present," in *The American Woman 1996–1997: Women and Work*, eds. Cynthia Costello and Barbara Kivimae Krimgold (New York: Norton, 1996), p. 35.

40. Ibid., pp. 37–38.

41. Roberta Ann Johnson, "Affirmative Action and Women," in *Women in Politics: Outsiders or Insiders?* ed. Lois Duke Whitaker, 3rd ed. (Upper Saddle River, N.J.: Prentice Hall, 1999), pp. 334–352.

42. The Civil Rights Project, "Joint Statement of Constitutional Law Scholars," (Boston: Harvard University), June 23, 2003, accessed at http://www.civilrightsproject. harvard.edu.

43. Janine Jackson, "Affirmative Action Coverage Ignores Women—and Discrimination: A Six Month Study of Media Coverage," *Extra!* (Americans for a Fair Chance, 1999), accessed at http://www.fair.org.

44. National Partnership for Women and Families, "Affirmative Action Helps Boost Women's Pay and Promotes Economic Security for Women and Their Families," accessed at http://www.nationalpartnership.org.

45. American Association of University Women, *Tech Savvy: Educating Girls in the New Computer Age*, AAUW Educational Foundation, Commission on Gender, Technology, and Teacher Education, 2000, accessed at http://www.aauw.org/ member_center/publications/TechSavvy/TechSavvy.pdf.

46. The National Partnership for Women and Families, *Women at Work: Looking Behind the Numbers Forty Years After the Civil Rights Act of 1964* (Washington, D.C.: National Partnership for Women and Families, 2004).

47. National Committee on Pay Equity, accessed at http://www.pay-equity.org/ info-time.html; WAGE Women are Getting Even, accessed at http://www. wageproject.org/.

48. Cynthia B. Costello, Shari Miles, and Anne J. Stone, eds., *The American Woman 1999–2000: A Century of Change—What's Next?* (New York: Norton, 1998).

49. Cynthia B. Costello, Vanessa R. Wight, and Anne J. Stone, eds., *The American Woman: 2003–2004: Daughters of a Revolution—Young Women Today* (New York: Palgrave Macmillan, 2003), p. 253.

50. Valian, *Why So Slow?* pp. 190–191.

51. Ibid., p. 198.

52. Alice H. Eagly and Linda L. Carli, "Women and the Labyrinth of Leadership," *Harvard Business Review*, September 2007, pp. 63–71.

53. *ibid.*, p. 67.

54. *ibid.*, pp. 69–71.

55. Del Jones, "2003: Year of the Woman Among the *Fortune* 500?" *USA Today*, December 30, 2003, accessed at http://www.usatoday.com.

56. "The Bottom Line: Connecting Corporate Performance and Gender Diversity," study conducted by Catalyst (2004), accessed at http://www.catalystwomen.org/ knowledge/titles/files/full/financialperformancereport.pdf.

57. "Women in the Labor Force in 2008" U. S. Department of Labor, Women's Bureau, June 19, 2009.

58. Catalyst, "Women and Men in U.S. Corporate Leadership: Same Workplace, Different Realities?" (2004), accessed at http://www. catalystwomen.org.

59. Ibid.

60. Lisa Trei, "Women Lawyers Continue to Battle Gender Bias, Rhode Tells Conference," *Stanford Review* (March 13, 2002), accessed at http://www.news-service. stanford.edu.

61. Ibid., quoting Deborah Rhode, chair of the ABA Commission on Women in the Profession.

62. Deborah L. Rhode, "The Unfinished Agenda: Women and the Legal Profession," ABA Commission on Women in the Profession, 2001, p. 5, accessed at http://www. abanet.org/ftp/pub/women/unfinishedagenda.pdf.

63. ABA Commission on Women in the Profession, "A Current Glance of Women in the Law 2003," accessed at http://www.abanet.org/women/glance2003.pdf.

64. Rhode, "The Unfinished Agenda," p. 14.

65. Valian, *Why So Slow?* p. 208.

66. Association of American Medical Colleges, "Increasing Women's Leadership in Academic Medicine," 2003 Report, accessed at http://www.aamc.org/members/ wim/iwl.pdf.

67. Ibid.

68. Diane E. Lewis, "Women Lose Ground in Science, Tech Jobs, Report Says," *Boston Globe*, July 18, 2001, p. D2.

69. Ibid.; Mary Thom, *Balancing the Equation: Where Are Women and Girls in Science, Engineering, and Technology?* National Council for Research on Women (2001), accessed at http://www.ncrw.org/research/iqsci.htm.

70. Active Duty Servicewomen by Branch of Service, accessed at http://www.defense link.mil/prhome/poprep2000/html/chapter3/chapter3_3.htm.

71. Ibid.

72. "Military Readiness: Women Are Not a Problem," *RAND Research Brief*, 1997, accessed at http://www.rand.org/publications/RB/RB7515.

73. "'Get Out of My Way': Women Soldiers, Making Quiet Progress, Now Hold Dangerous Combat Positions," *Newsweek*, October 29, 2001, p. 34.

74. Shauna Curphey, "1 in 7 U.S. Military Personnel in Iraq Is Female," *Women's eNews*, March 22, 2003, accessed at http://www.womensenews.org.

75. Mona Iskander, "Female Troops in Iraq Redefine Combat Roles," *Women's eNews*, July 5, 2004, accessed at http://www.womensenews.org; Lizette Alvarez, "G.I. Jane Breaks the Combat Barrier as War Evolves," *New York Times*, August 16, 2009, accessed online at http://www.nytimes.com/2009/08/16/us/16women.html.

76. Richard Sisk, "Gender Ban Ripped: Congress's Only Woman Vet Rips House Panel's Curbs on Troops," *New York Daily News*, May 21, 2005; Lizette Alvarez, "G.I. Jane Breaks the Combat Barrier as War Evolves," p. 2.

77. *Lioness*, http://www.lionessthefilm.com.

78. "Women Eyed for Combat," CBSNews.com, October 22, 2004, accessed at http:// www.cbsnews.com/stories/2004/10/22/eveningnews; Lizette Alvarez, "G.I. Jane Breaks the Combat Barrier as War Evolves," p.2.

79. Both quoted in Caryl Rivers, "Critics Aside, 'Military Moms' Are Here to Stay," *Women's eNews*, May 29, 2003, accessed at http://www.womensenews.org.

80. Linda Chavez, "Women in Combat Will Take Toll on Our Culture," Center for Equal Opportunity: Town Hall Column, 2003, accessed at http://www.town hall.com/columnists/lindachavez.

81. Ann Scott Tyson, "Woman Gains Silver Star—And Removal from Combat," *Washington Post*, May 1, 2008; A01.

82. Ann Scott Tyson, "Short Maternity Leaves, Long Deployments," *Washington Post*, February 18, 2008; A01.

83. Gretchen Cook, "Controversy Arising Over Female Combat Veterans," *Women's eNews*, November 11, 2003, accessed at http://www.womensenews.org.

84. Dorothy McBride Stetson, *Women's Rights in the USA: Policy Debates and Gender Roles*, 2nd ed. (New York: Garland Publishing, 1997), p. 317.

85. Lindgren and Taub, *Law of Sex Discrimination*, p. 217.

86. Susan Gluck Mezey, *Elusive Equality: Women's Rights, Public Policy, and the Law* (Boulder, Colo.: Lynne Rienner, 2003), p. 148.

87. *Doe v. City of Belleville*, 119 F.3d563; and *Rene v. MGM Grand Hotel*, 305 F.3d1061.

88. Institute for Women's Policy Research, "Fact Sheet: The Gender Gap by Occupation," April 2009, accessed at http://www.iwpr.org.

89. Marlene Kim, "Women of Color: The Persistent Double Jeopardy of Race and Gender," *American Prospect*, September 22, 2008.

90. "Fact Sheet: Equal Pay for Women of Color," AFL-CIO fact sheet (2004), accessed at http://aflcio.org/women/f_color.htm; Judy Goldberg Day and Catherine Hill, "Behind the Pay Gap," (Washington, D.C.: AAUW Educational Foundation, 2007).

91. Timothy S. Bland, "Equal Pay Enforcement Heats Up," *HRMagazine* 44, no. 7 (1999): 138–143.

92. Dan Ackman, "Wal-Mart and Sex Discrimination by the Numbers," *Forbes*, June 23, 2004.

93. Dana Milbank, "White House Men Highest Paid," *Washington Post*, July 14, 2004.

94. Diana Furchtgott-Roth and Christine Solba, *Women's Figures: An Illustrated Guide to the Economic Progress of Women in America* (Washington, D.C.: AEI Press and the Independent Women's Forum, 1999).

95. Ibid., pp. 18–19.

96. Claudia Goldin and Cecelia Rouse, "Orchestrating Impartiality: The Impact of 'Blind' Auditions on Female Musicians," *American Economic Review* 90 no. 4 (September, 2000): 715–741.

97. Kristen Schilt and Matthew Wiswall, "Before and After: Gender Transitions, Human Capital, and Workplace Experiences," *Berkeley Electronic Journal of Economic Analysis & Policy* 8 no. 1 (September, 2008): Article 39, available at http://www.bepress.com/bejeap/vol8/iss1/art39.

98. Alex M. Parker, "Portion of Gender Pay Gap Persists, Despite Workforce Changes," *Government Executive*, April 28, 2009, accessed at http://wwwgovexec.com.

99. Judy Goldberg Dey and Catherine Hill, "Behind the Pay Gap," AAUW Educational Foundation, April 2007.

100. Linda Babcock and Sara Laschever, *Women Don't Ask: Negotiation and the Gender Divide* (Princeton, N.J.: Princeton University Press, 2003).

101. Hannah Riley Bowles, Linda Babcock, and Lei Lai, "Social Incentives for Gender Differences in the Propensity to Initiate Negotiations: Sometimes It Does Hurt to Ask," *Organizational Behavior and Human Decision Processes* 103 no. 1 (2007): 84–103.

102. Hannah Bowles, quoted in Shankar Vedantam, "Salary, Gender and the Social Cost of Haggling," *Washington Post*, July 30, 2007; A07.

103. Furchtgott-Roth and Solba, *Women's Figures*, p. xx.

104. Denise Venable, "The Wage Gap Myth," (Washington, D.C.: National Center for Policy Analysis, 2002).

105. Furchtgott-Roth and Solba, *Women's Figures*, p. 19.

106. Lisa Belkin, "The Opt Out Revolution," *New York Times Magazine*, October 26, 2003; for a critical evaluation of Belkin's statistics, see Cathy Young, "Opting Out: The Press Discovers the Mommy Wars, Again." *ReasonOnline*, June 2004, accessed at http://www.findarticles.com/p/articles/mi_m1568/is_2_36/ai_n6196833.

107. Young, "Opting Out."

108. Donna St. George, "Most Stay-at-Home Moms Start That Way, Study Finds," *Washington Post*, October 1, 2009, page A-1; Judith Warner, "The Choice Myth," *New York Times*, October 8, 2009, accessed at http://warner.blogs.nytimes.com/2009/10/08/the-opt-out-myth/.

109. Ann Hulbert, "Look Who's Parenting: Will the Slacker Generation Improve Child-Rearing?" *New York Times Magazine*, July 4, 2004, pp. 11–12.

110. Federal Glass Ceiling Commission, *Good for Business: Making Full Use of the Nation's Human Capital* (Washington, D.C.: Government Printing Office, 1995).

111. Rebecca Traister, "The Truth About Carly," *Salon.com*, October 19, 2006, accessed at http://archive.salon.com/mwt/feature/2006/10/19/carly_fiorina/index.html.

112. Carol Hymowitz, "In the Lead," *Wall Street Journal*, July 8, 2003.

113. See Hesse-Biber and Carter, *Working Women in America*, pp. 163–173.

114. Francis A. McMorris, "Wall Street Women Gain Ceiling-Cracking Settlement," *Women's eNews*, July 16, 2004, accessed at http://www.womensenews.org.

115. Paul Rincon, "Women Looking Over Glass Cliffs," *BBC News*, published September 6, 2004.

116. Quoted in "More Women Join World's Workforce, Obstacles Persist," *Breaking Through the Glass Ceiling: Women in Management*, International Labor Office, updated 2004.

117. Gregory Northcraft and Barbara A. Gutek, "Point-Counterpoint: Discrimination Against Women in Management—Going, Going, Gone or Going but Not Gone?" in *Women in Management: Trends, Issues, and Challenges in Managerial Diversity*, ed. Ellen A Fagenson (Newbury Park, Calif.: Sage, 1993), pp. 219–245.

118. Albert J. Mills, "Organizational Culture," in *Women and Work: A Handbook*, eds. Paula J. Dubeck and Kathryn Berman (New York: Garland Press, 1996), pp. 321–322.

119. "The Glass Ceiling," *Economist*, May 5, 2009.

120. Suzanne Uttaro Samuels, *Fetal Rights, Women's Rights: Gender Equality in the Workplace* (Madison: University of Wisconsin, 1995), p. xi.

121. Ellen Goodman, "Equal Pay Struggle Continues," *Times-Picayune*, March 16, 1999, p. 5B.

122. *Lilly M. Ledbetter v. The Goodyear Tire & Rubber Company, Inc.* 550 U.S. 618 (2007), Justice Ruth Bader Ginsberg, dissenting, pp. 2–3.

123. Ibid., p. 19.

124. Robert Barnes, "Over Ginsburg's Dissent, Court Limits Bias Suits," *Washington Post*, May 31, 2007; A01.

125. "Pay Equity Pioneer Lilly Ledbetter Addresses the DNC," August 26, 2008. *PBS Online NewsHour*, accessed at http://www.pbs.org/newshour/bb/politics/july-dec08/ledbetter_08-26.html.

126. Kay Steiger, "Less Money, Mo' Problems," *American Prospect*, April 25, 2007, accessed at http://www.prospect.org.

127. U.S. Bureau of the Census, *Statistical Abstracts: 1997* (Washington, D.C.: Bureau of the Census, 1997), table 711.

128. Center for Policy Alternatives, "Women's Voices 2000: Women and Time" (2000), accessed at http://www.stateaction.org/programs/women/voices/time.cfm.

129. Ellen Goodman, "Who Gets Blamed for Matthew's Death? The Working Mother, of Course," *Boston Globe*, October 26, 1997, p. E7.

130. Susan J. Douglas and Meredith W. Michaels, *The Mommy Myth: The Idealization of Motherhood and How It Has Undermined Women* (New York: Free Press, 2004), p. 237.

131. See Janet C. Gornick, Marcia K. Myers, and Katerin E. Ross, "Supporting Employment of Mothers: Policy Variations Across Fourteen Welfare States," *Journal of European Social Policy* 7 (1997): 45–70.

132. National Women's Law Center, "Affordability: Women and Their Families Need Help Paying for Child Care," accessed at http://www.nwlc.org/pdf/AffordabilityFactSheet2004.pdf.

133. Children's Defense Fund, "The State of America's Children 2004," accessed at http://www.childrensdefense.org/.

134. Jaime Koniak, "Note: Should the Street Take Care? The Impact of Corporate-Sponsored Day Care on Business in the New Millennium," *Business Law Review* 193 (2002): 2.

135. Jennifer L. Glass and Sarah Beth Estes, "The Family Responsive Workplace," *Annual Review of Sociology* 23 (1997): 289–314.

136. Arlie Russell Hochschild, *The Time Bind: How Work Becomes Home and Home Becomes Work* (New York: Holt, 1997).

137. Glass and Estes, "The Family Responsive Workplace," p. 312.

138. P. Kingston, "Illusions and Ignorance About the Family Responsive Workplace," *Journal of Family Issues* 11 (1990): 438–454.

139. Labor Party, "Unpaid, Underused: Family Medical Leave Act," accessed at http://lpa.igc.org/lpv25/lp10.htm.

140. Costello and Krimgold, *Women and Work*, p. 85.

141. National Partnership for Women and Families, "Public Support for Family Leave Benefits Growing," news release, October 4, 2000, accessed at http://www.nationalpartnership.org.

142. See information from the Employment Policy Foundation, accessed at http://www.epf.org.

143. Ibid.

144. Heather Boushey, "Helping Breadwinners When It Can't Wait: A Progressive Program for Family Leave Insurance," Center for American Progress, May 2009, accessed at http://www.americanprogress.org/issues/2009/06/pdf/fmla.pdf.

145. Eyal Press, "Family-Leave Values," *New York Times*, Sunday Magazine, July 29, 2007.

146. Shelley J. Correll, Stephen Benard, and In Paik, "Getting a Job: Is There a Motherhood Penalty?" *American Journal of Sociology* 112 no.5 (March 2007): 1297–1338.

147. Steven Greenhouse, "Bill Would Guarantee Up to 7 Paid Sick Days," *New York Times*, May 16, 2009; Linda Meric, "Trying Times Call for Healthy Families Act," *Women's eNews*, June 8, 2009; National Partnership for Women and Families, "Support Paid Sick Days," http://paidsickdays.nationalpartnership.org/site/PageServer?pagename=psd_index.

148. Jody Heymann, Alison Earle, and Jeffrey Hayes, "The Work, Family and Equity Index: How Does the United States Measure Up?" The Project on Global Working Families, The Institute for Health and Social Policy, McGill University, 2008.

149. Madonna Harrington Meyer and Pamela Herd, *Market Friendly or Family Friendly: The State and Gender Inequalities in Old Age* (New York: Russell Sage Foundation, 2007).

150. Social Security Administration, "Fact Sheet: Social Security is Important to Women," October 2008, accessed at http://www.socialsecurity.gov/pressoffice/factsheets/women.htm.

151. Women 4 Social Security, accessed at http://www.women4socialsecurity.org.

152. Meyer and Herd, 2007, p. 2.

153. Social Security Administration, 2007.

154. Jeanne Sahadi, "Social Security Fund May Run Out Sooner," March 23, 2005, accessed at http://money.cnn.com/2005/03/23/retirement/2005_trusteesreport/.

155. Leanne Abdnor, "Social Security Choices for the Twenty-First-Century Woman," *CATO Project on Social Security*, February 24, 2004, accessed at http://www.cato.org/pubs/ssps/ssp-33es.html.

156. Marianne Sullivan, "Women Sharpen Views on Social Security," *Women's eNews*, March 9, 2004; National Women's Law Center, "Women and Social Security

Reform: What's at Stake," May 10, 2002, accessed at http://www.nwlc.org/pdf/WhatsAtStakeMay20002Revised.pdf.

157. "Women and Social Security Reform," pp. 1–2.

158. Ibid., p. 2.

159. Heidi Hartman, Catherine Hill, and Lisa Witter, "Strengthening Social Security for Women: A Report from the Working Conference on Women and Social Security," Warrenton, Va., July 19–22, 1999, accessed at http://www.irp.org.

160. Meyer and Herd, 2007, p. 37.

161. Ibid., p.67.

162. Mwangi S. Kimenyi and John Mukum Mbaku, "Female Headship, Feminization of Poverty and Welfare," *Southern Economic Journal* 62, no. 1 (July 1995): 44–53.

163. Randy Albelda and Chris Tilly, *Glass Ceilings and Bottomless Pits: Women's Work, Women's Poverty* (Boston: South End Press, 1997), p. 3.

164. Ibid., p. 6.

165. Bureau of Labor Statistics, "Employment and Earnings," January 2002.

166. Ibid., p. 9.

167. Economic Policy Institute, "Facts and Figures: Poverty," *State of Working America 2004/2005,* accessed at http://www.epinet.org; AFL-CIO, "The Current Minimum Wage Leaves a Family of Three 24 Percent Below the Poverty Line," *Myths and Realities: Minimum Wage,* accessed at http://www.aflcio.org/yourjobeconomy/minimumwage/myths/.

168. Ibid.

169. Holly Sklar, Laryssa Mykyta, and Susan Wefald, *Raise the Floor: Wages and Policies That Work for All of Us* (Boston: South End Press, 2002).

170. Economic Policy Institute, "EPI Issue Guide: Living Wage" (October 2001), accessed at http://www.epinet.org/content.cfm/issueguides_livingwage_livingwage.

171. Kathleen Maclay, "UC Berkeley Study Estimates Wal-Mart Employment Policies Cost California Taxpayers $86 Million a Year," *UC Berkeley Press Release* (August 2, 2004), accessed at http://www.berkeley.edu/news/media/releases/2004/08/02_walmart.shtml.

172. Gwendolyn Mink, "Welfare Reform in Historical Perspective," *Social Justice* 21, no. 1 (Spring 1994): 114–132.

173. Ibid., p. 117.

174. Heidi Hartmann and Roberta Spalter-Roth, "The Real Employment Opportunities of Women Participating in AFDC: What the Market Can Provide," *Social Justice* 21, no. 1 (1994).

175. Albelda and Tilly, *Glass Ceilings and Bottomless Pits*, p. 13.

176. Ibid., p. 100.

177. Ibid., pp. 102–103.

178. Jared Bernstein, *The Challenge of Moving From Welfare to Work: Depressed Labor Market Awaits Those Leaving Rolls* (Washington, D.C.: Economic Policy Institute, 1997).

179. Barbara Ehrenreich, *Nickel and Dimed: On (Not) Getting By in America* (New York: Henry Holt, 2001).

180. Wider Opportunities for Women, "Coming Up Short: A Comparison of Wages and Work Supports in 10 American Communities," July 2004, accessed at http://wowonline.org/docs/dynamic-CTTA-43.pdf.

181. Ibid., pp. 5–7.

182. Kristin Smith, *Working Hard for the Money: Trends in Women's Employment, 1970–2007.* Reports on Rural America, 2008, Carey Institute, University of New Hampshire.

183. Ibid., p.4.

184. Rebecca Blank, "Evaluating Welfare Reform in the United States," *Journal of Economic Literature* 40 no.4 (2002): 1105–1166.

185. Doug Lederman, "Welfare Reform and Women's College Enrollment," *Inside Higher Education* (November 14, 2008).

186. Peter Edelman, "A Call to Action: Taking a Stand Against Poverty and Inequality," remarks delivered as the keynote speaker at the Equal Justice Conference, Minneapolis, Minnesota on May 7, 2008, accessed at http://www.abanet.org/legalservices/dialogue/downloads/dialsu08.pdf.

187. Institute for Women's Policy Research, "Before and After Welfare Reform: The Work and Well-Being of Low-Income Single-Parent Families," June 2003, accessed at http://www.iwpr.org.

188. Dana Goldstein, "Pink Collar Blues," *American Prospect*, June 8, 2009, accessed at http://prospect.org.

189. Catherine Rampell, "As Layoffs Surge, Women May Pass Men in Job Force," *New York Times*, February 6, 2009.

190. Linda Hirshman, "Where Are the New Jobs for Women?" *New York Times*, December 9, 2008, accessed at http://www.nytimes.com/2008/12/09/opinion/09hirshman.html.

191. Goldstein, "Pink Collar Blues."

The Politics of Family and Fertility: The Last Battleground in the Pursuit of Equality?

The previous chapter examined the effectiveness of gender-neutral laws in ending employment discrimination and analyzed the limits of the legal equality approach to reconciling women's dual roles in the private and public spheres. Family policy and issues of reproduction and fertility pose the greatest challenges to feminists when choosing a path toward equality. Gender-neutral laws are nearly impossible to construct, considering the central role biological differences play in this area. Gender neutrality in family law or policies related to pregnancy often obscures the ways in which women are disadvantaged. For example, a law that prevents firefighters from breast-feeding their babies between calls only affects women, although it presumably applies to all firefighters regardless of gender. In *General Electric v. Gilbert* (1976), the Supreme Court ruled that a policy that distinguishes between pregnant and nonpregnant persons does not constitute sex discrimination against women.[1] This reasoning was overturned by the Pregnancy Discrimination Act of 1978. A legal equality doctrine is much more difficult to adopt in family and fertility policies because in many cases women's biological differences are paramount and are magnified by the socially constructed gender roles. Yet gender-specific laws that apply to women only and that are based on their biological functions are often discriminatory in their application. The debate over which path to equality is most advantageous for women is vividly displayed with regard to family and fertility issues.

This chapter surveys the laws that apply to the formation, maintenance, and dissolution of families constructed through marriage. Although nearly half of all marriages end in divorce, marriage remains the primary mechanism by which families are defined and recognized under the law. The issue of same-sex marriage has raised new challenges to the "traditional" family structure. The increase of female single-parent households challenges society to examine government programs that support children and women who must work outside the home. The presence of children in a woman's life directly challenges her autonomy. This chapter also examines reproductive policy. By regulating access to contraception and reproductive services, a state can regulate women's sexuality and reproductive choices. We will evaluate under what circumstances the state has a legitimate interest in regulating reproduction and how such regulations affect women's claims to autonomy. Should women be able to contract freely for their reproductive labor, just as men are constitutionally free to contract for their productive labor? Surrogacy, contract pregnancy, and *in vitro* fertilization present society with an entirely new set of issues. While sex is conceptually different from gender, emerging fertility technology may further blur or entirely erase the lines between sex and gender. Will fertility technologies liberate women from their biological role in reproduction in ways that promote equality, or will the science of fertility and reproduction serve as another form of patriarchal control? What impact will changes in reproductive technology have on defining and forming families in the United States? These broad questions form the basis of our examination of women's attempts to reconcile their role within families with their expanding role in the public sphere. As we'll see, public policy in this area both assists and hinders women's pursuit of equality.

THE DEMOGRAPHICS OF MODERN FAMILIES

American families are quite diverse in their forms. The traditional patriarchal family model of two parents—a male breadwinner and a stay-at-home mother—with two or more children characterizes less than a quarter (about 22 million) of all U.S. households. The 2000 census counted 105 million households in the United States, 27 million of which were headed by single men or women, making single-individual households more prevalent than the "traditional family" model. The most common type of household is the two-wage-earning married couple with or without dependents. These households account for about 34 percent of the total. The percentage of families with their own children living at home decreased to 46 percent in 2008, down from 52 percent in 1950. Female-headed households constituted 80 percent of the 12.9 single-parent families in 2006, with single males heading up about 4 percent of households overall. In 2008, 66.9 million opposite-sex couples lived together, 60.1 million (90 percent) were married and 6.8 million were not. Eighty-five percent of Asian children lived with two parents, as did 78 percent of white non-Hispanic children, 70 percent of Hispanic children, and 38 percent of African American children. About 9 percent of all children lived in a household that included a grandparent and 23 percent of those had no parent present. In 2005, for the first time, a majority of women reported living in a household without a spouse (51 percent).

Gay and lesbian couples account for just over 600,000 households, according to the U.S. Census Bureau's 2001 population statistics, but it is nearly impossible to get an accurate count of same-sex households because of the census question structure.[2] The number of same-sex households is an undercount of gay households since the census does not inquire about sexual orientation, and therefore gay singles, gay couples who live apart, and gay couples who did not complete a single form as a two-person household are not included in this figure. In a departure from 1990 procedures, however, census officials no longer count same-sex married households as "errors." Rather, "married" was changed to "unmarried" but counted as a single household.[3] Although it is too late to change the question wording for the 2010 census (the current survey has boxes designated for "husband," "wife," and "unmarried partner"), the way the data is received and reported will change. Rather than rejecting a survey from one household where two people checked "husband" for example, it will now be counted. The Census Bureau has previously collected data on same-sex marriages, but historically does not release the data. The Obama administration has directed the Bureau of the Census to release that information in the future. Data from the 2007 American Community Surveys showed more than 340,000 same-sex couples as being in marriages.[4]

American men and women are marrying later in life. In 2007, the average age at first marriage was 26 years for women and 27.7 years for men—the highest average age recorded in the twentieth century. In 2006, 24 percent of women and 34 percent of men in their early thirties had never been married. The divorce rate in 2008 for first-time marriages was 50 percent, but almost 80 percent of divorced people remarry, creating "blended families." The divorce rate slowed considerably in the early part of the 1990s, perhaps because men and women were marrying later.[5]

While all ethnic and racial groups have experienced changes in marriage and divorce patterns, the change has been particularly pronounced for African American women. In 1970, 62 percent of black women over the age of eighteen were married, 5 percent divorced, 16 percent widowed, and 17 percent never married. In 2000, 28.9 percent of African American women over eighteen were married, 12 percent divorced, 9 percent widowed, and 42 percent never married. In 2006, the percentage of African American women never married rose to 45 percent (compared to 23 percent of white women). The differences in 1970 among whites, African Americans, and Hispanics were relatively minor, yet the marital status of black women today contrasts sharply with that of both white and Hispanic women.[6]

CREATING FAMILIES THROUGH MARRIAGE

In 1976, the California Supreme Court ruled that actor Lee Marvin had to honor a prior agreement with Michelle Triola, who had been his nonmarital partner for seven years, that provided her with support and a share of their property should their relationship end. In issuing its ruling, the court took the opportunity to express society's view of marriage as "the most socially productive and individually fulfilling relationship one can enjoy in the course of a lifetime."[7] Marriage is both an individual choice and a social expectation. For women, the institution of marriage has historically been the most oppressive force in denying them the rights, privileges, and obligations of full citizenship. Chapter 1 reviewed John Stuart Mill's characterization of marriage as a form of slavery. Under coverture marriage, a husband's identity entirely subsumed his wife's. As a result, a woman was wholly subject to her husband's will and dependent on his willingness to provide support for her and their children. In entering coverture marriage, a woman relinquished control of all property and assets that she might have inherited from her family. Any assets that the couple might have accumulated during their marriage were considered the husband's property exclusively, including the household goods, the wife's clothing, and even the children. Coverture entitled the husband to expect obedience, maintenance of the household, supervision of the children, and unlimited access to the marital bed. Coverture obligated a man to provide the necessities, but nothing more. Should a wife rebel, common law provided for "mild correction." Throughout most of the nineteenth century, women's invisibility under coverture denied them political, social, and economic rights in the public realm. Although there were exceptions, such as prenuptial or postnuptial agreements that granted women control of their property, most laws that addressed women's property rights were not established until the late 1840s. Since property formed the basis of most economic and political rights in the United States, without property rights married women remained civilly dead.

Although coverture has largely faded as the standard for modern marriage, its vestiges remain in the patriarchal traditions and laws associated with forming a family through marriage. Family policy is not covered under the Constitution and has largely been left to the states to regulate. Most of the laws or court interpretations of statutes have evolved over time and do not express a coherent view of "family life" in the United States. Laws regarding marriage usually have to do with establishing a minimum age for males and females to marry, specifying property rights, providing for custody and care of children produced within a marriage, and setting the conditions under which a couple may divorce. In each of these areas, marriage policy is intended to promote social order and protect property interests. Therefore it can be difficult to talk about women's rights within a marriage or how marriage policy might either advance or hinder women's pursuit of equality. For the most part, the character of family life once the family unit is formed is considered a private matter and not subject to the intrusions of public policy in the same ways that education and employment were in the last two chapters. For women, the private nature of the family has left them largely unprotected from the power of patriarchy. Is it possible to talk about women's rights or women's equality within a family or are all individual rights subsumed by the interests of the family unit as a whole?

Men and women who come together in marriage, or even those who choose to live together without being married, can more or less negotiate their own set of gender roles with minimal interference from the state for as long as the union holds. However, they cannot escape the gender roles built into the U.S. tax code; the consequences of a largely absent family support system even in the face of women's increased participation in the labor force; insurance regulations; or divorce, child custody, and support laws. Legal marriage carries with it access to a variety of benefits: the right to share medical benefits, inherit a pension, or access spousal Social Security benefits. Legal marriage also carries a variety of social and cultural benefits as well as the privileges extended to individuals related by kinship. For example, if a friend invites you to a dinner party, you would not assume that the invitation includes your housemate, but you probably would assume that it includes your spouse. Legal marriage bonds two previously unrelated people in powerful ways. Privileges extended to "next of kin" go to a spouse before any blood relative. Other family constellations, while increasingly prevalent in the United States, have not been widely recognized by law or supported by public policy. Some large employers have granted access to employment benefits, such as health insurance, to "domestic partners" even in the absence of state laws. In 1996, Congress passed and President Clinton signed into law the Defense of Marriage Act (DOMA). The federal DOMA denies federal recognition to same-sex marriages and allows states to ignore gay marriages performed in other states. Prior to the federal Defense of Marriage Act, four states had laws banning gay marriage (Maryland, New Hampshire, Wisconsin, and Wyoming).

Vermont was the first state to pass a law that allowed full and equal civil legal status to gay and lesbian couples, although not the right to legally marry. Courts in Hawaii and Alaska attempted to recognize same-sex civil unions and give them the same legal privileges as heterosexual marriages; however, state constitutional amendments banning gay marriage overturned the rulings. In Massachusetts, seven gay couples filed suit, arguing that the Massachusetts constitution guaranteed them the right to marry. The state supreme court agreed and ordered the legislature to allow same-sex couples to marry by May 17, 2004. Eleven states had constitutional amendments banning same-sex marriage on the November 2004 ballot and they all passed. President Bush pledged to push for an amendment to the federal constitution defining marriage as the legal union of one man and one woman, and although an amendment was introduced in 2006, it never received a hearing in Congress. As of June 2009, gay couples can be legally married in Massachusetts, Connecticut, and Iowa; and by early 2010, gay couples will also be able to marry in Vermont, and New Hampshire. In November of 2009, Maine voters approved a ballot measure overturning legislative approval of same sex marriage. In May 2008, the California Supreme Court ruled that restricting marriage to heterosexual couples violated the constitutional rights of homosexual couples. The ruling took effect on June 16, 2008, and thousands of same-sex couples were married until the state constitution was amended by Proposition 8, passed on November 4, 2008,

Same-sex couple Del Martin (L) and Phyllis Lyon (R) are married by San Francisco mayor Gavin Newsom (C) in a private ceremony at San Francisco City Hall June 16, 2008 in San Francisco, California. Martin and Lyon, a couple since 1953, were active in the gay rights and women's rights movements. Del Martin died on August 27, 2008. *Marcio Jose Sanchez-Pool/Getty Images.*

to forbid gay marriage. Proposition 8 was challenged before the state supreme court, but upheld. In their ruling, the 6–1 majority said that the nearly 18,000 marriages that took place between June and November remained legal. Florida and Arizona amended their state constitutions to ban gay marriage with ballot provisions in November 2008, bringing the number of states that have passed bans on gay marriage to thirty-one.

Civil unions for same-sex couples are legal (or will soon be legal) in California, Colorado, the District of Columbia, Hawaii, Maryland, New Jersey, Nevada, Oregon, and Washington. New York and Rhode Island recognize same-sex civil unions and same-sex marriages performed in other states. In May 2009, the city council in the District of Columbia voted to recognize gay marriages performed in other states and subsequently voted against placing the question before voters on a ballot referendum. The District's decision to recognize gay marriages may yet be overturned by Congress. Under the Home Rule Charter, Congress retains the right to review policy passed by the D.C. City Council, but unless they act specifically to block the decision it will become law.

Public opinion on the issue of same-sex marriage varies by generation, ideology, and region of the country. Among those ages eighteen to twenty-nine in 2009, 59 percent favor same-sex marriage, but only 32 percent of those over sixty-five do. Among those of all ages self-identifying as liberal, 75 percent support same-sex marriage but nearly the reverse is true for political conservatives (80 percent oppose). By political party, 55 percent of Democrats approve, 45 percent of independents, and 20 percent of Republicans.[8] In 2004, 63 percent of southerners opposed gay marriage; but only 46 percent of those in eastern states shared that opposition.[9] The concentration of support for gay marriage in the Northeast has led supporters to mount a "6 by 12" strategy, hoping to win marriage equality rights in all six New England states by 2012. Gay and Lesbian Advocates and Defenders (GLAD), a nonprofit law firm, works to promote passage of gay marriage laws by providing legal expertise and information to state legislators and policymakers.[10]

Civil unions impose restrictions that legal marriage does not. For example, couples joined in a civil union may not file joint federal taxes or take family leave under federal law. President Obama signed a memorandum in June 2009 ordering that limited benefits (such as visitation and dependent-care rights) be extended to same-sex couples in the federal workforce. Although the president has urged Congress to repeal the Defense of Marriage Act, he has stated that he does not support a federal law granting same-sex marriage rights. Instead he prefers that the question be decided by each state. The change in federal practice, Obama said, "paves the way for long-overdue progress in our nation's pursuit of equality. Many of our government's hardworking and dedicated, patriotic public servants have been denied basic rights that their colleagues enjoy, for one simple reason: The people that they love are of the same sex." Gay rights advocates are angry that the president has not acted more swiftly in overturning the Clinton-era "don't ask, don't tell" policy that bans gays and lesbians from serving openly in the military, although he campaigned on the issue. Nor has he been willing to intervene in the military dismissals of gays and lesbians who face court-martial for disclosing their sexual orientation.

For many in the gay rights community, marriage equality is a basic civil right. If the right to marry is understood as a fundamental right flowing from the right to privacy, the question of same-sex marriages is far from settled. In *Loving v. Virginia* (1967), the Supreme Court struck down Virginia's antimiscegenation statute prohibiting interracial marriage, citing both the equal protection clause of the Fourteenth Amendment and the fundamental right to marriage derived from the constitutional right to privacy. Furthermore, the Court did not say that the Lovings had a constitutional claim to a mixed-race marriage, but rather a fundamental right to marry. Although several states had anti-miscegenation statutes and marriage between blacks and whites was culturally vilified, this did not dissuade the Court from supporting the right to marry.[11] This would suggest that it is only a matter of time before the constitutionality of same-sex marriages or state-enacted bans on same-sex marriages reaches the Supreme Court. In late November 2004, the U.S. Supreme Court declined (without comment) to accept a case challenging Massachusetts's same-sex marriage ruling. Several countries have national laws allowing same-sex marriage: Belgium, Canada, the Netherlands, Norway, South Africa, Spain, and Sweden. In Israel, gay marriages performed elsewhere are recognized. In another fifteen nations, civil unions or registered partnerships are legal for same-sex couples. The trend favors marriage equality rights in the United States and throughout the world.

THE DEVELOPMENT OF CONTEMPORARY MARRIAGE

Political scientist Dorothy McBride Stetson characterizes the development of modern marriage as the result of three theories: unity, separate but equal, and shared partnership.[12] Unity, defined by coverture to render husband and wife one legal entity, characterized marriage through the early 1900s and was slowly replaced by a theory of separate spheres that lasted throughout the 1960s. Within the "separate but equal" theory of marriage, each individual made a separate but equally important contribution to the union. This period was defined by traditional sex roles in which the male was the family breadwinner and the female was in charge of the home and children. Women in this capacity were glorified by the "cult of domesticity" and were urged to invest themselves in homemaking with the same fervor that a male invested in his paid employment. An explosion of consumer goods and new household appliances relieved women of much of the drudgery of housework and reinforced the primacy of the woman's role as household manager. While a woman was not considered a legal dependent of her husband within a marriage, she was severely disadvantaged by this theory should her marriage dissolve. Women who "stayed at home," as the theory prescribed, found themselves without adequate education or training, without an employment history or the job skills necessary to support themselves and their children, and without the credit history necessary to qualify for a mortgage or even to rent housing if the marriage ended in divorce. The courts most often required a husband to support his ex-wife with alimony and child-support payments, but her standard of living declined substantially, even with such court-ordered monetary support. Furthermore, most states granted a divorce only if one party was determined to have been at fault as a result of serious abuse, neglect, abandonment, or adultery. No-fault divorce, permitting a couple to part without publicly establishing blame, was first established in California in 1969. As more women entered the labor force

Encountering the Controversies of Equality

Domestic Violence Then and Now

Domestic violence is an issue that sits at the intersection of the private and public spheres. The context in which domestic violence is defined affects the remedy available. Under coverture laws of marriage, men were allowed to administer "corrections" to their wives since they were legally responsible for their wives' debts and conduct.[1] Just as parents were entrusted to discipline their children, a husband as the patriarchal head of a family was entrusted to discipline his wife. The phrase "rule of thumb" is said to have arisen in this context. A husband's legitimate authority to use force against his wife or children was limited to the use of a stick no larger in diameter than his thumb. One of the causes the temperance movement took up was to stop women from being physically abused by their husbands. Drunken husbands not only spent the family's wages but also often returned from a night of drinking to physically assault their wives and children. Activists urged reform of divorce laws to permit women to escape domestic violence.

In the 1970s, the battered women's movement reflected the divide among feminists. Some argued that the best way to help women end the violence in their lives was to provide them with services (e.g., shelter, police protection, legal aid, and counseling) within the conventional social service sector. Other more radical feminists believed that domestic violence stemmed from economic dependency and would not cease until the basic structural gender arrangements in society changed. They favored creating autonomous alternatives to the patriarchal family and economic structures.[2]

Addressing domestic violence must begin by moving the definition of the problem from the private sphere to the public sphere. When women's battery is defined as a family problem, public institutions are unlikely to interfere. Thus, police departments have been slow to intervene in domestic disputes until recently. A national coalition of feminist organizations successfully lobbied Congress to pass federal legislation on domestic abuse. The Violence Against Women Act of 1994 (VAWA) charges the Justice Department with collecting data on domestic abuse, provides money to state and local governments to fund efforts to provide services to victims and abusers, and identifies domestic abuse as a gender-based crime, which has allowed victims to sue their batterers in federal court. The VAWA has been reauthorized by Congress every five years since its passage and will next be subject to review and reauthorization in 2010.

In 2007, when NFL quarterback Michael Vick was indicted and found guilty of animal abuse for his role in a dogfighting ring, he was suspended indefinitely without pay from the NFL. Feminists are astounded that the NFL has not acted with equivalent outrage when players are charged with domestic violence against women.

Although some players have been arrested and convicted of spousal abuse, not one has been suspended from the NFL. In 2009, pop star Chris Brown was charged with domestic abuse in the beating of his girlfriend, the singer Rihanna. Shortly after the news broke and pictures of Rihanna's battered face appeared on the Internet, the *New York Times* ran an article about teenage girls' continuing support for Brown. In a survey of 200 teenagers by the Boston Public Health Commission, 46 percent said Rihanna was responsible for what happened; 52 percent said both bore responsibility, despite knowing that her injuries required hospitalization.[3] Both incidents prompted veterans organizations to call attention to a rapid increase in the incidents of domestic violence in military families as the stresses from war return home. Victims report that they encounter the "Camouflage Code of Silence" in attempting to report active duty abusers that is not pierced by the provisions in the Violence Against Women Act.

What do you think?

What are the causes of domestic violence? Are they different today than they were in the 1800s? Of females killed with a firearm, almost two-thirds were killed by their intimate partners. The number of females shot and killed by their husband or intimate partner was more than three times higher than the total number murdered by male strangers using all weapons combined in single victim/single offender incidents. In what ways does this statistic reflect the power of gender in society?[4] In at least one case, a California man has filed a sex discrimination suit because he was denied a bed in ten different battered women's shelters. The shelters claim that it is not clinically appropriate to house and treat male and female victims together.[5] Can domestic violence laws be gender neutral? How are males disadvantaged by the focus on women as victims? What would equal treatment look like in the case of domestic violence? How can the problem of domestic violence best be addressed today? Rather than falling, the rates of domestic violence are rising. How might society's seeming acceptance of violence directed at women best be countered? How can institutions like the U.S. military be called upon to do a better job in preventing domestic violence? Is domestic violence best eliminated with a legal equality or a fairness approach? Explain.

1. William Blackstone, *Commentaries on the Laws of England* (London: Strahan, 1803).
2. Gretchen Arnold, "Dilemmas of Feminist Coalitions: Collective Identity and Strategic Effectiveness in the Battered Women's Movement," in *Feminist Organizations: Harvest of the New Women's Movement,* eds. Myra Marx Feree and Patricia Yancey Martin (Philadelphia: Temple University Press, 1995), pp. 276–290.
3. Jan Hoffman, "Teenage Girls Stand by Their Man," *New York Times*, March 19, 2009; Stacy Bannerman, "Veteran Domestic Violence Remains Camouflaged," *Women's eNews*, April 13, 2009.
4. U.S. Department of Justice, Bureau of Justice Statistics, "Homicide Trends in the U.S.: Intimate Homicide," accessed at http://www.ojp.usdoj.gov/bjs/homicide/intimates.html/.
5. Elizabeth Zwerlig, "Suit Presses for 'Gender Symmetry' in Shelters," *Women's eNews,* July 23, 2003, accessed at http://www.womensnews.org/.

and increased their overall participation in the public sphere, the theory of marriage characterized as a shared, equal partnership became the norm. The equal partnership theory was defined in 1970 by a National Organization for Women task force as "an equal partnership with shared economic and household responsibility and shared care of the children."

The transition from "separate but equal roles" to "shared but equal roles" is hardly complete, as the previous chapter revealed, and most marital relationships remain asymmetrical. While the majority of state laws now recognize men and women as equal partners in a marriage, reality has not yet caught up with the law. Men and women both struggle to balance the need for two incomes with the problems created by the absence of a full-time family caretaker and household manager. Public policy has not kept pace by providing family support structures, even though the laws regarding marriage, divorce, child custody, and support have become, for the most part, gender neutral. In this case, gender-neutral policy does not disadvantage women's rights specifically but rather disadvantages women *and* men within the family unit.

Although the notion of a marriage contract is largely outdated, the concept of rights and obligations in a legal marriage retains some viability in the law. Originally, marriage contracts detailed the duties and obligations of both parties in a marriage. The husband was responsible for support, and in return the wife owed her husband household, domestic, and companionship services.[13] As we saw in chapter 2, anti-ERA forces objected to a blanket legal equality for women under the Equal Rights Amendment, fearing that husbands would no longer be obligated to provide financial support for their wives and families. Traditionalists then did not care that the presumption of marital support arose from coverture or that husbands and wives were already both liable in most states for joint debt—the war of public opinion is waged on rhetoric and image, not merely on fact. Today most courts obligate spouses to support one another according to circumstances rather than generalized gender roles. Although most marital obligations were unenforceable in court, there were and still are consequences for women stemming from this contractual conception of marriage and the theory of unity.

Until the Equal Credit Opportunity Act was passed in 1974 (and since amended in 1977 and 1988), women were routinely denied credit because lenders assumed that, married or unmarried, women were not economically responsible individuals. When a woman married, many credit card lenders automatically canceled cards that were in her birth name and reissued joint accounts in her husband's surname. If the marriage dissolved, through divorce or death, women did not qualify for credit since their credit history was based on their husband's. Women were often required to have a male (husband, father, brother) cosign loan agreements. When applying for a mortgage or joint credit with her husband, a wife was required to provide information about her birth control practices and her intentions to bear children. Only half the wife's salary was included in calculating assets to determine the size of a mortgage a couple could afford, based on the assumption by lenders that women were not autonomous economic entities. The Equal Credit Opportunity Act, as amended, requires lenders to base their credit decisions solely on an individual's ability to repay the debt, rather than on sex, race, national origin, or age. Further amendments in 1988 opened the door to commercial lines of credit for women entrepreneurs.

Coverture and the theory of unity rendered the husband and wife one person in the eyes of the law. As such, husbands and wives could not sue each other in civil court nor be compelled to testify against each other in criminal court. Over time, the private nature of family and marriage reinforced interspousal immunity, even though other legal changes granted women independent public standing, including the ability to make contracts. Courts did not want to settle disagreements between a husband and wife. In this sense, interspousal immunity has complicated a battered woman's ability to bring civil suits against her husband. Domestic violence has been ignored until recently because of the private nature of marriage. Because of the concept of "conjugal rights" inherent in the marriage contract, a wife could not charge her husband with rape. The "marital exemption" to state rape laws has only been addressed within the last decade.

Violence within a marriage raises questions of justice. Philosopher Susan Moller Okin argues that marriage and the family as currently practiced in the United States are unjust institutions.[14] While she acknowledges that talking about "justice" is difficult in such an intimate and private setting, justice nonetheless should govern marital unions and the families that result. Okin believes that the roots of injustice can be found in the vulnerabilities created by traditional expectations of women, both in paid labor and in the family. She argues that the "division of labor within marriage (except in rare cases) makes wives far more likely than husbands to be exploited both with the marital relationship and in the world of work outside the home." Traditional gender role expectations developed in childhood have led both men and women to anticipate a certain division of labor within a family, based on the "husband as provider, wife as full-time caregiver" model, which in most cases does not mirror reality. Since the majority of women (including mothers of small children) are in the paid workforce, they end up doing a disproportionate share of the labor at home and outside the home (since they work longer hours for less pay). They are disadvantaged in the workplace because the professions or occupations that provide the flexibility needed to raise children are often in traditionally female occupations, which pay less. Even if that isn't the case, women find themselves in professional settings that assume a full-time "wife" at home and do not support combining work and family in any sort of equitable manner. At home, they must deal with the unequal distribution of labor within the family. Even as wage earners, women assume the majority of child-care and household chores—the unpaid work of a family. In most cases, Okin argues, this imbalance of power, based on the traditions of gender, is a nondecision—assumed rather than decided.[15] The lack of a consensus on the norms and expectations of marriage makes avoiding vulnerabilities more difficult. Reality no longer reflects the expectations that born of traditional gender roles. Since what a family should be differs from what many families experience, we should strive to create diverse expectations that allow all types of families to flourish and do not make one sex vulnerable to power differentials that result from an asymmetrical division of labor.

THE LEGACY OF PATRIARCHY

American culture is devoid of public rites that symbolize the passage from childhood to adulthood, except for marriage. It is no surprise then that a lot is invested in the marriage ritual and ceremony. Young girls are socialized early to anticipate and plan for their wedding, a cost traditionally the responsibility of the father of the bride. The ceremony itself is a mix of civil and religious symbolism. White, the traditional color of a woman's gown, symbolizes purity, and the veil worn by many brides is a holdover from the days when the wedding was the first time a bride and groom met. The ring exchange originally symbolized the exchange of property that was negotiated in a marriage contract. Weddings are usually public celebrations where friends and relatives join in recognizing the new union by contributing money and gifts for the couple's joint household. Although weddings now come in all varieties—from very traditional to religious to purely civil ceremonies—the symbolism is an important aspect of joining two individuals—usually a man and a woman—in legal marriage. The symbols also reproduce the patriarchal culture that has oppressed women within marriage for centuries, although most brides and grooms would not recognize them as such today.

Names

Most people incorrectly assume that women are legally required to take their husband's surname. This habit, however, is a result of common law or tradition rather than a requirement by statute. A holdover from the days of unity in marriage, a woman's adoption of her husband's name signals a new identity in marriage for women, but not for men. It also adds a "social marker" to women's identities that men do not share. Women are known as Miss, Ms., or Mrs. Each carries social information about marital status or, with "Ms.," a refusal to be traditionally labeled. Men, regardless of age or marital status, are simply addressed as "Mr." Customarily (and in a few states, legally), children produced in a marriage are registered with the state under the husband's last name. The use of patronymics (father's names) was important in establishing the continuity of lineage and property rights. Some states, notably Kentucky and Alabama, have required that married women use their husband's name on such state documents as driver's licenses and tax returns. This sex-based requirement, which is for women only, was upheld by the U.S. Supreme Court in 1971.[16] Only about 5 percent of high school–educated women, 15 percent of women with college degrees, and about 20 percent of women with postgraduate degrees used a surname other than their husband's in 1990.[17] A 2004 study by Claudia Goldin and Maria Shim found that just under 20 percent of women kept their names in 2000, based on an analysis of wedding announcements in the *New York Times* and Massachusetts birth records. In reviewing Harvard alumni surveys, the researchers found that, ten years after graduation, 44 percent of the 1980 graduates who had married kept their name, while just 32 percent of the 1990 graduates kept their name.[18] In a separate study published in 2006, Michele Hoffnung found that 71 percent of the brides announced in the *New York Times* between 1982 and 2002 chose to adopt their husbands name, where as 29 percent chose to keep their birth name or to hyphenate. In a second study, Hoffnung has been following 50 women (half white and half women of color), drawn from five New England colleges and universities, since 1992. Among these women, 46 percent kept their birth name or hyphenated (labeled a nontraditional choice). Sixty-one percent of the women of color chose a nontraditional name, compared with 39 percent of white women. Women in each of the studies who chose to keep their birth name or to hyphenate their name, were better educated and married later than those who adopted their husband's name. In the longitudinal study of college graduates, about half of those with a nontraditional name had earned at least one graduate degree and they held more feminist attitudes. There was no difference between naming groups in marital role value or commitment to marriage.[19]

The public is not entirely comfortable with women who use their birth name, even when it is used in conjunction with their husband's surname. A 1993 *Wall Street Journal*–NBC poll found that while 74 percent viewed First Lady Hillary Rodham Clinton as a positive role model, only 6 percent favored her using Rodham in her name, and 62 percent were opposed to it. Another study conducted that same year found that 25 percent of southerners and 20 percent of people not from the South believed that the growing trend of women using their birth names "was a change for the worse."[20] The Lucy Stone League is an organization dedicated to equal rights for "women and men to retain, modify, or create their names, because a person's name is fundamental to her/his experience." The organization also advocates equality of patrilineal/matrilineal name distribution for children. Their primary mission is to educate women and men on the origins of name change at marriage for women and provide them with the knowledge to make individual choices.[21]

Domicile Laws

Domicile laws establish an individual's rights within a defined territory (most often a state) for the purposes of benefits and obligations. Since most laws regarding the family are state based, establishing permanent residency is significant. In a holdover from the days of unity in marriage, many states follow the common law that assumes that a husband's residence constitutes the primary residence of a family. In the days when men provided sole financial support for the family, giving them precedence in the choice of domicile may have made sense. As women enter the workforce on a more equal basis, where a family sets up residence is now subject to negotiation. A 1985 survey showed that 72 percent of women and 62 percent of men believed that a woman *should* quit her job and move to another city if her husband got a job there, even if she had a good job in the city where they were currently living. Only 10 percent of women and 19 percent of men said that the husband should turn down the job.[22] The rise of commuter marriages, initially necessitated by two professional careers and now most often borne of financial necessity, has caused domicile laws to begin to change. Demographic experts define commuter marriages as couples who spend at least three nights apart each week for a minimum of three months. The number of commuter marriages has increased in recent years as a result of the declining economy and rising unemployment. According to the 2006 U.S. Census Bureau, 3.2 million married Americans (including military families) live in different homes, a 26 percent increase between 1999 and 2006.

Property Rights

As we said earlier, coverture invested property rights entirely in the husband. The married women's property acts enacted in the1800s permitted women to acquire and control property. In response, unity gave way to "separate property" rights for men and women. In reality, however, because women were still relegated to the home and unpaid labor in the home by separate spheres ideology and tradition, laws that allowed them to acquire property, enter into contracts, or engage in business were initially limited. Even as women entered the paid labor force, their wages usually contributed substantially less to their family's income than their husband's did. By 1993, forty-one states had laws in which "property follows title." In common-law property states, husbands and wives are entitled individually to control property—that is, whoever holds the title, owns the property. In many cases, however, because full-time homemakers had no visible source of income, the courts ruled that jointly acquired property or assets (including a joint bank account) were the husband's property. In common-law property states, the courts also paid close attention to who paid the bills in two-income families. Women sometimes found themselves without assets if they assumed responsibility for such consumables as food and the husband paid the mortgage and purchased durable goods, such as the family automobile. In community property states, both the husband and wife equally control assets acquired in marriage. Nine states—Arizona, California, Idaho, Louisiana, Nevada, New Mexico, Texas, Washington, and Wisconsin—have some form of community property laws.

Although exceptions have been made for individual inheritance or assets accumulated prior to the marriage, the courts in community property states view a couple as one economic unit. In many cases, courts used to give husbands control over the ongoing management of community property. This has now changed to reflect the theory of marriage as an equal partnership.[23]

DIVORCE

Divorce contributes significantly to poverty rates among women; this stems from the interplay of private and public patriarchy. Within a marriage, women contribute their unpaid labor, and if they work outside the home, their earnings provide less than one-third of the family income in most households. When a marriage ends in divorce, a woman's standard of living falls because her single wage must provide for herself and her children. A ten-year study in California estimated that after divorce women's standard of living declined by 73 percent, while men's rose on average by 42 percent.[24] Men are also more likely to remarry and to do so more quickly than women. One study estimated that the total family income of a divorced woman and her children was less than 50 percent of the family income prior to divorce, but as the custodial parent she needed approximately 80 percent of the total family income before the divorce to maintain the family's standard of living.[25]

Since marriage is a state-sanctioned legal union, only the state can legally dissolve a marriage. Eighteenth-century feminists sought reforms to divorce law as a way of escaping abusive and dangerous marriages at a time when civil law did not recognize divorce. The state exercised its prerogative to encourage marriage even at the expense of women's physical safety and happiness. Prior to 1969 and California's adoption of no-fault divorce laws, most states required the party seeking a divorce to prove legitimate grounds for a separation. These most often included battering, abuse, abandonment, and (except for South Carolina) adultery. Evidence of fault was required even when both parties agreed to divorce. Reforms to state divorce laws began in the late 1960s and generally followed California's lead in adopting no-fault divorce laws. No-fault divorce is now available in all fifty states, although the application and disposition are very different. Irreconcilable differences or separation most often provide the grounds for contemporary divorce. States that recognize separation as grounds may require a couple to live in separate residences for a time (usually six months to two years) before granting a divorce.

In recent years, states have become alarmed at the rising divorce rates (over 50 percent of first marriages now end in divorce). In response, states have taken a renewed interest in legislating policy on marriage and divorce. For the most part, states have not returned to fault-based divorce, although some states have extended the waiting period for divorce or have required couples to get counseling when children are involved. Most states, however, have concentrated on encouraging couples to be more careful before entering into marriage in the first place. Some states now require couples to get "couples counseling" before issuing a marriage license. In 1997, Louisiana went a step farther and created voluntary "covenant marriages." Couples who choose a "covenant marriage" agree to seek counseling if problems develop in their marriage and will be allowed to seek a divorce only under certain severe circumstances (sexual abuse, adultery, abandonment) or after a two-year separation, very similar to the grounds of fault-based divorce. Arizona and Arkansas have since adopted similar legislation, and several other state legislatures have policies under consideration. Couples with a "regular marriage" may retroactively petition the state for a covenant marriage by declaring in a written affidavit to the court that "marriage is for life" and by agreeing to abide by the guidelines of a covenant marriage. In February 2005, Arkansas Governor Mike Huckabee and his wife converted their marriage into a covenant marriage during a mass ceremony held on Valentine's Day. Arkansas' marriage rate is nearly double the national average (15.1 per 1,000 population compared to 7.5 per 1,000 nationally), but the states' divorce rate is among the highest in the nation at 6.5 per 1,000 population). Governor Huckabee was a candidate for the 2008 Republican presidential nomination and is considering another run in 2012.

Property, Benefits, and Support After Divorce

While real property assets are fairly easy to divide and most states require an equitable division of real property, benefits awarded by a third party (health insurance, pension rights, stock options) or an increase in earning capacity derived from a professional degree are more difficult to divide. Since community property laws dominate most states, any assets or property acquired during marriage are subject to equitable division by the court. More than half of the states consider pensions marital property and subject to division. Federal law covers access to Social Security or military pension benefits after divorce as long as the couple has been married for ten years or more. An employer is required to continue health insurance coverage for a period of one year. The most difficult concept for the states to grasp, however, involves "human capital." In the 1970s and 1980s, the popular press was full of stories about professionally successful husbands who were divorcing their wives after several decades of marriage in favor of a younger woman, even though the first wife had often supported the family financially during her husband's years in law school or medical school. In almost all cases, the courts determined that earning capacity and educational degrees cannot be divided. However, several courts have used a man's earning capacity and a woman's contribution to developing his earning capacity to determine the amount of alimony payments. Others have required a husband to reimburse his wife for the cost of his education.

Alimony is yet another holdover from the theory of unity. A husband's obligation for financial support extended past the marriage if the husband sought the divorce or was determined to be at fault. During the marriage reforms of the 1970s, alimony laws were rendered gender neutral, allowing the courts to require support payments to either husband or wife. In *Orr v. Orr* (1979), the U.S. Supreme Court ruled that sex-based alimony laws violated the equal protection clause of the Fourteenth Amendment. The end to fault-based divorce also diminished the presumption that alimony is compensation for harm. It is rare that either spouse is now ordered to make support payments indefinitely. Short-term payments may be ordered to ease the transition from marriage to a single-wage status. Alimony may also be awarded to allow a spouse to receive job training or earn a college degree, or as a one-time financial award. In many cases, the trend toward gender-neutral, no-fault divorce laws has not benefited women, particularly those who pursued a traditional gender role within their marriage. These women suffer a dramatic loss of income and social status when their marriage ends.

Child support is different from alimony. Both parents may be ordered to provide support for their children, regardless of the custody arrangements. Noncustodial parents are much less likely to actually pay court-ordered support (and are more likely to be fathers). Congress has reacted by strengthening enforcement of child-support provisions. In 1975, Congress created the Child Support Enforcement program to collect unpaid child support from noncustodial parents. While billions of dollars have been collected and redistributed, that amount represents a very small proportion of what is actually owed. In 1996, as a part of the welfare reform bill known as the Personal Responsibility and Work Opportunity Reconciliation Act, Congress again strengthened collection provisions by creating state and federal databases to help locate noncustodial parents. Using motor-vehicle, tax, and public-utilities records has allowed authorities to track noncustodial parents across state lines. New penalty provisions revoke motor vehicle licenses, as well as professional and recreational licenses issued by the government, for nonpayment. In fiscal year 2009, the federal government is expected to provide $3.8 billion to the states for child-support enforcement efforts. In fiscal year 2007, nearly $25 billion was collected at a combined state and federal cost of $5.6 billion; more than $4.73 was collected for each $1 spent.[26]

TOWARD A GENUINE FAMILY POLICY IN THE UNITED STATES: WHAT WOULD IT TAKE?

Family policy, largely related to marriage and divorce laws, is administered almost exclusively by the states. This has resulted in an uncoordinated patchwork of laws and policies that are targeted at specific issues or problems. When federal legislation is layered on top of state statutes, the result is often more confusion than support for families. Determining what families need from government is made all the more difficult because of our inability to clearly define "family" or for women to agree on the nature of their role. Public and private employer policies aimed at parents and children necessarily exclude couples who choose not to have children. Does this unlawfully deny child-free couples a social or employment benefit? The debate over "family values" waged in a political context is laden with values regarding which type of family constellation should be rewarded or discouraged. Conservative Christians have entered politics in large numbers during the last decade to influence policy in favor of the "traditional family"—though the definition of the "traditional family," even according to this group, now includes two wage earners, meaning that nobody is home to care for the children or the elderly. The rhetoric of "family values" is designed to exclude single heads of households (whether single by circumstance or choice) and same-sex households. Given this political context, what type of family policy might we expect in the coming years?

Regardless of which political party controls the federal government, families of all types have put pressure on those in office for more help in accommodating the stresses associated with juggling work and family. The Family and Medical Leave Act (1993), discussed in the previous chapter, was the first parental-leave policy enacted in the United States. Most now believe it does not go far enough and should be strengthened. In spite of the fact that most American women are in the paid labor force, we have not taken full account of what that means. "We are operating as if they were still at home much of the time taking care of their families," and "some strong sense remains among Americans that women should be at home much of the time taking care of family life" because of the power of the idea that "women have a natural capacity for care of children and others, and that these natural gifts make it right, not simply convenient, for the woman of the family to provide or oversee its care."[27] Although the right of the mother to leave employment after pregnancy was affirmed internationally in the United Nations' International Labour Office Maternity Protection Convention, adopted in 1952, the United States lagged far behind other nations in even meeting the bare minimum requirement of twelve weeks of maternity leave. Of the 138 UN member nations, the United States was the only country that made this leave optional. In other countries, a mandatory minimum is enforced, and in several the minimum leave is compulsory.[28] Parental leave, entitling both mother and father to spend time with their children, is offered in 36 of 138 member nations. In twenty-five nations, including nine of the fourteen European Union members, parental leave is paid. The most generous parental- or maternity-leave policies offer high levels of compensation to offset a loss of earnings overall. In all cases, job guarantees are built into the policy so that parents are not penalized for taking time off. The barrier to paid leave in the United States is not economic but ideological.[29]

Internationally, support for families takes a variety of forms. Whether any one country has adopted a policy relating to family support depends on a number of factors, including structural economic factors (capitalist versus socialist economy), need created by changing social and economic factors, and the activity of family advocacy groups, employers and business owners, women's organizations, and religious groups. These "policy inputs" influence the "policy output" in each country and help explain why there are differences across national boundaries.[30] Family policy may take the form of cash benefits or assistance (health insurance, education, Social Security, or employment) to boost the family's standard of living; indirect cash transfers in the form of tax credits or deductions for dependent children, family allowances, and means-tested family benefits; employment benefits granted to workers with family responsibilities (maternity and parental leave, child-care leave); direct services to families (on-site child care, after-school programs); housing subsidies for families with children; or legislation that is consistent with the state's population policies (access to contraception, abortion services, infertility treatments, or adoption). The United States has a large number of policies at the state and federal levels that affect families, but the dominance of attitudes that support family autonomy and limited government involvement, as well as the reinforcement of traditional gender ideologies, has limited the coherence and reach of family policy. The issues associated with balancing work and caring for families loom large for individual families, particularly for women within families, but receive very little positive public attention. Mona Harrington, author of *Care and Equality: Inventing a New Family Politics*, argues that a serious politics of family care must "explicitly link economics and the function of caretaking. It must begin with a clear view of the unfair allocation to women of the major costs of caretaking and clear recognition of the critical deficits in the present care system. And then, with the whole picture of these systemic costs and deficits firmly in mind, the liberal community must work on the invention of a new care system."[31] Most important, she says, care must be thought of as a public issue—one of our national social issues. The need for socially supported care in the United States runs across all income levels, not just those at the bottom. Because of the focus on poverty programs as the only means of public family support, the idea of family care as solely a private responsibility goes unchallenged. Implicit then is the assumption that all of the other families are doing fine—that middle- and upper-income families can provide or, more likely, purchase all of the care services they require. The problem is that we have not devised any "equality respecting system to replace the full-time caretaking labor force of women at home."[32]

By comparison to other nations, the United States fares poorly on the Work, Family and Equity Index developed by the Project on Global Working Families to measure governmental performance around the world in meeting the needs of working families.[33] The United States performs well in equitable right-to-work policies, but falls short on supporting families. Out of the 173 countries studied, 169 offer guaranteed leave with income to women in connection with childbirth; 98 of these countries offer 14 or more weeks of paid leave. The United States, Liberia, Papua New Guinea, and Swaziland were the only four countries in the study that did not provide new mothers paid leave. Sixty-six of 173 countries provide fathers with paid paternity leave or guarantee fathers a right to paid parental leave; 31 of these countries offer 14 or more weeks of

TABLE 8.1 International Maternity Leave Benefits, 1998; Selected Countries from Each Region of the World

Country	Length of Leave	Percent of Wages Paid	Provider of Coverage
Congo	15 weeks	100	50% employer; 50% Social Security
Kenya	2 months	100	employer
Morocco	14 weeks	100	Social Security
Nigeria	12 weeks	50	employer
Somalia	14 weeks	50	employer
South Africa	4 months	45–60	unemployment insurance
Argentina	90 days	100	Social Security
Bahamas	13 weeks	100	40% employer; 60% Social Security
Brazil	120 days	100	Social Security
Chile	18 weeks	100	Social Security
Cuba	18 weeks	100	Social Security
Haiti	12 weeks	100 for 6 weeks	employer
Honduras	10 weeks	100 for 84 days	33% employer; 67% Social Security
Mexico	12 weeks	100	Social Security
Venezuela	18 weeks	100	Social Security
Bangladesh	16 weeks	100	employer
Cambodia	90 days	50	employer
China	90 days	100	Social Security
India	12 weeks	100	employer; Social Security
Iran	90 days	66.7 for 16 weeks	Social Security
Iraq	62 days	100	Social Security
Israel	14 weeks	100	Social Security
Saudi Arabia	10 weeks	50 or 100	employer
Australia	18 weeks	Fed. min. wage*	Social Security
Austria	16 weeks	100	Social Security
Canada	up to 50 weeks	55 for 50 weeks	unemployment insurance
Denmark	52 weeks	100 up to a ceiling	Social Security
France	16–26 weeks	100	Social Security
Germany	14 weeks	100	Social Security to a ceiling; employer
Italy	5 months	80	Social Security
Japan	14 weeks	60	Social Security; health insurance
Portugal	120 days or 150 days	100 80	Social Security
Spain	16 weeks	100	Social Security
United Kingdom	39 weeks	90 for first 6 weeks; flat rate for 33 weeks	Social Security
United States	12 weeks	0	

* Proposal pending approval; would take effect in January 2011.
Source: International Labour Organization, 2006, accessed at http://www.ilo.org.

paid leave. At least 107 countries protect working women's right to breast-feed; in at least 73 countries, the breaks required to breast-feed are paid. There is no such right to breast-feed, paid or unpaid, in the United States. A 2008 Catalyst survey of companies found that on a list of six benefits (including paid maternity leave beyond 6 weeks, paid paternity leave, paid family leave, family leave beyond the federal requirement and any ruling state statute, and paid adoption leave), the percentage of companies offering the benefits had fallen from 2007. In each case, no more than a quarter of the companies surveyed offered each benefit, and the decreasing share of companies offering the benefit in 2008 over 2007 ranged from a 17 percent decrease (paid paternity leave) to a 33 percent decrease (paid family leave).[34]

The next section of this chapter explores the link between population and family policy: the issue of fertility. Fertility and issues of population growth or limits even more directly target women and are rarely gender neutral. When policy is crafted to be gender neutral, it rarely benefits women in their pursuit of equality. The physical aspects of pregnancy, childbirth, and lactation render gender-neutral strategies largely useless because they focus first on sex and second on gender. Unlike education, employment, or family support, where socially constructed gender ideologies are most profoundly related to women's disadvantages, fertility issues focus first on sex and secondarily on gender.

CONTROLLING REPRODUCTION

A woman's individual interest in regulating fertility and reproduction is directly connected to issues of private and public subordination. Yet since human reproduction is also social and cultural reproduction, controlling the quality and quantity of reproduction has long interested the state. It is the social aspect of reproduction that gives women these socially constructed gender expectations that are not only related to childbearing but also have to do with child-rearing and motherhood. A state's survival depends on successive generations of children who have been properly guided to mature citizenship. A state's interest in regulating fertility and reproduction, therefore, is also directly related to women's subordination. In the United States, reproductive policy is not as explicitly stated as it is in other nations, yet it is present nonetheless. Such policies are complicated by the dominance of individualism and a liberal approach to policy creation. In most areas of U.S. constitutional law, the interests of the individual outweigh the interests of the state, unless the state can prove a "compelling state interest" that would warrant intruding on individual rights. In the area of reproduction, however, it is less clear whether individual rights reign supreme, most particularly women's individual rights.

The U.S. Supreme Court has extended the individual's right to privacy to some reproductive decisions (birth control, access to abortion in the first trimester), but has not required the states to support these "rights" if an individual cannot afford to purchase them on the private market. Some areas of reproductive policy and decision making do not conform well to a rights-based interpretation. Some people argue that the right *not* to reproduce is every bit as fundamental as the right to reproduce. Christine Overall contends that a woman has no moral obligation to have a child against her will. "Women who do not have access to contraceptive devices and abortion services are, as a result of 'biological destiny,' victims 'of a sort of reproductive slavery.'"[35] Alternatively, Sara Ann Ketcham argues that there is an inherent asymmetry between the right not to reproduce and the right to reproduce that stems from reproduction's inclusion of other people. Therefore, the rights and interests of others (father, child, society) must also be taken into account in protecting an individual's right to reproduce.[36] The first perspective is most directly relevant to contraception and abortion rights. The latter directly concerns the movement to endow the fetus with rights that are equal to those of the woman.

Individual Access to Contraception

The history of reliable contraception in the United States is a relatively short one. It has been only within the last forty years that women have had access to methods of contraception that are safe, reliable, and entirely within their control. The Food and Drug Administration (FDA) approved an oral contraceptive for women ("the pill") in 1960. While condoms and diaphragms were revolutionized in the nineteenth century as a result of changes in rubber manufacturing techniques, the pill represented the first new technology in contraception. The pill was followed by FDA approval of the sponge in 1983. Then came the cervical cap in 1988, and, in 1990, a long-acting, reversible contraceptive implant (known popularly as Norplant and effective for up to five years, although no longer available in the United States). Depo-Provera, an injectable contraceptive that is effective for up to three months, had been widely used in other countries prior to its approval for use in the United States. Additionally, the FDA approved the sale of female condoms in the 1990s. Sterilization remains the most widely chosen form of contraception for women. However, approximately 3 million women at risk for unintended pregnancy are using no form of contraception. Availability and cost, along with side effects and safety concerns, are the most common reasons women offer for not using contraception or using it infrequently.

New types of contraceptives include the vaginal ring (sold as NuvaRing), the patch, and a safer version of the intrauterine device (IUD). All three require a prescription. New contraception methods include Seasonale, an extended-cycle birth control that includes 84 active pills and 7 inactive pills. Lybrel, a second extended-cycle birth control, can be taken continuously without breaks for menstrual bleeding. These methods are not without critics and the most vocal are not from within the medical community. Some feminists argue that this method "medicalizes" normal body functions and that denying women regular menstrual cycles "infantalizes" them and robs young women of "that next stage of maturation."[37] Essure, a nonsurgical form of sterilization was approved by the FDA in 2002. A microdevice is implanted in the fallopian tubes and when body tissue grows into the insert, fertilization is blocked.

The most popular nonprescription contraceptive for women was the sponge until it was removed from the market in 1995 after problems were found in the manufacturing plant. The sponge's safety and effectiveness were never at issue, but the manufacturer (now known as Wyeth) discontinued it rather than upgrade the plant. In a 1995 episode of *Seinfeld*, character Elaine Benes searched pharmacies all over Manhattan for the sponge. Upon finding a case of sponges at a pharmacy, she rationed their use by setting "spongeworthy" standards for her boyfriends. A small pharmaceutical company in New Jersey bought the rights to Today's Sponge and in 2003 began selling it through two Canadian Internet sites. News of the sponge's return created waiting lists on both sites and has prompted women to travel to Canada, where contraceptives are not regulated as a drug, to purchase the device. The sponge is now available in the United States after a lengthy delay.[38]

The Guttmacher Institute estimates that the average American woman who wants two children spends about three decades of her life trying to avoid pregnancy and only a few years either trying to become pregnant or pregnant. Effective contraceptive use for sexually active women across three decades is problematic. By age 45, more than half of U.S. women have had one or more unintended pregnancies.[39] Development and dissemination of contraceptives depends in large part on the public's attitude toward sexuality, current birthrates, and the positive or negative consequences of population growth. Prior to the Civil War, many states permitted abortion until "quickening," but soon after the Civil War's conclusion most states banned abortions. Succumbing to the pressure to reproduce and new restrictive attitudes toward sexuality that were promoted by organized religion, Congress passed the Comstock laws in 1873. These laws were ostensibly designed to control pornography but defined pornography as any information or product distributed for the prevention of conception or for causing unlawful abortion. The statute, in effect, likened contraception to obscenity and made it illegal to distribute information on contraception or contraceptive devices. Various social sectors supported restricting contraceptives, including doctors. In their eyes, contraception violated nature, bred immorality, damaged health, and violated the sanctity of motherhood.[40] Many women, particularly those in the middle and upper classes, viewed contraception as a direct challenge to marital fidelity and their corresponding sphere of authority. Poor and uneducated women were most disadvantaged by unintended pregnancies and were especially vulnerable to public campaigns devoted to suppressing information or medical services. Middle- and upper-class women participated in an informal but extensive network of information, and had access to birth control devices illegally imported from Europe and to relatively safe, but still illegal, abortions.

Birth control advocates such as Margaret Sanger and Emma Goldman worked most directly with poor, working-class women, many of whom were recent immigrants. In addition to stressing that giving birth to too many children or not adequately spacing pregnancies was harmful to women's health, Emma Goldman, a socialist active in the labor movement, was also interested in limiting the influx of child labor, which drove down wages for everyone.[41] Immigrants were the targets of a robust eugenics (selective breeding) movement that thrived by promoting fears of "race suicide" if white, middle-class birthrates declined and poor immigrant populations increased unchecked. These seemingly contradictory interests forged a nascent birth control movement that directly violated the Comstock laws. By 1914, Margaret Sanger, who had been radicalized by her experiences with the left and a year in France, began to publish a monthly called *Woman Rebel*, in which she eventually promoted contraception as a woman's right:

> A woman's body belongs to herself alone. It does not belong to the United States of America or any other government on the face of the earth. Enforced motherhood is the most complete denial of a woman's right to life and liberty. Women cannot be on an equal footing with men until they have full and complete control over their reproductive function.[42]

Many issues of the *Woman Rebel* were confiscated by the post office under the Comstock laws. While the newsletter did not include information on contraceptive techniques, it did publish letters from desperate readers begging for information. In response, Sanger published a brochure entitled *Family Limitation: A Nurse's Advice to Women*. Between 1914 and 1917, more than 160,000 copies were distributed, although Sanger fled to England during some of that time to avoid further prosecution under the obscenity laws. In 1916, Sanger opened the first birth control clinic in the United States in Brooklyn, New York.

A court decision in 1918 allowed physicians to disseminate "advice to a married person to cure or prevent disease"—a clear reference to venereal disease and a cover for distributing contraception to married women. Medicalizing the birth control issue allowed Sanger to solicit support and cooperation from physicians, and in 1921 she formed the American Birth Control League (ABCL). By the 1940s, the ABCL gave way to the Planned Parenthood Federation of America in recognition of contraception's transformation into a "family planning" tool. Sanger's legacy extended into the 1960s, when Planned Parenthood challenged a Connecticut law that prohibited the sale, advertisement, or manufacture of birth control devices. The Connecticut law also prohibited married couples from using contraception. In 1965, the U.S. Supreme Court delivered its decision in *Griswold v. Connecticut*, declaring that Connecticut's law was an unconstitutional violation of the right to privacy of married persons. The Court extended the fundamental right of procreative choice and privacy to unmarried persons with the ruling in *Eisenstadt v. Baird* (1972). The fundamental right to privacy established in the *Griswold* and *Eisenstadt* rulings was extended to cover a woman's right to abortion services in 1973 (*Roe v. Wade*).

Individual Access to Abortion Services

The issue of abortion, much more so than contraception, has divided families, political parties, and the nation. Abortion "rights" were most clearly established in the Supreme Court ruling in *Roe v. Wade* (1973), although by the time *Roe* was decided more than thirteen states had reformed and liberalized their abortion laws. More than likely, state-level reforms would have continued had the Court not acted, but slowly and in a patchwork fashion. Almost everyone agreed that abortion reforms were necessary to protect women from physical injury and death at the hands of illegal abortionists. Just because abortion was illegal did not prevent it from occurring, and the dire consequences of botched abortions cut across all races and socioeconomic groups.

Justice Harry Blackmun, writing for the seven-vote majority in *Roe v. Wade*, used the trimesters of pregnancy as benchmarks to balance a woman's privacy interests with the state's increasingly legitimate interests in protecting a fetus as it approached viability outside the womb. In the first trimester, a woman's right to make private choices is protected from state interference (although later decisions have allowed the state to regulate the conditions under which a woman exercises her "right"). During the second (fourth through sixth month) and third (seventh month through birth) trimesters, the state gains grounds to regulate abortions "in ways that are reasonably related to maternal health" or to restrict its use entirely by the third trimester, except when necessary to protect the life or health of the mother. While the decision nationalized women's rights to a legal abortion within the first three months of a pregnancy, it also muddied other issues surrounding reproductive rights by rooting the decision in privacy doctrine. In *Harris v. McRae* (1980), the Court held that the right to privacy does not compel states to pay for poor women's abortions. The separation of public and private, enunciated in *Roe* and *Harris*, was used in 1989 (*Webster v. Reproductive Health Services*) to allow states to prohibit abortions from being performed in public facilities or by public employees. The public-private distinction was used again in 1996 to uphold the ban on the furnishing of abortion information and counseling to poor women by federally funded family-planning agencies (*Rust v. Sullivan*).

In other cases, the Court has allowed states greater leeway in establishing limits on a woman's right to abortion services as long as the regulations do not create an "undue burden" on the woman seeking an abortion. A state regulation is defined as an undue burden "if its purpose or effect is to place a substantial obstacle in the path of a woman seeking an abortion before the fetus attains viability."[43] In 1992, *Planned Parenthood of Southeastern Pennsylvania v. Casey* upheld most of Pennsylvania's regulations, including an "informed consent" provision, a twenty-four-hour waiting period, and parental consent for women who were minors. The only provision the Court declared an "undue burden" was the requirement that women notify their husbands prior to having an abortion. Thirty-one states enforce parental consent or notification laws for minors seeking an abortion. Forty-five percent of minors who have had abortions told their parents, and 61 percent underwent the procedure with at least one parent's knowledge.[44]

Two decisions delivered at the conclusion of the 1999–2000 term reversed the Court's trend in recognizing more active regulatory action by the states. In *Hill v. Colorado* the Court was asked to consider the constitutionality of a statutory buffer zone (in this case eight feet) around abortion clinics and around individuals who were entering the clinics. Antiabortion protesters set up human barricades around abortion clinics and harassed women on their way in and out of the clinics, urging them not to "kill their baby." In this case, the free speech interests of the protesters were weighed against the woman's right to abortion services. The six-to-three majority in *Hill* upheld Colorado's "zone of separation" statute, arguing that the law was a reasonable restriction on the First Amendment right of so-called sidewalk counselors to protest, educate, or counsel outside a health-care facility. While the Court recognized that the right to free speech includes the right to try to persuade others to change their views, "The First Amendment does not demand that patients at a medical facility undertake Herculean efforts to escape the cacophony of political protests."[45] The second case, *Stenberg v. Carhart*, dealt with the issue of late-term abortions and a state's ability to prohibit all late-term abortions (known as "partial birth" abortions by opponents). This case was more closely decided by the Court in a five-to-four decision and turned on the question of a woman's health. Justice Stephen Breyer, writing for the majority, said "a risk to a woman's health is the same whether it happens to arise from regulating a particular method of abortion, or from barring abortion entirely." This decision supports a doctor's determination of what is in the best interests of the woman's health over the state's outright ban of certain abortion procedures. However, this decision also demonstrates how vulnerable *Roe v. Wade* may be in the future. Justice Clarence Thomas wrote a dissenting opinion in which he detailed his fervent opposition to *Roe v. Wade*. During Thomas's confirmation hearings, he claimed that he had no opinion on abortion or the *Roe v. Wade* decision. As the youngest member of the Court (fifty-two years old at the time), he has clearly found his voice and seems poised to exert influence on this issue in the future.

Access to Abortion Clinics and Information on Women's Health Care

Although the first reported cases of violence at an abortion clinic occurred in 1977 (arson in St. Paul, Minnesota), clinics and providers have been regular targets of violence since the 1980s. More than 80 percent of all abortion providers have been picketed or seriously harassed. Doctors and other workers are subject to death threats, and clinics have experienced chemical attacks (for example, butyric acid), arson, bomb threats, invasions, and blockades. In the late 1980s, Randall Terry founded an organization called Operation Rescue and initiated a strategy of civil disobedience by blockading clinic entrances, engaging in "sidewalk counseling" in an effort to dissuade women from seeking abortions, and publicizing the faces of those entering clinics. Operation Rescue personnel displayed graphic photographs of aborted fetuses and chanted "stop the killing" as women tried to enter health clinics. Pro-choice forces countered with clinic escorts and human shields to protect women from harassment. There were thousands of arrests as clinics increasingly became political battlefields.

In the 1990s, antiabortion activists turned to intimidation and harassment of individual doctors and their families by picketing their homes, following them, and circulating "Wanted" posters. To date, over 200 clinics have been bombed or experienced serious vandalism. Dr. David Gunn was the first abortion provider to be murdered, in 1993, and since then there have been six murders and numerous attempted murders of clinic staff and physicians. The most recent killing was of Dr. George Tiller, described as the country's most prominent provider of late-term abortions. Dr. Tiller was killed inside his church in Wichita, Kansas, on Sunday, May 31, 2009. A suspect was arrested within hours. Although most antiabortion groups condemned the killing, Randall Terry called Tiller "a mass murderer who 'reaped what he sowed.'"[46] Tiller was also a frequent target of Fox News's Bill O'Reilly who referred to him as "Tiller the Baby Killer" and alleged he was guilty of "Nazi stuff." Tiller had been shot once before in 1993 and suffered injuries to both arms. His clinic, Women's Healthcare Services, had been bombed, blockaded, fired on, and vandalized. In the summer of 1991, more than 2,000 arrests took place outside of the clinic. One health-care provider describes the impact of the violence: "The fear of violence has become part of the lives of every abortion provider in the country. As doctors, we are being warned not to open big envelopes with no return addresses in case a mail bomb is enclosed. I know colleagues who have had their homes picketed and their children threatened. Some wear bulletproof vests and have remote starters for their cars. Even going to work and facing the disapproving looks from co-workers—isolation and marginalization from colleagues is part of it."[47] Despite immediate assurances to the contrary, Dr. Tiller's family announced in early June that the Wichita clinic will remain closed.

While abortion services may be legal within the first trimester, they are difficult to obtain for many women. In the United States, 87 percent of all counties have no abortion services, and 97 percent of rural counties have no abortion providers. Mississippi, for example, with a population of three million people has one abortion clinic in the state. Nine out of every ten abortion providers are located in major metropolitan areas. Medicaid funding has restricted abortions for low-income women for nearly thirty years, and eleven states now restrict abortion coverage in insurance plans for public employees. On November 7, 2009, the House of Representatives went a step further in restricting legal abortion by approving an amendment to the Affordable Health Care for America Act that would bar any insurance plan that is purchased with government subsidies from covering abortions except in cases of life threatening situations. Furthermore, individuals could not purchase with their own dollars private insurance that covers abortion if they receive a government subsidy to make health coverage affordable. Although this is not the final health care reform bill since the Senate has yet to act and the two chambers will have to reconcile any differences between the versions, the viability of the Stupak amendment (named for its primary sponsor, Representative Bart Stupak, a Democrat from Michigan) represents yet another potential restriction on legal abortion.[48]

Although abortion is the most common ob-gyn surgical procedure, almost half of graduating ob-gyn residents have never performed a first-trimester abortion—in part because only 5 percent of U.S. ob-gyn residency programs train future doctors to perform first-trimester abortions. A group of pro-choice medical students founded Medical Students for Choice in 1993 following the shooting death of Dr. David Gunn, a Florida abortion provider. The organization is a network of more than 10,000 medical students and abortion providers across the United States and Canada. Although the membership was "shocked" by Dr. Tiller's murder, the organization vowed that the killing has only strengthened its resolve to ensure that all women have a full spectrum of reproductive options. "Giving up would be a fate worse than death," said Miranda Balkin, a fourth-year medical student and board president of Medical Students for Choice. "My life is one life, but there are thousands of women who need reproductive choice."[49]

Forty-four states have minor consent laws that require women less than eighteen years of age to obtain written consent from a parent or legal guardian prior to an abortion. Thirty-four states enforce the provision, including Utah, where there is no judicial bypass option allowing women to seek a court order in lieu of permission from their parents.[50] Thirty one states require that a woman receive counseling prior to a legal abortion in the first trimester; six states require that the session be in person. Several states provide medically suspect information designed to be persuasive. For example, Mississippi requires that patients be told that "abortion may increase the risk of breast cancer" despite the fact that the claim is not supported by any medical science. In 1994, Congress passed the Freedom of Access to Clinic Entrances Act (FACE). FACE makes it a federal crime to use force, the threat of force, or physical obstruction to interfere with or intimidate clinic workers or women seeking abortion services. FACE does not prohibit peaceful protests that include prayer, singing hymns, carrying signs, or distributing antiabortion materials outside of clinics. The First Amendment protects these activities. However, if speech turns threatening, it is prohibited. For example, in 1996 a woman was convicted of a FACE violation for yelling through a megaphone, "Robert, remember Dr. Gunn. . . . This could happen to you."[51] Initial reports suggest that the law has been effective in maintaining access to women's clinics, but according to a recent report issued by the National Abortion Federation, the nations 2,000 abortion providers reported "14 arsons, 78 death threats, 66 incidents of assault and battery, 117 anthrax threats, 128 bomb threats,

109 incidents of stalking, 541 acts of vandalism, one bombing, and one attempted murder" during the George W. Bush administration.[52] Following Dr. Tiller's murder, Attorney General Eric Holder deployed federal marshals to provide additional protection to abortion providers and women's health clinics.

On January 22, 2001, President Bush's first day in office and the twenty-eighth anniversary of *Roe v. Wade*, the president reinstated the global gag rule (known also as the "Mexico City Policy") first applied during the Reagan administration, but repealed by President Clinton. The policy restricts foreign nongovernmental organizations (NGOs) that receive U.S. family planning funds from using their own, non-U.S. funds to provide legal abortion services, lobby their own governments for abortion law reform, or even provide accurate medical counseling or referrals regarding abortion. Organizations receiving U.S. funding are also prohibited from working to liberalize abortion laws in their own country. In a report titled "Access Denied: The Impact of the Global Gag Rule in Ethiopia," researchers document the impact the denial of funds has on family planning and HIV/AIDS prevention. Planned Parenthood of Zambia lost 24 percent of its funding as a result of the rule. In Kenya, for example, five family planning clinics have been forced to close.[53] Upon taking office, President Barack Obama issued an executive order on January 23, 2009, that repealed the global gag rule.

RU-486 Gains Approval

On September 28, 2000, the FDA approved mifepristone, also known as RU-486, to terminate early pregnancies (defined as forty-nine days or less). RU-486 was developed in 1980 and has been used in Europe and China by more than 620,000 women since it came on the market in 1988. The drug is administered in pill form in doses spaced two days apart. Women are required to return to their doctor fourteen days later to make sure that the pregnancy has been terminated. Mifepristone causes an abortion by blocking the action of progesterone, a hormone essential for sustaining pregnancy. The drug prevents an embryo from attaching to the uterine wall during the earliest stages of gestation. At this point in a pregnancy, an embryo is no larger than a grain of rice. This treatment regimen is effective in about 95 percent of all cases. Under the terms of FDA approval, mifepristone can be distributed by physicians who must also be able to provide surgical intervention in cases of incomplete abortion or severe bleeding (or they must have made plans in advance to have others provide such care). Side effects from RU-486 include cramping (sometimes severe) and bleeding over a period of nine to sixteen days. The advantages of mifepristone are that surgical complications are avoided and that it can be administered much earlier in a pregnancy than a surgical abortion, which is generally not performed until the sixth or seventh week of pregnancy. One disadvantage is that the process may take several days, rather than one visit to a clinic or hospital.

Opponents of RU-486 in the United States have cited the dangers to women using the drug. As Republican congressman J. C. Watts remarked, "Do-it-yourself abortion has no place in civilized society." Columnist Anna Quindlen observed that RU-486 is an exercise in self-determination for the woman who chooses to use it. "She is in charge of the decision, the mechanism and the process, not a dupe and not a victim; the choice is quite literally in her hands."[54] After twenty years, women in the United States now have access to a non-surgical abortion alternative. Considering the diminishing access to surgical abortions in the United States (over 87 percent of U.S. counties do not have abortion providers), this drug marks a major advance in a woman's right to choose. Medication abortions accounted for about 13 percent of all abortions performed in 2005 and 22 percent of all eligible abortions (those performed before 9 weeks). Women in 35 countries have access to mifespristone and it has been used by over 21 million women worldwide. In the first five years following FDA approval, there were four deaths attributed to septic shock arising from a medication abortion using mifespristone. The maternal death rate due to pregnancy is approximately 350 deaths per year. Medication abortion, which provides women with an additional option early in pregnancy is credited with a trend toward earlier termination of an unintended pregnancy. Fifty-seven percent of all known abortion providers offered medication abortion services in 2008, compared to only 33 percent in 2001.[55]

Despite the success and safety record of medication abortions, opponents renewed their efforts to have mifepristone removed from the market, arguing that the FDA acted hastily in its approval of the drug and ignored its safety concerns. In November 2003, two members of the House of Representatives introduced "Holly's Law," named for Holly Peterson, an eighteen-year-old California woman who died of a severe infection one week after taking mifepristone. Following the November 2004 election, the legislation was reintroduced and supporters vowed to renew their efforts to gain FDA suspension. The FDA has already required mifepristone's label to be changed to acknowledge that there are risks associated with any abortion and physicians prescribing the drug to instruct patients to contact them if they experience any excessive bleeding or bacterial infection. This is known as a "black box" warning and is the strongest warning the FDA requires. The drug remains available in the United States.[56]

The Demographics of Abortion

Today, as in earlier eras, whether legal or illegal, abortion in practice is not limited to a particular type of woman. Nearly half of all pregnancies in the United States are unintended and about 40 percent of these end in abortion. On the basis of current abortion rates, slightly more than one in three American women will have had an abortion by the time they reach forty-five years of age. Overall, the abortion rate in the United States is falling; in 2005 the rate was 19.4 abortions per 1,000 women aged 15–44, down from a peak of 29.3 in 1981.[57] Ninety percent of all abortions performed in the U.S. occur in the first trimester of pregnancy; 60 percent occur within the first eight weeks and 30 percent within the first six weeks. Each year, two out of every one hundred women from fifteen to forty-four years old have an abortion; 58 percent of them are in their 20s; 61 percent have one or more children; and 57 percent are economically disadvantaged. Fifty-four percent of women who had abortions were using contraception during the month they got pregnant. Nine in ten women at risk of an unintended pregnancy are using a contraceptive method.

Analysis of data on abortions between 1974 and 2004 identified several trends. Abortions declined overall, particularly among white women and teenagers, but increased among African American and Hispanic women, as well as those over 30 years of age. For example, the proportion of abortions obtained by women younger than 18 fell from 15 percent of all abortions in 1974 to 6 percent in 2004, while the proportion of abortions obtained by women in their twenties increased from 50 to 57 percent, and the share of abortions for women aged 30 and older rose from 18 percent to 27 percent. Thirty-four percent of all abortions in 2004 were performed for white women, 22 percent for Hispanic women, and 37 percent for black women. Put slightly differently, 5 percent of black women had an abortion in 2004, compared to 3 percent of Hispanic women and 1 percent of white women. The other substantial increase in abortion rates between 1974 and 2004 took place among women who already had at least one child, "reflecting the trend of women who cannot afford to have another child turning to abortion."[58] The inability to afford a child is indeed the most prevalent reason for seeking an abortion, given by 74 percent of women in a recent survey.[59] Catholic women are 29 percent more likely than Protestant women to seek an abortion, although their overall rates of abortion are comparable to the national abortion rate. Two-thirds of all abortions are performed on never-married women. About 13,000 abortions are performed every year following rape or incest. Of the 42 million abortions performed each year worldwide, more than 40 percent are obtained illegally.[60]

Worldwide, an estimated five million women are hospitalized each year for treatment of abortion-related complications, such as hemorrhage and sepsis. Complications due to unsafe abortion procedures account for an estimated 13 percent of maternal deaths (or 67,000) each year. In areas of the world where abortion is illegal or inaccessible, a variety of unsafe abortion methods are used by women in attempting to terminate an unintended pregnancy (e.g., drinking turpentine or bleach; placing foreign bodies, such as a stick, coat hanger, or chicken bone into the uterus; jumping from the top of stairs or a roof).[61] Compared to the abortion rates of other nations, the U.S. abortion rate is relatively high among developed nations at 19.4 per 1,000 women of childbearing age. While some opponents of abortion lay the blame on what they view as extremely "permissive" abortion policy, research conducted by the Alan Guttmacher Institute (AGI) and released in the report *Sharing Responsibility: Women, Society and Abortion Worldwide* attributes the high U.S.

Global Women's Health and Reproductive Care

Currently, 61 percent of the world's people live in countries where induced abortion is permitted either conditionally or without restriction. Twenty-six percent of people live in countries where abortion is generally prohibited. According to the World Health Organization, over 1,600 women die every day from causes related to pregnancy and childbirth. Unsafe abortions are estimated to account for at least 13 percent of global maternal mortality and a host of long-term maternal health problems. Incidence-of-abortion data are very difficult to collect. Many countries refuse to report such statistics, thus there is missing data in the table below.

World Economic Forum Health and Well-Being Indicator[1]		Restrictions to Abortion Access (2008)[2]	Incidence of Abortion (2003)[3]	Ratio of Abortion to 100 Live Births (2003)[4]
TOP TEN				
Sweden	1	18 weeks	20	34
Denmark	2	PA	15	24
Japan	3	SE, SA	13	28
Finland	4	SE, R, FI	11	19
Spain	5	WMH, R, FI	8	18
Iceland	6	WMH, R, I, FI	N/A	N/A
Switzerland	7	None	7	15
Netherlands	8	None	9	14
Norway	9	PA	15	25
Germany	10	14-weeks	8	16
United States	**42**	**12 weeks, FS**	**21**	**31**

abortion rate to a high unintended pregnancy rate. Citing developed countries in Western Europe with substantially lower abortion rates and more permissive policies (including full funding of the procedure under national health programs in many cases), AGI concludes that contraceptive availability and use accounts for much of the difference.[62] The Netherlands is consistently classified

BOTTOM TEN

Egypt	49	Prohibited	N/A	N/A
Turkey	50	8-weeks, SA, PA	12	10
Mexico	51	FS, R, FI, WPH	N/A	N/A
Colombia	52	WMH, WL, R, I, FI	N/A	N/A
Brazil	53	WL, R	N/A	N/A
Argentina	54	WPH, WL, R	N/A	N/A
Bulgaria	55	None	22	52
Uruguay	56	WPH, WL, R	N/A	N/A
Russia	57	None	45	104
Venezuela	58	WL	N/A	N/A

KEY TO ACCESS TO ABORTION ACCESS

FI allowed in case of fetal impairment

FS federal system, access to abortion varies by state

I allowed in case of incest

PA parental authorization or notification required

R allowed in case of rape

SA spousal authorization required

SE allowed on socioeconomic grounds

WL allowed in case of danger to a woman's life

WMH allowed in case of danger to a woman's mental health

WPH allowed in case of danger to a woman's physical health

1. Indicator is based on the adolescent fertility rate and the percentage of births attended by skilled health staff, adjusted by the number of physicians; maternal mortality ratio per 100,000 live births; and effectiveness of government efforts to reduce poverty and inequality. Source: Augusto Lopez-Claros and Saadie Zahidi, *Women's Empowerment: Measuring the Global Gender Gap* (Switzerland: World Economic Forum, 2005), accessed at http://www.weforum.org/pdf/Global_Competitiveness_Reports/Reports/gender_gap.pdf.
2. Center for Reproductive Rights, "The World's Abortion Laws," fact sheet, accessed at http://www.reproductiverights.org.
3. Gilda Sedgh, et al., "Legal Abortion Worldwide: Incidence and Recent Trends," *International Family Planning Perspectives* 33, no. 3 (September 2007): 106–116; incidence of abortion is measured as the number of abortions per year by women 15–44 years of age, per 1,000 population.
4. Ibid., ratio of abortion to live births is measured as the number of abortions per 100 live births.

among countries with the least restrictive abortion policies and ranks among countries with the lowest abortion rates per 1,000 women in the world.

In any given year, 85 of 100 sexually active women who do not use contraception will become pregnant, while only one in eight women who use an oral contraceptive (the most commonly used reversible method) will become pregnant. One of the major barriers to contraceptive use in the United States is cost. Cost for supplies alone can be approximately $15–30 a month for oral contraceptives, $400–800 for Implanon, the latest insert method that lasts up to three years, and $175–$500 for an IUD insertion that can last for up to 12 years.[63] Most women rely on employer-based private health insurance to pay for their health care, although most private plans do not cover the entire cost of contraception and many do not cover any of the cost. This more than likely accounts for women paying 68 percent more in out-of-pocket health expenses than men do. A nationwide poll found that 78 percent of privately insured adults would support contraceptive coverage even if it increased their costs by $5 a month (fourteen times the amount estimated for the additional coverage). Public funding is restricted to those who qualify for Medicaid or Title X coverage for care in publicly funded clinics. Public expenditures for family planning services totaled $1.85 billion in fiscal year 2006; Medicaid accounted for 71 percent of total expenditures, state appropriations for 13 percent, and Title X for 12 percent. In 2006, subsidized family planning services were provided at over 8,000 family planning centers; 33 percent were health department clinics, 27 percent were community or migrant health centers, 20 percent were other clinics, and 11 percent were Planned Parenthood centers. These services helped women avoid an estimated 1.94 million unintended pregnancies in 2006. AGI estimates that nationally, every $1.00 invested in helping women avoid unintended pregnancies saved $4.02 in Medicaid expenditures that otherwise would have been needed.[64]

On December 13, 2000, the Equal Employment Opportunity Commission (EEOC) ruled that employers discriminate against women when they offer insurance coverage for preventive health care, such as drugs to lower blood pressure, but exclude prescription contraceptives.[65] Although the ruling applies only to the two women whose complaints prompted the EEOC's ruling, the decision provides guidance to employers and the courts on interpretation of the Pregnancy Discrimination Act, which forbids workplace discrimination against women because of pregnancy, childbirth, or related conditions. "Contraception is a means to prevent, and control the timing of, the medical condition of pregnancy," the decision read. "In evaluating whether respondents have provided equal insurance coverage for prescription contraceptives, therefore, the Commission looks to respondents' coverage of other prescription drugs and devices, or other types of services, that are used to prevent the occurrence of other types of medical conditions."[66] The Equity in Prescription Insurance and Contraceptive Coverage Act has been stalled in Congress since 1997 without any significant action, but in the meantime several states have adopted new laws. Twenty-seven states require insurers that cover prescription drugs in general to provide coverage of the full range of FDA-approved contraceptive drugs and devices; 18 of these states specifically require coverage of related outpatient services. Twenty states allow certain employers and insurers to refuse to comply with the mandate, usually on the basis of religious objections.

Although an FDA advisory committee voted 23–4 to recommend approval of over-the-counter sale of emergency contraceptives (sold as Plan B), the FDA denied an application to switch Plan B to over-the-counter status in May 2004, citing concerns about its use by women under the age of sixteen. When used within 72 hours of unprotected sex or contraceptive failure, emergency contraceptive (EC) pills can reduce the risk of pregnancy by as much as 89 percent. Given that nearly half of all pregnancies in the U.S. are unintended and half of unintended pregnancies end in abortion, advocates of emergency contraception have promoted its use as a way to reduce the number of abortions. An analysis conducted by the Alan Guttmacher Institute estimates that 51,000 abortions were prevented by EC use in 2000, and that increased use of ECs accounted for up to 43 percent of the decline in abortions between 1994 and 2000 (despite the fact that only 2 percent of women reported having ever used emergency contraceptive pills and 73 percent had not even heard of emergency contraceptive pills). Nearly 6 percent of women in 2003 reported having used emergency contraceptive pills at least once in their lifetime. Access to emergency contraception is available without a prescription in thirty-three countries around the world. The American College of Obstetricians and Gynecologists and the American Academy of Pediatrics, as well as the majority of the mainstream medical community, support making Plan B available over-the-counter. Despite the fact that EC pills work by preventing pregnancy, and cannot interrupt or disrupt an established pregnancy (nor will the drug harm an existing fetus), antichoice advocates have been working to prevent wider distribution of the drug. On August 24, 2006, the FDA approved Plan B as an over-the-counter medication for those aged 18 and older. Sales to 17-year-olds were approved on April 22, 2009. Plan B is available by prescription in six states for minors younger than 17 years of age.[67]

A few states currently allow pharmacists to exercise their "conscience" and refuse to fill prescriptions for birth control pills and for emergency contraceptive pills. A K-Mart pharmacist in Wisconsin attracted legal and media attention when he refused to fill a woman's prescription for the birth control pill, claiming it would violate his religious beliefs to fill a prescription for a contraceptive that could cause what he believed to be an abortion, and refused to have the prescription transferred to another pharmacy.[68] Pharmacists' "refusal clauses" are not new, but following the release of Plan B more state legislatures have considered their adoption. The most targeted drug is Plan B, a time-sensitive medication that must be taken within 72 hours of intercourse to effectively prevent conception. Initially Wal-Mart refused to stock or sell Plan B following FDA approval in 2005, however by 2006 the company adopted a policy requiring all of its pharmacies to dispense Plan B in response to adverse consumer reaction and consumer demand for the product. Contrary to estimates that there would be no discernable demand for the drug, women spent $80 million on the over-the-counter drug in 2007. All of the largest chain pharmacies now have corporate policies guaranteeing that emergency contraception is for sale at all times. Women's rights advocates argue that pharmacists put women's lives in danger by refusing to dispense a legal and medically prescribed drug. A CBS News/*New York Times* poll, conducted in November 2004, found that 78 percent of the public believed that pharmacists who personally oppose birth control for religious reasons should not be able to refuse to sell birth control to women with a prescription for the drug.[69] Prior to leaving office in 2009, the George W. Bush administration adopted a series of federal protections for health-care workers who refuse to provide care that violates their personal, moral, or religious beliefs. This broad "conscience regulation" went well beyond pharmacists dispensing birth control; the Bush rule empowered the federal government to cut off federal funding for any state or local government, hospital, health plan, clinic, or other entity that did not accommodate doctors, nurses, pharmacists or other employees who refuse to participate in care they find objectionable. In February 2009, the new Obama administration moved to rescind the controversial "conscience regulation." The administration argued that the rule was written so broadly that could make it harder for women to get the health care they need.[70] The rule-making and rescission process on emergency contraception, the global gag rule, and "conscience regulations" demonstrate how quickly women's access to information, devices, and health care can change depending on the governing political ideology.

Public Opinion on Abortion

Overall, U.S. public opinion favors maintaining a woman's right to choose abortion, although support for abortion rights appears conditional. A 2009 Gallup poll found that 53 percent of the public supports legal abortion under certain circumstances, while 23 percent support abortion under any circumstance and 22 percent say abortion should be illegal under all circumstances.[71] Further, as social commentator Wendy Kaminer reports, "People seem inclined to prohibit abortions when women have them for the 'wrong reasons.'"[72] The public is most disapproving, according to a *New York Times* survey, of women who have abortions because they want to finish school or pursue a career; 70 percent said that they did not believe that abortions should be available to women who want to terminate their pregnancy for career-related reasons. Less than half of those surveyed (42 percent) supported abortion for teenage girls who wanted to finish school or continue their education. Only 43 percent said that abortion should be available to low-income women who could not afford another child. The strongest support was for women who terminated their pregnancies for health reasons or because there was a strong suspicion of fetal deformity.[73]

The public attitudes expressed in the *Times* survey appear to run contrary to recent state welfare reforms that withhold additional public support on the birth of an another child. These attitudes also seem to contradict economic rationality since women without an education cannot earn a sufficient wage to support a child and will be dependent on public assistance, private agencies, or family for support. Do romanticized attitudes toward motherhood account for these findings? Wendy Kaminer attributes the rather harsh attitude toward women who say they are not ready for the changes a child would require in their lives to an unwillingness to grant women autonomy: "The abortion debate is not simply about the nature of a human fetus; it is, in large part, about the nature of a woman. Is it natural for her to put motherhood second—or to choose not to become a mother at all? Is it natural for her to demand the same right to self-determination that fully democratic societies have always granted men?"[74]

In July 2004, freelancer Amy Richards elicited a huge response to her story, "When One Is Enough," appearing in the *New York Times Magazine*. Thirty-four years old and unmarried, Ms. Richards discovered she was pregnant. When she and her boyfriend went to the obstetrician, she discovered she was pregnant with triplets. "My immediate response was, I cannot have triplets. I was not married; I lived in a five-story walk-up in the East Village; I worked freelance; and I would have to go on bed rest in March. I lecture at colleges, and my biggest months are March and April. I would have to give up my main income for the rest of the year. There was a part of me that was sure I could work around that. But it was a matter of do I want to?" Ultimately, Ms. Richards decided to undergo selective reduction and aborted two of the three fetuses. She gave birth to a single healthy baby. On July 28, 2004, the *New York Times* published an "Editor's Note" saying:

> The Lives column in The Times Magazine on July 18 gave a first-person account of the experience of Amy Richards, who had been pregnant with triplets and decided to abort two of the fetuses. Ms. Richards, who told her story to a freelance Times Magazine contributor, Amy Barrett, discussed her anxiety about having triplets, the procedure to terminate two of the pregnancies and the healthy baby she eventually delivered; she expressed no regret about her decision. The column identified Ms. Richards as a freelancer at the time of her pregnancy but should have also disclosed that she is an abortion rights advocate who has worked with Planned Parenthood, as well as a co-founder of a feminist organization, the Third Wave Foundation, which has financed abortions. That background, which would have shed light on her mind-set, was incorporated in an early draft, but it was omitted when an editor condensed the article.[75]

Why did the *New York Times* feel compelled to offer this editorial note? Is there a reason the story cannot stand on its own? Is part of the reason expressed in the observation "she expressed no regret about her decision"? The column generated several hundred letters to the editor. Of the ten the magazine published, only two could be characterized as supportive of Richards's decision and males authored both. Most of the others led by commenting on the seemingly detached or cold-hearted manner in which she approached the decision to terminate two of the three fetuses.

Abortion played a role in the 2004 presidential election even though both candidates tried to avoid addressing the issue directly. For example, the American Life League's Crusade for the Defense of Our Catholic Church released an ad campaign featuring photographs of the so-called Deadly Dozen, twelve public officials from both parties "wanted for fraudulently claiming to be Catholic" because of their pro-choice policy stance. The ad implored Catholic bishops to refuse pro-choice Catholic public officials Holy Communion until they recanted their position. The abortion issue also more than likely mobilized a segment of the electorate in 2004. A Gallup poll of likely voters found that 19 percent are single-issue voters. Thirty percent of likely pro-life voters say they will only vote for a candidate who shares their view on abortion.[76] This is in stark contrast to the 11 percent of pro-choice voters who said they would only support pro-choice candidates. This "intensity gap" on the issue of abortion obviously favored George W. Bush. Nearly one-quarter of his voters were single-issue voters motivated by the abortion issue, compared to only 13 percent of Kerry's voters.[77] Having won the election with the support of ideological conservatives in the Republican Party, George W. Bush was expected by many to take action on the abortion issue. When Senator Arlen Specter, in line for the chairmanship of the Senate Judiciary Committee, commented that any Supreme Court nominee intent on overturning *Roe v. Wade* would probably not win Senate approval, he touched off a firestorm among Christian conservatives who claimed they were responsible for returning President Bush to the White House.

Abortion played a more muted role in the 2008 presidential contest, but was nonetheless present as an issue. Sarah Palin's addition to the Republican ticket created a decidedly pro-life visual. Palin frequently campaigned with her then four-month-old infant, born with Down's syndrome, and her pregnant, unmarried 17-year-old daughter. Palin's personal decisions regarding abortion seemed to inject abortion into the campaign without the usual vitriol and her presence on the ticket placated conservative Republican voters who were worried about Senator John McCain's credentials on reproductive issues and particularly embryonic stem-cell research. While 13 percent of Americans in 2008 said they would only vote for a candidate that shares their position on abortion, 49 percent said it was "just one of many important factors" and fully 37 percent said it was not a major issue at all.[78] Over 65 percent of Americans continue to express support for maintaining the principle holding in *Roe v. Wade*, allowing women to choose abortion virtually free from state-imposed restrictions in the first trimester. After the election, Sarah Palin spoke more openly about her decision to have a child at age 44 and to continue her pregnancy once she learned the baby would have Down's syndrome. Speaking at an Indiana right-to-life fund-raiser, she disclosed:

> I had found out that I was pregnant while out of state first, at an oil and gas conference.

> While out of state, there just for a fleeting moment, wow, I knew, nobody knows me here, nobody would ever know. I thought, wow, it is easy, could be easy to think, maybe, of trying to change the circumstances. No one would know. No one would ever know.

> Then when my amniocentesis results came back, showing what they called abnormalities. Oh, dear God, I knew, I had instantly an understanding for that fleeting

moment why someone would believe it could seem possible to change those circumstances. Just make it all go away and get some normalcy back in life. Just take care of it. Because at the time only my doctor knew the results, Todd didn't even know. No one would know. But I would know. First, I thought how in the world could we manage a change of this magnitude. I was a very busy governor with four busy kids and a husband with a job hundreds of miles away up on the North Slope oil fields. And, oh, the criticism that I knew was coming. Plus, I was old . . .

So we went through some things a year ago that now lets me understand a woman's, a girl's temptation to maybe try to make it all go away if she has been influenced by society to believe that she's not strong enough or smart enough or equipped enough or convenienced enough to make the choice to let the child live. I do understand what these women, what these girls go through in that thought process.[79]

Ruth Marcus, columnist for the *Washington Post*, concluded, "Except that, of course, if it were up to Palin, women would have no thought process to go through. The 'good decision to choose life,' as she put it, would be no decision at all, because abortion would not be an option." Like so much about Palin's candidacy, her decision about birth versus abortion proved to be a political Rorschach test for the politicization of the abortion issue. For Kim Lehman of Iowa Right to Life, her remarks demonstrate the strength of her convictions, "She was tested, tried, and chose life. It goes to show her character." For Elizabeth Shipp, political director at NARAL Pro-Choice America, it demonstrates the importance of the right to choose for every single woman, "If I didn't know better," she said, "I'd say Governor Palin sounds remarkably pro-choice."[80]

There was more action in the states on abortion issues in November 2008 and experts were divided on what role, if any, the controversial ballot initiatives would play in attracting voters. Jennie Drage Bowser, a policy analyst at the National Conference of State Legislatures, said that many of the social measures on the ballots were being pushed by evangelical groups to force McCain to pay closer attention to their agenda.[81] In South Dakota, voters soundly defeated a state constitutional amendment banning all abortions in the state except those performed because of rape, incest, or to protect a woman's health. The measure was defeated 55.3 percent to 44.7 percent. Initiatives in California requiring parental notification and a waiting period were defeated in 2008, as well as an attempt in Colorado to define a fetus as a "person" from the moment of conception and extend equal rights to the fetus. The "Colorado Equal Rights Amendment" was defeated by an overwhelming margin, 73 percent to 27 percent. Mark Meuser, a primary backer of the amendment and founder of the organization Colorado for Equal Rights, argued, "If the state or the federal government ever defined when life began, then the rights of the unborn would be superior to the woman's right to have an abortion. If personhood was ever defined, then the case for *Roe* would collapse." The issue of "personhood" for a fetus, particularly among those who argue that life begins at the moment of fertilization, clearly places adult women's rights to autonomy against those of a fetus.

Women's Rights Versus Fetal Rights

Liberal theories grounded on individual rights provide one philosophical basis for feminists to make equality claims in a number of areas, as we've seen in previous chapters. Liberal feminists have been both lauded and derided for their emphasis on gaining equal status with men within the current political, social, and economic system. Critics of liberal feminism often point to the limits of using a male standard of equality to judge women's status. Successful claims advanced on the basis of the legal equality doctrine are most often made under the banner of fairness—that is, if men retain certain rights, privileges, or obligations that further their status purely on the basis of gender, fairness dictates that women be treated equally by erasing gender/sex from the statute or policy in question. Alternatively, the other approach in pursuit of equality argues that fairness requires the law to treat men and women differently. How do these two paths to gender equality apply to pregnancy, reproduction, and regulating emerging fertility technologies?

The rulings in *Griswold* and *Roe* ground women's reproductive liberty in the constitutional right to privacy. Privacy in this sense is understood as a limit on government's intervention in personal decisions or conduct. Individuals have a fundamental "right to be let alone," according to the decision in *Griswold*. However, the Court's ruling in *Harris* raises questions about whether a negative view of privacy is sufficient to guarantee women the fundamental right to "personhood" (autonomy) in reproductive decision making. A right to obtain an abortion that cannot be exercised solely because of one's inability to pay rings hollow for many feminists. Does government have an affirmative obligation related to the exercise of privacy rights?

Feminist legal scholar Catherine MacKinnon has argued that locating women's reproductive rights in the privacy doctrine merely serves to reinforce the subordination women experience as a result of the public-private dichotomy. The assumption that women can exercise autonomy within the private sphere is faulty, she argues, and she cites as evidence the lack of support for a woman's right to refuse sex. If unintended pregnancy is a result of unintended sex (she argues here that men control sexuality entirely), then privacy understood as a negative right rather than a positive duty on government to provide termination of the unintended pregnancy merely reinforces women's subordination as a group to men as a group.[82] In this sense, ". . . *Roe v. Wade* presumes that government nonintervention into the private sphere promotes a woman's freedom of choice. . . . But the *Harris* result sustains the ultimate meaning of privacy in *Roe*: Women are guaranteed by the public no more than what we can get in private—that is, what we can extract through our intimate associations with men. Women with privileges get rights. . . .So women got abortion as a private privilege, not as a public right. . . .Abortion was not decriminalized, it was legalized."[83] MacKinnon charges that in the case of abortion specifically and reproductive rights more generally, "privacy" shields and protects the very source of women's subordination—the private sphere.

Within the private sphere, women are left to negotiate their rights as individuals who are segregated from the interests of women as a group. This, she argues, is why women cannot be effectively organized around the issue of abortion. "This is an instance of liberalism called feminism, liberalism applied to women as if we *are* persons, gender neutral. It reinforces the division between public and private that is *not* gender neutral. It is at once an ideological division that lies about women's shared experience and that mystifies the unity among the spheres of women's violation."[84]

Whether or not one accepts MacKinnon's line of reasoning, there is an interesting dilemma posed by *Harris*, in which the Court ruled that the government does not have to fund poor women's abortions through Medicaid. Privacy guarantees only the *decision* whether or not to terminate the pregnancy, not the ability to carry out the decision. The government in this case supports only one decision—the decision to continue the pregnancy. But how does this square with welfare reform provisions for a "family cap" or a limit to public assistance when an additional child is born? It would seem that government now supports neither decision—or rather the law may support both decisions, but for poor women, reality permits neither.

When Rights Are in Conflict: State Intervention

In recent years there has been a growing trend toward greater state intervention in the lives of pregnant women in the name of fetal protection. This intervention includes state-compelled medical treatment, arrest, and incarceration of drug-addicted pregnant women under child-endangerment laws or drug-distribution penalties, and workplace restrictions that apply to both pregnant and potentially pregnant women, and more numerous conditions placed by states on the right to seek a legal first-trimester abortion. Central to each of these areas is the competition of rights between the woman and the fetus. Some scholars have argued that the extension of "rights" to a fetus is possible due to advances in technology that have allowed the public to see the fetus as it develops recognizably human features long before viability.[85] *Roe* tips the balance from the interests of the individual (the woman) to the state at the point of fetal viability. As technology has gradually moved the point of viability earlier in the pregnancy, in both reality and public perception, the state has taken a more aggressive role on behalf of the fetus, often at the expense of a woman's autonomy. More often than not, the public has been supportive of increased state intervention, especially when it comes at the expense of personal autonomy for poor women and women of color. What many women do not acknowledge is that with each new form of state intervention, the autonomy of all women is placed at risk.

Compelling pregnant women to undergo medical treatment can be seen as enforcing the woman's duty to care for the fetus.[86] In the case of *In Re A.C.*, the court of appeals held that a trial judge's actions that compelled a woman who was twenty-six-and-a-half-weeks pregnant and dying of cancer to have a caesarean section violated a long tradition of an individual's right to accept or reject medical treatment and to maintain bodily integrity. At twenty-six weeks, the woman entered the hospital knowing that her illness was terminal and agreed to palliative care to extend her life until her pregnancy reached the twenty-eighth week (of forty weeks in a normal full-term pregnancy). Her condition worsened quickly and within four days she was intubated and unable to communicate further. The hospital immediately sought a declarative judgment from the court to intervene for the fetus as *parens patriae*. Doctors for the hospital testified that a fetus delivered at twenty-six weeks was viable (defined as "capable of sustained life outside of the mother, given artificial aid") and stood about a 50 percent chance of survival. There was no evidence offered that the woman consented to a caesarean delivery at twenty-six weeks, and her mother testified that she opposed intervention since she believed her daughter wanted to live to see the baby if delivered and that she would not have chosen to deliver a child with a substantial degree of impairment (fairly likely given the premature birth and the mother's medical condition). The trial court ordered the caesarean section, arguing that because the fetus was viable, "the state has an important and legitimate interest in protecting the potentiality of human life"; and further, that although there had been some testimony that the surgery would most likely hasten the woman's death, there had also been testimony that a delay would greatly increase the risk to the fetus.[87] The child died within two-and-one-half hours of the surgery, and the woman died two days later.

The appeals court based its reversal on several legal precedents, including an individual's right to make informed choices about treatment that includes the right to forgo treatment altogether and the court's inability to compel a person to permit significant intrusion on his or her bodily integrity even if the life of another person is at stake (e.g., compulsory bone marrow transplants for relatives). The court wrote, "It has been suggested that fetal cases are different because a woman who 'has chosen to lend her body to bring a child into the world' has an enhanced duty to assure the welfare of the fetus, sufficient even to require her to undergo caesarean surgery. Surely, however, a fetus cannot have rights in this respect superior to those of a person who has already been born. . . ."[88] Regardless of the appellate court's holding, forced caesarean surgeries continue. In March 2004, Utah prosecutors charged a woman with murder for failing to undergo a caesarean-section delivery, a decision that allegedly resulted in the death of one of her unborn twins. As Attorney Sherry Colb notes, this prosecution raises a significant question: "Are we, as a society, prepared to demand more of pregnant women than of anyone else?"[89] If we are sincerely committed to equality, the answer must be no; however, looking at trends in state and federal law, the answer appears to be yes. Parents of physically separate children are not required under penalty of prosecution to donate a kidney to save their child's life. Many do of course, but they are not legally obligated to do so. Ultimately, Utah dropped the capital murder charge against this woman, but not before she plead guilty to two charges of child endangerment for using cocaine during her pregnancy, placing her at risk of five years in prison. She was sentenced to 18 months' probation and ordered to seek drug treatment. A second area of states' attempts to regulate pregnant women's conduct is in regard to drug and alcohol use. Most often, drug- or alcohol-addicted women are identified for state intervention and punitive action after they have given birth to a child that tests positive for drugs or exhibits symptoms of fetal alcohol syndrome. Some states have required medical personnel in public hospitals to report such findings to law enforcement officials. These laws have a disproportionate impact on poor women and women of color because they are more likely to seek prenatal care and deliver infants at public hospitals. Dorothy Roberts argues that hospitals that serve poor minority communities have implemented infant toxicology tests almost exclusively. One trigger to testing is the mother's failure to obtain prenatal care, a factor highly related to race and income. In many cases, hospitals do not have formal screening criteria, but rely on hospital staff to identify women likely to be substance abusers and initiate testing on their infants. Racial stereotypes result in tests being performed almost exclusively on African American women and their babies.[90]

In Charleston, South Carolina, a "Search and Arrest" policy was instituted in 1989 at the Medical University of South Carolina (MUSC). Pregnant women who sought prenatal or medical care at the public hospital were targeted without a warrant or their consent for urine testing that looked for cocaine use. Positive test results were reported to local police, who arrested more than thirty women in the five-year period the policy was in effect. Some women were arrested and jailed while they were still pregnant. Others were handcuffed and arrested immediately after giving birth or while still in their hospital beds. A subsequent change to the policy provided women with the option of undergoing treatment in lieu of arrest, but treatment options were limited and no provisions were made to allow women to set their affairs in order or arrange for care of their other children before entering residential treatment programs. Women who refused immediate admission to residential treatment programs were arrested and jailed. Ten women (all indigent and nine of whom were African American) filed suit, charging that the MUSC policy violated their constitutional right to medical care, violated their Fourth Amendment rights against unreasonable searches and seizures, undermined the doctor-patient relationship, and ultimately endangered the health of women and their babies.[91] On March 21, 2001, in the case of *Ferguson v. City of Charleston*, the Supreme Court ruled the South Carolina policy an unconstitutional form of search and seizure.

In another South Carolina case, *Whitner v. South Carolina*, the South Carolina Supreme Court upheld the use of the state's child abuse and endangerment statute to prosecute cocaine-addicted pregnant women for child abuse. Although the word "child" in the statute is defined as a "person under the age of eighteen," the court held that a viable fetus met the definition and therefore warranted protection by the state. Generally, these policies are promoted as deterrents to adverse behavior among other pregnant women; however, there is little evidence that arrest and prosecution deters drug or alcohol addiction in any form. More likely, these policies discourage other pregnant women from seeking prenatal care out of fear of criminal prosecution.[92] The *Whitner* decision poses significant questions for all pregnant women. The state supreme court decreed that *anything* a pregnant woman does after viability that causes "potential harm" to the fetus is child abuse. "Anything" may include a list of activities that healthy pregnant women now take for granted—athletics, strenuous exercise, conditions of employment, diet, or travel.

In January 2009, a 28-year-old woman from Cameroon was arrested and jailed in Maine for having fake immigration documents. In May 2009, U.S. District Court Judge John Woodcock sentenced her to incarceration for 238 days. Normally, a forged-document offense would draw a sentence of "time served." In this case, the Judge extended Ms. T's sentence because she is both HIV-positive and pregnant. The length of the sentence insures that her baby will be born in prison. Judge Woodcock stated, "My obligation is to protect the public from further crimes of the defendant, and that public, it seems to me at this point, should include the child she's carrying. . .I don't think the transfer of HIV to an unborn child is a crime technically under the law, but it is as direct and as likely as an ongoing assault." He maintained that extended imprisonment would protect her unborn child; however, Federal Sentencing Guidelines do not permit a judge to take gender (and thereby pregnancy) into account in determining an appropriate prison sentence. Medical experts say that without any medical intervention, the risk of transmitting HIV from mother to child is, on average, 25 percent. Taking antiretroviral drugs during the pregnancy and birth or opting to have a caesarean section can reduce the risk of transmission to less than 2 percent. The woman, known in the proceedings as Ms. T to protect her privacy, expressly stated that she did not want to remain in jail in order to access medical care, nor did she want to give birth in jail. Working with her attorney and several advocacy groups, she had arranged for care at a local clinic. Judge Woodcock ultimately granted bail in June 2009 based on the argument advanced by her attorney and several women's advocacy groups that she would receive higher-quality care and more continuity of care outside of the prison system. The original 238-day sentence and the discriminatory logic behind it remain unchanged, however.[93]

Increased regulation of pregnant or potentially pregnant women can also take the form of workplace exclusions in occupations deemed hazardous to fetal development. Under the guise of protecting women's health, fetal protection policies have proliferated within the past two decades. The underlying philosophy of fetal protection policies is similar to that expressed in *Muller v. Oregon* (1908), a case in which the U.S. Supreme Court upheld a limited workday for women only. Limiting working conditions (hours, minimum wage, and the like) for men was considered an arbitrary infringement on the right and liberty of the individual to contract in relation to his labor. The Court's reasoning was based on what was termed "general knowledge" about women's physical structure, the injurious effects on the female body of long hours on her feet, and maternal functions: ". . . as healthy mothers are essential to vigorous offspring, the physical well-being of women becomes an object of public interest and care in order to preserve the strength and vigor of the race."[94] Contemporary fetal-protection policies also speak to the question of maternal duty and responsibility (as well as liability issues for the employer involved), although justification for maternal monitoring is now grounded in the "rights" and interests of the fetus rather than in broad social reproductive-policy goals. Individual women are viewed only within the context of reproduction in exclusionary workplace policies that bar women from certain positions designated as "hazardous." Ironically, fetal-protection policies are more likely to be in place in industries where women are not overrepresented, while the risks are greatest in industries where women constitute 75 to 80 percent of the workforce (e.g., semiconductors, textiles, and hospitals). Fetal-protection policies that exclude women from the highest-paying jobs are most often found in industries where women make up a small proportion of the total workforce. The scientific evidence on which exclusionary policies are based is subject to debate and rarely considers paternal risk factors, either genetically at the point of conception or the risk of a male exposing a pregnant woman to toxins that are on his skin or clothing. Critics of exclusionary policies directed solely at women charge that blanket policies that treat women as a class fail to recognize women as individuals capable of making autonomous decisions and evaluating risks in employment. This "romantic paternalism" is strikingly similar to protectionist policies of the progressive era that were declared unconstitutional under Title VII.[95]

State-Imposed Restrictions, Conditions, and Regulation of Legal Abortion

States have adopted an increasing number of restrictions and conditions on access to legal abortion in the United States as a result of the ruling in *Casey* (1992). Between 1995 and 2004, states enacted 409 antichoice legislative measures. In the 2005 legislative session alone, over 650 bills were introduced that would directly or indirectly restrict access to abortion and contraception or advance the legal status of the fetus as if it were separate from the pregnant woman.[96] A 2009 review of existing abortion laws by the Guttmacher Institute identified nine broad categories of regulations and limitations on whether, when, and under what circumstances a woman may obtain a legal abortion.[97] For example, 38 states require an abortion to be performed by a licensed physician and 19 states require an abortion to be performed in a hospital after a specified point in the pregnancy. Forty-six states allow individual health-care providers to refuse to participate in an abortion and 43 states allow institutions to refuse to perform abortions. Thirty-four states require parental involvement in a minor's decision to have an abortion, 22 states require one or both parents to consent to the procedure, while 10 states require that one or both parents be notified. Among the newest trends is a "counseling" requirement, imposed by 17 states, that may require information on at least one of the following: the purported link between abortion and breast cancer (6 states), the ability of a fetus to feel pain (9 states), long-term mental health consequences for the woman (7 states), or information on the availability of ultrasound (6 states). The veracity and accuracy of the information provided in these required counseling sessions is highly contested. For example, there is no medical science that supports a causal link between abortion and breast cancer and experts disagree over whether a fetus has the ability to register pain. On June 27, 2008, the Eighth Circuit issued a decision concerning a 2005 South Dakota law requiring doctors to inform patients seeking an abortion that the procedure will "terminate the life of a whole, separate, unique, living being." In a 7–4 decision, the court based its ruling in part on the majority opinion in *Gonzales v. Carhart* (discussed in detail below) expressing concern that women be protected from a decision they might "regret." A dissenting opinion noted that the law was not about giving women information designed to assist their decision making, but rather it "expresses ideological beliefs aimed at making it more difficult for women to choose abortions."[98]

Twenty-four states now require a woman seeking an abortion to wait a specified period of time, usually twenty-four hours, between an exam or mandated counseling and the procedure. Both the counseling requirement and most especially the mandatory waiting period require a woman to make repeated trips to the facility in order to obtain a legal abortion. As Rachel Benson Gold notes, "Many of these policies, at their heart, are premised on the notion that women who intend to have an abortion (and, to some extent, the public at large) do not fully understand what an abortion really is—and that, if they did, they would behave differently." Just recently, in *Gonzales v. Carhart* (2007), the majority all but invited states to reexamine the information they provide to women just prior to an abortion procedure, and specifically the information describing "the way in which the fetus will be killed," on the grounds that "a necessary effect of [such a requirement] and the knowledge it conveys will be to encourage some women to carry the infant to full term."[99] In the states that require women to receive specific information prior to an abortion, the Guttmacher Institute found only ten states in which the information generally conforms to the widely held principles of "informed consent," while information provided in the others was "designed more to influence rather than inform the woman's decision." There is no evidence that state abortion policies designed to persuade women to forgo a planned abortion are effective.[100] On the contrary, there is considerable evidence that the content of preabortion information mandated in several states is misleading and misrepresents current medical knowledge.[101]

Crisis Pregnancy Centers: No Health Care Available

Another tactic specifically intended to persuade women and prevent them from having an abortion is the so-called Crisis Pregnancy Center (CPC) found in many communities large and small. According to the National Abortion Federation, there are as many as 4,000 CPCs nationwide, compared with an estimated 2,000 clinics that provide abortion services for women.[102] Going by the names, Crisis Pregnancy Center, Pregnancy Aid, Birth Right, Open Door, or Pregnancy Counseling Center, these groups want to be the first contact a woman makes when she thinks she might be pregnant, so they can talk her out of considering abortion. CPCs often locate near high schools or near actual abortion clinics and advertise "free pregnancy testing" and "options counseling" to attract women who believe they might be pregnant. Women report that once inside the facility, it looks very much like a medical clinic, but CPCs do not provide information about abortion services or contraceptives, nor do they refer women interested in obtaining an abortion to an appropriate facility. Instead, while they await the results of their pregnancy test, women are asked to watch antiabortion videos and provided with antichoice literature. Having provided personal contact information when they first arrived, some women also report being harassed with phone calls or visits to their homes. Some state attorney generals have taken action against CPCs that appear to be intentionally misleading women. For example, in 2002 the New York attorney general reached a settlement with some CPCs requiring that they clearly disclose that they do not provide or make referrals for abortion or birth control and disclose in writing that the facility is not a licensed medical provider qualified to accurately diagnose or date a pregnancy.[103]

Federally Imposed Restrictions on Abortion

During the first George W. Bush administration, Congress passed two laws intended to narrow the scope of women's exercise of abortion rights by elevating the status of the fetus. On April 1, 2004, President Bush signed into law the Unborn Victims of Violence Act, also known as Laci and Conner's Law, after the Laci Peterson homicide. The legislation creates a separate offense for killing or injuring an "unborn child" while committing a federal crime against a woman. Although the measure excludes voluntary abortion, it defines an unborn child as "a member of the species homo sapiens, at any stage of development, who is carried in the womb." The specific language recognizes an embryo and fetus as a person distinct from the pregnant woman, thereby creating separate legal rights for the fetus. Because of this provision, opponents charge that it is a back-door attack on reproductive rights and threatens to undermine the central holding in *Roe v. Wade.*[104]

On November 5, 2003, President Bush signed a law banning so-called partial-birth abortions. The Partial-Birth Abortion Ban Act of 2003 makes it illegal for doctors to take overt action to abort a late-term fetus—one in its second or third trimester. The bill makes no exemption for a woman whose health is at risk by carrying the pregnancy to term, nor does it take into account ailments or deformities the child may suffer in life. The language in the federal legislation is very similar to Nebraska's late-term abortion law that was already declared unconstitutional by the U.S. Supreme Court in *Stenberg v. Carhart* (2000). Three federal judges in three different locations have issued injunctions against the act, citing the undue burden the law places on women's right to make their own medical decisions about abortion without interference from the government. U.S. District Court Judge Robert Kopf noted, "While the procedure is infrequently used as a relative matter, when it is needed, the health of the woman frequently hangs in the balance." Neither the Nebraska statute struck down in *Carhart* nor the federal law contains a health exception. In addition, each of the judges cited the law's vagueness relative to the procedures being banned. U.S. District Judge Phyllis Hamilton noted, "The term partial-birth abortion is neither recognized in the medical literature nor used by physicians who routinely perform second trimester abortions." She went on, "By referring to the procedure as 'infanticide,' Congress was being 'grossly misleading and inaccurate.' . . .Congress was aware that the abortion

Surrounded by lawmakers, U.S. President George W. Bush signs legislation banning so-called partial birth abortions in Washington November 5, 2003. The law will prohibit doctors from committing an "overt act" designed to kill a partially delivered fetus and allows no exception if the woman's health is at risk, or if the child would be born with ailments. From left are Rep. Bart Stupak (D-MI), Rep. Henry Hyde (R-IL), Rep. Steve Chabot (R-OH), House Speaker Dennis Hastert (R-IL), Sen. Orrin Hatch (R-UT), Rep. James Sensenbrenner (R-WI) Sen. Rick Santorum (R-PA), Rep. James Oberstar (D-MN), Sen. Mike DeWine (R-OH), and House majority Leader Tom DeLay (R-TX). *Reuters/Kevin Lamarque KL.*

procedure banned by the bill applied to fetuses that were too young to live outside the womb."[105]

On April 18, 2007, in a 5–4 decision, the U.S. Supreme Court upheld the federal Partial-Birth Abortion Ban Act of 2003 in *Gonzales v. Carhart*.[106] Justice Anthony Kennedy wrote the majority opinion and was joined by Chief Justice John Roberts and Justices Alito, Thomas, and Scalia. Justice Ruth Bader Ginsburg wrote a dissenting opinion that was joined by Justices Souter, Stevens, and Breyer. Justice Ginsburg again read her dissent from the bench, announcing her extreme displeasure with the majority's holding and it's basis. *Gonzales* marks the first time the Court has ever upheld a total ban on a specific abortion procedure, however the central holding in *Roe v. Wade* was not overturned by this ruling. The ruling upholds the law as written, but left open the possibility that the law could be challenged again "as applied." In other words, if it could be demonstrated that the law in its application constituted a substantial obstacle to the abortion right, the Court might reexamine the holding. Justice Ginsburg's dissent called the ruling "an alarming decision" that refuses "to take seriously" prior rulings and precedent. She wrote, "The Court's opinion tolerates, indeed applauds federal intervention to ban nationwide a procedure found necessary and proper in certain cases by the American College of Obstetricians and Gynecologists. For the first time since *Roe*, the Court blesses a prohibition with no exception protecting a woman's health. . . .A decision of the character the Court makes today should not have staying power." Since Justice Sotomayor replaced Justice Souter, it seems unlikely that the balance of the course will change on this question. As Justice Ginsburg notes, "The Court's hostility to the right *Roe* and *Casey* secured is not concealed. Though today's opinion does not go so far as to discard *Roe* or *Casey*, the Court, differently composed than it was when we last considered a restrictive abortion regulation, is hardly faithful to our earlier invocations of "the rule of law" and the "principles of *stare decisis*." In this, she suggests, the majority's opinion is political rather than judicial in nature. She writes, "In sum, the notion that the Partial-Birth Abortion Ban Act furthers any legitimate governmental interest is, quite simply, irrational. The Court's defense of the statute provides no saving explanation. In candor, the Act, and the Court's defense of it, cannot be understood as anything other than an effort to chip away at a right declared again and again by this Court—with increasing comprehension of its centrality to women's lives."

Particularly troubling to Ginsburg and to feminist legal scholars is the language Kennedy employs in defense of the government's intervention in women's medical decision making, even going to so far as to articulate a new government interest—protecting "the bond of love the mother has for her child."[107] The Court determined that abortion has serious harmful effects on women, including severe psychological consequences, even though this belief was based on "no reliable data," by the Court's own admission. Thus, the Court upheld the restriction as a way of protecting women from their own potentially harmful choices. Justice Ginsburg charged that this reasoning "reflects ancient

The Modern Comstock Era?

The Comstock Act (1873) likened contraception to obscenity and thus prohibited the distribution of any information on contraception or contraceptive devices. Supporters of the law believed that contraception violated nature—meaning that it allowed women to engage in sexual intercourse for purposes other than procreation. As a result, women were denied the ability to protect their health and control their fertility.

In this chapter, we have reviewed a number of developments regarding women's access to information and health care with emphasis on the many regulations and restrictions states and Supreme Court decisions have imposed on access to abortion and the procedures allowed, emergency contraceptives (Plan B), and medical abortion drugs (RU-486). Several other conservative trends pose threats to women's ability to control their fertility and protect their health today.

For example, during the Bush Administration (2001–2009), the federal government limited funding of sex education in schools exclusively to "abstinence-only" programs. Sex education programs receiving funding under this policy were prohibited from discussing condom use or other forms of contraception. In the last ten years, the federal government has dedicated $1.5 billion dollars to abstinence-only programs in schools. Critics charge that the abstinence-only focus is responsible for an increase in sexually transmitted diseases (STDs), unintended pregnancies, and abortions. Sixty percent of U.S. teenagers have sex before age 18; one in four teenage girls has an STD, and the U.S. teen birthrate is nine times that of the Netherlands, five times that of France, and three times higher than in Canada. Teen pregnancy is estimated to cost the U.S. government $9 billion a year.

The Bush administration also made abstinence a cornerstone of its international AIDS relief, deemphasizing condoms in favor of abstinence. The ABC policy—"abstinence," "being faithful," and "condoms"—was criticized in a GAO study that found that in many countries administrators were forced to shift U.S. funds intended to fight mother-to-child HIV transmission to support abstinence programs.

In January 2006, the FDA approved a cervical cancer vaccine (known as Gardasil). The vaccine works by guarding against the human papillomavirus (HPV), linked to cervical cancer in about three out of every four cases. Nearly 4,000 women die of cervical

notions about women's place in the family and under the Constitution—ideas that have long been discredited." Further, the majority's opinion uses rhetoric that demonstrates hostility to a woman's right to choose and disdain for the medical profession. Justice Ginsburg writes, "Throughout, the opinion refers to obstetricians-gynecologists and surgeons who perform abortions not by the titles of their medical specialties, but by the pejorative label 'abortion doctor.' A fetus is described as an 'unborn child,' and as a 'baby'; second trimester, pre-viability abortions are referred to as 'late-term'; and the reasoned medical judgments of highly trained doctors are dismissed as 'preferences' motivated by 'mere convenience.'" Legal scholars continue to warn, particularly after cancer each year in the United States and it is the third most deadly form of cancer worldwide. Ideally girls should be vaccinated before they become sexually active, thus it is recommended for girls beginning at 9 with a recommended window of 9 to 13 years of age. Several states considered and/or adopted regulations requiring girls to get the HPV vaccine as a part of the routine vaccinations required for entry into public school. Social conservatives objected, claiming that the public health mandate violated parents' rights and the vaccine would promote sexual activity.

More generally, social conservatives have expanded their anti-abortion focus to include an anti-contraception campaign. Judie Brown, president of the American Life League, described the mission, "We see a direct connection between the practice of contraception and abortion. The mindset that invites a couple to use contraception is an antichild mindset so when a baby is conceived accidentally, the couple already have this negative attitude toward the child. Therefore seeking an abortion is a natural outcome. We oppose all forms of contraception." Focus on the Family says, "Modern contraception inventions have given many an exaggerated sense of safety and prompted more people than ever before to move sexual expression outside the marriage boundary." The birth control pill, widely viewed as the most effective form of contraception, has been especially singled out. Albert Mohler, president of the Southern Baptist Theological Seminary, equates the pill with "the Fall" in terms of its impact on human history, "Prior to [the pill], every time a couple had sex, there was a good chance of pregnancy. Once that is removed, the entire horizon of the sexual act changes. I think there could be no question that the pill gave incredible license to everything from adultery and affairs to premarital sex and within marriage to a separation of the sex act and procreation."

During the Comstock era, contraception was outlawed under the prevailing cultural belief that there was only one reason for women to engage in sexual intercourse—procreation. Although men were not (and are not today) the target of the anticontraception campaign, the underlying message is that men must be protected from the danger of women's sexuality. Think carefully about the trends identified here. Abstinence messages targeted at children are quite different than many of the antisex messages directed at adult women, particularly married adult women. Have we returned to a Comstock-like era?

the Court's opinion in *Gonzales*, that we are perhaps one vote away from a majority decision overturning *Roe v. Wade*. The outcome of the November 2008 election elevating prochoice Barack Obama to the White House makes the immediate appointment of another antiabortion justice less likely, but as the history of judicial appointments demonstrates, no president can be entirely sure of an appointee's future opinions.

Because of the uncertainty of *Roe*, several organizations have undertaken analysis of the state of abortion rights in its absence. A number of states still have pre-*Roe* abortion bans on the books—several of which could, in theory, be enforced if *Roe* is overturned. In other states, policymakers are acting in anticipation of a day when *Roe* no longer limits the restrictions states can impose on abortion and writing legislation that bans abortion under all or virtually all circumstances. Still other states have laws declaring their intent to ban abortion to the full extent allowed by the U.S. Constitution.[108] Currently 20 states have laws that could be used to restrict the legal status of abortion. Four states have laws that automatically ban abortion if *Roe* is overturned (Louisiana, Mississippi, North Dakota, and South Dakota). Thirteen states retain, but do not enforce abortion bans enacted prior to 1973 (Alabama, Arizona, Arkansas, Colorado, Delaware, Massachusetts, Michigan, Mississippi, New Mexico, Oklahoma, Vermont, West Virginia, and Wisconsin—although some of these provide exceptions for rape, incest, and/or to protect the life or health of the woman). Seven states have laws that protect the right to choose abortion prior to viability or when necessary to protect the life and health of the woman (California, Connecticut, Hawaii, Maine, Maryland, Nevada, and Washington). A woman's right to choose abortion and to legally access abortion services is already heavily conditional on the policies adopted and enforced in the state where she resides. Given that 87 percent of counties in the United States (97 percent of rural counties) currently have no abortion providers, although abortion remains legal, it is also largely inaccessible to the majority of women. Rather than mitigating inevitable inequities in abortion access, current state policy exacerbates them.[109]

In each of these examples of increased government intervention in women's reproductive decisions and pregnancies, the intersection of race, class, and gender is unmistakable. Women of color and poor women are significantly more likely than middle- and upper-class white women to be prosecuted for drug addiction and child endangerment. Women of color and poor women are more likely to seek an abortion. The behavior and choices of all pregnant women are subject to intense scrutiny as fetal rights become a more prominent part of our public discourse. Women who do not fit the ideal of "motherhood"—those who receive public assistance, those who choose not to disrupt their careers with a pregnancy and opt for adoption or surrogacy, those who serve as surrogates or egg donors, and those who are battling addiction to drugs or alcohol—are all subject to public sanction at the hands of law enforcement, public opinion, and employers. In each case, pregnant women are hurled back in time to the days before women had access to the public sphere as fully responsible autonomous adults. Erosion of these rights and of support for women's autonomy poses significant threats to women's equality.

TECHNOLOGY, REPRODUCTION, AND GENDER IDEOLOGIES

Scientific advances in the technology of reproduction have increased the demand for applying such technology to infertility. Estimates ten years ago showed that nearly 15 percent of all married couples have fertility problems.[110]

It is estimated that the male sperm count has fallen by more than 30 percent in the last half century so that nearly a quarter of men now have sperm counts that are low enough for them to be considered functionally sterile. Similarly, the number of women experiencing fertility problems has also grown. Of those who are currently sterile, 40 percent attribute sterility to fallopian tubes scarred by pelvic inflammatory disease and other low-level gynecological infections. In addition to the physical aspects of consumer demand for fertility technology, changing social patterns have contributed to the trends as well. The wider acceptance of contraceptive use, abortion, and a growing trend among single women to bear and raise a child have all helped to decrease dramatically the number of infants available for adoption. The availability of fertility technology has increased the number of couples interested in producing "their own" child rather than having to navigate the complicated procedures involved with domestic and foreign adoptions. Finally, infertility increases with age in both men and women. People who have postponed marriage and parenting until after earning a degree and establishing their careers have, in turn, delayed childbearing until later in life.[111]

Consumer-driven demand for fertility technology, while presumably grounded in the most intimate desire for a child, has been criticized for "commercializing reproduction" and creating a market in women's reproductive labor. Treating women's reproductive labor as a commodity, similar to any other form of labor, presents society with a wide array of conundrums that are only now beginning to surface in the form of public policy. One of the first public exposures to contract pregnancy was the Baby M case, in which Elizabeth and William Stern contracted with Mary Beth Whitehead to have her artificially inseminated with William Stern's sperm. On delivering the baby, Ms. Whitehead was promised $10,000. The specific terms of the contract were drawn up to avoid "baby selling" under New Jersey law. Although the baby was initially turned over to the Sterns and Mrs. Stern was granted the right to immediately adopt William Stern and Mary Beth Whitehead's daughter, Ms. Whitehead subsequently changed her mind and sought custody of the child known in court documents as "Baby M." Whitehead argued that the bond between mother and child was more powerful than any contract. In 1988, the New Jersey Supreme Court sided with Ms. Whitehead and invalidated the surrogacy contract on the grounds that money exchanged for the purpose of adopting a child was illegal under New Jersey law and therefore the contract was unenforceable. The court invalidated Elizabeth Stern's adoption and restored Whitehead's parental rights, but awarded custody to William Stern. The outcome of this highly publicized case once again focused public attention on women's reproductive roles that conflict with social expectations. Those sympathetic to Whitehead's claims pointed to the Sterns' wealth, two-career status, and impatience with the adoption process as evidence that they were unfit as parents, compared with Ms. Whitehead, who already had children of her own and a stable marriage, and was motivated out of a desire to help infertile couples realize their dream. Ms. Stern, diagnosed with multiple sclerosis, was criticized for putting her own health interests ahead of having "their own" children.

Now, more than twenty years after the Baby M case in New Jersey, this area of the law is still largely unsettled. Nineteen states have passed surrogacy laws, New Jersey has banned surrogacy arrangements entirely, and still other states have prohibited any arrangement in which a surrogate is paid. In states without specific legislation, judges are required to interpret family law as best they can. About 22,000 babies have been born through surrogacy in the United States since the 1970s. Perhaps the newest area of surrogacy law involves embryo adoption. This situation arises when couples with viable embryos decide to allow them to be adopted by infertile couples rather than have them destroyed upon completion of their own assisted reproduction procedures. Unlike surrogacy, genetic parents relinquish all rights to the embryo prior to implantation. The child born of the implantation is the child of the recipient couple and no further legal action is required to perfect the parent-child relationship.

Sometimes fertility technology is news because of its unprecedented success. On January 26, 2009, Nadya Suleman gave birth to octuplets in California. Although the news was initially greeted with great curiosity and enthusiastic interest, the public's attitude changed when the identity of the mother and the broader circumstances became known. At the time of the birth, Suleman was single, unemployed and living with her mother, and already the parent of six children, including twins, ranging in age from two to seven. Whereas other women who have given birth to multiples have been showered with gifts from large corporations (a lifetime supply of free diapers or baby food, for example) or their own television show (*Jon and Kate, Plus 8* on TLC, for example), Suleman has seemingly only received criticism—that she is irresponsible and a "bad mother." All fourteen children were born with the assistance of fertility technology, raising a number of ethical questions within the medical community. "It was a grave error, whatever happened," said Eleanor Nicoll, a spokeswoman for the American Society for Reproductive Medicine. "It should not have happened. Eight children should not have been conceived and born."[112] Regulations covering doctors and clinics that provide fertility assistance are few, although there are guidelines promulgated by associations like the American Society for Reproductive Medicine and the Society for Assisted Reproductive Technology. Those guidelines call for no more than two embryos to be implanted in a woman in her early thirties; there is nothing in the guidelines about the number of previous children. The octuplets' birth led many in the medical profession to fear new legislation. "Legislation about how to practice medicine threatens doctor-patient relations and has unintended consequences that may be worse than the actual problem," said James A. Grifo, program director of the New York University Fertility Center and professor of obstetrics and gynecology at the university's School of Medicine. The United States does not regulate family size, but if it were to do so—how many? Who would decide and what would the implications be for women and gender equality? More importantly, what does this case and set of questions say about women's autonomy in the area of fertility?

The decline in the number of children in American families first accompanied industrialization and continued with women's permanent entrance into the workforce, making women with large families increasingly rare. In 2006, only 28 percent of women ages 40 to 44 had three or more children; 4 percent had five or more, and just 0.5 percent had seven or more.[113] The debate stimulated by Suleman's octuplets went beyond whether *she* should have fourteen children to whether the world can sustain 6.8 billion people. Some environmentalists advocate a universal one-child policy to return the world's population to twentieth-century levels and reduce the adverse impact on scarce and finite resources. Alternatively, the Quiverfull movement, a conservative Christian patriarchy movement in which submissive wives eschew all contraception in favor of the philosophy of "letting God give them as many children as possible—families of twelve or more children that will, they hope, enable them to win the religion and culture wars through demographic means—by reproducing more than any other social groups."[114] The Quiverfull philosophy is a conscious and direct opposition to feminism and gender equality. Some in the movement go so far as to advocate repealing women's suffrage in the pursuit of absolute patriarchal dominance. Women's highest calling in this vision is first as a "virtuous daughter" and next as a virtuous wife who subsumes her identity entirely in that of her husband, "her Lord," and her family's head. There are fascinating questions raised by the variety of attempts by the state, culture, and society to regulate and exert control over women's reproductive capacities reviewed in this chapter.

The policy status of surrogacy, contract pregnancy, and *in vitro* fertilization techniques that result in embryos being created outside the womb is unclear. Sex and gender are interwoven, but rarely consciously disentangled, in the public dialogue on the social desirability of decoupling traditional heterosexual intercourse from reproduction. Regulations are substantially behind medical technology and are largely driven by a reaction to events already unfolding (e.g., cloning). The question of whether reproductive technologies liberate women or serve as yet another tool of patriarchal control dominates feminist literature on the subject. While technology seems to have helped infertile women, single women, and women without heterosexual partners bear children, it directly challenges our definition of family, our understanding of the link between sex and gender, and women's biological and sociological role in reproduction. Should society set a limit on the number of children in a "family"? Is surrogacy exploitation akin to prostitution? Should women be able to contract for their reproductive labor as freely as they do for other types of labor? Do reproductive technologies devalue women's reproductive role or liberate women from the subordination inherent in biological reproduction? These questions and more will face future generations of men and women, as well as policymakers and politicians.

CONCLUSION

A variety of issues related to the family will face future generations of citizens and policymakers. The very definition of what constitutes a family is being contested today. Several states now recognize civil unions and give them something approaching the status of marriage so that same-sex couples can access state and employer benefits. Same-sex marriage is or will soon be legal in five states and is recognized by several more, even though the federal Defense of Marriage Act denies federal recognition to same-sex marriages and allows states to ignore gay marriages performed in other states. The trend in the states is toward a more inclusive definition of "family." New reproductive technologies have allowed same-sex couples, whether male or female, to genetically contribute to the conception of a "child of their own." Women's biological and sociological roles in relation to reproduction are less clear than they have ever been. How will these issues be resolved?

The policy process is not particularly well-equipped to deal with such intimate and complex issues. The same claim to privacy that gives women choices in reproductive decisions also surrounds and isolates them as individuals subordinated within families in the private sphere. Domestic violence, marital rape, and poverty conditions have all been beyond the scope of politics and government action until relatively recently in our history. More so than in other issues we've discussed in this volume, family and fertility decisions present women with direct challenges to their autonomy. When women were defined solely within the private sphere, they were virtually invisible. As women have become more active in politics and the public sphere, they have transformed previously private issues significant to their lives and livelihoods into issues legitimate for public policy. However, as government has become more involved in these issues, women's interests as autonomous individuals run the risk of being subsumed by larger social interests or by political ideologies that circumscribe their autonomy. Particularly in the area of reproduction and fertility concerns, women as individuals risk becoming an invisible interest in public policy debates. As we saw in chapter 5, electing more women to public office does not in itself guarantee that women's interests will be promoted. As Laura Woliver states, "If we honestly discussed abortion within the territory of gender politics and women's rights and health instead of centering on fetal life, we would have to answer questions about how abortion is singled out for regulations that presume incompetent, selfish, misinformed female decision making instead of simply regulating abortion with the same health and safety provisions for other medical procedures."[115]

How will women and men resolve these tensions created by the paradox of equality? There is no clear path to women's equality in the family and in reproductive choices. The legal equality doctrine's gender-neutral approach does not seem appropriate when the issues are tied directly to women's biological sex as well as socially constructed gender roles. The persistence of patriarchal culture, however, makes it difficult to determine what is fair treatment for women under the fairness doctrine. Betty Friedan has argued that the only way to resolve these seemingly intractable issues is to redefine the context of the problem from judging *equality* within a legal framework to judging it in the context of the substantive *quality* of men's and women's lives. This, she argues, calls for a reconceptualization of how to balance work (public sphere) and family (private sphere).[116] This new equality is not equality between men and women but in the substantive areas in which their lives converge. This is the challenge for the coming century as men and women continue their pursuit of equality.

Suggested Readings, Web Resources, and Films

Robert H. Blank, *Fetal Protection in the Workplace* (New York: Columbia University Press, 1993).

Robert Blank and Janna C. Merrick, *Human Reproduction, Emerging Technologies, and Conflicting Rights* (Washington, D.C.: Congressional Quarterly Press, 1995).

Jeanne Flavin, *Our Bodies, Our Crimes: The Policing of Women's Reproduction in America* (New York: New York University Press, 2009).

Anne H. Gauthier, *The State and the Family: A Comparative Analysis of Family Policies in Industrialized Countries* (New York: Oxford University Press, 1996).

Michelle Goldberg, *The Means of Reproduction: Sex, Power, and the Future of the World*. (New York: Penguin Press, 2009).

Kathryn Joyce, *Quiverfull: Inside the Christian Patriarchy Movement* (Boston: Beacon Press, 2009).

Ellen H. Moskowitz and Bruce Jennings, eds., *Coerced Contraception? Moral and Policy Challenges of Long-Acting Birth Control* (Washington, D.C.: Georgetown University Press, 1996).

Susan Moller Okin, *Justice, Gender, and the Family* (New York: Basic Books, 1989).

Susie Orbach, *Bodies* (New York: Picador, 2009).

Peggy Orenstein, *Flux: Women on Sex, Work, Love, and Life in a Half-Changed World* (New York: Doubleday, 2000).

Laura M. Purdy, *Reproducing Persons: Issues in Feminist Bioethics* (Ithaca, N.Y.: Cornell University Press, 1996).

Melody Rose, *Safe, Legal, and Unavailable? Abortion Politics in the United States* (Washington, D.C.: CQ Press, 2007).

Rickie Solinger, *Beggars and Choosers: How the Politics of Choice Shapes Adoption, Abortion, and Welfare in the United States* (New York: Hill and Wang, 2001).

Kate Conway-Turner and Suzanne Cherrin, *Women, Families, and Feminist Politics: A Global Exploration* (New York: Harrington Park Press, 1999).

Judith Warner, *Perfect Madness: Motherhood in the Age of Anxiety* (New York: Riverhead Books, 2005).

Susan Wicklund, *This Common Secret* (New York: Public Affairs, 2007).

Laura R. Woliver, *The Political Geographies of Pregnancy* (Urbana: University of Illinois Press, 2002).

Memoir: Martha Beck, *Expecting Adam* (New York: Berkley Books, 2000).

Novel: Margaret Atwood, *The Handmaid's Tale* (New York: Random House, 1998).

Novel: Richard North Patterson, *Protect and Defend* (New York: Ballantine Books, 2001).

ACLU Reproductive Rights: http://www.aclu.org/issues/reproduct/hmrr.html.

Alan Guttmacher Institute: http://www.agi-usa.org.

Center for Reproductive Law and Policy: http://www.crlp.org/.

Feminists for Life: http://www.feministsforlife.org/.

International Planned Parenthood Federation: http://www.ippf.org/.

MADRE: http://www.madre.org/.

National Advocates for Pregnant Women: http://advocatesforpregnantwomen.org/.

Susan B. Anthony List: http://www.sba-list.org/site/c.ddJBKJNsFqG/b.4009925/k.BE63/Home.htm.

Film: *If These Walls Could Talk* (New York: HBO Home Video, 1996).

Film: *Monday's Girls* (California Newsreel, 1993).

Film: *Very Young Girls* (GEMS Girls Education and Mentoring Services, 2007).

Film: *One Wedding and a Revolution: The Day San Francisco City Hall Said "I Do"* (San Francisco: Women's Educational Media, 2004).

Film: *When Abortion Was Illegal: Untold Stories* (Oley, Pa.: Bullfrog Films, 1992).

Blog: Our Bodies, Our Blog: http://www.ourbodiesourblog.org/.

Blog: (En)Gender: http://www.myhusbandbetty.com/.

Blog: MomsRising: http://www.momsrising.org/blog/.

Blog: myMADRE: http://madreblogs.typepad.com/mymadre/.

Blog: Nuestra Vida, Nuestra Voz: http://latinainstitute.wordpress.com/.

Blog: Womenstake, National Women's Law Center: http://www.womenstake.org/.

Notes

1. *General Electric v. Gilbert*, 429 U.S. 125 (1976).

2. Rosemary Radford Ruether, "Diverse Forms of Family Life Merit Recognition," *National Catholic Reporter* 36, no. 32 (June 16, 2000): 19.

3. David Whelan, "Do As, Do Tell: Same-Sex Households," *Forecast*, September 17, 2001.

4. Jake Sherman, "White House Looks to Include Same-Sex Unions in Census Count," *Wall Street Journal*, June 19, 2009.

5. Cynthia B. Costello, Shari Miles, and Anne J. Stone, eds., *The American Woman 1999–2000: A Century of Change—What's Next?* (New York: Norton, 1998), p. 190.

6. U.S. Census Bureau, "Table A1. Marital Status of People 15 Years and Over by Age, Sex, Personal Earnings, Race and Hispanic Origin," June 29, 2001.

7. Virginia Sapiro, *Women in American Society: An Introduction to Women's Studies*, 4th ed. (Mountain View, Calif.: Mayfield, 1999), p. 398.

8. Jeffrey M. Jones, "Majority of Americans Continue to Oppose Gay Marriage: No Change in Support from Last Year," *Gallup*, May 27, 2009, accessed at http://www.gallup.com.

9. Kavan Peterson, "50-State Roundup of Gay Marriage Laws," *Stateline.org*, November 3, 2004, accessed at http://www.stateline.org.

10. Melinda Tuhus, "Equal Marriage Push Intensifies in New England," *Women's eNews*, January 29, 2009.

11. William M. Hohengarten, "Same-Sex Marriage and the Right of Privacy," *Yale Law Journal* 104, no. 6 (April 1994): 1495–1531.

12. Dorothy McBride Stetson, *Women's Rights in the USA: Policy Debates and Gender Roles* (New York: Garland Press, 1997), pp. 178–183.

13. Sapiro, *Women in American Society*, pp. 392–393.

14. Susan Moller Okin, *Justice, Gender, and the Family* (New York: Basic Books, 1989).

15. Ibid.

16. *Forbush v. Wallace*, 341 F. Supp. 241 (1971).

17. Sapiro, *Women in American Society*, p. 392.

18. Alvin Powell, "A New Comfort Zone? Fewer Women Keeping Their Names on Marriage," *Harvard Gazette*, August 24, 2004.

19. Michele Huffnung, "What's In a Name? Marital Name Choice Revisited," *Sex Roles* 55 (2006): 817–825.

20. Nancy McGlen and Karen O'Connor, *Women, Politics and American Society*, 2nd ed. (Upper River Saddle, N.J.: Prentice Hall, 1998), pp. 214–215.

21. The Lucy Stone League, accessed at http://www.lucystoneleague.org.

22. Sapiro, *Women in American Society*, p. 392.

23. Stetson, *Women's Rights in the USA*, p. 192.

24. Lenore J. Weitzman, *The Divorce Revolution: The Unexpected Social and Economic Consequences for Women and Children in America* (New York: Free Press, 1985).

25. Hunter College Women's Studies Collective, *Women's Realities Women's Choices: An Introduction to Women's Studies* (New York: Oxford University Press, 1995), p. 249.

26. Office of Child Support Enforcement, U.S. Department of Health and Human Services, "Fact Sheet," last updated January 2009, accessed at http://www.acf.hhs.gov/opa/fact_sheets/cse_factsheet.html.

27. Mona Harrington, *Care and Equality: Inventing a New Family Politics* (New York: Alfred A. Knopf, 1999), pp. 21–22.

28. United Nations, *The World's Women 2000: Trends and Statistics* (New York: United Nations Publications, 2000), p. 133.

29. Ibid., p. 56.

30. Anne H. Gauthier, *The State and the Family: A Comparative Analysis of Family Policies in Industrialized Countries* (New York: Oxford University Press, 1996), pp. 3–4.

31. Harrington, *Care and Equality*, p. 48.

32. Ibid., p. 17.

33. Jody Heymann, Alison Earle, Jeffrey Hayes, "The Work, Family and Equity Index: How does the United States Measure Up?" The Project on Global Working Families, The Institute for Health and Social Policy, McGill University, 2008.

34. "Family Leave—U.S., Canada, and Global," Catalyst, March 2009, accessed at http://www.catalyst.org.

35. Robert Blank and Janna C. Merrick, *Human Reproduction, Emerging Technologies, and Conflicting Rights* (Washington, D.C.: Congressional Quarterly Press, 1995), p. 4.

36. Sara Ann Ketchum, "Selling of Babies, Selling of Bodies," in *Feminist Perspectives in Medical Ethics*, eds. Helen B. Holmes and Laura M. Purdy (Bloomington: Indiana University Press, 1992), pp. 284–294.

37. Tracy Clark-Flory, "The End of Menstruation," *Salon.com*, February 4, 2008, accessed at http://www.salon.com/mwt/feature/2008/02/04/menstruation/.

38. Emily J. Herndon and Miriam Zieman, "New Contraceptive Options," *American Family Pediatrician* 69 (2004): 853–860; birth control information and products accessible at http://www.birthcontrol.com; Linda Johnson, "After 8 Years, Today's Sponge Contraceptive Goes on Sale Again," Associated Press State and Local Wire, March 3, 2003.

39. Alan Guttmacher Institute, "Improving Contraceptive Use in the United States," 2008 Series, No. 1, accessed at http://www.guttmacher.org/pubs/2008/05/09/ImprovingContraceptiveUse.pdf.

40. Nancy Woloch, *Women and the American Experience* (New York: Alfred A. Knopf, 1984) p. 365.

41. Ibid., p. 367.

42. Quoted in Ibid., p. 369.

43. *Planned Parenthood of Southeastern Pennsylvania v. Casey*, 112 S Ct 2791 (1992).

44. Alan Guttmacher Institute, "Induced Abortion," *Facts in Brief*, 2000, accessed at http://www.agi-usa.org/fb_induced_abortion.html.

45. California Abortion and Reproductive Rights Action League, *"Hill v. Colorado*: Summary of the Court's June 28, 2000 Decision," accessed at http://www.choice.org/court2000/hillsummary.html.

46. Peter Slavin, "Slaying Raises Fears on Both Sides of Abortion Debate," *Washington Post*, June 2, 2009; A01.

47. Marlene Gerber Fried, "Excerpts from Chapter 17," *Our Bodies, Ourselves*, accessed at http://www.ourbodiesourselves.org/abortion.htm.

48. Eric Alterman, "The Truth About Abortion," *Daily Beast*, June 2, 2009; Ellie Smeal, "Fight back against Stupak," Feminist Majority Alert, November 11, 2009, accessed online at http://feminist.org/hot_topics/HealthInsuranceReformandWomen.html.

49. K. Aleisha Fetters, "Medical Students Fill Survivor Role for Dr. Tiller," *Women's Enews*, June 7, 2009.

50. NARAL Pro-Choice America Foundation, "Overview of States' Reproductive Rights Laws," accessed at http://www.prochoiceamerica.org/yourstate/whodecides/trends/.

51. National Abortion Federation, "Freedom of Access to Clinic Entrances Act," accessed at http://www.prochoice.org.

52. National Abortion Federation, "Clinic Violence," accessed at http://www.prochoice.org/about_abortion/violence/index.html.

53. Asjylyn Loader, "Report: Global Gag Rule Spurring Deaths, Disease," *Women's eNews*, September 25, 2003, accessed at http://www.womensenews.org.

54. Anna Quindlen, "RU-486 and the Right to Choose: Cheering, Wailing, Hailing, Damning— The Abortion Pill Is Important but No Panacea," *Newsweek*, October 9, 2000, p. 86.

55. Alan Guttmacher Institute, "An Overview of Abortion in the United States," January 2008, accessed at http://www.guttmacher.org.

56. Rebecca Vesely, "Teen Death Steers RU-486 Bill to Congress," *Women's eNews*, November 15, 2004, accessed at http://www.womensenews.org.

57. Rebecca Wind, "U.S. Abortion Rate Continues Long-Term Decline," Alan Guttmacher Institute, January 17, 2008, accessed at http://www.guttmacher.org.

58. Rob Stein, "Study Finds Major Shift in Abortion Demographics," *Washington Post*, September 23, 2008; A03.

59. Rachel Benson Gold, "All That's Old is New Again: The Long Campaign to Persuade Women to Forego Abortion," *Guttmacher Policy Review* 12, no. 2 (Spring 2009): 19–22.

60. Alan Guttmacher Institute, "Facts on Induced Abortion Worldwide," October, 2008, accessed at http://www.guttmacher.org/pubs/fb_IAW.html.

61. Alan Guttmacher Institute, "Facts on Induced Abortion Worldwide," October 2008, accessed at http://www.guttmacher.org/pubs/fb_IAW.html.

62. Alan Guttmacher Institute, *Sharing Responsibility: Women, Society and Abortion Worldwide* (New York: AGI, 1999).

63. Planned Parenthood, "Birth Control," accessed at http://www.plannedparenthood.org/health-topics/birth-control-4211.htm.

64. Alan Guttmacher Institute, "Facts on Publicly Funded Contraceptive Services in the United States," February 2009, accessed at http://www.guttmacher.org/pubs/fb_contraceptive_serv.pdf.

65. Tamar Lewin, "Agency Finds Many Health Plans Should Cover Contraceptive Costs," *New York Times*, December 15, 2000, p. A1.

66. Ibid.

67. The six states are Alaska, California, Hawaii, Maine, New Mexico, and Washington. Center for Reproductive Rights, "State Trends in Emergency Contraception," updated October 2002, accessed at http://www.crlp.org.

68. "Pharmacist Refuses to Fill Prescription for Birth Control Pill," *Feminist Daily News* Wire, March 23, 2004, accessed at http://www.feminist.org.

69. The Polling Report, accessed at http://www.pollingreport.com/abortion.html.

70. Rob Stein, "Obama Administration to Reverse Bush Rule on 'Conscience' Regulation," *Washington Post*, February 27, 2009.

71. Lydia Saad, "More Americans 'Pro-life' than 'Pro-choice' for First Time," *Gallup*, May 15, 2009, accessed at http://www.gallup.com.

72. Wendy Kaminer, "Abortion and Autonomy," *American Prospect* 11, no. 14 (June 5, 2000), accessed at http://www.prospect.org/archives/v11-14.

73. Ibid.

74. Ibid.

75. Amy Richards as told to Amy Barrett, "When One Is Enough," *New York Times Magazine,* July 18, 2004, p. 18.

76. The Gallup Organization, "Abortion Issue Guides One in Five Voters," October 26, 2004, accessed at http://www.gallup.com.

77. Ibid.

78. Lydia Saad, "Abortion Issue Laying Low in 2008 Campaign," *Gallup,* May 22, 2008, accessed at http://www.gallup.com.

79. Ruth Marcus, "Palin's Personal Choice," *Washington Post,* April 20, 2009.

80. Garance Franke-Ruta, "Palin Said She Weighed Abortion," *Washington Post,* April 18, 2009.

81. Ian Urbina, "Social Initiatives on State Ballots Could Draw Attention to Presidential Race," *New York Times,* August 11, 2008.

82. Catherine A. MacKinnon, "Privacy v. Equality: Beyond *Roe v. Wade*," in *Mary Jo Frug's Women and the Law,* eds. Judith G. Greenberg, Martha L. Minow, and Dorothy E. Roberts, 2nd ed. (New York: Foundation Press, 1998), pp. 737–742.

83. Ibid., p. 741.

84. Ibid., p. 742.

85. Robert H. Blank, "Reproductive Technology: Pregnant Women, the Fetus, and the Courts," in *The Politics of Pregnancy,* eds. Janna C. Merrick and Robert H. Blank (New York: Haworth Press, 1996), pp. 1–18.

86. Greenberg, Minow, and Roberts, *Mary Jo Frug's Women,* p. 772.

87. *In Re A.C.,* Court of Appeals of the District of Columbia, *en banc,* 573 A.2d 1235 (1990).

88. Greenberg, Minow, and Roberts, *Mary Jo Frug's Women,* p. 754.

89. Sherry F. Colb, "Crying Murder When a Woman Refuses a C-Section: The Disturbing Implications of a Utah Prosecution," March 16, 2004, accessed at http://www.writ.news.findlaw.com.

90. Dorothy E. Roberts, "Punishing Drug Addicts Who Have Babies: Women of Color, Equality, and the Right of Privacy," in Greenburg, Minow, and Roberts, *Mary Jo Frug's Women,* p. 772.

91. Center for Reproductive Law and Policy, "U.S. Supreme Court Hears Arguments in *Ferguson v. City of Charleston,*" (2000), accessed at http://www.crlp.org/100400ferguson.html.

92. Robert H. Blank, *Fetal Protection in the Workplace* (New York: Columbia University Press, 1993), p. 14.

93. Margo Kaplan, "Behind Bars for Being Pregnant and HIV-Positive," posted on *RHRealityCheck.org,* June 10, 2009.

94. J. Ralph Lindgren and Nadine Taub, *The Law of Sex Discrimination,* 2nd ed. (Minneapolis, Minn.: West Publishing Co., 1993), p. 39.

95. Blank, *Fetal Protection*, p. 99.

96. Center for Reproductive Rights, 2005 Legislative Summary, accessed at http://reproductiverights.org/.

97. Alan Guttmacher Institute, "State Policies in Brief: An Overview of Abortion Laws," June 1, 2009, accessed at http://www.guttmacher.org.

98. Gretchen Borchelt, "Eighth Circuit Allows Politicians to Interfere in Doctor-Patient Relationship," posted to Womanstake on June 27, 2008, National Women's Law Center, accessed at http://www.nwlc.org/.

99. Rachel Benson Gold, "All That's Old is New Again: The Long Campaign to Persuade Women to Forego Abortion," *Guttmacher Policy Review* 12, no. 2 (Spring 2009): 19.

100. Ibid., p. 22.

101. Harper Jean Tobin, "Confronting Misinformation on Abortion: Informed Consent, Deference, and Fetal Pain Laws," *Columbia Journal of Gender and the Law* 17, no.1 (2008): 111–153.

102. National Abortion Foundation, "Crisis Pregnancy Centers," accessed at http://www.prochoice.org/about_abortion/facts/cpc.html.

103. Ibid.

104. Keith Perine, "Fetal Protection Bill Cleared as Democrat's Substitute Fails," *CQ Weekly*, March 7, 2004, p. 744.

105. Sheila Gibbons, "Dim Coverage Given to Abortion-Ban Ruling," *Women's eNews*, June 23, 2004, accessed at http://www.womensenews.org.

106. *Gonzales v. Carhart*, 550 U.S. 124 (2007).

107. *Gonzales v. Carhart*, 550 U.S. 124 (2007).

108. Alan Guttmacher Institute State Policies in Brief, "Abortion Policy in the Absence of *Roe*," June 1, 2009, accessed at http://www.guttmacher.org/statecenter/spibs/spib_APAR.pdf; Juliette Terzieff, "If Roe Falls, States Ready to Curb or Ban Abortion," *Women's eNews*, November 9, 2007.

109. Melody Rose, *Safe, Legal, and Unavailable? Abortion Politics in the United States* (Washington, D.C.: CQ Press, 2007).

110. Robert H. Blank, *Regulating Reproduction* (New York: Columbia University Press, 1990), p. 13.

111. Ibid., p. 15.

112. Ashley Surdin, "Octuplet Mother Also Gives Birth to Ethical Debate," *Washington Post*, February 4, 2009; C01.

113. Kate Zernike, "And Baby Makes How Many?" *New York Times*, February 8, 2009, accessed at http://www.nytimes.com.

114. Kathryn Joyce, *Quiverfull: Inside the Christian Patriarchy Movement* (Boston: Beacon Press, 2009).

115. Laura R. Woliver, *The Political Geographies of Pregnancy* (Urbana: University of Illinois Press, 2002), p. 83.

116. Betty Friedan, *The Second Stage* (New York: Summit Press, 1986).

9

Setting the Agenda and Taking Action: New Challenges in the Pursuit of Equality

Our examination of women's pursuit of equality has focused on the complexities, tensions, and controversies created by the paradox of gender equality—that is, how to reconcile demands for gender equality with sex differences between men and women. Two major paths have been forged in attempting to resolve the paradox and improve the status of women. The difference between the two approaches lies in how the implications of sex differences are understood. Advocates of the *legal equality doctrine* believe that women can never achieve equality as long as they are treated differently from men. "Different" in this context always means inferior. By removing sex as a method of categorizing individuals, women will be free of the discriminatory institutional, legal, and political barriers erected purely on the basis of sex that have historically prevented them from full participation in society. Using the legal equality doctrine, women and men are made the same in the eyes of the law, and therefore cannot be treated differently (with a few remaining exceptions). Critics of this approach argue that since men and women are in fact biologically different, erasing their legal differences but not their real differences will merely burden women further. Advocates of the *fairness doctrine* believe that sex differences have significant and persistent consequences for how men and women live in the world. Women are disadvantaged and equality is not meaningful when their unique biological role is ignored as it would be under the legal equality doctrine. Using the fairness doctrine, laws that recognize and accommodate women's physical differences will thereby promote women's equality in reality. Gender, the evolving social construction of sex, complicates both approaches to equality.

As we have seen throughout this text, women do not agree among themselves on the meaning or even on the desirability of equality as defined by these two paths. Sex alone does not create a binding political identity among women, nor does it foster a group consciousness that mobilizes women around the issues of gender equality. Feminism, one manifestation of women's political conscious-ness, has not always provided an effective political mobilizing ideology because it too encompasses the paradox of gender equality. Feminism encourages unity among women even while recognizing and celebrating women's diversity. The same sorts of socioeconomic and political cleavages that divide men from one another also divide women and have proven difficult to overcome in adopting a single approach to resolving the gender paradox. Yet all women share one condition purely on the basis of their sex—a subordinate position within the gender hierarchy of *patriarchy*. Patriarchy privileges men over women, regard-less of class, race or ethnicity, sexuality, or political ideology. The pernicious influence of the separate spheres ideology has combined with patriarchy's male privilege to render women's pursuit of equality an enduring political challenge. Private patriarchy (families) combined with public patriarchy (economy, poli-tics, and public policy) creates a system that has historically submerged women in the private sphere, rendering them nearly invisible in the public sphere until the mid-1800s. The quest for women's rights can thus be characterized as a movement to gain women's autonomy and full citizenship in the public sphere. Gaining full equality in the public sphere requires a substantial reordering of the private sphere. Although the legal equality approach has been an effective tool in opening doors and dismantling barriers to women's full participation in the public sphere, the private sphere is far more impervious to legal man-dates for change. Within the private sphere, the fairness doctrine may be a more appropriate approach but still the notion of external forces impinging on the sanctity of family continues to meet fierce opposition, leaving the private sphere virtually unreformed.

This book has traced women's historical progress in their fight for autonomy and equality. Early women activists had obvious hurdles to overcome, starting with the debilitating fact that women were not permitted to speak aloud in a public forum. Without a public voice, women could neither articulate their own interests nor expect their interests to be represented in politics or policy. The first manifesto of women's rights, the *Declaration of Sentiments and Reso-lutions*, adopted in 1848 at the Seneca Falls Convention, included the demand for women's voices to be heard within their marriages, families, communities, and the larger political system. Today the *Declaration of Sentiments and Reso-lutions* provides a good framework for evaluating women's progress toward equality. Exactly how far have women come in the pursuit of equality? Partici-pants at the Seneca Falls meeting thought their demand for the vote was the most radical of the eleven resolutions that participants adopted. It was, as you recall from chapter 2, the only resolution that was not adopted unanimously. In retrospect, the third resolution called for an even more fundamental trans-formation. It read, "Resolved, That woman is man's equal—was intended to be so by the Creator, and the highest good of the race demands that she should be recognized as such." It is a simple declaration of equality between men and

Seneca Falls Women's Rights Convention Resolutions

On the morning of July 19, 1848, the *Declaration of Sentiments* (see chapter 2) was read, discussed, and approved by the convention. That afternoon, the following resolutions were then read and adopted:

Whereas, the great precept of nature is conceded to be, "that man shall pursue his own true and substantial happiness," Blackstone, in his Commentaries, remarks, that this law of Nature being coeval with mankind, and dictated by God himself, is of course superior in obligation to any other. It is binding over all the globe, in all countries, and at all times; no human laws are of any validity if contrary to this, and such of them as are valid, derive all their force, and all their validity, and all their authority, mediately and immediately, from this original; Therefore,

Resolved, That such laws as conflict, in any way, with the true and substantial happiness of woman, are contrary to the great precept of nature, and of no validity; for this is "superior in obligation to any other."

Resolved, That all laws which prevent woman from occupying such a station in society as her conscience shall dictate, or which place her in a position inferior to that of man, are contrary to the great precept of nature, and therefore of no force or authority.

Resolved, That woman is man's equal—was intended to be so by the Creator, and the highest good of the race demands that she should be recognized as such.

Resolved, That the women of this country ought to be enlightened in regard to the laws under which they live, that they may no longer publish their degradation, by declaring themselves satisfied with their present position, nor their ignorance, by asserting that they have all the rights they want.

Resolved, That inasmuch as man, while claiming for himself intellectual superiority, does accord to woman moral superiority, it is pre-eminently his duty to encourage her to speak, and teach, as she has an opportunity, in all religious assemblies.

women that is missing from the nation's founding documents. It took suffragists seventy-two years to win the elective franchise, but such a clear declaration of equality between men and women has yet to be embraced as fundamental U.S. law. The Equal Rights Amendment, although first proposed in 1923 and considered by the states between 1972 and 1982, was never ratified as an amendment to the Constitution. Moreover, its international equivalent, the Convention on the Elimination of All Forms of Discrimination Against Women (CEDAW), has yet to be ratified by the U.S. Senate since its adoption by the United Nations in 1979. Does that matter? Perhaps not if women have achieved equality by other means. Throughout the book we have examined a number of critical legal protections—the equal protection clause of the U.S. Constitution, Title VII, Title IX, the Equal Pay Act, the Pregnancy Discrimination Act, the Violence Against Women Act, and various U.S. Supreme Court interpretations

Resolved, That the same amount of virtue, delicacy, and refinement of behavior, that is required of woman in the social state, should also be required of man, and the same transgressions should be visited with equal severity on both man and woman.

Resolved, That the objection of indelicacy and impropriety, which is so often brought against woman when she addresses a public audience, comes with a very ill grace from those who encourage, by their attendance, her appearance on the stage, in the concert, or in the feats of the circus.

Resolved, That woman has too long rested satisfied in the circumscribed limits which corrupt customs and a perverted application of the Scriptures have marked out for her, and that it is time she should move in the enlarged sphere which her great Creator has assigned her.

Resolved, That it is the duty of the women of this country to secure to themselves their sacred right to the elective franchise.

Resolved, That the equality of human rights results necessarily from the fact of the identity of the race in capabilities and responsibilities.

Resolved, therefore, That, being invested by the Creator with the same capabilities, and the same consciousness of responsibility for their exercise, it is demonstrably the right and duty of woman, equally with man, to promote every righteous cause, by every righteous means; and especially in regard to the great subjects of morals and religion, it is self-evidently her right to participate with her brother in teaching them, both in private and in public, by writing and by speaking, by any instrumentalities proper to be used, and in any assemblies proper to be held; and this being a self-evident truth, growing out of the divinely implanted principles of human nature, any custom or authority adverse to it, whether modern or wearing the hoary sanction of antiquity, is to be regarded as self-evident falsehood, and at war with the interests of mankind.

Source: Elizabeth Cady Stanton, Susan B. Anthony, and Matilda Joslyn Gage, eds., *History of Women's Suffrage*, vol. 1 (Rochester, N.Y.: Charles Mann, 1881), pp. 67–74.

of law as it applies to women's equality. Yet, without that simple declaration of equality first proposed in the *Declaration of Sentiments and Resolutions*, the basis for women's equality remains nebulous and its very definition subject to variable interpretation, state and federal regulation, and intermittent enforcement depending on the character of the political climate. That said, where do women stand today relative to achieving the goal of equality?

This final chapter examines three areas in which women have demanded an expansion of rights, beginning with resolutions adopted at the Seneca Falls meeting. Each of the following sections briefly summarizes women's advances and identifies areas in which women are still struggling to define and achieve equality. In setting a future agenda for women's equality, we will evaluate the challenges that lie ahead in resolving the paradox of gender equality and identify ways for you to take action in the pursuit of gender equality.

ELECTIVE FRANCHISE AND POLITICAL REPRESENTATION

Although all women were enfranchised in 1920 with the ratification of the Nineteenth Amendment, it took more than seventy years and countless campaigns led by three generations of suffragists to win the vote. Having the vote is not synonymous with using the vote to promote women candidates or a women's political agenda. Women's votes have been highly sought after by both political parties, even though, as we have noted repeatedly, women rarely act as one homogenous bloc. For example, unique efforts were made in 2004 to mobilize single women voters who did not participate in 2000. Similar efforts were made to register and mobilize new female voters in 2008, particularly women of color and young women. Although men and women voted differently in the 2000, 2004, and 2008 presidential contests, we cannot say that women voters alone determined the outcome in these elections.

In 2009, seventy-three women serve in the House of Representatives and seventeen women serve in the U.S. Senate—a record high of 90 women out of 535 members, but still only 16.8 percent of the body overall. The rate of progress has been incremental and slow since 1992, widely hailed as the "Year of the Woman" because of the large gains women made as both candidates and officeholders in that single election cycle. Since 1992, women's share of representation in Congress has increased by just 6 percent. At this rate, it will be decades before gender parity is reached in Congress.

Whether "women's interests" will be more effectively advanced as a result of these modest gains remains to be seen. Descriptively, women are better represented in the 111th Congress than ever before by virtue of the increase in numbers of women *standing for* women. Role models are essential to attracting women candidates and convincing young women that a role in politics is key to charting their own futures. However, unless women in office also provide substantive representation by *acting for* women's interests, the status of women overall is unlikely to change. Until women occupy several of the available leadership positions within the institution, they are less likely to be able to shape the overall agenda to include women's issues. In this regard, women have made some progress. Representative Nancy Pelosi (D-CA) became Speaker of the House of Representatives in January 2007—the first woman to achieve that position. As Speaker, she is now two heartbeats away from the presidency in the constitutional line of succession and she plays a significant role in setting the congressional agenda. Upon accepting the Speaker's gavel she remarked:

> It's an historic moment for the Congress. It's an historic moment for the women of America. It is a moment for which we have waited over 200 years. Never losing faith, we waited through the many years of struggle to achieve our rights. But women weren't just waiting; women were working. Never losing faith, we worked to redeem the promise of America, that all men and women are created equal. For our daughters

Speaker of the House Nancy Pelosi (D-CA) takes the Speaker's gavel from House Minority Leader Rep. John Boehner (R-OH) after being elected as the first woman Speaker at a swearing in ceremony for the 110th Congress in the House Chamber of the U.S. Capitol January 4, 2007 in Washington, DC. Pelosi will lead House Democrats as the Democratic Party takes control of both houses of Congress. *Chip Somodevilla/Getty Images.*

and our granddaughters, today we have broken the marble ceiling. For our daughters and granddaughters now, the sky is the limit. Anything is possible for them.[1]

However, the fall 2009 debate over health care reform also makes clear that having a woman in the highest leadership position will not guarantee that she will always be able to *act for* women. Pro-choice Speaker Pelosi has been heavily criticized by members of her own political party as well as feminist organizations for allowing new restrictions on abortion rights to be added to the House version of the health care reform bill. *New York Times* columnist Judith Warner characterized the moment as "the false choice between women's self-determination and the greater good...the decision of whether to let health reform—desperately needed by children and families—move forward with such a considerable blow to women's rights embedded within it, or whether to let it die on the vine." [2]

The 2008 election cycle represents another significant advance for women in that Senator Hillary Rodham Clinton won 22 states during the primary, attracting nearly 18 million voters (47.8 percent of the total votes cast), and 1,896 delegates to the Democratic National Convention. Barack Obama clinched the nomination by earning 2,229 delegates (2,118 required) to the convention with a margin of roughly 152,000 votes in a contest in which over 35 million people participated[3] The race for the nomination was very close and either outcome represented "a first" for the United States. Although there are countless examples of the ways gender played a role in the campaign, there is no way to know to what degree gender trumped race as a stereotypical obstacle for voters to overcome in making their decision, nor can we truly parse out the ways in which Clinton's strategic campaign decisions were influenced by gender stereotypes in politics, only to run up against an entirely new political landscape than the one she anticipated (see chapter 4). Nonetheless, her successful candidacy opened doors for the next wave of female candidates and won her a place in the new administration as secretary of state. There are many who believe Senator Clinton's successful run at the nomination also led to Sarah Palin's selection as the Republican vice-presidential candidate—another first. Women's success and national visibility in both political parties in the 2008 presidential contest was unprecedented; unfortunately, the level of misogyny evident in the media was too. What impact will this have on women's willingness to wage a national campaign in the future? Does it represent a backlash against women's success and progress toward political equality, as some have suggested?

Future gender equality activists have three primary tasks: Recruit and elect more gender-conscious women to office and work to reelect female incumbents so that they will gain seniority and be eligible to assume positions of leadership. Given the recent research on the porous nature of the pipeline and women's inability to objectively assess their own qualifications for office, recruiting women as candidates will require sustained attention and intervention. Parity will require women to seek elected office as a matter of course and to run in large numbers in every election and at every level of office. However, there is evidence that the trend is going in the opposite direction. In 2008, 2,337 female candidates ran for state legislative seats, only 130 more than in 2004, but 31 fewer women candidates than in 1992. Of those who ran, 62.7 percent won seats. Similarly, in 2008 four women sought governorships (all Democrats, and all faced male Republican opponents); two won and two lost. In 2006, ten women ran for governor (5 Democrats and 5 Republicans) and six women were elected. Since about 70 percent of women in Congress have served in lower elected positions first, more women must declare as candidates and seek elected positions at all levels of government. As we've noted repeatedly and as empirical evidence confirms, when women run they have a better than even chance of winning—but, first they have to be candidates.

TAKING ACTION: WHAT CAN YOU DO?

- *Test the waters and gain some experience.* Run for a position in your campus student government or for an office in a club or organization you are involved with, to gain experience. Help other women see themselves as candidates for available positions on your campus and recruit them to run. Likewise, talk with your friends about running for future political office in your local community and in your state. The more you and other women envision yourselves as qualified candidates, the more likely you are to actually become a candidate.

- *Get some leadership training.* Many colleges and universities have leadership centers or programs to identify and train young leaders. Sometimes, there are leadership academic certificate programs or major programs of study that link course work with experiential internships, mentorships, or service-learning opportunities. See what is available on your own campus and get involved. Whether your issue is immigration, women's health, or environmental sustainability, there are community organizations that also need your talents and time. Once you get some training, put yourself to work!

- *Get some _political_ leadership training.* Chapter 4 includes a list of national political leadership and candidate training schools. Programs like The White House Project's "Vote, Run, Lead," and Running Start are designed for college-age women and open to women of all political ideologies and parties. You might not be ready to run for political office today, but the more training you get now and the wider your network of contacts, the more you will be prepared to run when you are ready. Look into local and state offices without age restrictions. Since most national officeholders gained experience in their local communities first, it is never too early to get started!

- *Invite a woman to run and support women candidates.* The most effective way to recruit women as candidates for public office is to *ask* them to run. The White House Project sponsors an e-mail campaign to "Invite a Woman to Run" (see chapter 4). You can do the same thing in your community. Look around you and identify women you respect and whose work in the community you value, and ask them to run for political office. Register to vote! Give candidates (male and female) who support gender equality your vote as well as your time and talents in their campaigns. All campaigns need good volunteers to spread the message and get voters out to the polls. While you are working for a candidate, you are also gaining experience and building a network of contacts for your own political future.

MARRIAGE AND FAMILY RIGHTS

The *Declaration of Sentiments and Resolutions* was primarily concerned with changing the common law practices associated with coverture that denied women the ability to exercise independent control over anything in their lives, including property, wages, household goods, and their children. Marriage reforms consistent with the legal equality doctrine now view men and women as equal partners in a marriage, yet new laws in a majority of the states classify marriage as legal only between one woman and one man, leaving same-sex couples in legal limbo. A few states now permit same-sex couples to marry, while a handful of others will recognize a marriage performed in another state or sanction civil unions. At the federal level, the Defense of Marriage Act still prevails.

Resolving the division of family and workforce labor will be a primary issue facing men and women in the future. Policies consistent with the legal equality doctrine are more problematic in this area than in any other because of the weight that biological differences have when assigning reproductive responsibilities. Beyond the physical implications of pregnancy, attitudes about women's sociological responsibilities for children and the home also complicate developing gender-neutral family policies. Gender-specific policies carry the danger of reinforcing attitudes about women's natural fit in the private sphere at the risk of further exclusion from the public sphere. The "mommy track," widely derided for downsizing women's ambitions, was actually first proposed as a way to make the workplace accommodate women's caretaking responsibilities at home consistent with the fairness doctrine. The "maternal wall" applies to all women whether or not they currently have or even plan to have children. Employers continue to recruit and place employees based on gendered expectations where men prioritize work over family responsibilities and women are expected to place family and children first. All women have the potential to be mothers and therefore experience a type of preemptive maternal discrimination. Aware of these forces, women act to cope rather than to confront. Felice Schwartz offers a poignant example in the "riddle of the rings."[4] A group of female Wharton MBA students told her that it was common practice for married women in the MBA program to remove their wedding bands before going to job interviews—"recruiters will not offer plum jobs to those women they believe will have commitments to their families." The students who told this story were not angry or outraged, but believed they were acting expediently and pragmatically to improve their job prospects. Thus women are significantly disadvantaged in the workforce because of the expectation that they continue to maintain the primary responsibility for the children and home. A substantial portion of the pay gap is attributed to differences in men's and women's length of employment experience. When children come into a family, their presence is associated with lower wages for women, but not for men.[5]

It may be that many of these issues cannot be resolved by public policy. The political culture in the United States has not supported government's intervention into the private domain of family and children until relatively recently. Even now, government's participation is limited to protecting the health and safety of individuals within families and does not include providing financial and programmatic aid to families struggling to balance work and family responsibilities. The Family and Medical Leave Act of 1993 is a pale comparison to family-support programs provided in many other nations (see chapters 7 and 8). Efforts to strengthen the legislation to provide paid leave funded by state unemployment insurance funds have been met with strong opposition. California is the only state that provides any form of paid family leave with the

California Family Temporary Disability Insurance program, funded entirely by employee contributions. There is little evidence that a national child-care policy is at the top of any legislative agenda, even though in forty-eight states the cost of center-based child care for a four-year-old is more than tuition at a four-year public university.[6] The Obama administration has signaled an interest in developing new ways to assist families in balancing work and caretaking obligations. The fact that the First Lady worked full-time as a lawyer until taking a leave of absence during the primary campaign, makes it more likely that any policy discussions will be grounded in the reality of first-hand experience. Until women and men reach the point where both are faced with the same challenges, it seems unlikely that a government policy will be the mechanism that produces real change. Policies that are designed to promote role equity (equality defined as fairness) have been more successful than policies designed to promote role change (equality defined as sameness). Balancing family with other public responsibilities presents a complicated case for this framework. Because men and women continue to hold traditional attitudes about the gendered division of labor within the family and private household (see chapter 7 on gender socialization and work), even women see their additional family responsibilities as "fair" up to a point. Until these attitudes change, it is unlikely that the public will pressure policymakers to produce solutions. Women must adopt change-oriented strategies of political participation rather than continue to privately cope as individuals. Throughout the book, the disadvantages women suffer as a result of children are clear. They have fewer job prospects, they are likely to be paid less than all men and women without children, they are less likely to be promoted to jobs with more responsibilities that also pay more, and they are less likely to have private pensions to support them in retirement. As a result, the best predictor of women's poverty is the presence of children. What does that say about gender, the prospects for gender equality, and for our culture in the United States?

TAKING ACTION: WHAT CAN YOU DO?

- *Think honestly about your own expectations of marriage and family.* Think now about what you expect from yourself and your partner when and if you create a family. Because you do not likely face the immediate pressures of a decision, this is a good time to write about what you expect and what you want your future life to be like. If you are not already in the practice of journaling or blogging, start one now to capture your expectations over time. Be sure that your expectations are grounded in empirical reality. Talk to your peers—both male and female—about their expectations. Armed with facts, confront myths and stereotypes about equality in the private sphere. Although people can argue over the source and the size of the wage gap, the difference in pay between men and women remains no matter who does the analysis or the number of control variables introduced. Women with children spend more hours per workday on child care and household chores than they did thirty years ago, and the United States is still among only four nations worldwide that does not guarantee paid family leave.

- *Lobby your state legislature and the Congress to adopt policies that support families and promote gender equality.* The Family and Medical Leave Act (discussed in chapters 7 and 8) is very limited in who is covered and in the unpaid benefits it provides. By comparison to other nations, the United States does not have a support system for working families. Do the research to identify promising approaches to supporting families and then lobby your state legislature and the Congress to pass appropriate policies. Our federal system of government allows the states to be policy laboratories and many of the most innovative approaches to assisting individuals in combining work and family can be found in the states or in the policies of private-sector employers. At the same time, states and companies differ and so before you decide where you will live and work, do the research. Organizations like the Institute for Women's Policy Research produce annual state-by-state report cards on gender equity.

- *Investigate the new activism around motherhood, fatherhood, and parenting.* Organizations like MomsRising and Mothers and More have been founded to promote the interests of mothers in the workplace. As we've noted repeatedly, parenthood has historically been located in the private sphere in the United States and too often parenthood has meant only "motherhood." As men make demands on the public sphere for more time with their families, they are also violating gender norms. A new father's movement has emerged to support men in doing so. If men and women worked together to put pressure on the public sphere, perhaps more generous family policy would result. There is a long history of politicized mothers' movements in other nations (e.g., MADRE) and there are signs that similar political action in this country might elevate private sphere issues to public policy attention.

- *Investigate the policies of companies before you go to work.* Not all companies have family-friendly policies in place. Each year, *Working Mother* magazine publishes the "Top 100 Best Companies for Working Mothers." *Fortune* and *Black Enterprise* publish similar lists. The Sloan Work and Family Research Network at Boston College is a another good source of information on workplace policies. Even if you do not plan to seek employment with one of these companies, research the policies that earned them a spot among the Top 100 Best so that you know what to look for when you pursue employment elsewhere.

- *Work to end unintended pregnancies.* Attempting to control fertility—whether through pronatalist policies or population control efforts—is an ancient and enduring political interest. Nothing affects a woman's autonomy more than her ability to decide if and when she will bear children, how many she will produce, and if more than one, how they will be spaced.

Contraception enables women to avoid pregnancy and yet nearly half of all pregnancies in the United States today are unintended. Educate yourself about reproduction and fertility, protect yourself from sexually transmitted diseases, and inform yourself about reproductive choices available in your community. Abortion remains legal in the United States, although it is increasingly difficult to access for most women, particularly for poor women and minorities. Promote education and fair access to health care for all women.

EDUCATION, EMPLOYMENT, AND ECONOMIC OPPORTUNITIES

Because women were legally excluded from all colleges and universities, as well as from most occupations, the *Declaration of Sentiments and Resolutions* demanded women have access to education and employment opportunities. Today, Title IX (discussed in chapter 6) and Title VII (discussed in chapter 7) guarantee that access to educational institutions and most occupations cannot be denied on the basis of sex. These two pieces of legislation have been powerful tools for women in developing the "human capital" necessary to broaden economic opportunities. Human capital, which includes education and experience in the labor market, is often viewed as the most important determinant of wages. Wages, of course, are an important determinant of security, health, and quality of life. As we have seen in the previous three chapters, gender-neutral access to education and employment does not necessarily ensure that the experience itself is comparable for men and women. Unless gender equity remains a priority in the changes that are being made to the way children are educated, gains in this area for women will be vulnerable.

The poverty rates for women in the United States, particularly among women with children and the elderly, remain startlingly high. Even as the nation has prospered, the proportion of women living below the poverty line has increased. There are a number of explanations for women's overrepresentation among the poor (see chapter 7). The 1996 changes to the nation's welfare policy likely impacted women's poverty rate. There is ample evidence that families relying on minimum-wage or low-wage jobs, even with two workers employed full-time, cannot attain self-sufficiency. The deep recession in 2008 and 2009 affected both women and men, although differently. Men were more likely to lose their job and to lose better-paying jobs, leaving many women as the new primary wage earner in their family. Because women are concentrated in low-wage occupations and because of the wage gap earn less than men, the recession's impact on women and their families has been severe. Although some communities have adopted living wage policies, they apply to very few workers and there is not currently a national debate on adopting a national living wage standard. Congress raised the minimum wage

Encountering the Controversies of Equality

Same Difference: Women and Abu Ghraib Prison

On April 29, 2004, the world learned of horrific abuses and torture that took place between October and December 2003 at Abu Ghraib prison, located about twenty miles outside of Baghdad, Iraq. CBS News' "*60 Minutes II*" broadcast graphic photographs of naked male prisoners in sexualized poses, hooded prisoners connected to electrodes, male prisoners piled naked in a jumbled human pyramid, and prisoners bloodied and beaten or worse—dead and packed in ice.

This torture did not take place at the direction of Saddam Hussein, but was perpetrated by U.S. military personnel and immortalized in photographs snapped by the same personnel while the abuse was taking place. There is the infamous picture of Private Lynndie England, a cigarette dangling from her smiling mouth, pointing to a naked male prisoner's genitalia. In another photograph, England is seen holding a leash attached to the neck of a naked male prisoner. Specialist Sabrina Harman is pictured smiling and giving the thumbs-up sign from behind a pile of hooded, naked Iraqi prisoners. Of the seven reservists from the 372nd Military Police Company who now face criminal charges, three are women. As the investigation unfolded, we learned that Army Reserve Brigadier General Janis Karpinski, commander of the 800th Military Police Brigade, was in charge of military prisons in Iraq. The top U.S. intelligence officer in Iraq, in charge of reviewing the status of detainees before their release, was Major General Barbara Fast.

This is an image obtained by The Associated Press which shows Pfc. Lynndie England holding a leash attached to a detainee in late 2003 at the Abu Ghraib prison in Baghdad, Iraq. *AP Photo.*

The images were horrific in their own right, but the visuals of women participating were especially jarring. Since the earliest suffrage campaigns, feminists have argued that women should be in positions of power because they would exercise it with more care, less violence, and more justice than men do. Women have advanced the notion that they are morally superior to men. What does Abu Ghraib teach us about these claims?

Journalist Barbara Ehrenreich wrote, "The photos did something else to me, as a feminist: They broke my heart. I had no illusions about the U.S. mission in Iraq—whatever exactly it is—but it turns out that I did have some illusions about women."[1] She is not alone in her disillusionment. Retired Lieutenant General Claudia Kennedy, the Army's only female three-star general, said, "I was surprised to see a woman there. One would traditionally think that women would be less likely to participate in something so completely unfair and really brutal."[2] Retired Brigadier General Wilma Vaught believed that women in uniform behaved differently from men. "Women were sometimes more thoughtful about how something ought to be approached than men were because men were just ready to charge off."[3]

In attempting to explain why women were so integral to the torture, Lory Manning, a researcher on women in the military for the Women's Research and Education Institute, said, "Women are human. I wanted them to be better, but that's not realistic." "They may be trying to be part of the majority groups that they belong to—to be like the men they serve with," according to Kennedy.[4] Some used this as an opportunity to argue again that women shouldn't be in the military at all. Linda Chavez, an opponent of gender integration in the military, wrote: "The men and women who engaged in this behavior abused and humiliated their captives, dishonored their country and deserve severe punishment. But if we want to prevent this type of conduct from ever occurring again, we not only need to punish those responsible but also look at all the possible factors that might give occasion to such abuses—including the breakdown in discipline and unit cohesion that have gone hand in hand with gender integration in the military."[5]

"What we have learned from Abu Ghraib, once and for all," wrote Ehrenreich, "is that a uterus is not a substitute for a conscience. This doesn't mean gender equality isn't worth fighting for for its own sake. It is. If we believe in democracy, then we believe in a woman's right to do and achieve whatever men can do and achieve, even the bad things. It's just that gender equality cannot, all alone, bring about a just and peaceful world."[6]

What do you think?

Are men and women really all that different? What did you think when you first saw women in the Abu Ghraib pictures and learned that a woman was in command of the prison system? How does this situation inform your thinking about gender equality? In what ways has your understanding about the differences between men and women been challenged by this event? Are men and women inherently different, or is behavior conditioned purely by circumstances rather than by gender?

1. Barbara Ehrenreich, "A Uterus Is No Substitute for a Conscience: What Abu Ghraib Taught Me," May 21, 2004, accessed at http://www.zmag.org.
2. Jodi Enda, "Female Face of Abuse Provokes Shock," May 10, 2004, *Women's eNews*, accessed at http://www.womensenews.org.
3. Ibid.
4. Ibid.
5. Linda Chavez, "Women of Abu Ghraib," *GOPUSA Commentary Corner*, May 10, 2004, accessed at http://www.gopusa.com.
6. Ehrenreich, "A Uterus Is No Substitute."

Point of Comparison

Measuring the Global Gender Gap—How Close You Are to Equality Depends on Where You Live

In several previous chapters, the World Economic Forum's (WEF) ranking of women's global gender equality has been employed to examine one or another critical area. In this final chapter, women's overall equality will be examined and ranked using the WEF data. "Gender equality refers to that stage of human social development at which the rights, responsibilities and opportunities of individuals will not be determined by the fact of being born male or female. In other words, a stage when both men and women realize their full potential."[1]

Recall that the WEF study employs multiple indicators in five areas: economic participation, economic opportunity, political empowerment, educational attainment, and health and well-being. The study assesses the status of women in 58 countries, including all 30 OECD countries and 28 others from the "emerging Market" world. Publicly available data sources as well as an original WEF survey are used to create a seven-point scale, with 7 representing the "best" or most "equal" condition and 1 representing the "worst" or most "unequal." Thus a country's overall score is an average of the scores in each of the five areas. Higher average scores represent a smaller gap and greater gender equality. No country has yet managed to eliminate the gap in gender equality (a score of 7), but some are closer than others.

The Global Gender Gap Rankings

Country	Overall Rank	Overall Score	Country	Overall Rank	Overall Score
Sweden	1	5.53	New Zealand	6	4.89
Norway	2	5.39	Canada	7	4.87
Iceland	3	5.32	United Kingdom	8	4.75
Denmark	4	5.27	Germany	9	4.61
Finland	5	5.19	Australia	10	4.61

in 2006, but at $7.25 (the new rate as of July 2009), it is still likely that a family of three would be 18 percent below the poverty line, even with both parents working full-time and year-around.[7] Addressing women's poverty will require attention to the impact of sex segregation in the workforce; disparate classroom experiences and counseling in grade and high schools; and the

Country	Overall Rank	Overall Score	Country	Overall Rank	Overall Score
Latvia	11	4.60	Argentina	35	3.97
Lithuania	12	4.58	South Africa	36	3.95
France	13	4.49	Israel	37	3.94
Netherlands	14	4.48	Japan	38	3.75
Estonia	15	4.47	Bangladesh	39	3.74
Ireland	16	4.40	Malaysia	40	3.70
United States	17	4.40	Romania	41	3.70
Costa Rica	18	4.36	Zimbabwe	42	3.66
Poland	19	4.36	Malta	43	3.65
Belgium	20	4.30	Thailand	44	3.61
Slovak Republic	21	4.28	Italy	45	3.50
Slovenia	22	4.25	Indonesia	46	3.50
Portugal	23	4.21	Peru	47	3.47
Hungary	24	4.19	Chile	48	3.46
Czech Republic	25	4.19	Venezuela	49	3.42
Luxemburg	26	4.15	Greece	50	3.41
Spain	27	4.13	Brazil	51	3.29
Austria	28	4.13	Mexico	52	3.28
Bulgaria	29	4.06	India	53	3.27
Colombia	30	4.06	Korea	54	3.18
Russian Federation	31	4.03	Jordan	55	2.96
Uruguay	32	4.01	Pakistan	56	2.90
China	33	4.01	Turkey	57	2.67
Switzerland	34	3.97	Egypt	58	2.38

[1]Augusto Lopez-Claros and Saadia Zahidi, *Women's Empowerment: Measuring the Global Gender Gap* (Switzerland: World Economic Forum, 2005, p. 1).

limits imposed by the maternal wall, the glass ceiling, the sticky floor; and, particularly, the pay gap.

The pay gap, although a strikingly consistent 20–25 percent across hourly and salaried occupations, remains the subject of debate. Some attribute the pay differential between men and women to "choices" each makes regarding employment, education, and family. The portion of the pay gap that remains unexplained by differences in education, occupation, union membership, and labor market experience, however, is estimated at roughly 12 percent.[8] This is the portion of the pay gap that is attributed to gender discrimination. This disparity, due purely to sex, is precisely the type of discrimination the Equal Pay Act of 1963 was designed to eliminate. But when "sex" is really "gender" with all of the stereotypes and traditional gender norms of society, can a legal equality approach embodied in the Equal Pay Act ever be effective in closing the pay gap? Recall the research on starting salary differences between men and women. Individual experiences are most similar upon application for their first job, and yet a salary gap is already evident between male and female new college graduates. Part of that gap has been attributed to men's willingness to ask for more salary and women's tendency to accept what is first offered (see chapter 7).

More than forty-five years after equal pay policy was enacted, women still earn less than men even when performing the same job in the same sector of the economy. The pay gap has indeed declined over the past three decades, but it has not disappeared. Women with college degrees will still earn less on average than men with college degrees ($10,017 less a year) and only slightly more ($4,772 more a year) than white men with high school diplomas (see Table 6.4). The more education, the wider the wage gap ($15,554 more a year for men versus women with master's degrees). Over a forty-year work life, a woman with a college degree will lose more than $713,000. Women who don't finish high school can expect to lose nearly $270,000 because of the wage gap. Like the wage gap itself, the amount of pay a woman can expect to lose over her working lifetime varies by state. The gap exceeds $300,000 in 15 states, $400,000 in 22 states, and $500,000 in 11 states. The career wage gap also varies by occupation, with greater gaps found in occupations requiring more education and training. Women in the legal profession, for example, can expect to lose $1.5 million in lifetime earnings compared to male colleagues. Across all occupations, the widest gaps are found in finance and management while the smallest gaps are found in construction and maintenance.[9] Although the EEOC suffered a reduction in both staffing and resources during the Bush administration, new attention to the wage gap is likely during the Obama administration. A cosponsor of the Lilly Ledbetter Fair Pay Act as a Senator, Barack Obama made it the first bill he signed into law as President. However, that law merely restores the pre–*Ledbetter v. Goodyear* conditions under which an individual can file a claim for pay discrimination. It does not enhance the equal pay guarantees of the Equal Pay Act like the Paycheck Fairness Act would, nor does it move toward a pay equity model often referred to as "equal pay for comparable work" in recognition of persistent occupational gender segregation. Class-action pay discrimination suits, such as *Dukes v. Wal-Mart*, are currently winding their way through the court system. A more vigorous defense of equal pay standards by the EEOC would include more class-action suits filed on behalf of women in occupational sectors other than retail.

TAKING ACTION: WHAT CAN YOU DO?

- *Make choices now that will improve your salary prospects later.* In chapter 6 we reviewed the statistics on women in STEM disciplines as undergraduates and later as graduate students and researchers in science, engineering, and technology fields. Think carefully about your choice of major and why you have selected it. Does it accurately reflect your career interests and will it allow you to move into a career that pays wages sufficient to support you and your family? Might your choice of major have been conditioned by stereotypes and gendered expectations at any point in your life? Not everyone has an interest in science or the technology fields, but everyone can improve their math and technology skills now in a way that will expand their choices of occupations later. If you are majoring in a field in the humanities, social sciences, arts, or education, explore cognate majors or minors that will improve your earning power even as you explore your true interests. If you find that your major does not reflect your genuine interests, but instead represents a gender-default choice, make an informed decision to change it!

- *Research the wage gap and identify resources that will allow you to fight for wage equity.* The information on the wage gap can seem overwhelming. Look for research and information sources from nonideological sources and recognize the perspective of the authors of research you consume. The Institute for Women's Policy Research issues regular reports on the wage gap and makes research on its sources available on its Web site. The AAUW (American Association of University Women) published "Behind the Gap" in 2007 and it is available online. The WAGE (Women Are Getting Even) Project and AAUW have a collaborative project called $tart$mart that sponsors workshops to teach junior and senior college women basic salary negotiation skills and how to benchmark the salary of the job they want when they graduate. The sponsors' goal is to conduct workshops on over 500 college campuses in the next three years. Bring a $mart$tart workshop to your campus!

- *Protect Title IX.* Stay informed about the status of Title IX, the legislation that opened doors for women in education as well as sports and ended discriminatory quotas in professions like law, engineering, and medicine. The AAUW, founded in 1881 to advance equity for girls and women in education, is an advocacy and research organization with information on a wide range of Title IX issues. Likewise, the National Women's Law Center tracks legislative issues and court challenges related to Title IX. If you play sports, volunteer to coach a girl's sports team for children in your community. Although the law now provides the opportunity for girls to play sports, only supportive adults can translate opportunities into reality. This is particularly important if you live in an urban area.

- *Advocate for gender equity in tax reform and Social Security reform.* The National Council for Research on Women (NCRW) provides information, research, and publications on the impact of the tax code on women and tracks the implications of tax-law changes for women. The National Women's Law Center and the AAUW (as well as others) provide information and sound research on Social Security, private pensions, and women in retirement. Educate yourself and start planning for your retirement now. Although it seems a bit absurd, now is the time to start investing for retirement even though you may not yet have secured your first "real" job! Financial security across the lifespan is a gender-equality imperative.

WHERE DO WE GO FROM HERE?

As we reach the end of this volume and our analysis of the gender paradox, where do men and women stand after more than 150 years of effort toward a resolution of the paradox? We must conclude that men and women are more equal today than at any other time in U.S. history, but the paradox has not been entirely resolved. In a variety of contexts, men and women lead very different lives and, in some cases, women are decidedly disadvantaged because of their gender in addition to their sex. Public attitudes about gender roles in society have changed to support women as participants in the public sphere, although, as we've seen, there are limits to the autonomy women are extended. Feminism remains the most significant ideological challenge to the gender hierarchy that limits women's full participation and autonomy, but feminism faces a direct challenge to its own legitimacy as an organizing philosophy for women. There is a self-identified "third wave" of feminism underway. Notable for its decentralization and concern for a wide range of social justice interests, including many with a global scope, this branch of feminism is less focused on an advocacy consistent with the legal equality doctrine and more interested in humanist approaches that are consistent with, but not identical to, the fairness doctrine.

Now, in the early twenty-first century, young women find themselves heirs to their mothers' and grandmothers' unfinished equality agenda.[10] That agenda is likely to include many of the same issues addressed by women at the Seneca Falls Convention in 1848—equality in work and wages; an effective public voice; political parity; accessible, quality child care; reproductive freedom; and educational equity. What is old is also new. Today's feminist agenda must be reshaped by the experiences of contemporary women, building on past successes and overcoming the remaining barriers to full participation in public life. Young women will need to craft their action strategies, choose their political leaders, and gain even greater entrée into the places where decisions are made. The opportunities are boundless, but not without challenges. As Lady Astor, the first woman to be elected to the British parliament, chimed, "When I came in, I left the door wide open!" The challenge of gender equality is now in your hands—and the door is wide open.

Suggested Readings and Web Resources

Jennifer Baumgardner and Amy Richards, *Manifesta: Young Women, Feminism and the Future* (New York: Farrar, Straus and Giroux, 2001).

Lia Larson, ed., *Skirting Tradition: Women in Politics Speak to the Next Generation* (Hollis, N.H.: Hollis Publishing, 2004).

Carolyn B. Maloney, *Rumors of our Progress Have Been Greatly Exaggerated* (New York: Modern Times Books, 2008).

Marie C. Wilson, *Closing the Leadership Gap: Why Women Can and Must Help Run the World* (New York: Viking, 2004).

AAUW (American Association of University Women): http://www.aauw.org/index.cfm.

AAUW, "Behind the Gap": http://www.aauw.org/research/upload/behindPayGap.pdf.

Center for American Women and Politics, NEW Leadership Program: http://www.cawp.rutgers.edu/education_training/NEWLeadership/index.php.

The White House Project, "Vote, Run, Lead": http://www.thewhitehouseproject.org/voterunlead/trainings/.

The White House Project, "Invite a Woman to Run": http://www.thewhitehouseproject.org/tools/ecard/.

Institute for Women's Policy Research, Status of Women in the States: http://www.iwpr.org/States2004/SWS2004/index.htm.

Institute for Women's Policy Research, Women and Social Security: http://womenandsocialsecurity.org/Women_Social_Security/.

MomsRising: Breadmakers and Breadwinners: http://www.momsrising.org/.

Mothers and More: http://www.mothersandmore.org/.

National Council for Research on Women, "Taxes ARE a Woman's Issue": http://www.ncrw.org/publications/taxes.htm.

National Women's Law Center, "Education and Title IX": http://www.nwlc.org/display.cfm?section=education.

Running Start: http://www.runningstartonline.org.

Sloan Work and Family Research Network: http://wfnetwork.bc.edu/.

$mart$tart Workshops: http://www.wageproject.org/content/get_even/aauwenlist.php.

Third Wave Foundation: http://www.thirdwavefoundation.org/.

Veteran Feminists of America: http://www.vfa.us/.

Notes

1. "Rep. Nancy Pelosi's Remarks Upon Becoming Speaker of the House," *Washington Post*, January 4, 2007.

2. Judith Warner, "'Mad Men,' Maddening Times," *New York Times*, November 12, 2009, accessed at http://warnerblogs.nytimes.com/2009/11/12/mad-men-maddening-times/.

3. Real Clear Politics, "Election 2008," accessed at http://www.realclearpolitics.com/epolls/2008/president/democratic_delegate_count.html.

4. Felice Schwartz, *Breaking with Tradition: Women and Work, the New Facts of Life* (New York: Warner Books, 1992).

5. The Council of Economic Advisors, "Explaining the Trends in the Gender Wage Gap," 1998, accessed at http://www.whitehouse.gov/WH/EOP/CEA/html/gendergap.html.

6. Children's Defense Fund, "The State of America's Children 2004," accessed at http://www.childrensdefense.org.

7. Liana Fox, "Minimum Wage Increasingly Lags Poverty Line," Economic Policy Institute, January 31, 2007, accessed at http://www.epi.org/economic_snapshots/entry/webfeatures_snapshots_20070131/.

8. Ruth Leger Sivard, *Women: A World Survey* (Washington, D.C.: World Priorities, 1995), p. 9.

9. Jessica Arons, "Lifetime Losses: The Career Wage Gap," Center for American Progress Action Fund, December 2008, accessed at http://www.americanprogressaction.org.

10. Cynthia B. Costello, Vanessa R. Wight, and Anne J. Stone, eds., *The American Woman 2003–2004: Daughters of a Revolution—Young Women Today* (New York: Palgrave Macmillan, 2003), p. 179.

Index